THE GREAT MAN

Contemporary Political Comment and Satire
The Senate of Lilliput
Hummingbirds and Hyenas
Looking Down on Mrs Thatcher
The Shooting Gallery
The Quiet Rise of John Major
Election Rides
Machiavelli's Children
The Lost Leaders
Lines of Most Resistance
Denis Healey: A Life in Our Times
Reform! The Fight for the 1832 Reform Act
The Diaries of Charles Greville (editor)

THE GREAT MAN

Scoundrel, Genius and
Britain's First Prime Minister

EDWARD PEARCE

JONATHAN CAPE
LONDON

Published by Jonathan Cape 2007

2 4 6 8 10 9 7 5 3 1

First published in Great Britain in 2007 by
Jonathan Cape
Random House, 20 Vauxhall Bridge Road,
London SW1V 2SA

www.randomhouse.co.uk

Addresses for companies within The Random House Group Limited
can be found at: www.randomhouse.co.uk/offices.htm

The Random House Group Limited Reg. No. 954009

A CIP catalogue record for this book is available from the British Library

ISBN 9780224071819

The Random House Group Limited makes every effort to ensure that the papers
used in its books are made from trees that have been legally sourced from well-
managed and credibly certified forests. Our paper procurement policy
can be found at: www.randomhouse.co.uk/paper.htm

Typeset in Sabon by Palimpsest Book Production Limited,
Grangemouth, Stirlingshire

Printed and bound in Great Britain by William Clowes Ltd, Beccles, Suffolk

For
Alistair Stead

CONTENTS

LIST OF ILLUSTRATIONS

INTRODUCTION

Robert Walpole is, by convention, the first Prime Minister of Great Britain, an office which evolved across four reigns – from Charles II's 'Ah, Mr Godolphin, never in the way, never out of the way!' to Walpole's immediate predecessor, James Stanhope.

Godolphin in the 1680s was essentially a King's Minister, but unlike the medieval and regressive figure of Strafford, less than fifty years before, he was not a henchman of royal absolutism. Stanhope, 35 years on, was less a King's man than someone whose independent opinions converged with those of George I. An internationalist wanting peace with France and alert to German questions, he was rather the King's ally. But Stanhope was also the leader of a clearly defined political group commanding both houses of Parliament. His Tory predecessor 1710–1714, Robert Harley, had been all of that, in the Commons at least and in his relations with Queen Anne, even though he fell at the very end by losing her good will. Either man might with propriety have been called 'Prime Minister'.

The fact that Walpole was able in 1727 to survive the death of the approving George I and the accession of the hostile George II can be cited as distinguishing him as more of a Prime Minister. But without the good offices of George II's wife, Caroline, it is doubtful that he actually would have survived. We call him the first Prime Minister because he combined an exceptionally long span of office, happily never again equalled, with a delight in parliamentary management, conducted with exceptional success through good sense, lucid argument and dedicated corruption. We call him many other things, but the term, 'The Great Man', a derisive expression in his day, contains truth. He ran bribery and corruption on an industrial scale; the system which began to be dismantled in the Reform Act of 1832 was, if not his creation, his life work of perfection and augmentation. Against all that, he kept the country solvent and out of foreign wars and, quite simply, he commanded his times.

There is a great body of Walpole scholarship, the names of J.H. Plumb, Paul Langford, Betty Kemp, Jeremy Black, and Paul Fritz among the many distinguishing it. But a modern, completed, full-length life has never quite happened. There have been excellent synoptic lives and outstanding intense studies of aspects of his career, like Paul Langford's investigation of the excise crisis and the account by Paul Fritz of the Jacobite question and how Walpole handled (or manipulated) it. However, since Archdeacon William Coxe's two volumes of 1799, (today a vital primary printed source), there have been, at length and covering his whole life, only Sir John Plumb's volumes of 1956 and 1960. Whatever the Master of Christ's reasons for calling quits, something discussed in the final chapter here, it seemed reasonable, with proper respect, to go back to the beginning and make one's own effort.

On a personal note, I have never enjoyed historical research and writing so much. To sit in Cambridge University library, where thanks are due to Mrs Polly Harris, and view the treasures of an incoming post, more than 7,000 letters strong, was a privilege and fun. It might be a letter from the great mephisto, John Law, that one picked up, or a dark brown scrawl by the Duke of Grafton complaining from Ireland about the troublemaking of Dean Swift, or any of those from the start of the century, in which the young squaderbug is begged by his factor, John Wrott, to pay at least some of his creditors.

At the British Library, also owed thanks, the great mines were the microfilm records of the vividly abusive press of the 1720s and 30s, dominated by Bolingbroke's opposition paper, *The Craftsman* and the prim, nagging and judgemental diary, in a decent handscript, of Sir John Perceval. Overall, the judgement of David Starkey that 'the justification of history is that it is fascinating' never seemed more true.

I must acknowledge debts to those who have read this book, in whole or part, and made welcome and important criticisms. Lord Rowlands, a student of the early period with a special interest in Robert Harley, concentrated very helpful comment on the opening section, while Dr David Carlton of Warwick University, an old friend, gave very good advice on the conclusion. The Right Reverend Christopher Hill,

Bishop of Guilford, has kindly read and commented on the chapter about Walpole and the Church. I must also thank Professor Robert Giddings for open-handed loans of valuable and essential books which, in the fashionable style, he later converted into donations. Dr Perry Gauci of Lincoln College, Oxford, has read and commented on the full text, guided the author with shrewd points and given enormous encouragement. Richard Collins for Jonathan Cape has been his customary friendly and impeccable self, elegantly editing a far from flawless text. (The distinction between Hanover and Hannover is intended.) Final thanks are due, as in respect of every book I have published, to my wife, Deanna, who has done everything else, which is to say a great deal.

Edward Pearce
Thormanby
North Yorkshire
October 2006

THE STATE OF PLAY

In 1685, when Robert Walpole was nine years old, the Earl of Argyll, arriving on the Kintyre peninsula, raised his standard against the new king, James II, with the proclamation, 'No Prelacy, No Erastianism'.[1] Even by the standards of the theological seventeenth century in theologically minded Scotland it sounds a bit odd. But the disputes which whirled about Britain over the forty or so years between the Popish Plot and the early days of George I were grounded in religion. And it was the sort of religion which bubbled over through the doctrines of divine right and non-resistance into raw politics of the Humpty-Dumpty sort: 'Who is to be master?' And Robert Walpole, forty years after Argyll had been beheaded for his serious-minded presumption, would make that question his chief concern.

There is no way of understanding the cool, political manager of the eighteenth century without understanding the unmastered, passionate and violent years of the late seventeenth in which he grew up. In 1685, 'erastianism', the primacy of government over the Church, meant conformity to a king's notion of God and how to worship him. The Whig party, which Walpole would turn into an engine of control, derived its name from the Scottish word 'Whiggamore' or 'Whiggamer', meaning 'driver'. The original Whigs, driving hard against God's anointed, were essentially an armed and fighting resistance to the view of Charles II and James II that Scotland should be subdued from her own notions of religion and governed by bishops deferring to the central power.

Such government would be enforced against revolt, brutally by the Earl of Lauderdale, mercifully by the Duke of Monmouth and with peculiar ferocity by the troops of James Graham of Claverhouse, otherwise 'Bonnie Dundee' and yet otherwise 'Bloody Clavers'. He invoked penal confinement on the Bass Rock and in Dunottar Castle, torture involving thumbscrews (a Muscovite innovation), the leg-crushing mechanism called 'the Boot' and quite enough hangings to make his point. It was a definition of erastianism to give Argyll's motto distinct immediacy.

These first Whigs might be narrow and overzealous Calvinists, but they made up a genuinely popular movement and were the bitterest opponents of imperious central government. The intended smear of using their name to describe the English supporters of Lord Shaftesbury, opponents of the crown as worn by Charles II, was accepted with pride. Religion came into the English conflict too. A subordinated Church went naturally with an imperious government. The Stuarts were erastians whenever they got the chance, and whenever they got the chance they were absolutists as well.

Charles II is a man hard to pin down, clever, intellectually curious in a lazy way, kindly and vindictive by turns, devoted to responsive ladies and little dogs and remote from serious religious conviction. Tolerant until driven by provocation to intolerance, Charles was as corrupt in a corporate way as parliamentary underfunding could make him. And needing the money, he signed up pridelessly to the secret Treaty of Dover (1670) and to Louis XIV. That undertaking gave him hard cash and a degree of independence from Parliament. Though if Charles, in his cynical way, could help it, there would also be independence of Louis. If the King of France, a man sweatingly devout, wanted in return both Charles's own conversion and every effort to save England for the True Faith, such things could be promised for delivery when the time was right, which would be some other time.

If Charles's opponents, the new-named English Whigs, had grasped the depth of his all-round agnosticism, they would have breathed easier. The sanest of all the Stuarts (not a high distinction), he was nearer the deism of the next century than any earnest Catholic or Protestant of his day could imagine. But against such coolness, in an age of royal absolutism, it would have been an odd king who did not hanker after getting some of it for himself. The King of England, financially fettered by an elected assembly, argued at by pamphleteers and with the events of 1642–60 everywhere resonant, was an odd king out. But the acts of opponents pushed him in the direction of self-help.

Opposition which reasonably feared the intentions of Charles's brother and heir, James, Duke of York, and wished to exclude him from the succession, had in 1678 taken the discreditable turn of the so-called Popish Plot. Titus Oates, an uncomplicated villain, had exploded centre stage like a demon king, claiming knowledge of a Catholic plot to suborn the nation, kill the King and generally take over. Affinities with Senator Joseph McCarthy in the United States of the early 1950s have been made to the point of tedium, but ready conviction that the Russians were coming did match parallel broad belief in an imminent Catholic conquest.

When, by pure luck, one of Oates's random charges – against James II's secretary, a zealot and convert, Edward Coleman – turned out to be true, nonsense acquired plausibility and a course of inquisition, pursuit and the judicial murder of several perfectly innocent Catholic priests and laymen followed. The intellectual Jesuit, John Wall, the Irish priest, Charles Mahoney and the well-loved eighty-year-old Nicholas Postgate, ministering to the moorland villages behind Whitby, all died during the hysteria, essentially for being Catholic priests, and in Mahoney's case for the further aggravation of being an Irishman.

But the fear so readily lit by Oates's false witness was not altogether irrational. Catholicism threatened, not through the Pope, however often the English burned him in effigy, but in the person of Louis XIV, who, triumphalist in religion and foreign policy, turned periodically in his lurching way to invading his neighbours, with the Netherlands first in line. This was done for the glory of Louis of course, but where they were not Catholics, with a further hope of bringing the consolations of that faith vigorously to them. In 1684 this same Louis had revoked France's guarantee of toleration, the Edict of Nantes,* proclaimed by Henri IV, and commenced a persecution of French Protestants more wholesale and longer lasting than the Popish Plot.

The *dragonades*, forced billetings of dragoons in wrong-believing households, and the small, savage war fought in Languedoc to turn Calvinists into the wilderness, produced a flight from France of perhaps 100,000 very often creative, entrepreneurial people, not balanced by any Catholic flight from England. It was a further measure of what absolutism could do in religion that Louis turned his wrath upon the Jansenists, good Catholics, mostly priests or monastics, with certain

---

* The revocation was itself the Edict of Fontainebleau.

interesting uncanonical thoughts, and razed their little centre of reflection, the Abbé of Port Royale, to the ground.

It was a further irony of the time that Louis, devout beyond the
requirements of bigotry, found himself, for reasons of pure politics –
who would command the priests? – in a descending spiral of bitter
conflict with the Pope. Innocent XI (Benedetto Odescalchi), reckoned
the ablest pontiff of the century at his death in 1689, was within a step
of excommunicating the King. Innocent disliked the brutalities of Louis's
dragonades and, while welcoming James's accession, was, in the words
of a papal historian, 'suspicious of his subservience to Louis XIV and
disapproved of his ill-judged methods of restoring Roman Catholicism
in the country'.[2] But the quarrel which would lead Louis to seize the
papal city of Avignon hung again upon mastery. The King was determined to choose (and control) all the French bishops and called the
system 'Gallicanism'. This too was a policy entirely erastian.

English dislike of Catholicism was not the prerogative of a mouthing
mob. George Savile, Marquess of Halifax, who would show James
personal loyalty until his collapse was self-evident, and the philosopher,
Locke, were anti-Catholic as an extension of being anti-absolutist. In
the last decades of the seventeenth century prejudice and political liberalism touched fingers by coincidence, with Whiggism at its high point
containing the materials of full freedom of conscience. Halifax later
told Gilbert Burnet, another, more pious Whig (he was after all Bishop
of Salisbury), that 'He was a Christian in submission; he believed as
much as he could, and hoped that God would not lay it to his charge
that he could not digest iron as an ostrich did.'[3]

Financial circumstances and inclination had made two successive
heads of a not very important country the dependants and pensioners
of the greatest King in Europe. If the details of the Treaty of Dover or
the correspondence of the French ambassador, Paul Barrillon, had
become public, Charles, for all his endearing insincerity, would have
been esteemed a traitor. As it was, opposition had overreached itself
during the exclusion crisis. It stumbled, and the opportunity for Stuart
absolutism was grasped. For the last four years of his life, Charles II
had instituted a direct form of personal government with no Parliament
and thus no parliamentary restraints, calling in town and city charters
to intrude royal power there. (In Scotland, under James's rule there,
the physical repression, which Professor Ogg thought worse than the
dragonades,[4] was stepped up.)

There are academic arguments as to how far the new diktat was inspired and pushed by James with a French contribution, and how far Charles was acting, in anger and design, on his own account. But acting he was; opposition was dispersed, Shaftesbury fled to Holland, dying there soon after. The Whiggism, to which Robert Walpole's father ardently subscribed, was discredited, the politics of Outs who might now be out for ever. Centralised monarchical government and a subordinate role as the brisk, fond lackey of a France ready for another round of Continental invasions seemed assured.

The death of Charles on 6 February 1685 removed a lazy, clever man, resorting late to despotic means, and brought in one not actually unintelligent but lacking judgement, compassion or sense, to whom they were the only proper form of government. James was also more Catholic than the Pope, certainly than this Pope. In Scotland he continued 'thorough', James's term for his own earlier ungentle governorship there. Defeat of the precipitate rising in the west of England led by the Duke of Monmouth, Charles's son by his first serious mistress, Lucy Walter, was followed by the hangings, quarterings and boilings of the quarters in tar before public display of 350 rank and file men, miners, cloth-workers and small tenants, around an assize circuit of Salisbury, Dorchester, Exeter, Taunton, Wells and Bristol. It was garlanded by the burning alive of an elderly lady, Alice Lyle, who had given refuge to two men in flight. Attempts have been made at revision of the odious reputation of James's instrument in this, Lord Chief Justice Jeffreys. The first response was right; this was a man whom no revision can mend.

The Assize was an assertion of power and inducement of fear. It would have worked – atrocious acts commonly do. James was in no danger. As an outstanding historian of the period argued[5] in December 1687, a year before James's downfall, he would nowhere have been thought in danger. He was irritating people and being silly, but the normal props of a king – gentry, army and Church – stood at any rate three and three-quarter square behind him. The cruelties of the western circuit would count against him only in rationalised retrospect. But crimes were compounded by mistakes, aggressive mistakes.

James brought religion and religious politics back into contention by threatening the institutional powers of the Church of England. The language was that of toleration. The King's Declaration of Indulgence offered to Roman Catholics and Dissenters alike something of the liberty which the modern Western mind cannot imagine any faith being denied. But the Declaration did not simply derogate from the primacy of the Anglican Church; it came from James whom nobody quite believed and it came on behalf of the Catholic interest which had just revoked the Edict of Nantes. Halifax, who actually believed in toleration, was unimpressed.

> This alliance between Liberty and infallibility is bringing together the two most contrary things which are in the world. The Church of Rome doth not only dislike the allowing liberty, but by its principles it cannot do it . . . the continuation of their kindness would be a habit of sin, of which they are to repent, and their absolution is to be had upon no other terms than their promise to destroy you. You are therefore to be hugged now, only that you be the better squeezed at another time.[6]

James talked toleration, but his proposals did not have the connotation of toleration in the comfortable contemporary sense of living and letting live, the co-existence of faiths. The Test and Corporation Acts which he proposed to suspend were iniquitous in principle. But once removed and with a driving activist pushing Catholics into the influential places from which they were no longer barred – local magistracies, Lord-Lieutenancies of the counties and commissions in the army and militia – he was talking the infiltration of power. In the early days it was only talk, green paper stuff, a scouting of the ground and thoughts about policy. But Tyrconnel, his man in Ireland, had filled officers' places with Catholics, something which had everything to do with military leverage and nothing to do with fair play for the Irish.

In England, the royal dispensing power would shortly set aside the barrier against a similar operation there. In practice it would have been too great an undertaking for the limited and distinctly leery Catholic population to cope with. But any bogey was of the King's own making. And with his Minister, Sunderland, setting an example, the conversion of rising men, the sacrament of the career was feared and expected. The role of Samuel Parker, fellow traveller, Catholic convert and holder of the Anglican See of Oxford, had pushed toleration to a precipitous height.

Such developments were seriously feared in all the rural places which would have given James simple traditionalist Tory loyalty. No one actually said 'The Country is in danger' but it was a profound and perfectly rational assumption. And the King had been busy about an extensive programme, working through a commission to place busy Catholic activists, cadres rather, in the high places of education, government and the army.

The evidence was coming all too specifically home. A questionnaire had been circulated among justices and militia officers asking if they would support the Declaration of Indulgence and serve as, or support, MPs implementing such change. The answers amounted to a collective body swerve of evasion and abstention which James chose to see as outright defiance. The consequence was a burst of activity by the commission so that between February and April 1688 a massive cull of local office holders took place across the shires, and a bloc of Catholics and those hugged Dissenters was brought in.

The territory where Robert Walpole's father was an active participant shows startling figures. In the two counties of Norfolk and Wiltshire, the 143 JPs at the start of the reign (almost all Tories incidentally) had dwindled, leaving only eighteen still in place by the summer of 1688. This was an attack on the ruling class, a humiliation and demotion of greater and lesser noble and gentry families whose voices were customarily heard with respect in Westminster and St James's because they were heard as immediate authority in the county town. The people through whom a king ruled were being turned into ones who, owing him nothing but their degradation, now contemplated the option of not being ruled by him at all.

As with the gentry, so with the clergy. The leaders of the Church of England were preponderantly Tories, James's own men to the death if he had possessed an atom of tact or manners. And in setting them to proclaim the undermining of their own ecclesiastical state from their own pulpits, he was testing them to destruction, or rather its Anglican equivalent, resistance! Those familiar with the Vicar of Bray will recall that 'When royal James possessed the Crown, / And Popery grew in fashion; / The Penal Law I hooted down, / And read the Declaration'. Seven Anglican bishops did not give as sharp a lead to their clergy as legend proclaims. Nominally headed by Sancroft of Canterbury, they refused, with a profuse elaboration of reverence, to obey a king bent more frantically than most kings upon obedience. It was an act in defence of an interest, the Church established supreme by law. But it took the doctrine of non-resistance, so much preached from Anglican pulpits, and broke it into several pieces.

And by bringing James as prosecutor to court, their consequent trial brought another of the institutions and interests of England into play. When the judges acquitted Sancroft, Lloyd, Ken, Turner, Trelawny and Lake, they ranged the settled and not-to-be-meddled-with institutions of England against a king whose acts began now to be weighed only as aspirations. It would take the desertion of his leading general and the inactivity of his naval commander to complete the circle of James's self-destruction.

The inclination of William of Orange, Stadhouder of the Netherlands and James's nephew directly and by marriage, to invade England derived from his very reasonable fear of the alliance between James and Louis. The King of France had attempted the conquest of the Netherlands in the 1670s and his chief Minister, Colbert, had stated the realities then with wonderful succinctness: 'If the king subdues all the United Provinces of the Netherlands, their commerce will become the commerce of the subjects of His Majesty, and there will be nothing more desirable.'[7] He hadn't succeeded, but Charles II had been France's ally. And in 1688, with James as a French creature, William was determined to get his retaliation in first.

His opportunity came from the preoccupation of Louis with extending his quarrel with the Pope by invading the Rhein-Pfalz in a campaign of outstanding cruelty, the outcome of furious disputes with Pope and Emperor, one of them over appointing a new Archbishop of Cologne. The territory and the long-simmering dispute with the Emperor in Vienna were at the forefront of Louis's mind. Otherwise, having some intelligence of William's possible intentions, he might have reflected that the Rhein-Pfalz is a long way from the Dutch border. Making an incursion there was an unwise move for any ruler who thought that his retaliatory power protected the King of England.

William's *occasion* came on 30 June with an invitation from a group of English notables, also as it happens, seven, grandees of title and landholding, that he should come into England with an army. But even before they wrote, James, rebuffed by bishops and court, had already started back-pedalling at speed, dissolving his commission and restoring town charters, suggesting the weakness and vulnerability which, more than oppression, provokes attack. He had managed over forty months to frighten, offend, alienate and unite against him the ruling classes of England.

But in June a happy event quite did for him. The birth, after fifteen years of marriage to the apparently barren Maria Beatrice of Modena, of a son, perfectly cleanly and legitimately, implied a Catholic dynasty and a political godson to Louis XIV. (It also closed off William's prospects of legitimate succession through his wife and his own rank as a grandson of Charles I.) The doctrine of non-resistance to the King's most sacred Majesty was all very well, but even to the ardent Tory loyalists, who talked of little else, its implied consequences no longer seemed worth the candle. Non-resistance could be taken up later, a shadow game in comfortable retrospect with a safer sort of monarchy properly established. As for the baby, he was instantly libelled as a lowborn changeling brought in, hidden in a warming pan, by the midwife, Judith Wilkes, and was destined to live a pale life as the pious and diffident repository of a losing side's graceful legend, James Francis Edward Stuart, the Old, and increasingly tired, Pretender.

Having chosen Torbay* in preference to Bridlington and benefited from the English naval commander Dartmouth's careful deference to delaying winds, William landed and made less a march than a progress west to east, part way through which John Churchill, the general sent against him, when he was already in conversation with the letter senders, changed sides and entered his camp. The reaction of James back in London was one of panic and prayer. 'The Virgin Mary is to do all' said his profane Lord Chancellor, Jeffreys.

It has been seen as a sort of nervous breakdown, but his failure of will had an inspirational effect. Desertion was widespread and included the defections of the King's daughter, Princess Anne, her husband, George of Denmark, and Henry Compton, the one bishop who knew exactly what he was doing, which, in this case, was ushering the Princess to Nottingham and the forces of Lord Devonshire's non-loyalist muster. No reliance was placed upon the soldiers of what, a few months earlier, had been looked upon as the King's standing army to subdue the nation. James fled by water, was stopped in Faversham harbour, was robbed, returned, his second escape contrived by the new authorities and fled again, inevitably to France.

What would be called the 'Glorious Revolution' had been a combination of slow-motion coup, bluff-calling and implosion of authority. If legitimacy turned upon inheritance, there was no legitimacy. And to many people of the day, inheritance, even if strained, did matter. It was very important that William's wife, Mary, James's Protestant daughter

---

* Paignton actually.

by a first marriage, had a claim as next in line, something which made the warming pan nonsense a vital fiction, a lie of state. James was initially described as having 'abdicated', something the Church and King men disliked, so he was said to have 'deserted'. There had been no invasion, no coup, just a vacuum which nature on this occasion had rather liked. To fill it, the Tories would have preferred Mary as sole Queen, with William as Regent. William, a claimant in his own right, indicated that there was urgent business in the Netherlands to which perhaps he should return immediately. And the negotiators settled, happily enough, for William and Mary, joint sovereigns, justifiable in different ways to different consciences, the consciences of Whig and Tory.

The lines of early eighteenth-century politics were being drawn in the last decade of the seventeenth, but drawn very loosely in terms of groups of interests and opinions. There would now be stability by the lights of the shuddering, pre-crisis days of James, but it was as volatile as stability gets. The opposition had been calling across the century for regular parliaments, something better than prorogation tempered by supply. 'Annual parliaments' said radicals, something echoed long after by the Chartists. The solution, agreed to eventually in 1695, was the Triennial Act. That appealed to the left and principled wing of Whiggism. It made for vigorous politics, ready changes and an excitement which managerial politicians, and the King, at first resisted.

That liberal wing looked to wider liberties, fuller representation and, among Protestants at least, something better than toleration, a wide and accommodating church roof with the tests drawn faintly. That put them at odds with the reflexes of the Church of England as vested interest, body corporate and institution wonderfully preoccupied with itself. 'The Church in Danger' was a proposition as dubious as the warming pan, but paranoid anxiety that the heirs of Cromwell and the Levellers hid behind the plain people worshipping God with few cere-monies and no bishops, prospered in every second rectory.

The Comprehension Act, proposed in 1689 and never to be, is one of the great might-have-beens of history, a Church settlement without the fine filters of doctrinal allrightness of the Test and Corporation Acts. In fact, the bitterest quarrels dividing Whig and Tory would involve legislative attempts to keep Dissenters out of place and office by imposing tests of orthodoxy. Similarly, there were thoughts of wider representation and about resisting the systemic corruption of rotten boroughs and their patrons. The thoughts of 1831 stirred in 1690, but they were not encouraged.

About one thing Whigs were agreed: they were the war party. If William feared the France of Louis XIV, so did they. Louis would do what he could to restore James to the throne, at first through the campaign in Ireland and prospectively through incursions. He was also approaching the European campaign against the Emperor in north-west Germany and the Spanish Netherlands which menaced William in the United Provinces. Fear of subordination to the dominant power, hope for trade and obvious shared interests with the Continental alliance against Louis brought Britain in 1692 into the first of two wars. Any politician hoping to make his way in the Whig interest would be clear about two things: France must be resisted and war was the patriotic interest and should be pursued. It was the commanding doctrine of the next two decades and the young Robert Walpole, later to rejoice at continuous peace founded upon close and amiable understanding with France, agreed to it as strongly as anyone.

But in the 1690s the war party were recurringly sustained in, or brought back to, power by the eccentricities of the King of France. Louis was making war on and off, harassed by domestic misery, the destituting crop failures of 1693-4 which had peasants in some areas eating grass. If Louis went to war, he rushed to do it; if he wanted to get out, his scramble to end it involved him in weak terms, a fire sale of his original objectives. He also had a weakness for the grand, cost-disregarding gesture. The Peace of Ryswick which ended the first conflict in 1697 had stipulated French recognition of William's full status as King. When the former James II finally died on 16 September 1701, the Pretender was hastily recognised as James III, florid sweep of the arm rather than considered *démarche*, but one seen in Britain as the clearest declaration of hostile intent.

The English succession had been resolved in 1700 after another death, that of Princess Anne's only surviving child, poor William of Gloucester, ailing all his short, calculated-over life. A decision about the succession after Anne's then remotely projected death had been postponed in the deliberations over the Bill of Rights because of his birth. William dead, and his mother, who even at thirty-five was far from healthy, it was made in the Act of Settlement. The inheritance of Sophia of Hanover and her heirs was proclaimed. Louis might/might not think the claims to the crown of James's son worth sponsoring, but the gesture had drawn him in. Arguments from the pacific Tories about costly wars in far away countries on behalf of Johnny Foreigner were doomed by all the fears of suborning and invasion implicit in that chevalieresque gesture. The element of damn fool in Louis XIV should never be underestimated.

But the Whigs needed all the patriotism they could get. The fact of the revolution and 'their' king on the throne had not made them the national majority party. Only James's Roman Catholicism and French sympathies kept them respectable. They could be identified, like all parties of change, with their furthest left wing, and according to the Grub Street journalist Ned Ward, a *Sun* columnist out of his time, with the suppositious Calves' Head clubs, widely alleged, nowhere proved, to meet in celebration of the execution of Charles I. The Whigs were the heirs, it was said, of rebels and traitors, Cromwell, Commonwealth Men, Monmouth, the Rye House plotters. Worse, they were a bunch of meddling intellectuals. Luke Milbourne, a Tory preacher, made himself clear about the Calves' Head clubmen – 'O, may our souls never come into the secrets of such men, nor our honours be united in their assemblies' – before going on to identify them with 'all our Knoxes, Buchanans, Miltons, Sidneys, Lockes and the like Agents of Darkness'.[8]

Not for nothing did the Reverend Milbourne make that speech on 30 January. It was the anniversary of the execution of Charles I, or, to any Tory clergyman, his martyrdom. It was solemnly kept as a day of fast and humiliation in such circles, also as a pulpit opportunity for fulminating clergymen. Whig clergy, fewer, and for the most part, calmer, reserved their *festa* for the good Protestant anniversary, 5 November, Captain Fawkes's attempt at parliamentary combustion *and* William's landing at Torbay. But there was an inherent strength in the Tory position which they were not fully able to exploit. For all the quality of the leading Whig minds, including Algernon Sidney and John Locke whom Dr Milbourne had consigned to Hell, they did not have extensive currency.

Arguments for a contract between King and people were put with more persuasive intelligence by lay pamphleteers like James Tyrrell and the outstanding Low Church Bishop of Bangor, Benjamin Hoadley. But the national temper was conservative, and the conservatism reflected the prevailing view of the Church. Anglicanism was as hierarchical as Roman Catholicism. It stood upon obedience rather than developing argument. Being hierarchical, it was profoundly royalist, a royalism translated into the doctrine of non-resistance, a sort of truculent servility, and one they urged upon their flocks. The most influential political theorist of the day was not Locke, Sidney or Halifax, but the long-dead cavalier apologist, Sir Robert Filmer, whose *Patriarcha; A Defence of the Natural Power of Kings against the Unnatural Power of People*, a candid title, had been dug out and published in the absolutist eighties. Filmer urged that the obedience of children to fathers echoed and exampled all the obediences from Adam (literally) through Jewish prophets and Roman Emperors down to the very latest Most Sacred Majesty. John Locke was for the future, Filmer, who had written it in the 1640s, for the here and now. *Patriarcha* was a text mightily alluded to, and Filmer himself, in the words of Peter Laslett, 'that extremely rare phenomenon, the codifier of conscious and unconscious prejudice'.[9] In the war of pamphlets which would rage across the years after the Glorious Revolution, the commonest coin was a more glorious submission.

The problem for the Tory churchmen, or High-Flyers, was that the logic of their own position was Jacobitism. Non-resistance meant non-resistance to *any* king, including James, against whose intrusions into the privileges and autonomy of the Church of England they had petitioned. Once they had indeed resisted the King who tried to pack the Masters' lodgings in Oxford, the only argument left to them was exceptionalism, resistance in emergency which, as the foundation for an absolute dogma, lacked all credibility. This brought a bright thread of absurdity into the phenomenon of the non-jurors, Anglican clergy refusing the oath of loyalty to the usurper, William. Such was the intellectual confusion of the High Church party that five of the seven bishops whose trial had triggered James's fall became non-jurors, with Archbishop Sancroft topping off the nonsense by briefly hanging on to Canterbury and its revenues and hiring suffragans to consecrate new bishops. They would be consecrating Whigs; non-juring was as bad politics as logic. The takers of this high and self-defeating line were deprived of their sees and new low-flyers appointed.

The King, at war from 1692 to 1697, was rather too busy to be overly troubled by baroque consciences, and politically he sought governments functioning on a non-party or all-party basis. But the Whigs, specifically what were called the Junto Whigs, clear-cut and hard-driving partisans, were so definitely the war party, a group whose members had warned of French aggression for twenty years, as to be his natural, unavoidable allies. Ironically, the Machiavelli urging their advance was Robert Spencer, Earl of Sunderland. Sunderland of course had been for most of the previous reign at James's ear, engaging in, where he did not instigate, the worst affronts to constitutional practice and the Anglican interest. And he had underwritten his credentials by turning Catholic, before deserting just ahead of the Revolution, when he fled with discernment, not to the long doom of French exile, but to Holland. Having recycled himself in the Anglican confession before demonstrating his usefulness to a sceptical William, he was a vivid measure of just how flexible the late seventeenth century could be.

The Junto, though they worked untrustingly with the new, improved Sunderland, were, as the saying goes, tightly knit. Their core – Somers, Wharton, Montague, Edward Russell – functioned, often away from London at a member's country house, more like a cabinet than any group of ministers seen so far. They were able to do so precisely because they were doing something quite new – relying upon and commanding a majority in Parliament. The beginnings of the conscious, systematic parliamentary management of which Robert Walpole would be the triumphant and finished master were stimulated by the deft Tory opposition of Harley and Foley.

Wharton is almost a first and extravagant draft of Walpole, a coarse, uncourtly election agent and machine politician of a very high order. The Junto ministry of the mid-nineties were, in a rough way, efficient, engaged in naval reform and war finance, not to mention the creation of the Bank of England, and persuading William in 1695 to accept a declaratory Triennial Act. A measure enhancing Parliament by requiring elections every three years was the logical act for men on terms with the King but holding further power in Parliament. They might be a war party and anti-French, and they were clearly empowerers of the Commons. But they were also defining Whiggism as an organisation, something to be run in the fullness of time by a Walpole determined for peace and friendly to the French. In the longer term, institutions would be more important than policies.

But the Whigs of the nineties were less well placed than their successors of 1720 to consolidate power. Nothing is more fallacious than casual belief in the smooth, assured creation of a Whig and 'constitutional' century. The Junto Whigs were in a coincidence of interest with William, able to give him support in a foreign policy that, with Dutch advice, he largely conducted himself. Having them as his domestic government in England made unsentimental sense to him. But their grounding in natural popularity was thin, only strengthened by the war, which, like most wars, was a wasting asset. To so much of the Church and many people beyond it, the Whigs were not a party but a faction, and a rebellious faction at that, which, startlingly, had managed to rebel successfully.

All politics moved on a sea of ambiguity. The consensus was glad James had gone but wished that he had not been removed, wanted in kingship what it idealised, a son of the Church of England, blessed by God and long practice; didn't like what it had just had, a zealot upsetting long practice and the Church of England. William was necessary and clearly well above an evil, but still foreign. Lacking grace in either sense and precipitously come upon them, he deserved and got the cool loyalty owing to the least worst option, a loyalty he as coolly returned.

But the people loved his wife. Mary was one of them, as English as British royalty got to be.* Childless, she was a responsive, affectionate, for want of a better word, good, woman who disinterestedly loved her country which responded in kind and would grieve deep at her sudden death of smallpox at thirty-two. Mary II was a mirror of the English: knowing that her father had to go, sincerely opposed to his purposes, but guilty at having helped dethrone him, exactly the way they felt. The union with William had been a marriage of convention and, on his part, of rather perfunctory and preoccupied infidelity, but with a reticent, understated strand of love. It was expressed beautifully. Knowing that Mary had a sympathy above the age's for the broken victims of glorious war, William made over the grand new building at Greenwich to be a naval hospital, because she would have wanted it.

William himself was necessary, accepted, nothing stronger, though the clarity with which the necessity was seen showed vividly in reactions when a serious conspiracy against his life, the Turnham Green plot, was unearthed. The position of a political party or faction might be lifted by an act of treason against King and government, but the Whigs remained a ministry against the grain, an opposition fortuitously in power. And the Tories, in their own eyes a government in opposition, were developing aptitudes for exactly the management, electoral and camaral, accomplished by Wharton. This sort of leadership would come from the moderate wing of Toryism, former Country Whigs, unhesitating takers of the oath, supporters of the war within reason, men fit for office.

The chief figure in this circle, Robert Harley, was the oddest combination of tortuous intriguer and civilised statesman, not so much library

---

* Her mother, James's first wife, was Anne Hyde, daughter of Lord Clarendon.

squire back in Herefordshire as raging bibliophile, source of the Harleian. Pleasant, unranting, free from corruption but compulsively devious, Harley overtly preached moderation and, given a free run, wanted it. In ideal circumstances he thought, rather in the way of monarchs themselves, of coalitions of reasonable people in the centre, shading to Tory indeed but not hung with the sectarian clogs of the heavy Anglicans, like Sir Edward Seymour or his future nemesis and temperamental opposite, Henry St John.

He was a moderate man in an immoderate time. He not only derived from the old Country Whig opposition which had taken on Charles II in the seventies, and surfaced again to harass the Junto, but came originally from Dissent. One of the Junto leaders, outraged at 'the motley affair' of a coalition, spoke of it as the doing of 'a r[at] like Harley'. At the outset in 1696–7, Harley was running a Country and Tory alliance, but as time passed over the first decade of the new century the Tory identity, growing in frustration and rage, would come to dominate, not on merit or quality of leadership, but from numbers and the strength of its primitive purpose.

Party was forming, and it would not be a matter of clans and family groups with a thin political laminate. Academic argument has been through some bitter conflicts of its own when the ideas of Sir Lewis Namier (*The Structure of Politics at the Accession of George III*) were pushed by disciples into a mechanistic reduction of everything to a Lebanese or Scottish norm of kinship and clan alliance. Family links and friendships were important, of course, as the Walpoles would link upwardly with the Townshends and, a little below, with the Turners, but only as part of the woodwork of party, the way Norfolk Whigs organised themselves inside the Whig party. It is now generally accepted that politics, full-dress party politics under the meaning of the act, was alive and rather unnervingly well in the 1690s.

The effect of the Triennial Act of 1694 had been to set the pot bubbling even more busily and to make long periods of consolidation (or inertia) impractical. Politics, meaning patronage, elections, programmes, things done with voters in mind, was continuous. And party members functioned socially, with Whig and Tory coffee houses and taverns, party colours and, at the parliamentary level, increasing coordination and planning of government business. Substantial numbers engaged happily in what Soviet spokesmen would call 'Party Life'.

The political efficiency and cohesion of the Junto Whigs accompanied their run of domination; and the idea of a one and a half party state, what would actually happen across Walpole's twenty-one-year stewardship, was already hoped for and feared. The exertions of Harley and his kinsman and ally, Paul Foley, were a reaction to such excess of mastery. They lacked the Anglican paranoia of so many Tories, but they needed allies much as the High Tories, lacking warmth towards such sophisticated and moderate-minded men, needed intelligent leadership.

The two sides were distinguishable over the wars, Whigs ardently for, Tories acquiescent and looking for ways out. They divided more bitterly on the Dissenters, who to the Whigs were well-regarded allies for whom the Toleration Act had been passed at the outset of the Revolution. Failure to get a Cohesion Act, itself a consequence of churchly fears and selfishness, had left not just the working-class Baptists and theologically impossible Quakers and Unitarians, but the large, rich congregations, Independents and Presbyterians, outside the National Church, free to start building their meeting houses and doing so at a violent rate. The Dissenters were also offering better, because more modern and focused, education in their mushrooming academies than was available to the children of Church people. They were a concentration of business and money, influential in the City, with a couple of Lord Mayors at this time, one of whom took his procession, swordbearer and all, back for service in a dissenting chapel.

The Church of England, always sorry for itself, cherished as less a grievance than a profound wound the practice of 'Occasional Conformity'. This was a device, not unlike tax avoidance, for staying gracefully within the letter of the law while ignoring its imperious spirit. One qualified for civic office and full rights by taking the Anglican sacrament, but there was no specification of how often. Once a year would do and for large numbers of the less pedantic Dissenters, once a year did. The Church was enraged and obsessed, and a large part of Tory business in Parliament would be legislation to outlaw occasional conformity.

Though the real intensity was to build up later in the reign of Anne, the five bishops who refused the oaths had been joined by four hundred clergy, often making large sacrifices of comfort and wellbeing. There was a neurotic, self-martyring strain in all this, for no one was trying to hurt them; the oath had been softened with their consciences in

mind. Sophisticated Tories like Sir Simon Harcourt, a confederate of
Harley, would devise a form of oath to the 'King in Parliament'. He,
a monarch panoplied in law and assembly, should indeed not be resisted,
whereas a king *solus* was a fallible man, capable of being wrong.[10] But
despite best efforts, the Church, through its lay and clerical membership, was still a great body of discontent, in other words a political
resource.

The extent of unhappiness within the Church of England is beyond
dispute. Wearing their hats as Tories, which is to say upwards of three-
quarters of the parish and lesser cathedral clergy, they accepted William
of Orange through several differing degrees of limpness. For the High-
Flyers, influenced by the ideas of Charles I's dervish-like Primate, William
Laud, this order was the binding together of throne and Church into
a sacred union with obedience to the first intimating, at the very least,
deep deference to the second. As members of one authorised organisation, they were horrified to find that the Toleration Act had set free
competitors, those other Protestant congregations, using their new
legality to build meeting places and fill them.

Still privileged, Anglicanism was no longer compulsory. Back in 1662,
shortly after the Restoration, 1800 clergymen had been driven out of
their benefices for Presbyterian leanings. A public set free to worship
where it wished was now following them, abandoning the parish church
in unmistakable numbers. In areas where Puritanism had flourished in
a subterranean way, people walked away from the parish church in the
same unmistakable numbers. Beyond such tribulations, the career landscape of the established Church showed hillocks, ridges, hills and small
mountains of lush benefices above a great plain of parish clergy, poor
in a ground-down way still true when Trollope wrote about the Perpetual
Curate of Hogglestock.

The response to all these tribulations showed in the bitter hostility
of Tory chapters to Whig bishops; and increasingly, of course, bishops
were Whigs! In Convocation the Lower House was simply unmanage-
able. It had wrecked the Comprehension proposals, set itself with much
virulence to block the designs of bishops and demand autonomy from
them. Non-resistance hardly described it. The bishops responded in
ironical echo of the Stuart Kings to Parliament by indefinite prorogation! The feeling existed among such turbulent, resentful men that they
were living in an occupied country. One clergyman, admittedly an
extremist, put it plainly to a friend. The death of King William in 1702

was 'the most joyful day he had seen in thirteen years'.[11] But we shall hear more from Dr Henry Sacheverell later.

This was the savage far edge of clerical discontent. But the general High Church malaise articulated a Tory quality – ambiguous feelings about the Revolution and yet more the succession. People unwilling to swear to William, objectionable as a Calvinist as well as a Dutchman, would be loyal to the churchwoman, Anne, but a sentiment for the Pretender lay there. It tied in with notions of the monarch as the immediate and particular servant of God and of the almost sacramental duty owed to him. A James Edward Stuart heeding this-worldly Catholic priests and making his own act of symbolic conformity with Canterbury would have been very serious politics.

But in 1700, with William of Gloucester dead and no accredited Protestant heir, something had to be done. And in the Act of Settlement, the long contemplated Electress of Hanover, chatelaine of Herrenhausen, but granddaughter of James I, was, with her heirs, so designated by Parliament. Here, before High Churchmen and strong Tories, was God's Regent appointed by a legislature! A response of overt Jacobitism was not to be discounted. It had violent and intimidating street support by way of a London mob, the Jacks. It had substantial sympathetic roots, and it had a future. No one would quite have guessed in 1701, when Robert Walpole entered Parliament as Member for Castle Rising that that future would be as the greatest liability of the Tory party.

'I WAS IN HOPES YOU WOULD HAVE . . . PAYED'

If background matters, and it is generally reckoned to, then Robert Walpole was very lucky. He was born on 26 August 1676 into a county family. It was not an aristocratic one, though his grandfather had been knighted. He was born to no current title, but to a manor, a position high in local precedence and one holding, for when he needed it, a web of cousinage whose writs moved within the county. His grandfather, Sir Edward, had been a Member of Parliament for the port of King's Lynn. His father, also Robert, known as Colonel Walpole from a militia rank, handsome as the son would never be, did anticipate that son's intelligence. Although he would buy a pack of hounds to gain good-will with neighbours, Colonel Robert was by inclination a library squire, a reader of the classics, of Edmund Spenser and, in particular, of the dry ironies of Francis Bacon, of almost all of whose works he had copies.[1]

Young Robert's maternal grandfather, Sir Jeffrey Burwell, came from the same happy niche, a knight, but trained in the law, with land near a Walpole property in Suffolk and, on the strength of his taste in sermons,* something of a Puritan. It fitted a pattern. This was Eastern Association country; radical Cambridge was its university. The abso-lutist aspirations of Stuart kings had many opponents there, and though the Walpoles had a remoter Catholic history, including a late sixteenth-century martyr and a couple of Jesuits,[2] all that had been put behind

---

* Sir John Plumb relates in *Sir Robert Walpole*, vol. I, p. 83, that he gave his daughter three volumes of the sermons of the Calvinistic William Perkins of Christ's College, Cambridge.

them and their religion was unambiguously Protestant. In the contests, political and religious, related above, conflicts dimming only very slowly over the sixty-eight years of his life, Robert Walpole knew where he would stand.

The Walpoles were not rich, and Colonel Walpole lived sparely, with wine and books the only luxuries, looking for economies despite the instincts of an intelligent but careless wife, and applying himself to agricultural improvement in the hope of betterment. It has been reckoned that progress in agriculture from the late seventeenth until deep into the eighteenth century ran down a diagonal line from striving Norfolk to pre-wheel Cornwall. Sea-born proximity to dynamic Holland, doing wonders on the same flat, rich, often reclaimed, land, had given the county, in an age of laborious communication, a lead, together with Cambridgeshire, Northants and Leicestershire, over remoter western areas. Crop rotation, marling and winter fodder crops were quickly taken up here. Devotion to the doubly useful, soil-enriching, winter diet-providing turnip would tag a neighbour, colleague and brother-in-law 'Turnip Townshend'. Jonathan Swift's remark about the man who made two blades of grass grow where one grew before being more meritable than the whole race of politicians, though aimed at Walpole and his circle, had long been pre-emptively embraced by Walpole's people, the land-improving politicians of Norfolk.

This was also an area where enclosure advanced most swiftly. A Walpole neighbour, Thomas Coke, 'Coke of Holkham', as well as being a fervent improver was the leading encloser in the country. The strong farmer, to use an Irish term, benefited from the legal costs and general burden put upon small and captive participants in the enclosure of common land. Bankruptcy and distressed sales recurringly did their Hobbesian thing. At the end of his life, Coke remarked, 'I am become the ogre at the feast. I have eat up all my neighbours.' Robert Walpole was entering a time in which competition, the business of going down and going up in the world, would accelerate. Politically, he would be a noted encloser and eater-up himself.

Colonel Robert had a different standing. He was small gentry, financially stretched, though moving slowly up, mortgaged but buying land. But he was chiefly respected for himself, trusted as honest and capable and accordingly sought out and consulted on other people's business, as in the complex probate problems attaching to the will of Sir Thomas

Hare of Stow Bardolph.[3] And he was rated highly enough toward the end of his short life to make a successful bid for Parliament. Observing that Castle Rising, formerly a fief of the Howards, was vulnerable, and having some house property there, he bought more. This was a burgage borough, one where the vote belonged to householders or occupants, and a very small burgage borough at that.

He would be accepted by the Howards as someone tolerable for the junior seat, almost all constituencies being two-Member affairs. With that noble family slackening control, the Colonel, in 1695, formed a syndicate with friends, the Turners, the Hostes and his brother, Horatio, despite his being a Tory. He made enough running for the Howards to concede him nomination of the town mayoralty in alternate years, but not the second seat which, by way of a nominee, would have begun a connection and the gratifying rewards which accompanied it.[4] But he had made a start. The younger Robert would have a seat to inherit and the first family essays had been made at a parliamentary grouping. The Walpoles were acquiring consequence, small gentry very much on the rise. Humphrey Prideaux, Dean of Norwich, who watched trends in local politics like a psephologist, identified the two interests in Norfolk politics, and in January 1700 identified the faction 'which now prevails',[5] that of the Duke of Norfolk allied with the elder Robert Walpole. The Dean was also very much aware of the prospective influence in the county of the Townshend family. The prime candidate for Lord-Lieutenant on the death of the current Duke of Norfolk was the young Charles Townshend, 2nd Viscount. With a family electoral base in Great Yarmouth, he was seen at the end of the century as a soothing compromise, to 'remove all manner of divisions out of the countrey [*sic*] . . . which for 25 years hath been continually harassed with them'.[6]

Meanwhile, Robert himself was acquiring education, first at a local boarding school in Great Dunham, then as a commoner at Eton, already a pre-eminent school, if one with overtones of a learned borstal. He had been intended for the Church and one can only try to imagine the lesser career which a Reverend Robert Walpole might have made. In a time of political religion and religious politics, he would have been Low Church, perhaps Latitudinarian, a clergyman with the very best of Whig connections in Norfolk and beyond, which he would have played upon remorselessly. He had the mind as a young man for essential reading, huge talents for disputation; and instead of pithy political pamphlets, he would have written sermons and broadsides quite as pithy in defence of the Church policy of the Whig ministers who would have managed his preferment. One can contemplate a key chaplaincy in, say, a Russell household, a living by the advowson of such a family for income, with a curate to run it, a prebend for more income, access to a fashionable pulpit and an early archdeaconry for status. After which, a procession of smaller and greater sees, with Lincoln reached via St Asaph and Lichfield, might very readily have produced Archbishop Walpole.

As it was, while he was at Cambridge, inevitably King's College, his elder brother Edward, who was to have owned the land and been Member for Castle Rising, abruptly died. In spring 1698, Robert was recalled to Houghton. For the interim he would be concerned with the estate, with turnips and fodder grasses. But Walpole, the sound farming gentleman, getting moderately rich by husbandry and financial restraint, is less imaginable than his ascent to the papacy. During this interim a marriage was arranged with Catherine Shorter, dark-eyed and beautiful in Sir Godfrey Kneller's portrait, but someone whose vivacity would turn almost at once to bitter accusations, gently met in Walpole's only surviving letter to her of 17 July 1702, to discontent and eventual instability within the limits of sanity.

Briefly delightful after a ceremony on 30 July 1700, it would prove a profoundly unhappy marriage marked by routine infidelity on Robert's part and probably some excursions by Catherine. It brought money, £7000, the bride's father, John Shorter, being a Baltic merchant and her grandfather a former Lord Mayor of London. Fortunately, neither Robert nor Catherine, both spendthrifts, could seriously get at the cash, various family mortgages having usefully bespoken it.

But the interim shrivelled to three months. Walpole's entry into Parliament would begin in sadness and develop into a scramble. Colonel Robert, whose own parliamentary career, delayed by the need to pull round and expand the estate, was looking increasingly hopeful, did not outlive the seventeenth century. He fell mortally ill and, after lingering a little, died on his birthday, 18 November 1700, exactly fifty years old. His heir wasted no time on retarding grief; his letter of self-recommendation to Thomas Howard, patron of the seat, was sent before the Colonel's funeral. Election itself followed unopposed in January 1701 and, before making away to London, he gave orders for the expensive demolition of rambling Tudor Houghton and its improvement in the latest and more expensive manner.

The debts created by this uncosted operation may have been the greatest of the burdens which Walpole bestowed upon friends, neighbours and tradesmen. The evidence of financial embarrassment strews the record Vallombrosa-style. So does the evidence of spending hard and whistling. The guide to the labyrinth is John Wrott, factor, steward and financial longstop to the young squire. He tells him in a letter of 21 May 1703, 'There is nearly thirty workmen about at Houghton & how they will come to be paid I can't tell for I have no money by me nor can I get any.'[7]

Robert Walpole would always live high, and in office he could usually afford to. At twenty-four, an unpaid backbencher, married to a wife at least as extravagant, he lived, as he would for a number of years, at or near the edge. He had ambitions for the widest influence within the county and already, in 1701, stood not only for the family borough, but for one of the more prestigious county seats, a knight of the shire being something demonstrative of greater standing than the occupant of a borough seat owned or fought over. It proved premature. Roger Townshend, younger brother of the Viscount, took one seat, the moderate Tory, Sir Jacob Astley, the other. The Townshends were friends, but Walpole learned here that their writ ran further than his. The preferred Raynham candidate for the county, Ash Windham, would be a future Walpole partner at the hustings.

But bills and debts would cloud the short term. Thirteen days into the new century, 13 January 1701, Wrott writes of a Mrs Polworthy who 'is very uneasy. She expected forty pounds more and hoped she should not fail of it by Candlemas.' (As that date, the feast of the purification of the Virgin Mary, falls on 2 February, she would be lucky.) John Wrott, who demonstrates the qualities of an East Anglian Figaro, is fully up to the sort of persiflage needed under such pressure: 'I told her the lowness of the price of corn and the great payment to the Taxes occasioned a great scarcity of money among the tenants, the way the wagon payment could not be assured so soon as some expected.'[8]

Along with the demands of creditors like Mrs Polworthy, doomed to be anxious for long periods of time, are those of tenants and here perhaps a servant, seeking favours. Thomas Carter sends notice of the Walpoles' firstborn: 'Little Master Robert is very well and runs about and eats like anything', before telling and asking, rather feudally, that 'Thomas, set ashore sick coming home by London, humbly begs the favour of you to help with twenty or thirty shilling so that he may have the wherewithal to subsist while he can reach home'.[9] Was Thomas another servant sent on a journey or Carter's own seafaring son? Had help been reliably available from Colonel Robert such that it was now hoped for from his successor? And did it come?

Will Ryder of Dedham was anxious too. 'I was in hopes you would have . . . payed long before this time as I know you promised. Sir I would advise you to take speedy steps about it for I have great want of it. I thought I might have done you a kindness by paying in part, but as you desired to pay in ye whole, I desire you to paye me in whole between this and our Lady next [Annunciation, 25 March].' Writing on 9 December, he was being lenient or realistic, adding, 'I pray sir, let me beg you favour of a line or two by first appointment, otherwise it will occasion me a journey.'[10]

Re-elected for Castle Rising in the general election of 1701, Walpole would toy with ideas of expanding his influence by importing some obliged colleague to the second place there. But he would soon be giving up his own seat, making way for his uncle, Horatio Walpole, something of a brute and everything of a Tory. It looks like Namierite evidence: blood thicker than water, clans manipulating together, political parties of no account. It was nothing of the sort. Walpole was frantic for money and needed to raise some by selling a large property, Hesset, in Suffolk, for which he would also need Horatio's consent. And *that* required valuable consideration. It was a move out of all consistency with the good party man and undeviating partisan, something to raise eyebrows in Whig coffee houses. And with Walpole behaving like a Hogarthian apprentice, and elections falling like snow, he seemed anyway to have every prospect of being out of the next parliament elected in 1702.

Fortunately, he had used his early months in Parliament busily and helpfully on behalf of his friends in Lynn, serving as chairman of the committee handling a private member's bill to authorise the building of a poorhouse in that town. He was brisk and attentive to their business. The Turners who commanded there were appreciative; one of the seats was coming open and, though it was widely sought after, the influence of Charles Turner, head of the family and dominant local landlord, was used to see competition off and young Walpole in. Blessed by Uncle Horatio, the Suffolk sale went through (to the MP for Bury St Edmunds, Captain Porter).[11]

But Walpole was still living above his income, keeping tradesmen at the stave's end and everlastingly putting off people like his distant cousin, Roger Pepys, 'touched', as Sir John Plumb puts it, for £100, and now, like so many people, writing insistent and unrewarded letters.[12] Roger's letter of 3 December 1703 gives an idea of the elastic quality required in any financial concession to this young man: 'Not having heard from you since mine in September last to Houghton when I told you I was willing to stay to Christmas for ye money as you wished & drawing near this time makes one send this to desire you would accordingly pay the remaining five hundred pound and interest to Mr Fra; Long in the Close at Norwich . . .' and as if delay by contrived non-receipt of demand were feared, Roger adds, 'I desire you would tell me of receiving this and please prevent my jumping to conclusions!'[13]

Walpole was also the husband of the expensive Catherine. And in January 1703, Wrott, respectfully avoiding comment, tells him of the delivery of 'two gowns in a box wherein is a parcel of fine lace from Holland for my lady'.[14] These might well have been smuggled goods, about which an older and more Treasury-minded Walpole would try to take severe measures. Meanwhile Catherine's requirements continue through Wrott: 'My lady writ to me yesterday from Wareham that she Expected [money] the week after you went for London & £100 more at Midsummer. For my part, I can't tell where it is to be had nor is there much in any tenant's hands except Sherwood's and he can't pay till after the Lamb Faires,'[15] says Wrott on 21 May 1703.

Meanwhile, a Mr Bell writes on 16 March of the same year, 'Mr Brown is with me at this time . . . and hopes you would pay the money herewith.'[16] Wrott's letters tell of a rural establishment, which, whatever Walpole's ambitions for it, functioned on the steward's ingenuity and market credit. On 7 May 1703 he was

> at Swaffham Fair where I bought as many hoggs as my money would command which was about 300 & there is better than a hundred still wanting to fill up the Flock which for want of money I can't do. For the same reason I did not go to Thetford fair . . . Mr Mostyn came to me at

Swaffham Fair and desired me to let you know Mr Pell is very uneasy for want of money & and that he had writ you about it . . . As soon as you were gone from home, Mr Joynes comes to me for money which he told me you said I should pay him.[17]

On top of the Walpoles' extravagance there was a quite literal shortage of money, a constant practical problem throughout the century. Wrott told Walpole in his next letter, 'I have not yet had any demands from Wareham, and very well I have not, for I have none by me nor can get none. Scarcity of money is the general complaint in the country.'[18] Yet at the same time Walpole was a busy, active MP, witness the King's Lynn poorhouse business. And more important than that, he used the best efforts of an active MP to obtain convoys for the commercial flotillas putting out of Lynn harbour. And despite the advancement of a Tory into his own original seat, his party indulged the new Member with minor responsibilities. In his first session he was three times a teller in a division, in the session 1701–2 seven times, and across 1702–3, six. He was also marked for favour by election to the Kit-Cat Club. Politics goes, always has, always will, with food, wine and good talk. Dining clubs just happen and they make excellent vehicles for anything from mild mutual promotion to criminal conspiracy. The Kit-Cat Club, named for Christopher Catling, its original caterer, was the Whig elect at dinner.

Most British political dining clubs have been confined to Members of Parliament. The Kit-Cat not only boasted the key men of the Junto like Somers, Montague, Somerset and Wharton, but welcomed too the likes of Jacob Tonson, the outstanding publisher of the day, Joseph Addison (who *was* an MP), essayist and playwright, William Congreve, less political, better playwright. Another member, Godfrey Kneller, painted the Kit-Cat portraits, forty-two of them now hanging in the National Gallery.[19] Robert Walpole quickly became a member. Back in Norfolk, letters were being written asking him to pay the interest on loans, and he came near to arrest for debt before contracting a new, large, but tolerantly managed one from Thomas Gibson, his scrivener.[20]

Not all of Wrott's letters pass on the demands and movements of creditors. There is factual and innocent news too, small purchases and hopeful husbandry. In the new year of 1702, 4 January, come 'two turkeys and three brace of partridge and, by the wagon, Pudding', while the same letter advised 'weather much abated so that we do not now feed 40 fat sheep – a tedious time for cattle and turnips & esp. sheep'.[21] In May of the same year, he relates 'I have drawn off the French wine which held out very well; the strong ale I intend to bottle off in a day or two and believe will be very good.'[22]

There is also news of the Great Storm of 1703, one not equalled until 1987. 'As to the damage sustained by the violent storm of winds, the greatest loss you had was at Sydeston, most of Sherwood's barns were blown down and the tiles of the granary and barns.' But happily, it was neighbours who suffered most. For 'the damage in the neighbourhood is considerable. Mr R. Gallup's new barnes at Massingham are down, one of Humphrey's Wind Mills shattered all to pieces & the miller's son killed.'

Away from such rural anxieties, Walpole was moving in the company not only of the most influential men of his party, but (and there is some overlap) among the cleverest, most interesting people of the time. A loan to Robert Walpole was a long-term investment; it had to be. The creditors were men of the world who should have known all the maxims beginning with *Caveat*. But one letter a good deal later from an Elizabeth Richardson, if taken at face value, has a sinister ring: 'I have given you frequent trouble on this occasion [topic] . . .' she writes on 26 January 1704,

> the money left by my son in your hands remains there for anything I know, having no account of its being paid to the person I once ordered to receive of you. You may consider I am a poor widow left with four children. Whatever it was my poor boy left with you for me, be it more or less, can do you no good but may be very serviceable in my family, therefore pray be pleased to let me have it. Mr Smales will be in London ere long when I have desired [him] to wait on you . . .[23]

Mrs Richardson sounds muddled. She might, very remotely, be operating some sort of begging device. But the strong likelihood is that this imploring letter relates to money entrusted to Walpole, and then kept, by negligence or cynicism, from people poorer than himself, a species of conversion beyond excuse.

Broke and untrustworthy he might be and very much enjoying himself, but whatever the appearances he was not, in Lady Bracknell's phrase, living entirely for pleasure. The Townshend connection inherited from his father was of course an essential start. Charles Townshend mattered a great deal. He had just become Lord-Lieutenant and left the stump electioneering to Walpole. Indeed, at this stage he kept rather in the shadows, and certainly did not maximise his influence. But the dawdling Townshends were bigger fish in Norfolk than the busy Walpoles, as well as being, at this stage, a step or two back from complete identification with the Whig leadership.

By most accounts, their young head of family was hugely popular in the county. A Major Houghton of the County Militia thought that 'none would desert serving under the Lord Townshend, though I found few willing to serve under any other, especially a stranger'.[24] And Townshend's attitudes within the county were lazy and tolerant. Unlike Walpole in either particular, he was happy, as Lord-Lieutenant, to leave most Tory occupiers of local offices and appointees of the Duke in place. But the alliance of the two men, later reinforced by the marriage of Townshend to Walpole's sister, Dorothy, would become a central fact of British politics. In many ways, Townshend was the perfect partner for Walpole. Despite his local roots and the Lord-Lieutenancy, he was never an avid player of the local detail. With no constituency experience as a Member – he had inherited in 1687 as a minor – he did local business as a duty rather than an enthusiasm. He was a metropolitan man mindful of the metropolis. From Raynham in 1704 he would write to Walpole in pursuit of political news, 'tho' I am extremely fond of the country . . . I cannot keep my thoughts entirely from Westminster'. He was quite interested enough to exert influence at Great Yarmouth, even after his sick brother Roger's withdrawal, to get two approved Whigs securely in.

From the start, Walpole was assembling a circle which he would later dominate. Like the Tory leader Robert Harley, with whom he had otherwise only talent in common, Walpole had a gift for friendship. James Brydges, Paymaster General (1705–13) and later Duke of Chandos, described his as 'the most friendly nature I have known'. Good humour joined with leadership qualities acquired a following, and Walpole could soon count on circles beyond the family group of Walpoles and the Townshend connection, a local nucleus which, before long, included his brother and lifelong lieutenant, Horatio Walpole, as well as William Feilding, Ash Windham of Felbrigg and Thomas De Grey, a Windham cousin, at Thetford and the two Whig candidates for

Norwich, Waller Bacon and John Chambers. *They* would suffer the chicanery of the Tory Mayor, William Bythe, who voided their election being non-freemen for a freeman borough.

These were all Norfolk men, but the group was not limited by the Fens. Walpole had no compunction about doing favours upwards. The Devonshires almost defined the term 'Grandee', but it was at Castle Rising that William Cavendish, Marquess of Hartington, heir to the Duchy and ardent Whig, was found a seat under Walpole's immediate patronage in 1701. In James Stanhope he found a man of equivalent talent to Spencer Compton, the lifetime occupant of his shadow. Then there were Sir John Holland, General Earle, Richard Temple of Stowe, Sir John Cropley down in Dorset and Jack Smith who would soon occupy the Speaker's chair. As early as 1708, Marlborough would be acknowledging 'the personal friends of Mr Walpole'.[25]

The larger events in which the Kit-Cat diners busied themselves favoured the Whigs. In King William's time they had been the war party. Louis XIV now did his very best to justify them. The War of the Spanish Succession is not simply a musty old story. It was the contest for who was to be master. If the Bourbons, through Louis's grandson, Philip, inherited Spain on the death of the decrepit Carlos II, without major countervailing and binding conditions, they would inherit the Spanish American options, most of the world's gold and a dominant share of vast, anticipated trade. Imperially, they could threaten the Empire, based in Vienna, but ruling in the Spanish Netherlands, half the Low Countries. The beginnings of overseas empire, what had been won by neighbouring Holland, ruled by King William of England, what England had won, the places where they both traded and, ultimately, Holland itself, could fall subject to a France able to exploit so many assets.

The sharing of a ruler by the two countries, something which ended with William's death from fever induced by a fall from his horse, was more than symbolic. It marked a common defensive interest of these conspicuously Protestant countries, yet one drawing in the Empire and its narrow, tenacious and extravagantly Catholic emperor, Leopold I. And that interest would be pursued despite William's death in March 1702. Peace had held since the Treaty of Ryswick (1697), but that rested upon an impudent plan involving Louis and William, for the redistribution of Carlos's lands overseas before he was dead, with the

Spanish Americas and the Spanish Netherlands going to an Austrian archduke. The Spanish crown itself was to pass to Josef Ferdinand, Elector of Bavaria.

When Josef Ferdinand incontinently died within fourteen months, on 14 November 1698, earnest attempts were made by all the parties to put an acceptable succession and peace together again. The Spanish Netherlands was the key to any peace; and Louis in another of his lurches, calculated or not, destroyed all hope for peace by taking over fortresses there and asserting that his candidate in Spain, Philip, could also inherit the crown of France. This would combine with something noted above – recognition in 1701, by Louis, of the Pretender's claim to the English throne. His words to young James Edward were calculated to make every English Protestant prejudice seem common prudence: 'I will subordinate all material and political considerations for the sake of true religion. Remember that it is your religion that makes you King.' The war which followed this ring of circumstances would begin as patriotic and consensual, an English war. But by the end of the next ten years, it would become a Whig war.

Government would lie in the early years of Anne with what were called the Duumvirs (co-rulers). Sydney Godolphin, a fussing, ubiquitous financial specialist, was a man around since Charles II, who had observed, 'Ah Mr Godolphin, never in the way, never out of the way.' He was partnered by the great Achilles, John Churchill, Duke of Marlborough. The General was about to enjoy enormous Continental military glory in a sequence of battles won over the French which 'every schoolboy' of legend could once recite: Blenheim, Ramillies, Oudenarde and, more problematically, Malplaquet, actually a bloody draw. Neither man had strong inherent political colours, though Marlborough's ferocious wife, Sarah, would become a sort of Whig Boadicea. They were there because there was a war to be fought, an administrator working with a soldier who either corresponded or commuted. Otherwise the Ministry was mixed. But with military victory, the Whigs, as supporters of the war, advanced. By April 1704, the year of Blenheim, most of the High Tories, Rochester, Nottingham, Jersey and Sir Edward Seymour, were gone, replaced by the moderate Harley and the very young Henry St John, the beginning of a ten-year alliance working its way to misalliance.

Walpole's first chance came in 1705. The Junto Whigs had made an advance in the elections and were able to put in a Whig, William Cowper, as Lord Keeper (later Lord Chancellor). Walpole, who enjoyed the personal support of Edward Russell, was appointed to the council of the High Admiral, Prince George of Denmark, amiable consort of the Queen and described by Sir John Plumb with his usual briskness as 'stupid and drink-sodden'.[26] Russell was a brave sailor, victor of La Hogue, a Junto Whig and a Norfolk man who had taken his title, the earldom of Orford, from what was then, before silting up, a Suffolk port.

At this time the Whigs were riding high but only tangentially connected with office. They were supporters of Marlborough, but not holding places in what was a mixed Ministry, its Duumvirs served by moderate Tories like Harley from 1704, joined next year by middling Whigs like Newcastle,* balanced by a Tory, Buckingham. Marlborough, a difficult man but a wonderful soldier, in May 1706 added Ramillies to Blenheim, while Lord Peterborough was winning a battle in Spain and the main imperial soldier, Eugène of Savoy, was defeating the French outside Turin.

Walpole's appointment reflected the Junto's ability to put their men into junior jobs. They were not Marlborough's choice of friends, but they supported him in his work. The Tories, rooted in the country gentry, touched by a soft spot for the Stuarts and resentful of wartime taxes, could not be counted on to see the war through. The post on the council, though junior, allowed him to demonstrate his hardworking efficiency, especially over finance, something he always handled better for other people, to meet the full Cabinet (and the Queen) at the weekly Naval Council meeting and establish himself as a reliable supporter of Marlborough.

He did this notably by defending the General's heavily criticised brother, George Churchill, a conspicuously inept commissioner of revenue to the Council.[27] He was also breaking the law at a steady rate. Sir John Plumb speaks indulgently of 'the small perquisites which he could extract from his office'.[28] This is to say that, conspiring with John Burchett, Secretary of the Admiralty, Walpole had claret, champagne and linen smuggled from Holland to the Pool of London or a Norfolk port, using, when necessary, an Admiralty launch.

Walpole, though advanced by the Junto, chose, when they and

* John Holles, 1st Duke.

Marlborough began to differ, to stick by the General. And the Whigs, seeing their war succeeding, looked for more in the way of high places. The Godolphin/Marlborough government came under criticism, despite Ramillies, when the Spanish part of the war began to go sour. They were also faced with difficulties in 1706 over the Union negotiations with Scotland and indeed, the mistakes of George Churchill over naval revenue. With the problems, Whig criticism intensified. Walpole, as noted, was staunchly for the Churchill interest on the last count and as reliably onside with ministers on all the others.

Such imperfect party spirit stirred some irritation. Jacob Tonson, printer, publisher and good party man, when elevated one evening and sitting between the lawyer Sir Robert Dormer and Walpole, remarked that he 'sat between the honestest man in the world and the greatest villain; and explained himself that by the Honest man he meant Dormer, the other was a villain for forsaking his patrons and benefactors, the juncto . . .'[29]

The Whigs had felt under-rewarded and in 1706 had tried to knock down doors to admit their man, Sunderland, as Secretary of State. They were denied for one of those purely personal reasons with which the Queen's relations with ministers were flecked. She couldn't stand the man. Balked, they became ever less supportive. But the Junto was the rising force and Walpole was not the man to miss an upward curve. In 1708, as his friends, notably Townshend and Devonshire (the former Hartington), began the move back to orthodoxy, Marlborough was warning his brother that Walpole would no longer defend the Board against Whig attacks. He was back in the central grouping of post-Revolution Whiggish politics and was sufficiently highly rated to suffer no pains for straying.

But he was rejoining as the market price fell. Slowly widening across the years 1706–10 was public disillusionment with the war and the taxes it imposed. Robert Harley, a colleague in these days, would lead the opposition which would bring the Tories to power in 1710 and the peace and disengagement policy which would flower as wisdom or grand betrayal in 1712. Harley regarded Walpole as a catch and, in his flexible way, would much later make overtures. Walpole, promoted Secretary at War in February 1708, in anticipation of the Junto men coming in, would welcome Somers and Wharton into government in November of that year. And with his following, he would stick solid with them all the way to defeat, opposition and resurrection. Great problems were coming up for the Whigs, but Walpole's identification with them was settled for good.

THE CONSEQUENCES OF DR SACHEVERELL

Walpole's career at this time was one of straightforward and early advancement in step with the progress of his party. There was no reason to think that the Secretary at War, in good standing with the people comfortably in power, would now do otherwise than move on and up with them. His political partner, Townshend, had received a post hardly of less standing and perhaps more immediate usefulness. He was sent abroad as ambassador to Holland to work directly with the increasingly impossible Duke of Marlborough for the preliminary diplomacy of what might have been a *Whig* peace treaty. But political security has a way of being upset by what Harold Macmillan much later ruefully called 'Events, dear boy, events'. Fewer events were more abruptly destructive of a clear sky than those triggered by Dr Sacheverell.

We have met Dr Henry Sacheverell before, rejoicing at the death of William III. It takes a strange personality to talk like that, to think like that. But Sacheverell, perhaps because he was the cadet of a family noted for devotion to the Puritan and parliamentary cause, of all High-Flyers flew the highest. Notwithstanding his fellowship at Magdalen College, Oxford, he had no distinction as a scholar. His strengths, by contemporary accounts, were those of style. His voice was 'his greatest excellency'[1] and he had the clerical afflatus, 'a bold man and a good presence, and delivered a thing better than a much more modest man, however preferable in learning, could do'.[2] We should say that he had charisma, alas.

He also swelled and took colour in unfeigned and intimidating rage. That shone out of his words: the Dissenting Academies were 'illegal

seminaries' which would 'propagate a generation of vipers that will eat
through the very bowels of our Church and perpetuate their dissension
to posterity'.[3] Interestingly, Sacheverell would be defended by counsel
(Sir Simon Harcourt) educated in such a seminary, as (by Sir Peter King
and Sir Joseph Jekyll) he would be prosecuted! When it came to occasional conformity, that was the doing of 'double-dyed practical athe-
ists . . . who can betray and sell their Saviour for money and make the
Blessed Body and Blood of his sacrament, the seal and sanctuary of the
worst of iniquity'.[4] The Whigs received similar treatment in one of his
pamphlets: 'a base, treacherous and undermining set of fellows . . .
public blood-suckers that had brought our kingdom and government
into a consumption'.[5] The greatest enemy of all was the other Church
party, 'shuffling, treacherous latitudinarians', moderate men, keen to
throw as wide a roof as possible over as many fellow Christians as
they could, otherwise 'These temporising hypocrites' and 'associated
malignants'.[6]

Like many fanatics before and since, Sacheverell was quick to proclaim
the fanaticism of others. The annual taking of an Anglican sacrament,
prudential avoidance of an irksome regulation excluding a talent out
of a career, something chiefly done by the more worldly Dissenters,
was lashed in a university sermon at Oxford in 1707 as 'that quintessence of fanaticism, Occasional Conformity'. A growing idea that the
doctor might be a little off his head was supported in the same para-
graph when he estimated this venial dodge level in iniquity with 'lying,
fornication, adultery, perjury and murder'.[7]

This, then, was the cleric, Fellow of Magdalen, Rector of St Saviour's,
whom a Tory Lord Mayor, Sir Samuel Garrard, mischievously but with
mounting unease, had invited to give the 5 November sermon at his
own inaugural service. Sacheverell had been rattling about the Midlands
cities on a circuit with Oxford as its base for a decade. The sermon,
entitled 'In Perils among False Brethren', citing Second Corinthians XI.
26 and exploding at St Paul's in November 1710, was essentially a
rehash of one delivered years before in Oxford. The Whig politicians
had heard of him, but with no indication of anxiety. Why should such
a sermon, delivered now, set the chief men of the Junto into furious
action and their lawyers to work advising over prosecution?

For a long time the puzzle of the Sacheverell impeachment which
would set off such calamitous consequences has been written off as an
irrational response to irrationality. What Defoe had said at the time

was so obviously right, that 'the roaring of this beast ought to give you no manner of disturbance. You ought to laugh at him, let him alone; he'll vent his gall, and then he'll be quiet.'[8] However, Geoffrey Holmes took the trouble to reason through the political context which left the rantings of a clerical bigot so charged with political implications as to drive ministers on to action.[9]

For a start, Sacheverell had incited the mob. And the Tory mob, the Jacks or Church and Queen, was a frightening affair. John Tutchin, a lay Low Church controversialist and publisher, had been beaten to death by one in 1707. Gloating over his death, another High Church parson, the Reverend Charles Lambe, observed, 'The fellow indeed, had an honest dry drubbing, just as much as he deserved and no more', adding that he must have been poxed 'or else he would have lived, thrived well and mended like a walnut tree after a beating'.[10] And alongside the violence lay a pattern of virulent political activity by the High Church party. What Sacheverell had said *was* seditious. Timed on a Whig red-letter day, the 5 November celebrations, delivered at London's cathedral in the presence of a great tranche of the political class, on the invitation of a Tory Lord Mayor, it spoke politically of a coming struggle 'against principalities, against powers, against the rulers of the darkness of this world, against spiritual wickedness in high places'.

It was a mad sermon, raging at fellow Anglicans and the government, those 'false brethren in Church and State' who 'put it in the power of our professed enemies to overturn and destroy the constitution and establishment of both'. And the gall might well not be vented. Certainly in the fortnight of deliberation over prosecution, Sacheverell showed no sign of being quiet. The mad sermon looked like spilling over. It had been printed, was selling heavily, and great overflow crowds attended the doctor's next sermon at St Margaret's Lothbury. These were violent times, and this sermon had mingled the politics of incitement with his bloodshot doctrine. The risk, evident to the ministers taking the decision, was that unpunished assault upon the authorities would inspire the whole party of the High Church, carrying the nervous official Tories along with them, into open-ended revolt. The doctrine of the High Churchmen was 'non-resistance' and the irony was not lost on James Stanhope, who called him 'this juring non-juror', that Sacheverell was doing a dangerous amount of resistance.

There were less good reasons too, like the sensitive Godolphin's personal affront at a reference to 'Volpones' when, as was well known, the nickname 'Volpone' had been attached to him by enemies. But to dismiss the impeachment as arrogance or irresponsibility is to miss the gunsmoke in the air, the partisan gloating of the *ad hoc* following which now gathered around Henry Sacheverell. He had made himself a political leader with a mob and a faction happy to be led. Pure party politics underlay everything. Robert Harley, with his Dissenting background and taste for coalitions or 'motley Ministries', would despise the whole demagogic, abusive and unchristian performance. But as leader of the Tories, he could see nothing but advantage; and Harley's hand would be suspected in much of the printed ephemera which flooded out later in the crisis.

It was, of course, still a profound mistake to impeach Sacheverell. A lesser step, like summoning him before the bar of the Commons, would have done all the necessary tricks. We know that from hindsight, and both Defoe and Lord Chancellor Somers knew it then, but at the time the large action taken to frighten the crowd had a certain anxious rationale. Certainly there is no suggestion that Walpole doubted the course. Trial before the House of Lords was a solemn thing and it carried greater penalties. The Whigs were looking for a life ban from the pulpit, (a cruel and unnatural punishment in this case), a prison sentence and perhaps unfrocking. One backbencher, with Titus Oates perhaps in mind, spoke wistfully of whipping at the cart's tail!

Ironically, impeachment made ever less sense as supporters and enemies engaged in what politicians now call 'a big conversation'. Sacheverell was not the only pamphleteer. White Kennet, the Low Church's regular advocate and a much better theologian, took him apart on scripture and used the dedication of his quick pamphlet addressed to the Aldermen of London to flatten the Magdalen man with graceful ennui: 'I have tired myself more than I can do you by searching a place that affords nothing but what is offensive to any senses that are in a right order. You laid it upon me, but I hope one such penance is enough for a man's life.'[11]

George Ridpath, a Whig journalist and future editor of some quality, did a serious and damaging analysis of Sacheverell's case in 'The Peril of being Zealously Affected but not Well'.* And while the doctor's sermon sold furiously, it stood alone. He was distinctly short of champions. It was only after his arrest and detention by the Sergeant at

---

* 'Well-affected' at this date signified 'loyal'.

Arms, that, in the new year 1710, the friendly pamphlets came. But by then he was a martyr. When legal process and its publicity had done, he would in all his brutal demerits have become a cult.

The bill which impeached Sacheverell in the Lords charged him in effect with libelling the Revolution and alleged three things. He had said 'that the necessary means used to bring about this happy revolution were odious and unjustifiable', that William III had disclaimed the least imputation of resistance and, finally, 'that to impute Resistance to the said Revolution was to caste black and odious colours upon his late majesty and the said revolution'. Put crudely, as such heavy talk needs to be, what they meant was that Sacheverell was a Jacobite who was stirring up people to hate the Revolution as much as he did.

So he was, but the case turned for much of the time into a debate on resistance and non-resistance. And Walpole, given the chance to function as one of the government managers, in effect a battery of parliamentary prosecutors behind the lawyers, went to the heart of it. Never slack in business, he took his commission very seriously, studying the London and Derby sermons and turning up for the preliminary hearing against Sacheverell and his printer, Clements. And instead of giving himself head notes, his usual practice, he wrote out the speech in full.[12] When the trial began in Westminster Hall on a set designed by Christopher Wren, who had given Sacheverell his new St Paul's for a stage, and with the Queen in her box and the galleries packed, Walpole, when his turn came on the second day, showed no sign of doubt or of distancing himself from the undertaking, and the quality of his discourse is striking. Walpole also had an executive loathing of cheeky journalists which we shall see again:

> The great licentiousness of the press in censuring and reflecting upon all parts of the Government, has of late given too just cause of offence; but when only pamphlets and common libels are matters of complaint which none but mercenary scribblers and the hackney pens of a discontented party are employed to vent their malice, 'tis fit to leave them to the common course of the law, and to the ordinary proceedings of the courts below. But my Lords, when the Trumpet is sounded in Sion, when the pulpit takes up the cudgels, when the cause of the enemies of our government is called the cause of God, and of the Church, when this bitter and poisonous pill is gilded over with the specious name of loyalty, and the people are taught for their souls and consciences sake to swallow these pernicious doctrines, when instead of

sound religion, divinity and morality, factious and seditious discourses are become the constant entertainments of some congregations; the Commons cannot but think it high time to put a stop to this growing evil, and for the authority of a parliament to interpose, and exert itself in defence of the Revolution, the present government and the Protestant Succession.[13]

It was splendidly put, formality but incisive formality. And Walpole's next point contains the crux of the reasoning behind this dangerous undertaking. For, he said, 'if the doctrines advanced by Dr Sacheverell are not criminal in the highest degree, it will follow that the necessary means us'd to bring about the Revolution were illegal, and consequently that the present establishment and Protestant Succession, founded upon that Revolution, are void and of no effect'. It was necessary to make things clear. He could not say that 1688 and all that had been resistance, and a good thing too. To argue for resistance and do so in the reign of Queen Anne, he said, one risked 'being misconstrued and misrepresented as maintaining anti-monarchical schemes. But surely my Lords, to plead for Resistance, that Resistance which can alone be concerned in this debate, is to assert and maintain the very being of our present government and its constitution.'[14]

He was also happy to imply, accurately enough, that the High-Flyers were fellow-travelling with the Pretender. For 'so awkwardly do they speak well of what they do not in their hearts approve, that in vindication of His late Majesty (for that's a part that sometimes they think useful to add), they declare his most glorious enterprise, to save a sinking nation, utterly illegal'. Not giving any imaginable Jacobite sympathy the benefit of any doubt at all would be a thread running through Walpole's life to its end in, ironically, 1745. With damning brevity, he stressed the High Church party's entirely genuine devotion to Anne: 'To recommend themselves to the Queen, they condemn the revolution without which she had never been Queen, and we a most unhappy people.'[15]

He took the key principle of the sermon 'The utter illegality of Resistance upon any pretence whatsoever is the general position laid down in the Sermon', before running briskly through all the illegalities and corner-cuttings of James II:

. . . which if it be strictly and in the most extensive manner true, the assuming and exercising a power of dispensing with, and suspending, the laws, the commitment and prosecution of the bishops, the erecting a court of Commissioners for Ecclesiastical Causes, the levying money by pretence of prerogative, the raising and keeping a standing army without consent of parliament, and all the grievances enumerated in the Bill of Rights, were all meer pretences and not sufficient to warrant and justify what was then done in defence of the true, ancient and indubitable rights and liberties of the people of this kingdom . . .

That is, in the manner of the day, a long sentence – so long that I have dissolved it in a line of dots. But it is not the less effective. It did not necessarily prove a high crime, but it demonstrated past answering the massive self-contradiction at the heart of the High Tory case. If resistance were wrong then the enforced departure of King James was also wrong. And that admitted, the implicit question was 'You want Jacobite rule with all its illegalities, now, don't you?'

Pure scorn having its forensic uses, he called up the professional politician's trope of giving the enemy his words back in the teeth, in the process demonstrating his own unrelenting, saw-edged style. This was a '*seditious, discontented, hot-headed, ungifted, unedifying* preacher (the Doctor will forgive me for borrowing one string of epithets from him, and for once using a little of his own language) . . .'[16]

Walpole was also happy to give his own defence of resistance. It was the proper resort in high emergency of men facing the overthrow of law. But it was also incapable of being cut and dried in statute: 'When and upon what never to be expected occasions, it may be exercised, no man can foresee; and it ought never to be thought of but when an utter subversion of the laws of the realm threaten the whole frame of a constitution and no redress can otherwise be hoped for.'[17] However exceptional the resistance, to deny it would be fatal. For 'the doctrine of unlimited, unconditional passive obedience was first invented to support arbitrary and despotic power.'[18] As for Sacheverell's claim that the Revolution had involved no resistance, that was 'rubbage'.

For this preacher 'had no hopes of distinguishing himself in the world, but by a matchless indiscretion'. And such a man should 'not advance with impunity doctrines destructive of the peace and quiet of Her Majesty's government'.[19] Shrewdly, Walpole kept out of the narrowly legal argument, paying a compliment to counsel 'who are more proper, and a great deal more able, to manage that province', and relying on plainer matters. For 'if we remove the rubbage with which the doctor

has an excellent talent at puzzling common sense, and bring together
the several sentences that can only be relative to one another, 'tis impossible for the art of man to make any inferences or constructions, so
close and strong, as the plain and genuine sense of the whole scope of
his sermon must, at first view, suggest to every man's understanding.'

And what Sacheverell was saying was that during the Revolution no
resistance took place. Surely it was not necessary now to prove that it
did take place? 'I should as well expect that your lordships would desire
me for form's sake to prove the Sun shines at Noon Day.'[20] The position was clear. If resistance were all the high-flown things Sacheverell
said it was, then 'it is a sin which, unrepented of, by the doctrine of
the Church of England, carries *sure and certain Damnation*'. In which
case, all they could do was to repent and make restitution.

Having made his points on the logic of a theological proposition,
Walpole turned, man of the world to the men of the world occupying
the House of Lords: 'I beg your Lordships to consider what a duty is
here pressed . . . and what must be the consequences, if these doctrines,
without any reserve or exception, are, without impunity, preached
throughout the Kingdom.'[21]

But if Walpole was elegant and effective, Stanhope, speaking soon
after and rising step for step with him among the younger Whigs, was
equally so, notably in taking on non-resistance. 'My Lords, if this
doctrine of Non-Resistance be true . . . It doth involve the greatest part
of this nation in the guilt of rebellion and treason.' As for Sacheverell,
'This man is an inconsiderable tool of a party, no ways worthy the
trouble we have given your Lordships', but his doctrines must be
defeated and the doctor himself be so punished 'as may deter others
from the insolence'.[22]

And he defined the underlying objects of Sacheverell and his friends'
loyalty with dramatic impact. They could not 'deny that the true and
real object of their darling Doctrines, such as *Jus Divinum, Non-
Resistance, the Undefeasible, Unalienable Hereditary Right*, that, (I say)
the true object of their Doctrines is a Prince on the other side of the
Water.'[23]

Stanhope went further than Walpole or any other manager in advancing
a new political principle. He openly avowed John Locke's theory that
a contract or, as he put it, 'compact', existed between ruler and ruled:
'I believe one may . . . venture to say that there is not at this day subsisting
any nation or government in the world whose first original [origin] did

not receive its foundation either from Resistance or Compact. And as to our purpose, it is equal if the latter be admitted. For wherever Compact is admitted, there must be admitted likewise a right to defend the rights accruing by such Compact.'

What was taking place, parallel with the necessary but less interesting argument about whether Sacheverell, cloudily ambiguous in places, had said in citable terms what he had undoubtedly meant, was a grave disputation about the moral foundations of government. What would take place in central London on the night of 1/2 March was something else.

It was never proved in court that the rioting, fire-raising and murderous violence of those hours was organised by greater folk than the porters, watermen and bricklayers who from Blackfriars Street to Lincoln's Inn to Hatton Garden, then as far west as Drury Lane, stripped out, looted and burned down six Dissenting chapels before being driven off without a fatality, by troops sent by the Queen's personal authority, but witnesses described the giving of instructions by the occupants of coaches. The London mob, whomever its victims, was rarely more than semi-autonomous. The objective was to do all imaginable physical harm, with murder a lightly taken risk, to Dissenters and their places of worship.

There was a line, but not a secure one, separating the virulent hatred which was Sacheverell's regular discourse from acts in the Kristallnacht mode. The time would come when Robert Walpole in power would show himself an unrelenting pursuer of Jacobites, and he would not then be notably willing to make refined distinctions between High Church enthusiasts pickled in non-resistance, Jacobite fellow travellers and the full, treasonable thing. There was doubtless an element of opportunism in this, but surely also a larger one of loathing and distrust illuminated by the doctor's words and the fires they lit.

But the trial had been a clumsy undertaking, the breaking of a black beetle rather than a butterfly upon a wheel, all too heavy an instrument to work. The House of Lords had to be persuaded on a straight vote, peer by peer; and though the Whigs enjoyed majority enough there to get a finding of 'Guilty' by a modest nineteen votes, the proof of this pudding would be how hot it was. The Lords had to vote on 21 March, by competing motions for the punishment as well as the verdict. The hoped-for unfrocking was not proposed. The government's own favoured sentence, one said to have the Queen's support, proposed now by the Earl of Carlisle, a ministerial junior, involved seven years' peace and quiet (no preaching), a short term (three months) of imprisonment and a bar from preferment during the ban.

That was itself a pre-emptive toning down on the life bar originally expected. But the House of Lords, itself a crowd, however benign, reacted in collective sympathy to a speech by the Duke of Argyll arguing in a very cricketing way that what had mattered had been to bring in a guilty verdict, not to punish fiercely, and prompting the idea of a single year's suspension. There was sufficient response for ministers to settle for a compromise which kept Sacheverell from thumping his lectern cushion for three years. This carried by six votes, but a motion for a bar from further preferment during this suspension suffered from rebels and absentees and was lost by one.

Sacheverell might be brought to the bar of the House to make submission on his knees. But Walpole, like his colleagues, knew the score: 'This day has put an end and a most disagreeable end to Dr Sacheverell's trial for though he was voted guilty yesterday by a majority of 17, his punishment was reduced very low this day by a majority of one, that I think they had as good as acquitted him.'[24] The £200 living in remote west Shropshire thrust upon Sacheverell by a crypto-Jacobite squire, Robert Lloyd, was the least of his glory. He would proceed to a round of celebratory Tory dinners, to a positive progression via an Oxford which had never actually liked him very much but now hung out its flags, on through the sympathetic Midlands shires, where, amid bonfires and more dinners, he enjoyed all the pleasures of a platonic martyrdom with the advantage of being floridly alive. 'He showed,' said the Low Church Gilbert Burnet, 'as much insolence on that occasion as his party did folly.'[25]

But the government had suffered more than a humiliation. It had sensed a loss of support before this: the war went on, the costs of the war went up, and the land tax which was to pay for it ground down. Robert Harley might benefit from the temporary vindication of a buffoon, but he was going to win power as the champion of a prospective peace.

And as Burnet remarked of the Sacheverell demonstrations, 'all this was like a prelude to the greater scene that was to be acted at court'.[26] Within a government of many strands recognition of the mood would show. Harley was a pollster and focus group user before the letter. His intelligence network, spread across a modest-sized electorate, told him good news without flattery. The steps pre-conditional to seeking a peace began with new authority within the government, authority to reshuffle in slow motion. Moderate men, like Shrewsbury and Somerset, came closer. Argyll, whose intervention may have swung the Lords, picked an ostentatious quarrel with the Commander in Chief. And at a time when the Court had its own politics parallel with Parliament's, Marlborough was losing purchase there.

Queen Anne and his Duchess, heroines of so many bad novels, had reached the point of screaming fissure. Sarah's greed and mania beat down upon Anne, already dying at forty-five, until dismissal reduced her to a remote voice railing sexual slander from the bottom of a well. The Harley cousin Abigail Masham, who had been infiltrated into court, had soothed the Queen as she damned the Marlboroughs. Abigail had done her work but so had they. Walpole, as Secretary at War, found himself a channel of communication between the Commander in Chief away in Holland and a dominant Minister who was trying in small, provocative steps to undermine a man whom Anne would now probably have gladly dismissed.

That would have been bad politics and not the style for Harley who favoured an induced resignation. Abigail wanted a colonelcy for her brother, Jack Hill, whom Marlborough, detesting the man, had tried to keep out of reach of the rank. Harley insisted, and the Queen, quite alienated from the pair, insisted too, indeed, wanted to issue a peremptory command. An enforced gazetting could have been the trigger of a resignation, very much Harley's idea. Walpole, as he told Marlborough by letter, had persuaded the Queen to hold her hand until she had the General's own response. He now had to persuade Marlborough not to indulge in pique and throw his hand in. And he needed the urgings of colleagues like Godolphin and Shrewsbury to restrain him. The compromise was to make out the commission but leave the conferring of it to Marlborough at his own time during the campaign. And to be rid of wrangling, the Duke gave it out at once.

Humiliation and explosion had been avoided, though not Marlborough's ultimate departure. But Harley registered the cleverness of Walpole and made no secret of his professional respect. But he demonstrated his own arts by attacking a man whom Marlborough trusted and relied upon, his son-in-law, Sunderland.* Trust and reliance

---

* The 3rd Earl, son of James II's Minister, who had gone on to serve William.

were no part of Anne's response to her Secretary of State, whom she detested. As Sunderland's successor would relate her comment, 'Lord Sunderland always treated her with great rudeness and neglect & chose to reflect in a very injurious manner upon all princes before her, as a proper entertainment for her.'[27]

Harley being an incremental politician, the departure came by way of those advance leaks which our time thinks peculiar to itself. The sacking was murmured about, underlining Marlborough's isolation and serving Whig ministers a cocktail of fear and uncertainty. Walpole joined colleagues at a meeting on 14 June in sending a message to Marlborough begging him not to resign. But with the unpopularity of the war manifesting itself in militia mutinies and with the Queen in total assent with Harley, whom she also liked best of all her ministers, events were taking their course.

Bishop Burnet describes Anne telling her ambassadors 'that they should assure her allies, that she would make no other changes; and said this herself to the minister whom the [allied] States had here; all these concurred to express their joy in this resolution . . .' But as the Bishop laconically added, 'Two months after the change of the secretary of state, the queen dismissed the earl of Godolphin from being lord treasurer.'[28] Marlborough had protested furiously at the removal of Sunderland, but at Court his writ no longer ran.

He was Sarah's husband and it did Godolphin no good with the Queen that he was her loyal friend. As Lord Treasurer, he held the post most nearly analogous to Prime Minister, but the power had drained away. Of his actual dismissal, Burnet wrote, 'Mr Harley was the person with whom the secret was lodged; and it was visible he was the first minister: and now it appeared that a total change of the ministry, and the dissolution of the Parliament were resolved on.'[29]

In fact, a near complete clean-out of the Ministry would take place, with Somers, Devonshire, Boyle and Lord Derby being removed for Tories of various colours, including one whose presence Harley would regret, the glittering cynic and player of the Jacobite card, Henry St John. Robert Walpole was the last man of consequence to fall, and he lasted long enough to congratulate a colleague on an achievement which, coming before the Sacheverell case, would have reinforced the Ministry.

For now, six months after the trial, the allies had won at Saragossa, an important battle in the otherwise dismaying Spanish theatre of the war. The victor, returned from his parliamentary duties, would be

General James Stanhope. The victory would be too late and too far away. Hatred of the war had become hatred of the war party, and Harley was able to persuade the Queen to advance the date of a general election. And in so far as the eighteenth century did landslides, this would be one. The election was a rout. Stanhope's friend, the retiring Secretary at War, wrote on 19 September, his last letter in that post, 'We are in such a way here that I cannot describe, but you can imagine nothing worse than you will hear . . . Dear Stanhope, God prosper you and pray make haste to us that you may see what you would not believe if it were told you.'[30]

Stanhope would have this bleakness brought home personally. The measure of a sweeping Whig defeat in the elections would be the result in the open, almost democratic, contest in his constituency of Westminster, where 'The Tories and High Churchmen concentrated all their forces against him, accused him of nameless vices and "with having profanely defiled the altars".'[31] Stanhope, admittedly with a proxy representing him, was massively defeated, and, hero or no, fled to Cockermouth, pocket property of the Duke of Somerset. By this time Walpole and Townshend, despite the latter's continuing ambassadorial sojourn in Holland, had all the Whig candidacies in Norfolk to dispose of. Ash Windham, Townshend's cousin and effectively his proxy, met with Walpole and Sir Charles Turner and determined candidates for all the Norfolk constituencies. Samuel Fuller and Horatio Townshend were to fight Great Yarmouth, the incumbent Whig, Robert Bayliss, and a son of Sir Henry Furnese were offered to Thetford, Sir Charles Turner chose himself and Robert Walpole (with Horatio Walpole as first reserve if Robert won the county) for King's Lynn. Sir William Feilding retained the little committee's confidence at Castle Rising where he might be joined by Sir John Holland, demoted from Knight of the Shire. But it was to be understood that Walpole prudentially reserved the family jewel of Castle Rising, having poor expectations of the county seat.

There was a splendid insolence about the operation, carried out, of course, in London, but the precaution was a good idea. This was to be a terrible election for Whigs, however selected. Failure was general despite Horatio Townshend's obeying instructions to 'go down to Raynham and kill a sheep or two . . . lay aside the merchant, and spend and speak like a gentleman'.[32]

In fact, the preferred seat of King's Lynn did return Walpole, but in Norwich, 'they pelted Mr Walpole with dirt and stones and drove him out of his tent,* spoiling his fine laced coat which they told him had come out of the Treasury'.[33] Walpole not only came last in the County of Norfolk, he came bottom of the poll, and not only came bottom of the poll, but lay with his 2391 votes almost four hundred below his Whig colleague, Ash Windham. This perhaps distinguished a prosecutor of Sacheverell from a mere voter against (the view of Geoffrey Holmes), but also perhaps marked off a prominent member of a war government from an obscure one.

* A candidate's marquee, pitched at the site of the hustings.

4

GO TO JAIL

It was Walpole's misfortune that while this undertaking was being painfully and as quietly as possible pursued, reckless Tory back-benchers should stir on their own account, looking for suitable candidates for lynching. Harley, now Earl of Oxford, was plagued by the October Club and all it symbolised, friends of the Sacheverell cause, crypto-Jacobites and the sort of primitive country gentlemen Vanbrugh may have had in mind when fashioning Sir John Brute. Yet to this rough constituency, peace negotiations were an admirable undertaking. This had been their war only for so long as Louis constituted a threat and the costs were limited. It had turned into a grand triumph for John Churchill, who had abandoned James II and was now Duke of Marlborough. And the cost fell unequally, too much of it they thought, on the heads of land tax-paying Tory country gentlemen.

At the same time the achievement of peace by treaty was, at the high point of Tory fortunes in the Commons, threatened by Whig predominance in the Lords, something reinforced by a shift among moderate Tory peers, men now demanding stiffer terms in any treaty. This group were known rather endearingly as 'the whimsicals'. More accurately, they were solid Hanoverians, mistrustful of Toryism's undeclared second fork, the return of the Pretender James Edward Stuart.

And naturally, the Whigs, dusting themselves off, turned energetically to opposition. This took the agreeable form of scrutinising the unseen *possible* treaty for all the blunders and betrayals it might contain. They would make a particular point of insisting that a war begun to keep the King of France from ruling Spain and its empire through his grandson should not, after so many allied victories, end with Bourbon control of these territories.

Harley was engaged upon his life achievement, at a moment past the high point where we would have negotiated from strength, but with the conflict still shaded in our favour. Britain held a strong hand despite military failure in the Spanish theatre and Marlborough having run out of triumphs in the Low Countries and Germany. The peace to be finally agreed at Utrecht was a more honest affair than the cavalier private arrangement with France which St John, in his short-sightedly selfish way, had wanted, one ignoring and cheating the allies. But even so, it would make enemies enough among those allies, not least and fatally, the Electoral family of Hannover.

Harley's immediate and apparently hopeless problem was a dire shortage of votes in the Upper House. He had hoped from a conversion of Scottish peers* into the real, vote-in-the-Lords thing but was denied by a rebellion of the new opposing coalition. It looked as if the peace gained so painfully at Utrecht might be balked in a Whig Upper House. The war had been undertaken in the first place to prevent the succession of Louis's great grandson as Philip VI of Spain. That could not now be done without a longer, dearer, bloodier war. A compromise which simply kept the French and Spanish crowns from unification would pass the Commons and make few enemies in the country, but in the Whig-shaded Upper House a single important defection threatened the whole undertaking.

The Earl of Nottingham could be called a Church and War Tory, favouring every privilege and exclusion serving the Anglicans but as ready as any Junto Whig to carry on fighting the French. On 7 December, 1711 Nottingham put up a motion in the Lords proclaiming the slogan 'No peace without Spain'. With ardent Whig support, it passed. Robert Walpole came forward next day with an identical motion in the Commons which was, of course, heavily defeated.

Public opinion was almost certainly with the Tories, making them at this period the popular party, almost, indeed, the people's party. *Per contra*, involvement with Nottingham induced a step downward in the coming decadence of Whiggism. The threat to substance and conviction when greedy politicians are tormented by opposition is familiar. For Nottingham's support, probably available free anyway, the Whigs,

---

* Sixteen Scottish peers only went by nomination to Westminster.

thrashing about in the misery of defeat and deep opposition, rushed to pay the price of surrendering a central principle, religious toleration. This embodied a whole future of enlightened belief, such prospects as universities and public posts free of religious tests, the liberalism latent in Whiggery at its best. But when, subsequently, Nottingham came forward with a new Occasional Conformity Bill, the Whig leadership offered no resistance. A fifty-year tradition of sympathy with Dissent and support for its liberties had been thrown over to achieve a frantic little fix.

Daniel Defoe, whose politics were back to front of Nottingham's, an anti-war tolerationist, addressed the Whigs with a cry of grief and contempt: 'Never open your mouths after this about public faith, the honour of treaties, justice to allies and standing fast to confederacies and the like; whoever may speak of these things, it is not for those I am speaking of to open their mouths about it now.'[1]

It was opportunism and short-sighted opportunism at that. Nottingham would have joined anyway and nobody came with him. The Queen was dying. Georg of Hannover, himself a Lutheran, well to the theological left of the Church of England, was also a friend of religious toleration, a better Whig than the leaders of that party. In return for making no real concession, Nottingham had done more for the privileges and *Nomenklatura* rights of the established Church than a dozen Sacheverells. And to round off the bitter irony, reneging did not even give the Whigs political reward; submitting to that Occasional Conformity Act in 1712, they would lose, by a yet wider margin, the election of 1713.

But while Walpole and his colleagues made their peace with High Church primacy, he, the maker of so much high-quality trouble in opposition, was found out in a small but tangible dishonest act and nailed up for it by vengeful Tories. If an example were to be made, Walpole as a new man was perfect: not absolutely established and about the right size to be picked on, as pushy as talented, so already detested.

The Tories' laureate, Jonathan Swift, would be suitably horrid:

Walpole was a person much caressed by the opponents of the Queen and ministry, having been first drawn into their party by his indifference to any principles, and afterwards kept steady by loss of his place. His bold, forward countenance, altogether a stranger to that infirmity which makes men bashful, joined to a readiness of speaking in public, hath justly intitled [*sic*] him, among those of his faction, to be a sort of leader of the second form. The reader must excuse me for being so particular about one who is otherwise altogether obscure.[2]

This should be seen as an example of the onlooker's partisanship exceeding that of the players. Both Oxford and St John admired and valued Walpole. He was the last Whig to leave the government when, in January 1711, he was relieved of his surviving subsidiary post as Treasurer of the Navy. And that loss came in response to clamorous Tory backbenchers pressing Oxford to a universal purge. But if in fluid times, when his party's fortunes were on the river bed, he and his ally, Townshend, could have been brought across, they would have been a brilliant acquisition. Walpole's letters to Oxford have not survived, but one from the Lord Treasurer of 26 November 1711 addressed to a 'Lordshipp' (presumably Townshend), but found in Walpole's papers, says nothing very much in the best, opaque, soothing Harleian way, but proposes a meeting shortly, with the Minister as caller.[3]

But if one party panicked, so did important supporters of the other. When Nottingham's Spanish motion had carried against the government in the Lords, Swift, as much a Harley friend as Defoe, feared, so he told Stella Johnson, that such a 'mighty blow' to the Lord Treasurer 'may end in his ruin'. The vote seemed important at the time, just as, to the Whigs, the shabby deal with Nottingham seemed a price worth paying. But Swift was reckoning without his leader. Oxford's enemies called him 'Robin the Trickster', but the Whig blockade of the peace treaty was frustrated rather by his boldness. With a sudden break from his serpentine caution, he used his influence with the Queen for the brilliantly simple expedient of creating a dozen Tory Lords, quite enough in a small House to secure the treaty. Robin the Trickster had played his supreme trick.

Persecuting a former Whig minister now looked apt. It could serve as several things at once: red meat for the booby squires, a warning shot at the opposition and proof of the Ministry's clear dominance. St John seems to have been the chief mover. The Committee of Accounts, ministerially packed, had been looking at the books of Walpole's old department and had come up with evidence of the former minister cutting his financial adviser, Robert Mann, into a good thing. This amounted to two pieces of an army forage contract for Scotland, out of which the contractors had bought him at 500 guineas the one, £500 the other. By what seems like psychic error, one of the departmental cheques had been made out not to Mann, but 'Robert Walpole'. And on 17 January 1712, the Commons proceeded against Robert Walpole.

Assuming what lawyers call 'blameless inadvertence', which the Tories didn't, the deal with Mann was still culpable. Walpole owed his man of business any number of favours, not least in return for help in illegal acts. Mann had helped him pass wines, duty unpaid, through the customs, something which, done by a rough Sussex sailor, was called smuggling and often ended at the gallows. Mann was being given part payment for services to Walpole with public money. This is usually called corruption. The question of Walpole's honesty will come up again as his career and opportunities advance.

There is no point in moralising across nearly three hundred years, but no point either in suggesting that Walpole was merely conforming to the age in his corrupt acts. Not Stanhope, nor Townshend, nor, for all his deviousness, Harley, turned their offices to profit. Harley, offered a bribe by a place hunter, William Brenand, returned the answer,

> I must tell you very plainly I resent your going about to offer me money, and much more your continuing to insinuate it in your last letter even after I had told you so plainly before I would hear nothing of it. I told you before that you did not know me when you went that way to work . . . I repeat to you that until you are cured of thinking to bribe me, I shall never think myself capable to serve you.[4]

It is a letter which Walpole could not have written. He had different standards and would set an example to the century.

Even so the charges were made for party purposes, the doing of Bolingbroke and eager groundlings. Walpole, the party man, had across 1711 been an effective critic of the peace negotiations. The Tories controlled the Commons and meant to use it for effect. They did; when read today the official report of the proceedings, though elliptical, is dramatic: 'Then the order of the day was read, for taking into consideration the report from the said Commissioners the 21st December last, whereupon the House proceeded to take into consideration that part of the said report which relates to forage depositions of Mr Man [sic] . . . Ordered that candles be brought in. And they were brought in accordingly.'

Then came the motion 'That Robert Walpole esq. a member of this

house, in receiving the sum of 500 guineas and in taking a note for
500l more, on account of two contracts for Forage of her majesty's
troops quartered in North-Britain, made by him when Secretary at War,
pursuant to a power granted to him by the late Lord Treasurer, is guilty
of a High Breach of Trust and notorious corruption.' His friends tried
to have the last three words omitted, but were defeated by 207 to 155.
The substantive motion then carried 205 to 148. When it came to what
might be called the rhetoric of punishment, a much smaller majority,
168 to 156, agreed to commit Walpole to the Tower while a final vote
of 170 to 148 expelled him from the House of Commons.[5]

It was probably the low point of his career. Imprisonment was the
least of it. The age's combination of minimal administration and class
distinction, even in prison, meant that Walpole could hire comfortable
rooms, indulge his taste for the table, write pamphlets against the government and have as many visitors as he wanted. It was also true that his
vacation of Lynn would not mean permanent loss. The seat was quickly
occupied for him by Jack Turner, a member of the leading family in
the circle of his closest allies in Norfolk.

There was a flurry of sympathetic pamphlets, including one by
Walpole himself, defending the European alliance from Swift's deadly,
if specious, *Conduct of the Allies*, making, as well as his own,
Godolphin's and Marlborough's case against the Tory batteries alleging
wall-to-wall peculation. And at the election of November 1713, otherwise disastrous for the Whigs, he would return to Parliament. Above
all, sentence and expulsion had at all times been accepted as political
by the people practising politics. Walpole had been 'disgraced' only in
inverted commas.

But things still looked unhealthy for the Whigs. Nottingham's motion,
for which so much had been sacrificed, had not stopped the progress
of the Treaty in Harley's improved House of Lords, and Whigs in opposition had continued suffering all the pains of a losing side. Marlborough,
who had been removed from all his posts, had been censured in
Parliament for his financial conduct, as had two other important Whigs,
Somerset and General Cadogan. Meanwhile, after the electoral triumph
of 1710 had been confirmed in 1713, the Whigs, for all their ditched
principles, had now a mere 150 seats in the Commons.

Walpole responded to all this by turning pamphleteer. *A Short History
of Parliament* naturally defended his own conduct but shrewdly shifted
on to territory where Harley dwelt least happily. The Tory party didn't

want to talk about the succession to Anne because it knew that the question broke them wide open. Walpole, attacking the commercial treaty with France which was in the making, was telling everyone, including the voters of Lynn, that the government meant to frustrate the Hanoverian succession.

He was not long back before he was called upon to conduct the parliamentary defence of a colleague, singled out not for flexible accounting but something more enjoyable: seditious libel. The defendant was the MP for Stockbridge, Sir Richard Steele. Playwright, essayist, producer with Addison of the original *Spectator* and *Tatler*, Steele was an Anglo-Irishman of great sweetness and charm. As a journalist he could stand as a paradigm for the trade: disorganised, but able to write thousands of words at instant notice, devoted to company and alcohol, at permanent right angles from solvency, but blessed with the ingenuity which often protects the hard-up. He would die in 1729, comfortably out of reach of his creditors, in Carmarthen! Such plays as *The Conscious Lovers* are not performed today and only dutifully read since. Though graceful, they lack the sting and sexual snap of Wycherley and Etheredge. He was the sort of man to whom happy endings come naturally, and his good humour even extended to the creation of a sympathetic Tory squire, Sir Roger De Coverley.

But Steele was serious about his politics and a dedicated, partisan Whig, neither soft-centred nor reticent. As a pamphleteer he said what he thought, and what he thought in *The Crisis* was expressed in a well-judged header, 'The Protestant Succession in the House of Hanover is in danger under Her Majesty's Ministers'. This was set out as a shilling pamphlet. It sold forty thousand; copies appeared all over the country and, as it came close to the truth, infuriated the Tories. Since he also wrote that he wouldn't put it past them to assassinate the Queen,* the very last thing they would do, the text fell neatly into the category of seditious libel.

Defoe, who had a private grudge, wrote to Oxford to say as much and share in the wild talk. 'If, my lord, the virulent writings of this man may not be voted seditious none ever may, and if thereupon, he may be expelled, it would suppress and discourage the party . . . It is far from me to move your lordship to personal resentment. It is the

---

* While this was absurd, it has to be remembered that only two years earlier, in March 1711, a man called Antoine de Guiscard, representing himself as a French agent, had attempted the assassination of Harley by stabbing him and had inflicted serious injuries.

party, not the man, and I see such black designs in their view that if possible they will run things up for blood . . .[6]

But Steele had touched a nerve. It was a time of intense, hysterical politics. John Toland, another Whig writer, talked darkly, but in evident earnest, of Ireland and Scotland being poised for rebellion and of the Pretender gathering support in London. Meanwhile Bolingbroke, godless stirrer-up of the Church wing of the Tories, had pushed his and their luck by bringing in a Schism Act designed to destroy the best, most useful schools in the country, the Dissenting Academies. Running ahead of Oxford, Bolingbroke was playing a straight Jacobite hand. The idea of James Edward taking the Anglican sacrament to qualify for the resumption of Stuart kingship, by inheritance, divinity and the rest of it, was being more than canvassed. The Queen was a dying woman. Through the time of Sacheverell's triumph and Walpole's confinement to the Tower, that had been the Whigs' one great, unacknowledged consolation. When she should die, the Electress Sophia, thirty-five years older but far fitter than Anne, with son, grandson and great-grandson in waiting like the line of Banquo, stood anointed by Parliament through the Act of Settlement.

So much that was exactly right for the politics of 1710 was terrible for the day Anne died and the Act of Settlement came into operation. Enough people in the country wanted peace, numbers beyond the country gentry paying four shillings in the pound land tax for war. The Tories were still popular when peace was delivered through Bolingbroke's agent, Matthew Prior. As for the countries which made up the Alliance, they did not lie near the conscience of the voters. Celebrations were marked by 'great bonfires and illuminations throughout the cities of London and Westminster, and magnificent fireworks were played off on the Thames over against Whitehall'. The Queen was personally prominent, authorising 7 July 'for a public Thanksgiving for the safe and honourable Peace lately concluded and invited her Parliament to attend her to St Paul's; Both houses went with the usual state.'[7] But symbolically for so much that was happening, Anne, ill again, could not attend the solemn service. As for her Loyal Opposition, the record puts it deftly: 'The Whigs were absent for another cause.'

The Emperor, the Duke of Savoy, the Dutch, whom most Tories particularly hated, could go hang. But Hannover was part of the Alliance and couldn't go hang. A good deal of Whig effort was put at this time into establishing a record of speaking, writing and making public demonstration of their entire dedication to, and identification with, the dynasty in waiting. Hannover had been slighted and her gains by the war put in jeopardy. The Tories were being watched very coolly from Herrenhausen. Already, a tactless envoy, Baron Schütz, had pushed hard for the summons to the House of Lords of a certain Duke of Cambridge, otherwise Georg August, second heir to the Electoral throne of Hannover and the hereditary Arch-Treasurership of the Holy Roman Empire. Whether or not Sophia outlived Anne, Hannover was about to become Hanover, and Georg August would eventually succeed his father, Georg Ludwig, as George II of Great Britain. And the Tories had offended the whole family! On top of which, the partial secret of Oxford's success had been his coaching of Anne in all her many residuary powers as monarch. Up to a point, peace had been a very good thing, but ministers were perilously close to that point.

Accordingly, the idea of combining the rapprochement with France flowing from the peace treaty (and the enmities made among former allies, now slighted) with an approach to James Edward had begun to make a certain dangerous logic; and conversations with the Pretender and his entourage had started. Steele, editing for the Whigs one of the milliard short-lived periodicals of the day, *The Englishman*, was, despite the overkill there and in *The Crisis*, close to at any rate Bolingbroke's real intentions. The mood of early 1714 was the overture to an unperformed drama, a shuttlecocking of accusation and indictment in a phase of pre-coup. A second Steele pamphlet, alleging French betrayal of treaty terms in delaying the slighting of fortifications at Dunkirk, underlined England's endless suspicion of France. Many Tories, feeling more at ease, would have ignored such fulminations, but ministers found making a case against Steele the means of defending themselves.

By degrees, starting with backbench indignants and through the motion of one of them, Joseph Hungerford, followed by a formal complaint from Harley's close ally and cousin, Thomas Foley, the House was moved in the next few days to a motion condemning him. Reasonably enough, Steele asked for time; his case needed to be prepared. As reasonably, the Tory managers put examination off from Monday till Thursday (18 March). On the Monday, Steele stepped up with a move of his own, an address to the Queen making all the points in his Dunkirk pamphlet about French failure to comply with treaty terms over its fortresses and harbour. The address was blocked, but Whig determination to do a Sacheverell and turn an indictment against one of them into charges against the government was clear.

Everyone liked Steele. But no one on his own side wanted him first up defending himself; the crockery wasn't quite safe. His *Spectator* colleague, Joseph Addison, cooler, smoother man and future office holder, was encouraged to write his speech. Meanwhile the party's most effective debater was on hand and delighted to undertake the case. It was a major moment for Robert Walpole. He had just returned from parliamentary exile, elected again for Lynn in the 1713 election, a beneficiary of the Triennial Act which the Whigs, back in power, would soon abolish in the name of stability. It was a chance to shine in debate and to carry fire to the Tories.

For Walpole, then at his most militant, there was nothing excessive in *The Crisis*. 'This extraordinary and violent prosecution struck at the liberties of the subject in general and the members of that House in Particular.' It 'justified Mr Steele in all the heads of the accusation raised against him'. Getting very near to Bolingbroke's particular knuckle, Walpole invoked 'the visible encouragement that was given to the Pretender's friends'. And what about the matter of Sir Patrick Lawless? Lawless was James Edward's secretary and close adviser. He was a Catholic and, obviously worse than that, an Irish Catholic. He had borne arms against the Queen. 'If,' said Walpole, 'such a man be not only permitted to come into England, but to appear at Court, in the Presence Chamber: If he be caressed by ministers; nay, I speak it with horror, if such a man be admitted to Her Majesty's private audience in her closet, will not every good subject think Her Majesty's person in danger?' It was in danger, as Walpole knew and must rationally have hoped, only from the congeries of sicknesses which would kill her very soon. But Sir Patrick Lawless *had* been at court so things must be very bad.

It was a cool man's employment of hysteria. To defend Steele, one attacked the government. That other pamphlet of his, also giving offence, had made a great issue of the detail of the Treaty of Utrecht not being followed through. The French, Walpole now argued, had signed up to the demolition of fortresses and decommissioning the harbour at Dunkirk. That 'ought to have been finished five months after the signing of the Treaty: But instead of that the French had, yet only pulled down part of the outward fortifications . . . instead of ruining the harbour, they were actually repairing the sluices and working on a new canal'.

But there was also a touch of sly humour. Steele, in suggesting a threat under these ministers to the Protestant succession, had been speaking generally. Walpole compared the pamphlet to a sermon: 'General invectives in the pulpit against drinking, fornication or any particular vice, have never been esteemed a reflection on particular persons, unless these persons are guilty of the darling sin against which the preacher inveighs.' Harley drank, Bolingbroke picked up whores on the street. Walpole, neither abstemious nor chaste, pinked them and moved on. Importantly, as Sir John Plumb pointed out, he also shifted the subject of debate/indictment from Steele's enthusiasm for pursuing the war to his concern for the succession, asking, 'How comes writing for the succession to be a reflection on this Ministry?'

Steele would produce what the record calls 'Mr Steele's apology'. Rather it was an *apologia*, a putting again of the arguments which had offended. He was not, of course, going to escape, though the debate wound furiously along until midnight. The Tory majority would see to that; he was condemned and expelled by a vote of 245 to 152, though his finances were very quickly improved after a whip-round among the more affluent Whigs. It was money well earned. The Whigs had a good deal to congratulate themselves on, having been joined in this crucial encounter by Nottingham. The whimsical Tories had signified their position on the succession and they knew what time it was: the last months of Queen Anne's reign.

But Tory domination, so strong in the Commons, by no means denied support in the country, was faltering. Their central policy, even without hindsight, made little sense. They owed their current power to the peace policy which had got them a brilliant election result in 1710. That policy was in the long-term British interest, but strewn with mines for the immediate future. Popular it might be in the country, but ministers also needed the support of the monarch. With reservations, they had it from Anne. But every move they made offensive to paid-up members of the Continental alliance, every conversation with the Pretender's adviser, the Abbé Gaultier (now urging Anglican conversion upon James Edward), increased the loathing for them felt by their future King. A policy disastrous for the quite near future was predicated by the fatal appeal to most Tories of lower land taxes through disengagement.

A dabbling Jacobitism delightful to a noisy faction of that party was something else. The triumph of Dr Sacheverell may have contained the doom of his patrons. For the Tory party was split. The so-called whimsical Tories – Nottingham, Shrewsbury, Sir Thomas Hanmer, Speaker of the Commons – were wiser than Oxford, who could never resist a side option, much wiser than St John, who, having flattered the High Church zealots with all the facility of an atheist, became the prisoner of their love. The Tory Ministry had been brilliantly created and advanced by Oxford, the peace as brilliantly achieved with St John prominent, (rewarded for his efforts by ennoblement as Viscount Bolingbroke).

A slower peace, ostentatiously looking after Hanoverian interests and not so ruthlessly selfish towards the rest of the alliance as to warrant the term *Perfide Albion*, could have been pursued by a Tory party openly and consistently Hanoverian. As it was, Bolingbroke, gambler, temperamental extremist, rider of crazy horses, made war upon Oxford, a moderate dragged by his own schemes from his moderation. Some of Oxford's failure of judgement in the last stages was occasioned by his heavy drinking. But anyone who had Bolingbroke for a lieutenant *would* drink heavily.

Harley had lost much of his influence with the Queen over her private pique at his son Edward's call on the title possibly flowing from his marriage. Trivial Court stuff but fatal: he had also lost the closet influence of his cousin, Mrs Masham, moving to the higher bidder, Bolingbroke, before making off into oblivion with her winnings. He was finally ambushed at a Council meeting on 27 July and deprived by Anne of the Lord Treasurer's white staff. But his one concern over this last term, not to relinquish office to his unstable colleague, had been accomplished. Bolingbroke had meant to effect his Jacobite coup through a purge of local administration, very much a return to the ways of James and of Charles II's late days, to make the movers of toasts who passed glasses over the finger bowl into Lords-Lieutenant, and pack the magistracy and army command. The conventional judgement is that for such an operation he would have needed a full six weeks. Having less than a week, he was reduced to lighting bonfires in celebration of King George.

The last thing any Tory Minister should have been doing was to please his rank and file. Bolingbroke, who needed to evict Oxford if he was to pursue his extreme course, would be left when Anne died, something in narrowing prospect for years, with a policy only to be achieved by a new, full-dress military coup. As it was, interim power had been passed in Anne's last act of state to the moderate and

Hanoverian Tory, Shrewsbury. Recognising the winning side, the Commons, notwithstanding its large Tory majority and great body of high, crypto-Jacobite members, passed a measure putting a price on James Edward's unremarkable head. The Lords, despite the treaty enrolments of Tories, declared it high treason to enlist soldiers in his service. Then, at the last, on 1 August, poor Anne, sick all her modest length of life, finally, at forty-nine, died.

'THE OLD ORDER CHANGETH'

'Dear Dean,

The Earl of Oxford was remov'd on Tuesday, the Queen dyed on Sunday . . . what a world is this & how does fortune banter us?'[1] So wrote Bolingbroke to his and Oxford's friend, Jonathan Swift, adding, 'I have lost all by the death of the Queen.'

He had, as others had gained. Another correspondent, Charles Ford, told the Dean of St Patrick's that 'Stocks never rose so much in so few days. This is imputed to hatred of the old Treasurer and the Popularity of the new one.* Stocks had indeed risen. South Sea went up from 81.5 on 30 July to 89.5 on 5 August to 92.5 on 6 August. It had, of course, as we shall see, barely started. Oxford's perfectly responsible scheme for exploiting Spanish-American trade would become the South Sea Bubble in other and Whiggish hands only toward the end of the decade.

Less ephemeral gains would be made here and now by the party of Hanover men who, having had a good war, now looked to do even better out of the peace they had furiously opposed. Lord Chancellor Harcourt arranged for Shrewsbury, the last-gasp royal choice of Lord Treasurer, to be confirmed by oath. The Regency Council list, prudently arranged years before, was unsealed and, at one o'clock on the day of the Queen's death, 'George, by the Grace of God, King of England, France and Ireland . . .' was proclaimed. The new King took his advancement without rushing, not leaving the Electorate immediately, marking time with diplomatic business in Holland when delayed by winds, and

---

* Respectively, Oxford and the ring-holding Duke of Shrewsbury (*The Correspondence of Jonathan Swift*, p. 102).

finally arriving in Greenwich seven weeks later, on 18 September. But when he arrived in London, the public reaction, this in the city of Jacks and meeting-house burners, was one of delight. The Duke of Berwick, illegitimate son of James II and a far abler man than his chastely born brother, observed scrupulously that he 'was received with every possible demonstration of joy'.[2]

George, whom casual English opinion, including that of distinguished historians, has consistently slighted, was a shrewd man, very conscious of the sensibilities of his new subjects. As far back as 1706, when the idea of his eldest son Georg August's going to England for show and reconnaissance had been proposed, he had persuaded his mother, the Electress Sophia, against the visit. And when a later request, of April 1714, for a summons of the younger George, already Duke of Cambridge, to the House of Lords, upset Anne, George, despite originally initiating it, pulled out and blamed his envoy, Schütz.

The new King also had a good idea of the argumentative, non-absolute nature of the British state. George, whom Plumb characteristically calls 'stupid', took advice from a *Justizrat* called Gottfried Wilhelm Leibniz. And the philosopher had written to an English friend, 'How perfect is your constitution and how in accordance with the dictates of reason.'[3] The dictates of reason gave George a good deal of power, as they had Anne, and he fully intended to have as much British sympathy shown to the interests of Hannover as the Tories had denied them. Foreign policy was an area where he was quite plain about exercising influence.

Something else: George was *not* the man of fond island memory who 'did not speak a word of English and therefore gave up attending the Cabinet'. No doubt he was shaky at the start, but, *not* being stupid, he learned it, learned it till he was capable of annotating an English memorandum in English. In 1723 he wrote across a paper submitted by Townshend, 'I agree with you in everything contain'd in this letter and desire you to communicate your opinion to the Duke of Newcastle or H. Walpole* that the instructions to the ambassadors may be sent according to your opinion. G.R.'[4] There was also the international language option of all educated persons, French.

The English politician most attractive to the new King was Stanhope – General Stanhope – committed to honouring the alliance throughout

---

* Robert's brother Horatio, later ambassador to France.

the conflict, and, like George, a former serving soldier. Stanhope's party, or rather the party to which his faction adhered, was, of course, the Whigs. And George was ready enough to work with a government preponderantly Whig. He distrusted Oxford entirely and snubbed him in public. Utrecht was a betrayal of the allies and George had been one of the allies. Accordingly, the key appointments made Stanhope and Townshend Secretaries of State; Halifax (Montague) First Lord of the Treasury; Sunderland (resentfully) Ireland; and Cowper Lord Chancellor. Marlborough was swiftly restored to glory as Captain General and Robert Walpole became Paymaster General.

Very foolishly, the Hanoverian Tories, Nottingham, Hanmer and Sir William Bromley, declined the offices held out to them by George himself.* A place from which to reason with and please the King and the opportunity for doing service and give the lie to Whig smears of covert Jacobitism were passed up. George was left to be coached in the English niceties by Lord Chancellor Cowper, whose brazenly titled 'An Impartial History of Parties' explained to the poor foreigner how support for the Protestant succession had been, since 1679, a wholly Whiggish undertaking. Cowper's wife claimed that George kept the memorandum by him so that he was 'as we wish on the subject of parties'.[5]

Also, and particularly importantly, the Lord Chancellor impressed it upon George that royal favour shown to this loyal party would enable them to win the elections necessary to give him a loyal government. Whig advancement in the Lord-Lieutenancies and magistracies started here. An election, then and long after, required after a monarch's death had already swung them back into power, though they had not reached the Tory total of 1713. Then the Tories had 364 men in the Commons from England and Wales, a number which had risen through by-elections and petitions challenging returns to 376. The Whigs held no more than 137. That majority came crashing down in 1715. It involved the gaining of fifty-three seats not held by Whigs during their earlier triumph in 1708 and twenty-three never held by them throughout Queen Anne's reign. The Whigs had got so far by doing notably well in the open contests where seats were not under proprietorial lock and key. But they improved the shining hour with the petitions in which fifty defeated Whig candidates were declared by the Whig-packed committee to be the winners. It was

---

* Nottingham would later take up the post of Lord President.

an extreme example of a familiar fixing and in 1741 it would come back and bite Robert Walpole.

As for Walpole, he had in a sense been kept in his place. Sunderland, Stanhope and his own Norfolk comrade-in-arms, Townshend, were greater men in the ministerial firmament. Paymaster General was no great leap from Secretary at War. But Walpole needed money very badly and his job provided it. He was entitled to invest all surpluses and, at the end of the accounting year, keep the interest. The practice denied the return of interest to the state, whose money it was, and wrote up as a lawful convention the plea in mitigation of every defaulting solicitor or army officer privately applying mess funds, 'I was only borrowing the money. I always meant to give it back.'* For Walpole it was the perfect post. Wholly within the law, he could now pocket public money. In fact, he did rather more. Plumb acknowledges that the sums of money passing into Walpole's accounts at this time go beyond this explanation. Between 10 January 1716 and 11 May of the same year he lists as 'Reced of your Honour in Bank' (meaning banknotes) eleven entries of between £300 and £5000 to a total of £16,600, £800,000 at the most conservative modern conversion. As Plumb says 'where Walpole obtained the bank notes will never be known'.[6]

He distinguishes between such possible sources as Chelsea Hospital funds, used for speculation before return, and large sums for which there is simply no explanation. Even the invested surpluses which he is willing to excuse 'by the standards of the day' had produced widespread protest in the past when Lords Ranelagh and Brydges, as Paymasters, had taken advantage of such standards. The advice which a French Premier would give, two hundred years later, with no suggestion of peculation, perfectly characterises Walpole's conduct. 'Enrichissez-vous,' said Guizot. But the last, latent words must remain with Sir John Plumb, a consistent overall champion of Walpole: 'Although the mystery remains, the facts of Walpole's sudden wealth are impressive and important.'

Money was only one reward of power; quite as important was revenge. The Tories, pressed by backbench clamour, had been bent upon systematic exclusion of their enemies from local office. They had also, at Bolingbroke's cynical instance, passed the Schism Act. So when it came

* If no longer permissible under convention, this can still be done. The late Edmund Dell, Paymaster General 1976–8, quirkishly delayed signing the waiver for twenty-four hours in order to pass one night in the fantasy of having all that money to spend.

to rooting out the last remnants of Tory place-holding, little distinction would be made. Revenge would go into gear through the King's proclamation to the new Parliament and a vivid response made to it. And Walpole, least forgiving and most Hobbesian of the Whigs, had inserted a passage into that proclamation alluding to past threats to the Protestant succession from the late government. He then, probably in concert with Stanhope,[7] moved an address saying that the government should 'trace out those measures whereon he [the Pretender] placed his hopes, and to bring the authors of them to punishment'.

It was a declaration of inquisitorial and persecuting intent. And not altogether surprisingly, Bolingbroke drew the conclusion that he was its first object and that the bell, book and candle of the English way with high treason might be reserved for him, a procedure going all the way to Tower Hill and the not quite obsolete axe. He was warned of the prospect by the Duke of Marlborough, himself a correspondent with the Pretender. Characteristically, he panicked. On 6 April he slipped out of a theatre before the play finished, and, dressed in the plainest clothes, with a bob wig and the alias of a valet,[8] made his way to the coast, landing at Calais next day.

From his own point of view there was a good case for flight. He had been in deep. But the flight was taken as admission of guilt. In circumstances where working to set up one head of state against a constitutional statute which had established another, he *was* guilty, and if Walpole had anything to do with it, guilty of treason. He had also said, written and done enough to satisfy the unfriendly judges he could expect to find. But from the point of view of his party, it was the worst act in the world. Bolingbroke not only fled, he made straight for the Pretender's court, was embraced and for a brief interim served in the melancholy office of Secretary of State in exile. The perfectly thinkable possibility of Hanoverian Tories working through a king more pluralist than the Whigs was blown to the winds.

All Tories would now be damned, far beyond whatever sneaking and ineffective regard some of them might have for treasonable Jacobites bent upon crowning James III and helping the Pope in his designs. The scenario which Walpole, more than any other Whig, could now follow was straight up and down Ulster Orange. As for Bolingbroke, he had brought flamboyance to cowardice, adding one more betrayal to a fair list, and had made his last great contribution to the Whig interpretation of history.

Walpole was almost as keen to get Oxford. Though the Lord Treasurer had argued against his prosecution for Robert Mann's contracts, if it were possible to inflict anything upon him, through ruin and imprisonment down to death, Walpole would try for it. Oxford, despite his correspondence, fundamentally sceptical about Jacobitism and everlastingly discreet in talking to *anyone*, reckoned that he had nothing to fear. On top of which, he was in his quiet way, as Plumb fairly concedes, a much braver man.

His persecution was launched in the Commons as soon as Walpole's motion against Bolingbroke had carried *nem. con.*, by his Herefordshire neighbour and old enemy, Coningsby. It did not have backing from more thoughtful Whigs. But when Sir Joseph Jekyll, good party man and prosecuting counsel against Sacheverell, told Parliament that the case was 'slightly founded and straining the law', he needed the chair's protection from the rabble element on the backbenches.[9] The motion carried by 280, at which Walpole was reported saying 'that if 280 would not make him fly, the Devil was in him for there was no such man living in the world'.[10] The House of Lords was another matter, the impeachment being thrown out there with Anglesey, a whimsical Tory, creating more Whig rage by remarking that proceedings like these 'would shake the sceptre in the King's hand'.[11] But after celebratory demonstrations in his favour, revenge was had with an order carried eighty to fifty-five, committing him to the Tower where he stayed (nearly dying) for another two years.

The Walpole line of universal suspicion and general pursuit of opponents was, of course, massively reinforced by the odd sequence of episodes known to romantic novelists as 'the Fifteen'. How seriously we take that rising and the general mood of the country towards the Pretender will affect judgement of the conduct of the Whigs. For Sir John Plumb it was a profoundly serious affair, mismanaged indeed but giving King and ministers good reason to fear for the survival of their power, though he acknowledges that the relentless assault on the Tories helped provoke it.[12] He sees Bolingbroke's flight as more than a breaking of nerve, rather an opportunity to be grasped. He credits the Tory with far greater sensitivity to public mood than Walpole and quotes the disturbances created by Jacobite mobs in Lancashire, Shropshire and Essex. Bolingbroke, in this view, was 'aware of the extent and depth of anti-government feeling. Locked up in the Tower, he could not exploit this to his purpose. To stand his trial would be a fruitless gesture. In person he might persuade James to cast aside his religion and appeal to the common people against the greed and graft of the Hanoverian court.'[13]

With the utmost respect to a great historian, this strains at the evidence. When that modest event 'the Fifteen' came, a single English notable, Thomas Forster, MP for Newcastle, threw in his hat and raised a modest troop of men.* The argument is surely a form of back rationalisation, crediting the Bolingbroke of the habitual wild streak and weakness of nerve in a crisis, with an improbable thought-out schedule of reasonable action. Perhaps it also puts Walpole's long, flesh-creeping exploitation of the Jacobite threat into a more plausible light.

Any thoughts in Bolingbroke's head about seizing an opportunity existed at the same febrile level where, in the Queen's last days, he had invited the Whig leadership – Wharton, Craggs and all (Walpole was back in Norfolk) – to dinner and proposed a coalition to them. Bolingbroke had lived exclusively in the short term, originally seeing advantage in an appeal to Jacobite *feelings* which were quite unbankable when all sense for the Tory party lay in its relations with the future and not very distant King. After all, Thomas Tenison could see this and he only occupied the See of Canterbury and was not supposed to be worldly-wise. But the Archbishop had been in steady correspondence with Hanover (and at deliberate arm's length from the Ministry) from 1711 onwards.[14] The best view of Henry St John in all his contemporary and posthumous charm is probably a variant of Sellar and Yeatman. He was romantic *and* wrong.

The rising, which itself owed something to the hopes held out to James Edward by Bolingbroke, was a piece of unexampled good fortune to the Whigs. It was ultimately, against all intentions, entirely Scottish, and anti-Scottish feeling was more potent in England than any distrust of Germans. It lacked serious foreign assistance, with the dying Louis passing the contract on to Spain. It was wretchedly managed. Yet it scared everybody, ministers included, quite enough to set up a legend to be tapped at will. Walpole in particular would take up the threat of Jacobitism with a nagging, lifelong insistency, whose element of sincere belief is past judging.

Everything in the way of muddle and improvisation was foreshadowed

---

* In the city of Newcastle itself Forster had singularly little success. The legend is that the universal name of Tynesiders ever since came about when they were described (in Sunderland) as being 'Aal for Geordie'.

in August by the Duke of Ormonde who panicked at the prospect of arrest and fled, taking up a position coordinating (from France) troops too remote to be coordinated. By contrast, Stanhope's response was lucid and immediate. The taking of the rising seriously was never in doubt. Habeas Corpus was suspended and six thousand Dutch troops brought over. At home, twenty-two regiments were recruited and troops sent westward to garrison Bristol, Plymouth and Southampton. Admiral Byng* was despatched with a squadron to patrol the Channel, and incomers at all ports were examined by customs officers as potentially dangerous. London, with its Jacks and High Church mobs, was watched over by a body of the Guards bivouacked under canvas in Hyde Park. All this was the work of Stanhope and Townshend, Secretaries of State, and Robert Walpole who had been promoted, just before the rising and on the death of Halifax, to the Chancellorship of the Exchequer. And with the government fearful about the west, a group of political figures suspected of Jacobite sympathies, one including Lord Lansdowne and Sir William Wyndham, future long-service parliamentary opponent of the Whigs, was detained without trial.

The revolt was to have been driven by several undertakings, two of them Scottish, a march into the English north-west and the Lancashire Catholic enclaves, with distant hopes of taking Liverpool and reconnaissance with a Welsh rising, and a drive by the Earl of Mar in Scotland upon Edinburgh. The third was to have been a descent upon the south coast of England by James himself while Ormonde organised a diversionary assault upon Devon. If plans had been fulfilled with reasonable timing and efficiency, 'the Fifteen' might have been rather more than a debacle fading into legend. There was enough Jacobite feeling in London to cause concern, notwithstanding the Guards in Hyde Park. High Church mobs had celebrated Queen Anne's coronation day, 23 April (also of course, St George's Day), with pointed chants of 'God Save the Queen'.

After the rising had started in Scotland, a succession of gang fights between London Jacks and supporters of the King had marked Stuart anniversaries. Attacks on loyalist taverns to echo those made on Dissenting meeting houses in 1710 were made by Jack gangs, up to five hundred strong. This went on until July 1716, when, after an assault on Read's Mugg House in Fleet Street, five Jacks were tried and hanged.[15]

---

* Not the one shot in 1756, but his father.

In the real world of military campaigning, distance was making nonsense of Ormonde's plans. Two small stabs at Devon had no effect. James, waiting, disappointed and delayed, now sought a foothold where at any rate some activity was afoot, going instead to Scotland. By this time it was 22 December; Mar's rising, though nowhere crushed, was stalled, the English expedition had been stopped at Preston and the march on Edinburgh had failed as a result of the encounter with Argyll at Sheriffmuir, a draw when Mar, fighting it, had needed a victory. As for James, in a way which symbolised his whole life, he was too late, even though he had useful numbers, ten thousand men. Honourable, decent, stiff, unimaginative, in so many ways a perfect constitutional monarch, he was reported by Scottish rebels as a desperate disappointment. And being a decent, honourable man and seeing the certainty of a bloody defeat and a great cull of his followers, he withdrew in February. There would be no Culloden to end 'the Fifteen'.

By contrast with such management, the London government led by the former serving General, James Stanhope, had known about plans since he had received a despatch from Paris on 20 July. He maintained near daily contact with his field commander in the English theatre, General George Carpenter.[16] Argyll, descendant of the Earl who had risen against prelacy and erastianism in 1685, knew his Scotland and was certain that a rebellion without momentum and victories would see its troops quietly slip away. Fraught people in London damned him for a faint heart and doubtfully loyal, sending their own man, Cadogan, in his place, only for Cadogan, when he took up that place in February, to find that the Highland troops were slipping, or had already slipped, quietly away.

The rising had failed. In Harrington's laconic phrase, treason had not prospered, and the winning side dared call it treason. The issue quickly became one of punishing the losing side. George I, though this is not said very loudly, was generally inclined to magnanimity. As there had been no Culloden so there would be no bloody assize. Cadogan had set the tone by deliberately looking the other way while rebels did what Argyll had known they would do – went home. And this king had anyway no stomach for gibbeting foot followers. Against the 350 executed across the west under James II, twenty-six serving rebel officers were executed and seven hundred men sent into colonial servitude. As for the aristocratic leadership, there was a list of seven rebel Lords who had borne arms against the crown who might, in law, all go to

Tower Hill. Mar was not among them, having done his own slipping away early.

Left to himself, King George would have spared all. As it was, he managed to be a mitigating influence against those, very much led by an inflamed Walpole, who wanted every head. Walpole's authority for revenge lay in a clause of the Act of Settlement stating 'that no pardon under the Great Seal of England be pleadable to an impeachment by the Commons of England'.[17] The House of Lords, 'motivated', as Ragnhild Hatton deftly puts it, 'by class solidarity', was sufficiently with George to helpfully petition him 'to show mercy to such as might deserve it'.[18] Seven Lords engaged in the rising and taken after Preston were tried and condemned; four were reprieved and two, Kenmure and Derwentwater, beheaded. The last, Nithsdale, denied mercy, with his wife's aid helped himself and escaped from the Tower in the best tradition of a nineteenth-century novel about a Highland rising. At George's instance much of the money taken in forfeitures was spent upon local schools.

Jacobitism was to be the curse of the Tory party. It would be the text for a succession of Whig sermons starting in 1717 with one from Charles Townshend, Walpole's closest collaborator. He feared 'that the fire of the whole rebellion is rather smothered for a time, than wholly extinguished, and that it is ready to catch hold of the first convenient matter that shall be offered it, and may break forth with fresh fury'.[19] The implacable nature of the men in charge was signified by the case of Nottingham, one Hanoverian Tory in a Whig government. He had openly supported general clemency and as the price the King paid for his own clemency, was dismissed for it.

The immediate effect upon the Tories, despite their large innocence, or prudence, in the matter, was to cow and inhibit them in opposition. They hardly protested at the four-shilling land tax demanded by Walpole to cover costs occasioned by the rising. For the time being, the Whigs had the stage to themselves, and, in the way of such triumphs, mastery would turn quickly to private quarrels. It would not do so, however, until the holding of power had been ruthlessly consolidated. Parliamentary elections, once a matter of royal necessity for obtaining supply, had been given a legal term by the Triennial Act of 1694.

Frequent elections are expensive; they are also a check on the executive. The Junto Whigs who had passed that bill were not more pluralist than the generation of 1716. They had very recently been the opposition and had seen Charles II in the mid-1680s try his hand at open-ended suspension of Parliament. Frequent elections were a guarantee to oppositions, and in 1716 the Tories were the opposition. Seven years of assured Whig power with no voters to sweeten could be defended as stability – stability in power for the winning side. And given the patronage now in the hands of any government, it might be the foundation of a very pleasant stability for more years than seven. Even the dying Lord Somers, now facing a termination of his own, could applaud something extending life to the party. One Whig, Sir John Perceval, had his own candid gloss, finding that 'the only way to destroy Toryism will be to establish the present Parliament for some years to come'.[20]

Tories and old Whigs opposed the move, notably Shrewsbury, initiator of the Triennial Act and the same militant Whig, Perceval, who spoke of a long-life Commons as 'departing from Whig principles and perpetuating a Ministry though they serve their country ever so ill'.[21] Speeches were made about the extension of powers of patronage, prophecies which Walpole in person would soon justify up to the armpits. Not surprisingly, he was an enterprising advocate of the change, claiming characteristically that the Pretender was the chief beneficiary of less stable government, along with foreigners who were always taking advantage of us. The votes were there, among them forty-five representing Scotland by way of the government's purchasing arm, and, despite the votes against of forty-three Whigs resisting such modernisation, the bill passed by 122. The Tories were a party programmed for smear, defeated anyway, barred from patronage and their thin electoral prospects now heavily postponed. The Whigs were free to get down to a more interesting conflict with other Whigs.

Walpole would be at the heart of this. For a long time he would function as 'Walpole and Townshend', in the closest factional concert with his brother-in-law and Norfolk neighbour. None of that needed to have mattered but for Walpole and Townshend losing their sense of proportion, never a strong point, and picking a quarrel both with Stanhope's France-assuaging foreign policy and the King's German ministers. Atavistically, he demanded inclusion of Protestant Holland in the French treaty. This was a way of fighting the last war and completely ignoring the pacific and godless cynicism governing French policy under the Regent Philippe d'Orléans. Furthermore, he objected to the possible use of the British fleet in the Baltic, and both he and Townshend rounded upon and generally put blame upon the King's German advisers.

The immediate quarrel centred upon King and court. George, as Elector, had anxieties in the Baltic territories acquired from Sweden which Sweden might unaccountably want to get back. This created circumstances where having a French alliance at his back made very good sense to him. England being England and all foreigners resented on a non-discriminatory basis, the fear was that the helping of Hanover and making friendly terms with the French would alike be seen as a betrayal of John Bull. Stanhope, a foreign affairs man, appreciative of George's concerns, in his biographer's words, 'had not the inestimable advantage of having been born and bred in England and so under-standing almost instinctively the needs and innermost feelings of his countrymen'.* Unencumbered by such lumber, he looked coolly at foreign policy, understood the advantage to England long term of the French concord and conducted policy accordingly.

As briefly as possible, George's objective was to make a treaty between Britain and Holland on the one hand and France on the other. Work on this was done in the second half of 1716, from July of that year through to January 1717 to be precise, while George was chiefly in Hanover and Stanhope with him, and while Townshend, Walpole plus Walpole's aspirant diplomat brother, Horatio, Townshend's under-secretary, remained at home. Essentially, the treaty intended to confirm the status quo since the Treaty of Utrecht, but with certain points insisted upon or hardened. The French foot-dragging over reducing the Dunkirk harbour defences was to end and the Pretender should not remain on French soil, while the Dutch should have a barrier treaty to protect them from future French incursions. All this could be got from the Regent, Orléans, who had given neither men nor money for 'the Fifteen'. But the Emperor in Vienna had an objection that the general treaty recognising the status quo in Italy would bar him from the revision by which he hoped to recover Sicily, ceded unwillingly at Utrecht to Victor Amadeus of Savoy. A compromise was worked out with Vienna which left Italy out of the reckoning and settled for the rest of the treaty.

It was all sensible, peace-securing diplomacy, but it also left for later matters affecting Holland and the barrier treaty which should protect them in law against French ambitions. Time was needed to bring round

* Basil Williams, *Stanhope: A Study in Eighteenth-Century War and Diplomacy*. This is unfair to Williams who says this in the context of Stanhope's Suffrage Bill, dealt with later in the chapter.

the Emperor, an interested party in the Austrian Netherlands. This was too much for Charles Townshend. He jumped to the conclusion that the old system of the wartime alliance was being broken up, that the Dutch were either being cut out or, alternatively, as non-signatories, set free to benefit as traders in future British wars, in which she would have no obligation against poaching. As Townshend and Walpole were in London and the negotiations conducted on the Continent by George and Stanhope, some of the communication problems besetting Ormonde and his Scottish commanders applied here.

But a new crisis added to the confusion and resentment brewing over the French treaty. Hanover had benefited at the end of the war by way of territory – Bremen and Verden – won from Sweden. Charles XII of Sweden, having amazed Europe by his expansion eastward and subsequent collapse, was back – in Scania, Norway, actually, and threatening. He was restrained from self-help by the threat which a British fleet under Admiral Norris represented. Meanwhile the Tsar, Peter the Great, having some years earlier stopped Charles in his tracks at Poltava (1709), was emerging as a new European factor, something vividly illustrated by ambitions to turn Mecklenburg, near Hanover, into a client state, a very disturbing development for the Elector. A war was very seriously contemplated, and George and Stanhope considered ordering Norris to spend the winter in the Baltic and encourage Peter to retreat from his foothold.

Townshend, not a tactful man, wrote to Stanhope on 4 October (New Style), begging him 'not to consent to Sir John Norris staying any longer than the first of November in the Baltic, nor to the King's engaging openly in the affair of the Tsar. The Northern War has been managed so stupidly, that it will be our ruin – would it not therefore be right for the King to think immediately how to make peace with Sweden even tho' he should be obliged to make some sacrifice in obtaining it?'[22] George was pushing his luck by using the British navy in fact or *terrorem*, though he had the excuse of threat as well as hope of gain. The devil was in the adverb: 'stupidly' was certain of giving enormous offence. It did. Saying that he should simply take good British advice and give way over these tedious German territories pleased quite as much.

However, the whole north European element in foreign policy, its serving of German interests contradicting, as it did, tight particulars laid down in the Act of Settlement, had explosive potential in a country where Jacobitism was still a force and affection for the new royalty temperate in the extreme. Walpole, himself almost neurotically concerned about a Jacobite threat, understood this, but was in no position to exploit it. But plotting, real if oversold, sent a long shudder of anxiety into politics, one which would be renewed across the next five years and be part of politics longer yet.*

Only a little earlier, in August, negotiations over the French treaty had proceeded very well between Stanhope and the Abbé Dubois, first at The Hague then in Whitehall. Essentially, the Pretender was to go to Italy, the French alliance with Sweden, made by Louis, would be dropped, the Protestant succession in England be so phrased as to guarantee Bremen and Verden, the Empire left free to seek Sicily back by exchange and the Regent offered military support if the senior Bourbon King of Spain should make a claim on the French crown. The draft was signed on 24 August and sent to London where Townshend set about resisting the terms of the negotiations.

Not only did he reasonably enough inform the Dutch through Horatio, but added his own unauthorised and mutinous gloss that they were 'conditional upon Dutch consent'. In fact, it was a good treaty, specifically good on the Dunkirk harbours, something over which the French had played a long delaying hand for five years. Stanhope was told on 9 October to sign the treaty and Townshend, already at odds with King and first Minister, could not expect to remain in office. He had not understood the larger dimensions, and in pursuit of a superfluous anxiety about Holland, rooted in the circumstances of 1702, had presumptuously exceeded his authority.

The best construction that can be put upon Walpole's resistance to all this, which would spark a long course of defection and obstruction in domestic parliamentary politics, is that he had the Commons to manage and expected serious resistance there. Alternatively he saw a weapon and used it. If so, Sunderland in Stanhope's camp, a professional *frondeur* keen to make a quarrel out of a disagreement, stood ready to respond.

Parallel with the diplomatic differences lay a great pettiness occasioned by the matter of Melusine's Duchy. Ehrengard Melusine, Graefin von der Schulenburg, is commonly called the mistress of George I. For reasons which have nothing to do with political correctness, it makes

---

*This is dealt with in company with Jacobite enterprises generally in Chapter Eight.

better sense to see her as that contemporary thing, his partner. Sophia Dorothea, adulterous not without provocation, had been locked up in a castle at Celle since 1694 and Melusine, who had come on the scene in 1691, had been George's wife in all but priest's and registrar's terms for better than twenty years, and they were steadily devoted. Walpole would later describe Melusine as Queen in all but name. Keeping her onside was an elementary pre-conditional step of British statecraft, something Stanhope properly understood. Obtaining for the King's consort an *Irish* peerage, as Duchess of Munster, equivalent in terms of comparative nobility to a plastic mac instead of a Burberry, was not clever, but it was what Townshend had done. Walpole would famously say, while regularly paying it, that 'Every man has his price'. Melusine had hers and Townshend had underbid.

She was not a malicious woman but all courts are preoccupied with precedence, whether or not the younger son of a Viscount comes into dinner before a Master in Lunacy. And, anyway, she detected scorn, rather a Townshend speciality, in the fobbing off. He (and Walpole) had made an enemy; she was also a busy correspondent recording the small coin of court ill will. An enemy whom they had anyway had been making busy nearer the King. When George went to Hanover, Sunderland, who *was* a malicious woman, had organised his own holidays to get from Aix-la-Chapelle (Aachen) and its waters to Herrenhausen and the trouble he could make there.

Not that the King was an enemy. George was grown up in his political dealings and he fully recognised Walpole's great abilities. But beyond anything stirred up by Sunderland or Melusine, Townshend had not understood the King's foreign policy. Even the most narrowly Hanoverian part made good sense; it did not conflict with British interests and it concerned issues and necessary checks appropriate to the present and the immediate future. There was too much disagreement for continuation in a Secretaryship of State (Northern Department) stuck full of all these points at issue. Townshend had to go, but he was fired only in the lesser sense of becoming Lord-Lieutenant of Ireland. George cushioned the horror of it by saying that he didn't actually have to go there! Peace was then formally made up with the King earnestly seeking it.

But what stood naked behind the civilities was bubbling enmity between Walpole and Townshend on one hand and Sunderland on the other, with Stanhope, because of the strategic issues and his own comfortable understanding of the King, drawn into concert with Sunderland. George called the parties together on 16 January 1717 to attempt conciliation, using Stanhope to convey harder words separately. He wanted to keep all his ministers, with Townshend's notional exile to be made short, six months or so and followed by promotion.

Walpole and Townshend submitted, with Townshend kissing hands for the Irish post and Stanhope taking over his (senior) secretaryship. Dinners were given by different parties to mark reconciliation, but between Sunderland and Townshend at any rate there could be no peace. The Duchess of Munster, as Melusine would remain until 1719, informed the chief Minister in Hanover that Sunderland was 'hated' by the pair and that they would neither receive nor visit him.[23]

In foreign affairs the two men had been out of their depths. But both would have argued that, domestically, they understood the temper of the Commons and that a pro-French policy which neglected the vital ties with Holland would weaken King and government in the Commons. This was a flimsy argument. The rising had only just been defeated. The Hanoverians who, together with their government, had come well out of the conflict, were the country's main shield against a Jacobitism now manifestly a minority culture even in the Tory party, itself bedraggled and bruised by recent events. Crown and government were in no danger, least of all over arcane points of foreign policy.

But fear was always Walpole's weapon of first resort. The brothers-in-law, defeated at court, went back to Parliament to look to their strengths and assemble a weapon for themselves. Stanhope was playing to the King; they would take aim from Westminster. The early months of the new year, 1717, were spent in gathering support – support among Whigs and Tories, support to be used against Stanhope and George. The idea of a strong, united party, held together despite differences by common principles, was about to be blown to atoms by the ultimate good party man.

Peace lasted through the early months of the year only to be threatened when George went again to Hanover. Notoriously that royal house maintains dynastic bad relations, successive fathers denouncing a line of sons rebelling on the hour against them. The Prince of Wales, now Englished to George Augustus, had married a wife, Caroline of Ansbach, handsome, pneumatic and intellectual, one holding him in awe in each department, a wife by whom, despite his infidelities, he was generally directed. Caroline liked politics, liked intrigue and dragged George

Augustus into both. To that taste Walpole and Townshend gave savour, themselves intriguing against the Duke of Argyll, insisting that unless he were dismissed, something which further blocked off his succession as commander in chief to the sinking Marlborough, he would represent a general threat. Argyll, justifiably angry at being superseded in Scotland for sensibly letting a winning course take its way, might, they argued, work against ministers while the King was away. The ploy succeeded and George and Caroline, friends of the Duke, submitted unhappily. The King, though capable of pepperiness, genuinely sought domestic accord, giving George Augustus most normal powers of regency.

But by now they were bent upon a larger quarrel, the Prince letting it be known in a crude piece of disloyal populism, as the Duchess's brother reported in another letter, that he 'thought little' of Bremen or Verden.[24] George Augustus had a little following in Parliament and he could attend the Lords as Duke of Cambridge. He did not, of course, come there to vote against his father's ministers, but his supporters knew that they should do so. The whole tenor of things was profoundly childish. Caroline disliked Townshend.

They were friends of Argyll, whom the Norfolk men had brought down. They had no natural ties to the Tory party with its historic regrets and pale acquiescence in the new dynasty. But it was Tories who came to the Princess's salon. It was the Tories who moved in Parliament for £100,000 to be paid on the Civil List to the Heir, the Whigs who had to vote it down. Lady Cowper who had been so pleased at the correctness of royal sentiments over the British parties, asked Caroline sourly 'if she continued in the resolution of being a Tory?'[25] And bad blood being thicker than water, George Augustus, following his Princess, did everything he could to encourage the Townshend faction against his father's Minister. Townshend and Walpole had the same enemies as the Tories and the same friends at court. It was a case of the greater spite prevailing over the lesser.

On 9 April 1717 there was a vote on supply, always an occasion for talking about most things. Attacks were made on Bernstorff and Bothmer, the King's German advisers at court, both of whom had made serious attempts to reconcile all parties earlier in the year. Bremen and Verden were brought up, foreign fripperies of no interest to Britain, upon which good British money was being spent. What Walpole had said he most feared in Parliament he was conjuring up there. He voted for the government motion but deliberately held back his interest – the votes he could deliver in a division. The Prince of Wales absented himself, but his men, tipped the wink, voted against, reducing the majority to fifteen. In all, fifty-three Whigs had voted against Stanhope. Next day with identical tactics of nominal loyalty and dedicated back-stabbing, the majority was down to four.

There, wrote a German correspondent, went a parliament lost to the King.[26] Townshend was dismissed with civility. Walpole, invited to stay and cooperate, said that he couldn't work with the people in office and resigned. They were followed by a close circle of allies, *inter alia* Lord Orford, Paul Methuen and William Pulteney, respectively First Lord, Southern Secretary and Secretary at War. It looked briefly as if the Ministry might fall. But the King put his best efforts and interest behind his ministers, the placemen sat tight and a thin ministry was reconfected, with Joseph Addison, Pope's derided Cato*, given the junior secretaryship, Sunderland the senior one while Stanhope himself took the Treasury.

The effect of the revolt was to paralyse government policy, a paralysis which fell briefly upon essential measures like the Mutiny Bill and lastingly upon liberal measures which Stanhope was promoting. The general amnesty which the King wished to issue to Jacobites – perfect political wisdom having won the fight, not to grind the shoe in the throat – was threatened. As we shall see, plans to give greater rights to Dissenters, a group to whom Walpole had always paid court, would be postponed out of sight, along with plans for toleration of Roman Catholics and Jews and for liberalising universities from their present status as particularist Anglican institutions. There were ideas here which would be lost until the 1830s.

All these measures lay at the heart and head of thinking, principled Whiggism. To oppose them was to take sides with Squire Booby and Dr Sacheverell, something about which Walpole and Townshend, in their determination to wreck Stanhope and affront the King, would do without reflection. Ironically, bad ideas of which Walpole approved were also jeopardised. The persecution of Lord Oxford, of which he was the virulent instigator, was current government business so it had to be opposed. This pleased Walpole's new Tory allies who were told

---

* 'Like Cato give his little Senate laws / And sit attentive to his own applause', *Epistle to Dr Arbuthnot.*

that the government were planning to try him by attainder. The Earl left the Tower in July 1717 for his estate in Herefordshire, occasional interventions in the Lords and an affable correspondence with the Pretender, by no means treasonable, but, not surprisingly, more sympathetic than anything said or written when he was in office.

The Commons grew rough-mouthed and, a word it would not have recognised, 'racist', regularly abusing Germans for being Germans and for being here, and when it was feeling properly unpleasant, damning the King for both. 'A Mecklenberg Squire' William Pulteney would call him. The Walpole group were working with the Prince's men, but also with the Tories. And a volume of anti-Hanoverian abuse and wholesale financial slurs gave the impression that that party, utterly worsted electorally and weighed down by the rising, had assumed the leadership of Commons opinion. So far did things go that the Court made clandestine contact with the exiled Bolingbroke, now sacked by the Pretender, for fear that Walpole might not scruple to find him a congenial ally. Yet such was the absurdity of polemic that Walpole's people were accusing Stanhope, and by implication the King, in respect of their accord with France, of behaving like Bolingbroke.

Two quarrels were taking place side by side with considerable overlap – the deepening conflict of George Augustus and Caroline with the King, one whose futilities, like the choice of a name and a godfather for the Prince's new son,[27] are too fatuous to list; the other, of Townshend and Walpole against Stanhope and Sunderland, far more important, very little less mean.

However mean, the quarrels were drastic, and in November/December 1717 had blazed up into a sort of small war between the King and George Augustus who had got himself into a shouting match with a courtier, the young Duke of Newcastle, allegedly threatened a duel and got himself expelled from the Palace. It was the source of a good deal of unhappiness, especially for the King, but politically he stood firmly by his own measure and his own men. Stanhope, who had been keeping the shop uneasily at the Exchequer, was brought back into the full panoply of foreign affairs, Anglo-Hanoverian style, when, without losing Sunderland to the Ministry, he resumed the Northern Secretaryship, with the younger James Craggs, very much Stanhope's and the King's man, relieving the littérateur, Addison, at the Southern Secretary's post.

This was now, without reservation, a Stanhope Ministry, consolidating a more tentative position first taken up in October 1716, and would remain so until his sudden death in February 1721. Walpole and Townshend had demonstrated enormous nuisance value and had set back indefinitely plans to make the country a more open, secular and tolerant one. But they had not budged King and Minister from the foreign affairs stand they had taken, or weakened their general command. The attack upon colleagues and disruption of the party had been abortive, but it went on.

On 4 December, Walpole moved for a reduction in land forces by 12,000 men, failing to carry his motion by fifty votes. So-called reductions in numbers to 16,000 men had actually left it above 18,000 'which was one third more than the number of Land Forces amounted to formerly in time of peace'.[28] They had, of course, increased during 'the Fifteen', and the implication of the motion was that forces giving military strength to a monarch with his own Hanoverian agenda should be denied him. And anyway they amounted to a standing army which good Englishmen were against. In taking this stand, Walpole was keeping company with William Shippen, a live-and-die, declared Jacobite who denounced a foreign policy conceived 'by the meridian of Germany'[29] by a king ignorant of the English people or country.

'It is the only infelicity of His Majesty's reign,' Shippen had argued, 'that he is unacquainted with our language and constitution; and it is therefore the more incumbent upon British ministers to inform him that our government does not stand on the same foundation with his German dominions which by reason of their situation, and the nature of their constitution, are obliged to keep up armies in time of peace.' His speech against the expenditure on land forces had come after Walpole's, and he spoke of it admiringly. 'I will not trouble you sir with my remarks on the fallacy of those reductions. They have been sufficiently exposed by a gentleman, (Mr Walpole) who is better informed of the secret of the affair and who, I am glad to find, when he is contending for the service of his country, is no more afraid than myself, of being called a Jacobite, by those, who want other arguments to support their debates.'[30] But Shippen *was* a Jacobite and it was a measure of the situation that Walpole found himself *en cette galère*.

However, his speech was full of echoes of the 1630s and the disputes over ship money and a standing army, the sort of thing which the rulers of less happy countries needed. This promising anxiety was being worked, just a little less provocatively, by Walpole. The Member for King's Lynn returned to the debate just before Christmas. In the practice of the time, ministers had asked for money (£681,618) for the King. Speaking on 9 December 1717, he made an elaborate analysis of the costs of various kinds of regiment, foot, horse and dragoons. They, especially the dragoons, were 'most grievous and oppressive to the country'.[31] He suggested that by cuts in this area nearly £100,000 could be saved – 'for the country', as he put it. These were, of course, the sort of troops likely to be used in the threatened Spanish conflict. Effectively he was engaged in a plea for hypothecation, the focusing of money granted upon specific objects with Parliament to do the specifying.

Craggs for the Ministry argued that it had been the practice to grant what was necessary to maintain troops, not to go into such regimental detail, but with Members 'contenting themselves with fixing the whole number, [they] had wholly left the regulating of the matter to the crown; and he hoped they would not shew less regard to His Majesty or repose less confidence in his wisdom . . .'[32] The best way, replied Walpole ironically, 'for the Commons of Great Britain to acknowledge His Majesty's most gracious intentions for the good of his subjects was to point out to him the means of rendering those intentions effectual; that this might be done by disbanding or dismounting eight or nine regiments of dragoons, whereby the country would be eased of a great burden and oppression'.[33] Fashionably for this period, William Shippen had been sent to the Tower earlier in the month for his candid animus. But Walpole came within fifty of winning the vote and, having nagged about the cost, did bring about a concessionary reduction in army pay. As war with Spain was looming, this could be called an example of constructive defeatism.

The recurring theme of opposition to the Ministry was demonstrated over the Mutiny Bill. Oxford, cheerfully dabbling in a little politics after his acquittal, made a point in the tradition of Hampden which, against a German king, Tories were now making their own. 'The keeping up a standing army in time of peace was not the way to gain the hearts, but rather to increase the disaffection of the people . . . all good and wise princes had ever chosen to rather depend upon the affections of their subjects, than on a military force.' He added a little less mildly that 'none but bad and corrupt ministers have need of troops to maintain their authority and unwarrantable proceedings'.[34]

Walpole under the same business advocated withdrawing the death penalty for desertion. He was not remarkable in his compassion for the common soldier, but some Whigs were decently sympathetic and were ready to vote for such an amendment, bringing Stanhope's majority down to eighteen. In time, Walpole would follow a distinguished policy of avoiding foreign wars as expensive, open-ended and futile. In the early months of 1718, he was, by contrast, opposing specifically the *King*'s war, one undertaken in part to support the Emperor in his dispute with Philip VI of Spain. The Emperor was another German: what did all this have to do with the sovereign English? And anyway such involvement left us vulnerable at home. He particularly objected to sending a fleet into the Mediterranean 'whilst Great Britain was left naked and exposed to the insults of a provoked enemy abroad'.[35] Unfortunately for such a ploy, Admiral Byng soon after defeated a Spanish fleet at Cape Passaro in the approved, patriotic 'Hearts of Oak' manner, and a motion deploring the absence of a formal declaration of war failed by sixty. Whether as stratagem or longer-term principle, the Walpole who had sought to extirpate the Tories was busily replicating Tory policy. The Walpole who had sought to prosecute Oxford for treason now followed Oxford's pacific thinking.

It was at this point that Stanhope brought forward his plans on religious toleration. A man who had read his Locke and actually believed in religious toleration, he proposed that everything remaining on the statute books of the Tories' punitive Anglican triumphalism should simply go, the Occasional Conformity Act, the Schism Act and parts of the much older, Caroline Test and Corporation acts. George, a broad-minded Lutheran who had no bigotry toward Dissenters or indeed Roman Catholics, strongly approved.

In rebelling against this, Walpole, though he contradicted all his earlier positions, was acting in line with certain shifts among Whigs generally. The trial of Sacheverell had taken place only nine years earlier. The Church of England might be an unnecessary enemy. And although the bishops' vote was split now that the Whigs had made a number of them, the Church had, if anything, hardened in defence of its rights, rents and general supremacy. To the Bishop of Winchester, Trelawney, reformers were 'Phanatigs', saying that if they 'can get a bill to their minds, farewell to episcopacy'.[36] Nicholson of Carlisle spoke of repeal of the Occasional Conformity Act as 'Readmission of Occasional Hypocrisy'.[37]

Walpole saw the bill late, as it had commenced in the Lords, where fifteen of the bishops had opposed it. His arguments were from party. The bill ran 'against the judgment of half the Whigs'.[38] They were supplemented by an observation speaking the bronze mentality of the machine politician with breathtaking complacency. Stanhope meant to open public offices to Dissenters, but, said Walpole, 'there were people enough to fill all offices without capacitating any more disqualified'.[39]

He also put on enough of the Church-in-danger Tory style to claim that what was being attempted 'would in a scandalous manner have evaded the Test Act', and would be 'a handle to the disaffected who would inculcate into the minds of the people that many of the measures which occasioned an unfortunate prince's abdication were now renewed'.[40]

Opposition to the original Test and Corporation Acts as they affected Dissenters had been the core of Whig belief and purpose in its early seventeenth-century days following Shaftesbury. The bill passed with an underperforming majority of eighteen, but the opposition had done enough to convince Sunderland, to whom Stanhope yielded, that the key clauses which undid the Test Act would not carry in committee. They were dropped and the purposes of the legislation defeated.

The last measure of factional zealotry taken up by Walpole's faction was directed against Roman Catholics. Stanhope, true to his general liberalism, wanted in a quite separate manoeuvre to remove the penalties of taxation, inheritance, education and liability to unconscionable oaths, under which they stood. The essential pre-condition was to persuade Rome through leading Catholic aristocrats like the Duke of Norfolk to withdraw its endorsement of the Pretender. The Catholic noblemen dithered and, according to James Craggs, they did so after the intervention of Walpole's lieutenant, William Pulteney, giving 'mighty assurances that they would destroy the present Ministry with the King, and so discouraged them from engaging themselves in a falling house'.[41]

Craggs was on the other side, but for such things even to be said and suspected gives a startling idea of the dark mood to which Walpole, in pursuit of revenge and advancement, had brought things. On one issue, however, his factionalism had point and validity: the legislation to which Stanhope turned his hand in 1719. The peerage has historically been many things, not least a commodity. But in the mixed constitution of England in the early eighteenth century, they were votes, votes in a chamber at least equal with the House of Commons. Peers could initiate legislation and they could terminate it. Practice might involve much forbearance and holding one's hand, but the reserve power, even in repose, was a great thing.

The King's first Minister commonly sat in the Lords or, like Harley, went there during his time in the highest office. Harley had also demonstrated at the high point of his influence with Queen Anne that, in order to get the right result, endorsement of his peace treaty, the Lords could be packed. The twelve peers made for the purpose in 1711 lingered in Whig nostrils even after the effect had been incrementally reversed. In 1719 they themselves had a majority in the Lords. The temptation existed to take the ball home while they were ahead of the game and freeze the score.

There were other reasons. The Prince of Wales, having made a cave at Leicester House, where he kept a shabby court with a clutch of anti-ministerialist politicians, put those enjoying office into disagreeable reflection on the coming ability of George II to undo the servants of George I. A lavish creation of Leicester House men upon accession would, beyond the withdrawal of other royal favours, quite undermine a government. There were also objections to the traffic in which the present King's Hanoverian ministers, his lady and close courtiers availed themselves of a trade in titles, something to be deplored or at any rate restricted to true-born Englishmen.

The outcome of such thinking was the Peerage Bill. The motion introducing it proposed 'That the number of English peers should not be enlarged beyond six above the present number, which upon failure of male issue, might be supplied by new creations; That instead of the Sixteen elective peers in Scotland, 25 might be made hereditary in that part of the Kingdom, whose number, upon failure of heirs male, should be supplied by some other Scotch peers'. The bill was backed by the King who gave Stanhope for publication a statement waiving his right to create peers.

George's thinking was personal; his son had provoked him deeply. When reconciliation came, it would not go deep. The idea of waiving his own powers in order to waive those of George Augustus was to impose posthumous restraint upon a foolish posterity. The larger, ministerial, notion was for a hard peerage, hard in the way of a currency, a sort of monetarism in strawberry leaves. Given the powers of the Upper House, it was the setting of an elite in ice, proof not only against purchase and royal favour, but talent. It was oligarchic in theory as the century was to be oligarchic in practice, but to work oligarchies need to be flexible. This bill, essentially the product of Sunderland's peremptory mind, with Stanhope accepting and cooperating, pointed toward

a Venetian concept of nobility, a closed conspiracy of the inheriting. It
was not a good idea.

Walpole returned to his alternative outlet in controversy, the pamphlet.
He had a good, vigorous, uncluttered style and got to his point in
'Thoughts of a Member of the Lower House' by arguing that 'the House
of Lords will be a fixed, independent body, not to be called to account
like a Ministry, nor to be dissolved or changed like a House of Commons
... [We should see] King and Ministry entirely at the mercy of the
Lords and the Commons more dependent on the Crown.' And with a
snap of irony he added, 'I presume no one will suggest that all merit
is exhausted by their present Lordships.'

He enquired 'why any number of Men, who enjoy themselves the
highest Dignities and Privileges in a Commonwealth should shut the
Door upon all others who may have equal Births, Deserts and Fortunes'.[42]
This last point was pertinent. It was a time when men, having made
their way up by getting rich – through marriage, trade and land values
– then acquired more land to the point of qualification for nobility.
People coming up, like the Walpoles, bought land and married into
peerage families. Dorothy Walpole, Robert's sister, was married to
Viscount Townshend. And there were scores like them, but Robert
Walpole was acquiring status (and getting rich) through the House of
Commons. The trouble he had made in the last three years was a
measure of his influence, the clan web of connection and the actual or
prospective reward which might be held out. Reward might be office,
might very well be membership of the peerage.

The Peerage Bill raised a public furore. Publications mushroomed in
opposition or support, one form being the serial pamphlet. Over two
weeks and two issues, Addison and Steele long estranged, fell further
out as the former Secretary responded snappishly in the pro-bill *Old
Whig* to his former friend's anti-bill *Plebian*, the first of three. 'The
House of Peers,' wrote Steele in that publication, '... may in time
become corrupt and offensive, like a stagnated pool which hitherto has
been preserved wholesome and pure by the fresh streams that pass
continually into it.'[43] He also added pointedly that 'the great Business
is always carried on by Men created in their own Persons; and if all
such were now to be excluded, I need not say what would be the ability
of the House'. Addison, who had married a countess, maintained that
the bill would prevent a superfluity of lordships.

After these two long-distance men, single pamphlet followed upon single pamphlet, though Walpole succeeded himself with *The Moderator*. It was a quarrel which made strange allies. Walpole had desisted from pursuing Oxford to disoblige Stanhope. He now found himself the uncomfortable ally of Oxford who opposed the bill as Walpole accused him of seeking amnesty and a return there. Oxford in turn was cheerily encouraged by the Steele whom he had had expelled from the Commons a few years before. Disputes had so far divided Walpole and his following from Stanhope and the King. But the Peerage Bill and the ideas attendant upon it chiefly reflected the personality of Charles Spencer, 2nd Earl of Sunderland.

In a letter to young Newcastle, he announced imperiously that the King was determined to go on with current legislation which he listed as 'the Peerage Bill, the university Bill and the repeal of the Septennial Bill [*sic*]'. No bill to end the terms of Parliament was ever tabled. But the judgement of Basil Williams, Stanhope's biographer, drawing from one of his letters, is that what was intended was a simple extension of Parliament, a reward to Members who voted the right way on the peerage, a tantalising increment of the exclusivity promised in that legislation to peerage families. James Craggs, the Younger was on record at the same time canvassing the opposite idea, the threat of snap election to bring recalcitrants into line. As Williams says, there is a whiff here of Cromwell and the sent-away Long Parliament.

Newcastle warned against meddling with the parliamentary term: 'Should this parliament be continued [i.e. extended], it would show a great distrust of the king's interest in England, and look as if our past conduct wd not be approved of, when on the contrary, we have all the reason to think it before this parliament ends, the King's affairs will be upon so glorious a foot it will [be] almost impossible to oppose him.'[44]

So much of what Stanhope was trying to do was tolerant and enlightened, and Walpole had been its opportunist and not very creditable opponent. The Suffrage Bill and the Parliament-stretching ideas floating unconsummated about it made Walpole, as automatic critic of the Ministry, a champion of pluralistic politics and a society open to the rise of merit. In fact the idea of meddling with elections, already thinned out, was quickly dropped by Stanhope, probably at the sensible instance of Newcastle who had offset the unparliamentary instincts of Sunderland.

Even so, it increasingly began to look as if the Peerage Bill on its own would pass. Newcastle's talk of glory had not been bombast. The foreign end of George and Stanhope's policy was coming vividly right. The prospect of an extended Swedish war had ended in a peace, and on 23 November, the day before Parliament was due to meet, the chief advocate in Spain of a continuation of the war, Cardinal Alberoni, had been dismissed. Everything was falling into place; the foreign war, inspiration of Townshend and Walpole's quarrel with the King and his ministers, had succeeded. When the Peerage Bill was brought before the Lords, they supported it with all the enthusiasm of club members contemplating an exclusivity ever more exclusive. It was questionable if the opposition Whigs, Walpole's own constituency, would offer real resistance. The Whigs had by tradition usually dominated the Upper House, hence the anger at Oxford's intrusion in 1711. Why should not this happy state of affairs be institutionalised by statute?

The very difficulty of resistance only enhances what Walpole would now achieve. There was, first of all, a meeting of the opposition Whigs at Devonshire House, the Duke being a conscientious opposition Whig. As Walpole's first biographer, Archdeacon William Coxe, put it, he 'found the whole body luke warm, irresolute or desponding: several of the peers secretly favoured a bill which would increase their importance'.[45] It was also argued that the Whigs, having attacked Oxford's creation of peers in 1711, thought it inconsistent to oppose legislation against further such abuse of the prerogative. According to Coxe, Walpole was alone in his determination to fight the bill. But his word for it was 'dastardly'. He had recognised 'the only point on which he could harass the administration with any prospect of success; that he would place it in such a light as to excite indignation in every independent commoner'.[46]

Walpole now set about shifting the mood of the meeting to attack, raising the consciousness, one might say, of the lesser men. Doing something he did very well, Walpole talked common, Norfolk plain, quoting 'a plain country gentleman, of about eight hundred pounds a year . . . with heat and some oaths (which was what Mr Walpole overheard and catched at), "What! Shall I consent to the shutting of the door upon my family ever coming into the House of Lords?"' Walpole took this up. 'The same sentiment might easily be made to run through the whole body of country gentlemen, be their estates then what they would; for my part I am determined that if deserted by my party in this question, I will singly stand forth and oppose it.'[47]

All this was done, says Coxe, 'with uncommon vehemence, occasioned much alteraction, and many persuasions were made to deter him from adopting a measure which appeared chimerical and absurd; but when they found that he persisted, the whole party gradually came over to his opinion and agreed that an opposition should be made to it in the House of Commons'.[48] As a general rule, Walpole being bluff is a signal to count one's spoons. He was an artful metropolitan sophisticate who did a very passable Good Old Squire. But even if his whole object was to get his enemies, the Stanhope Ministry – and on the strength of his performance on religious toleration, he might have spoken against if Stanhope had offered seats in the Lords for election – he was at least at home in talking such language. He was a grandee leading hayseeds, but he knew how hayseeds felt.

The speech was good enough to rally his own faction and its friends. And when he came to speak in the House on 18 December, he flattered legislators with their own virtue, upon which Stanhope was making an assault. 'The usual path to the Temple of Honour has been through the Temple of Virtue; but if this bill is passed into a law, one of the most powerful incentives to virtue would be taken away, since there would be no arriving at honour, but through the winding sheet of an old decrepit lord, or the grave of an extinct noble family . . .'[49]

Virtue was something in which, without rhapsodising about it, country gentlemen did believe, and thought themselves possessed of. Quite why it should dry up for the lack of viscountcies is not clear. But Walpole, invoking it, asked the central question: 'How can the Lords expect the Commons to give their concurrence to a bill by which they and their posterity are to be for ever excluded from the peerage?'[50] On the legislation's larger, higher purpose, he conveyed a sepulchral gravity: 'That this bill will secure the liberty of parliament I totally deny; it will secure a great preponderance of the peers; it will form them into a compact, impenetrable phalanx.'[51]

Walpole's concluding evocation of medieval oligarchy was meant to frighten. Gentlemen should not 'shut their ears to the dreadful example of former times; let them recollect that the overweening disposition of the great barons, to aggrandize their own dignity, occasioned them to exclude the lesser barons, and to that circumstance may be fairly attributed the sanguinary laws which so long desolated the country.'[52] Meanwhile, his earlier point, that Stanhope, having only recently acquired a peerage himself, was 'now desirous of shutting the door after him',[53] was, if obvious, no less effective. But perhaps the most lucid, if arguable, argument in a clear and penetrating speech concerned the emerging constitutional balance. 'The Crown is dependent on the Commons by the power of granting money; the Commons are dependent on the Crown by the power of disso-lution: the Lords will now be made independent of both.'[54] 'The present view of the Bill,' he added a little later, 'is dangerous, the view to posterity personal and unpardonable; it will make the Lords masters of the king.' Such vacancies as would occur would be ministers' own creation. 'And the new peers will adhere to the first minister with the same zeal and unanimity as those created by Oxford adhered to him.'[55]

As for the enlarged Scottish peerage, Walpole wasted no civilities. 'The sixteen elective Scotch peers already admit themselves to be a dead court weight, yet the same sixteen are to be made hereditary and nine added to their number. These twenty-five under the influence of corrupt ministers, may find their account in betraying their trust.'[56] What mattered though was not the speech, however well turned. It was the fact of rebelling when there had been no organised mood for rebellion. Walpole had rallied opposition to something wanted by ministers at the height of their success and authority. He had talked opposition up and it had flown. The bill was defeated by 269 votes to 177, a degree of revulsion nowhere expected.

Walpole had been done a great favour in being given a case which could give him nothing but credit. It was one, moreover, in which natural Tory support could not taint his opposition to the government. This was a good faith question and he had personally insisted on the stand, having spotted ahead of his supporters the latent strength of resistance, not so much to a concentration of power as to the road block erected against the ambitions of knights, baronets and the heads and heirs of country families. Famously, Walpole proclaimed, 'Every man has his price.' He could imagine nothing less wise in a minister than to remove every man from the market.

The time was now right for reconciliation. The war and its atten-dant alliances, which Townshend and Walpole had in so insular a way rejected, had ended in victory. The King's interest had been looked after, the links with France had worked, a whole mindset in foreign policy had been created for the future – Walpole's future. Most of the pair's factitious revolts had failed, but the last firework had exploded in the most satisfactory manner. Over the whole match, Whig government and Whig opposition had played something very like a draw.

There was still the option of the Stanhope people doing business with the Tories, but once again that party deployed its genius for counting the teeth of a gift horse. Sir William Bromley, a former lieutenant to Oxford, was approached by Harcourt, himself a former Tory who had moved smoothly to the winning side. His response was to turn about and, followed by his party, temporarily boycott Parliament. His explanation spoke the reflexive fearfulness, the positive inferiority complex of the Tories at this time: 'We could only have joined with them and no further than they thought fit to go, in whom we could have no confidence.'[57] Fearful of being picked off, as Harcourt had been, they would only go in as a whole party. The idea of key men entering a Ministry in return for specific measures, and using as a weapon the ability to withdraw what they had held out, required a confidence they did not have. And by staying out they redoubled the appeal of floor-crossing to individual Tory talents.

Stanhope was also under assault from one of the King's famous German ministers, Andreas Gottlieb, Graf von Bernstorff, who, with revenges of his own in mind, had begun to agitate against what he called 'the Cabal', the Stanhope cabinet. In letters sent abroad (and intercepted), he had described how a better government from the point of Vienna's foreign policy might be obtained. Imperial pressure should be put upon the King to bring in Townshend and Walpole, to appoint five or six Tories and relegate Stanhope and Sunderland to subordinate posts. Whether this sort of talk flowed from conversations with either man is not known. Given George's solidarity with Stanhope, the whole notion sounds wild and whirling. But discovery of the letter had apparently put the flaky Sunderland 'into not a little fright'.[58] The response, according to this narrative, was to pre-empt any such manipulation of the King and to reconcile Walpole and Townshend from a position of strength.

It sounds remote, unlike the obvious pressures of parliamentary reversal, but Stanhope was a man preoccupied with foreign policy and the doings of courts, foreign and British. Jealous fear of the German advisers for the King's support meshed with those advisers' jealous fear of ministers. Whatever the compulsion, settlement of the court wars of King and Prince would be a precondition of reconciliation. It was one thing which both Walpole and Stanhope thought as necessary as desirable. King and Prince were worked upon, something easy for Walpole whose special care had been the Prince of Wales.

George Augustus, as the patron of an opposition group wanting a return to the mainstream, was very vulnerable. The mere possibility of being deserted by his supporters was humiliating. Whereas in return for submission and apology he would escape the dead end of disreputable public conflict even if Cowper, as so often a great nuisance, was urging the Prince to conditions and resistance. The King, upon whom James Craggs was working for the Ministry, was more difficult. He had come close to hatred for George Augustus as the squabble was extended. But he was persuaded. The conclusion of the more important quarrel between Minister and opposition leader was heralded in the essential but lesser accommodation of King and Prince.

A farce of royal reconciliation was enacted on St George's Day 1720 with the Prince kneeling before his father and the King positively gagging at the grace appropriate for a returning prodigal, and getting out only the words, 'Your behaviour, Your behaviour', in the customary French. Drums were beaten, bonfires lit and the population encouraged to cheer as the humiliated Prince left after declaring insincere reverence to his unforgiving father. It deserved the pen of Jonathan Swift and in *Gulliver's Travels* would receive it.

'I WAS OFFER'D A PRESENT BY THE SOUTH SEA COMPANY'

The South Sea Bubble would cause certain politicians and financiers to go in fear of their lives. It would straightforwardly ruin many people. A modest few, individuals like the Duchess of Marlborough and Thomas Guy, miserly founder of the hospital named for him, sold out near the top of the market and lived insufferably ever after. Even so, these were not the chief beneficiaries. A marginal gainer on stock sold very early, then pulled back by his lawyer from calamitous late re-investment, Robert Walpole did best out of the South Sea Bubble. It made him first man in his party, Prime Minister and, at several contingent removes, rich enough.

But at the Bubble's beginnings lay a concern for sound finance. Seventeenth-century royal and government finance, a shaky, unsophisticated affair, had, from Charles I's Ship Money crisis onward, underlain most of the crises of that unstable century. As Geoffrey Holmes points out,[1] notions of a permanent national debt, prudentially managed and periodically eased, but not too much worried about, did not exist. The Micawber rules of debt as ruin oppressed ministers as much as individuals. And government had grown more expensive, especially a government running Marlborough's wars. But taxes alone did not suffice. There had to be loans, new and more sophisticated but still inadequate, making up over the twelve years of Queen Anne, 1702–14, less than 40 per cent of a bill of £99 million.[2] Taxes had risen between 1689 and 1714 by an average of £5 million (a figure to be multiplied by something between fifty and sixty to be even guessed at in today's terms).

And further and better taxes had to be found as the wars progressed, the newest, most effective and unpopular of them being Land Tax. A call to reduce it would be the recurring plaint of landowner, small or large, paying it. And tackling Land Tax would be the policy motif of the two shrewdest politicians of the half-century, Harley and Walpole. It was, though, indispensable, 'the flower of the funds',[3] bringing in £2 million a year at top rate. Tax and loan worked together and, as a result of the needs of war, the system became more flexible and capable of expansion. The creation of the Bank of England in 1694, lending half its subscription of £1.2 million to the government in return for incorporation, was a private device for coping with state requirements which, despite early scares and crises, had worked. Funded debt, the citizen's loan to the state via the Bank of England for which he was paid annual interest, came into existence. These were 'the funds' in which men of means, the yeomen of rent, placed their money, and from which they drew it across succeeding centuries. We had a national debt which worked, but it was not quite believed in yet.

There was another, purely political, problem. The Bank's stock was sought after, it had great influence with its client, the government; and striving to finance a Whig war, it was a Whig institution. All its leading figures, from its creator, William Paterson, the Chancellor, Montague (Lord Halifax), who supported him, and vital names in its management, John Houblon and Gilbert Heathcote, were solid party men, supporters of the Revolution and King William. The Bank of England was an important part of the Tory squire's inferiority complex.

So, to be a little unfair, the Bubble had Tory origins. If the Bank of England (and the East India Company, another source of financial support) were Whig creations with an eye upon Dutch practices (established in the reign of William III), should they not be at least offset? What could have been more natural for Robert Harley than to establish a financial and trading organisation with Tory credentials to run against such Whiggish things? Tory propaganda was as heavy with dislike of finance capital and its practitioners as a Marxist seminar. The party of the country gentleman and High Church rector was not much involved in manufactures, not at all in finance.

In 1705, Lord Justice Holt had declared the air of England too pure for slaves to breathe. But between 1720 and 1729, British ships took 243,000 souls as slaves from Africa and delivered up 210,000 to the American colonists. It was already a piece of the South American market to which this country had access. The Catholic Church, whatever its other failings, had and has a good name as protector of the native people of the southern continent. Such protection did not reach an Africa not yet seriously settled above the Western Cape, and slaves were in great demand in South America and the Caribbean. Britain was the chief slave trader of the day, taking a little above half the business.[4] Profits in the Jamaica trade of £200,000 a year had been recorded over 1698–1708. When the title 'South Sea Company' was agreed, it was in the mood which preceded the end, in 1712, of what was, after all, the War of the Spanish Succession. No successful war is without its spoils, and the takings of this conflict included the *Asiento*, access to the general trade of South America, about which, then as later, golden and fallacious expectations had been formed.

In fact, little South American trade materialised. Losing the Spanish part of the war was one cause, fighting a subsequent, quite separate, war against her was another. But in 1718, a limping trade company took the interesting step of offering to service the national debt, a financial venture heavily dependent upon confidence and other ephemeral things. But political as well as financial motivation played its part. There were roots in the old Tory antipathy to the Bank of England going back to the last years of the seventeenth century. The South Sea Company would merge with something called the Sword Blade Company which had tried its hand at this undertaking, on a smaller scale, before.

Originally created for the manufacture of rapiers, hollow-bladed in the French style, it had done respectable manufacturing business until about 1713, turning out the product at a steel works in Shotley Bridge, County Durham.[5] But the company had come into hands wholly financial which would convert it into a species of bank. As early as 1702, the Sword Blade, able under its charter to issue stock, had been using it to buy pieces of government debt, army debentures, issued on favourable terms by the Paymaster of the Forces. It now functioned as a rival to the Bank and organiser of a virulent, pamphleteering lobby against renewal of its charter.

Fortunately, the Bank's services to government during the financial strictures of wartime enabled it to keep the Sword Blade at arm's length, extending its charter until 1732, but had only been able to achieve this after lowering its rate from 5 to 4.5 per cent on a new loan increased in volume to a million and a half, a huge sum in the early eighteenth century. The Bank of England was a little like the BBC today: a fairly well run organisation deserving altogether more trust than its rivals, but enjoying privilege and primacy by charter, a charter sourly resented, railed at and conspired against. The South Sea Company created by Harley had many purposes, slavery being one, finance on easy terms for the hard-pressed Tory voting squire another. It was also authorised to run the first ever national lottery, but the purpose truly yearned for was the one to which the Sword Blade had aspired, the servicing for its own profit of a national debt now handled in a drably conservative and unspeculative way by the despised Bank of England.

The two private companies would have more than aspiration in common. The moving spirit of the Sword Blade was John Blunt, an unfastidious, bullying man, originally a scrivener. He had a line to the Harleys at precisely the moment when, in early 1711, they were preparing the way to end the war. Robert Harley, bent upon what today is called an 'exit strategy' to a conflict decelerating in success but not expense, was able to present to the Commons a horrific list of bills, the cost of subsidising our military allies from the Archbishop of Trier to the King of Prussia, 'an *extra* charge of £11,141, 2s, 3d, he has been at in recruiting the body of his troops in *Italy*'. Harley wanted to discredit the war. He was already turning the hand of his friend Swift to writing *The Conduct of the Allies*. Spelling out the costs to a horrified Tory Commons at a low point in the Spanish campaign the day after news broke of the gratifying defeat of a Whig general (James Stanhope in his military hat) at Brihuega was every bit as good.

The immediate mechanism necessary for paying Marlborough's troops was a lottery. It was not the first. The Bank of England had run one with limited success in 1710, but was slow and unwilling about a second. Blunt and the Sword Blade men jumped in with a scheme marked by more showmanship. Their prizes were not the dull annuities of the Bank, but, first, the interest upon large cash sums of up to £12,000 (perhaps £600,000 in current money), then, later, the cash itself. It was a rousing success and met the pay schedule completely, encouraging Blunt and his associates to come up with another, bigger, better one, with £100 tickets and a top prize of £20,000. With tickets at the equivalent of £5000 in our money, this was not aimed at the fluttering general public. It sought to raise money from money on the chance of very much more money. Money replied: the second lottery was an even bigger success. Blunt, jobbing for himself, sold almost a million pounds' worth of tickets.[6]

With so much government goodwill and with a scheme pointing expectations where Harley wanted them to go, to the rewards of peace, it was possible to sell a scheme for the South Seas. It would, after all, require an organisation on the lines of the East India Company. This one should make money on its own account, and there was a sympathetic ear for a scheme to take debts from a government otherwise obliged to do everything with a hike in land tax. Tory MPs, the current majority, might not like flashy finance, but they liked *this*. Both politically and as business, everything was going like a fully rehearsed ballet.

In such circumstances Blunt was able to advise the Lord Treasurer's brother, Edward Harley, the Auditor, on important details. Together they quietly settled plans for the creation of a South Sea Company to take on the nine million sterling of unsecured debt, about which the government had worried and had taken steps to see everyone with a vote worried too. The founding document, having established this undertaking, went on virtuously about trade. The company should conduct

the sole trade and traffick from August 1st 1711, into, unto and from, the Kingdoms, Lands etc of America, on the east side from the river Aranoca, to the southernmost part of Tierra del Fuego, on the west side thereof, from the said southernmost part through the South Seas to the northernmost parts of America, and unto and from all countries in the same limits, reputed to belong to the crown of Spain, or which shall hereafter be discovered.

Against such a roll of eloquence one should put the words of a failed tile manufacturer. Daniel Defoe, despite his closeness to Harley, was an early unbeliever. He thought that

Unless Spaniards are to be divested of common sense, infatuate and given up, abandoning their own commerce, throwing away the only valuable stake they have left in the world, and in short, bent on their own ruin, we cannot suggest that they will ever, on any consideration or for any equivalent, part with so valuable, indeed so inestimable a jewel, as the exclusive power of trade to their own plantations.[7]

However, that was to worry about the long term when there was an immediate preoccupation. Harley, for all his political manoeuvring, was personally incorruptible, as was his brother. But they were dealing with

men who had been their backers and, politically, they were looking for
a counterpoise to the Whig-dominated Bank and East India Company.
Accordingly, like privatisers in the late twentieth century, they wanted
to shift the state's debt burden from the taxpayer to somebody else. In
return for relief of those nine millions, they were prepared to pay out
annually 6 per cent of it, pedantically calculated at £568,279 10s. The
government had achieved a coup, the Bank had been badly slighted
and, according to how the new South Sea Company was managed, it
would create profit or loss.

As the historian of the Bubble, John Carswell, remarks, the moving
spirits of the Company were very little interested in trade, not one of
the directors having knowledge or experience of South America. What
they understood was finance – creative, manipulative, confidence-
exploiting finance. With the status of a state-created and state-endowed
company on a level with the East India Company, they were placed to
do that wide and deep. The men doing this were taking a lead from
John Law, whose Mississippi Company in France had initially rather
more to do with the Mississippi than the British group with the South
Seas, but whose thinking was anyway large and imaginative rather than
fraudulent.

Broadly, Law could see the enormous potential for economic expansion in a seemingly poor country like France if investment capital were
released. As early as 1713 he had made a fortune of over £100,000 at
the values of the day (at ours, perhaps five million!).[8] Despising gold
as a superstition and a shackle on trade, Law favoured a national paper
currency kept stable by banking rules and the underwriting hand of
the state. This could not immediately be had from the government of
the French Regent, Orléans. But, in 1716, Law was allowed to create
a private venture with known government approval, printing and issuing
a currency convertible at the quality of coin measured at time of issue.
He correctly guessed that confidence in his issue would keep demands
for redemption to a level which could be met when, inevitably, the
chaotic national finances required the currency to be debased. His
Banque Générale, blessed with public confidence and royal/governmental
favour, demonstrated its clout by obtaining a decree, of 20 April 1717
(New Style), that all tax collections should be passed to the Treasury
in Banque Générale notes.

Having created a national private currency, Law moved on to the
international scene by a device extraordinarily like the South Sea

Company. The Mississippi Company had been floated in 1712 for the trade of the area in the vast south-western part of North America known as Louisiana. It was in a lingering and unhealthy condition, but Law intended it for exploitation of the American West, long before transcontinental railways, cattle drives, gambling cities or the film business had been contemplated. His official name for it, inspirational but never much in circulation, was the Company of the West.[9] Again, he would canalise the resources of the state so as to use its money productively. A quarter of the company capital, 100 million livres (about £150,000 sterling), would be subscribed in hard cash, the rest in state bonds which at that moment, autumn 1717, could be bought at a discount of 80 per cent.

In effect, Law was taking up a great part of the French state debt in return for an annuity paid by that same state to his company. In these early stages, he bribed no one with dividends, telling investors to wait for trade to earn profits; meanwhile, serious trading, notably in furs and tobacco, was undertaken. What he was doing was closely followed abroad, not least in Whig Great Britain. The men coming to the fore in that country after 1714 were business-minded and, if not drunk on greed, felt that they could get to like it.

Law would ultimately be confounded by market pressure from men less rational than himself. But his was a sound and creative idea which would be corrupted. The British imitation began with the day trader's instinct for making something out of nothing. The trade of Louisiana might be less than Law hoped for, but it was a real venture for something tangible. The South Sea Company did not even make much of a fist of selling Negro slaves. There might be a contract with Madrid for providing 4,800 a year to seven ports on the continent, but they ran into the sullen bureaucracy of the colonists who blocked the first ship (its shackled cargo discounted cheaply in the West Indies), on the grounds that not all the formalities over the *Asiento* had been completed. The slave trade never made the directors much money, but it was perhaps symbolic of their whole cunning but unreflective approach to business that South Sea ships had a higher mortality rate among their valuable cargo than was usual. They were regularly and lethally overloaded.

And after three years of cooling relations with Harley's government, the South Sea men found themselves obliged after the end of Tory rule and the Stuart dynasty, to make new friends. They wasted no time.

Joseph Addison, a senior Whig without the means of his grandee colleagues, wrote to Lord Halifax in November 1714 about the job he had hoped for and not received and the payments expected for work done, also unforthcoming. Complaining of 'the unhandsome treatment I have received from some of our new Great Men in every circumstance of that affaire', Addison grumbled that he had been offered nothing except that 'I was offer'd a present by the South Sea Company. I never took that nor anything else for what I did, as knowing I had no right to it.'[10] Addison could be insufferable about virtue but he did try to practise it.

In the same letter he describes his rejection for the Board of Trade and the bearer of the news: 'Young Craggs told me about a week ago that his Mty, tho' he did not see fit to gratifie me in this particular designed to give me a recompense for my Service . . .'[11] Addison, who insisted that he was worth a job paying £1000 a year, was writing at the end of November 1714. By Christmas the names of Craggs *and* the Earl of Halifax, whom the essayist had solicited, were listed among those holding more than £10,000 of South Sea stock!

Young Craggs would be placed rather to offer South Sea bribes than take them. He and his father would become close enough to the directors of the South Sea Company to be regarded as their confederates. The Craggses, father and son, were as keenly observant of what was going on in Paris as they were to the front of the new British regime, close to George's court and deeply committed to James Stanhope. The elder Craggs, rich anyway, grew richer as Postmaster General where he supervised the decoded correspondence between the (mostly very poor) Jacobites and the Pretender's little court in Avignon. The younger Craggs had risen via a court position with the Prince of Wales (before the royal split), to Walpole's old job as Secretary at War, to the splendour of junior Secretary of State. Craggs senior kept himself very fully informed of the Company of the West, the money it raised, the way it was raised, through a transfer of indebtedness from the state to a private company as, far more heavily than cash subscriptions, state bonds were taken for the purchase of stock. It all seemed to have handy application in Britain.

As one of the first monitors and enthusiasts for the Law system, he would be drawn early into patronage of South Sea undertakings. But at this stage, inducements refused or accepted existed for the pursuit, at least as ministers saw it, of a high and aspiring purpose. The mood late in 1719 was euphoric. The new Spanish war had been a success, and at home the defeat of 'the Fifteen' had been followed by the complete fiasco of a projected rising earlier in that very year. It was the time of the Peerage Act, about which Walpole had been so unhelpful, and of projected and defeated university reforms. It was time to think big.

The state, in the way of states, had a debt, which, in the way of debts, had to be serviced. If somebody else was competent to take up all or most of this in return for a large privilege and immediate working cash, the government politicians would be able to talk in the virtuous way of politicians about economy and reductions in expenditure and look to tax cuts and public gratitude. There was no particular reason why the South Sea Company should qualify for this role. It had not been a spectacular success as a trading company. It was run by businessmen, many of them connected with the Sword Blade, who had handled lotteries well enough, but whose personal reputations were not of the highest. Their old nay-sayer, Daniel Defoe, said that 'these men with a mass of money which they command, of other people's as well as their own, will in time ruin the jobbing trade'. He then added prophetically 'But 'twill only be a general visitation . . . like a common calamity . . . that drowns lesser grievances in a general deluge.'[12]

Careful orthodox thinking in government would have wanted such an undertaking, if it were to be done at all, safe in the prudential hands of the Bank of England. The Bank thought so too and would bid for it. The men who ran the South Sea Company rated the opportunity and bid higher. They also spread largesse like silage, leaving several ministers, as already noted, holding pleasant amounts of equity. And they worked through congenial ministers – Aislabie, Chancellor of the Exchequer, Sunderland, second in the Ministry only to Stanhope, and the elder Craggs.

The largest single part of the burden was war debt, money raised to pay for Marlborough and Louis XIV, debt raised at high interest and being repaid by long-term annuities. Service on these amounted to £800,000 annually. Combined with an armful of smaller obligations, some of them going back to Charles II, at only a little less, total yearly service stood at around £1,500,000. This was represented as a capital sum. The redeemable debts worked out realistically at £16 million, the non-redeemables, by a variety of elaborations which generally disadvantaged the holders of longer and more recent annuities, at £15 million.

The government for its part undertook to pay the company by annuity a pound for every pound of debt relieved, but in the case of one group of debts, they needed to pay only 14s, a saving for the Treasury of £40,000 a year. And if, after seven years, the South Sea Company's operation had fully succeeded, the percentage on which the annuity was calculated would fall from 5 to 4 per cent, saving the Treasury £400,000 annually. This, as Carswell stresses, was a dazzling induce-ment, only a little less than the annual cost of the armed forces.[13] The purpose was to establish a sinking fund, by means of which, as the South Sea Company achieved its ends, a sixth of the national debt would be cleared in seven years and the debt as a whole in twenty-five. What Blunt and his associates offered ministers, what the Sword Blade had done modestly and Law so far splendidly, should be under-taken now by the South Sea Company.

The operation was to work by way of rising value in the stock of the South Sea Company, an increase good enough to persuade the holder of a government annuity to convert to South Sea stock. The company would have authority to create more stock. The exchanger of annuity income for stock would benefit by the Company's rising dividends as its value rose, and, as that stock rose, he could also look to capital gains. This was a stock which could not work through ordinary good trading, one which, never on the most hopeful terms, would answer and about which the company's Court of Directors had no illusions.

Confidence was to do all. It would contribute the higher price at which stock would be attractive; and, as a gap opened between the par value at conversion and the market value, the surplus could be sold as profit. It was to be, in Ramsay MacDonald's famous rambling phrase, 'On and on and on and up and up and up' . . . until it wasn't. The effect of a puff operation was to put all resources into the inducement of sale, few if any into valuable trade. The effects were what they always are, inflationary, money with nothing to do injected into a boom.

As for the directors of the company, Blunt, Clayton, Knight (the Cashier), Caswell and Jacob Sawbridge and the like, they would within a month be neatly epitomised by Sir Richard Steele in his latest short broadside, A Nation a Family: 'The Managers . . . acting without trading . . . are only so many people about a potful of English beef; they stand around with ladles as it boils, and skim off the fat for themselves while those who were to have their proportion in the meat, as it was bought, must be contented with the lean offals for want of it being in favour with the providers or in fee with the cooks.'[14]

Once ministers had made their compact with Blunt and his crew they sprang it upon the political world as a *fait accompli* not worth the tedious delay of serious debate. Aislabie, the Chancellor, set out the scheme to the Commons on 22 January 1720 and was followed to the floor by Craggs who spoke with glib assurance of an immediate parliamentary assent to such a splendid scheme without a division. An Irish Whig, Thomas Brodrick, got up and demanded that the undertaking be subjected to tendering. In doing so, he confused Aislabie, who talked about brooking no delay and acting 'with spirit'.[15] The House engaged in a couple of hours' unresolved debate before adjourning.

The Bank of England had been horrified at what was happening, and a very good friend of the Bank was Robert Walpole. He was party political on the subject. The Bank was a Williamite creation come from the hands of the Junto. The South Sea Company's disreputable roots in the Sword Blade may have been a lesser count against them than their respectable connections with Lord Oxford. Walpole had the historic good fortune at this time still to be an Out, and he opposed the terms. He was a strong supporter of the Bank and pointed out that the South Sea Company was free to vary its price for the annuities it bought up while the Bank was subject to a fixed ratio of £1700 for every hundred in the long annuities. He called for the rise of their stock to be similarly limited. This was a central anomaly about the South Sea Company's position. The terms left the Company free, as the Bank was not (and should not have been), to create a surplus and the capital gains going with it by offering less than the market price for its script.

Political alliances apart, this was the sort of thing that a shrewd financial head, advised by a yet shrewder one, could see. And Walpole had the services of the second in his financial adviser, and at this time his right arm, Robert Jacombe. A banker who had worked for Walpole during his time as Paymaster General, he was also, professionally, the holder of his personal account. Walpole was certainly pro-Bank; he was a friend of its directors. We have, however, no printed parliamentary record of his contribution to the general debate. And as his biographer, Coxe, also has Walpole not only denouncing stockjobbery, but dwelling 'on the miseries and confusion which then prevailed in France from the adoption of similar measures' at a time, February 1720, when Law's scheme was riding high, there is a suggestion of the historical airbrush about the Archdeacon's account.

Brodrick, a man of sixty-six who had sat for twenty years in the

Irish Parliament and had been since 1713 Member for Stockbridge, also very usefully took a note of the proceedings. Brodrick was a genuine independent, very much respected, not obliged to Stanhope, but declining three years earlier to join Walpole's guerrilla war against him. And on his account, Craggs's introduction was met by 'a full quarter hour of silence' while Members looked at one another and wondered who would speak first in this open space of arcana and fast-talking. Eventually, Brodrick made his own contribution: 'I hoped in order to make the best bargain wee could, every other company, nay any other society of men might bee at full liberty to make proposals as the South Sea company, since every gentlemen must agree this to be the likeliest way to make a good bargain for the publique.'

As for ministers, 'Our great men lookt as if thunderstruck, and one of them in particular, turned as pale as my cravat.'[16] What Brodrick says next makes a pretty nonsense of Archdeacon Coxe's heroic account even though he actually quotes it: 'Mr Walpole applauded the designe, and agreed in general to the reasonableness of the scheme, wherein however something wanted amendment . . .'[17]

And indeed, as Brodrick tells it, Walpole's intervention, with its critical comparison with the Bank's rules, followed a private provocation by Nicholas Lechmere. Lechmere, Member for Tewkesbury, a former Solicitor General and follower of Sunderland, was a quarrelsome fellow generally. Described as 'a good Lawyer, a quick and distinguished orator, much courted by the Whig party, but of a temper, violent proud and impracticable',[18] Lechmere was on the worst possible terms with Walpole, having, as Sunderland's adherent, engaged in frequent encounters with the rebel against the Ministry.

He was himself much involved with the South Sea people who were alleged to have settled their plans in his chambers. And in the debate of 22 January, he indulged, according to Brodrick, in 'invectives against Walpole's former scheme giving great preference to this'.[19] 'Walpole's former scheme' was, of course, his sinking fund of 1717. Whatever the rights and wrongs of Walpole's own financial planning, and despite the excellent points he made about lack of South Sea constraints, his intervention came only after an attack by a personal enemy on his own earlier work, and the critique he did make of the South Sea scheme was practical, governed in part by his sympathies for the Bank. It was in no way an attack on the whole undertaking, about which he showed himself perfectly relaxed.

As Sir John Plumb points out, he had been a fierce opponent of the South Sea Company's creation in 1711. A judgement cannot leapfrog over nine years and become credit for having seen the dangers all along. In 1711 he was attacking an idea of Robert Harley's and the advancement of a Tory financial grouping, something the good party man would be against. He had made no further criticism in the intervening years, as when the South Sea took up more public credit in 1713. Indeed, he demonstrated his confidence in the Company's *Asiento* slaving interest, buying into the South Sea in 1717 to the tune of £1000. And in the January 1720 debate, as we have seen, the independent Brodrick recorded privately and conclusively, 'Mr Walpole applauded the designe, and agreed in general to the reasonablenesse of the scheme, wherein however something wanted amendment . . .' (*q.v. supra*).

For three years Walpole had attacked everything of consequence, wise or foolish, which the Stanhope Ministry had done. By 1720 he was on the way back to peace with the leadership. So, as across 1720 the price of South Sea stock inflated towards implosion, no criticism of the deal or the company came from Walpole.

Meanwhile, Brodrick's intervention and the embarrassment of ministers had obliged a withdrawal of the attempt at having immediate enactment gaily waved through. The Bank, already alerted by the City grapevine about what was up, rushed to the politicians with a scheme of its own. It undertook to make available £5.5 million for a franchise to exchange Bank stock with debt holdings. This was put to the Commons on the same day, 27 January, that the South Sea made an improved offer in this frantic bidding skirmish. The South Sea, led by Blunt, came up with a larger sum totalling £7 million. Against this brass insolence, the Bank, though it made further adjustments, had no defence. And South Sea stock rose 31 points. But it would be a delicately ironical footnote to this debate at the start of everything that, when the whole speculative adventure fell apart and a parliamentary select committee was formed to pick its way through the debris, its chairman would be Thomas Brodrick.

It was now necessary for Parliament to give its approval. The Bank might not be able to meet Blunt's wild throw, but it could still summon argument in the chamber against the sense of the authorising legislation. There would be a debate of six hours, during which Walpole argued, with the support of his brother, Horatio, and the slightly eccentric Richard Steele, against acceptance and in favour of the Bank's proposals. The opposition in principle was defeated on 21 March by 201 to 131.

That was inevitable, but a motion was also entertained to compel the Company to fix its conversion rate and put this into its statute. This, as Walpole had argued, was the essential thing; the handicapping of the Bank by a monopoly of flexible conversion to make South Sea stock rise with the conversion rate was arbitrarily reduced. The chief supporter, or, in American language, booster, of the South Sea was John Aislabie, Chancellor of the Exchequer, and now receiving at the hands of the South Sea Cashier, Robert Knight, £20,000 of stock on top of his earlier holdings.

Knight, younger son of an old Warwickshire family, was far more important than the slightly minionish title of 'Cashier' suggests. One cannot put it more plainly than to say that he was the holder and transmitter of the stock which would be issued to politicians to make them think the right way. William Yonge,* a future Walpolean office holder who seconded Aislabie, would a few days later be credited with £3000 of stock in the green book in which Knight kept his dealings. Twelve MPs were credited with a total of £39,000. These were not precisely bribes of a subtle kind, though there were ways of making such holdings advantageous.

It was for the Company in the person of Knight to determine the profit made per point rise. The friend of the Company held stock for which he did not pay now, but which he could sell back direct to the Company in return for a points rise multiplied by agreed unit profit. The biggest friend of all, the Earl of Sunderland, often called Duumvir (co-ruler) with Stanhope, was assessed at £500 per point above 175. The elder Craggs's original keenness to have the scheme go through on the nod is better understood in the light of a similar undertaking. The outcome of the March debate was not the purpose of such distribution; that was secure enough. These were expressions of gratitude to the Treasury. But the Court should also be made happily complicit. Postmaster Craggs took into his special care the obtaining for Melusine and her daughters by the King, £120 per point above a mere 154. This was a matter of private contracts privately arrived at. They involved

---

* According to Lord Hervey, 'his name was proverbially used to express everything pitiful, corrupt and contemptible' (quoted in Romney Sedgwick, *The House of Commons, 1715–1754*, vol. I, p. 567).

not only no money but no actual physical share certificates, only the scrupulous entry in Knight's green book. But with stock trebling and quadrupling, the arrangement would seem like a paradise of ready cash. Certainly it gave new and beautiful meaning to friendship.

The role of Robert Walpole in the coming months, if not precisely improper, hardly shines with credit and shows exactly no understanding at all of the South Sea scheme being a risky affair. The details became apparent to Sir John Plumb from the books of Robert Jacombe wearing his hat as Walpole's private banker. In June 1719 – i.e. before the debt-clearing scheme was established – Walpole held £18,760, 7s in the South Sea, probably, thinks Plumb, money from those surpluses left at profitable discretion to the Paymaster General, remaining from his time in that office and not yet required back. He sold in June, then September, respectively £6000 and £1000, transferring the proceeds to his brother, Horatio, before selling another £2000 at the end of October. Meanwhile, aware of the bidding soon to start under one scheme or another, Walpole was buying government annuities.

On New Year's Day 1720 his holding stood at £9760 7s. This did not stop him, on 25 January, *selling* £18,000 worth and getting £24,383 15s for it, clearly a bold operation, something made clear by the payment *to* Walpole by a Mr Sloper, a Treasury official, of £9000 of ante-dated South Sea stock, securities no longer bearing interest (bought now for £8770), which the statesman had already sold. His last dealing in South Sea paper came in March 1720 and had a value of £760 7s. It stood at the time at 194.5. However pleasant his operation in selling forward on a rising market stock he did not yet own, he was showing overall no real understanding of this market. The whole point about the South Sea operation was that its stock had to go up. The very freedom to manipulate its price ratio which Walpole had so penetratingly criticised was directed to this end, and, in the short term at least, the stock was very nigh certain to rise. Patience at the base of a bubble, readiness to jump as it swells, are the marks of the shrewd player of such markets.

For whatever reason, Walpole, out in the last week of January at 194.5 in a stock which would clear 1000, does not qualify as anything but a dabbler unnecessarily nervous at the edge. When the full South Sea Bill went through its second reading by a majority of 201 to 131 on 21 March, the stock would touch 400 before settling back on 330. All sorts of shrewd but not greedy men and institutions, led by Hoare's bank, sold then and took sweet profits. By the beginning of June, the

Reverend William Stukeley was recording: 'Surprising scene in Change Alley. S Sea in the morning above 900 . . . professions & shops are all forgot, all goe thither as to the mines of Potosi. Nobility, Ladies, Brokers & footmen all upon a level. Great equipages set up, the prizes [prices] of things rose exorbitantly. Such a renversement of the order of Nature as succeeding ages can have no idea of.'[20]

As much was true in France where the exiled Bolingbroke, acting, so he said, on John Law's own advice, had gone into Mississippi stock and was telling a friend that their rise obtained for him 'at least as much as I have been hitherto robbed of', and he had acquired a house, La Source, near Orléans on the proceeds. Swift referred to him as 'Our Mississippi friend'.[21]

Walpole played no part in any of this, getting out not just early but far too early. To surrender the last five rungs of a twenty-rung ladder likely to collapse is wisdom, jumping off with fifteen to go understandable miscalculation. To propose getting on again at the eighteenth is something else. Yet this is precisely what the former and future Chancellor of the Exchequer did in June, putting in £9000 when the South Sea debt stock reached 1000. He was pressing his bad advice generously at this time upon friends and connections. His circle at Lynn, Sir Charles Turner, James Hoste and William Allen, were so guided, while Lady Cowper reported that he was encouraging the Princess of Wales, his closest royal acquaintance, to join the play.[22]

But Walpole had, in the spring of 1720, other and better things than bubble-chasing to do. Now by events, whose oddness still perplexes historians, Walpole would move back into formal, if still peripheral, office. Walpole's admirers have made a great deal of his Englishness and staunch resistance to the machinations of the King's 'hated German ministers'. Against which stood Stanhope; the internationalist, soldier on foreign campaigns, welcome visitor to many courts, awake to the refinements of the map of continental Europe, was supposed to be at home with bloody foreigners. But Andreas Bernstorff, the most important of the Hanoverians, had fallen out with Stanhope; losing badly to him in the complex matter of the Prussian Treaty. And having lost caste with the King in that affair, Bernstorff was minded accordingly to make common cause with Stanhope's enemies, for which read Townshend and Walpole.

They might be narrow Englishmen, might be involved in the formal rebuke issued by the House of Commons to the German ministers, but Bernstorff seems to have thought that the 'disgusted Whigs' were convenient allies. The Stanhope/Sunderland Ministry had enjoyed foreign triumph and it was presiding over a financial blooming. Despite the reversal on a closed peerage, it stood very high, too high, argued Bernstorff, for the King's own authority. Their foreign policy would be one of renewing war, and the financial schemes which they sponsored would help them to 'establish themselves & be able for the future to give laws to the King & his son & even remove them when they shall think proper'.

Against all this, an alternative strategy to be adopted by Walpole and Townshend is sketched. They would put up money to help George's ally, Augustus of Saxony, take hereditary hold on his elective Crown of Poland, money also being made available for George to buy land in Germany. There would be a general reshuffle of ministers, with Sunderland and Stanhope demoted respectively to the abominated Irish Lieutenancy and either the Privy Seal or Generalship of the Horse, while Walpole took the Exchequer and Townshend the Paymastership. The brothers-in-law also had it in mind, readers were told, to admit half a dozen Tories to dilute Whig dominance. This ultra-cynical proposal was supposedly communicated in these words to Graf Sinzendorff, Vice-Chancellor of the Empire in Vienna.

According to Stanhope's biographer, writing in the early 1930s, the memorandum 'bears all the marks of having sprung from Bernstorff's German brain'.[23] And Basil Williams goes on to say, 'It is hard to believe, in spite of Bernstorff's assertion, that Walpole and Townshend really countenanced this fantastic scheme.'[24] History is more cynical and less Anglo-centric than it was in 1932. And however gratified Sinzendorff might have been at such correspondence, no copy exists in the imperial archives.

Perhaps because no such memorandum was sent. We are probably up against a classic example of the transitive leak, one *meant* to flow out. The text, neither recorded nor remarked upon in Vienna, went the rounds in London, the French ambassador, Lord Oxford, Townshend himself. A more usual conclusion today is that somebody (Bernstorff in collusion with Walpole? Walpole and Townshend without Hanoverian help?) was trying to make ministerial flesh creep. At this time, mid-April, the South Sea was riding high and ministers with it. But the Disgusted Whigs had registered any amount of parliamentary trouble and one great victory. The memorandum, breathing menace and invitation, sounds as if its intended readership was the King and the government. Certainly ministers were unhappy, Sunderland being put 'not into a little fight'.[25]

The idea seemed to have been to make a compromise with the Norfolk faction, stuffing mouths with office, though below the level pitched at in the reshuffle sketch. Walpole, known to need money, was by a return to that office offered another gulp of the Paymaster's semi-legal rights of creaming off the income of invested public money. Townshend became President of the Council, with a third associate, Paul Methuen, made Comptroller of the Household. Since Walpole was coming back on board, there was a task waiting for him to prove goodwill. The quarrel between father and son had been an acute embarrassment and source of derision for too long. Walpole was on excellent terms with another player, the royal daughter-in-law, Caroline of Ansbach, Princess of Wales. The quarrel of the Waleses had been his quarrel; his and his faction's withdrawal from it on admission to the Cabinet would leave the little court at Leicester House without political allies worth having. George Augustus, a man under the thumb of a wife upon whom he lasciviously doted, would do as she said.

Caroline may not, says Plumb, awarding a beta plus, have been as bright as she thought herself, but she was brighter than George and was quickly persuaded by Walpole that cutting losses with a burst of public insincerities to the King was the least worst course. It would cost him the grudging resentment of the Prince for some time, but the Prince's submission to his father, however ungracefully received between clenched teeth, ended for form's sake a long, sour, self-destructive family quarrel. Walpole, who had done much to keep the family throwing things, now took implausible credit as peacemaker. He and his faction were back in office, perfectly happy with the false prosperity of the South Sea venture, yet back far too late to take serious blame when it went explosively wrong.

Indifferent to political adjustments, the merry speculative dance continued. Walpole *had* made money this time, by getting into other stocks, notably the Royal African Company which, like many others, was carried up in the Bubble mood. He was also buying land in Norfolk, and this during, rather than after, the Bubble period, paying more rather than cashing in on the fall after the city crisis. He was, however, saved from buying South Sea at the top only by the constructive inaction of his friend Robert Jacombe.

Jacombe smelt burned bull and sent off gloomy letters to Houghton as the summer advanced with no effect whatever. Walpole, back in Norfolk, was oblivious to the hints he was getting from an acutely shrewd banker based in London watching the first crinkling of financial leaves. From a far corner of the kingdom in an age when a letter could take a week to arrive, Walpole in late August would give his friend William Allen, who was setting out for London, a letter telling Jacombe to invest £5000 in the Company. His own correspondence immediately afterwards included a letter full of political doubts about Company policy from Townshend, currently one of the Council of Regency while George was in Hanover. A Bubble Act aimed at restraint among secondary flotations had been proposed with obvious intimations of unease.

Luckily for Walpole, Jacombe was too worried to obey instructions without question and he summed up his message to Walpole in the succinct comment, 'Ready money is a valuable thing'. Walpole was grateful for that, but thought only in terms of the last issue of stock. He wanted to sell what he held and suggested too high a negotiating price; and he also wanted, incredibly, to be in on the next and fourth South Sea issue. But when that packet of orders came, it came too late. Walpole's credit as a shrewd man in the markets would be saved by chance and Jacombe's wisely dragging feet.

Walpole sent off a new order to buy on 24 August, one worth £6500 and involving the money of local friends. It arrived, as Jacombe delightedly reported, too late. Walpole was saved by circumstance from his own naïve judgement and the consequences spread around country friends relying upon its sophistication. Walpole would have credit in his own time and long after for a financial perception which he never displayed.

But involvement in the market was not merely directed at making money. It involved politics. He was a supporter of the Bank, its directors were friends over some years, men whom he could trust. As long as there was a chance of the Bank playing a hand in the enterprise, he had to stay at arm's length from the South Sea. His selling out in March, just before the second major debate, served to demonstrate his allegiance. But at the same time, Walpole, close for so long to the royal opposition, prevailed upon the Princess of Wales to get into what was so obviously a good thing, probably, thinks Carswell, by way of Knight's private list of favoured politicians, his green book.

Almost certainly George I was also a holder of stock under this

hypothetical, almost metaphysical system.[26] But while Walpole show-
ered the royal Outs with bad, well-meant advice, he was engaged in
bringing his great *fronde* with ministers to an end. They had won the
large military/strategic argument. He had defeated them over the closed
peerage. He couldn't destroy the Ministry, but he had demonstrated
his trouble value to it. Ironically, the intermediary for such a reconciliation was young Craggs. But reconciling Whig factions had to be
synchronised with reconciliation of royal parties, George and George.

But this third subscription came at the high point of the optimism
and hysteria. If Walpole was deluded at this stage, he was in wide and
glittering company. From its inception as a proposal in Parliament, the
scheme had caught fire. It moved from March to June at a rapid,
lurching pace. By mid-June it had reached a high point; a lavish honours
list included the master planner and head of the South Sea, John Blunt,
now Sir John Blunt, Baronet, a title which survives today in the blameless person of Sir David Richard Reginald Harvey Blunt, twelfth holder.
Plans were on foot to design and build, on a site now prosaically occupied by St James's Underground Station,[27] a grandly imposing South
Sea Square. Stock was being quoted at between 715 and 780, but
Thomas Guy, shrewdest investor of all, had sold out below par at 600
– probably for cash! He had been selling quietly since April, un-
encumbering himself of £54,040 of stock in small parcels of £1000 or
less, clearing £254,000 (perhaps £15 million in today's money).[28]

The House of Commons was less shrewd. Having swallowed the
South Sea scheme, it began to worry about the imitative small schemes
for development which flourished under its inspiration. Famously, Swift
imagined the project to produce moonbeams out of cucumbers and
there were actual proposals for woad and imported broomsticks which
had the natural ring of satire. But the list of ninety or so bubbles set
before the Commons at this time is full of proposals which, however
doubtfully financed or managed, sound intrinsically useful: for supplying
London with sea coal; for making of muslin; for an engine to fetch
water to the town of Deal; for improving land in Flintshire; for
purchasing and improving fenny lands in Lincolnshire; for the more
effectual making of baize in Colchester[29] and so on. Land drainage in
Lincolnshire and weaving muslin are projects with better prospects than
making money out of a South Sea trade extensively barred and wholly
uncomprehended, better yet than levitating an equity on expectations
incapable of fulfilment.

But a mass of smaller speculations – a hundred in six weeks (May/June), promoted in a costerish way on what was called Lower 'Change', projections in insurance, turnpikes, land, gold mines (in, ironically, 'Terra Australis', not the Australia which had not yet been discovered, but presumably the South America bitterly guarded by Spain) and the fixing of quicksilver – turned upon a belief that what went up would never come down. Against such thinking, the law made the establishing of an unauthorised joint stock company a common nuisance.

Even so, the legislation was directed to protect, not restrain, the only begetters of mass speculation. The new projectors were users-up of money which South Sea directors wanted invested in their own projection. And it was not altogether accident that exactly as the Bubble went through, the South Sea Company had moved on to the third subscription, one of unlimited size and on yet slighter security. The effect was spasmal. In two days at the start of June the market leapt from 610 to 870, taking the Royal African, where Walpole had put money, with it – 105 to 190.[30] As for the Bubble Act and its supposed restraints, though Lower Alley would soon shrink, it was immediately followed by the announcement of twenty-four new projects.

The act would do long-term harm by discouraging serious financial operations, but in the short term it was hardly going to matter. The South Sea market was approaching its zenith, the Bubble was fully distended. The Chancellor of the Exchequer sold out with a profit of £86,000[31] and Aislabie was as near to the directors, though Blunt heartily despised him, as anyone outside the Company's own inner ring. The King, a deep player under the name of Aislabie's brother-in-law, Vernon,* was earnestly urged to sell by his Chancellor but for once justifying Plumb's description of him as 'stupid', refused, calling Aislabie 'a timorous man'.[32]

The King was throughout under the impression that Aislabie would use his discretion to sell his South Sea stock for him. Aislabie would subsequently argue that he could not sell 'without increasing the public clamour upon myself or without prejudice to the king's affairs'.[33] George, who had come back from Herrenhausen to find the stock down to 300, kept a stiff upper public lip and remained in his patron's place with the Company.

---

* Subsequently expelled from the House for attempted bribery.

Drawing upon its chief banker, the Sword Blade, the Company, in anticipation of the credit card operators, had always been a ready lender in order to create the demand which bought into its operation. That was the immediate and insistent need as the date of the fourth subscription approached. The holders of annuities were now outnumbered by the straight buyers-in, but a last pitch at those remaining was a success and, by now, the South Sea actually held nearly 90 per cent of redeemable debt. But the price faltered at the start of August, falling below 900. The sun blazed down on London in the late summer of 1720 with Walpole, as we have seen, blithely unaware, out of town literally and figuratively, trying to sell third subscription to buy fourth subscription, the sort of blameless confidence which Sir John Blunt would have liked to see maintained all round.

But the Company had overloaned, about £5 million against revenue, since April, of £3.5 million. It had raised expectations which the practice of anything so tricky as prudence, however slight, would annihilate. And so soon as the stock failed to go up, it would begin to fall, no tragedy to a well-run wholesale grocer or maker of cotton cloth, but to a company selling expectations, the profits available on a rise, the prospect of imminent implosion. There were problems abroad, in the Netherlands, in the activities of one Case Billingsley whose companies were triumphantly pulling in badly wanted speculative capital and who stood ready for a wounding court fight if any attempt were made by a Treasury, always helpful to the South Sea, to use the Bubble Act against him. Finally, problems for John Law in France, compounded by a trade-inhibiting outbreak of plague in that country, deepened general anxiety.

The fourth subscription opened on 22 August, St Bartholomew's Day, apt for a massacre. If the price fell back, destroying the capital gains motive, something had to be done to sweeten the yields. Recklessly, but he was hardly placed for prudence, Blunt held out the promise of a dividend of 30 per cent this year, with a guaranteed dividend of 50 per cent across the next ten. It was, like so many late and flailingly improper company practices, something done to get cash in at stage C to pay out on stage D, but only performable over any longer period with money beyond the dream of ever being earned.

Upon such improbabilities, the King of Spain, guarding the gates to any truly substantial intrinsic South American trade, announced, like rulers of Spain for the next 286 years to the time of writing, that

Gibraltar must be returned. War threatened, and Blunt's nephew, Charles, retreated to an upper room and cut his throat.[34] The price went quickly in a few days from 750 to 700 to 575; Blunt was shot at in the street.[35] On 16 September, the directors of the South Sea Company who so very recently, even if it seemed a lifetime past, had humiliated the Bank of England, turned in this black hour to the Bank of England.

The sequence of events had worked very well for Walpole, though he may not have appreciated the fact. He had been suffering throughout the summer from deep distress at the slow, held off, but unrelenting death by inches of his cherished daughter, Catherine, born in 1703 and to die in 1722.[36] But after much absence, he was on hand when he was wanted and he was very much wanted. He was a Bank of England man and a Whig politician, and his is the handwriting which records the undertaking reached at an urgent meeting on 20 September that the Bank of England should act as agent for selling South Sea bonds and convert a part of its own public debt holding into South Sea stock at a price of 400. To do this, the Bank undertook to raise £3 million in instalments, the first of which would be lent to the South Sea Company for a year. The debt incurred would be settled by a transfer to the Bank of South Sea stock.

It was a large undertaking, to hold the interim, and one which failed – even in the interim. On 29 September stock fell to 190 and the Sword Blade bank stopped payment. The Sword Blade had been for nearly twenty years the enemy of the Bank. Gilbert Heathcote, former governor of the Bank and ungenial house ghost, took a vengeful and myopic view. Nothing would be done to save the Sword Blade, but the South Sea had a promise which good opinion would call a binding contract. The whole business, he clearly thought, was one of those rescues which involve pushing the drowning man under.

This was not wisdom: intended recovery turned into vertical panic. South Sea reacted by falling from 370 to 180. The price of Heathcote's revenge on the Sword Blade was the vitiation of his intention to save the South Sea and the market itself. Politically, Walpole was in the position of a man who had done everything wrong, but not in any way damaging to himself. He had not seen through Blunt, he had had expectations of the South Sea identical to those of any uninstructed member of the crowd; he had tried to lose money on it and been rescued by the financially far shrewder Jacombe. And now the memorandum embarrassingly in his handwriting, probably at the dictation of Gilbert

Heathcote, had not only made matters very much worse, it made or implied a rescue which rapidly showed itself unaffordable. He had taken part in drawing up the memorandum, had concurred with the bad judgement and not seen the fairly obvious consequences to a company if its bank goes under. The legend of the financial wizard dies hard but, candidly, as a man on a white horse, Robert Walpole had been strictly infantry.

But this was nothing politically. He was on the record defending the Bank with which he was known everywhere to be fast friends, he was *per contra*, and very handily, untainted by personal ties to Blunt, Knight and Caswell. For that matter, he was only very recently a member of a government, several of whose members were head, heels and elbows into the whole calamitous *Ding an sich*. He was clean. Stanhope was even cleaner, but Stanhope's purity was cognate with Stanhope's ignorance. He was a foreign affairs man, a large forward thinker who left the soiled business of money to other people, in this case to John Aislabie, if not quite a crook then not quite not. Since Stanhope was also the head of government, the King's Minister or perhaps Prime Minister, this was something of an omission, honest negligence where the noun outweighed the adjective.

Walpole, by contrast, was placed like Cincinnatus, the known and distinguished figure withdrawn from government who should now splendidly return to it. The fact that he had been there since 11 June didn't count. Throughout the zenith and fall of the South Sea he had been a silent auxiliary of the Ministry, making no trouble and incurring no blame. And this was, after all, summer, a time of rural retreat for most of society, especially for that dedicated East Anglian. Spending so long in Norfolk had conferred no intrinsic merit upon Walpole. It had kept him ignorant with only the lifeline of Jacombe to keep him from ruinous embarrassment. Nevertheless his own reaction to so many things, that it would be a good idea to go back to Norfolk, had never been more wise.

After ten days, which included the Bank consultation and the memorandum, he did go back there, taking money which he had drawn from Jacombe.* In Norfolk he stayed through the rest of September to October. But he was beginning to be talked about. The poet and peace

* 1,000 guineas' worth, withdrawn on 27 September (C(H), quoted in J.H. Plumb, *Sir Robert Walpole*, vol. I, pp. 321–2, note).

treaty negotiator, Matthew Prior, noted on 4 October 'Walpole and Townshend sent for that they may settle matters',[37] and talked *to*, notably by the hovering Robert Jacombe who, on 13 October, said, 'Everyone longs for you in town' and, on 1 November, added, 'They all cry out for you to help them.'[38] Jacombe was a friend and partisan. But his words may have inspired Archdeacon Coxe who was both, only more so, to the benign Stalinism of his account of a grateful nation turning to its saviour. Charles Realey, the American historian who, in 1931, first put Walpole into a decently cautious perspective, points out that even more ardent messages came from several hands to Harley who, at sixty and lately recovered from his fevers in the Tower, stayed sensibly in his garden and bowling green in Herefordshire.

Eventually Walpole chose a great Whig festive day, 5 November, for his return to London. He was raising his price in the political market. There was nothing lofty about the Walpole of autumn 1720, but he *looked* lofty. He was by no means clean in his own general dealings, but, lit by expectations, he would pass for clean. However, by no means was he met with universal hurrahs. There was distrust of his Bank connections since they underlined the factionalism between the institutions. And the modest recovery in stocks over this period, which to the loyal Coxe was a simple reaction at the great man's return, was put down by contemporaries as relief that all ministers were now on the same raft and pulling in the same direction. 'This happy union brought up the stock again' says a letter of 24 November. He was coming back, indeed, but there was everything to do as one of a team.

For, as we have seen, the supposed meddling of the Germans had helped bring about limited conciliation between the double acts of Stanhope/Sunderland and Walpole/Townshend. Over three years, he had been their factitious enemy. They had responded in kind, treating him as an enemy to be suitably done down. They had been happily quarrelling politicians; now fear of what the Germans might be up to, followed by a financial slump moving into its throat-cutting phase, required them to be politicians making up.

The political importance of the crash could hardly be overstated. There were spectacular losers at the top of society: the Duke of Portland reduced to the humiliation of governing Jamaica; Lord Irvine seeking similar degradation in Barbados;[39] Sir Isaac Newton losing £20,000;[40] Lord Londonderry £50,000;[41] the bankruptcy of the Sword Blade Company; the near failure of two leading insurance companies, the

London and the Royal Exchange; a major fall in the building trade as villas in town and country became a burden; properties not bought; houses not finished nor taken up; builders bankrupted; workmen thrown out of work and a fall in land prices.

In Holland where the South Sea appeal had had takers, rioters burned down a coffee house frequented by the damned English.[42] The prospect of other rioters nearer home, of ruin begetting fire in the streets, was no fancy. The horrific prospect of the Pretender flourishing on English soil followed close behind. It was a very comforting thought that Stanhope's providential diplomacy had put James Edward beyond the Alps among the congenial pieties of Rome.

Walpole, who had returned to London on 8 November, was placed for a central role. George, unable to escape one, arrived on the 10th. In attendance was the Paymaster General who, the day before, had had another meeting – with colleagues in the Bank and their dependants at South Sea House. The Bank's undertaking to the South Sea had been set out in Walpole's hand in September, the so-called Bank Contract. But all thought of re-sparking the market by taking that company's stock had been dispersed by abandonment of the Sword Blade and the deepening of the market fall which it had precipitated. The men who had set the terms were in position to play by them. Having made bad very much worse, the contract would now be curtly, if formally, repudiated.

Walpole would make enemies for life by the way in which the Bank Contract affair had been conducted in the weeks after September. The Bank directors and their favourite politician had held out a deal which they quickly learned was incapable of delivery. They had undertaken to buy £3 million in shares at 400. They had delayed across early October, making excuses and postponements. The Bank had great problems of its own, needing a cash delivery from Amsterdam to keep going, but the promise, vitiated by its own downing of the Sword Blade, was kept in the air and the almost daily requests from the South Sea for the support promised, shiftily evaded. Meanwhile, Walpole was making his own plans for recovery, or, rather, preparing to take up plans made by Robert Jacombe.

Then came the announcement of 9 November. A party from the Bank appeared at the South Sea offices and set out what should now be done. Payment out would amount to £340,000 and nothing more. The contract had been held out, expectations raised. Bank directors and Walpole, fully and early aware of having promised too much, had held their tongues in politic fashion. The word was 'repudiation' and the next word was 'deception'. The South Sea price fell to 135. In the judgement of an eminent lawyer, Serjeant Chesshyre, the agreement was 'binding on the Bank of England'.[43] The view of John Carswell is unambiguous: 'It is difficult to acquit either Walpole or the Bank of systematic and masterly duplicity over the whole affair.'[44] Having played his part in deepening the crisis, then breaking a contract, Walpole had inadvertently cleared the ground of any alternative to Jacombe's plan which he now unveiled, first to his returning colleagues, Sunderland and Stanhope, then, with some noise, to the public, as Walpole's plan!

7

'ODIOUS INQUIRIES'

The South Sea Bubble had rested upon confidence, recovery upon the same interesting foundations. The reality across the country was frightening. The South Sea directors had done by stumbling inadvertence what John Law had fully intended to do in France. They had met the problems of an economy full of activity and short of currency with a supply of paper money.

What was accepted as payment at the height of the Bubble was not a formal paper currency backed by specie, bank and government; it was transactional paper like the packet, said to be worth £60,000, taken in a coach robbery between Slough and Colebrook in August or the package stolen from an Oxfordshire maltster.[1] This last was made up of shares in a flax plantation in Pennsylvania and an Essex company engaged in land development. The list of bubbles printed for Parliament during legislation of the Bubble Act – for 'Drying malt by hot air', for 'Carrying on a trade in the river Oroonoko in America', for 'Insuring all masters and mistresses against the losses they shall sustain by servants' (this one seeking a subscription of three million) and ominously, for 'Lending money on stocks, annuities, tallies etc.' – were, once running, capable of generating unofficial exchange. And all of it would go to worthless printed matter.

The paper had been very useful in both countries, sparking sane and practical enterprises along with the moonbeams, but useful only to the far point of general credibility. And credit had now collapsed, not just credit in the Sword Blade or South Sea, but the credit which decently covers a ninety-day transaction and keeps gold out of socks.

What was needed was a counter-confidence, a belief that somehow

heroic stock losses and all the contingent ruin in property and manufactures were, in that twentieth-century Chancellor of the Exchequer
Nigel Lawson's phrase, 'a blip', and that all would soon be for the
Panglossian best. For the moment, at any rate in the mercurial world
of London politics, such optimism actually seemed in order. The Whigs
had their majority, the opposition was feeble, the weasel dream of
'drawing a line' and 'moving on' would surely flourish. Walpole would
bring in his scheme and all would be well. That wasn't actually wrong.
All that was wanting in this judgement was the word 'ultimately'.

Meanwhile, a ballad circulated, the penultimate verse of which ran:

A race of men who t'other day
Lay crushed beneath disasters
Are now by Stock brought into play
And made our lords and masters,
But should the South Sea Babel fail,
What numbers would be frowning?
The losers then must ease their gall
By hanging or by drowning.[2]

Parliament was angry. Viscount Molesworth, who had lost £2000
of borrowed money,[3] was livid, so livid that he invoked the Roman
response to parricide. They 'adjudged the guilty wretch to be thrown
alive sewed up in a sack into the Tyber . . . and since he "looked upon
the contrivers and executers of the villainous South Sea Scheme, as
the parricides of their country, he should be satisfied to see them
undergo the same punishment".'[4] Such bar-parlour snarlings might
be discounted, but it was the breadth of public anger rather than its
florid highlights that thoughtful politicians feared. Blunt and the rest
would soon enough be convicted of a series of improprieties and
impositions on the public, but it was improbable that opinion would
confine a discriminating focus upon the directors of the South Sea
Company.

Parliament had passed the enabling legislation in a champagne spirit.
Ministers and Members, led by the Chancellor of the Exchequer, had
been players and investors, takers of inducements and profits, perhaps
confederates and, if confederates, why not conspirators? The list of
those who had blown on a flame which had burned so many was
eminent and long. So very many people had a common interest in

muffling the explosion, tempering the wind, keeping the lid on, every cliché of scoundrelly discretion.

Talk of heavy retribution might help a man in a rage feel better. But there was no South Sea director who, if threatened, did not have a tale to relate which would bring Honourable and Right Honourable Gentlemen, long-descended nobility and better to the same fire. The reaction to Heathcote's self-defeating short way with the Sword Blade had been a warning. This was a crisis which could spill beyond Parliament into the court and beyond both, on to the streets. Already in the days before Christmas 1720, the people who, with every government assurance and encouragement, had exchanged annuities for the latest issue of South Sea stock were swirling about Westminster expressing ungrateful sentiments. A petition to Parliament from Worcester on 23 December complained that trade had dried up and blamed the financiers.

It was the first of so many. Cobbett's *Parliamentary History* prints nine and a half columns of them. New Sarum (Salisbury) catches the mood: 'That the late South Sea Directors and their black accomplices, by their insatiable covetousness and ambition, supported by the base arts of fraud and dissimulation, have brought the trade and public credit of this kingdom under the most languishing condition, as they have also done to the petitioners: and praying relief.'[5]

The sorrowing petitioners of Agmondesham (Amersham) spoke of 'the sad circumstances wherein all sorts and degrees of men amongst them are involved; and of those piercing cries and loud complaints which diffuse themselves far and wide; and are heard with grief in every corner of our once happy island, does constrain them to implore the House to continue its endeavours that all possible reparation may be brought to the poor sufferers . . .'[6]

Bristol, distinctly rougher, demanded that Parliament bring 'to condign punishment those voracious Robbers of their Country and Mismanagers of the South Sea stock who, to aggrandize their families, have unjustly amassed vast sums of money, destroyed our credit and ruined many thousands of their fellow subjects' and required 'that no man's greatness, ill-gotten riches or flight from justice may screen him from public punishment'.[7]

This is an early use of the word 'screen' (or more commonly at the time, 'skreen') as noun or verb in this historic context. We would say 'whitewash' or 'cover-up'. But all the words describe ancient and comfortable practice by every government answerable to anyone. The conduct of Samuel Pepys, Secretary to the Navy, during the Brooke House inquiry of 1669–70 involved getting the King, the Naval Board (and the Secretary to the Navy) out of the blame for negligence which had let Michael De Ruyter burn the British fleet at anchor in the Medway. His defence worked through the structured tedium of vast circumstantial detail, rich in red herrings, the cost of Riga hemp and the shortage of Eastland timber. A delighted Charles II would speak of 'Mr Pepys that must be Speaker in the Parliament House'.[8] When government actually *is* culpable, the spokesman playing out time and minimising excitement is treasured above 3 per cent stock. If Walpole could screen a great gathering of variably involved personages, he would be placed for a great reward.

However much ministers deprecated the pursuit of 'Guilty men', they were not placed to resist pressure. Sir Joseph Jekyll, former minister and leading lawyer, now Master of the Rolls, struck a quiet, lethal note, saying: 'That as he doubted not but among the South Sea Directors some might be innocent and others criminal, so he was of opinion that there were those who were not Directors, no less, if not more, criminal than the Directors themselves, and who therefore deserved an equal if not a severer punishment.' As for how to do it, Sir Joseph was clear, adding, 'That upon extraordinary emergencies where the laws are deficient, the legislative authority may and ought to exert itself; and he hoped a British parliament would never want a vindictive power to punish national crimes.'[9]

The meaning of 'vindictive' has changed since 1720; even so, this was an observation to induce executive stress. Both the Walpoles argued against vain pursuit and for concentration upon 'the remedy'. Walpole's contribution is pure oil of discretion: 'if they went on in a warm passionate way, the said scheme might be rendered altogether impracticable; therefore he desired that the House would proceed regularly and calmly, lest by running precipitately into odious inquiries, they should exasperate the distemper to such a degree as to render all remedies ineffectual'. Jekyll was not for smoothing. He stressed 'the necessity of examining without the least delay into the conduct of the South Sea company; to see whether they had made good their engagements and strictly followed the rules prescribed to them by the act passed last session of parliament . . .'. And when he tacked to the government's vague motion on investigative powers, the words, 'and for punishing the authors of them', ministers did not dare resist.

'Vindictive punishment' and 'odious inquiry' were not to be entirely escaped. In the meantime, government men must push on with 'effectual remedies' and 'the said scheme'. Walpole, whatever the hatreds between him and established ministers, had the locus of a saviour. He was more than ordinarily shrewd and very interested in money. And if not certainly a first-rate financial mind, he talked like one. He had gambled in the Bubble and done so unskilfully, but without being badly burned or much noticed. He was an insider with the style and address of an outsider. But his real core gift was to be a lucid, plain-seeming kind of debater, inspiring confidence in his nerve and grasp, and optimism about his honesty. And at this point, confidence and optimism were the only things.

It was just as well. Jacombe's donation to his client, communicated in October, which Walpole would outline to the Commons on 21 December, wasn't actually going to work. He called it 'engraftment'. It had existed in draft since 28 November and proposed

> That nine millions of the capitall stock of the South Sea Company with an annuity of £5. per cent per annum issuing from the Exchequer and payable weekly, be ingrafted into the Bank of England and added to the present capitall stock of the Bank amounting to £5,560,000 or thereabouts. That every proprietor of the said nine millions so ingrafted, be entitled to a share in the capitall of the Bank at the rate of £120. per cent viz. For every £120. in the nine millions to be ingrafted, each proprietor to have £100. stock in the Bank. The remaining £20. per cent, part of the nine millions, making in the whole one million and a half, to be referred for the common benefit and advantage of the Bank.[10]

Put in terms of plainer arithmetic, the Bank and the East India Company would convert nearly half the paper of South Sea (£18 million out of £38 million) to their respective stocks and issue it slightly above market rate to the holders of South Sea paper. In selling the plan, Walpole was keen to talk anti-monopolism. The power and capital of the South Sea would be divided three ways, what was held would be made sounder by following the principles of a modern unit trust, here a basket of three assets. It was a horse and water scheme, with the Bank and the East India Company as the distinctly hesitant horses. And it was small consolation to the late entrants, urged by the government to surrender annuities charged to that government in return for stock, now rubbish and, even on fruition of the scheme, worth half the thirty-six-year purchase of their original holdings.

There were now two considerations: getting the scheme accepted – by Bank and Parliament – and, more problematically, having it work. The Bank, where Walpole had an enviable collection of friends and contacts, was the easy part, its assent coming early in the narration. He also won access to the King, an early sign of his rising political star. Mere talk of the Bank's acceptance pushed up South Sea stock by 75 points to 215. On 28 November, Walpole was, by way of encouragement, minuting interested parties that the Court of Directors had 'authorised the committee to meet and treat upon' his proposal.[11]

The immediate effect of trying for parliamentary approval was, as we have seen, quite different. Parliament heard Walpole out, but seems to have been far from understanding him. It was, anyway, too angry at the damage done, the public enraged and the fraud practised, to respond in the genial way of his friends at the Bank. The scheme's want of remedy for the late-entering annuitants was recognised; Walpole, knowing better than to push his luck, held back.

The South Sea's battered staff worked on the demands Parliament had made. It must have set out for it the loans undertaken and the rules broken when making them. It wanted, and quickly, details of the £774,000 of stock greatly exceeding what the Company had to issue yet nevertheless, by one means or another, put about. The fountain of this information, so far dry, was Robert Knight, white-collar criminal on a transcendental scale. Knight was custodian of the famous green book of individual stock transactions, so often on such advantageous terms, to people of such high public standing. Anything he might say was terrifying.

Meanwhile, the Court of South Sea Directors met and begged its shareholders to accept the engraftment scheme, but also begged for time to seek the modification demanded by enraged holders of paper now horribly crumpled. But it was too early for a smooth progress of the Walpole/Jacombe scheme to be contemplated. Pursuit, punishment and revenge were the preoccupation of the street where a director of the South Sea Company, Lambert Blackwell, had to be rescued from an impromptu lynching party,[12] and in Parliament, where after furious exchanges and invitations to settle matters by duel, the respected, independent (and anti-South Sea) Irish MP Thomas Brodrick was elected on 29 December into the chair of a Committee of Inquiry. In the words of the chronicler of the Bubble, 'It was the talk of the town that they would be hanged whether there was law for it or not.'[13]

In Parliament, which resumed on 4 January, for much of 1721 two undertakings were proceeding, the legislation of Walpole's engraftment scheme and the inquiry of the Brodrick Committee. The scheme, always and with reason, looked upon sceptically, was nevertheless put through; first voted on next day, a motion was supported 173 to 130. A formal bill passed first reading by 165 to 118 on 3 February, second reading on 7 February, by 237 to 139. It passed the Commons without recorded vote on 22 February. And similarly, on 22 March, it passed the Lords.[14]

The scheme was unreal. It made demands on the Bank and the East India Company in terms of growth beyond what could be expected of them. But it was formally law, something seeming to be done. And the ablest parliamentarian of the time was speaking regularly about the central issue of the hour. The entrance to power did not need to be a triumphal arch. On the other count, pursuit and punishment, the Brodrick Committee was hard at work. From Saturday 14 January onward, it met for three weeks, six days a week, 9 a.m. to 11 p.m.[15] On the Monday it examined Blunt and Knight notably about stock 'taken for particular persons' and not recorded, and about Knight's green book. This volume was acquiring mystic properties. But essentially, it was recognised as the record of stock issued, free or advantageously, to important people by way of bribes. On the Thursday, privately, Theodore Janssen, one of the most reputable people associated with the South Sea, urged Knight to come clean on what he knew. 'If I should disclose all I know,' said the Cashier mildly, 'it would open such a scene as the world would be surprised at.'

On Saturday with the committee still diligently sitting, Knight and his son went quietly to Dover pleasantly ahead of the pursuit following when Parliament was told. A chartered yacht took him by way of Calais to Brabant, today a province of Belgium, then a territory of the Holy Roman Empire, resented and appreciated by different parties as being free from all extradition. It was everything at which opposition and rank-and-file MPs would rage, and ministers, very quietly, celebrate. The name of the yacht was the *Joyeuse Entrée*!

Knight left a letter to the directors dated Sunday the 22nd. With stupefying aplomb he spoke of 'self-preservation' having 'obliged me to withdraw myself from the resentment against the Directors and myself, yet I am not conscious to myself of having done any one thing I can reproach myself for, so far as relates to an honest, sincere intention and zeal for the Company'. Having a little homily about the directors pulling together more than they had and some assurances about his own holdings, Knight signed off 'I am prest for time, so can only assure you that I am, with all respect in inclination, though not in power – Gentlemen, your most obedient, humble servant, Robert Knight'.[16]

The Commons was furious, so furious that on 24 January it sent addresses to the King 'to issue a proclamation with a reward for discovering, apprehending and detaining the said Robert Knight that he may be brought to justice' and, as ineffectually, 'to give orders forthwith to stop the ports, and to take effectual care of the coasts, to prevent the said Mr Knight or any other Officers of the South Sea Company from escaping out of the Kingdom'. The King complying, a proclamation was published offering £2000 reward.

In the same spirit of doing and being seen to do *something*, the House summoned four South Sea directors who were MPs, Sir Theodore Janssen, Sir Robert Chaplin, Francis Eyles and Jacob Sawbridge. General Charles Ross, a Scottish member of the committee, said that it had already discovered 'a train of deepest villainy and fraud that hell ever contrived to ruin a nation'[17] and successfully urged their expulsion, detention and seizure of their papers. In fact, Janssen and Eyles were at the furthest margin of wrongdoing, no part of the inner conspiracy. Expulsion took place at once and on the next day the Lords examined five men, Houlditch, Hawes, Gibbon, Chester and Chaplin, and all were put in custody. The serious malefactors here were Houlditch and Hawes, the second of whom was a close confederate of the Chancellor, John Aislabie.

Parallel with these hearings, the Brodrick Committee was conducting private examinations. And interesting overlaps and catch-ups occurred between them and Lords and Commons activities. So Charles Joye, deputy governor of the Company, and its only man of any account still free to walk the streets, recklessly offered the clean (and incredible) version of Knight's account, saying that it was 'as received from the Committee of Treasury who never laid any account before the Court of Directors of stock sold until after the receipt of the order of the House'.[18] On the same day, Blunt had told the committee, as he afterwards reassured Joye, that he had said nothing incriminating about ministers or royal ladies. But there being no honour among thieves and Blunt having decided to oblige Parliament with full, or any rate well-chosen, details, he spent the next day (still in private) reversing his evidence and spelling out horrid details, names and all.

In a few days' time, the Commons would be given the full account, but ministers guilty, innocent and bemused, fell into warranted relief. Brodrick was mocked by the Secretary of State, young Craggs, at the delay, not much of one, in presenting his first report. Oddly enough, considering that further Lords examination of Blunt was due next day, ministers held a party, attended by a very good-humoured George Augustus, which went on for a very long time. It may have been held in connection with James Stanhope, as soldier, succeeding the lately deceased Marlborough as Captain General, supreme military office of the kingdom. Certainly it was a good party, at which 'they drank excessively of new tokay, champagne,* visney and barba water, thirteen hours it is said'.[19]

When it came to questioning Blunt, the Lords was not the forum where he proposed to peach. And, having refused to answer a question, he was told to withdraw while the peers debated the next procedural step. Philip Wharton, Duke of Wharton, a sexual activist and odd, flighty, politically unstable person en route from the Junto Whiggism of his father, Thomas, to Jacobitism and Roman Catholicism, launched an attack on ministers. It was not the sort of invective a modern, stripped-down, demotic politician would use or recognise. He compared Stanhope with Sejanus, the ambitious Roman minister who had created a split in the imperial family in the time of Tiberius.

Stanhope, of course, had been notably caught up in the quarrel between King and Prince of Wales. He, at once, responded, seized by a rage which took him to his grave. He invoked the elder Brutus who had sacrificed his worthless son. That was a stroke at Wharton, rake-hell and betrayer of the family creed, but it was Stanhope whom it struck. He suffered 'an apoplexy', (what sounds like a cerebral haemorrhage), collapsed, was taken home, seemed to recover, took tea with Sunderland and the Duke of Newcastle next day, went back to bed and died.

Robert Walpole never had better news. Stanhope might be surrounded

---

* Champagne as we know it, albeit somewhat sweeter, had only existed since 1700 when the great Dom Perignon, Cellarer of Hautvilliers Abbey, had perfected his experiments.

by trouble, but he was a victor in the war, the King's trusted ally, a man of enormous distinction. Vanbrugh, the architect, thought him 'quite clear in the eyes of all parties in regard to this devilish South Sea affair that is like to taint the greatest part of those who were otherwise fit to do business'.[20] He was not in fact *quite* clear: sales of stock to one 'Stangape', the name 'Stanhope' having been changed, would be revealed by a South Sea employee, Daniel Watkins, a little later. But overall, he was cleaner than Walpole ever had been or would be. But events, mostly deaths, now fell in line to make Walpole master.

On 16 February, Brodrick reported for his committtee, beginning with the information exacted from Blunt, quoting him and Houlditch as to Sunderland's involvement, the discounted terms offered to the Duchess of Kendal and another court lady, the Graefin von Platen Hallermund, the role in the market of the Chancellor of the Exchequer, Aislabie, and a very large bribe paid to Charles Stanhope, Secretary to the Treasury. Brodrick very reasonably wanted his report printed. Walpole gave a first instance of his skill at cushioning fraud when he persuaded the House not to. But the knife came close to ministerial ribs when, on 28 February, Charles Stanhope, unwise cousin of James, became the subject of inquiry and parliamentary vote. The first question concerned £250,000 in his name in the Sword Blade Company books. He avoided further pursuit when a director of the Sword Blade gave assurances that Charles Stanhope's name had been used without his knowledge. As the money was generally recognised as a bribe fund and the word of a Sword Blade director, even by way of self-incrimination, lacked credit, he was hanging on.

The second charge concerned £10,000 held by Knight for the benefit of 'Charles Stanhope Esq., one of the secretaries of the Treasury and a Member of this House, without any valuable consideration paid or security given for the acceptance of or payment of the said stock; and that the difference arising by the advanced price thereof was paid to the said Charles Stanhope Esq., out of the cash of the South Sea Company'.[21] Charles protested that he had employed Knight as a private banker. As for any stock bought for him by Knight, 'he had paid valuable consideration for it', in other words, bought it with his own money.

This had all the qualities of a likely story. But heaven, earth and the royal influence were moved to get him off, George writing to two committee members, Jekyll and Molesworth, 'desiring it as a favour that nearly concerned him that they would not vote against Mr Stanhope'.[22]

In fact, Jekyll, Molesworth and William Sloper on various pretexts slipped quietly away. Sloper, once deputy Paymaster to Walpole, had handled his accounts at the period when the sale of £9000 of South Sea stock had made a profit of nearly £3700. He would, though, be an opponent of the engraftment scheme.[23] Charles Stanhope, benefiting from a moving speech invoking the late first Minister, from his cousin, Philip, later the epigrammatical Lord Chesterfield, scraped through because on one reckoning, 'between forty or fifty who could not bring themselves to give negatives, were however prevailed upon to withdraw before the question'.[24]

The prevailing upon was the doing of Robert Walpole who had spoken in defence and exerted himself in all the other available ways. And when the motion charging Charles Stanhope was lost by three votes (180 to 177) anger (and appreciation) were directed at Walpole. Brodrick said that the outcome had 'put the town in a flame to such a degree as you cannot easily imagine'. Matthew Prior, hero of Utrecht and, as a substantial poet, apt for a striking phrase, told his friend Swift that 'conditions were wilder than St Anthony's dream'.[25] St Anthony's dream concerned temptation. And at the back of all minds lay the figure of its modern custodian, Robert Knight.

About Knight certain essentials need to be understood. The House of Commons officially wanted him back. Thomas Brodrick, his committee and the opposition, really and earnestly did want him back. The Ministry in which Walpole, closing on power, and recognising the rescue of the Ministry as the means by which he would get it, wanted nothing of the sort.

Knight had been at the centre of things. Modern research, chiefly that of John Carswell, in his heavily revised history of the Bubble,* has established that he was at least as important in the South Sea scheme of things as the bombastic figure of Sir John Blunt. Without breaking the law a step further, Knight had Moriarty potential. He knew, and his green book would corroborate, who among ministers, courtiers, royal mistresses and King George I, had received stock on fictional terms, and which other ministers had been flatly bribed for the legislative slipway laid to launch South Sea. Whoever held that ledger could

---

* This tells us how, in the early 1990s, John Carswell, advised by the actual finder, Peter Barber of the British Library, obtained this outstanding material, an account to which what follows is wholly indebted.

convict or blackmail half a government and a wide circle of the best people.

The Haus-, Hof- und Staatsarchiv in Vienna revealed to scholars in the early 1990s exactly where Knight was and how representatives of a government dominated by Walpole kept him there.[26] Knight had early been arrested by Officers of the Governor of the Austrian Netherlands and kept in amiable detention in the citadel of Antwerp. The person answerable for him was Ercole Turinetti, Marquis de Prié, deputy governor of the Austrian Netherlands, a cool, professional diplomat following the book. Part of that book was the inviolability of Brabant to foreign extradition.

The first request for Knight's return came from Stanhope just before he died. Stanhope, whether or not he had received stock, being essentially honest, the request was probably in earnest. De Prié urged the Austrian ambassador in London, Johann Philip Hoffmann, to represent to British ministers that if they thought this one over, they might well find such a return not in their best interests. Hoffmann, conveying news of Stanhope's death, agreed, adding that 'a highly placed personage'* close to the King had made known what he stated to be George's wishes . . . that on no account should Robert Knight return to England.

Hoffmann also recounted the general fury and prospective ministerial breakdown in Britain: 'Turbulence and animosity now prevail in Parliament and the consequence is an attack without any reservations on everyone who is found to have gained by the bribery and corruption which the Directors of the Company extended to persuade them to use their votes and influence in the establishment of this recent operation of the Company.'[27]

Yet the first message was to be quickly contradicted by William Leathes, British Resident, who, following a time-honoured practice, had not been residing. After prolonged leave on his Suffolk estate since August 1720, Leathes had come from the King, and to the amazement of de Prié, furiously demanded the return of Knight. He was politely put off while the deputy governor consulted Vienna. Leathes was imperious and unsilken, a recognisable sort of Englishman abroad. De Prié was amazed, but in no hurry. He had taken custody of Knight's papers, including the green book, confiscated when he was arrested. These, in

---

* Carswell's guess is the Duchess of Kendal.

accordance with the proprieties, had been sealed and given to the British chargé d'affaires. Unsurprisingly, they exist in no British archive.

The threat from Knight would be little diminished. Surely he had the choicest names in his head? But assuming that Walpole and Townshend *did* see them, blackmail potential could now be shared. Not merely would Walpole almost certainly be armed against his chief surviving enemy in government, Sunderland, but his relationship with the King would acquire a certain texture. Walpole had benefited at once from the investigations which, by turns, he hindered and encouraged. During the examination of Aislabie by the Commons after his questioning by the committee and Lords, Brodrick, accustomed to opposition from that quarter, observed that 'Walpole's corner sat mute as fishes'.[28]

Aislabie was done for and he knew it. He was Chancellor in name only and for some weeks had played no part in financial debates. On the day that the *Gazette* announced the reward for taking Knight, it informed its readers of Aislabie's resignation. Walpole quietly succeeded him, now doing officially what he had been doing unofficially.

On 25 February, the second Brodrick report was very specific about this minister's dealings, quoting a witness, the broker Matthew Wymonsold, about '£20,000 of South Sea stock bought by Mr Wymonsold for Mr Aislabie on 1st March 1719 at several prices, amounting in the whole to £35,357', also 'that Mr Knight, late Cashier of the South Sea Company, paid the examinant the money for such stock and placed the same to Mr Aislabie's account'. The bribe had been self-evident. There was also evidence from the director, Francis Hawes, that 'he had caused the Book of Accounts between them to be burnt and given him a discharge for the balance amounting to about £342,000'. To the Commons this 'appeared so heinous and so home a proof' that they drew up and approved twelve resolutions on the purchases of stock, improper advice given on the conduct of the company and other assorted villainies, and concluded by ordering, among other unpleasant things, 'That the said John Aislabie be committed prisoner to his Majesty's Tower of London'.

Another Member of Parliament, the Sword Blade man Sir George Caswell, had been revealed as a channel for bribes. Monies in the books, £250,000, representing profit on £50,000 South Sea stock, were recognised as part of the £574,500 appearing on the South Sea's books as sold to persons unknown as Company legislation proceeded. This, said the committee, was done 'for the benefit of persons, whose names were designed to be concealed with intention to make an interest in favour of the Company and to facilitate the acceptance of the South Sea proposals and the passing of the bill which was at that time depending in parliament'.[29]

The defensive exertions of Walpole's whips for Charles Stanhope were not repeated. Caswell's defence, that the Sword Blade had bought stock as simple speculation, was not accepted. There had been no current payment, and Caswell's further defence, that another £70,000 of Sword Blade stock, in pawn with the South Sea, represented valid security, was also rejected, though Jekyll saw merit in the argument. A series of resolutions condemned Caswell and his partners. They were 'guilty of a corrupt, infamous and dangerous practice'.

Caswell was expelled from the Commons, sent after Aislabie to the Tower, and legislation introduced compelling Sword Blade directors to refund the £250,000. Caswell complained bitterly to Walpole that he had been treated worse than a South Sea director and that he 'would be utterly ruined by it if not prevented by the intervention of just men'. He had a case against this clawing-back bill which went far beyond his liability as a co-partner in the Sword Blade. Instructively, though Walpole had not intervened to save him during the hearing, the confiscatory bill, though read a second time, made no further progress in the Commons which Walpole would control. Passivity under attack and inertia in pursuit were his natural weapons.

That control was coming about. James Stanhope was dead, Aislabie in jail. On 6 February, the day after Stanhope's death, young Craggs, popular, likeable, not a taker of stock, advancing the South Sea project more from naïvity than serious wrongdoing and, at thirty-five, already a major player, developed the early symptoms of smallpox. He continued working, not least signing letters to diplomatic missions in pursuit of Knight's return. And on the 17th, the day after Brodrick's first report, he died. A month after his son's death, James Craggs the Elder, worth a million and half in the values of the day and very much deeper into the South Sea, described in the official report as 'the principal agent for the Administration in the *whole* transaction of the South Sea project',[30] also died, 'not without very strong suspicion of having used violence to himself'.[31]

Facing a hearing on 18 March, James Craggs had taken enough laudanum to kill himself on the 17th. Quite what support and screening he had hoped for from Walpole nobody knows. Charles Stanhope, guilty as charged, had benefited from every parliamentary skill of that minister. Aislabie, also guilty, had been written off. But thick-skinned and self-cherishing, the ex-Chancellor would thrive, leaving the Tower in due course and taking back to his estate near Ripon quite enough money for the pleasant life of a country gentleman. Clearly, the elder Craggs, despite talents to make a million and more, lacked the coarse fibre of survival. With the dead and discredited piled all round, the path taking Robert Walpole to the head of affairs was being cleared. He was not chief Minister, but the former chief Minister was dead and, with a single exception, there was no one to resist this last stretch of his assent.

That exception was Charles Spencer, Earl of Sunderland. But Sunderland was horribly implicated in the Bubble. He was in Brodrick's full focus and vulnerable to King's evidence given volubly by Sir John Blunt. On 15 March, the Commons debated a motion flowing from the latest report. It recognised that after South Sea proposals were accepted, but before the bill passed, '£50,000 of the capital stock of the South Sea company was taken in by Robert Knight, late Cashier of the said Company, for use and upon the account of Charles, Earl of Sunderland, a Lord of Parliament and first Commissioner of the Treasury, without any valuable consideration paid, or sufficient security given, for payment for, or acceptance of the same'.[32]

Even for the insouciant eighteenth century, this was a great matter – the head of the government charged by a responsible parliamentary committee with taking payment to advance the scheme which had ruined thousands. It gave Walpole no problems at all. There followed what the record calls 'a warm debate that lasted till eight at night'. But it came a day later than expected at the 'pressing instances of Mr Walpole' so that witnesses should verify their statements to the House. A straight vote would probably have finished Sunderland. Prevarication was the last line of defence.

Everything was now done that could be to soften the impact of clear evidence. Walpole and Henry Pelham, Sunderland's man but on improving terms with Walpole, acted for the Earl. As Brodrick later told a correspondent, they assured the House that 'no stock had ever been taken in for him by Knight or note given, so that the question in truth was neither more or less whether we should give credit to that assertion or Sir John Blunt's oath'.[33] Blunt was the most unpopular man in the country. Initiator and chief mover of the corrupt selling of the South Sea scheme, he was now ratting wholesale on old confederates and clients. But he had every motive for sticking to his story and he knew more about the South Sea than anyone except Robert Knight.

Other ploys were used by Walpole's team against innocent witnesses, quibbles about how many people had been present and whether Knight, whose earlier remarks they had quoted, had spoken to them in the presence of Blunt. But, as Brodrick told his correspondent, 'Such trifling stuff would never have been insisted upon in any other case, and would in any other have been the strongest proof of the fact.'[34] But Brodrick, who recognised a ploy when he saw one, summed it up in pure political terms: 'If you come into this vote against Lord Sunderland, the ministry are blown up, and must, and necessarily will be, succeeded by a Tory one.' And, he added wryly, that he 'had never heard any thing better debated on one side or more weakly on the other'.[35] Walpole got his majority; Sunderland was exonerated of the charges by 233 votes to 172.

Of course Brodrick was right. The Commons with its Whig majority feared the political implosion if Sunderland followed Aislabie to the Tower. Probably Walpole feared it too. He wanted above all things to supersede Sunderland as head of government, but he needed there to *be* a government, needed a Whig majority intact in Parliament. Sunderland was also known to be talking to Tories like Archibald Hutcheson, the economist, whose South Sea recovery scheme had been a rival to Walpole/Jacombe's. He had also given a position in the Ministry to Simon Harcourt, historically Oxford's man. Walpole understood that a deal with the Tories, taking them out of the romantic futility of crypto-Jacobitism into an all-party government, would have made excellent sense to the King. It was one of several things which he needed not to let happen. He did need, and would very soon get, coalition with Sunderland. Acquittal and the continuation of a Whig administration made that inevitable. The acquittal got court and government into easier water, but, as Edward Harley astutely remarked, there were too many Members voting his guilt and voting against the Court for Sunderland to remain as first Minister.

On Stanhope's death, in early February, he had been replaced as Secretary of State by Townshend, a big advance for the Walpole camp. This, following the death so soon after of young Craggs, had been offset by the appointment to the other secretaryship of John Barnum Carteret, very old nobility, friend of young Craggs, also close to Sunderland. Walpole's own formal

accession to the Exchequer came on 3 April, and, with it, the office of
First Lord of the Treasury which Sunderland now resigned. Walpole had
his coalition but he was nothing like supreme minister.

Sunderland kept the secret service money, ironically free after acquittal
on charges of *being* bribed, to continue bribing. He also kept the empty-
sounding, but important, post of Groom of the Stole which underlined
his continuing credit at court. Lesser offices were cheerfully divided up.
That spy's paradise, the Postmastership General (free steam-access to
the mails), was split, an act of screaming blatancy, between two men,
not only partisan but family, Edward Carteret, brother of the Secretary
of State, and Galfridus Walpole, brother of the First Lord. For a period,
Walpole would now operate with colleagues, on a sort of exalted proba-
tion, their man of business, whose scheme should rescue the financial
situation. He would also continue in the ungazetted role, already in
circulation, of Skreenmaster General.

In his hands, business with the Austrian officials holding Knight took
on a quite new direction. King George's instructions to Leathes for
urgent extradition make no sense given his own involvement and the
message sent, probably by Melusine. John Carswell points out that
Leathes described himself as instructed by the King at a large gathering. George probably had no alternative but to give, through clenched
teeth, instructions against all self-interest. Stanhope had been either
innocent of wrongdoing or sincerely believed himself so. But by mid-
March, with Stanhope dead and George able to give briefings more
discreetly, there appeared in Vienna a certain Colonel Charles Churchill,
about whom one thing is vividly certain: he was a devoted friend of
Robert Walpole. Member since 1715 and until his death in 1745 for
Castle Rising, the Walpole family borough, his illegitimate son later
marrying the no more matrimonial daughter of Walpole, he was party
comrade, bottle-splitter and family!

Records do not survive in the Staatsarchiv of requests made, messages
from London conveyed. All is conjecture but some sorts of conjecture
are better than others. Churchill, around whom bastardy cheerfully
swirled, was Marlborough's bend sinister nephew, had served in the
War of the Spanish Succession and come to know Austria's own
Marlborough, Prince Eugène. He was also present at a meeting chaired
by Sinzendorff, imperial foreign minister, and attended by a personal
representative of King George, the Swiss, François de Saint-Saphorin.
This meeting is known to have discussed the message for de Prié.[36]

Churchill's official letters to the official government are described by Carswell as 'totally mendacious'. If anyone was placed to come from Walpole to tell the Austrians not to send Robert Knight back to give unwelcome evidence, it was Charles Churchill.

As for official channels, Leathes was singing a different tune. The bullying envoy making ungraceful demands for Knight's instant return now suggested *two* correct lines. Officially, Knight was a fugitive from justice and should be returned to face it. Unofficially and urgently, he begged the Marquis de Prié so to arrange matters that the prisoner should *not* be handed over. He also requested that the Austrian would do nothing to help Parliament get itself caught up in the truth, nothing, that is, to 'have the British parliament or the British people to doubt whether the representations being made for extradition were sincere and unreserved'.[37]

The cynicism is precipitous. Leathes, by the old tag, had been 'sent to lie abroad for his country', and he was hard at it. Walpole, conducting foreign policy direct or through Townshend, had to assuage an Austria which did not feel that it owed Great Britain special favours. But through Leathes and de Prié, the King was telling Charles VI that 'favourable management of this affair . . . would be regarded by his Britannic majesty as the most conspicuous mark of friendship the Emperor could possibly confer on him. Which he would always bear in mind, and one for which he would demonstrate his gratitude at all opportunities.'[38] This, behind the stately prose, spoke of a frantic anxiety.

Getting the Austrians to do the decent thing when presumably they had read Knight's papers and knew just how frightened the English establishment was, would be something of a drawn-out campaign. But anger at Britain's brutally self-seeking role at the end of the war should not get in the way of the Empire's interests. The Pretender, James Edward Stuart, might have been incrementally demoted by France, from Paris to Avignon to Rome, but ultimately he was France's card to play if it suited, exactly what would happen in 1745. A Britain governed by an Elector of the Empire and good ally in the war made sense to Vienna. Religion was no longer an issue. Louis XIV was the last man to have thought otherwise. George's and Britain's unsoundness over the Real Presence was neither here nor there. The Emperor was not going to use bribes taken by George to make a French pensioner King of England.

Even so, this was a fearful time for Walpole. Clichés about powder kegs were the simple truth. Getting the Austrians onside through intelligent professionals like de Prié, by way of Leathes, doing as he was told, and Churchill, his closest friend, was an essay begun just short of the highest office and the first great undertaking of what might now be called his Prime Ministership. The shift was now in its last phase. Officially, Sunderland was a reconciled good colleague of his former opponents, Walpole and Townshend. Facile civilities abounded, social occasions like an excursion to Richmond to call on the Prince of Wales were pursued. Walpole was not engaged in a stroll to the top, nor Sunderland alone in detesting him. Carteret was not an admirer; the calm was frightening. The situation had become simple Humpty Dumpty. Who was to be master?

This was, to use a politician's banality, a time of continuity and change – continuity in fixing the investigating committee, not least by way of conspiracy with the Austrians, change in getting his men into government and Sunderland's friends out.

Westminster had been engaged since December in debates and pursuits largely flowing from the activities of Brodrick's committee, activities best understood by the headlines in Cobbett's *Parliamentary History*: 'Progress of the South Sea Scheme', 'List of Bubbles', 'National Infatuation and Despair', 'Account of the Bank Contract', 'Six reports of the Committee' and 'A Petition for Justice on the Authors of the Present Calamities'. John Aislabie would have a whole debate to himself before committal to the Tower.

The grand finale following scrutiny of the estates of the South Sea directors would be an inquisition into their assets, and a judgement, delinquent by delinquent, of what should be recovered. Walpole would be active in all this, shocked and deploring with the best, but keeping heads off poles and minimising the political effect. The committee, apart from the scrupulous Brodrick, was dominated by more partisan Tories. And though they did not show fierce political edge, Walpole viewed the process as he viewed everything, in party terms. He was present in the chamber for one thing: to make the least of the calamity.

He was also engaged through diplomatic channels to see that the star witness never appeared in court. In this he would be fortunate in his foreign colleagues. De Prié, the imperial foreign minister Sinzendorff, and ultimately the Emperor, were asked very civilly to keep Robert Knight (and his well-informed son) away from questioning which, if answered, would send things up in flames. De Prié first of all did a little exercise on behalf of the official, 'Send him back', British position. He circulated the states of Brabant with a petition from Leathes (written by de Prié), asking for return. This was done with the British Parliament very much in mind. Its language proclaimed in a familiar, spurious ministerial manner, 'Everything possible is being done.' The inevitable polite refusal by the local municipalities, Brussels, Malines and Antwerp, gave a sturdy burgherly defiance to the frustrated representatives in Westminster.

Viscount Molesworth, the throw-them-in-the-Tiber man, had toned down his act, moving that Knight be offered a full pardon in return for coming home and giving an equally full testimony. This was not at all what Walpole had in mind. Knight, who had rather liked the idea, was quickly sent an (untruthful) message that no pardon could protect him from the committee's fury. That committee was, *au contraire*, quite sophisticated enough to look after a decently communicative Knight. Beyond that, the Walpole machine, representing a government noisily pursuing truth, organised the defeat of Molesworth's motion. The committee sent the indignant General Charles Ross to the Austrian Netherlands in hopes of an interview with Knight. At urgent British request, the Knights were secretly moved on 23/24 May from Antwerp to Luxembourg. When someone, *un esprit inquiet*,[39] unkindly questioned their continued presence in Antwerp, they were returned there. By such heavy ingenuity, time was spun out. It spun until 20 August when Parliament rose.

The unlucky man in the middle during all this was Resident Leathes. George had changed his mind in mid-rhetoric, and he must have realised that politics had anyway made him the servant of two masters, one to be pleased, the other obeyed. At the same time, he was dealing with a clever Italian bureaucrat whose mind, especially in diplomatic French, worked quicker than his. Carswell is satisfied from its complex style that the next important letter given by Leathes to him for the attention of Sinzendorff, Prince Eugène and the Emperor had been drafted by de Prié. The deputy governor had already briefed his principal, the great Eugène, who, among other things, was the actual Governor of the Austrian Netherlands.

Now, on 31 August/11 September,* Leathes made the climactic request of the Emperor. He wrote floridly that HMG was terribly grateful to

* This indicates the Julian Calendar followed in Britain, and eleven days advanced on the Gregorian version, adhered to on the Continent. It was changed, provoking riots, in 1752.

the Emperor for trying so hard to expel Knight, but that, of course, if autonomous states stuck to their rights, there wasn't much that could be done about it, so we wouldn't push things. But the letter, written on behalf of King George, broke out of flummery to speak the wishes of that king 'pleased to express the wish that Your Excellency should order the Governor of Antwerp Citadel to enlarge Knight from confinement, allowing him not only to have liberty to walk on the Citadel but to escape'.

The final sentences, as expressly, trusted that de Prié would do the necessary 'in such a manner that it shall not appear that this escape is authorised by His Majesty or this government'.⁴⁰ It is difficult to imagine even the dullard of Leathes's first and unimproved letter producing such a naked horror and then piling Pelion upon Ossa by identifying King George as principal. As an invitation to shocking revelation it ranks with the US Republican presidential candidate James Blaine's unhappy postscript, 'Burn this letter'.

Prose style apart, it carries all the motivation of an Austrian text, done as reinsurance and leaving the English government no weaselling room about what they had wanted and why the Austrians would do it for them. This accomplished, Robert Knight and his son were shortly afterwards dropped off on the other side of the French border. Although Parliament would confiscate what he had not been able to take with him, Knight was comfortably enough placed, settling down at Vincennes, than which there are worse places, going into business and striking up a friendship with Bolingbroke, also exiled. He was not, however, permitted to return to England until 1742, the year of Walpole's fall. His parliamentary property at Grimsby was looked after by a nominee and later inherited by the younger Robert. But from 1747 to 1754, the son would sit for, of all imaginable constituencies, Castle Rising!*⁴¹

But through summer 1721 urgency had diminished, the political threat retreated. The central arithmetic of the Commons stood where it had, a body of Whigs, of opposed factions perhaps and sometimes inconvenienced by genuinely disinterested men, but usually able to outface an opposition essentially Tory. If pursuit of the guilty slowed to a ritual, it was no fault of Brodrick's committee. They had worked very hard, producing six reports after the first and doing so in three

---

* The doing, allegedly, of Walpole's son and successor who shared a couple of actresses with him.

months. The idea had been to make the operators pay what were called, reasonably enough, 'the sufferers'. At the end of May, a sort of reckoning had been staged, at which penalties were handed out. Some were large, as a string of directors were subjected to the question of what they must repay, but no one was stripped naked, no one, after the early sendings to (and quiet releasings from) the Tower, was put in prison. There were saltings away and inspirational accountancy where money was not trapped in land.

The one person upon whom serious revenge descended was Sir John Blunt, and for a reason. Blunt had turned King's evidence, done everything to accommodate the committee. Walpole, essentially working for the South Sea directors, was very happy to make an example of him. He shifted in this case from defence to prosecution, suggesting that no more than £1000 should be left to Blunt from an estate notionally identified at £183,000. The final deal was not much better – £5000 – though Blunt did manage to retire in decent comfort to Bath.

There was a lengthy debate about Aislabie enlivened by General Ross excitedly entering the chamber to announce that Thomas Vernon, the ex-Chancellor's brother-in-law, had attempted to buy his support. The full weight of Vernon's expulsion is expressed in the laconic language of Romney Sedgwick's *The House of Commons, 1715–1754*, which notes of Vernon that, after expulsion, 'defeated at the ensuing by-election for Whitchurch, he recovered his seat at the next general election'. At the end of all the fuss, Aislabie, a taker rather than a maker of bribes, the holder of a high office who had behaved like a share pusher, got away with a remarkably light penalty. He was docked £45,000 from an estate of around £160,000. He had been an inveterate enemy of Walpole. But the new First Lord, who never let either vindictiveness or justice get in the way of self-interest, rated Aislabie's two seats at Ripon far above satisfaction.

At the back of the minds of party managers, Robert Walpole's most of all, lay a calculation for the future. Seats were effectively property. Just as the Walpoles owned Castle Rising, Sir George Caswell owned Leominster (his nickname was 'the Lem Knight'), Jacob Sawbridge had a handy interest at Cricklade in Gloucestershire, and John Aislabie, as we have seen, determined which two members would represent Ripon. The huge estate of James Craggs the Elder would soon enough create an alliance of sons-in-law investing in manageable boroughs, people to be cultivated. And it would be wrong to say that there is no gratitude in politics.

Anyway Parliament itself, as the summer advanced, was a rapidly diminishing asset, something Brodrick understood very well. He was conscious of a House of Commons drifting away. Against the Russian experience, Walpole would benefit from General Summer. The eighteenth-century Parliament was not manned by professional politicians living if possible in London, whatever their responsibilities for Dumfries or Exeter. The Tories in particular batted deep in country gentlemen with seasonal agricultural considerations. As time and men slipped away, Brodrick realised that he had done everything he now could, and resigned the leadership of his committee. On 25 July, there were hardly a hundred MPs left to whom the King could make a perfunctory dissolution speech.

Beyond the business of the screen, Walpole's own undertaking, Jacombe's engraftment scheme, having been legislated for with some celerity, rather lost its point. Sir John Plumb speaks of a conspiracy against it by the South Sea directors, upon whom it made heavy demands, and of Jacombe's 'panic' after an unrewarding conversation with a key director, Francis Eyles. But although he talks about Sunderland being behind it all, as he may well have been, he gives no hard evidence: 'Details of the plot have never come to light . . .'[42] The reality was that, independent of political machination, the engraftment scheme was not going to work. It had made the assumption that the Company had a debt to the Exchequer. But there was no possibility that the South Sea could ever meet it. There was also a crying need, not recognised by Jacombe, to give priority to the late converters of annuities to South Sea stock. They had the worst terms and had been most directly encouraged by the government. Very quietly the engraftment scheme was allowed to lapse, the powers conferred by legislation not taken up.

The serious business of a financial settlement of a vast enterprise called into being to relieve the state of most of the national debt had been delegated very early to a capable, elderly man with no political cards to play, William Lowndes. He had worked in consultation with Walpole and, having done the key work, could count on the political machine to put it through. Pursuit of the irredeemably lost being pointless, the seven million undertaken by the South Sea to government was now written off, Company loans were cancelled and subscriptions marked down in value. A distribution of surplus stock was made among buyers who had converted on government advice for the August subscription, providing they still held the stock, and for contracts to buy stock not settled before 29 September.[43]

A point widely taken, but not trumpeted, by the government was that the initial reason for accepting the South Sea scheme, that by clearing the debt they might end the Land Tax, was no longer operative. Keeping land tax as low as possible would be the career-long preoccupation of the politician who had succeeded to, and come through, the greatest domestic crisis of the century.

The Lowndes scheme arrangement was swiftly put through as law at the end of the session. By this time, 25 July, the House was disgracefully thinned. Parliament might sit till late in the year, but it would sit without most of its Members. This hiatus to a government machine with a core of loyalists kept in town was seriously helpful. This might be particularly true if things got rough as, in August 1720, they most certainly did. The discontents of many creditors still ran high, and as the parliamentary record puts it, 'A tumultuous Concourse of the Annuitants assembled in the Lobby pf the House of Commons'. The concourse involved, again as the record puts it, 'several hundreds of the proprietors of the Short Annuities and other redeemable public debts of both sexes'.

And the Commons, learning 'that a crowd of people were got together in a tumultuous and riotous manner in the lobbies and passages to this House', it was ordered 'That the Justices of the Peace for the city of Westminster, do immediately attend this House, and bring the constables with them'.[44]

Sir John Ward, a director of the East India Company, presented a petition arguing that money had been lent 'upon parliamentary security' and that in February the Commons 'had thought fit to leave the validity or invalidity of their subscriptions to be determined by the common law: But being informed that by the Bill now depending, they were tied down to take South Sea stock at £300, they now therefore prayed that they might be heard by themselves or their counsel against the said bill.'[45] The response came from Walpole, bureaucratic, offhand and final: 'He did not see how the petitioners could be relieved.' The reduction of the House to about a sixth of its full complement gave him a handle. The resolutions on which the bill rested had been laid, had gone through King and Privy Council. So 'they had given their word of honour to the members that were gone into the country that they would not alter a tittle in them', at which he moved the resolution. It was in vain for Brodrick, the straightest man in all this oblique dealing, to wonder why Walpole wanted to put the resolution without hearing the petition 'which he thought would look as if they could not answer the allegations contained in the said Petition'.[46] Walpole had the numbers and Brodrick's motion to hear the petition was voted 78 to 29 in a House long emptied by harvest and holiday. The bill itself passed all stages in three days in a Commons reduced to fifty.

Walpole had done what he wanted to do. A far from perfect settlement had been made, leaving behind a legacy of resentment, much of it directed at the man who had acquired the soubriquet Skreenmaster General. But there was financial order and he had established his authority. The Walpole management team had lost a few votes, abstained from one or two contests but had won most points, demonstrating that the man giving it instructions had a power in Parliament through which he could govern the country. It was now a time for the putting of knees firmly beneath the ministerial desk.

'TREASON DOTH NEVER PROSPER'

The greatest opportunity for securing those knees came from the Court of his Majesty King James III, now in Rome and then in Urbino, which is now Bologna. James Edward Stuart was a remote and ineffectual looker-on, a man trying to conjure nostalgia into substance, almost, if not quite, a cleared-out racing man still watching the horses. If it was 'not quite', that was because there were still many friends willing to stake him. Small amounts came at different points in the diplomatic circuit from countries and rulers in passing conflict with British policy. Too much came rather pathetically from country gentlemen, heirs of those other country gentlemen who had melted down the family silver to fund Charles I in his dogmatic incomprehension of men and events. 'When the King enjoys his own again' was a royalist carousel song from the 1650s, but it spoke forlorn feelings after 1714 very well.

Even so there were quite enough Jacobites. And the idea, derived from historical fiction, that this was a largely Scottish phenomenon, is misleading. The Scottish dimension was there, of course, and owed something to the Catholics scattered in highlands and islands, though they were a minority among fierce Calvinists even here. Scottish Jacobitism owed at least as much to dislike of the Union with England, one of those pragmatic, long-headed things always railed at. It had a following in Wales, notably in the North Walian fiefdom of Sir Watkin Williams Wynn, a long-dedicated opponent of Walpole and the Whigs in Parliament. Lewis Pryse, expelled for not taking the oaths in 1716, is described as having 'near seigneurial authority in Cardiganshire'.[1] The cause had followers in the Marches: in Shropshire, where Dr Sacheverell had been given a living, and in Herefordshire. Catholic

gentry made Lancashire and Staffordshire notable centres. Jacobitism
also had a large and flammable following in London, heirs of those
same Jacks who had rioted for Sacheverell and been hanged for riots
at George's accession.

Again, the Catholic aspect always risks being overplayed. So
Protestant a country as early eighteenth-century England could not have
sustained a credible counterforce deriving only from Roman Catholic
allegiance. The centrally important Jacobite, Bishop Atterbury had no
theological sympathies with Rome whatever. And the too-Catholic
nature of the Pretender's court was brought home to James Edward by
English well-wishers.

One estimate, drawing on information in Sedgwick's irresistible *The
House of Commons, 1715–1754*, lists 137 Members of Parliament
either Jacobite, or suspected of being, over that period. (A calmly drawn
list of Labour MPs seriously likely to have been Soviet supporters during
the forty-four years after 1945 would not have exceeded twenty.) The
inner core of fully acknowledged Jacobites working together in the
Commons and marshalled by the likes of William Shippen and Sir John
Pakington, numbered around forty, twice as many.[2] And one must
remember that no acknowledged Roman Catholic sat in the Commons
over Sedgwick's era (or for another seventy-eight years beyond it). The
suspected Jacobites in Parliament were (had to be) Protestants.[*]

The number in Parliament after the good Tory election of 1713
having been judged by the outstanding historian of that era as 'at least
80', he adds, 'It is impossible to be precise as to the correct figure, but
it was undoubtedly in the region of 100,' and as one of their members
noted, it undoubtedly included 'a great many young members, keen
and eager and wanting only to be led to action'.[3]

There had been several moments since 'the Fifteen' when Jacobites
had stirred, notably a plot involving Sweden, whose quarrel with
Hanover had created a circumstantial sharing of interest with the Stuarts.
But on these occasions, with the foreign affairs specialist and King's
man, Stanhope, in charge, the situation had been fraught. The Elector,
Georg Ludwig, seeking Swedish territory, had leagued himself with Peter
of Russia as he engaged in a war of threats and manoeuvres against
the Swedes. Meanwhile, George Lewis, King of England, had wanted,

---

[*] For all the pleasures of Sedgwick's career sketches of eighteenth-century politicians, modern
scholarship reckons that his quota of Jacobites is too high.

as early as 1715, a fleet of British ships under Admiral Norris sent to the Baltic to serve that Hanoverian purpose, exactly the sort of thing against which lines had been pre-emptively drawn in the Act of Settlement. In the process he stirred up wide resentment readily conflating with Jacobite activity.

In which case, the Swedes, however remote from the Pretender's well-springs, saw no reason why people with a common enemy should not join hands in giving him a hard time. A credible Jacobite threat, everyone agreed, rested upon a continental sponsor putting up an army, and, as was shyly admitted, helping to pay for it. France had pulled out of the game, but Charles XII of Sweden, impossible romantic and outstanding soldier, squeezed hard between the Elector and the Tsar, had excellent motives. George wanted the Swedish territories of Bremen and Verden. The Swedish ambassador in London, Karl, Graf Gyllenborg, had certainly been talking to all sorts of undesirables; and if the Whig Ministry was devoted to a single piece of statecraft, it was the inter-ception and deciphering of other people's letters. So Gyllenborg's corre-spondence with Baron Goertz, Swedish ambassador at The Hague, was read here. Consequently, Townshend, Secretary of State, could tell Stanhope on 23 September 1716 that King Charles was 'treating with the Jacobites in order to join with the Pretender'.

A later letter from Goertz's secretary had spoken promisingly of a rendezvous and money. With George back in the country, the tem-perature rose and the government moved. Gyllenborg himself was arrested. The warrant said that he was 'carrying on a treasonable corres-pondence against His Majesty's government and hath endeavoured to engage several of His Majesty's liege subjects to execute and stir up a rebellion, towards the support of which he had promised them foreign assistance'.[4]

The British next, on 4 February 1717, extended their arm to Holland, trying to have Goertz arrested there, and, after a chase from The Hague to Amsterdam, succeeded. Three British subjects, Major Boyle Smith, Sir Jacob Bankes and Sir Charles Caesar, an MP, were also arrested at this time. There was a general froth of panic and activity, ships made ready, sailors frantically sought and pressed, one Admiral sent to the North Sea, another to the Scottish coast. Something with a contempor-ary ring to it was the quartering of troops, first in Hyde Park, then Blackheath. More recently, tanks have been sent to Heathrow in a similar spirit of manipulative patriotism.

Then ministers fell into a fright of their own when it was reported that Swedish men o'war had been sighted off Great Yarmouth. A full parliamentary show and public reading of the letters was staged before a very responsive House. It produced a fulsome address to the King deploring 'the obstinate and inveterate rancour of those who are again endeavouring to embroil their native country in blood and confusion'. The House also proclaimed in a sort of early eighteenth-century Stalinese that 'We adore the watchful eye of Heaven that has so wonderfully guarded and protected your sacred person and cannot too much extol the wisdom and vigilance that have been used in so early and seasonably discovering this desperate attempt.'[5]

But Count Gyllenborg, before his arrest, had been conducting a highly successful pamphlet war pointing out that the British fleet's function in the Baltic, supposedly protecting Denmark, was strictly to the King's private purposes and aimed at expansion of 'his Dominions in GERMANY at the expense of BRITISH blood and treasure, by involving those nations in foreign quarrels'.[6] If he had also been waiting for the post from Avignon and discussing Jacobite finance for Swedish military action, it was done in response to the constitutionally forbidden and illegal acts of the King Elector against the sovereign territory of Sweden.

In fact, Swedish activities, although hostile to Britain, were exploratory. The Swedes, after a heroic, legendary and ruinous war, needed money to fight the campaign that kept their Continental territory. Goertz's job had been the raising of finance for this last effort. He personally had sought it everywhere, and now, without the knowledge of Charles XII, tried to get it from the Jacobites, not themselves oversupplied but perhaps able to get their hands on some. The deal, which he candidly spelt out as his own speculative notion, subject to royal assent, was that if money came on offer, Goertz would do everything he could to persuade the King to provide the troops. Involvement was treason for the English Jacobites, but very much hypothetical treason, to be committed in the future conditional tense.

No change would be got out of the British arrestees. Gradually, the public mood deflated, and both the Englishmen and the Swedes were released. But a policy triumph had been won by Sunderland and Stanhope over Walpole and Townshend. Both of these had been unhappy at the Baltic purposes of the King. Townshend had stated that he simply would not get supply if he brought a request for the costs of a Baltic action into the House. He 'would be in great danger from such a step of ruining his credit and influence in both houses'.[7] That spoke the real differences between the Whig factions. And the brothers-in-law would soon be gone from office.

But now that Swedish dealings with Jacobites were public, the King's credit – credit to get supply for a fleet in the Baltic – was restored. Ministers had a plot of sorts on their hands; they showed evidence of being genuinely frightened of an invasion. But it was a highly thera-peutic fear. For on the back of it, Stanhope could now argue to the Lords about British interests in the Baltic – trade purposes. And the word 'Jacobite' worked like a charm upon Townshend and Walpole. Out, though they were, to get ministers on any issue and in the teeth of past commitments, 'Jacobite' froze them rigid. It was not just a matter of rebutting ministerial smears about a *tendresse* for the Pretender. This was an area of perfect conviction and real fear. 'The subduing and eradicating of this evil is what ought principally to be aimed at and intended,' said Charles Townshend.

But when, on 3 April, the Commons was asked for supply without conditions, supply which would cover action in the Baltic, Will Shippen and Tories less Jacobite than he spoke scornfully of the open-ended, detail-free commitment. Despite the enthusiasm of Walter Hungerford, an otherwise silent loyalist demanding a declaration of war on Sweden, this was still not a popular cause. But with Walpole and Townshend onside, it was granted – by four votes. The Swedish plot had not been a government confection, but ministers went to great trouble with the icing.

Before the Swedish option was ended by something entirely unfore-seen, another plot, likely to dovetail with it, was being eagerly promoted. In the tragi-comical way of Jacobite activities at this time, the Swedish conspiracy of 1717–18 overlaps with the Spanish conspiracy of 1718–19. The combined opportunities, appearing at one moment, glistened with more practical hopes than most of these losing-side chimeras. They arose from the Continental foreign affairs of this period which only specialists know about. The War of the Spanish Succession, that Whig triumph soured into a tax bill, out of which Harley's Tories had got the country in 1713, concerned a French threat to dominate Europe at the expense of the Empire by commanding Spain through a Bourbon heir. In effect, she had inherited the thing, with Philip VI, the Bourbon occupant of the Spanish throne, but had lost the war. And with Louis XIV dead, the grand design had collapsed. The Empire had meanwhile

emerged from Utrecht much strengthened, not least with large pieces
of Italy taken from Spain.

Spain was forbidden to take action by the *Asiento* treaty and a second
agreement reached in January 1717. But with an Italian Queen in
Elizabeth Farnese and an Italian Prime Minister in Monsignor Alberoni,
circumstances might change. Alberoni was at first unforthcoming, but
when James Edward, with more vigour and astuteness than usual,
successfully canvassed the Pope to elevate him to a Cardinal's hat, the
Jacobite representative in Spain, Sir Patrick Lawless, had something to
work on. Vienna, a German power, English ally, on good terms with
the Elector of Hanover, was the enemy. Her friends were Spain's enemies
by association. The thought of obtaining a different King of England,
one grateful to Spain, was highly attractive to these dominant figures
in Madrid, which city was awash with underemployed Irish soldiery
owing Hanoverian England no favours at all!

But the key to everything was the Papacy, important here not for
doctrine but money. Thirty years earlier, Pope Innocent XI had wasted
any amount of disregarded restraining advice on James II. A successor
might come into play and, in the process, spark Spain to action (fulfilling
the darkest notions of English atavism). The current Pope, unsurprisingly another Italian, and an extremely angry one, was Clement XI.
Giovanni Francesco Albani, under this title a long-serving Pontiff, in
office since 1700, had supported the Emperor and been rewarded at
Utrecht with patronising contempt. As a papal historian succinctly puts
it, 'Sicily and Sardinia, Parma and Piacenza* were disposed with cynical
disregard of the Pope's overlordship'.[8]

Clement was willing to put up hard cash to finance a restoration.
He was also a sharp spur to Spain through a grateful Cardinal Alberoni,
now happy to disregard tedious treaty obligations. In terms of the
Victorian jingo song, Spain had got the ships, Ireland, at one remove,
the men, while, curiously, the Pope had got the money too. James
Edward might attribute such favour to his pious devotion. Clement,
the last of the fighting Popes, wanted in the best temporal tradition to
get back papal and Italian territories from the hands of the Emperor
and his protégé, Victor of Savoy.

Alberoni was ready to fight the Emperor in Italy by sending thirty
thousand troops to Sicily and giving every assistance to a Stuart bid to

---

* Alberoni was a native of Piacenza.

effect a restoration in England. That nation's government, now given to sophisticated foreign involvements, kept to its treaty commitments and did itself a favour when Admiral Byng shattered the Spanish fleet at Cape Pesaro, close to Messina. It was a debt which will have weighed heavily in Vienna two years later when Robert Knight's green book fell into imperial hands in Antwerp.

Spain was expected in London to be stopped dead by this reverse. Instead, Alberoni, something of a gambler for an ecclesiastic, doubled his efforts. Spain had still the means and a much greater motive for the English invasion. The talks between Jacobites serving a hypothetical power and the ministers of a real one intensified. Ormonde, ablest and most disinterested of Jacobite soldiers, engaged and frustrated over alliance diplomacy in Sweden and Russia, now alerted to developments, went to Paris then Madrid. At the same time, the diplomacy meant to involve Sweden, but so lately going nowhere when Ormonde failed to get an audience in Stockholm, came to sudden and fascinating life. Lawless was sent there by Alberoni to try the Swedes again in the light of acquiring a committed ally in Spain. And on the day Ormonde started out from Paris to Madrid, a Swedish diplomat arrived in Paris to tell the Spanish ambassador of the readiness of King Charles XII to join Spain in invading England!

When Ormonde reached Madrid in November, he was among active friends, treating with real means and real authority. He had his colleague, General Arthur Dillon, appointed Captain General of the invading army. After some wrangling, it was agreed that Spain would give '5,000 men, of which 4,000 are to be foot, 1,000 troopers, of which 300 with their horses, the rest with their arms and accountrements, and two months pay for them, 10 field pieces and 1000 barrels of powder and 15,000 arms for foot with everything necessary to convey them'.[9]

For a few weeks, October–November 1718, England, the Hanoverian regime and the Stanhope/Sunderland Ministry were in furious danger of a double-pronged attack from two nations, Sweden and Spain, respectively alienated by George's ambitions in Bremen and developments in Sicily. The word 'crisis' was an understatement. Then, in a season of sudden things, Charles XII, thirty-six, healthy, survivor of triumphs and disasters, a soldier not less brilliant than Marlborough and Eugène, laid siege to Halden in Norway, where on 1 December, a sniper shot him dead.

One fork was gone, for only the reckless brilliance of Charles would have contemplated the English adventure. Because Alberoni kept his nerve, the other remained: 5 warships, 22 transports, 500 troops and ammunition for 30,000,[10] sailing from Cadiz late in February and due to collect Ormonde at Corunna. At which point, the Protestant winds which had saved English governments and puffed English conceit in the past – the Armada, William's descent on Torbay – were augmented by a third, a Protestant storm rather, which on 18 March, off Cape Finisterre, scattered what part of the Spanish fleet it did not destroy. Some ships fled home, a fraction made a hopeless descent on northern Scotland. Either the God in whom Jacobites put faith could not be trusted or no one had told them about seasonal weather.

While so much excited activity was afoot, ministers in London were busy finding out about it. The spy system at home and abroad, which Walpole was to make his province for twenty-one years, was up and running at this time when he was either in opposition or minor office. The Earl of Mar had been secured as an (unreliable) agent at the Pretender's court. Edward Willes's cipherers, so important in the next crisis, were busy. The government also had its friends abroad. Friendship with France, which Walpole would make the staple of his foreign policy, had already been established by Stanhope. And from another political ecclesiastic, Abbé Guillaume Dubois, head of the Regent's government in Paris, ministers heard of James Edward's intention to leave Rome for Madrid to join Ormonde.

The Stanhope/Sunderland reaction to a foreign undertaking was defensive and prompt: ships to the western coast, troops to the western counties. It was in respect of this area that the French ambassador, representative of a friendly power and so not engaged in wishful thinking, wrote 'If the Duke of Ormonde, whose name is ever dear, came at the head of 6,000 men with arms, ammunition and money, God only knows what would be the outcome in the west of England where there are more than 30,000 workers in mines who pass for Jacobites and a large number of tinners unemployed because of the interruption of commerce.'[11]

There was separate evidence of discontented clothiers in Devon engaged in a tax strike. A discreet traveller to Bristol and the west on the government's behalf, Samuel Buckley, spoke of a majority of the people of the West Country being 'judged to be disaffected'.[12] The government had ships out and troops lined up on the land behind them, generals were sent to Scotland, Ireland and the west. The one in Scotland, Weightman, faced with the forlorn landing in Glenshiel, thought best 'to terrify the Rebells by burning the houses of the Guilty and preserving those of the Honest', something unthinkable today.

The fear had been real that a landing would be followed by a rising, that sympathy for the Pretender and dislike of the government made a reversal of 1688–9 by similar means a serious prospect. Only the chance of a storm had prevented it. And ministers, notably Robert Walpole, walked in expectation of renewal, when they would pursue native Jacobites with relentless and vengeful attention. Walpole had been at the sidelines of these episodes. But the King's first Minister would be better placed to exploit the events of 1722, the Atterbury Plot and the pitiful Layer Plot, and to play them for all they were worth. In fairness, Walpole had an unamended record as doctrinaire Whig and Hanoverian. Disloyal to colleagues he might have been on a sweeping scale, but he had plumped hard for the House of Hanover. And though he played between King and Prince during their dispute, his concern was to serve and enjoy the patronage of both Georges. He was sincere enough also in his abhorrence of the Jacobites and his readiness to take them at their own deluded word as serious, conspiring enemies, served by a network of sinister agents. Not for nothing had he been one of the managers at the trial of Sacheverell ten years before, something which made him view High-Flying Churchmen, non-jurors and all the sneaking regarders of Jacobitism in the rectory with a perfectly sincere loathing.

No one embodied that sort of mentality, for all that he had swallowed hard and taken the oaths, than Francis Atterbury. Dean of Christ Church, Oxford, itself a thieves' kitchen of reminiscent disaffection, he had been close to Harley who had put him there and, months later, advanced him to the joint honours of Dean of Westminster and Bishop of Rochester. But his natural sympathies were with Bolingbroke. He embodied in more feline, better educated form, Sacheverell's sort of triumphalist, *Anglicani contra et super mundum* churchmanship. Vain, prelatical, enchanted by his purple, very far from stupid, but short of long-view judgement, he carried his own destruction within him.[*] Atterbury had been dissuaded at Queen Anne's death when, as Dean

---

[*] It is a melancholy irony that the author of the excellent biography of Atterbury, widely quoted here, had too great an affinity with his subject. Gareth Bennett, of New College, Oxford, made in *Crockford's Clerical Directory* an anonymous and wild assault on the liberal Archbishop Runcie. With nothing worse to fear than distant mutterings in cathedral closes, but at the end of his personal tether, he killed himself in 1987.

of Westminster, he was in charge of the funeral arrangements, from going to Charing Cross and proclaiming King James.

By temperament, he was a conspirator. Dryden's words for the arch-Whig Shaftesbury fitted him to perfection: 'For close designs and crooked counsels fit / Sagacious, bold and turbulent of wit.'[13] He makes a complex contrast with the chief spokesman for Jacobitism in the House of Commons. William Shippen was candid in his beliefs, bitingly rude, thoroughly downright in everything he said, close to the clever Bishop, but ultimately shrewder or luckier. Shippen had, though, been lucky in having recently been sent to the Tower. It was only for saying that the King's speech was 'rather calculated for the meridian of Germany than of Great Britain' and adding that George was 'a stranger to our language and our constitution'.[14] But as he had been entrusted by Atterbury at just this time with raising the money to finance a Swedish invasion, Shippen, helpfully removed from the temptations of treason, had smelled the fire and would never be burned again. The frantic trawl after Atterbury's fall would not find a farthing's worth of evidence against 'Honest Will'. He would die in 1743, still Member of Parliament for Newton, uncorrupted and unsoftened in his antipathies but able to say of Walpole, 'Robin and I are two honest men; he is for King George and I am for King James; but those men in long cravats [assorted careeristic floor-crossers] only desire places, either under King George or King James.'[15]

There was a distinct Atterbury set: the Earl of Arran, the Duke of Norfolk, Lord North and Grey, the Earl of Orrery, Sir William Wyndham, Sir Charles Caesar and Shippen. It worked, on and off, and in poor harmony, with another group identified with the Earl of Oxford. Perhaps the characteristic which explains distinctions best is that most of the Atterbury set, and none of the Oxfordians, ended up in the Tower. But then Oxford *had been* in the Tower, and, always careful, he was not encouraged by the experience, drawing around him in Poulett, Mansell, Bingley and the Bishop of Hereford, as well as a family group of Harleys and Foleys, men who would take his lead in maintaining Stuart contacts but not rushing forward. The groups squabbled to the point where James Edward, with whom they all corresponded, complained of '"diversity of opinions", "endless disputes, and a multiplicity of useless letters"'.[16]

Atterbury cherished his preferments enough not to hurry into plots. Indeed, on getting suggestions for activity before the South Sea crash in letters from James Edward who was writing to him directly, he did not deign a reply for seven months.[17] But the South Sea crisis provided an irresistible temptation. Some members of the Jacobite inner circle, General Arthur Dillon, Lord North and Grey, Sir Charles Caesar, and of chief importance to Atterbury, the Jacobites' best soldier, the Duke of Ormonde, responded with a proposal for an unsupported modest-sized invasion. Atterbury's objection was to the limitations: 'the time is lost for any attempt which shall not be of force sufficient to encourage people to come into it'.[18] This was true enough. It was a given among serious Jacobites that no rising not backed by serious money, foreign men and a foreign state would get anywhere. The unconsummated Swedish talk was at least based on this sound assumption, and the Spanish affair had come to an assembly of men, weapons and ships for invasion. The model was, of course, the Dutch-backed invasion of 1688–9, the treason that men dared not call treason.

But the South Sea undertaking and implosion seemed, by its grand scandalous excess, to perhaps cancel out this obvious maxim of sense at least for a while. The future Speaker, Arthur Onslow, good Whig that he was, had talked about the Pretender being able to walk to his throne had he arrived alone in the autumn of 1720. In April 1721, Atterbury wrote to James Edward that 'a less assistance is requisite whilst this disposition lasts'.[19] He was leaving it late. The screen was in operation, the settling of major South Sea obligations pledged. Even if the plot had been managed with far more reticence and professionalism than it would be, 'this disposition' was *not* going to last. But Jacobitism lived on its imagination. It was thought essential that James Edward should show his anti-charismatic person at the head of his troops. Were he to do that, Sir Henry Goring assured him, and on the day of his landing, a thousand men would join him and, within another day, swell to five thousand.

Just how unsuitable the Pretender was for practical business would be shown by his appreciative response to a visitor to Rome that summer. Christopher Layer, ironically a Norfolk man, also a Roman Catholic, a barrister, very young and one floating on a remote and beautiful cloud, had a plan which involved presenting to James Edward (and Walpole) a list of 114 named 'persons of fortune' in Norfolk 'now desirous to show their loyalty and affection by joining in any attempt that shall be thought advisable to bring about a speedy and happy restoration'.[20]

Layer should have been recognised at once by any competent observer as a mildly crazy fantasist, unvouched for and unstable, blowing bubbles of a different kind to the South Sea directors. But it was the measure of the circle around the Pretender and of James Edward that they lacked any sort of hard, realistic grasp. Accordingly, thanks to the Pretender, impressed by his passionate support, Layer was authorised to approach either Orrery or North and Grey as proxy for James Edward as godfather to the young man's baby daughter. This fantasising innocent now had access to the circle of serious English Jacobites. He would meet them and proudly acquire new names which, when apprehended, terrorised under interrogation and in a state of breakdown, he would pour out. In less than twelve months' time, on 17 May 1722, all the plots, grave and risible, would be dispersed to the winds and Christopher Layer's head would be barbarously displayed on the South Gate of London Bridge.

Just as Stanhope and Sunderland had been rescued by the Swedish episode from the consequences of an unpopular and literally unconstitutional adventure in foreign policy which they should not have countenanced, so Walpole would have his path made smooth by the Layer Plot and the larger conspiracy with which it overlapped. In 1720, the Bubble had brought the Jacobites back to the plotting table, but the Bubble had brought Robert Walpole to the direction of government which, in his case, meant yet more ready and generous investment in a corps of highly professional spies and cryptographers, allied to a near fanatical loathing for the enemies of the Hanoverian settlement.

The immediate thinking of the Jacobites in France and Italy followed the Duke of Plaza Toro who led his regiment from behind, in judging that first action should come from the Jacobites of England. This wasn't cowardice. The opportunity provided by the Bubble was not matched by the professional army that they all, English and foreign-based Jacobites, knew to be essential. Nor immediately did they have the money. Nobody had suggested to the Pretender's following that they might have had a fund invested in the South Sea before getting out when Thomas Guy and the Duchess of Marlborough did. Frustrated over Sweden and Spain and with the Regent Orléans declining all involvement, they perhaps began to despair of the one thing they all agreed to be essential. And when the crash came, Jacobites as much as ministers and directors were nonplussed. James Edward was in Urbino, beautiful but remote even by the standards of Stuart exile, where slowly delivered messages about a brilliant opening to be taken quickly rather mocked themselves.

And there were other options, especially for Tories not buying the whole Jacobite ticket. On Stanhope's death, Sunderland was conscious both of his vulnerability and of needing new allies. The old Ministry had functioned as a militant Whig affair, secure on its own base, but financial crisis and death altered the case. The enemy now was Walpole. What was wrong with an accommodation with, at any rate, moderate Tories? The obvious man was William Bromley, prominent in Oxford's day, Speaker of the Commons 1710–13, Secretary of State 1713–14. Such, however, was the fluidity of Tory politics that his moderation was not anyway so very moderate. Bromley had helped raise money for the Swedish undertaking. And if Sunderland could talk to Bromley, he could surely talk to the Bishop of Rochester. This was pure crisis; Stanhope dead, Aislabie disgraced and done for, Walpole, his inveterate enemy, everywhere, including engagement in Sunderland's own defence on South Sea charges.

There were griefs for both parties. Atterbury's wife was dying, he was hobbled by gout, the idea of mutual support had charms. The meeting between the two faced brutal realities. Sunderland needed Tory votes immediately to free himself of the corruption charge debated in the Commons. Sunderland could do the Tories the greatest possible favour by calling an immediate dissolution and an election they could enter with real hopes. Perhaps neither man mentioned the Jacobites. It was an unsayable and unnecessary word.

Atterbury could negotiate as a standard Tory; and, to Tories, a quick election in which they might wave the bloody scrip of the South Sea, plus Sunderland's talk of posts to be taken by men as involved with the Pretender as Atterbury himself and Lords Trevor, Strafford, Orrery and North was immensely tempting. A share in government for fellow travellers of the cause had every kind of advantage to them over the military options. Foreign armies didn't happen, conspiracies were reported to Walpole's thought police, risings fell. Why not take the legal, risk-free path? Into the bargain, Sunderland was also talking prelacy to a prelate. Rochester was a modest see. Winchester was magnificent, and its old Bishop, Jonathan Trelawney, one of the seven troubling James II thirty and more years before, had died on 19 July. At some point either Sunderland offered Atterbury the see or Atterbury thought he did.

The effect of a Tory alliance with the Sunderland element had already been suggested in the vote on Sunderland's own impeachment. Ironically, while Walpole, for obvious party and ministerial purposes, had through clenched teeth to do everything to clear Sunderland in the Commons, the majority for that acquittal included a substantial number of Tory votes. And as can easily be overlooked, Jacobites at this time took a full part in ordinary parliamentary politics. In particular, they threw themselves into the debate opened on 13 November on the Royal Navy with all it implied about fleets sent on Hanoverian errands. Atterbury himself, at that time juggling high treason and ministerial cooperation, spoke forcefully in the Lords against George's foreign policy as having no constitutional sanction. Incidentally, during another debate on allowing Quakers to affirm rather than take the Anglican oath, he also demonstrated his own brand of churchmanship. The parliamentary record says it succinctly: 'Bishop of Rochester, who according to his former assertion, endeavoured to prove that the Quakers were no Christians.'

Unfortunately for the purpose of making progress, nobody trusted anyone. Could Sunderland be relied upon to use machine money to elect what Tories called 'a good parliament'. Could the Tories be relied upon, in their rustic directness, not to start a Jacobite scare? If Sunderland said in his cups he so disliked George Augustus that, rather than see him as George II, he would welcome James III, it looked altogether too much like a crude snare. Bromley later observed that 'wanting faith, I absolutely declined the opportunities offered and pressed upon me of receiving all possible assurances . . . Promises were made to me so extravagantly large that it was affronting me to imagine I could think them sincere and be imposed on by them.'[21] And as summer turned through autumn, it became clear that Sunderland had been unable or unwilling (and who knew which?) to deliver his talk of early elections; this parliament would complete full legal term.

The truth was that the Tories were wretched politicians, honest, optimistic, short of *Sitzfleisch*, and perfectly incapable of compromise, half-loaves and flair. What unfitted them for government equipped them wonderfully for romantic charm, posthumous charm. Lord Bathurst declared himself 'sick of some late transactions'[22] and decamped to the country. William Shippen told a Scottish friend of his anxiety: 'how far some of their number might be taken off the right scent, in case, as the consequence of such conjunction, they found the sweets of power and preferment'.[23] It was terribly like the Labour Party in the late 1950s.

Perhaps minds would not have been quite so high if Sunderland's overtures had come before, not after, the giving of promises to James Edward. And while the English Jacobites reproached one another and dithered, a messenger came from the Pretender's court urging action and talking detail, all the evidence which a hungry minister, breathing treason and gallows, would wish to know. The messenger was George Kelly, improbably to English prejudice, at once a clergyman, Protestant, Irish and Jacobite. His message, though, was a sort of Annunciation; a small invasion to be commanded by the Duke of Ormonde was proposed. James Butler, 2nd Duke, Anglican, *preux chevalier*, represented the Jacobite cause as human ideal. To snub him and have the Pretender, so delighted with the first response, now writing to ask about uncomprehended delay while the English end of the group took up the Privy Seal and the bishopric of Winchester, would have been a low, patient, cunning, indeed Whiggish, thing.

The alternative, a rising against an armed government able to conjure Dutch and German forces, was against everything Atterbury and Lord Orrery, the consistent possibilists of the movement, had ever argued. Orrery was unmoved by the proposal. This was still a war without an army; the idea was nonsense and suicidal, it should not be touched. Elections were the thing. If you lost them, you were not executed or stripped of your estates. But the impulse among Jacobites to be wrong and romantic, to qualify for representation in a novel by Robert Louis Stevenson, was too great for such sense. And, against his better judgement, perhaps through sensing that he was losing caste with old friends, Francis Atterbury went along with the adventurists.

A plan was drawn up in consultation and sent back by way of Kelly. The Duke was to come by ship to the Thames, accompanied by enough Irish officers and weaponry to make the core of the army of twenty thousand which should be raised, Lord Lansdowne was to land independently in Cornwall and raise the west. Lord Strafford, with his Yorkshire connections, should do as much in the north. Meanwhile, almost as if they were dabbling in that constitutional second option they had renounced for ever, the conspirators with a place in Parliament returned to energetic involvement in debate, joining the former Whig Lord Chancellor, Cowper, in a furious assault on the government. They also made preparation for elections now coming about under the Septennial Act.

If the Jacobites made poor politicians, they made worse conspirators. In this, Atterbury was better than most. His reply to the Pretender was dictated for the Reverend Mr Kelly to write down. He kept all treasonable business out of the Westminster deanery, allowing discussion only at his Bishop's residence in Bromley, where servants and chaplains were to be trusted. Consequently nothing in his hand was ever transcribed from code for Walpole's eyes by the government's chief cryptographer, Edward Willes. Evidence, when the reckoning came, would be dubious and second-hand, quite inadequate to take him by way of a normal court to the scaffold.

But the conspirators and their water carriers were a muddled, innocent lot. Atterbury insisted on messages and money going by trusted courier. Impatient and careless in the way of the whole circle, the men so charged put all their faith in the cipher and used the ordinary mails, subject to opening and inspection since Walsingham's time. Worse yet, Christopher Layer, though Atterbury would not have given him a glass of wine, had the Pretender's imprimatur, and was excitedly and devotedly skipping around serious activists and innocently picking up the information which he would convulsively divulge when his own folly drew him to Walpole's remorseless attention. Layer's dreamings, wishful thinking and treble counting of latent support in the grumbling shires had already done their bit to rouse James Edward and his court to a pitch of uncalled-for optimism. Always badly informed, they were now, thanks to Layer, even worse informed.

Everything was going wrong that could go wrong. Money was needed, money was not coming in; Atterbury's old dubiety flooded back, so did his cunning. He persuaded the ardent-for-action colleagues that a letter be sent in order to be intercepted. It would be full of gloom about the lack of support, the unreliability of the Tories in Parliament and the country. The backbenchers, he wrote, were 'a rope of sand; there is no union, no spirit among them, and few of them are men of any capacity or courage'.[24] The letter, he argued at home, would be read by the intercepting ministers who would be put off their guard. But it was recognised by the Pretender's men for what it was. As the Earl of Mar put it to James Edward, this was Atterbury's 'real opinion of things, and he took that pretext only of showing to his partners as if he intended it to be intercepted, but truly to let his real sentiments be known [to us] . . . If it was all as the Bishop said,' he observed, 'any undertaking on that foot, against the government were almost madness to be attempted.'[25] Such threat as there was to the government of George I was in retreat.

The threat to the Jacobites was opening up, as was the coming triumph of Robert Walpole.

Atterbury had done everything he could to warn his friends overseas against action. He was playing his English colleagues out long to the point where action could be put on long-term hold. And being sensible, if unworthy of the RLS spirit, he was looking after his own survival. But April was to be the cruellest month for Atterbury. He had been drawn into an enterprise he did not think capable of success; he attended at Bromley that dying wife, now near the end of her struggle. On top of all of which came a message from the Pretender's court, again by way of George Kelly, full of zeal for action. It was, however, tempered by the wish to put everything in the hands of Oxford. Atterbury knew that Oxford, the Baldwin of his time, ageing, still sick from his long time in the Tower where Walpole had put him, was too cautious and too shrewd actually to do anything. But hardly had Kelly been sent away, naïvely excited at a cunningly upbeat response from the Bishop, than on 19 April he was back with terrible news.

Like Stanhope and the younger Craggs, Sunderland had, very suddenly, died. Imperfect ally he might be, but Sunderland was a man happily ambiguous and, at his most Hanoverian, never the restless, obsessive, hunting-down enemy of the Jacobites Walpole was. And Walpole was now chief man in more than contested precedence. His great enemy and obstacle was dead. His other enemy, the whole Jacobite cause, about which he was distinctly manic, would now be pursued *ad inferos*. His first act, in the face of protest from the Duchess of Marlborough, Sunderland's mother-in-law, was to break all seals to the dead man's rooms, seize his papers and institute another of his searches.

On 26 April, Catherine, Atterbury's wife of twenty-six years, died. It would soon after be his further misfortune that a message should come *to* him through which he would be apprehended. In their world of adventure and cipher, the Jacobites all had code names. Atterbury's was 'Illington'. Kelly had been careless about despatches, putting his latest messages under single cover through the ordinary post where, of course, it was picked out and read. Walpole did not know for certain whom this name covered and couldn't prove anything in court yet. But he did know that 'Illington' was somebody important corresponding with leading Jacobite circles.

And he held in reserve a player whom no one could trust but over whom Walpole held quite a weapon. This was John Erskine, 3rd Earl of Mar. Mar, inept leader in 'the Fifteen', who had been semi-disgraced once before at the Pretender's court, had then entered into a Faustian relationship with the British government. They were paying him a substantial pension for services rendered by way of intelligence and a negative influence. Mar, forlorn and wanting a role, tried to play both sides and had managed to get himself back into serious favour with the Pretender. He did not plan to betray the English faction, but he had recovered his place largely by urging an optimistic, activist line.

When intelligence of his role reached Walpole, there descended upon Mar in Paris on 29 May the ubiquitous Colonel Churchill, not, in his booming way, a natural Mephistopheles, but quite able to take delivery of a soul. The threat of cutting off supplies obliged Mar, in the way of multiple agents, to a betrayal in order to stay in play. The betrayal was simple and central. Unable to name Atterbury in an English court, he would instead, using his own cipher name of 'Motfield', write a letter on 11 May – a letter to Mr Illington.

This was a taut and nervous time. The military camp had been set up in Hyde Park, 7 May 1722, government stocks were falling, enemy spies were everywhere advertised, government spies everywhere active, a terrible time for indiscretion. On 19 May, Walpole struck at the messenger. The letter came by the hand of George Kelly. Kelly might not be discreet, but he was, in a nice, old-fashioned way, brave and true. When Walpole's men came for him, he put up a heroic resistance, suddenly amazing the men searching his room by setting about them with a drawn sword, driving them out and, before armed troops could get to him, burning his papers.

But for a blameless little dog and an innocent landlady that might have been it. Walpole had had a very good idea for some time that 'Illington' was the Bishop of Rochester, had even visited him on the 16th, and there was no one he would sooner hang. But he had so far no case. However, interrogation, by both Walpole and Townshend, shifted to Kelly's landlady, Mrs Barnes, who, questioned about the likely authors of the letter, gave nothing away, probably having nothing to give away. She did, however, talk about a little French dog called Harlequin, whose leg had broken on the journey. This signified nothing until she said that Kelly had promised, if it should remain lame, to get it for her – from the Bishop of Rochester! As Walpole wrote to his brother Horatio, this 'served to fix the certainty of the names'.[26]

The story was soon out, and the general public excitement mounted.

A dangerous hiatus followed. Walpole knew a good deal, but for the sort of show trial based on sound evidence which he planned, both to scarify Jacobite sympathisers and make a display of Robert Walpole's strenuous loyalty to the King, he needed much more. What had, of course, been accomplished was the collapse of any threat from a Jacobite landing. That game was up and under lights. If Sunderland had lived, not much more was likely to have happened. Walpole, for a variety of reasons, few of them creditable, favoured, in Housman's phrase, 'Jail and gallows and hellfire'.

Next, while Atterbury was lying very still, known about as a correspondent, but not adequately incriminated, and with Dennis Kelly, a key courier, proving as resolute as his near-namesake, George, in destroying all his papers, the correspondence of one 'Rogers' came into intercepting hands. They were addressed to General Arthur Dillon and had been written in terms of the things which should be done in a rising as imagined by Christopher Layer. 'Rogers' was James Plunkett, Layer's companion on his earlier journey to the Pretender in Rome and no wiser than Layer himself. Then, on 28 July, Walpole had yet more of the luck in which, through the mortality of his colleagues and the folly of the Jacobites, he was currently rolling. A friend of George Kelly, another Irish, Protestant, clerical Jacobite and another poor man in need of employment, one who had been used by Atterbury as a copyist and with links to Lord Orrery and another important Jacobite, Thomas Carte, walked, fly calling upon spider, into the London house of Robert Walpole.

This Irishman's name was Philip Neyno and he seems to have hoped to make a little money by telling Walpole nothing very much. He was shown a surviving, inherently unhelpful letter retrieved from Dennis Kelly's bonfire. It contained the names 'Illington', 'Hatfield' and 'Digby'. Anxious to improve his earnings by a show of credibility Neyno identified the Bishop, George Kelly and General Dillon. This at once enlightened Walpole and as there was no cipher in Dennis Kelly's letter, Neyno was incriminated as a man whose knowledge implied deeper involvement. As interrogator, Walpole seems to have combined the rubber truncheon and cup of coffee approach in his own alternating personality. Threatened with the gallows in a cycle of cross-questioning which, according to Walpole, also varied to £350 worth of bribes,[27] Neyno broke. What he knew Walpole now learned: Ormonde's incursion, the names of major participants and the role of George Kelly serving Atterbury.

The attempt to arrest Thomas Carte failed. Forewarned, he had fled to the Continent, but, on 24 August, Francis Atterbury was arrested. To Neyno's examination was added that of John Sempill (or Sample) to whom Neyno's questioning had led them.

Sempill was abusively handled by Townshend, Carteret and Walpole who threatened him with 'gibbet, racks and fire' and with Newgate, which in the 1720s was very little improvement.[28] This was done in pursuit of corroboration and further detail in respect of names which Neyno had given. The inquisitors were particularly anxious to know whatever might incriminate Cowper, the former Lord Chancellor, who had moved to the Tory side and was on close terms with Atterbury.

Both lines of pursuit came to nothing for the good reason that the examinees disappeared. On 4 August, Sempill risked the drop from the room of the messenger's house where he was detained and got clean away. The Canadian scholar Paul Fritz would establish that the same Sempill would one day turn his hand to betrayal by the other hand, informing on Jacobites abroad for Walpole. Whether his escape, like many before and since, was connived at by the authorities can only be conjecture, but it would be par for the prideless course of counter-intelligence.

In the case of the Reverend Philip Neyno, it does not arise. Subjected to endless verbal abuse and threats, he had escaped once and been recaptured. He was now promised the worst of Newgate in all its filth, infection and company. At three on the morning of 26 September, he attempted a descent from his third-floor room to a walled garden by the river, then in flood, into which he leaped, his body being taken from the Thames by watermen the next day. On the body was a memorandum of Walpole's requirements demanding, *inter alia*, incrimination of George Kelly and Carte and 'What I know or believe concerning any persons of High Rank, and who I think had the chief conduct and direction of the whole affair'. A good deal of tragedy attaches to many of the players, fools like Layer and high players like Atterbury. But Neyno is, of all the conspirators, the saddest. A poor man, he had tried to sell low-quality, unhurtful material to the other side, been trapped, then furiously and repetitively bullied over many weeks. His death, like Sempill's escape, warrants conjecture. Was it an escape miscarrying or a halfway suicide? Certainly it was the running of a risk in which the odds on death were the shortest. And by dying he had removed a cherished witness against Atterbury and the other

Jacobite leaders. In that miserable end there is perhaps a touch of half-advertent nobility.

Atterbury was in the Tower under the unsympathetic supervision of Colonel Adam Williamson, a narrow military Whig with no sense for what might be owing to a Prince of the Church. (His treatment of poor Layer was less subtle; with the full authority of Walpole, he clapped him into irons.) But for all his pride, Atterbury was a very capable man and he boxed clever.* In the Tower with him was a full cast of players great, little and suppositious: Captain Dennis Kelly, a Mr Cochrane, Layer, the Earl of Orrery, Lord North and Grey, all joined in late October by John Plunket, George Kelly and the Duke of Norfolk. By means of a Privy Council warrant, Walpole gave himself powers of a faintly contemporary sort to keep them all in detention for the next twelve months plus suspension of that moveable safeguard, Habeas Corpus.

In fact, the key evidence would come from little the prisoners would say, but rather from Layer's papers, to which ministers could make a perfectly legal claim. Whatever possibilities of invasion and rising had been cloudily discussed in the future conditional tense by Atterbury, Orrery, North and the rest, those of Christopher Layer, a dream child doodling, had been laid out as perfect policy: capturing the Prince of Wales, setting the London mob to work and, that done, the taking of the King into protective custody. The fountain of Layer's wishful thinking was played at full during his trial on 21 November and brought him to conviction and sentence involving the full castrating, eviscerating and quartering reserved for treason.

But he was kept back from these delights for another seven months in the hope – Walpole's hope – that, flattered with talk of reprieve, he might help bring Atterbury to similar conclusions. It didn't work. Layer was useful for whom he knew as belonging to a circle tentatively sympathetic to treason. His own plans were his own plans: they could not be attached to anyone else. He was an orange squeezed dry, for whom credible betrayal was impossible for want of knowing anything to betray.

The measure of Walpole's combined obsession and power playing was that he took his work home with him, bringing a case full of documents back to Norfolk in pursuit of evidence against all and any which would maximise sensation and punishment. Over the discreet Earl of

---

* He boxed altogether, on one occasion, knocking the officious Williamson down.

Orrery, Lord North and Grey and the evidence-vandalising Captain Kelly, there was no case acceptable even for the most sympathetic court. Against Atterbury and George Kelly and against Layer's associate, Plunket, who had been less given to writing things down, the case was too thin for ordinary procedures. They had acted in highly suspicious ways, used ciphers, communicated with the Pretender's court. (This was not a crime though it would soon be made one.) Although this whole affair was and is always referred to as 'the Atterbury Plot' and he was indeed party to treasonable conversations and preliminaries, it never had been 'the Atterbury Plot', but the one he had been inveigled into. He had been through his whole course of action in a state of grave doubt, one deepening with events. From such doubt had followed an equivalent caution. Where was the autograph evidence of planned insurrection, mobs raised, country gentlemen solicited to the flag of rebellion?

Walpole was driven to lesser charges and punishments and to a different form of trial. A select committee of the House of Commons should sit on the question, a very select committee, not to say packed. The committee was to examine what Walpole and his assistants, the lawyers Poyntz and Delafaye, had put together. What was done, however convincing, however true, was still done without witnesses and upon circumstantial evidence, on its own, unacceptable in a court of law. Conclusions were instead to take the form not of a verdict but a combined Commons vote and a bill. It was to be a bill of Pains and Penalties. The Commons voted Atterbury's guilt and he was to suffer dismissal from all his preferments, an unpurpling of the proudest Bishop in English Christendom, and banished the country on pain, if he returned, of a common felon's death. This having been formally proposed by the Commons, he was put, on 6 May, to formal trial by his peers in the House of Lords. His prosecution was in the very symbolic hands of a former Tory and personal friend, Robert Raymond, who had crossed the floor and discarded sentiments to become Attorney-General, rising later to be Lord Chancellor. Raymond would be despised for his mobility but his move to the obvious winning side sent its own demoralising message.

Atterbury was impressive and specific, condemning

the reading of extracts of anonymous letters without suffering any other parts of the same letter though relating to the same subject, to be read . . . excusing the decypherers from answering questions asked by me and which

I thought fit for my defence, lest they should reveal their art . . . reading examinations neither dated, signed or sworn to . . . reading letters supposed to be criminal, writ in another's hand and supposed to be dictated by me without offering any proof that I either dictated them or was privy to them.[29]

What was alleged, said the Bishop, was that 'I have had consultations to forward the conspiracy.' The first charge was that 'I traitrously consulted and corresponded with divers persons to raise an insurrection &c. in this kingdom, to procure foreign forces to invade it.' But their Lordships would observe 'that there is not one overt act or circumstance of time and place mentioned, proved or alleged. I have not therefore consulted or conspired at home.'[30] His case was that the trial was improper by all the evidential rules of English law, and so it was. Under the less demanding rules of historical examination, Atterbury was guilty of enough preliminary acts and consortings to warrant lesser charges. But he was incapable of being convicted under the common and customary rules of law. Justice would be very rough, Parliament employed to usurp the law.

This was a time which exactly fitted Sir John Harrington's mocking comment: 'Treason doth never prosper. What's the reason? / For if it prosper, none dare call it treason.' But the defeat of Atterbury and his associates, however arrived at, marked a long defile of retreat for English Jacobitism. It would acquire a chimney-corner quality, and become a losing side attracting few new or younger recruits. The notion of Hanoverian Tories was strengthened. The more zealous or eccentric fled abroad to share the tenebrous retreat of the Stuart court. When, like Philip Wharton, one of them turned Catholic, Jacobitism lost credit with the sustaining core of country gentlemen. Men like Sir William Wyndham and Lords Bathurst and Gower made their peace with Hanover if not with Walpole. And in 1728, Atterbury in his exile received a letter from his son-in-law, William Morrice, about the decline of Jacobite finance: 'Several of the Benefactors are dead; several weary of such incumbrances; & the whole Club, (from whence greatest parts of the Bounty came) is in a manner dissolved.'[31] Tories, once thought of as at least Jacobite fellow travellers, would use the succession of George II as an occasion for a display of conspicuous, not to say overdone, loyalty. They would merit Will Shippen's later scornful remark about himself and Walpole being the only honest men. By contrast, Lords such as Lichfield, Scarsdale, Stafford, Gower and

Bathurst, would, in Lynda Colley's phrase, set an 'example of unabashed toadying'.[32] The rising of 1745 would be something else, the product neither of Walpole's demise nor a strong and thriving Jacobite tradition. The sudden availability in that year of an army of invasion, always talked about in the eight or so years after 1714, would be to what remained of English Jacobotism a surprise, pleasant or otherwise.

But essentially after 1722, whatever the noises off and the conjuring of scares, lines were laid down between winners and losers. 'If it prosper, none dare call it treason.' Atterbury had been engaged in the preliminaries of an unconsummated treasonable plot, the Whig leadership of 1688–9 in the successful execution of one. *They* had prospered to the point of becoming His Majesty's ministers. His was a bankrupt conspiracy, its main man stripped and banished, briefly to serve the Pretender in exile. It was, as auctioneers say, 'all done'.

Except that it was never done for Walpole. Spying on Jacobite and Jesuits was a flourishing, out-of-door trade and source of steady income to the likes of John Macky whose crisp letters scatter the archive. Cooperating much of the time with the Postmaster of Louvain, a Monsieur Jaupain, Macky comes over as neither consultant parasite nor hysteric, but as a hardworking professional spy writing to Walpole in pleasingly man-to-man fashion, even arguing with him about authentication of pictures. Employing fewer flourishes than most correspondents, he told the minister what he has to tell. But he does not relax. On Christmas Day 1725, he is writing to Walpole that Jaupain 'hath found out the channel [the courier?] of Paris as well as Rome' [to the Pretender], adding cryptically, 'and you need not doubt (though he hath some qualms about Spinelli), he will go through both'.[33]

Letters from Jacobite to Jacobite also appear, like one from a J. Rochefort expressing hope that, after the death of Orléans, 'our King and his family will soon return to France', a belief also picked up by Macky. The English spy in Antwerp on 3 January has more information: 'I have come here under pretence of buying pictures, to find out if possible by what conduit the letters pass here from Holland and to England; it's certain that Pennington in Rotterdam sends them hither and receives them from hence.'[34]

Writing on the 8th, he reckons that Walpole would want to know from enclosed materials 'the vast efforts the Pretender is making at the severall Courts of Europe against the Irish Popish bill'. But Macky is not concerned with make-work. 'The Duke of Grafton will soon tell you whether this correspondence is worth keeping up for it may last a year.' And in the next letter of 19 January, he guesses, surely correctly, Walpole's indifference to Ireland, something about to give him serious grief (see *post* Chapter 9 *passim*): 'I am afraid that this Irish story is no material service because you take no notice of it in any of your letters.'[35] On the 26th, along with a new cipher from the helpful M. Jaupain, and with matter-of-fact bleakness, he gives Walpole something close to his preoccupations: 'The Bpp removes to Lille and is without hopes.'[36]

Such information about the despair of Atterbury should have soothed Walpole and let him enjoy Macky's cultivated sideline to spying demonstrated in a letter of 5 February from Brussels: 'I saw at Mechlin a large picture of Snyders . . . finely disposed which will serve as a chimney piece in the room where you hang the others. I can have it for near thirty pounds . . .'[37] It was doubtless necessary to know what the other side, however fading, were up to, and the straight-speaking Macky seems to have done that impressively well, but the Prime Minister's concerns were not so utilitarian.

The measure of the unrelenting, graceless zeal of Robert Walpole was that when Atterbury died in France ten years later and his body was brought to England for Anglican rites of burial, orders were given for the coffin to be stripped of its lead and opened. This being by foresight empty, officers had authority to search a separate crate in which the body had in fact been hidden, then to examine closely the body itself and the caskets which, in the way of eminent interments of the day, contained respectively his heart and entrails. They were to be searched (in vain) for evidence of letters written ten years before.

Vindictiveness was one thing, ferocious repression another, and the victims of Walpole's ferocity would not be Bishops, however unsound, but criminals already covered by law, poor men, small offenders, the gallows procession which Walpole and lawyers assembled in the aftermath to Atterbury's aspirational treason. Perhaps the single finest piece of original research in eighteen-century studies of recent years appears in the late Edward Thompson's *Whigs and Hunters*. It concerns the response of Walpole and his lawyers to the activities of armed and disguised poachers in the early 1720s, notably in Hampshire and Berkshire.

It is a fascinating account, not least of the tribulations of the Bishop of Winchester in his episcopal game lands. What happened immediately was violent and criminal, but all the deeds done did not begin to be a national emergency. The state was not threatened. They had nothing to do with the Jacobite cause, though one or two Jacobite gentlemen like Sir Henry Goring[38] may have fantasised on the possibility. The poachers were disguised, commonly by blacking their faces. And with a nice touch of ambiguity, the legislation against them quickly became known as the Black Act.

The preamble, a sentence of about four hundred words, is heavy quoting, but we can get the drift: *That if any persons, from and after the first day of June in the year of our Lord one thousand seven hundred and twenty three, being armed with swords, fire arms or other offensive weapons and having his or their faces blacked or being otherwise disguised, shall appear in any forest, chase, park, paddock or grounds inclosed within any wall, pale or other fence wherein any deer have been or shall be usually kept, or in any warren or place where hares or conies have been or shall be usually kept, or in any high road, open heath, common or down* . . . The act then lists a series of offences which might be committed by such *ill-designing and disorderly persons.* They involve, in addition to the deer poaching already mentioned, damaging fish ponds, killing or wounding cattle, cutting down trees *in any avenue or growing in any garden, orchard or plantation; setting fire to any house barn or outhouse, or to any hovel cock, mow or stack of corn, straw, hay or wood*; shooting at anyone in a dwelling house, sending unsigned letters with demands for money or venison, rescuing anyone in custody or persuading another person to join him on any of these activities.

The conclusion is bleak: *every person so offending, being thereof lawfully convicted, shall be adjudged guilty of felony, and shall suffer death as in cases of felony, without benefit of clergy.*[39]

The bill was put through Parliament in four weeks in May 1723. No debate took place on a piece of legislation which added fifty capital offences to the statute book. Thompson quotes the pre-eminent criminologist Sir Leon Radzinowicz:

There is hardly a criminal act which does not come within the provisions of the Black Act; offences against public order, against the administration of criminal justice, against property, against the person, malicious injuries to property of varying degree – all came under this statute, and all were punishable by death. Thus the Act constituted in itself a complete and extremely severe criminal code . . .[40]

Indeed, under one part of the law, a man sworn against to the Privy Council and proclaimed by the Council, who did not then surrender himself, became automatically guilty and could be sentenced to death without trial, a notion which might without impropriety or anachronism be termed totalitarian.

As law against criminal gangs, this statute would be savage, and, as Sir Leon pointed out in the same study, it had no known equivalent in the laws of supposedly less liberal European countries. Yet, in Thompson's words, the Act, coinciding with 'the years of Walpole's final political ascendancy, signalled the onset of the flood tide of eighteenth-century retributive justice'.[41] Additional legislation would bring such offences as the cutting of reeds within its compass.

In Winkfield, in the Forest of Windsor, a centre of Black activity, there had been rights granted a hundred and more years before 'to digg, carry away turf, gravel, sand and loam, heath, fern and furzes wherever they shall be found in Lord's waste'.[42] Laws against violent poaching would now be augmented to punish the taking of a traditional share in the economy of the owner's waste and open land. Despite the burst of ordinary criminality which took place and provided the pretext, there is a great temptation to see the Black Act as an accompanying statute of intimidation to accompany the enclosures of common land distinguishing the era.

The timing is also important. Walpole did not invent an emergency out of the deer raids in Berkshire and Hampshire either, but he certainly raised the profile of crimes perfectly capable of being punished severely enough under existing statutes. And an emergency, like a Jacobite threat, was something which a man settling into power could turn to account. *Contra* President Roosevelt, a certain kind of politician has everything to hope from fear. The need 'to do something' exalts a leadership and makes everything from hanging despoilers of trees to imprisoning accused men without trial proof of vigilant leadership.

This was the time of the collective fine levied upon Catholics, of the imposition of an oath of allegiance, the time of the grand Jacobite scare, based, as we have seen, not upon nothing but upon plans from which the conspirators had already backed off and upon the blabbering fantasies of Christopher Layer. The South Sea had created public anger, the screening of the South Sea had made Robert Walpole an object of loathing outside the financial world. A display of resolution through strong measures, measures in defence of property and property's expansion, the legislating of what a fair-minded non-Marxist would recognise as class laws made all Walpole's points. Easier access to the gallows for intruders upon property went down well among Lords and Commons, all of them men of property.

PLOTTING IN FRANCE, STUMBLING IN IRELAND

To anyone other than Robert Walpole it was now clear that the secure head of government was Robert Walpole. But a partial explanation of his long success and occupancy was a continuous nervous conviction that he was *not* secure.

He had been more nearly right to fear the Jacobites than our hindsight fully understands. But he would continue in that fear until it became absurd, anxious about them beyond their merits and prospects: so also with his civil opponents, other politicians and parties. Many of the principles of Whiggism would be put aside by Walpole, but the notion that only the Whig party should ever hold power was held to like a spar in the sea, even when his feet rested on hard sand. It was not simply greed for office. Fear of losing power caused him to take ever more of it. A belief that every man not bought, naturally subordinable or blood-related was untrustworthy would sustain in office a tight ring of minions and family connections.

> Should such a man, too fond to rule alone,
> Bear, like the Turk, no Brother near the throne
> View him with scornful yet with jealous eyes,
> And hate for arts which caused himself to rise . . .
> . . . Like Cato give his little senate laws
> And sit attentive to his own applause.

Pope's comment in the *Epistle to Dr Arbuthnot*, though directed at Joseph Addison (as literary cham rather than second-line politician), applies perfectly to Walpole and may have been written with that sly ambiguity left trailing. Walpole gave, in the first two years of his power, a demonstration of his two chief ways of proceeding. Carteret, he set himself to undermine and destroy. In the Duke of Newcastle, he recognised a born lieutenant, a man whose limited but real abilities and bubbling, diligent energy were topped off with an impulse to devotion, a henchman, however quartered and descended, brisk and fond, fetching and carrying beyond even Walpole's capacity to suspect. Until very late they enjoyed a political marriage without a cloud.

Newcastle has come down to posterity in the bitchy account of Lord Hervey, under-Queen at George II's court, whose malice described a fussing ninny. But Newcastle was not a fool. Stanhope in 1719 commented that in electoral matters he 'can judge as well as anybody'.[1] The abilities were adequate and supplemented by intense application. He was also a kindly man, witness a letter to Walpole in 1727 about the British consul in Cadiz who has run up worrying debts, strictly in the King's service, one which, though it attempts no more than elementary justice, rings well: 'I send you enclosed poor Cayley's bill. If you knew how necessitous he was, I dare say you would be compassionate his case. I therefore beg you will think of some way, if there be any, to make him easy for I am told the poor man is in the greatest financial difficulties.'[2]

The defects were those of confidence and assurance. The son-in-law of old Marlborough, heir to vast political influence through the Holles and Pelham estates, he had neither grandeur nor delusions of it and was always looking for a man to be grateful to. He had found one in Stanhope. And as long as Stanhope lived, Newcastle spoke scornfully of Walpole who, with his friends, rebels against the Stanhope/Sunderland Ministry, were 'the most abandoned kind of men, the most abandon'd to all pretence of principle'. When both men had died, Newcastle simply wanted to go on being busy in politics.

His cousin, Henry Pelham, less than fascinating, but a quicker, sharper man, had already made peace with Walpole. Newcastle was available, Walpole recognised the type of a second rank, unthreatening colleague, incapable of obstruction or designs. The relationship deepened. Newcastle wanted to serve and be useful; Walpole wanted to be secure against the knives and mounting ambitions of which Newcastle was essentially innocent. He was to be an artful man's artless servant.

Carteret wasn't like that. He was not more aristocratic than

Newcastle, the Granvilles having been in the Channel Islands, Devon and Cornwall only a century or two longer than the Pelhams and Holleses had been in Sussex. Carteret was related to Sir Richard Grenville of the *Revenge*. A Pelham had captured the King of France at Poitiers. (On an altogether smaller scale, the Walpoles had been on the Norfolk scene since Henry II.) But where Newcastle lacked a sense of what was owing to him or any high notion of his worth, Carteret was everybody else's idea of a grand Englishman, a milord *avant la lettre*. He had put in for the Lord-Lieutenancy of Cornwall at the age of twenty-two.[3]

To social position and its assurance, he added large intellectual gifts. He had not bothered with a degree at Oxford, but, as Swift noted, 'with a singularity scarce to be justified, he carried away more Greek, Latin and Philosophy than became his rank; indeed more than most who are forced to live by their learning will be at the unnecessary pains to load their heads with'.[4] To this, he inexcusably added excellent French, the language of diplomacy, which Walpole spoke only adequately, and decent German, thought an exotic excess in Coleridge eighty years later. This established a channel to the King/Elector calculated to jangle nerves less taut with paranoia than Walpole's.

A handle and a genuine occasion were granted to that glintingly suspicious mind by Carteret's antecedents. He had been something of a Tory, his family having been on good terms with both Oxford and Bolingbroke. But annoyingly, he had quickly established himself as a 'Hanover Tory'. Even so it was a measure of Carteret's unsuitability for Walpole's team that his appointment was greeted with delight by the Dean of St Patrick's. Swift sent Carteret a letter of congratulation. He also enclosed a copy of the first of *The Drapier's Letters*, his satires on the copper coinage to be provided for Ireland by William Wood, of which more anon. Carteret, clearly on the wrong foot since that copper coin affair was already embarrassing the government, delayed replying, then wrote in apology, hoping that their old friendship might be renewed.[5]

He was also very wealthy, his wife bringing him £12,000 a year, and young, born in 1690, fourteen years after Walpole. Young, gifted and rich, he was not the material of which a Walpole colleague might be constructed. 'So young, so fair, they say, seldom live long': the sentiments of Richard III echoed in platonic form, only the career to be smothered, in the first Minister's mind.

They were intensified by the expertise of young Carteret in foreign affairs. With his languages, a wide knowledge of history and natural affinities with James Stanhope, Carteret was a classic natural for the diplomatic circuit. At the unforgivable age of twenty-nine, he had been sent as ambassador to Stockholm in the middle of the chaos following the death of Charles XII, where a Russian siege, latent with menace to the Elector of Hanover's territories, was expected to become a Swedish surrender.

Carteret's job was to square and stiffen the vacillating chiefs at the Swedish court, Queen Ulrika Eleanora, Charles's sister, and a Polonius-like ditherer, Chancellor Kronhjelm, and tie them into a British treaty and protection before the Tsar could tie them into anything else. He was met with no coherent answer, so he set a deadline for which the Swedes failed to turn up. Carteret promptly turned to the one person willing to make up his mind, Ulrika's husband, Fredrik, later King Consort. Fredrik was in the field waiting in company with his senior soldier, Marshal Ducker, for the Russians.

Backed by the old soldier, Carteret persuaded Fredrik to sign up to the British alliance, backed as it supposedly was by the ubiquitous Admiral Norris and a fleet. He then sustained a month of plausible bluff to cover the delay imposed on Norris by Stanhope's concern not to offend the Danes by unauthorised passage in the sound and the customary problems with weather. Just before the Swedes could lose their nerve and make terms with the Tsar, Carteret was able to conclude four weeks of graceful prevarication with a letter sent ahead by Norris assuring Stockholm that the fleet was close. A damn close run thing, it was also a triumph of brilliant diplomacy and one close to the King Elector's heart and interests. This was no colleague for Robert Walpole.

Since Carteret held one Secretaryship of State and Townshend the other, it was upon the field of foreign affairs that Carteret, the rival, the too-distinguished talent, was to be stabbed. In January 1721, after the Swedish triumph and at the instance of Stanhope, he had been sent as ambassador to the Congress of Cambrai which was intended to resolve outstanding international differences. The appointment came just before that minister's sudden death at the beginning of February. In March of the same year, the smallpox which then killed James Craggs the Younger made Carteret Secretary of State. At this time, of course, there were *two* Secretaries of State dealing with, respectively, the northern world and the southern. Stanhope (who had held the Northern seals himself) having died, Townshend had come in to take them up, having held that responsibility before (September 1714–December 1716). Carteret undertook almost simultaneously the southern responsibility – Spain, Italy and France.

Administratively, it was not the best of ideas since all Carteret's recent experience had been in the north, in Sweden, Denmark and Russia. That post might also have allowed closer and more advantageous contact with the King, to a German-speaker, expert in matters from Vienna to Stockholm, dealing with the King's neighbours and opponents. He was also coming to office shattered by the death of Stanhope. The death which had advanced Walpole to unexpected thresholds had deprived Carteret of more than a patron; it had killed the man he most revered. Years later, with no reason to embroider, he would tell the House of Lords that where Stanhope spoke 'there was no occasion for counsel; he talked, my Lords, like a statesman, a lawyer and a merchant at once; I do not know my Lords, if we ever had a greater man in his way'.[6] The other good thing about Stanhope was that he could be trusted.

Carteret had been first appointed by Sunderland, but he was Stanhope's man, heart, soul and intellectual persuasion. He had incontestably first-rate abilities and now, under Walpole, he had to share responsibilities with Walpole's brother-in-law and suffer the hostile machinations of Walpole's younger brother. Foreign policy at this time would remain very much the thing Stanhope had set out to make it, a pacific stance, though highly, if calmly, alerted to the country's interests and security, at whose heart stood an accord with France and a contingent positioning at non-belligerent distance from the Empire. It was a policy with which Walpole and Townshend had no quarrel. They would pursue it themselves, abhorring international quarrels and taking all possible credit for avoiding them; all conflict would be strictly personal.

Carteret had been at first burdened with French apprehensions, following the South Sea Bubble and the feuding of the two Whig factions, that England was losing her political edge in Europe and that a less complacent deference might be in order. He met this by concentrating on serious understanding with, and the sympathy of, Cardinal Guillaume Dubois. He got it; each of them wanted the same thing for his country in relation to the other's country. What would, ironically, be Walpole's domestic triumph – the crushing of the Atterbury Plot under lights before it had got beyond talk – was the result of friendly information relayed through Carteret by Dubois.

Walpole's return for this helpfulness from a Prince of the Catholic Church was in line with his sullen offshore mentality, the imposition of a £100,000 punitive tax on the entire English Catholic community for the grave offence of being the English Catholic community. This was Walpole at his bigoted, vengeful worst, and Carteret had to make the best fist of it that he could with a Cardinal who, however this-worldly, took such sectarian spite rather amiss.

But Dubois was yet another of the ungodly clergymen who abounded in Continental chancelleries during the early eighteenth century. Described by Basil Williams as 'a foxy intriguer if ever there was one',[7] Dubois was also a walking illustration of the folly of confusing the Roman Catholic religion, to which he adhered in his French, eighteenth-century fashion, and support for James Edward Stuart. The Cardinal detested the Jacobites, a nuisance running at an injurious tangent to his policy of accord with Hanoverian Britain. He carried this dislike to the length of denouncing the British ambassador, Sir Robert Sutton, as a Jacobite fellow traveller. Carteret, though defending his man against the Cardinal's charges, was the prisoner of them and accordingly obliged to withdraw Sutton and leave affairs in the hands of Sir Lukas Schaub.

Sutton, almost certainly innocent of this, became better known ten years later as, at best, a monumentally inefficient trustee, under whose chairmanship the Charitable Corporation suffered major losses through fraud. He was very much Walpole's man and, by the time of the scandal, an MP defended by the Walpole interests until the affair got too hot. He was then expelled from the Commons. Even so, in the great Walpole tradition, he was successfully screened from the looming prosecution and able to come back at the next election for Robert Knight's wholly corrupt family fief, Great Grimsby.[8]

As for the new ambassador, Schaub seems to be one of the fall guys of history. Drawing a low number in the lottery of life as a foreigner, commonly described as 'the Swiss, Schaub', he enraged Walpole's brother, Horatio. Horatio's letters drip with hatred. Schaub is a 'coxcom' [sic] who is 'fitter to turn a spit like a fox, in a wheel than be a Minister'.[9] An uncritical Plumb descants to Horatio with wildly extravagant charges that 'Reckless and arrogant, he was blind to reality and busy digging not only his own grave but his country's as well'.[10] Basil Williams, cheering less hard for the Walpoles, merely has him 'as an ambassador of very light weight'.[11] Certainly he seems to have talked too much, assured, as seemed reasonable, that good relations could be made better and his master brought great credit by the accomplishment of a single trivial but difficult thing.

The handle given to Walpole and Townshend was the frivolity of royalty, in this case, slightly off-royalty, Amalie, Graefin von Platen-Hallermund. She was the daughter of the Sophie Karoline described by Plumb in his slashing way as 'the King's Roman Catholic mistress'[12] and by George's biographer Ragnhild Hatton as no such thing, it being more likely[13] that George's father, the Elector Ernst-August, had also fathered Sophie's brother. The young lady was making what seemed a good marriage in France. She was wedding Henri Philippeaux, Comte de St Florentin and son of the Marquis de la Vrillière, which might perhaps have been enough, especially as the Marquis had, in 1723, been made Secretary of State. But the von Platens were deathly keen to have the Vrillière family title edged up a notch to a dukedom.

George, showing a customary kindness within the family, for which he would be rewarded in sour England only with a charge of double adultery, was keen to indulge the girl. Carteret and Schaub were asked to do their best, but it was the sort of thing which ministers and ambassadors should have tried to play down. And it was happening at a bad time. Good relations had been sustained for nearly three years, with Carteret and Schaub making it their business to give the Cardinal the earliest intelligence of any intrigue against him by his many enemies. With so much accord at the top, relations between England and France had continued on the very best of terms. But in August 1723, the death of Cardinal Dubois at the hands of the killer surgery of his day removed their key ally.

Meanwhile, the ducal campaign gave Walpole the chance of an arm's length operation against a colleague. His instrument against the man he had nominated as an enemy was his brother, Horatio. Horatio, quite apart from being family, fitted the model of the perfect Robert Walpole creature. He was second-rate, perfectly serviceable in a distinctly jittery way, dull but comprehensively loyal, a sort of less likeable close-kin version of Newcastle. And Horatio, writing about the match from Versailles on 1 December 1723, has hopeful bad news: '. . . the Duke of Orleance [sic] was under the greatest difficulty and embarrass on account of the letter Sir Luke had delivered to him from his Majesty [sic] desiring a dukedom for Mr de la Vrillière . . . and his Royal Highness apprehended that his Majesty, as well as himself, may have been imposed on in this affair'.[14]

The real trouble was that, contrary to English prejudice, French dukedoms were not traded like cigarette cards, there being enough prejudice about differentials in the local nobility to satisfy members of a particularly narrow-minded craft union. The Vrillières were not fully accredited members, semi-skilled at best, people whose elevation 'would incense to the highest degree the nobility of France, as well as all those that are not Dukes, as an unusual and unheard of thing . . . it is a Family Bourgeoise and looked upon as such by the nobility'. And as for that important office held by the groom's father:

> a Secretary of State in France is considered in a much lower Degree and is Employment too mean for a man of quality to accept . . . If the Countess of Plat [sic] desired to have a Daughter settled in a family of France suitable to her merit and condition, there was no need to have recourse to so mean a one as that La Vrillière and have it dignified for that purpose, for nothing could be so easy, or might be so still, than to find out a proper match for her in a family that might have a just pretension to a Dukedom without the least difficulty or uneasiness to any Body [sic].

Indeed, he had a candidate ready and willing: '. . . the Duke de Verajnas has let him know that he would offer himself to the young Lady if it was proper'.[15]

At the same time, Orléans, who had not yet actually read George's letter, was profuse in his willingness to oblige him if this was really what the King wanted. Horatio was being told what delighted him. Schaub presumably was hearing a less candidly brutal account, strong on the wish to oblige, softer spoken on the Vrillières being the sort of people who have china ducks on the wall. He responded by wanting to push briskly on 'to secure forthwith the execution of what was desired before too great an opposition formed against it'.[16] Orléans told him that he had heard that Horatio was against the undertaking. To which Horatio, in his teeth, 'told him that what was said of me was false'.[17]

Horatio was, however, clear sighted enough to recognise that 'if the Cardinal was still alive, he would have underhand conducted this affair in such manner as to have freed the Regent to have done it in spight [sic] of all the nobility'.[18] What Dubois would readily have done and the Regent, with much embarrassment, might have done for Carteret and George, the next Regent, Bourbon, would ultimately find impossible.

Amalie von Platten-Hallermund's social ambitions might have been gently evaded, even given the King's goodwill towards her, if Carteret had pleaded the extreme difficulty, after losing such excellent connections, of still running a court intrigue. But though too professional a diplomat and too grand a nobleman to be any sort of ready intriguer himself, he was very well aware of the hostility of Townshend and Walpole from the start and had taken the view that something done to seriously please the King would be worth the trouble. But on the pretext of the Cardinal's death, Horatio would be sent as a special envoy to Paris, a glorified tourist, a superfluous act in terms of doing the job, but an effective marking down of Schaub in the eyes of Orléans and the court. He was there precisely for that – to attack Carteret through Schaub and to report on the ambassador, whom he calls 'the little gentleman' to Townshend, the other Secretary of State and to his brother, the Prime Minister.

The purpose of the mission was savagely clear. Archdeacon Coxe, first and devoted biographer of Walpole, puts it all with admiring candour, acknowledging that

> it became a matter of great concern for Townshend and Walpole to have their own confidential embassador [*sic*] at Paris which was now the centre of the secret negotiations for all foreign affairs, and by these means, to prevent their opponent from preserving his weight in the cabinet, which he principally derived from the supposed credit of his creature, Sir Luke Schaub. It was in their interest therefore to obtain his removal, and to substitute some person in whom they could place implicit confidence, and whose appointment should prove to the Court of France and convince both friends and adversaries in England of their ascendancy in the Cabinet.[19]

Everything turned upon whether it was to be the future Duchesse de la Vrillière or not the future Duchesse de la Vrillière. Would Schaub's best efforts and contacts pull off this coup and strengthen Carteret and himself with the King? Schaub's worst fault was optimism. He had his own line through a certain Madame de Prié and Orléans did stress his wish to oblige King George. Told what he wanted to hear, he believed it and told Carteret so with far too much conviction. Expectations were being built up in Hanover, not wisdom.

At the same time, Horatio was writing exultantly to Townshend about the equivalent of riots in Grosvenor Square:

... this thing began to break out all of a sudden, and like a great cloud gathered at once on a Summer's day, burst with a surprising violence, the whole Nobility being in an alarm at Paris and Versailles spread to insolent Reflections ... In short, my Lord, the weakness of the Regent in giving alway [*sic*] civil answers even in matters that he has an aversion to, and the forwardness, sufficiency* and particular views of Sir Luke's in doing vast matters by concluding this Affair, made him, I believe, interpret what the Regent did not directly refuse as a consent and take his measures accordingly, both in acting here and in writing to Hannover, and 'tis strange that Sir Luke does not perceive that Cardinal Dubois is dead.[20]

Not just Dubois: for almost at once a shell exploded in the embassy trench. On 3 December, Horatio sent a frantic follow-on note to a despatch, announcing that 'ye D. of Orleans dyed yesterday between 7&8 in the evening suddenly of an apoplexy'.[21] The hedonistic, clever and Anglophile Regent was now replaced by the Duc de Bourbon, the new man to brief over the futilities of a noble intrigue. Superficially this might have been an improvement for Carteret and Schaub. Bourbon was as amiable as Orléans but rather more respectable, with only one principal mistress, and that, the same Madame de Prié with whom Sir Luke was on excellent terms and through whom he would now apply his campaign. The death of Orléans encouraged other people: 'The Jacobites are very full here of the pretender's return with his Court to St Germain.'[22] They had been pushed by the Regent and his ministers first to Avignon then Rome. They now dreamed, rather pitifully, of returning to their exile of first choice.

Horatio, meanwhile, had spent Christmas canvassing the aristocracy, applying himself notably to Fleury, not yet Cardinal, only Bishop of Fréjus, but, at seventy, the coming man.† Fleury was against the dukedom and 'has treated Vrillière with a great deal of freedom upon it. All the men of quality,' added Horatio, 'as it came in their way, showed their aversion to it'.[23] He was also keeping at arm's length the overtures of Bolingbroke, still in exile though long sundered from the Pretender's court and bidding to ingratiate himself with the new British power base.

The former Minister of Queen Anne, then briefly of James Edward

---

*A word which has changed meaning and at this time signified not 'adequacy' but 'self-assurance'.

† He would be made chief Minister in 1726, ruling until his death in 1743.

in exile, was making his way on a strange curve which would bring him to inspired journalism in opposition to Walpole and a book, *The Patriot King*, whose notions would charm the future George III. At that moment, Paris/Versailles 1723, he was working a laborious passage back to recovering his estates by way of briefing Walpole's brother on the doing-down of Walpole's enemies. As sharp as he was erratic, Bolingbroke knew what Walpole wanted and 'with great vivacity and pleasure, told me I never could have such a glorious foundation of merit and confidence with His Highness [Bourbon] than to show him his Majesty [*sic*] has been imposed upon and deceived by Schaub and destroy the credit of Lord C-[arteret] who must have been at the bottom of the whole matter'.[24]

Horatio declined the gambit. 'The incovering [*sic*] his L'ship's discourse joined with the general precaution I had formed to myself not to be led into any matter of moment under His L'ship's management . . .' Accordingly, he 'let him know the opportunity he proposed was of too nice a nature for me to make use of for that purpose, that I was not intirely [*sic*] convinced that Schaub has deceived H. Majest. to M. le Duc's disposition toward the Dukedom for la V . . . I took the case to be that the ladies had ingaged [*sic*] him before the late Duke of Orleans's death to give his consent, at least to acquiesce in it.' Horatio, discovering depths of deviousness he had not suspected in himself, watched Bolingbroke crumbling before him 'with the air of a person the most disconcerted and disappointed I ever saw.'[25]

The struggle continued into the next year, with Horatio an immediate personal gainer, writing to his brother on 20 January to profess that it was 'with a heart pierced with the greatest sense of duty and gratitude that I ought to acknowledge the honour intended me by his majesty in giving me the character of envoy extraordinary and plenipotentiary'.[26] The appointment would be resisted as it amounted to a stroke at Carteret, still dear to the King, following the sidelining of his trusted servant. But at Westminster, Walpole was riding a year of easy legislative success and readily forthcoming parliamentary monies. His obvious authority in that place subtly and silently diminished the royal prerogative. It became convenient for George to defer to the man who ran the Commons and had so few problems in the Lords. Carteret hit back by way of the despatches now sent as priority to Schaub – who should discuss their content with French ministers – and only then shown to Horatio. It was no way to run a chancellery.

Horatio, glorying and worried by turns, feared that the new French ambassador to Britain, the Comte de Buy, had 'an acquaintance with Schaub's friend, Madame de Prié', also about 'his brother, the Abbé de Broglie's, familiarity' with the same lady. This connection 'has been the real means of procuring the Duke of Bourbon's nomination of him as a person who they hope by his conduct and dexterity in England may still bring about that great point of the dukedom which meets with such insufferable difficulties'. Horatio then cheered up to add that Vrillière was 'in the vapours about it and like to go downright mad as his father did'.[27]

Mistresses were on the whole bad politics. Ultimately they got nowhere, even with Bourbon who had been well disposed and had almost certainly raised hopes, before finding himself assailed by a chorus of disapproval from the French nobility, obnoxiously particular about everything from Amalie's mother's uncertain genealogy to Schaub's own commoner origins and his not being a proper Englishman. Absurd Swiss aspirations were being destroyed by absurd French objections, by means of which Walpole's monopoly of English power was screwed further in. Horatio was able, on 15 February 1724, to describe to his brother the tortured statement of the Duke of Bourbon as Schaub pressed the Vrillière case which was in turn the von Platen case and King George's case.

Bourbon said that he 'had met great difficulties in the affair, and the more he thought of it, the greater he found them every day, but would do everything in his power to oblige his Majesty and in two or three days he should be able to know what he should do'. This sounded hopeful to Schaub, but the next words were deadly: 'But I am sure it is not expected that I should embroil the office of my administration for the sake and the intrigues of women.'[28] Heckled by his peers, Bourbon would finally refuse the elevation, setting off a train of misery through Amalie, now marrying beneath her, via her mother, to the King to Carteret. (The dukedom did not come to the family until 1770.) That part of the game was almost up. Schaub, Amalie and the Vrillières had lost it.

Horatio, who had been promised the status of ambassador in advance of Schaub's recall, giving England a double representation, nagged home for formal credentials for unpleasing reasons about which he had been asking the all-informed Bishop of Fréjus. 'I took it for granted that he would have been able to let me know when my little friend would be recalled and when I would be in a condition to pass him by and make him appear as contemptible as he deserves.'[29]

But Walpole and Townshend, happily conspiring to destroy someone through their family envoy, now instructed Horatio to write what the Archdeacon deftly calls 'an ostensible letter'[30] damning Schaub's conduct. Horatio, for all his virulent dislike of Schaub, bridled at what he was asked to do. 'I am now to draw Sir L. Schaub's picture in colours he deserves to be sent to Ld. Townshend, to be layd [sic] before the King, to be shown by the King to Carteret and Schaub's particular friend Lord Antrim.'*[31] Horatio had clearly been roundly knocked about in elder brotherly fashion in the previous letter. He is distressed and at a loss: 'I protest to God that I can't comprehend what you mean by it.' But he knew who was master and submitted in a rather snivelling fashion: 'I will do everything to comply with my friend's wishes however different mine may be and escape all occasion of reproach for [word illegible] and selfishness.'[32]

The letter was written, the letter worked, and Schaub, though permitted to return for the marriage of the mere Comtesse de la Vrillière, was effectively recalled and Horatio made ambassador in his place. Schaub had been a proxy for Carteret; with Schaub's authority gone and the King briefed, the Secretaryship of State was lost to Carteret. Their investing such efforts in a bagatelle which should have been represented to the King as a desperate long shot, but had instead been promoted as almost accomplished fact, had removed more than an exceptional talent; it demoted a non-member of Walpole's circle.

Carteret's replacement as Secretary of State spoke for everything Walpole did and stood for. It was, of course, the Duke of Newcastle, inferior to Carteret on every count except obligation to Walpole. Newcastle's merits were those of a decent applier of limited talents. His brother, that other and abler Walpole loyalist, Henry Pelham, would be Walpole's ultimate successor, the Duke would be Secretary of State for thirty years. The whole mean-spirited operation seems pointless except for the very Walpolean point that it pushed down a man of comparable talent.

However, at his best when dispassionate and not politicking, Walpole could get serious business right in foreign policy. Russia had gained a great deal of ground against Sweden as Fredrik had lost control to 'a

---

* Unclear in the original.

defeatist council of ministers and senate'.[33] There was a departmental tendency to overstate Peter the Great's menacing potential, planning Scandinavian conquests with which to 'make Russia able to terrify and distress all the coasts of Britain'.[34] This could have been the trigger for granting the King open-ended funds for his Baltic purposes when, in fact, Peter had been conducting minor naval manoeuvres. Fortunately, Walpole's prejudices cut the other way; his alarm bells only rang for Jacobite plots. The Treasury allocated a modest sum to cover an extended royal stay in Hanover, but treated the whole scare with a mixture of doubt and economy.

A great irony about Walpole is that his least attractive acts of ruthless self-aggrandisement and catch-all nepotism largely succeeded and have found historians to applaud them, while his acts of thoughtful, constructive statesmanship frequently ran into deep trouble. The failure in 1733 to realise his sensible plans for an efficient excise scheme is the business of a later chapter. But at roughly the same time that Walpole was cold-bloodedly blighting the career of a colleague with whom a more balanced man could have worked happily, his proposals to give Ireland a sound coinage ran into the clever malice of a master propagandist and a prolonged episode of general public unreason.

A building in Wolverhampton carries a plaque telling us that on that site there once stood the Old Deanery, home of William Wood (1671–1730), ironmaster of the town. This writer, having seen it, for mischievous interest asked around a dozen of his acquaintance, politicians and political journalists, who they thought this might be. None of them had the least idea, something which may be a reflection on the standing of history in political circles. It was this Wood who, in 1722, obtained a licence to mint small copper coin for Ireland. He won the contract by buying it from the Duchess of Kendal, George's Melusine, who had been granted it by Sunderland for just such a purpose. Discreditable only as a general post-dated principle, it was the way of the world they both inhabited. Melusine was wife and consort in all but name, with the costs that accompanied the role. She supplemented whatever came to her unofficially from the King's income by cheerful deals of this sort. Had she been granted a generous Civil List of her own, the same patriots who damned her trading would have damned *that* with an additional fusillade of moral reproach.

One thing has to be made clear. The copper coin which Wood manufactured, an order of £108,000, was assayed by Sir Isaac Newton and found to be of mint quality; apart from some variation between individual coins, there was nothing wrong with it. This has to be said as there are authorities, like *The Cambridge Guide to Literature in English*, which, commenting on *The Drapier's Letters*, insouciantly remark that this work 'effectively prevented the issue of debased coinage'. The literary world has long celebrated the victory of one of its own partisans over the dreadful men of politics. And how could a low tradesman from the West Midlands be right in a dispute with a canonical author?

When a contemporary politician/writer was found who *did* recognise William Wood, unsurprisingly Mr Michael Foot, author of a well-known biography of Swift, he knew what he had always known, resolutely refusing to believe what was reported in the official assay of 28 March 1724: 'very good copper, and taken one piece with another full weight, yet the single pieces not so equally coined in the weight as they should have been'.[35]

There was room for a less unreasonable anxiety. Small as the sum seems today and confined to small coin, it represented a 25 per cent increase in the volume of Irish coin. Fear of inflation might have seemed a genuine risk if the general complaint had not been a shortage of currency for all commerce. In truth, shortage of coin would be a problem and a restraint on commercial expansion not just in Ireland, but in England, and would remain one throughout the eighteenth century. Forgery was not looked upon as a crime at all by traders, especially in the Midlands and North of England, where men like Thomas Lightowler and David Hartley were looked upon as benefactors. Everything was wrong with the currency system: overvalued silver, poor quality even in official coinage and dependence on random commercial paper.

Every kind of official or high-sounding financial document served as unofficial currency, not least (see *supra*) the share certificates of the South Sea Company. And specifically in Ireland, the small coin already circulating was so debased that thirteen Irish pence made a shilling.[36] Getting decent quality copper coin into circulation in Ireland was a completely constructive act, likely only to benefit Irish commerce. Whatever the many injuries done to Ireland by England, the work of the Wolverhampton metal master was not one of them. But prejudice governs the record because in the years 1722–5 prejudice won a great battle against Wood and Walpole.

But there were complications in Ireland. Walpole's enemies in Ireland were led by the Brodrick family which included the Irish Lord Chancellor, Lord Middleton, formerly Alan Brodrick. These were people with serious authority in the Irish Parliament which, for all its clogs, could still make very serious trouble. Some of the antipathy went back to 1720–21, the time of the Walpole screen, which had frustrated the inquisition into the South Sea chaired by another Brodrick, the irreproachable Thomas. The Brodricks were Irish trouble, in part at least as honest government men who saw Walpole as the South Sea Screenmaster, in another part, people in complicated relationships with both Carteret and Walpole. Being essentially friends of Carteret, as the intrigue of Townshend and Horatio gathered momentum in London and Paris, Lord Middleton and his connection saw no occasion to discourage trouble in Dublin. Their true point of departure was less metallurgical than constitutional. The Irish Parliament had played no part in respect of Wood's patent. Granting it was a non-consulting paternal act, something done for the Irish without asking them.

The crisis expanded, starting at Wood's first undertaking in mid-1722, and running nearly three years. The Irish Parliament rebelled; Middleton, as Chancellor, with a good deal of Irish *schadenfreude*, made no serious effort to check it. The Lord-Lieutenant, the Duke of Grafton, stood in a classic, not to say apostolic, succession of uncomprehending Englishmen who put their genius into not understanding Ireland. Lord Hervey had spoken of 'the natural cloud of Grafton's understanding' making 'his meaning, always as unintelligible as his conversation was unentertaining'.[37] A second choice for the job after the Duke of Bolton had refused it, Grafton dug the hole deeper by losing his temper full time, turning cheeky resistance into a three-year running feud, stroking no hair and making no friends. Instead, he dug his own trench for a war of attrition with Parliament, signing up to an internal Irish quarrel, working closely with Connolly, Speaker of the Irish Commons and Middleton's rival, getting the English House of Lords to pass a vote of censure against Middleton and demonstrating a general peremptoriness where charm, not to say blarney, would have served better.

His letters to Walpole say a good deal. 'Unwilling to trouble you with my private letters' on 17 December, he goes on for ten pages of bold, brown scrawl, complaining of 'the behaviour of a certain family here to which is chiefly owing the great obstruction which has been given to the King's business this session and my own continued diffi-culties since the beginning of it'.[38] He is talking about the Brodricks and simply does not know how to handle them. Grafton is a moaner, complaining that he was 'never favoured with one line from my Lord Townshend since my arrival in this Kingdom'.

He has, though, had plenty to moan about: 'the chief topic which has occupied debates in each of Houses of Parliament since ye recess has been His Majesty's answers to the Respectful Addresses relating to Mr Wood's patent'. Except that 'respect' didn't seem to be quite the word for it, and the person showing hardly any at all was the Lord Chancellor, showing 'great partiality on the Woolsack in shifting and putting the question . . . From many instances, for some years past this principal has governed his politicks. He throws himself among the majority and then resumes to himself the Honour of being Chief of yr party.'

It is, of course, all you can expect if you let the natives help run the colony. 'L. Sunderland carried the compliment to this country too far by choosing out of the natives the Chief and most of the other judges, and the Bishops too, which has been attended with very mischievous consequences for the English interest . . .'[39] Grafton is not talking about the Catholic Irish. His problems lie with lawyers, clergy and politicians conforming to the established Church, Anglo-Irish, but not respectful. He is defeatist: '. . . in plain terms while the Chancellor is in power prejudice prevails, all influence is lost. I can expect no good from them and heartily wish I had done with them till which time I shall continue to live in a kind of fever.'[40]

The impression of the Englishman abroad seeking to be understood by shouting was exactly achieved. Walpole himself lost his temper and usual judgement, violently abusing the Irish parliamentary opposition, accusing Middleton of 'treachery and low cunning'. But he also person-ally drew up a statement setting out details of the patent, the assay of Wood's coins, as the good copper they were and put that sensible judge-ment to his Irish public.

Not that fact or sensible judgement mattered where Jonathan Swift was concerned. The Dean of St Patrick's entered the argument early in 1724, addressing a series of pamphlets 'To the Shopkeepers, Tradesmen, Farmers and Common People of Ireland'. Notionally, it was the work of a draper, known only as 'M. B', supposedly keeping a shop in St Francis Street. It is known to literature as *The Drapier's*

Letters. Swift knew nothing of business or economics, but knew very well that he was not going to get a bishopric out of Walpole, certainly not the English bishopric he craved. And Wood notwithstanding, this was a campaign directed at least as much against Walpole, 'Flimnap', villainous Lord Treasurer of Lilliput, in Swift's subsequent *Gulliver's Travels*.

In 1720, on the death of Lindsay, Archbishop of Armagh, the see held by the Primate of All Ireland under both confessions, Swift had hoped to see his friend and patron, William King, Archbishop of Dublin, advanced to it. But Walpole had been warned against him by Grafton. King was indeed a fine man, 'charitable, hospitable and a despiser of riches and an excellent Bishop', but you couldn't count on his politics. He had made trouble over Grafton's vice-regal speech: '. . . he urged some very indecent expressions objecting to the words "a happy people," ' . . . This could not be esteemed such for since the King's accession, by an act of another kingdom, they were in some respect put under slavery, with other unguarded expressions.'[41] The trouble with King was that, having such virtues, 'he has generally the love of the country and a great influence and sway over the clergy and all Bishops who are not natives'. Contrariwise, 'to those who are sent over from England he does not show much curtesie'.[42] Grafton adds that he 'thought it proper to lay this information before you'.[43]

It was laid to good effect. In 1724 Walpole organised the translation of Hugh Boulter, Bishop of Bristol, Englishman, safe pair of hands, sound chap, Whig. By all accounts, Boulter would be a devoted, reforming Bishop, open-handed in giving relief, but 'committed to upholding what he considered the English interest in Ireland'.[44] With all his genius, Swift was a bitterly, and at last, dementedly, disappointed clergyman.

He was much else beside. Along with the talents which produced *Gulliver* and *The Tale of a Tub*, he held the Irish people in an odd mixture of contempt and compassion. From such a congeries of impulse and opinion stemmed the literary champagne and economic nonsense of *The Drapier's Letters* where the protagonist tradesman 'M.B.' writes, 'You may take my word, whenever this money gains footing among you, you will be utterly undone . . . Do you think I will sell you a yard of tenpenny stuff for twenty of Mr Wood's halfpence? No not under two hundred, at least.'[45]

The Drapier's Letters has been praised more often than read. It is successful journalism, brilliantly successful at paralysing a colonial administration which had been behaving with thick-headed reasonableness. But reading it cold today, amid those scatterings of capital letters and italic type, one encounters a shouting, bullying rant: 'First Observe this little Impudent *Hardware Man* turning into ridicule *the Direful apprehensions of a whole Kingdom*, priding himself as the cause of them, and daring to prescribe what no king of *England* ever attempted, how far a Nation shall be obliged to take his brass coyn.'[46] Alternatively we have 'while there is a *silver* sixpence left these BLOOD-SUCKERS will never be quiet'.[47] Much of it seems to be written in green ink.

Ireland had every kind of justified complaint against England. She was ruled well or ill by Englishmen or Irishmen accommodated to England. But Swift was digging down to unreal miseries to induce despair, playing to the gallery of suspicion and unhappiness. The Irish were miserable? The English were conspiring to make them more miserable yet: 'England gets a million sterling by this nation; which, if this project goes on, will be reduced to almost nothing. And do you think those who live in England upon Irish estates will be content to take an eighth or tenth part being paid in Wood's dross?'[48] The fact that it wasn't dross and that Swift had no way of knowing, that he was writing out of his own rage at all things English, makes the whole exercise a cruel piece of personal irrationality thrust into the manufacture of popular discontent.

What had first carried the general agitation forward was Wood's patent being an English act, indeed an invocation of the royal prerogative, leaving Irish representatives unconsulted. It was not calculated to be popular with the Protestant Anglo-Irish, over whose parliamentary heads it had also gone. What Swift achieved was to rouse Catholic Ireland, shopkeepers and the street. The high-toned part of his argument was that 'government without the consent of the governed is the very definition of slavery'.[49] But dropping the grand manner, he was talking fear to get panic. Coupled with factual untruth – that Ireland was being supplied with 'brass money'[50] and that Wood, a major industrialist with large national interests in copper mining, was 'a low mechanic come to cheat them'[51] – the appeal was explosive. As Grafton noted, 'Many people in Dublin come through weakness, others through malice, flocking to the Bankers to withdraw their money or to alter their notes with an express condition, to be paid in gold or silver', adding that 'many other ridiculous extravagances have prevailed, not worth your notice'.[52]

A major crisis had blown up quite beyond the abilities of the fulminating Lord-Lieutenant, unsubtle even by the standards of Dublin Castle. Walpole didn't understand Ireland, a foreign country which apparently could not be managed. For, as Grafton now told him plainly, 'I must say as I formerly hinted, there was no making any impression on them in its [the coinage's] favour.'[53] *The Drapier's Letters* were directed at the Prime Minister who defended the coin in his statement, and clearly hit home. He was angry and quarrelsome, lashing out even at the stepping and fetching Horatio. The 'ostensible letter' about Schaub had been written at this time, and Carteret destroyed in his office and the King's mind turned against him. Yet the irony was that the only man who could talk Ireland out of worse trouble and negotiate Walpole's surrender was the Brodricks' friend, Carteret, the whirligig of time doing its customary thing.

Where Walpole had struggled on with a policy, good in conception but incapable of being sold politically, relying on a mediocre representative who reinforced his own uncharacteristic inflexibility, Carteret, sent out to Dublin as the new Lord-Lieutenant, put himself about, meeting Swift face to face and allegedly answering his reproach about 'persecuting a poor draper' with a line of Virgil, *Res dura et regni novitas me talia cogunt moliri.*[*][54] The only politician who could look Swift coolly in the eye as an equal, he allegedly, according to an unreliable later account by Sheridan's father, provoked him to the words 'What vengeance brought you among us? Get you back, get you back, pray God Almighty send us our boobies again.'[55]

He instituted a financial audit which, in a country whose funds were given to wandering, put the Dublin political scene into a froth and thereby diverted attention from the climb-down on Walpole's currency problem. This, long inevitable, had, almost as long, been thought impossible. But it was Walpole's face which Carteret was losing, something he found himself cheerfully able to do. After which, he rapidly established himself as an efficient, sympathetic and extremely popular Lord-Lieutenant, a thing so inherently improbable that an Irish Bishop was heard to murmur 'A Daniel come to Judgment'.

---

[*] Hard necessity and my newness in office require such acts.

The judgement upon Walpole in the early twenties must be that he pursued the concentration of power with brilliant and unhealthy success, while, in respect of a sound policy deserving better management, his defeat at the hands of a provincial assembly and a pamphleteer had been total.

'SIR BLUE-STRING'

For a couple of years following his victories of 1724 Walpole would enjoy a triumphal period, something gratifying to a triumphalist. The demotion of his ablest Whig rival had concentrated power into the narrowest circle of family and subservience. With its currency reform aborted, Ireland had actually been a defeat, but in the fashion of Ireland it had gone away, and the Brodricks were out of place, so that was all right. Control of the Commons was delivering whatever was asked. The King, who had never liked either Walpole or Townshend, was content that they were performing to his requirements and, having accepted the 'ostensible letter', was, if by no means estranged from Carteret, happy to see him demoted. Now was the time for showing favour to his Minister. George would accept hospitality at the Richmond Lodge which Walpole had recently acquired, would indeed, on one occasion, drop in for dinner without notice, affability in a Guelph-Wettin far beyond the customary limp norm.

From affability flowed honour. Walpole was clear about the House of Lords. Harley, St John and Stanhope, while still in office, had become respectively Earl of Oxford, Viscount Bolingbroke and Earl Stanhope. Walpole had as great a taste for glory as any of them, but the instinct which allowed no serious talent to flourish in government would allow no one capable of becoming a rival to run the House of Commons. But on the other hand, a loyal mediocrity could not be relied upon to run it smoothly or speak to it with the authority, charm and menace of Robert Walpole. The strawberry leaves could wait.

Instead, Walpole solicited the King for a dormant honour. His father had held no title, but his grandfather had been Sir Edward Walpole,

Knight of the Most Noble, but dying out, Order of the Bath. It was a characteristically dynastic touch for the Prime Minister in 1724 to ask the sovereign to conjure this defunct body of chivalry back into life by creating Sir Robert Walpole KBE. Its red riband was charming, and identification with the most successful man of the day created quite a market for a reissued line. Walpole, always humourless about jokes against himself, reacted characteristically to a joshing squib from Chesterfield:

Tho' a bauble I call it
It must not be slighted
'Twas one of the toys
Bob gave to the boys
When first the chits were knighted.[1]

On the appearance of this in April 1725, Chesterfield was instantly dismissed from his post as Captain of the Yeomen of the Guard. The Bath, in all its nobility, was yet another instrument of favour and control, one of those free bribes in which the British specialise. Chesterfield was a refined intelligence, a drily witty speaker and a persuasive influence in the Lords. All sense was for keeping him onside, and the attempt to get him back would be made with the embassy to The Hague in 1727, but the ravelled sleeve never was properly knit up and he became a cool, injurious critic in the thirties. A tolerant urbanity was not one of Walpole's many qualities.

He ought to have been too strong to fear or mind leg-pulls. For the measure of George's confidence was that he soon after opened to Walpole the highest order of all, Edward III's creation, the Garter. It had, in fact, been given to Townshend, an accredited nobleman, a year earlier. Even so Walpole was overwhelmed and proceeded to behave in a somewhat arriviste way, having this order's still prettier blue ribbon included in every picture of himself, even the one surrounded by his dogs as Richmond Park Ranger. It was everywhere incorporated into the stucco of his new mansion, Houghton. The dazzlement was noticed, and in an age of healthy and eloquent disrespect, the mounting list of disobliging nicknames for the head of government was augmented with 'Sir Blue-String'.

But it was a good time. His enemies were confounded, Atterbury in exile was despairing, and, in 1723, Walpole had enjoyed a wonderful run of episcopal deaths. London was mortally vacated in April of that year, but for the bench of bishops, May was the cruellest month: Ely died on the 4th, Winchester mid-May, Chichester at its end, while St David's hung on until October. With Rochester stripped from Atterbury, the King (suitably advised by his ministers) was able to put in pure party men. Of these by far the most important would be Edmund Gibson, translated from Lincoln to London, and subsequently made ecclesiastical adviser, a sort of Chief Whip among the higher clergy, with special responsibility for assembling a loyal Episcopal vote in the House of Lords. (See *post* Chapter 13 *passim*.)

Meanwhile in Ireland, the blocking of the too nativist William King and the transfer of Hugh Boulter from the impoverished See of Bristol to the Irish primacy (see *supra* Chapter 9) would have long-term benefits for party rule. Boulter improved upon his genuine charitable merits by notifying Newcastle of every vacancy in every Church place throughout Ireland. In February 1727, for example, he reported that only nine out of the twenty-two Bishops in Ireland were English and urged that the good work of what might be called episcopal settlement should be redoubled.[2] Sunderland's too-great tenderness for employing natives would be reversed for an age to come. In England, Gibson, as a dedicated Whig, would run the Church in these interests, and for ten years 'Walpole's Pope', otherwise Bishop of London, outreached unsound and aged Canterbury and unsuitable York. But a man of outstanding gifts, with serious plans for reform, notably more extensive education and advancement of earnest merit to the snug livings, he would, as we shall see, like so many first-rate men, break, however quietly, with Sir Robert.

Walpole was even happy in his private life. The long, ever-distancing marriage to Catherine Shorter had dwindled into estrangement. One of its last events had been the death in October 1722, following the drawn-out misery of tuberculosis, of the couple's daughter, also Catherine, to whom Walpole in his strong family fashion was sincerely devoted. The active sexual life, about which he was reticent and gossip busy, seems, this side of actual whoring, to have been of a socially unequal and impermanent nature. It included the unidentified mother of one acknowledged illegitimate daughter, Catherine Daye. But that personal life would brighten into affection and real happiness in the person of Maria, or Molly, Skerrett.

The daughter of an Irish gentleman from Galway who intensely disapproved of both Walpole and the relationship, she would be no more a mistress in the derogatory sense than Melusine, the King's Duchess, was to George. He wooed her in Catherine's lifetime, but with the marriage dead to all but the clergy. He won her, but not quickly, to his bed, and a child was born before wedlock. But as both gentle-woman and object of devotion, Molly Skerrett too was a partner, not a concubine, something to be underlined by the couple's marriage, unhypocritically soon after the death of Walpole's wife in 1738.

Walpole had the Rangership of Richmond Park, nominally for his son, and spent £14,000 (£750,000 of our money) knocking down and putting up in the approved fashion. Walpole, whose complicated character embraced furious hedonism as readily as it sought out low motives and went for ever in fear of the hands of enemies, had a delightful time, freely spending on himself: the paintings sought abroad by agents, including that particular agent, John Macky, parties, held in Chelsea and Richmond, a hospitality in wine and food never calculated. But Walpole's generosity could not be reliably counted upon to encompass compassion.

Even Plumb, so very much Walpole's partisan, is a little shocked by the case of Sir John Fryer. Back in 1721 when, according to taste, Walpole was anxiously screening fraud or calming unreason, Fryer, as Lord Mayor of London, had taken on the angry movers of an address from the Court of Common Council. At that time, the City of London involved craftsmen and small tradesmen; it was by no means today's white-tied assembly of corporate accumulation. There was a lower-middle-class, often dissenting, radicalism still about which went back in its sentiments to the early seventeenth century.

Fryer had, there and then when needed, been a good loyalist standing up to, and heading off, furious addresses to Parliament, without which, in those explosive times, harassed and frightened ministers could very well do. His business had then suddenly gone under and he was desperate for any sort of lowly job to keep him from actual destitution. He wrote to Walpole that after 'two years five months attendance on the Treasury it will be needless to repeat the many applications I have made or the frequent promises I have had from your Lordship for a Tidesman's place in the Port of London. I am now reduced to that extremity that I must either soon participate in your Lordship's favours or change my liberty for confinement in a gaol . . .'[3]

A tidesman or tidewaterman was a small official of the docks, a post familiar in the archive as one regularly applied for by small agents looking for small berths; Fryer had been Lord Mayor. He now spoke of his 'extremitys which are such as to render your Lordship's personal help only serviceable . . .'. Nothing came; Fryer had performed a service but could never perform another. The only tide which came to him was destitution, and 'the unfortunate, humble and respectful servant', as he signed himself, died unobliged by ministerial favour eighteen months later.

The only grief afflicting Walpole at this time, but it was a great one, was the death on 29 March of Viscountess Townshend, his Secretary of State's still quite young wife. She was, of course, Walpole's much younger sister, Dolly, the young flirt who had got into a scrape with Lord Wharton twenty years before, someone peculiarly dear to him and happy in a faithful, close marriage to Townshend. As wife and sister, she had been a sort of graceful hyphen between men joined otherwise rather by interest than affinity. Townshend was a man of general rectitude who carried his nobility heavily. He was incapable of Walpole's philandering and, despite his secondary part in the Carteret intrigue, not much happier in the world of fixing and knowing men's price in which his brother-in-law delighted. The family alliance had a deal of ruin in it, yet was indeed good for another four years. But Dolly's end took the affectionate, reconciling humanity out of it, leaving the ties to be frayed by events and differences.

There was at this very time, March 1726, something more than a spat between the two. Money was sought, by the King and by Townshend, to pay Hessian troops at a time when war with Spain looked possible. Walpole was against all of it: the troops, the money and the war. In fact, nothing happened, and Walpole's instincts are very attractive here, but observers drew conclusions about relations between the two men. Pozzobueno, the Spanish Minister, writes 'that misunderstanding between Townshend and Walpole daily increases'. And he cites Baron Palm, representative of Vienna, saying 'that the division between Townshend and Walpole was very great'.[4]

Things would settle down for some time yet, but the combination of a genuine difference of outlook, one man an internationalist, ready, if necessary, for military action, and another, commercial, Treasury-led and pacific, was real. And with Dolly gone, there was no persuasive intermediary to offset Walpole's instinct to rule alone. Eventually, in 1730, Townshend, like Carteret in 1723–4 and the Bishop of London in 1736, would no longer fit near what was becoming something of a throne.

Instructively, Pozzobueno quotes another member of the diplomatic corps, Fabrice, who 'imagines that Walpole is so desirous of getting rid of Townshend that he is capable of reconciling himself with William Pulteney and placing him in Townshend's post'. He wasn't, but the name Pulteney introduces a new strain into the politics of the mid-1720s, the modest down slope following the victory ridge of 1723–5. Walpole had enjoyed an open road for his triumphs in the preceding two years because a proper opposition did not exist in the House of Commons. With Oxford dying and absent, Cowper, a fugitive from the Whig camp of victory and a real organising force in the Lords, also dying in October 1723, the Tories had lacked a leader. As working ruralists, they were wretched attenders, frequently mustering a vote between the sixties and nineties against major measures. Meanwhile, the successful conclusion of the Atterbury case had demoralised Tories as it had given the Whigs cohesion and Walpole standing with the King.

But these smooth waters were about to be disturbed, notably by this Pulteney. William Pulteney, a rich, well-connected man of serious talent, was a Whig, another of those people whom Walpole tried to keep down and succeeded only in driving out. He, reasonably enough, rated himself above the court post of Cofferer of the Household with which his mouth had been inadequately filled. His slowness to rise owed something to the fact that he had no significant electoral clout. He wanted the Secretaryship of State which had gone to Newcastle.

However, where Newcastle was reckoned to have sway over sixteen parliamentary seats, Pulteney could only share the two-seater family borough of Hedon with a single colleague. But Pulteney was a serious force. As Chesterfield put it, 'He was a most complete orator and debater in the House of Commons; eloquent, entertaining, persuasive, strong and patriotic as occasion required; for he had arguments, wit and tears at his command.'[5] And Arthur Onslow who, becoming Speaker in 1727, was a regular witness of their encounters, thought that Pulteney 'certainly hurt Sir Robert more than any of those who opposed him'.[6]

The beginnings of trouble had appeared in January with an attack on the government for corruption, contained in a petition brought by the Earl of Oxford (Edward, the 2nd Earl, Robert Harley's son) and Lord Morpeth, complaining, with good reason, about the administration of 'the estates of Elizabeth, Duchess dowager of Montague, a lunatic . . .'.[7] The charge was that money which should have been invested through the offices of Masters in Chancery on behalf of the poor woman had dematerialised.

Immediate focus fell upon Thomas Bennett, one of the Masters. The petition charged that Bennet 'has not deposited, pursuant to orders of the said court, several Mortgages for large sums of money belonging to the estates of the said lunatic; neither hath he deposited nor secured pursuant to orders of the said court, 9,000l and upwards of his balance of cash . . .' To all this, the parliamentary record adds in its own under-stated way the fact that 'a great debate arose thereupon, in which some severe animadversions were made on the conduct of the Earl of Macclesfield, late Lord Chancellor'.[8]

Effectively the charge against Macclesfield was that he had turned his Chancery Masters into embezzlers by driving up the price of their places as paid to him. And Macclesfield, in Sir George Oxenden's words, 'in order to pay to him those high prices and gratuities for their administration, had trusted in their hands large sums of money belonging to suitors in Chancery'.[9] Than which one can't speak plainer, except that no one thought such corruption remarkable. A contemporary wrote, 'It is hard to judge of his fate as yet, although the Court love the man; we have found guiltier men find out a back door.' And the King, regretful at the decision, saw him to a pension and contributed to the fine.[10]

The instinct of the government, meaning Walpole, had been to accept cheerfully the likely guilt of Macclesfield, someone he disliked and owed no favours, by moving for his impeachment. Macclesfield, after all, was George's man, not Walpole's. This narrow focusing would skip neatly past a more general and dangerous inquiry into corruption starting at the top, an irresponsible parliamentary kicking of stones to see what might be under them. When Pulteney rose to support such an inquiry, something forlorn given Walpole's majority, it was an act significant beyond the attempt itself. He thought that 'it little became the dignity of, and was even derogatory to, the prerogative of that House which is the grand inquisition of the nation, to found an impeachment upon those reports without a previous inquiry and examination into the proofs that were to support it'. Accordingly, he moved 'that this affair might be referred to the consideration of a select committee'.[11]

What the Tories wanted – and it *was* the Tories, for Pulteney was followed in support by Wyndham, Sir Wilfrid Lawson and Thomas Pengelly, regulation Tories – was the chance to ask difficult questions about corruption generally, which a committee of inquiry would provide. Inevitably, the opposition was defeated, but the vote, 164 against 273, was good by opposition standards. As it should have been, for Pulteney was backed here, and in his future career, by a personal following of similar discontented Whigs, most notably Samuel Sandys, Phillips Gybbon and Sir John Rushout. Ministers might proceed serenely to a full impeachment of Macclesfield, the King might meet part of the bill for the fine in which the impeachment ended. But they had all seen a group of disaffected Whigs pick up a richly satisfying pretext and set a pattern for reinforced, better directed opposition.

The fight against Walpole would henceforth be dominated by men more politically astute than most Tories, and the Tories were delighted. Things were changing in Parliament. Walpole's long ride would continue but it would be a rougher one and marked with reverses. Opponents of the government on this issue would form the nucleus of 'the Patriots', a term to be used forty years later by John Wilkes and his following, and a phrase usefully covering people reliably agin the government. It was not a particularly pure opposition. Pulteney was disappointed of office; Samuel Sandys, 'a tall, thin young gentleman' from an old Worcestershire family,[12] effectively his lieutenant, had applied the year before, at the age of twenty-nine, for the post of Secretary at War. But then Sandys already had standing: he had been one of the group of Whigs invited to meet at Walpole's house to hear the text of the King's speech ahead of delivery. He would now be a regular, assiduous and effective speaker against the Ministry. 'Every man has his price' is too famously Walpole's definition of his own realism. It was perfectly true of both Pulteney and Sandys. By not paying it, the Prime Minister made a great volume of trouble for himself in the next decade and a half.

Having made up his mind to go into opposition, Pulteney went. His next excursion was made against the requirements of the King. Walpole had made it a rule to keep the Civil List at a level agreeable to the King whatever the parliamentary pain. But it was never agreeable when, as on 8 April, 'Mr R. Walpole [*sic*] acquainted House that he had a Message to relate from his Majesty', one which informed members that 'The necessities of his Majesty's government having rendered it impracticable for his Majesty to make any considerable retrenchment in the expenses of his Civil List; and having engaged his Majesty in some extraordinary expences [*sic*] which he is persuaded his loyal Commons will believe have been employed, not only for the honour and dignity of the crown but for the interest and prosperity of his people' and so on for several more sub-clauses before reaching 'may be enabled to make use of the Funds lately settled for the payment of the Civil List annuities . . .'[13]

In the high tradition of the early seventeenth century, a king's need was Parliament's opportunity, in this case the opportunity of the Tories and the newly emerging Patriots, His Majesty's extremely polite but not particularly loyal opposition. Relishing the fact that the supplicant was in fact coming back for more,

> Mr Pulteney took notice that it was not long since (viz. July 1721), a Fund was given to discharge the debts of the Civil List; and therefore it was a matter of surprise that so many new ones had been contracted in so short a time; that if things were carried on at this rate there would be no end of it; that it was incumbent upon them to enquire into the causes of this growing evil.[14]

After 280 years, Pulteney's next words still glow off the page. He wanted to ask the King for details or, as he put it,

> that an address be presented to His Majesty that he would be graciously pleased to give directions that the proper officer or officers of the Exchequer, Excise, Customs and Post Office do lay before the House an Account of all Monies which have been issued and paid out of the said offices to any person or persons on account; for the Privy Purse, Secret Service, Pensions, Bounties; or any sum or sums of money to any person or persons whatsoever without account from March 25th 1721 to March 25th.[15]

It was a good question. It called for a grand inquisition into every place, pension, bribe, votesworth, sinecure, sweetener and misappropriation, discerningly scattered as political consideration by a government widely thought to do rather a lot of that sort of thing. It wasn't going to happen, of course. Walpole had the votes, many of them secured by pensions and bounties, to stop anything so discordant actually taking place. But it meant debate and publicity and the leaving of high-quality mud. So did Pulteney's other observation: 'He wondered how so great a debt, viz, 508, 667l 19s and 4d could be contracted in three years time, but was not surprised that some persons were so eager to have these deficiencies made good since they and their friends had so great a share of it. And desired to know whether this was all that was due or whether they were to expect another reckoning.'[16]

A pension was being paid, said a minister, probably Walpole himself, to Lord Godolphin. 'But then Godolphin and his father had so well deserved of the government that they could not handsomely remove him without a gratuity; and therefore they gave his lordship a pension of 5,000l to make room for the worthy gentleman, (meaning Mr W. Pulteney) who now occupied that post'.[17] It is the sort of riposte which makes loyal backbenchers make loyal backbench noises. But in respect of Pulteney's question, about how such a large volume of debt had been contracted in such a short space of time, as the Record says, in its muted way, 'To this, no direct answer was given.'

While there was no way that Walpole's system of inducement and payrolling would collapse beneath parliamentary fire, the fact that it was made the centrepiece of a newly assembled opposition signifies that bought and sold politics was not yet universally accepted or thought unworthy of raising. There had been places and placemen before, but Walpole was the most systematic and unfastidious player of that game electorally and inside the House of Commons itself. The sort of thing which a hundred years later would be assailed successfully by new Whigs and Radicals, by Lord Durham and Francis Place, and defended by Ultra Conservatives invoking the sacred rights of property, became the ordered system of things in Sir Robert's hands. And both parties learned to play it. As the Whigs would discover under George III, patronage was a ball which, once lost, was phenomenally difficult to recover. The politics of 1689–1715 were fluid, elections were lost and won, parliamentary groups mobile. The stability of Walpole, like the stability of Pitt and his Tory successors, depended upon systemic corruption, innovative in the 1720s, an aspect of the sacred and perfect constitution of 1831.

But immediate opposition did not stop at Pulteney and the Patriots. Viscount Bolingbroke, born in 1678, was two years younger than Walpole. The brilliance which had brought him to the threshold of mastery when still in his thirties could be, and was, called febrile unprincipled careerism.

Nobody set out this dualism more ferociously than Walpole's apologist, Hervey:

> As to Lord Bolingbroke's general character, it was so mixed that he had certainly some qualifications that the greatest men might be proud of, and many which the worst would be ashamed of: he had fine talents, a natural eloquence, great quickness, a happy memory and very extensive knowledge: but he was vain much beyond the general run of mankind, timid, false, injudicious and ungrateful; elate and insolent in power, dejected and servile in disgrace: few people ever believed him without being deceived or trusted him without being betrayed . . .[18]

Hervey, who would be damned blacker yet by Bolingbroke's friend, Alexander Pope,* is enjoyable, if biased. Certainly the febrile aspect of Bolingbroke had been demonstrated in 1715 when, in contrast to the steady scorn with which Oxford had met impeachment and possible execution, his nerve had broken at once and, doing all that his enemies might have hoped, the High Tory had gone higher yet, fleeing to France and taking shadow office with the Pretender.

Flight was not necessarily a mistake. Bolingbroke was more vulnerable than the tracks-covering Oxford to having a capital case made against him. As it was, Oxford spent three ague-inducing years in the Tower and emerged shrewd as ever, but too ill for activist politics. Bolingbroke was fit and well, but had given over a good deal of the too much spare time on his hands writing facile, untruthful defences of his former precipitancy. He was then a rasher, younger, less well-rooted man. Before 1714 he had flattered the squires and parsons with legislative persecution of Dissenters and their valuable academies while holding religion in the filtered light of scepticism.

Having been at once embraced and, in July 1715, given one of James Edward's hypothetical earldoms and made his 'Secretary of State', he busily involved himself in plans for that year's rising. It was not a lucky time for him – 'the Fifteen' failed, yet he had bemired himself with treason in its support, and, on the death of Louis XV, the Orléans Regency had shown itself determined to conciliate England and push the Pretender into extra-galactic exile. A lot of sympathetic ink has

---

* 'Yet let me flap this bug with gilded wings / This painted child of dirt that spits and stings'. *Epistle to Dr Arbuthnot.*

been spent on Bolingbroke posthumously, much as sympathy was spent on the man in his lifetime. He had, incontestably, a first-class mind, capable of serious philosophical reflection. One did not become the intimate of Pope and Swift on shallow politician's charm. His thinking would influence another generation as Pitt, Bute and George III read his writings. The return he had now made from what had seemed bottomless oblivion was remarkable in itself.

Yet in contrast to the business-minded and intellectually incurious Walpole, he had all the qualities for failure, even if it was brilliant failure. Having terrible short-term judgement, no patience and a brittle nerve, he had joined all the wrong sides. Bolingbroke had played his cards so quickly that he was looking for another table. He accordingly prepared himself not only to leave the Jacobite cause, but to betray its members to the Whigs. In all this and in his too-seldom resisted charm, there functioned, surely, a personality flaw with a hint of the criminal. He rattled round contrary politics like the projectile in a pinball machine. And his immediate concern in 1716 had been to work his way back into English politics by way of Stanhope and Sunderland. The winning side had a fascination for a busy loser.

Walpole, dourly impervious to the charm, would have sent him to Tower Hill like braver, duller men such as Derwentwater who had taken up arms in the rising Bolingbroke helped organise. But Stanhope, easier tempered and recognising the uses of men, wanted him drawn on. Stanhope's envoy, Lord Stair, very much charmed, wrote privately to the Duke of Marlborough:

> He orders me to tell you, that he will have no reserve of any kind with you, that he will tell you all he knows, that he will depend upon your protection and be entirely governed by your advice. He will likewise freely tell the King everything he knows, and do everything to deserve His Majesty's pardon . . . He speaks to me already with a great freedom, and tells me he will give me an account of everything he knows as soon as he hears from England that he may hope for the King's mercy.[19]

The choice which E.M. Forster famously indicated, between betraying one's country and betraying one's friends, did not apply to Bolingbroke, gaily available to do both.

Essentially he set himself up as the honest Tory who would rescue that party from the error of Jacobitism. Given such light-hearted abjection in the man, Stanhope had been happy to make accommodations. Rebels in the field had had their estates sequestered; the Catholics would shortly, in 1722, be surcharged by Walpole for being Catholics, however loyal. But Bolingbroke was allowed to send his agent, John Brinsden, into England to look after his estates and interests. Modestly secure (he had married good French money), Bolingbroke responded in a friendly spirit by attempting to bribe the Secretary of State, James Craggs the Younger, to have his Bill of Attainder of 1715 set aside.

Craggs was genuinely outraged. 'I take it in the plain sense that somebody supposes that I have credit enough to get this matter through the house of commons, but am such a rogue, that notwithstanding all my promises and professions, I will take no pains in it without a sum of money as likewise I am judged to be susceptible to such an offer.'[20] It was a double example of Bolingbroke's frivolous, instinctively amoral nature. As in 1714, he prejudiced a sound position by an extreme act – of treason then, of dishonesty now. It would take him much longer to recover his position than he had assumed when he turned Queen's evidence to Stair in 1716. The deaths of Stanhope, Sunderland and Craggs left him without great men for friends in Parliament. He paid court to Carteret who responded in a kindly way. But having Carteret for an ally when he was being undermined by Walpole was no sort of advantage.

As for Walpole, he is seen at the core of his nature on this question. The party's correct line and its attendant bigotry, which made Walpole such a sectarian in politics, served him well. So did his broad streak of vengefulness. We have seen Horatio Walpole being paid court to by the exile and assuring his brother of the full frosty dubiety with which he treated the former Minister and describing Bolingbroke's frustration. Indeed, with Walpole and Townshend in power, there ought to have been no prospect of a return. But there was one person always good for valuable consideration. Melusine Ehrengard, Graefin von der Schulenburg, Duchess of Kendal, was never known to refuse money or, in fairness, not to give value for it. And in his wife, Marie-Claire de Marcilly, Marquise de Vilette, married months after the death of his mistreated first wife, Bolingbroke had another victim of his charm, and a rich one with assets in England, willing to go in person, draw on them and see Melusine right to the value of between £11,000 and £12,000 (half a million and above in our terms).

Walpole was never at liberty to freeze Bolingbroke into the perpetual exile at which, next to the block, he rated him. He was obliged to compromise with a king now nagging his Prime Minister, as we may assume Melusine nagged him. Anyway George, given the chance, was a generous man who annoyingly never quite took English political quarrels altogether seriously. Even so, Sir Robert gave away as little as possible. The Attainder should be withdrawn in respect to his estates, but his place as a peer in Parliament was not restored. Even with royal backing, Bolingbroke's legal return through a parliamentary bill was something less than rapturous. There were both Whigs and Tories who for complementary reasons objected to the return of a scoundrel. 'An enemy of God and man' was how the Whig Sir John Cope put it. Captain Vernon, interestingly, called him 'a complicated villain'.[21] And the complaints did not all come from the fulminating backbenches. Sir Paul Methuen, a serious and ranking office holder, drew breath from conformity to run through all the charges previously made against Bolingbroke before his flight. Oxfordite Tories held him in contempt for his backstabbings in 1714, Will Shippen and his friends for the betrayal of Jacobites to the government in 1716.

But more dangerous than such protest was the intervention in committee of Lord William Pawlett with a clause barring Bolingbroke from ever sitting in either House or holding any office or place. As this stated expressly what Walpole had done by omission (withholding the title and with it the right to sit in the Lords), Walpole was able to talk implausibly about not being vindictive. Even so, the clause attracted eighty-four votes. There had been promises (for the future, made in the past by other men) that he would have access to an open political road. Not getting it, he rightly blamed Walpole. If he were now, in 1726, to play a political hand from outside Parliament, it would be played against Walpole. In a government headed by Stanhope, certainly in one led by Sunderland who was always well disposed, Bolingbroke might readily have been a ministerial supporter, one with hopes of office. Under Walpole, he was perforce to remain a Tory.

And given that his betrayals coexisted with a formidable theoretical intelligence and fine literary style, the Tories received at roughly the same time as they were making their loose alliance with Pulteney and the Patriots, a sharply effective addition to their strength. At the house he had bought, Dawley Farm, near Uxbridge, Bolingbroke entertained, gathered his friends together and planned opposition moves. For not only was he back, he had allies. Pulteney's quarrel with Walpole had, of course, been one of career. That lesser man, Newcastle, was Secretary of State, the post he thought right for himself. But he was to give that opposition a gloss of principle, arguing that he was an old Whig, true to the party's resistance to despotism; and here in the Walpole system was a form of fine-thread electoral control, and a greater one of place disposal, quite despotic enough.

Bolingbroke had been the persecutor of the Dissenters, legislating for the theocratic ambitions of the Sacheverells, the man planning, if Queen Anne had lived a few weeks longer, the ejection of all Whig magistrates and army commanders, to effect a coup for the Pretender. Pulteney prided himself on being an Old Whig devoted to the liberties and breadth of tolerance distinguishing that outlook. Yet here was Bolingbroke saying 'I have much esteem for Mr Pulteney. I have met with great civility from him, and shall on all occasions behave myself toward him like a man who is obliged to him.'[22] Events were dictating affinities and an enemy's enemies were coming together. As his biographer Professor H.T. Dickinson says, Bolingbroke was telling the Ministry either to treat with him or see him and his circle join in arms with Pulteney and the Patriots.

The Tories had been in a sad way. If Walpole, with his determination to hold down the Land Tax, had not shot their fox, then certainly he had taken it off their property. The Church could not be said to be in danger when Dissenters complained that, instead of their full rights and liberty of conscience, all they were given by the Whigs was an annual amnesty for avoiding regular communion. On top of which, the Tories were more of an archipelago than a continent: Jacobites like Shippen and Hynde Cotton, and three kinds of Hanoverian Tory, Oxfordians like Bromley and Lord Strafford, another group around Sir Thomas Hanmer and Bolingbroke's own circle.

But there was a final group about which they needed to worry most, the men – Sir Robert Raymond, Sir Edward Knatchbull and Lord Finch – whose frustrated abilities pushed them in the opposite direction to Pulteney, a discreet journey over the hill of independence into Walpole's luscious valley. The challenge of putting the remaining Tory bits together again in shrewd consort with disappointed but able, out-of-place Whigs was very much Bolingbroke's sort of thing. For all his distinction as a political theorist, he was a happy and gifted maker of mischief, and mischievous oppositions are more effective than solemn ones.

Barred from speaking in Parliament, he turned to debating in print.

Journalism of a high order in the form of a newspaper, *The Craftsman*, would now be financed. Edited by a talented young man out of Oxford (literally – sent down for insubordination!), Nicholas Amherst, it would have Pulteney as contributor. And, opening with a few lines under the humble pseudonym 'Will Johnson', Bolingbroke began a career which would involve writing, by general consent, about a fifth of all the pieces over nine years.

The Tories had always been rather good at journalism, having been served, through the darkest times, not without courage and verve, by Nathaniel Mist's publication, known as *Mist's Weekly Journal*, which, after his exile as a Jacobite, continued through a (humorous) deputy as *Fog's Weekly Journal*. Mist was vividly *ad hominem*, something which readily affronted the readily affrontable Walpole, by treating the Whigs in 'Lectures against the Muggletonians', like the followers of an unfortunately named preacher, Lodowick Muggleton, who had proclaimed himself messiah in waiting for the Day of Judgement. As for Walpole in his pride of day, Mist had also produced a 'Dialogue between Ulysses and a Hog'. The hog speaks:

> I affected modesty to be contented in an under-office, yet I absolutely disposed of all the rest, to my slaves for servility, to fools for my profit and thus I arrived at full power . . . back'd with immoveable impudence, I became First Minister, General, Admiral, High Priest, Chancellor, Treasurer and everything to the King. My name was Harpages . . . [the King] was surrounded by my tools, and kindred, and besides was prepossessed by my calumnies and assurance that whoever inveighed against me intended to abuse him, that censuring my conduct was a reflection on him and whoever was not my friend was an enemy to his country.

Ulysses asks, 'Were the people contented under such administration?' and receives the reply, 'The People! I never regarded them.'[23]

The Craftsman was top of the market, assured and scornful rather than angry. The paper started up on 5 December 1726, appearing twice weekly and expanding from a single sheet to a four-page affair. It had immediate effect, being denounced as 'the alarum bell of sedition'.[24]

Bolingbroke early hit a note to which his readership could respond. As in Anne's reign, the Tory party was against City finance. And Walpole's England ran over with financiers and financiers' runners, like the detested stockjobbers, doing far too well and now moving into politics. Where a seat had belonged to an old county family with yeoman voters content to vote in Sir John's wise choice, the money men were making a market, upping the price, corrupting the yeomen with a better offer. In fairness, Bolingbroke, for all his tergiversations, was following here a thread which could be found in his earliest writings and speeches. He was by sentiment a Tory in the old, land-based and social pyramid sense. For all the doubtful motives, in opposing Walpole he was doing his true, natural thing.

Walpole had responded to the vivacity of his critics in the press with all the weapons which an imperfectly libertarian constitution afforded: suits for libel and, in the case of the Jacobite, Mist, proceedings which made him flee the country. He also tried to mount his own press barrage. He was not actually very good at this. *The London Journal*, *The Corn Cutter's Journal* and *The Free Briton* went to press on behalf of the all-powerful minister. But William Arnall, his chief writer, had little flair and less humour. A notion of a laborious, literal-minded defence falling over into absurdity is demonstrated in the loyalist *Daily Courant* in reply some years later to *The Craftsman*'s biting invocation of an old Whig principle, rejection of a standing army (Walpole had one and was hiring Hessians for it).

This wasn't a standing army, argued the *Courant*, it was a land force. 'A standing Army is such a body of men as are kept up contrary to the Constitution, modelled at the will of the Prince . . . an instrument of arbitrary authority by which slavery may be introduced. A land force, on the contrary, is a national guard raised, paid for and regulated by parliament for the defence of our country against unforeseen accidents such as domestic sedition or foreign invasions.'[25] Not actually nonsense, it denied and explained, was heavy and tedious, not the way in polemical journalism.

The importance of newspapers, even though circulation might be modest, was that they extended debate beyond Parliament. There, Walpole had his majority, his payroll, his personal domination. Eighteen months after it was started up, the busy Tory correspondent Dr Stratford wrote, 'I would desire the continuance of *The Craftsman* as well as *The London Evening Post. The Craftsman* is the chief support to our spirits in the country.'[26] The mailing list, as put together four years on in 1730, indicated fifty-eight politicians subscribing regularly to the issue which was being redistributed by groups of them to their friends. Sir William Wyndham, doyen of Tories and perhaps the most respected

In the latter days, the full commons shortly before Walpole's fall

Ribbon and star displayed: Walpole resuscitated (and traded) the Bath
and was overjoyed at the Garter

The alternative
First Prime Minister,
James Stanhope, Earl Stanhope

The last barrier to Walpole's
ascent, Charles Spencer,
Earl of Sunderland

Unstable, extravagant, estranged:
Catherine Shorter,
the first Lady Walpole

A clever, managing wife:
Caroline of Ansbach,
George II's Queen

Speaker Onslow in the Chair.
Sir Robert close by

Dr Codex or Walpole's Pope,
Edmund Gibson, Bishop of
London, de facto Head of
the Church of England

'Amongst False Brethren.'
Dr Henry Sacheverell.
Incitement to sedition?

Mourning? The Tory leaders,
Bolingbroke and Oxford, with
(inset) the exiled conspirator
Bishop Atterbury

DIGNITY AND
IMPUDENCE

'A Peppery Little
Lieutenant-Colonel Retired.'
King George II

'The Craftsman.'
Nicholas Amherst,
writing as Caleb
D'Anvers, mocked
Walpole in that Journal

Walpole's equal in Debate
heads the Opposition.
William Pulteney,
Earl of Bath

City man and steady expert.
Critic of Walpole,
Sir John Barnard

figure on that side of the House, took a regular forty copies for reissue, with other Tories, like Sir Watkin Williams Wynn, also chipping in as bulk buyers and circulators. The papers sold as readily to Whigs of all colours, the Outs, friends of the Sunderland connection, radicals like Sir Thomas Aston and members friendlier to Dissent and toleration than Walpole thought prudent.[27]

Though not forbidden by law, there was a touch of *samizdat* about the hand-to-hand circulation of vigorous anti-government propaganda. And *The Craftsman* was good at what it did. As the arch-Walpolian Hervey said through clenched teeth, 'All the best writers against the Court were concerned in The Craftsman which made it a much better written paper than any of that sort that were published on the side of the Court. The two best of these writers were Lord Bolingbroke and Mr Pulteney.'[28] But the highest compliment came from the Law Courts where eight writs were issued over four years. The writers, perhaps because they were the ones taunting and stirring up, kept their tempers better than the Court and Ministry men. Though a duel was fought when Hervey abused Bolingbroke in a scurrilous pamphlet, he generally replied in a high, polite and reasoned style.

The precise purpose of the opposition which gathered round Pulteney, Bolingbroke and *The Craftsman* was like many oppositions, nebulous, at least at the edges. Toryism, as noted, implied the Church protected from the danger she was said to be in, the country gentleman relieved of land taxes, a cool view of finance and, up to a rhetorical point, less corrupt government. On the first two, Walpole had cooled controversy by only amnestying the Dissenters who conformed occasionally, instead of going the full liberal distance of a proper reforming Whig. And the country gentleman he kept beneath his special care; his starving of the nation's periodic impulse for war was directed at shielding the payer of Land Tax, hit so hard to fund Marlborough's glories. As for finance, with all its rogues and runners, it was here to stay, opposition to it only rhetorical. As for cleaner government, there was certainly resentment at the systematic and cold-eyed use of places, jobbery and appointments to sweeten and secure a majority. There were place bills in Parliament and talk of more frequent parliaments, the Septennial Act of 1716 having screwed ministerial chairs soundly into the floor boards. But as would be demonstrated when Walpole eventually fell, his system would have an enormous charm for an opposition tasting power and was becoming institutionalised.

As for Bolingbroke himself, though effective and giving Walpole his first prolonged hard time since the South Sea crisis, he was as much a part of the world of letters as of politics, and some of his ideas had a whiff of premature romanticism. He was certainly influential, as he contrasted the corrupt present with the wholesome past, in helping to start up the gothic fashion. Queen Elizabeth and the Anglo-Saxons were appealed to. Not unsuccessfully, the taste went into the theatre and one production, James Ralph's adaptation in 1731 of a play written fifty years earlier during the Exclusion crisis, which drew the character of a scheming, low Lord Burleigh 'who builds his rule / Upon the Vices of a venal World', was a clear Patriot hit at Walpole.[29] Even 'Rule, Britannia!' was the catchy hit number of a rather later Patriot product, the masque *Alfred* by James Thomson and David Mallet, music by the (Roman Catholic) Thomas Arne, proclaiming, in the year of Walpole's fall, that Britons never, never, never would be slaves.[30] In itself, such stuff was very miasmal, but talk from the late twenties on, of the Norman yoke and indeed, the catch-all term 'Patriots' itself, was very widespread. Indeed 'Patriots' served well enough to mantle what was a very disparate coalition involving men who had been at each others' throats in the reign of Queen Anne. Like *The Craftsman* itself, it was highly subversive of the people in power. It was the fate of opposition to win the cultural conflict as they lost the political one.

But such reservations in the longer perspective should not minimise the extent to which Bolingbroke, Pulteney and their loose alliance did change politics. The Walpole who had screened the South Sea and convicted Francis Atterbury had, Ireland excepted, been coasting since late 1722. He was legislating at will, delivering what the King desired financially and, despite deferring to what the King wanted in foreign policy, creating that consolidated personal power which history has saluted as our first Prime Ministership. But he now faced an intelligent, active and, most objectionably, eloquent opposition. What he did would be resisted in the Commons. What he was would be mocked and derided in print; the forces able to inflict later actual defeats were being laid up. And since Walpole could never be easily tolerant of contradiction and resistance, he almost certainly magnified his predicament.

However, the one thing in which he knew himself secure was the support of the King. George might have had inclinations to a more mixed Ministry, and certainly the opposition were persuaded that he might have sought something along those lines. But Walpole buttered the royal bread and assured stability. Without an excess of affection, the two men offered each other reassurance. They were each other's familiar and comfortable source of stability, something once fully achieved, to be tested again.

OH, DEATH, WHERE IS THY STING?

At 7 a.m. on 3/14 (Gregorian/Julian calendar) June 1727, the King set out on his annual visit to Hanover, planning to call at Osnabrück, his birthplace, to meet his brother, then at the family home, Herrenhausen, to be joined by his daughter, now Queen of Prussia, and embrace his twenty-year-old grandson, Frederick, with whom he enjoyed a mutual affection and for whom he had marriage plans. After a slightly weather-delayed departure from Gravesend for Schoonhaven, the journey was resumed by carriage to Varth, near Utrecht, then, by the next night, Velden. An hour and a quarter out of Velden, the King displayed the symptoms of a stroke and soon after collapsed. He was bled and taken unconscious to Osnabrück. He briefly recovered consciousness here, but on 11/22 June, King George I died.

If Walpole and George I had reached a good relationship, George Augustus, now informed of two equally delightful things, his father's death and his own standing as George II, was no part of it. Back in the days of Walpole's opposition to Sunderland and Stanhope, he had played court to the Prince, busy in his parallel quarrel with the King. When, as sense required, peace had been made up in both disputes, the Prince of Wales was the last, late and unwilling party, his submission to the King sullenly resentful and recognised as sullenly resentful. George Augustus, in the best tradition of the family, levelly hated his father and son who, as observed, were on the fondest of terms with one another. Walpole came into the equation as a former friend who had defected to the enemy.

Interrupted at dinner in his Chelsea home, the Prime Minister hurried to Richmond where he found George in bed. The succinct sentence, 'I am come to acquaint your Majesty with the death of your father', elicited the no more elaborate reply, 'Go to Chiswick and take your directions from Sir Spencer Compton.'[1] Compton was Speaker of the Commons and, more pertinently for the new King, Treasurer to him as Prince of Wales. He was not an opponent of Walpole: no such person could have occupied the chair. He had gone into opposition with him in 1717 and was precisely the sort of amiably inferior politician flourishing without offence under the Robinocracy. Arthur Onslow, his successor and deemed a great Speaker, put it nicely: Compton was 'very able in the chair but had not the powers of speech out of it'.[2]

His reaction to the King's injunction was related with his usual bitchiness by Hervey: 'a plodding, heavy fellow with great application, but no talents . . . his only knowledge forms and precedents and his only insinuation bows and smiles . . . dazzled with the lustre of so bright a prospect.'[3] He was told by the King to prepare a royal address to Parliament, but feeling unequal to the task, he turned to Walpole for a draft. Walpole, having done this in an accomplished way, at the same time obtained a letter from the French Premier, Cardinal Fleury, offering continuing inviolate adherence to the friendly status quo between the countries. Meanwhile Horatio Walpole, ambassador and brother, brought sprinting from Paris to stress the importance of such good relations, underlined the case for keeping hold of nurse.

But despite these shrewd acts, we should not see cool resourcefulness triumphing with masterly insouciance. Walpole had been unnerved. Arthur Onslow is a truthful, unmalicious witness:

> . . . he took me into his arms with a flood of tears that came immediately from him, crying out that the kindness of his friends had drawn a weakness from him which his enemies should never do. He then made me sit down by him, for I was going away, and entered into a long discourse of his ministry, justifying his measures and defying any charge that could be made against him, ending by saying, that everything he had been employed in would devolve upon Mr Compton (which indeed everyone believed, and people crowded during these few days in their resort to him accordingly), [and] seemed to like this destination for Mr Compton, better than for any other person, and declared he would never leave the Court if he could have any office there, and would be content even with the Comptroller's staff.[4]

This is the Walpole of all the anxieties, convinced that his night-mare has become reality. But Compton's own action when he specif-ically declined the Treasury, the fulcrum of power, as he must have understood, fits perfectly the measured judgement of the Treasury Secretary, John Scrope: 'he was frighted with the greatness of the undertaking and more particularly as to what related to money matters'. There being no one to tell Sir Spencer what Lord Stanley would tell Disraeli in 1848 – 'Oh they give you the figures' – Compton faded from George II's calculations. He was also, according to Hervey, supposed to have been made to engage, in the way of the duels of organists fashionable at the time, in a speech-writing competition with Walpole which he, unsurprisingly, lost. Much more important and something equally unsurprisingly omitted by Hervey, is the role of the new Queen.*

Caroline of Ansbach was a clever woman. Sir John Plumb, some-times resembling Hervey in his denigrations, says that she was not as clever as she thought she was. But she appreciated Walpole, who made himself a fast friend. More mature than George, she had long before shrugged off resentments at his compromising with the old King seven years earlier. She thought him the best man around and looked forward to more of his company. The relationship between George II and Caroline was perhaps a better natured (and highly sexual) version of the one enjoyed by the Proudies. George, fulminating in all directions, lacked the Bishop's dithering mildness, but had no more real resolution. Caroline, calmer, subtler than the Barchester lady, but bent on making the decisions, issued few commands, doing it all through her guile and his infatuation.

Any speech contest, if it ever happened, would have been the choice (her choice?) of an obvious territory demonstrating Walpole's superior abilities. Indeed Plumb sensibly doubts how far the nomination of Spencer Compton had gone and how serious it had been. It was an instant response to precipitate information. George needed second thoughts and Caroline was undoubtedly providing them. The first sign of Walpole being back in play came when the King called him in for informal talk about the Civil List. It put both men at advantage, Walpole to make a bid, the new King to get very much improved terms.

---

* Pope described Hervey as her courtier in terminal language: 'Or at the ear of Eve, lasciv-ious toad / Half froth, half venom, spits himself abroad.'

And when, eventually, Walpole resumed his duties, he proposed a pleasant Civil List for the new reign. It augmented George I's £700,000 by the £100,000 already paid to him as Prince of Wales, with another £100,000, found as provision at the King's discretion, for the new heir, Prince Frederick. The opposition had not at this stage counted themselves out of the contest. Pulteney had not denounced Walpole's use of negotiable exchange as inducement for nothing. He made a serious pitch at finding the new man's price. Indeed, he was allegedly the highest bidder, but the bid was not accepted. For a start, there was no guarantee that Walpole's parliament would find the King's money to please Pulteney. And he was badly placed at court, having made the bad mistake, in a serious politician who had to play the court, of having in the old King's lifetime sought to square the younger George by way of his mistress.

This set of Waleses, not the last, had conducted an open marriage, but Caroline, being thoroughly grown up, made no trumpeted difficulties. Fond of George but not of his boring military man's company, she was happy with the hours he spent daily (not necessarily in serial congress) with Mrs Henrietta Howard, an oddly clever woman for a king as patronisingly handled by historians as George II. But this lady of charm and intellect had little taste for political intrigue while Caroline, who did have such interests, had resented Pulteney bypassing her politically.

Walpole took her seriously, talked policy and, like all clever politicians, he listened. When Caroline talked to George she talked Walpole's views and Walpole's interest. The pressures on the new King need no great leap of the imagination. He will have heard her strong-minded case for the status quo on one side, Walpole talking serious money on the other and an intensely uncomfortable Spencer Compton demonstrating his unsuitability in the middle; George's way to retreat and the unsaying of hasty things was clear. Across the period 16–27 June, the crisis cleared itself. Walpole made minor adjustments to his Cabinet, ostentatiously keeping his son-in-law, Malpas, sacked from his Court post, Master of the Robes, as it was George who had sacked him. He also submissively accepted August Schulz, a royal German favourite, in his place, as well as taking on the Court-favoured Chesterfield, too clever and critical-minded to be borne, but employed now with Cabinet rank, if at arm's length, as ambassador to The Hague.

Finally, the restored Premier saw to it that everything ended happily for Compton: Paymaster General with its free money option and a barony as Lord Wilmington. But he was shrewdly taken out of the chair, which fell to the consoling Onslow. At something slightly more than a bound, Jack was free/Robert was back. But he was in a game with new players, a rejuvenated opposition and with many conflicts in store, the first of which, in accordance with the practice of the day, was the general election, following the death of a monarch.

> I am to acquaint you that Parson Bedford has secured one hundred and fifty votes at Tregony (for one vote) at £5 each vote; I find he has been tampered with and some overtures have been made to him by a merchant in London who purposes to disburse the money, making his wife a present of plate and preferring his son, Thomas, to the command of a ship of 40 guns; this proposition is so far agreeable. I see he is fixed in the single resolution (viz.) if his son Thomas Bedford cannot by you be made a lieutenant of a man of war, you must put an equivalent in his hands, in lieu of the lieutenancy; otherwise ... he will not now trust to any man's honour and this he tells me he wrote to you about.[5]

Something of the flavour of the 1727 election, indeed of all Walpolean elections, is caught by this message from his agent, Wolbridge, to the Prime Minister after working Tregony, an open and wonderfully corrupt borough in Cornwall. He goes on to mention a comptrollership 'of the coynage of *illegible* which if you had not before now given away, would the grant of that office do?'[6] The election was conducted on a straightforward market basis, with the agent listing his expenditure. Mrs Bedford had been seen right with a piece of government plate costing £20. At Michell (St Michael's?) thirty-four voters had been purchased for £30 each, total expenditure coming to £1620. At Grampound, forty-one votes had been bought, again at £30; while the purchase of three magistrates had cost twice the rate while the soul of the Mayor had come at £100.

Politicians fighting general elections were obliged to be in the giving mood, something which put people of influence into the spirit of asking. John Fortescue, an occasional correspondent of Walpole's, relates from Dorsetshire that he had dined yesterday at Puddletown and that in the company was a Mrs Harris who 'I find, would be glad to have it mentioned to you whether among any alterations that may or may hereafter be made, there may not be something or other you might purpose for Mr Harris.' This lady, in asking for things sideways, had a deft touch which speaks the playwright who might have invented her. 'There are, she thinks, Places which must be given to somebody, and which if you thought of it, perhaps you would rather chuse to give to him than another.'[7]

Meanwhile, in Buckinghamshire, Lady Fane has a clear understanding of the Church's true purpose, writing to a friend, Mrs Phillips, who has the Minister's ear, telling her 'that Mr Fane stands for this county. The favour I beg of you is to ask Sir Robert Walpole to speak to Dr Clare, Dean of St Paul's, to give Mr Fane his interest, he having an estate belonging to that Deanery in this county.'[8]

A subsequent footnote to this spiritual enterprise was that Charles Fane's most important backer in Buckinghamshire had been Lord Cobham. In 1733, Cobham would oppose Walpole's most contentious measure, the Excise Bill (see *post* Chapter 12) and be promptly dismissed from his colonelcy of the 1st Life Guards. It was offered to Fane who had voted in favour. 'It would have been,' he said, 'the last thing in my thoughts to have desired a succession arising from the removal of my Lord Cobham, with whom I have lived in the most perfect friendship and from whom I have received several obligations . . . nevertheless . . . I understand it in such a manner as that my duty calls upon me to bury all my scruples in a perfect obedience to his Majesty's gracious disposition.'[9]

Sometimes a local politican sent a practical message explaining that an election had been managed very sweetly in the ministerial interest, coupling this information with a brief résumé of his own credentials and excellences. Sir George Treby, Member for Dartmouth, had been edged from office as a friend of Carteret into a tellership of the Exchequer, and had just been removed, with characteristic ruthlessness, from that remunerated post on George II's accession. His letter from Plympton of 4 August 1727 exemplifies the patient usefulness of an Out working his way back in.

Walpole wants Dr Sayer as his candidate in Totnes. Very well, Sir George 'will recommend Dr Sayer to be chosen at Totnes . . .'. At Plympton, his own family seat, 'I think it is certain I shall be able to bring in Mr Cavendish with myself, tho' my calculations say that he is about four score behind me as matters now stand, they agree Mr Cavendish has a majority likewise, and as I shall be able (if occasion

requires) to fling some second votes on him . . . and as the Mayor is a
tenant of mine and struggling in our interest, you may conclude Mr
Cavendish is safe.'*[10] Having spelt out the extent of Walpole's indebtedness,
Treby concludes by listing his own and his late father's credentials as
elemental Whigs. In 1730 he was returned to his tellership and given the
Mastership of the Household and, having run another, wider, set of seats
at the 1734 election, ended his days as a Lord of the Treasury.

Another of the pleasures of Georgian electioneering related to freemen
boroughs, where the vote lay in the hands of freemen of the town,
something splendidly pure and democratic sounding, apart from the
disposition of local interest brokers to create honorary freemen, portable
voters who, in return for pleasant temporary residence and an agreed
sum, would declare for the right candidate on the hustings. This was
a time when candidates could move easily about between options and,
if they chose to, go for more than one. John Verney, another Whig
candidate, reports that Salisbury did not look good for his brother-in-
law, Anthony Duncombe, Whig candidate in a deplorably honest
constituency which took only those offers helpful to the city. This makes
Verney 'the more solicitous for Radnor' and its eleven hundred freemen.

He seemed to be doing quite well. 'I am already sure of an equality
of legall votes.' But at this point, the two-way dubiety of eighteenth-
century politics asserted itself: 'the returning officer who is Mr Lewis's
Brother [-in-law], has declared that he will return him right or wrong.
They have made two hundred Burgesses[†] within the fortnight and I
dare say will make a thousand if necessary.'[11] Verney wanted Walpole
to warn Lewis off: 'I am persuaded that the least word from you will
make him desist, for he has a place at the Customs House which was
granted to his father for thirty years, and since the death he has enjoyed
the profits of it . . .'

But either Lewis's nerve held or Walpole saw no advantage in discour-
aging a steady loyalist. Lewis's brother-in-law elected him for New
Radnor boroughs and Verney fell back on the family seat. Anthony
Duncombe, having been elected in Salisbury after all, Verney was
returned for the spare family seat of Downton by his brother-in-law.
Meanwhile back at Tregony, the man who had 'tampered with Parson
Bedford', John Goddard, a Portugal merchant, was elected as an

---

* He wasn't
† In fact, freemen.

Independent Whig to drive his own bargains with the Ministry.[12] In fact, generally supportive of the government, he would be rewarded with a remunerative diplomatic mission to the Seville Congress over 1730–31.[13]

The situation at Radnor is instructive. It had been a fief of the Harleys. But with the loss of royal favour and with Oxford in the Tower for three years at Walpole's instigation, his local rival, Lord Coningsby, moved in, but real power slipped to the town bailiff who created the honorary freemen in 1722 to get Thomas Lewis elected. Coningsby's successor, Chandos, had the power to outcreate him, but for whatever reason it was never used, and after desperate chicanery in the 1734 election, Thomas Lewis turned to the Ministry in 1739 seeking a new charter to reshape the borough and its practices to suit himself. The money for this expensive legal undertaking was found from the secret service fund by Robert Walpole. Throughout a dull, remorseless career which lasted till 1761, Lewis remained an undeviating ministerial supporter never once found on an opposition voting list. Effectively he became a franchisee of Walpole and his successors, a man with a licence to print voters. It was a step far beyond the older fiefdom of a local great lord, a deepening and sophistication of corruption, denial of the frailest ghost of representation facilitated with public money.

There were, however, places and men beyond fixing, even by Walpole served by great numbers posting and hasting, like Milton's God, at his bidding. On 7 August, the Duke of Rutland laments to Henry Pelham, rising inoffensively within the system, about 'how ill our affairs go at Preston and how obstinately the whole body of the town is upon chusing Pulteney,* even the officers of the government, so that no way remains, but that of proposing Mr Mordaunt which I apprehend will be difficult and on which head it will be proper to consult Sir Robert Walpole to receive his directions'.[14]

The Duke was Chancellor of the Duchy of Lancaster and Mordaunt was his man, sufficient in many parts of the country to assure respectful election. Realistic despair came from Thomas Ashurst who had found the votes cheap in Preston but already sold: 'May it please your Grace we find the voters generally engaged on one side or the other . . . notwithstanding all the effort we could make, there is not the least probability

---

* This was Daniel Pulteney, William's equally combative brother.

of success. Voters had been given two or two and a half guineas before
we came down.'[15] Mordaunt himself was succinct: 'All I can assure
your grace is that no sum of money can compass this affair . . . and
that bestowed in the most plentiful manner would not gain forty votes.'[16]

The local gentry, nearly all Tory and including significant numbers
of Catholics and Jacobites, had bought early and at an easy price votes
which the men of Proud Preston, strong in such sentiments, would
probably have cast anyway. There was discussion across the correspondence, heroically brazen among the lieutenants of Robert Walpole,
of entering a petition for corruption. But the fact that the other assured
victor, the Dissent-connected Whig, Sir Henry Hoghton, was 'rather
inclined to Pulteney', discouraged the thought. Mordaunt withdrew and
Pulteney and Hoghton were returned unopposed.

In the Pelhams' own territory of Sussex the case was quite otherwise. 'We are here,' he added at the end of a gloomy letter of 10 August
to Walpole about Preston, 'in full joy as to men's minds in this county,
no opposition appearing in any one place where we are in any way
concerned.'[17]

Overall, Walpole did, of course, win again and win with an increased
majority. The Tory part of the opposition had been reduced to less than
130 from 180 seats held previously. And in the county seats, where the
eternal honest country gentleman, saluted by Bolingbroke, stood tall,
they were down from 58 to minority status with 37. Walpole was
playing by rules which allowed of no other result. But it is arguable
that the result was less important; certainly it was less interesting, than
the election. The opposition was no longer one of Queen Anne-fixated
memorialists; it had come to terms with new and different talents which
would make themselves briskly felt.

And during the election they had, all of them, actually been an
opposition, had run a vivacious and injurious press and pamphlet
campaign. There had been indentations wherever any sort of
autonomous electorate subsisted, including a furious shared contest
in the City of London. There would be important defections to come.
What mattered about the 1727 election was that it sent Walpole's
enemies back to Westminster with their morale in a far better state
than their numbers and assured that they could give Robin, as their
ballads cheekily called him, a worse time yet. For reasons which had
been brewing for some time in Vienna, then Madrid and finally Paris,
they would be proved right.

Foreign policy is continuous even when nothing much happens; a trend or long-term shift in that policy is no respecter of returning officers. It goes on before and after elections, sometimes running through them, had in fact been a ministerial obsession for years before the death of George I. Walpole, though he did not, like a later monarch, 'hate abroad', definitely wished that it would go away. Failing that, though too sharp-minded not to keep an eye on things, he never claimed expertise. He relied heavily on a group of people: Stephen Poyntz, a roving man of business with a gift for turning up where things were happening; his ambassador in Vienna, Sir Thomas Robinson, about whom Plumb is unkind, but who seems to have been able to engage the glacial Austrian establishment well enough in helpful dialogue; his brother Horatio, dishevelled, hurried and under-dignified, but at any rate dedicated to the job and devoted to him in the way of a younger brother. Walpole accepted a good deal of what they reported, usually followed uneasily, but reserved to himself a right of intervention, a right which would ultimately precipitate a final crisis with the guide he would choose to follow no longer, Charles Townshend.

The crisis developing for government in the new parliament of 1727, wholly unpleasant as it was, should have surprised no one. Supposedly new developments were only the continuation of a conflict in Europe, simmering nicely for some time, impinging themselves upon Walpole well before the King's death and the election. The pattern of foreign affairs had been determined from 1716 on by George and Stanhope. Marlborough's wars, the Whigs' wars, the wars which the Tories had ended at Utrecht, had been fought in alliance with Austria, otherwise the Holy Roman Empire, the Dutch United Provinces and other, chiefly German, states, Hanover vigorous among them, all in opposition to France. They had been fought because Louis XIV was bent upon expansion by Bourbon inheritance in Spain, hence the name War of the Spanish Succession. And that threat had been enhanced by the option of his expansion north-westward against Flanders.

Getting a north German Protestant king in 1714 meant for England getting a high official of that elaborate structure, the Holy Roman Empire. As noted, George I was High Treasurer of it. As Elector of Hanover, he Pickwickianly elected the Holy Roman Emperor, always by a convention the head of the Habsburg family resident in Vienna.

This Emperor was first among unequals, but not master of them. Relations, especially those of the Protestant states, with their titular and touchy overlord, were delicate and the parties inordinately sensitive. And with Louis repulsed, then, in 1715, dead, the need among them for huddling up with Vienna declined. As for England, the Empire, Austria, whatever it was called, was a remote country whose language nobody, except Carteret, spoke. Marlborough and Prince Eugène had been genuine comrades. But England and the Empire were cold-eyed pragmatists thrown together for an interim which, with precious little notice, the English had ended in 1713.

The war over, Stanhope had seen what Walpole, in opposition after 1717, for his own factitious reasons, had refused to see, that a lasting and mutually comprehending peace with France made most sense for a commercial state. It was equally apparent, given the antipathies *vis-à-vis* the Empire, that relations between those two countries should be correct but very little more. Ironically, this was very much the conclusion reached and the foreign policy looked forward to by Oxford and Bolingbroke when, with a brisk wave, they bought themselves out of Marlborough's war at Utrecht. Equally ironically, Walpole would completely accept this policy on readmission to Stanhope and Sunderland's government; and once he won full power, he showed no hint of wanting to resile from it. As for Horatio, having won the embassy through his campaign of denigration against Carteret and Schaub (see *supra*) he had, if not gone native, certainly become the close and admiring associate of Cardinal Fleury, effective ruler, in his eighth and ninth decades, of France.

Any shift of alliance would be disturbing and Walpole, primarily a domestic politician, relying heavily on his brother's regular intelligence, was loath to make it. *Quieta non movere*, 'Let sleeping dogs lie', is routinely given as his motto. But the kingdoms were not quiet, and the dogs stirred. Commoners like Walpole and Fleury might rule, but royalty meddled. International politics in the first half of the eighteenth century was dynastic: whose son might marry whose daughter in return for what secret protocol, to secure annexation of what province, win succession to whatever throne and do down which neighbour. Not for nothing were the wars of this era named for a succession of successions, Spanish, Polish and Austrian.

It was with such manoeuvres that the British, reliably paranoid and not necessarily wrong, were most concerned. Being done down was something they rather counted on. What to do about it had been a preoccupation of ministers, especially Townshend, in the latter years of George I. The English succession had provoked nothing worse than an election. Borough patrons rewarded, voters paid on the nail, ministers went back to worrying about the foreign threat.

WARS AND RUMOURS OF WARS

A recurring anxiety for British foreign policy had been the dynastic marriage. There had already been an anticipatory infant compact made between the daughter of Philip V and the still underage Louis XV. That had been done by Orléans, himself a potential heir. But when Orléans suddenly died, his successor, the Duc de Bourbon, had eventually reversed policy, dropping, in February 1726, an arrangement provocative to those fearing a personal union of France and Spain, about which Bourbon had his own doubts.

The betrothal had postponed the begetting of an heir to the throne of France which, given the Infanta's age of nine, had been highly theoretical. The termination of the betrothal had in fact been discussed back in 1724.[1] Instead Louis Le Bien Aimé, when ready, would be found another lady, a wife of his own physical maturity, Maria Leszczynska, daughter of the Pretender to the throne of Poland.

By this act, Bourbon had so enraged Spain, in particular Elizabeth Farnese, mother of the ditched Infanta, that she began an elaborate and distinctly eccentric course of diplomatic adventure. Very suitably, its conduct had been entrusted to a semi-freelance diplomat, himself quite eccentric enough. Jan Willem Ripperda, a Dutchman, had already begun much vaguer conversations in Vienna about Austro-Spanish rapprochement. He would now have authority to turn this into a full-scale Treaty of Alliance. It was something accomplished through undertakings of financial subsidy to the strapped and rapacious imperial court, one resting upon unreal ideas of Spanish resources.

This was to be a large and ambitious affair, calculated to break glass in a number of chancelleries, notably the one occupied by Viscount

Townshend. There were to be large commercial understandings, most notably a green light to the accursed Ostend Company to do business on the Spanish Main, *Asiento* country. There would be support for Russian claims in the Baltic, this at a time when the Tsarina Catherine I was talking of using George I's cherished trophies, the counties of Verden and Bremen, as pawns in northern deals.[2]

If this were not provocation enough, the Emperor endorsed, and offered military support in the little matter of Gibraltar. Finally, to round off the diplomatic excess, there was to be another child betrothal, between Don Carlos, younger son of Elizabeth and Philip, and Maria Theresia, daughter of Charles VI. This was a secret clause, meaning that Horatio Walpole, returning from ambassadorial duties to brief the Commons, announced in his review of developments that there was a secret clause.

Maria Theresia was no ordinary princess. She was, despite the Salic law excluding women, the *only* Habsburg candidate. And Charles, denied a son, now lobbied the courts of Europe to have her accepted as heiress presumptive. Under the same treaty, a grateful Spain gave her solemn support for just such an agreed succession, the famous Pragmatic Sanction which would rattle like the chains of Marley's Ghost through the middle decades of the century. One threatened dynastic union was replacing another, something offensive to Lord Townshend and all right-thinking English prejudice.

Actually, the English probably smelled in the prospect of an Austro-Spanish rapprochement more trouble than would ever be made. But they were naturals for overreaction. Spain was an old and valued enemy. Austria, paralytic with protocol and precedence, was an actively intolerant Catholic power, over grand towards the German Protestant states, leaving Protestant minorities ill-treated in her own territories. The 'poor Palatines' were known to the English as refugees come to this country, like the Huguenots, to escape worse intolerance than was ever visited upon the double-taxed English Catholics. A multiple hanging – of ten Protestants in the Polish town of Thorn after riots provoked by the suppression of their schools – did not create a good impression and put English intolerance in perspective.

This factor worked both on street opinion and two successive Kings. Both Georges had been loyal to the Empire, the younger George, an ardent soldier when he got the chance, having fought for them in the late war. But even in George I's time, the Elector of Hanover had become 'one of the acknowledged leaders of German Protestantism and was bound to resist'.[3] The refinement of the Whigs having been at all times the war and alliance party was noted only as a pedantic point. In the distended nostrils of the Schoenbrunn, despite the efforts of Sir Thomas Robinson, England, all of it, was the disloyal ally of Utrecht, also a distinct outsider, a country devoted to commerce and tainted with social mobility. England at this point was an arriviste, risen through trade, Austria, the Lady Catherine de Burgh of Europe.

The quarrel with Spain essentially concerned trade. The British idea of the *Asiento* had been demonstrated by the South Sea Bubble. Sir John Blunt and his associates had pulled in vast, scurrying investment because the purchasers anticipated, with the rest of Britain, huge augmentation of trade, in selling slaves, and acquiring gold, sugar and tropicana from the Spanish Indies and main coast. The fraud of the company's spin and self-promotion did not end a general, slightly more sober belief that in that territory we would do wonderful business.

To Spain, treaty or no treaty, nothing was less welcome. The British, in Spanish eyes, were interlopers, pirates and thieves, Protestant thieves at that. Again, in an age of faith and unreason, it mattered gravely that the takers and keepers of Gibraltar were heretics. It mattered quite as much that Spain, cleansed of Muslims and Jews by Ferdinand and Isabella in the late fifteenth century, should in this small region see Jews invited back by English Protestants. That England should use her usurped position in Gibraltar and (actually more valuable) win Port Mahon in Minorca for all sorts of deals with Spain's Muslim enemies, the rulers of Algiers and Morocco, was one more thorn in the pious crown.[4] The two countries were natural and impassioned enemies whose interests and prejudices worked in comfortable contra-sync.

Essentially the Walpole/Fleury view was that this was all rather silly. One operated quietly and commercially, getting richer and keeping out of fights. To the activist, Townshend, a Spanish–Austrian rapprochement seemed altogether more fearful, a foundation for the sort of military power and interest to threaten quiet and fall over the dogs. Townshend, upholder of the French connection, was also mindful of Austria's freedom, since recent victories over the Turks, from any useful enemies south and east. He envisaged the Austrians concentrating their ambitions in the west, anticipating a large and lasting Spanish–Austrian alliance to recreate the late medieval domains of Charles V. In a midnight fit of the horrors he outlined this scenario in a letter to Newcastle.

Don Carlos, the bridegroom in waiting, was only the younger son of a father in good physical if not mental health. But Townshend liked a nice funeral.

> You know how weak in health king Philip is, and is not likely to be long lived and the Prince of the Asturias [the heir] is in a hectical and consumptive way, so that in all probability, Don Carlos will come to be king of Spain by the time the intended marriage takes place, and being sent to Vienna to be bred up there and having the Austrian dominions joined to the vast territories of Spain may become more formidable to the rest of Europe than ever Charles Vth was by reason of this relation to the Crown of France. The life of the present Christian King is the only direct obstacle to his laying in his claims to that kingdom; if he should dye without heirs as his state of health is far from strong, it is easy to see what resistance the Duke of Orleans and his party will be able to make to the party of Spain and the Austrian territories.[5]

Townshend's mind was working like that of Great Aunt Ada Doom who had seen something nasty in the woodshed and had never been the same since. Philip V, though he would go mad, lived until 1746, outlived by the Prince of the Asturias, while Louis XV would not die until 1774.

Townshend looked to make England secure against the Spanish and Austrians through a preventative alliance, something he would consolidate in 1725. Spain and Austria having come together in the Treaty of Vienna, the Alliance of Hanover would involve Britain, France and Prussia, and employing the cash methods which won elections, Sweden, Denmark and some small German states. Townshend was thinking on a grand scale, fearing in a large way too. The Hanover Alliance was seen as a great coup; it would turn into a burden and one that need never have been taken up.

It looked like insurance, but the premiums were horrid, and preparation for war to keep the peace in pre-nuclear times readily induced preoccupying fear of war itself. What was happening was that Europe was divided between Austria and Spain on the one hand, England and France on the other. But there would linger a recollection, whatever France's current antipathies to a Spain dominated by Elizabeth Farnese, of a family compact – Spanish Borbón with French Bourbon – for which Louis XIV's wars had been fought.

It was also tricky politics at home, playing first into the hands of the steady, sullen resentment of Hanover and Germany – a political constant – Walpole defended his brother-in-law's undertaking. But as its provocative potential grew more evident, he gradually came to resent both – alliance and brother-in-law. The alliance involved an expensive pursuit of those professional escorts, Sweden and Denmark and the soon to be bilking Prussia. And was it not, anyway, an alliance confected against a chimera? Spain and Austria were not going to make a grand Habsburg union. This pre-contract between children was not going to last either. The Emperor Charles would, at a later date, see to that. A writer in *The Craftsman* put the threat of Don Carlos, Emperor from Transylvania to Peru, in delightful perspective. It should be rated, he said, on a level with the Welsh lady who, if an uncle, three brothers and two sons happened to die, might be left a considerable fortune.[6] But it seemed very different and far more menacing at the time.

Events were behaving very badly towards Walpole. He had run into the clamour and costs of war while the opposition, who might otherwise have made speeches about Old England and her older enemies, shook their heads at this dubious imbroglio. They talked instead about restraint and deplored the fearful military expense. The hired Hessian troops in particular made a splendid, two-handed weapon for any opposition. They would cost money and taxes; and though excellent troops, they were undoubtedly foreigners and German foreigners at that.

Furthermore, the country was now to support a standing army, something which, by all their household gods, the Whigs were sworn to resist. Nothing could have been more galling for Walpole than to hear William Shippen in the debate on the Treaty, 24 January 1726, using his own pacific language on this specific point: 'Tis therefore unintelligible to me, how the keeping up an army in time of peace which had formerly been thought criminal advice in Ministers, as being incompatible with our constitution, should now be annually recommended to Parliament by our modern patriots, as the only method of securing us in the possession of our laws and liberties.'

Shippen was speaking against the raising of what the government now euphemistically called 'Land Forces'. He continued in Walpole's own best vein. Great Britain enjoyed at present 'a happy and perfect tranquillity which seemed firmly secured by the late disarming of the highlands of Scotland and, on the other hand, it having been unanimously resolved to enable his Majesty to have a strong fleet at sea early in the spring, this, they thought sufficient for the safety and defence of the kingdom'.[7] He was voicing Walpole's own secret thoughts and, following his consistent instincts, something the Prime Minister denied in his teeth. Too grown-up for such futilities, he had been compelled to make more than a show of readiness. Those mercenaries must be hired, hearts of Hessian oak, money found and the country prepared for a high-tax, trade-losing war.

It was all very vulgar, but there was something in both the geography and the preliminary hysteria, premonitory of the lead-up to the War of Jenkins's Ear (1739), not least in a situation involving a British Admiral (Hosier this time, Vernon on the later occasion) off the South American coast. Francis Hosier was placed to be neither privateer nor proper combatant, only to stand watch while the Spanish Fleet brought back its silver and England's claims on *Asiento* trade grew ever more rhetorical. And there was a key difference. The bellicose talk came from the Ministry and would be nicely echoed in the loyal address of the House of Lords on 20 January at the start of the 1726 session:

> It is no surprise to us that the enemies to your Majesty's person and government are labouring to disturb the peace of this kingdom, if they can flatter themselves with the prospect of any new troubles or commotions in Europe. We can easily believe that at such a juncture, new schemes and solicitations are daily making by the most profligate and abandoned of them to revive the expiring cause of the Pretender; all of which we assure ourselves can have no other effect than to hasten his destruction and the utter ruin of his perjured adherents.[8]

This was fighting talk, and, for the present, Walpole was the prisoner of Townshend's actions, actions endorsed by no one more vehemently than his man in Paris, Ambassador Walpole. Horatio had bought the whole Austrian threat line and would speak fervently upon it to the Commons. The treaty of Peace at Vienna

> was soon followed by a treaty of Commerce, the main design of which was to support and countenance the East India Company some years before established at Ostend by granting to the inhabitants of the Austrian Netherlands greater privileges both in the East and West-Indies than were ever granted to the English or Dutch which visibly tended to the entire ruin

of many valuable branches of our trade and was contrary to several solemn
treaties still in force . . .

And, of course, when our people had protested in Vienna and Madrid,
they had been snubbed. For

> at the court of Madrid, these complaints were received with coldness, and
> at that of Vienna, with stiffness and haughtiness, even to such a degree that
> the imperial Ministers did not stick to insinuate that if his Britannic majesty
> persisted in his resolution to take measures in opposition to the Treaty of
> Vienna, his Imperial Majesty would not only think himself disengaged from
> the guarantee of the Protestant succession to the Crown in Great Britain;
> but that the same might be attended with consequences in relation to his
> Majesty's dominions in Germany . . .

As for the 'match between the Emperor's eldest daughter and the
Infante Don Carlos', Townshend's nightmare went public:

> . . . it was easy to foresee the consequences of such a marriage. For the issue
> male that might come of it, might in time be possessed not only of all the
> hereditary dominions belonging to the House of Austria and of the imper-
> ial dignity, but also of all the dominions of the Spanish monarch which
> would entirely overthrow the balance of power and render the liberties of
> Europe very precarious.

The Hanover Alliance had been created, said Horatio in high style,
'to give a timely check to the further progress of such dangerous
designs . . . to maintain and preserve the public repose and tranquillity of Christendom'.[9] But such expenditure, undertaken in semi-panic,
lent itself to opposition ribaldry and invested the Tories with the
Whig virtues, the party for the moment of, at any rate, peace and
retrenchment.

And unfortunately, the wild swerve into war-readiness was taking
place precisely as the opposition was being augmented. Shippen was
now joined by more polished and injurious talents. Pulteney's split from
Walpole was complete, Bolingbroke was hovering in the background, a
demon king in waiting. And it was Pulteney who intervened (9 February
1726), demanding a Committee of Inquiry into Public Debts, specifically to state the public debts as they stood on 25 December 1714 as

against 25 December 1724. The purpose was to distinguish 'how much of the said debts have been provided for and how much remains unprovided for by Parliament'. That, said a rattled Walpole, was 'unseasonable and preposterous . . . it might give a dangerous wound to public credit at this critical juncture when monied men were already but too much alarmed by the appearances of an approaching war . . .'.[10]

He was supported by Barnard, one of the City Members, an independent, spokesman for the small traders of London and no friend of the Prime Minister, who said that 'stocks were within a few weeks fallen 12l or 14 per cent'.[11] The exchanges then grew satisfyingly personal, Pulteney saying that he had raised the motion 'with no other view than to give that great man an opportunity to shew his integrity to the whole world which would finish his sublime character'.

Walpole, baring his teeth, thought that 'this compliment would have come out with a better grace and appeared more sincere when the fine gentleman had himself a share in the management of the public money than now he was out of place'.[12] So there! He had no trouble getting his majority, 285 to 107. But the men who would strengthen Pulteney's hand in future, Samuel Sandys, Sir Joseph Jekyll, Master of the Rolls, and Pulteney's clever brother, Daniel, had joined him. As we have seen, Daniel Pulteney would soon be the object of intense efforts to separate the stubborn voters of Preston from him.

And anyway, a parliamentary triumph in an imploding cause is an uncertain victory. The conflict behind the financial anxieties and the personal knockabout was the product of misperception. Townshend was a distinguished specialist in foreign affairs, Horatio a hard-working diplomat, but both had indulged retrospection and projection. They confused Charles VI, who had limited means and aspirations, with Charles V who, two hundred years before, had dominated Europe.

The Pragmatic Sanction, assent by the powers to Maria Theresia's right to inherit an elective crown, was no more than that, a keeping of things in the family. It was not the foundation of European domination. Charles had anyway intended a marriage between Carlos and Maria Theresia only if he had had a son to remove her from the direct line of succession. Prince Eugène, elder statesman, conscious from his long wartime associations of the value of a British connection, now began to assert himself in Vienna.[13] The Spanish Alliance rested upon wild financial promises from Ripperda to the Austrians which he had no right to give and Spain no means to pay. This Dutch wild card was discarded in disgrace, at one stage bizarrely seeking asylum in the British embassy. There had been, all along, a fantastic quality to the whole undertaking. But its discomfiture did not end the Anglo-Spanish state of war.

There was something which Pulteney could exploit in the Commons and in that recently launched (December 1726) busy, much-talked-about and distinctly classy *Craftsman*. He had had contacts of his own which the government, with its penchant for opening other people's letters, knew about. He was close to Baron Palm, the Austrian Minister, from whom he learned of the limitations of the Treaty of Vienna, readiness for negotiation over the Ostend Company and, importantly, the significance of George I's interest in acquiring the small but agreeable duchies of Berg and Julich. Like almost everything else at this taut, war-threatened time, that was less important than it was made out to be. But 'Julich and Berg' were words to be set to a favourite Tory tune: the German King, servile ministers in attendance, dragging sovereign Englishmen into German quarrels over his exclusively German interests, the Alliance of Hanover – an alien imposition confected by foreigners for foreigners with help from the Walpoles.

All that had to be said obliquely if one were not to be sent, as Shippen had once been, to the Tower. But that was unnecessary; the trick was to ask embarrassing questions quite politely. Were not the imperial court pretty indifferent to the Pretender with whom Walpole was always threatening everyone? Would the government please make available papers from their representatives in Spain and Austria? Had the King promised to give up Gibraltar back in 1721? (He had come pretty close.) This last impertinence came from the troublemaking Samuel Sandys in a separate debate on the 'Land Forces'. Sandys moved that

> an humble address be presented to his Majesty that he would be graciously pleased to communicate to this House copies of the Declaration, letter or engagement which in the Marquis De Pozzobueno's letter to the Duke of Newcastle of the 21st of December last, is asserted to be a positive promise upon which the King of Spain founds his peremptory demand for the Restitution of Gibraltar . . .

Sir Thomas Hanmer, Hanoverian Tory, spoke the language of sceptical moderation, observing:

> if the dangers they were threatened with were so real and so imminent as
> some people pretended, he would be one of the foremost in the most speedy
> and most vigorous resolutions. But that he thought those dangers yet extreme
> distant, to say no more – that indeed some foreign Princes may make a
> political use of the Pretender as a state bug-bear to frighten and alarm us
> and thereby make us subservient to their ambitious designs; but in his
> opinion, his [the Pretender's] interest was never so low, nor to his party so
> inconsiderable and so despicable as at present and therefore in this day's
> debate he ought to be left intirely [sic] out of the question . . .

The mistakes, said Hanmer, were really our own (he might have said
'the King's' but didn't), adding:

> that he was apprehensive the acquisition of some dominions abroad had
> sown the seeds and were the true causes of the divisions and distractions
> which now threaten the tranquillity of Europe, by drawing us into unac-
> countable compliances with the emperor on the one hand and into a promise,
> at least a conditional one, for the restitution of Gibraltar on the other hand,
> both which had brought us at last into the present difficulties.[14]

Sir William Wyndham got quickly enough to the point when he
compared foreign policy with the labours of Odysseus's wife: 'Penelope-
like, we were continually weaving and unravelling the same web; at
one time to raise up the Emperor to depress France, and now we were
for depressing the Emperor which could not be done without aggran-
dizing France . . . under pretence of holding the Balance of Europe, we
should be engaged in continental wars.' That would prove true in the
middle distance with the wars of the early forties and the Seven Years
War, begun 1756, though England would do very nicely out of them,
especially the latter. But Wyndham was telling the secrets of Walpole's
heart, relating his own deepest fears.

The Prime Minister got his majority safely enough in the debate on
the address, with only eighty-one unpatriotic enough to vote against.
But this was the sort of support attaching to any government close to
war, the customary rallying ardently round in the face of the evidence.
His own speech was thin, a distancing of himself personally from any

offer on Gibraltar, effectively passing the charge to the King and a
defence against charges that he might have moved diplomatically over
the Ostend Company.

It would, he said, have been 'highly imprudent and impolitic in us
to quarrel with the emperor', something which came strangely from a
man rearming for a quarrel with the Austrians *now* when they insisted
that, at all relevant times, they had been open to negotiation. And like
many a man in a fix, Walpole jumbled time sequences, conflating recent
bellicose Austrian talk during the Ripperda episode into a debate about
our earlier secret compliance with them. Patriotism, always a handy
refuge around dinnertime, got him through. In fact, there had been
such an offer, one made by Stanhope; though with typical brass neck,
surrender of Gibraltar had been contemplated in terms of a swap,
perhaps for Florida! And George I, not being properly British, had
talked to the Spanish about possibly giving the Rock up without a deal
– at some time in the future, if the Lords and Commons should agree;
a likely story.

What did resonate to Walpole's advantage was a memorandum from
the Austrian Minister, Palm, in Latin, but not less offensive for that,
denying British charges of secret articles supporting the Pretender in
the Treaty between Spain and Austria. Unhelpful phrases swam there,
'. . . with what view, on what motive and to what purposes these infor-
mations, founded on the falsest reports, is not only easy to be understood by his Imperial and Catholic Majesty, but is obvious to the
meanest capacity'.

As the comedian says, 'It's the way you tell 'em.' And Palm's grandil-
oquent scorn directed at the King of England was Vienna at its least
gemütlich. Denunciation of Palm by the Commons on 15 March and
his expulsion from St James's followed pleasantly. But the victory was
parliamentary. The actual crisis continued, as did the prospect of war.

The land siege, however ragged, continued behind Gibraltar. Hosier
was still annoying a Spanish fleet, but not actually succeeding in his
purpose of blocking the carriage of treasure from the Americas. But
there was, too, a problem for Charles VI. If the Hanover Alliance was
a burden in England, his own growing Vienna grouping rested upon
Spanish subsidies which were not going to happen.

There would also be, in June 1726, a decisive shift in France. Cardinal
Fleury had been a major player at the French court for some time. But
shortly after Ripperda's fall in June 1727, Fleury, to the delight of

Horatio Walpole, replaced Bourbon as First Minister. Fleury was the complete player of the diplomatic game without ever thinking it anything so trivial as a game. Letting everybody down in the nicest possible way was his chief art. Given power, he would combine maximum humouring of the English through the susceptible Horace with an elaborately polite refusal to get involved, Hanover Alliance or not, in a British war with Spain. At the same time, while being equally pleasant to Spain, he did not actually do anything for Spanish war aims over Gibraltar.

Fleury was also mindful of the Emperor's isolation and wanted to add to it. Charles was fearful of Spain settling without him and with Maria Theresia's crown unresolved. Charles knew that Fleury knew it and knew also that the Cardinal could influence either way the immature rulers of Spain: Philip who, in 1727 would go mad, and the mercurial Queen Elizabeth Farnese. If England's conflict with Spain became war, it ought under the terms of the Alliance of Hanover to have brought in France. Walpole personally would have settled for loud military music, Fleury was even less disposed to war and had anyway neither good reason nor intention even to contemplate fighting the Spanish to please the British. He played on his excellent relations with Horatio and did everything to direct British greed overseas.

Was not the British interest in the East Indies, with those profitable trading posts threatened by landlocked Vienna, cutting itself into the eastern trade which everyone knew to be finite? The British really should worry about the Ostend Company. Through the golden filter of hindsight (and free trade) the Ostend Company was no sort of threat; as for Gibraltar, it was at least as much hostage as foothold. Sense had so far been an option. However, by concentrating on it, Fleury did two things. He intimated non-compliance in action against Spain and invited the English to push at a door standing ajar. They were invited to ask for what they would get.

Charles wanted the Pragmatic Sanction above all things and would give up without grief those lesser matters which, so Townshend had persuaded the House of Commons, the British nation and himself, were the pillars of his diabolic plot. Time was passing; by the spring of 1727, the Hanover–Vienna standoff of alliances would have been running, expensively, for two years. What was wanted, thought Fleury, was a conference and what better place for a conference than Paris?

He knew what he was doing, which gave him a distinct advantage over everybody else. The Emperor just knew that he was badly overextended. The English wanted assuagement of their anxieties and justification for the taxes they had raised. The Ostend Company was perfect. It had originally been undertaken in the interests of certain Jacobites, for whose fortunes imperial concern was minimal. It didn't matter. Which was why Fleury made so much of it. Perhaps to a central European imagination less comfortably landlocked and to a ruling court less scornful of trade, it would have mattered. But it had never been the spear aimed at England's commerce (and thus heart) as Fleury had slyly suggested and which the more frantic Englishmen had always supposed. Suspending it for seven years was easy for Charles and a great, deft contribution to peace. It was sufficient then to wrap this up in 'the Preliminaries of Paris' and agree on a grander, more comprehensive congress, to be held, still in honest-broking France, at Soissons. All that was agreed and signed on 31 May (New Style) 1727. On 11 June (New Style) George I died. But however much George II disliked his father, he had no quarrel with events.

Unfortunately, the next events were less encouraging. The insanity of Philip V, coming soon after, did nothing to help, putting in authority, as official governor of the kingdom, Elizabeth Farnese. This was the same Italian lady who wanted the Italian territories of Parma and Piacenza returned to her adoptive country, a point to which she kept coming back. But she concentrated for the moment on her quarrel with the English, valiantly increasing the stakes, seizing, aptly enough, the *Prince Frederick*, one of ours, about which we were understandably agitated. It was intended as ransom for Hosier removing himself from Spanish waters. The Spanish quarrel now looked like a war crisis in draft.

Britain was in conflict with Spain as an unwelcome Mediterranean power, Gibraltar plus Port Mahon in Minorca, the best harbour in the sea. She was no better regarded for her semi-piratical role in the West Indies and off the coast of South America. Tit for tit may be a foolish game, but the Queen of Spain was inclined to it. Spain made ready to blockade Gibraltar. Seizing the *Prince Frederick* simply deepened the risk. This was, in England, the sort of thing to fire up opposition news sheets and alert the permanent party for war, any war.

Nor did the arrival as French Foreign Minister of Germain-Louis Chauvelin extend good feeling. Replacing the Comte de Morville, long serene on £4000 a year of British bribes,[15] Chauvelin was fashioned to make English headlines. A bristling adventurist and French patriot, he was never a patriot for us. Though how far he was hired by Fleury to do aggressive things over which the Cardinal could shake his head to Horatio, a Jorkins run by Spenlow, is a nice point.

For Chauvelin, the *Prince Frederick* was diplomatic real estate; it enraged the British by demonstrating their impotence and kept Anglo-Spanish ill will just below combustion. Nothing would do for British opinion, parliamentary and public, but that the ship was returned to this country. Fleury's private attempts to have a neutral take it were rejected here. Hosier was staying where he was – not that he was having much effect – until we got it back. As for the Preliminaries of Paris, they could stay preliminary. War now looked vastly more likely, driving Walpole to the political equivalent of spitting in his own soup. To pay for it, he raised the Land Tax paid by his beloved country gentlemen to four shillings in the pound.

Relations with Spain during what has been called 'the Cold War of 1727–1729'[16] were as bad as relations get. British consuls had been withdrawn from every Spanish city where they had served, and the South Sea Company's single annual ship to the Main had been arrested. On the other hand, the British cheerfully kept up the trade based on our own West Indian islands with those of Spanish America, working the prevailing winds through Cuba, Puerto Rico and Hispaniola, whose governors organised coastal protection against such trade. This was intensified with police actions by the Spanish against the larceny of Britain's unilateral free trade.[17] As for bringing the Spanish siege of Gibraltar and non-compliance on *Asiento* trade to an end, in 1727, Hosier, most melancholy of British naval heroes, on watch for so long outside Portobello as well-protected bullion ships sailed past, finally, with most of his sailors, died of yellow fever. He would be commemorated wittily and at the Ministry's expense in a rollicking piece, 'Admiral Hoiser's Ghost', by the Hamburg merchant, opposition supporter and balladeer, Richard Glover.

It is the way of drawn-out conflicts to damage judgement and do political harm. And the Soissons Congress was one of the ways in which conflict would be drawn out. It left English ministers frustrated, economically pressed and looking ineffective, as indeed they were. Meanwhile, the sharp and pertinent opposition comments, chiefly in *The Craftsman*, make an excellent chronicle of events and mood. They highlighted pacific rhetoric and burdensome war-spending coming to resolution neither by treaty nor engagement. Though we had flattered ourselves that with prospects of accommodation and have talked nothing but Peace for almost a year past, yet we have actually been under most of the Calamities of a War, not only with regard to the expense of it, but also by the loss of a multitude of ships and the interruption of a most beneficial trade which can only enable us with any tolerable ease to bear the burthen of a war.

Whereas our allies, the French, have all this time been talking nothing but War, and yet have continued in a state of almost profound Peace, and the Dutch who have not seem'd in their speeches much less forward for hostilities, have never the less remained in the same happy state of tranquillity, uninjured in their Manufactures at home and unmolested in their commerce abroad.[18]

Whoever wrote that essay was at once blaming Walpole as principal dragger of military feet and proclaiming Walpole's own deepest discontent at endless expenditure. The author was also making hay in a favourite Tory meadow by blaming the French: 'But if the conjectures of the world are true with regard to our French Allies, it were to be wished that this matter might be brought to hastie *éclarcissement*, for the whole turn of these affairs depends entirely on the sincerity or insincerity of those in whom we have so long confided.'[19]

The French dimension was Townshend's inheritance from Stanhope. Its advocate, not to say cheerleader, was Horatio Walpole. But look, said the paper, how long Fleury's supposedly friendly diplomacy is taking. *The Craftsman* wanted things brought to a crisis. 'Keeping off the Bad Day,' it added sententiously, in the same piece, 'was always a dangerous maxim.' Also, that crisis should be forced before the opening of Parliament mindful of the estimates, 'because if we remain in the same uncertain state at this time, we shall be obliged to keep up the same Forces by sea and land for another year, and consequently the same heavy taxes will be continued to us . . .'.

Not content with all this, *The Craftsman* went fishing. Anticipating the furious parliamentary explosion which would throw Walpole back on his heels in 1730, it slyly hinted on 30 September at possible problems over that God-given harbour for French naval invasions of England, Dunkirk. 'Private letters from Dunkirk,' it murmured inconsequentially, mid-column, 'take notice that the harbour of that Place is so far opened (by the tides, it is said) as to admit vessels of a considerable Burthen.' 'The fortifications of the city of Dunkirk,' so the ninth article of the

Treaty of Utrecht had recorded in menacingly pedantic detail, were to 'be razed, the Harbour to be filled up and the sluices or Moles which serve to cleanse the Harbour to be levelled.' The terms had been negotiated fourteen years earlier by Matthew Prior, the plenipotentiary sent to Utrecht by the then Secretary of State, a Viscount Bolingbroke. The thought of a war Whig, as Walpole had been, a denouncer of Utrecht as betrayal of our victories, actually letting its terms lapse through negligence was an irony not lost on the former exile at the Pretender's court.

The role of *The Craftsman* was, in concerned terms, to torment the government, alternating a shocked appraisal of mounting costs with the sounding of a new, hard-to-switch-off alarm. Perhaps conflict with the Empire had not lapsed. 'Letters from Vienna bring advice that his Imperial Majesty hath ordered new levies be made in all his hereditary countries, and commanded his whole army ready to contest the field by April next in case of an open rupture; and it is added that they talk no more of peace there or of sending plenipotentiaries to the Congress [of Soissons].'[20]

Pulteney and Bolingbroke had another device to make ministerial flesh creep. In 'the latest Amsterdam *Gazette*', the writers had found 'an expedient upon the carpet'. It was

> for terminating all the differences between Great Britain and Spain which retard the public negotiations of these matters by intirely [*sic*] demolishing Gibraltar and razing all its fortifications, and that the Emperor, King of France and the States General be appointed guaranties [*sic*] that they shall never be repaired and that the Road shall be open for all the trades of Europe'.[21]

The mood of low, bubbling belligerence which the Tory/Patriot alliance wanted, both to undermine market confidence in Walpole and keep up taxes, involved a nice balance of foreign dastardliness and gallant island provocation. So they related how Spain was threatening us in the Americas. 'The King of Spain hath trumpt up new difficulties concerning our usurpation, as it is called, of the island of Providence over building a fort on the coast of Florida and possessing ourselves of a Settlement in the Bay of Campeachy . . .' On the other hand, British tars were pulling Spanish noses. 'Sir Charles Wager with the British squadron under his command keeps cruising in the Bay of Cadiz which gives great unease to the inhabitants of those coasts.'[22]

But when peace loomed at the end of the year with Spanish ratifi-
cation of the Paris Preliminaries, *The Craftsman* hid its regrets behind
a scatter of brilliant light fire. Its envoy took a stroll through London,
finding

> Exchange Alley a mere Babel of Noise, Hurry and confusion – The BULLS
> tossed their heads on High and roared in triumph for the Victory . . . whilst
> the poor humbled BEARS sank their miserable crests and bit the ground
> with extremity of anguish . . . yet I observed a general Discontent and
> Lamentation about the place upon the prospect of peace which would, by
> ending the fluctuation of stocks, in a great measure put an end to their
> game and would not serve their ends half so well as either an actual war
> or that uncertain precarious state which we have been in for above these
> two years past.

The writer next looked in upon his friends near the Temple

> where I popt [*sic*] my head into Dick's Coffee House [a noted resort of
> Tories] where I found a cluster of honest Country Gentlemen smoking their
> pipes round the great table, expressing themselves in highest raptures on
> the present pattern of affairs . . . They seemed to make no doubt that the
> Empire and the king of Spain would be obliged to refund us all the expenses
> which we have been at and make full restitution . . . that the Army would
> be immediately reduced, the four shillings in the pound taken off from the
> Land and perhaps some part of last year's subsidies remitted to the people
> as it was in the golden days of Queen Elizabeth.

Finally, on visiting 'several military coffee houses near Charing
Cross', the traveller checked the mood of 'the gentlemen of the Blade',
finding that 'several gay young volunteers (who have for this year
past constantly attended Mr Figg's Amphitheatre*), have, all of a
sudden, laid aside their terrible faces and discharged the Fencing
Master'.[23]

The plague of the late 1720s was one of conflicts moving laboriously to resolution with costs mounting and taxes imposed while fears
suddenly rang out like faulty alarms. *The Craftsman*, cheerfully pursuing

---

* James Figg, bare-knuckle prize-fighting champion of all England, also a celebrated stave
and sword fighter, kept an academy to teach these refinements.

its own agenda, was quick to publicise them, greeting the congress at Soissons with another bite at the Dunkirk cherry, announcing:

> an affair of the utmost importance to Great Britain in every respect viz. the Reparation of the Harbour at Dunkirk to which we hope his Most Christian majesty [Louis XV], our faithful ally, did never give the least countenance since his great predecessor thought fit to consent in the most solemn manner to its demolition and stipulated that *it should never be a harbour again*; but as we some time ago saw an article which said in one of our newspapers, that the inhabitants of the Town have petitioned their Sovereign for this purpose . . . and as we have repeated intelligence from persons coming from thence that the harbour is actually open'd so much as to receive ships of considerable burthen and that the inhabitants take all opportunities to clear it. I hope it will not be thought improper to take notice of it and recommend it to the eyes of my superiors as a matter which ought to be looked into.[24]

Bolingbroke had good French sources and was widely suspected of having excellent contacts among French ministers. He might mock the Ministry for failing to resist French incursions, but his great friend and frequent guest at Dawley Farm was Théodore Chavigny, the French ambassador, a good friend of the unspeakable Chauvelin. Chavigny was moreover constitutionally allergic to Walpole. His closeness to Bolingbroke and the opposition put Horatio into a rage: 'He lives, eats and drinks with the enemies of the King's government and after a bottle, carries his liberty as far as to joyn with them, as we are informed, in talking treason . . .'[25]

As for Dunkirk, at this time it amounted only to a few paragraphs of graceful trouble-making. But its day would come; that coastal town was already, in 1728, a matter of quiet concern to ministers. Newcastle, Secretary of State for the Southern Department, had directed the engineer, Colonel John Armstrong, in earnest detail to check everything. His letter of commission required Armstrong 'to repair forthwith to Dunkirk and there in conjunction with such engineers, officers and pilots as we shall appoint for your assistance as you shall think proper to advise with, take the best measures for seeing the 9th article of the Treaty of Peace between us as above recited, executed in all things according to the true intent and meaning thereof'.[26]

Every complaint about the deviousness of Fleury and the French way

of graceful non-compliance would be illustrated in the correspondence
between Secretary of State and examining engineer. Armstrong was, by
agreement of both governments, to work with a Dutch engineer,
Cronstroem, and a French one, Riccoumel, to check the condition of
the harbour and fortifications. (Cardinal Fleury had been very emphatic
about the complete openness of the undertaking.)

The French technique was a mix of Kafka and 'I can't do that without
authorisation'. Armstrong found himself 'not a little surprised this
morning when I went to make my compliments to the Marquis
D'Alemba, Commander of the Garrison . . . when he asked the occasion of my being here . . . He had no knowledge of M. Riccoumel's
orders, nor had he communicated the least little of them to him that
was commandant of this place and his department being in that of M.
D'Argenvilliers, Secretary of State.'[27]

Armstrong, evidently a sensible, good-tempered, practical man, an
engineer in fact, reported on 5 September reassuring information. The
channel was 'not above half the Breadth that it formerly was and in
many places not above one third, and it is not above one ten feet deep
upon the Niep [neep tide] and thirteen in the spring tides so that a ship
drawing ten foot of water on the Niep cannot come in'.[28] But he would
later report new fortification and sluices contravening the treaty.
Ministers began at once to send off letters to Armstrong himself and
to their embassy officials who in turn set imperiously about French
ministers, to, it seems, no great effect.

The long-running British ministerial/official conversation involving
Newcastle, Horatio Walpole, Harrington (Townshend's successor),
Stephen Poyntz, Lascelles (Armstrong's close colleague), with Fleury
and assorted official Frenchmen hovering unhelpfully, had the qualities
of eternity. Demolition work was demanded, the demand transmitted
and pondered. Compliance was something else. The actual work of
demolishing anything proceeded on the basis of 'Right, said Fred', with
M. de la Blandinière, the contractor, as Fred.

'On the 14th [April 1730],' says Harrington to Poyntz, nearly two
years after Armstrong's commission, 'we spoke to the Cardinal in the
strongest terms about M. de la Blandinière's not having yet begun to
execute his orders by Demolishing [sic] such works as appeared by his
own report to be contrary to the Treaty'.[29] The Duke, writing to
Harrington and Poyntz a fortnight later, says optimistically, 'You will
insist that immediate and effectual order for their being forthwith

demolished.' He adds, 'It is now 2 months since the order was given to M. de la Blandinière and nothing material has yet been done in consequence of it.'[30]

Lascelles writes to the Duke two days later: 'I continue daily to importune and press M. de la Blandinière to put his orders in execution, but with no better success than I have hitherto had, he pretending that he hath received no further orders from the Court, without which, he says, he cannot begin the demolition.' It goes on. As late as 1733, there is a note in the archive from Lascelles about difficulties over the sluices.

The overall picture at this time, mid-1728, was of the Soissons Congress grinding its elaborate way to little effect, the opposition making hay, ministers laughed at, a sense of futility and mounting costs. And if there was a loser in all this, it was Townshend. He had been both dogmatist and alarmist, taking the Bubble at full proclaimed value. As both the expert and Walpole's intimate, his nightmare perceptions had been taken up and followed. The Austrian conflict had receded, but that was the one which he had overstressed. As the fizz of early war talk ran flat in a bottle opened too soon and Prince Eugène's good sense gained ground with the Emperor, any credit Townshend might have won was diminished.

He had been the internationalist, heir to Stanhope's large-visioned policy, but with an edge of decisiveness, the resolute approach. And much good it had done us. The Welsh lady would not indeed inherit a considerable fortune, but an elaborate undertaking, expensive in bribe money to petty rulers, had been erected for a side issue. Peace had been proclaimed at Paris but the Spanish struggle for the gains of Utrecht, the *Asiento*, slaves and gold, went on. And as we settled into this treacle marsh, the abominable Chauvelin was laughing up his sleeve. Townshend's hostility to Austria had almost certainly strengthened her ally, Spain. He was guilty of too much foresight. In consequence, never mind international treaties, understandings between kings and emperors, a domestic alliance of Norfolk men going back to Queen Anne's time had frayed till it snapped. In May 1730, Townshend went.

It is not necessary to accept Hervey's judgement – sycophant putting down dropped colleague – that 'a great mortification to Lord Townshend's pride was the seeing and feeling every day that Sir Robert Walpole who came into the world, in a manner, under his protection and inferior to him in fortune, quality and credit, was by force of his infinitely superior talents, as much above him in power, interest, weight, credit and reputation'. There is an arguable case that Townshend's active foreign policy had worked, however painfully. The Ostend Company would be discontinued, the dynastic marriages would not take place. In terms of heading off everything that Spain or the Empire might have done faced with a passive Britain, preoccupied with domestic tax levels, Townshend had a case. But it had all been too uncertain, taken too long, cost too much and cut too deep against the conflict-avoiding, surplus-accumulating grain of Sir Robert Walpole.

There was another unexpected factor. The Duke of Newcastle, whom George II, when Prince of Wales, had called 'not fit to be a chamberlain in a second-rate German court',[31] had started to shed the deference to Townshend which had made the Viscount treat the Duke as a discountable cipher, not to be consulted on things that mattered even when, like the Spanish negotiations, they fell into Newcastle's own southern territory. Newcastle was a younger man, only thirty-one when he had been appointed after Carteret's demotion. He was courteous and kindly, his letters full of concern for subordinates, and he lacked self-esteem, something which, rather than sycophancy, explains his whole style.

But he had put up with a very great deal from the seigneurial Townshend. And Newcastle could think for himself. He was moving away from Townshend's certainties. In a paper of 1727 he had characterised Austria's behaviour as, though objectionable, much less so than that of Spain. Townshend, by contrast, was describing the Emperor's rule as 'Despotick'.[32] Newcastle was mildly alert to Fleury's combination of eloquent assurance and practical inertia, observing in 1728 that 'He may not always act with that vigour and firmness with which he sometimes talks.'[33]

And, increasingly, Walpole was at odds with Townshend. In 1729 they had almost come to blows. Friendship was breaking up for sure, but their *policy* dispute was not simply a matter of costs and delay. Walpole, like Newcastle, worried much more about France than Townshend, for whom the French understanding was a fixture. Walpole, fearful that Chauvelin's Anglophobia would find an outlet, was ready for friendly gestures toward the Emperor who, not getting her subsidies, was cooling towards Spain. In such a climate, the idea of Britain (and Hanover) actually endorsing the Pragmatic Sanction, which Townshend saw as commitment to a future war, became a serious prospect, the price of separating the Empire from Spain.

Townshend was right, of course. Prussia under Frederick William I had already, in 1726, double-crossed the Hanover Alliance and changed sides on getting a better price from Vienna. She would double-cross Vienna again in 1740 when his son, Frederick II, set about getting his hands on Silesia, driving all accepters of the sanction to war. In 1731, when Townshend was back at Raynham improving turnip yields, Walpole would authorise signature of the second Treaty of Vienna which accepted the Sanction.*34

But that was in the future, 1742. Being prescient was no help to Townshend in 1728–30. And he had shown no prescience at all in treating the Duke like a badly designed footstool. Newcastle might be a worm, but he had a worm's-eye view of who was winning. And putting himself solidly behind Walpole, he turned. Townshend tried to dismiss him as 'utterly unqualified and an intolerable incumbrance [*sic*] in public business'35 and substitute the much cleverer Chesterfield. That was no way to work with Walpole who disliked Chesterfield intensely for *being* clever, also as a friend of the poets and playwrights with whom the Premier had a comfortable relationship of mutual loathing.

Anyway, trying to manage that sort of intrigue involved working the court where George II, who had told Newcastle, 'You are von rascal' during the great family quarrel, had in the same conflict called Townshend 'a choleric blockhead'. He was comfortably brought in line by Queen Caroline's determination to back Walpole and resist any move against Walpole's man. Everything was turning towards a British deal with Vienna which left Spain on her own where Townshend would have reached an accommodation with Spain and threatened the Austrians. In 1729, with England talking softly to Vienna and contemplating conflict with Spain, policy had shifted out of sight. 'The Cardinal,' said Newcastle, 'is not dead, but dead to us', adding that he 'had long been of the opinion that nothing could be so much in the interest of the King and Nation as a thorough reconciliation with the Court of Vienna'.

That shift in policy worked for all immediate concerns. The Treaty of Seville, 1729, with Austria onside, affirmed the right of the British to make money selling black slaves to the South American territories, the Annual Ship of the South Sea Company, lately detained, was

---

* Chavigny would warn Bolingbroke against the government's undertaking at Vienna. It risked, he said, Great Britain being dragged into a Continental war.

acknowledged, and facilities which Spain had offered to the Ostend Company were withdrawn. What had made Spain compliant, apart from her isolation, was what strictly mattered only to Elizabeth Farnese. Her Italian ambition to establish the Italian duchies of Piacenza and Parma as the territory of Spain, with her son Carlos as their ruler, was recognised – as an eventuality. That meant 1733 when, through the so-called family compact, another deal would elevate Carlos, (now 'Carlo') to rule over Naples, its great south Italian hinterland and Sicily. Though British recognition of the Pragmatic Sanction did not come formally until 1731 at the second Vienna Congress, it was plainly understood and had long-term consequences.

Even in the short term there was trouble to come. *The Craftsman's* little digs about the local people at Dunkirk wanting their never-to-be-enlarged harbour enlarged exploded as a parliamentary bomb in 1730. The instrument was not Pulteney, but Sir William Wyndham, dignified, grumbling, old-style Tory, who, on 10 February, at the conclusion of a speech complaining of the decline in trade, notably woollens, proceeded to foreign affairs, the mismanagement of which had left the French free to encroach on plantations and refuse recognition in harbour of the union flag. On top of which, said Sir William, whose timing was very good, the harbour at Dunkirk had been restored and he had expert witnesses, ships' master no less, on immediate call to give evidence.

Parliament was in uproar territory. Horatio Walpole objected, as well he might, to Wyndham's witnesses; much better to wait for the government's papers and their own representative in Dunkirk, still Colonel Armstrong. What followed was classic Robert Walpole, a holding action, letting hot iron cool before the opposition could hit it properly, time played for, detail then supplied in a great volume of official papers. Time was duly wasted, procedural mistakes were made by the opposition and Walpole took elaborate trouble to treat uncertain Members with tender care. But at the end of all this, he had in his hands a letter from Fleury, promising, for what it was worth, to give an order to destroy whatever it was that might have been erected.

It was also the case that Newcastle's assiduity and the fussing insistence with which he had bombarded embassy, engineer and French ministers, should, if found among the papers, have done the government some credit. Again, fears of French plans, however solemnly both opposition and Walpole presented them, were not declaration of war material. Fleury was a sharp and devious servant of French interests and no minder of legal requirements inconveniencing them. But he was not an enemy and he was not going to war. The good sense of both premiers ultimately counted for more than the political bubble of a partly fortified harbour. The reality was that over Dunkirk, British ministers, resting their authority upon a document, sought to impose something the French would not submit to. Yet British outrage in no way reached the going-to-war point, something both they and the French knew. It would take Lord Shelburne, decades later, to come to terms with the realities and, by writing it off, end a long course of ineffectual fulmination.

But Walpole's thinking was badly flawed. Refusing to make a five-act tragedy of Dunkirk ought not to have been translated into an underestimation of the long purposes of Cardinal Fleury. And in 1733 they would be manifested. France had lost face and territory in consequence of having lost the War of the Spanish Succession. Four years after Dunkirk had been shelved as an issue, she would make another succession the occasion for recovering ground. Spain had a French King. Might not Poland have a creature of France?

This frail territory in the east, a titular and calamitously elective monarchy with a nobility from which parties and *frondes* could be shaped, was the perfect object of outside domination, something which, with the three famous partitions, would, across the century, become gradual national extinction. But when, on 1 February 1733, August of Saxony, the latest franchisee of Poland, died, it was a racing certainty that the powers would contend, if necessary by way of war, in a contest of rival nominees. Austria wanted a good status quo for Austria by replacing August II with August III. France, spotting possibilities, had in Stanislaw Leszczynski a proper, eight-consonantal Polish candidate, a former King, deposed long since by the Swedes, who happened to be the father-in-law of the young Louis XV. There was going to be a war.

The view in Norfolk in the 1730s was phlegmatic. This was another remote, foreign business in which England could only lose money and get horribly tied up. And, oddly, Walpole's foreign policy followed the first draft of Townshend's. France was not a threat. Chavigny might be a prancing fool and house guest of Bolingbroke. His Minister, Choiseul, might be a spitting Anglophobe, but the Cardinal was all right. André Hercule de Fleury was a French Walpole, a keeper-out of wars.

Rather, he was a keeper-out of wars he couldn't control and a much better diplomat than Townshend, Horatio Walpole or, indeed, Sir Robert Walpole. The Prime Minister's aversion to war is very attractive to a modern British reader, but in the slow-moving chess game of the eighteenth century, allies were there to be retained or conclusively swapped with an eye on the future configuration of the pieces. *Not* to support Austria when under treaty obligation to follow quite recent undertakings at Vienna was to risk being without her when France or Spain, perhaps France *and* Spain, attacked British interests. Walpole's mistake was to think short term and to think too lightly about France.

His instinct was to stay out of the conflict whatever the betrayal of allies or the consequences in the longer term of such desertion. Walpole would emulate the Pharisee in the gospels walking resolutely on the other side. The war itself had little or nothing to do with the Polish succession. Austria and the Russia she now cultivated were on the spot and on the borders, able to require the Polish nobility and Diet to elect the father's son, the approved German and imperial candidate. British troops were never going to be asked to do intrepid things along the Vistula, but British ships would be sadly missed in the Mediterranean. The first prize was what Spain, client of France, might pick up in Italy, the second, the fee, injurious and humiliating to Britain, taken by France.

In the teeth of the Treaty of Utrecht and all the reasons why the War of the Spanish Succession had been fought, Fleury had established the Family Compact, Bourbon and Borbón, working together. It was an anti-Austrian compact also injurious to Britain. France would engage by sieges at 'Kehl and Phillipsburg in Upper Germany to prevent any diversions of the Imperialists from the east',[36] and would support any Spanish claim on Gibraltar. Spain wanted territory around Milan, which Britain, under the Treaty of Vienna, was obliged to defend, in practice by naval intervention. If she did send ships, Spain was to renege on the *Asiento* treaty and its South Sea trade concessions to England, making over half of them to France.

Meanwhile, the Kingdom of Sardinia which, based in Turin, could have handily supported Austria, was bought off with the (unkept) promise of its own piece of the Lombard cake. A British navy, rebuffing Spanish landings on the Italian mainland, would have met treaty commitments and frustrated the complex French gains sought from an isolated Austria. Spain might or might not withdraw from the *Asiento*, though a Spain roundly defeated in the Mediterranean would hardly have risked conflict with Britain in the Atlantic.

Walpole wanted to worry his head about none of these contingencies. He was a man of few and certain fixities. One of them was that wars drove up the Land Tax. Another was that the chief beneficiaries would be the Jacobites. However, his policy of bilking treaty obligations did not move smoothly into inaction. He had a fierce opponent in the King. Quite apart from enjoying soldiering quite as much as he did extra-marital sex, George II was, as George I had grudgingly conceded, '*un homme honnête*'. He was outraged at the prospect of betraying both a solemn international undertaking and his obligation to the Emperor as a Prince of the Imperial Court. He didn't greatly like Charles VI, but abominated the idea of letting him down.

And honour and duty were not George's only motives. He was not impressed by Fleury's charm. France had been the great aggrandising state in Europe; recovering strength, she would be so again. All the rest was humbug. This was a plain man's rough judgement which Walpole wouldn't and couldn't see. It was also very much the conclusion of the Duke of Newcastle. The Duke, through the running sneers of Hervey and the lectures he endured from Horatio, did a lot of work as Secretary of State.

His ambassadors were a variable lot, from hardworking Keene in Spain and Waldegrave in Paris to idle Essex in Turin and quarrelsome Kinnoull at the Ottoman Porte.[37] But in his gentle, effusive way he requested and got a great deal of information and read every word of it. He knew very early about the deal with Sardinia and the Family Compact. He had expressed personal inclinations for a British tilt towards Charles through Robinson in Vienna. And he thought that 'we have nothing to wish from France or to do with them'.[38] He lacked the confidence and character to be happy with betrayal, but, at this time, also the confidence to take on Walpole. Oddly in a Duke, Newcastle had too much deference.

Typically, Walpole would approach the problem of George II through Queen Caroline who initially also supported the Empire. (But for a strong-minded, liberal Protestantism, the young Caroline might, by a strategic conversion, have become the imperial consort.) She had seen off the Jesuit sent to convert her then, but the flattering consultations with Walpole won the Queen round. And Caroline could cajole George almost as readily as she had been cajoled.

Walpole now took the conduct of all relevant policy into his own hands, sending his brother to deal in secret at The Hague with Fleury's envoy.

Thus Britain reneged on her undertaking in the Treaty of Vienna. France, Spain and Sardinia could attack the Empire in Italy with the Mediterranean free of the British navy. The fighting done, Emperor and Cardinal reached conclusions, also in secret. Stanislaw, a non-starter in Poland, was bought off by Charles with life tenure of his personal territory in Lorraine, while being compensated with Tuscany and French recognition of the ultimate succession of the Pragmatic Sanction. It was, anyway, a sanction which France would later, just as pragmatically, disregard.

England, having played no part, had, unsurprisingly, no rewards, but what really mattered, no consultation. Walpole had gone behind the Emperor's back to give Fleury a free hand. He now had a steady enemy in Charles, but more important yet, when Lorraine passed on Stanislaw's death to become an integral part of France, Louis XV would rule 'a larger self-contained territory than she possessed in the days of Louis XIV's greatest glory'.[39]

Walpole had known what to do, known better than George, better than Newcastle. Knowing better, he had become a spectator to the creation of power, lands and aggressive assurance for the French state, the prevention of which had been the preoccupation of British, and especially Whig, opinion for fifty years. Fleury was mischievous and active where Walpole was static, more expert in foreign affairs and more awake. Unchastised, Spain, with her several grievances against Britain, would, in the shade of France, eventually create conflicts which even the most resolute Pharisee could not pass by.

TO HEEL BUT SNAPPING:
WALPOLE AND THE CHURCH

The flavour of early eighteenth-century clerical life is best seen through a case study. Dr Jacques Sterne was the finished example of a Walpolian clergyman. His career and the early activities of his nephew, Laurence, perfectly display the political scent on the ecclesiastical breeze. Jacques was, and had always taken care to be, a Whig and a Walpolian Whig. He did not lose by it. Rector of Rise in the East Riding of Yorkshire, at twenty-six, in 1723, he would add, in 1729, the benefice of Hornsea-cum-Riston, then a fortnight later, the York Minster prebend of Apethorpe. He exchanged this in 1731 for Uskelf (worth more), acquiring in 1734 a further prebend, at South Muskham (attached to distant Southwell Minster), before finally, at forty, emerging as Archdeacon of Cleveland and Precentor of York. His income by then was £900 a year from his Church livings alone (double that of one of the humbler bishoprics), and he resided in the wing he had purchased of one of York's great buildings, the Treasurer's House.

As a good party man, Sterne was a leading presence in electoral business, working in the 1727 election for Cholmley Turner, successful candidate in the Yorkshire county seat, and in the bitterly disputed election of 1734 for the defeated Sir Rowland Winn. And after the failure of the 1745 rising, he would sit in unmerciful judgement. On the Special Commission of 1746 which indicted seventy-five persons from the losing side, the Archbishop of York (Thomas Herring), the Marquess of Rockingham, Viscount Irwin, Sir Miles Stapylton, Mr Turner and Sir Rowland were joined by Archdeacon Sterne. Seventy prisoners were sentenced to death. Forty-eight had their sentences commuted to transportation for life, while twenty-two, one of them a piper bearing no arms, would be hanged in groups on the Knavesmire on three successive Saturdays.

The Archdeacon worked hard to bring a local Tory physician and possible Jacobite, Dr John Burton, to a similar conclusion, making it clear that he was also trying to break the Tory/Country party in the City. He claimed at one point to have proof that the Country interest in the City was involved with a Jacobite conspiracy. Dr Burton would survive through failure of evidence, emerging, drastically transformed, as Dr Slop in *Tristram Shandy*.

The Archdeacon's first requirement of his nephew was that he apply his writing talent promoting a Whig candidate.[1] The young man cheerfully dedicated himself and his talents to straight-up-and-down electioneering. In January 1742, just over three years into his incumbency as Vicar of Sutton-in-the-Forest (£100 a year plus glebe land), Laurence had one objective during a bitterly fought by-election – that Cholmley Turner* should be elected.

In 1741 Laurence helped set up *The York Gazetteer*, in opposition to the Tory *York Courant*. Its purposes were emphatic. 'As this paper is partly set on Foot to correct the weekly poison of *The York-Courant*, 'tis hoped that well-wishers to the cause of Liberty and Protestantism will give it Encouragement.'[3] *The Eatanswill Gazette* could hardly have described *The Eatanswill Independent* more vividly. Sterne was accusing the *Courant*'s management, Caesar Ward, John Jackson (and that same Dr John Burton), of Jacobitism and Roman Catholicism. Ward responded with a reprint from a London paper, *Common Sense*, which attacked 'political hirelings'. Sterne took on the London publication and described its editor Charles Molloy as 'a bigoted Papist'.[†]

Laurence next accused the Tory candidate, George Fox, of being an Irishman, a serious allegation in those days; and when this charge was attacked by a correspondent signing himself 'J.S.', Laurence was directed by Jacques to identify him as having, on account of the recent

---

* Turner was nothing like as uncritical a Walpole Whig as the Sternes. He spoke against the government in a foreign affairs debate in 1729 and voted against it over the Hessian troops in 1730, the army in 1732 and the excise in 1733. Walpole complained that 'he was so wrong headed, there was no holding him' and wondered solicitously if the red ribbon of his own beloved Order of the Bath might sweeten his inclinations.[2] The task was sweetened with a prebendary stall in York Minster worth another hundred.

† Papist or not, Molloy, earlier a moving spirit behind *Fog's Weekly Journal*, did have distinct Jacobite sympathies.

commercial treaty with Spain, denounced Walpole as having 'forfeited the name of Englishman'. Laurence, not being a demon investigative journalist, wrongly identified another local clergyman, James Scott. It was not an edifying episode and so seriously had the Reverend Mr Sterne aroused political feeling that, one night, he was beaten up on the streets of York.⁴

Laurence Sterne, apart from being the subsequent author of a work of eccentric genius, was a fairly typical cleric of his time. He was a Cambridge graduate when the universities were close to being seminaries, and Cambridge loyalist Whig while Oxford was clenched in Tory resentment. He had his family Church connection, but no immediate help from territorial authorities. And when, in 1742, disgusted with the quarrels politics had got him into, Laurence refused further services as a propagandist, favour dried up. As his biographer, Ian Campbell Ross, puts it, 'He would have almost two decades in which to count the cost.'⁵

The goodwill of the local squire could be important, but at his first benefice, the squire, Philip Harland, had no freehold to bestow, which was just as well since Harland was a Tory. They did not get on, but with the Whig, Stephen Croft, at Stillington, where Laurence acquired a £50 living through his wife, he enjoyed the best of highly convivial relations. And much later, as a famous author, he enjoyed the interest of a local magnate, Viscount Fauconberg.

But national political favour determined advancement. A Tory squire owning that clerical freehold, the advowson, could put his man into the rectory readily enough. And one leading study reckons upon more than two thousand livings being controlled through the advowsons of Tory landowners.⁶ But many others, as well as all the prizes for senior churchmen, were disposed of at the top. So were the places and pensions desired for themselves by lay patrons. The longer the Whigs held office, the better could the holders of advowsons see the point of compliance. The upper ranks of the Church were well supplied with Whigs, even before Walpole's advent. By September 1721, nineteen of the twenty-six bishoprics were, on Sunderland's reckoning, already in their hands. With the instincts of the parish clergy widely and deeply Tory, the Church was becoming a tribe of plumed chiefs and sullen Indians.

During his brief early prosperity, Laurence had enjoyed, through his uncle, the goodwill of the Archbishop of York since 1724, Lancelot Blackburne, a parody of a corrupt Walpolian cleric. He had attracted a pamphlet, 'Priestcraft and Lust, or Lancelot and his Ladies'. Walpole's son, Horace, would later write of the Archbishop having 'all the manners of a man of quality though he had been a buccaneer, and was a Clergyman, but he retained nothing of his first profession except the seraglio'.[7] Latitudinarian in theology, luxurious in private life, a pluralist in so many ways, thoroughly idle, yet adventurous enough in early life to be seriously reputed a former chaplain on a pirate ship, a good party man without restraint and snugly suited at court, Blackburne was the very model of a bad episcopal example.

Court rumour ran a long way ahead of historical probability. But it was the measure of his disgraceful and envied reputation that he was whispered to have earlier officiated in a secret wedding bringing together George I and his Melusine. Whatever the truth, Blackburne had achieved warm goodwill at court and, in 1717, had become Bishop of Exeter. When to the steep bill of episcopal mortality for 1723 was added, in April of 1724, Sir William Dawes, Archbishop of York, Blackburne was agreeable to George and no problem for Walpole. As he grew older, the Archbishop did not take the tedium of administration and visitation too seriously, giving up confirmation altogether in 1733, leaving the young faithful to deputies for the next ten years. One of them, his chaplain, was that other good party man, Dr Jacques Sterne.

The world of Blackburne and the Sternes was underwritten by a hard-handed erastianism which said that the state, otherwise very roughly Robert Walpole, the Duke of Newcastle and the Lord Chancellor of the day, called the shots and the Church submitted. But that power had to be held in the teeth of a majority of Anglican clergymen, its ranks heavy with Church and King men, Tories cool toward the King of 1714. Walpole would make the decisive move against the Tory interest in the Church after an earlier experiment in guided cooperation, begun by Stanhope and Sunderland, had been bitterly resisted by the very man they had appointed.

The Whigs had always wanted specific reforms which weakened the aggressive primacy of the Church against other Protestant Christians. The reigning Primate between 1694 and his death late in 1715 had been Thomas Tenison, moderate, genuinely liberal and much loved. In his last years, coinciding closely with the Harley/Bolingbroke regime, he had resisted Bolingbroke's vicious drive against Dissenters, enshrined in the Occasional Conformity and Schism Acts. Tenison had been overridden and sidelined in favour of the Tory Archbishop of York, John

Sharp. However, surviving Anne and the Tory government by sixteen months, he lived to crown George I before dying in December 1715, requiring the Whigs to choose another Whig.

Unfortunately for enforcement of policy, they chose William Wake. The Bishop of Lincoln, now translated, was indeed a Whig but also a High Churchman, and a stiff-necked one, especially in areas where the new masters wished, quite properly, to move. Everything came back to Occasional Conformity. This practice, touched upon earlier, was the ecclesiastical version of tax avoidance. Since the seventeenth century, Dissenters had got round the ban denying them place and office by turning up for an annual communion by the Anglican rite. If that was a fix, it was a fix provoked by the vengeful particularism of the ruck of Anglican clergy denouncing it.

Bolingbroke had curried favour among country gentlemen, at Oxford high tables and especially in the rectories, with an act outlawing the practice and laying large penalties upon Dissenters for dissenting. The Whigs, with their excellent connections in Dissent and links via Shaftesbury to the Parliament men of 1640, were supposed to dismantle the whole thing. Indeed, they meant to get rid also, at least for Protestant Dissenters, of the Test and Corporation Acts of Charles II which had imposed the ban in the first place.

But Wake would have none of it. Such was the clerical closed-shop mentality that even the Whig bishops were split on the subject. Stanhope and his colleagues found a task heavier than they had envisaged, and one made more tedious when their own Archbishop of Canterbury stood sullenly in the way. The period of Whig rule before Walpole succeeded was marked by two-sided bitterness in Church affairs. Not only had the Whigs inherited a Tory Church, but being Whigs, they did not much like the Church of England. Latitudinarianism, a broad, many syllabled word for tolerance about doctrinal detail, was smiled upon. And deism, the polite term covering unbelief before Thomas Huxley coined 'agnostic', quietly defined the free thinking of so many new men. There flourished among Whigs, along with liberality and electoral considerations, a degree of anti-clericalism and secularism. The Whigs not only wanted power over the Church, they wanted the Church demoted and deprived of authority.*

---

* But the low view, however enjoyable, does not do justice to the sincere intellectual moderation of many serious people.

One mighty row reflecting the Church at its most dogmatic was the so-called Bangorian controversy. The most dedicatedly Whiggish *and* Latitudinarian of the higher clergy was Benjamin Hoadly, also a sharp and effective political controversialist. So when the Whigs, unsurprisingly, made him a bishop (of Bangor) in 1715, there was, in the best unchristian spirit, much muttering about an unsound sermon he had published in 1706. Hoadly, an honest and intellectually brilliant man, was no covert unbeliever, but he was distinctly cool about the Church's special role. In another sermon, preached before George I, he said in terms that Christ had not given divine authority to ecclesiastics. They served God but did not carry his personal aura or authority; the truth was his, not theirs. To that, a sensible Lutheran, this anapostolic view was unremarkable sense. To the Tory clergy, it was Church treason. The Bangorian controversy followed.

It gained more space than it deserved through Convocation, a church parliament, turned in Anne's time into a hellish fire zone by the hatreds running through the clergy. It had been, and was again in George I's earliest days, the chosen arena of Francis Atterbury, as furiously orthodox about the Church's pre-eminence as he was loyal to the one, true, anointed King, James III. A high-flying clergyman's belief in non-resistance did not apply to the monarch to whom he had sworn an oath in which he did not believe. Hoadly was in danger, in Sydney Smith's phrase, of being torn apart by wild curates, with Atterbury attempting, in 1717, to turn Convocation into a clerical riot. The new Bishop of Lincoln, a Dr Gibson, of whom more later, begged that 'no business . . . be entered upon in Convocation till the present jumble was over'.[8] But the clergy jumbled venomously on until crown authority was invoked to prorogue Convocation . . . until the next century.

Probably a majority of benefice holders accepted the elevation of the priesthood and the institutional Church above all except the King and perhaps God. This was the doctrine taught by William Laud, spiritual ideologist to Charles I, and one of the comparatively few Archbishops of Canterbury to have been beheaded. The running quarrel was inherited and historical. Given a disputed crown and the shallowness of clerical allegiance to the Hanoverian settlement, this often seemed like a church against the state. And Whigs found that, for dealing with it, William Wake was no use at all.

On Occasional Conformity, he had opposed the original Tory bill in Queen Anne's time and may have owed his present appointment by the

Whigs to that. But now, in 1717, he informed George I 'that eighteen or nineteen bishops would be against reforming the Act . . .', making the limp plea of its having been 'so lately and unanimously agreed to'.[9] This opposition helped delay formal abolition of the repressive Acts out of sight, and appeared to demonstrate the power of a high and militant Church. In practice, Wake provoked a very willing Whig leadership into finding other ways of killing an ecclesiastical cat. Walpole would, as remarked, give the Dissenters the form if not the substance through annual Amnesty Bills starting in 1728.

The new first Minister inherited the problems, but met them with his customary good luck. As noted above, in 1723 Death busied itself with the episcopacy. To the deaths of Stanhope, both Craggses and Sunderland, the Minister found himself happily obliged between May and October of that year to find new and suitable incumbents for Ely, Winchester, Chichester and St David's, while vacation of the See of Rochester after the disgrace of Atterbury completed the bag. All had been Tory bishops; indeed, given the extremity and dedication of Atterbury's opposition, Rochester counted as what football commentators call a 'six-pointer'.

But the move which counted for most in 1723 was the translation to London of that restraining voice in Convocation, Gibson, Wake's successor (from 1716) as Bishop of Lincoln. In fairness to Walpole, and against the Dionysiac image of the eighteenth-century clergyman, the Prime Minister, though concerned for the political soundness of appointments, would be able to make proper choices of decent candidates, having first taken advice from a sober and earnest man. The history of Church affairs for the next thirteen years would be bound up with Dr Edmund Gibson.

A son of Westmorland, born in 1669, and risen from modest farming stock, Gibson had first-rate intellectual gifts and went via Bampton Grammar School (recognised there by its master as 'this miracle')[10] to Queen's College, Oxford, in May 1687. He had proved at Lincoln a devoted and efficient pastoral bishop. Since this was the largest see in England with 1312 parishes,[11] he carried out triennial visitations, separating visitations from confirmations, two functions usually combined, in order to do the confirmations with greater care. A measure of the work undertaken survives in a letter dealing with a confirmation tour 'at Beaconsfield, Wicomb [sic] and other places in Buckinghamshire and Bedfordshire', for which he required stops at 'seven places in Buckinghamshire and four in Bedfordshire in hopes that his repairing to so many places might reduce the numbers to 300 or at most 400 at each place'.[12]

To such, literally, hands-on work, Gibson added the reputation of the greatest Canon lawyer of the century. As a younger man he had laboured, under the patronage of Archbishop Tenison, at the *Codex Juris Ecclesiastici Anglicani*. It drew upon all the clerical legislation, English and Legatine, and all subordinate regulation penned since the time of Archbishop Langton in 1222, ecclesiastical law comprehensively surveyed. Published in 1713, the two-volume work was still being praised in 1900 by the historian Stubbs as 'the standard work and treasury of all sorts of such lore'.* This labour, which inspired the dubious nickname of *Dr Codex*, had been undertaken in 1710, and had involved four years of minute work which seriously set back his health. It had been composed during the bitter Church and state, Whig and Tory quarrels of that period of Convocation, and set out just what the powers of the Church might be. It was an irony that so much authority and so many decisions would now pass through the hands of Dr Codex under heavy pressure from that most demanding of laymen, Robert Walpole.

There were reasons for this and other reasons leading to impasse and his long-growing unhappiness at conflict. Any large experience in the late teens or early twenties is said to mark a character for life. Gibson had arrived at eighteen at Oxford University at the very moment, in 1687, when James II, with princely stupidity, would attempt (see *supra*, Chapter 1) to pack the colleges with Roman Catholic heads of house, employing nominees held in general disesteem: Obadiah Walker at University College, Anthony Farmer at Magdalen, John Massey at Christ Church and Samuel Parker, advanced to the actual See of Oxford.

The whole operation, conducted in the most royalist, Tory and High Anglican institution in the kingdom, was folly without fellow. Oxford and Cambridge were very different places. The Oxford Martyrs, Ridley, Latimer and Cranmer, were all Cambridge men. Cambridge had not been Cromwell's and Milton's university for nothing. A Protestantism close to Dissent flourished in the Fens, and that university was as easy with natural or experimental philosophy (science) as with republican thinking. Oxford had been Charles I's temporary capital, and the university yearned for the King and absolute royal authority, something

---

* Not just Stubbs; the report leading to the major Canon Law reform of 1964–69 found Gibson's Codex 'absolutely indispensible' and its preliminaries 'the best accounts of the sources of the law of the Church'.

to be met by non-resistance. Along the High, Divine Right was preferred to the laws of physics flourishing off Trinity Lane.

But though Oxford wanted desperately to be loyal to James II, it drew the line at Romanising its own Church of England. Impossibly, James had alienated them. But there lingered long after a masochistic urge for Sacred Apostolic Majesty. Still, non-juring (refusal of oaths to William III) would prove such bad economics in a trade dependent upon state favour that very few clergymen stayed the full course. However, to use a good Catholic expression, many remained non-jurors *in pectore*. Edmund Gibson, Oxford man, Fellow of the Queen's, had been affected. He would be hostile to Rome all his life, but he had spent a year (July 1690–June 1691) holding back from his degree by postponing a decision on the oaths before taking them. He had been burned by Jacobitism, had shared the impulses of the non-jurors, then sharply and decisively rejected them.

He became by honest *political* conviction a devoted Whig, but he would always be a High Churchman. This, in eighteenth-century England, had nothing to do with rituals or Roman leanings, and every-thing to do with a jealous exaltation of the institution of the Church of England, with little friendly to say to Old Dissent (Quakers and Independents) or the New Dissent of John Wesley emerging in the last decade of Gibson's life. A Whig High Churchman, earnest in both professions, was an odd confection, one which ultimately led to the Bishop's semi-amicable divorce from Walpole's regime through incom-patibility. But 'ultimately' can take a while, and for a very long interim (1723–36) Gibson and Walpole would work well and effectively together.

High Churchman or not, the Bishop of Lincoln could offer civil toler-ance. He had few political problems during the Occasional Conformity conflict about distancing himself from Wake and his friend, William Nicholson of Carlisle, and accepting a much-tempered reform bill. He informed Wake in November 1717 that he was going into discussion with five bishops over 'the abolition of the sacramental test so far as it concerned Corporations'.[13] Which, as Walpole wanted dissenting support inside those corporations, was helpful.

The bill came to the Lords in modified form, repealing the excesses of the Schism Bill, ending the actual criminal penalties for attending a Dissenting place of worship and giving Dissenters (Whig voters one and all) access to borough corporations. It was noted succinctly that 'the Archbishop of Canterbury spoke most materially against the Bill, the Bishop of Lincoln for it'.[14]

Credit with the Whigs would be doubled by Gibson's role in the Bangorian controversy. Hoadly's views on the Church as a body of free servants of Christian doctrine exercising private judgements was seen by the high-flying clergy as putting 'the Church in danger' and deadly heresy. Gibson used practical arguments about Church cohesion to modify the Hoadly view. If the apostles had 'meant to establish churches as societies of Christians', then 'a power of admitting, governing and ejection would follow of course and from the very nature of Society'. On the other side of the argument, he affirmed a very Protestant definition of the Church of England, rejecting infallibility and 'presuming not to offer any doctrine or interpretation of her own as an absolute Rule of Faith, but for ends of order and government only'.[15] Amid the mystical buzz of a clerical randy, this was such good administrative (and Whiggish) sense that the Bishop of Lincoln's attractiveness to ministers grew irresistible.

As the rational voice and compromise-making negotiator for the established Church, Gibson was noticed and his name written down. The Duke of Newcastle, for whom Church preferment would be a life-long hobby, put it succinctly: 'Our man must be the Bishop of London. He has more sense, and, I think, more party zeal, than any of them.'[16] His biographer, the pre-eminent ecclesiastical historian Norman Sykes, heads one section of a chapter 'The Admission of Gibson to the Firm of Townshend and Walpole'. His appointment as 'Adviser' sounds humdrum, but it marked the supersession of Archbishop Wake. The customary role of the Primate in guiding the chief Minister over Church appointments was decisively transferred to Gibson. Wake held the See of St Augustine but not the ear of Robert Walpole.

The first chapter of the present study actually began with a reference to the cry of 'No Erastianism' made during Argyll's rising of 1685. What Argyll meant by erastianism was Charles II's attempt, through bishops, to impose Anglican forms and state rule upon the Presbyterian, which is to say democratic and Calvinistic, Church of Scotland. This abomination of erastianism was at the core of the Scottish opposition which gave the word 'Whig' to politics. Walpole's determined management of the Church from 1723 was *Whig* erastianism, another contradiction and one which, as ministers picked loyal bishops, suited the pragmatic Minister to perfection.

Gibson, coming in at the start of 1723, was ideally placed to meet that clutch of deaths with as many entrances. The vacancies at Ely and Winchester came very close together, Fleetwood dying on 4 August and Trimnell on the 15th, when the King, Townshend and Carteret were all in Hanover. But it was to Gibson that the two men, neither trusting the other, both wrote asking advice. Gibson took his duties very seriously, but understood the political requirements. And as lesser bishop was translated to greater bishopric, the business and authority of the modestly named adviser expanded.

Richard Willis of Salisbury, with him in the group supporting reform of the Occasional Conformity Act, was successfully recommended to the great See of Winchester. While probably drawing a breath over a man well to his own theological left, he pleased court and activist Whigs by accepting Benjamin Hoadley for Salisbury and replacing him at Hereford by an Oxford moderate, Henry Egerton, Canon of Christ Church. For Ely, a see of great resonance and value (£2300 pa), he suggested Thomas Green of Norwich, which see was filled by a Cambridge academic, Dr John Leng. As for Atterbury, now languishing at the court of the Pretender, the bishopric which he had seen as almost a principality was to be filled by a friend of Gibson, Dr Bradford.

As the dead accumulated, Gibson would successfully promote a reluctant Edward Waddington for Chichester and, on the death of the Bishop of St David's, a close friend, Richard Smallbrooke, later his biographer, took up the West Wales diocese. Significantly, Willis, a like-minded man and ally, added to Winchester the Clerkship of the Closet, a court appointment, a sort of political high chaplaincy. This was a personal and political move. It meant that, at the lowest, he could keep Gibson's back covered with the King. But there was a better, less self-interested purpose.

It is very important not to be cynical about Gibson. He lacked the humour for it. He was, over this twelvemonth, appointing men who were loyal to the Hanoverians and politically right for the government and the party governing in violently contentious times. But all were men of good life and decent learning and, by the standards of the day, conscientious attenders to their duties. A semi-exception to this was Hoadly who had combined controversial views with rare attendances in his remote North Wales diocese. But Hoadly was a savagely crippled man, barely mobile. He preached from his knees, not from any affectation of piety or 'enthusiasm', but because he was physically unable to stay standing up, and a rota of episcopal brethren quietly stood in for him over visitation duties.[17]

Gibson had dutifully met an immediate requirement in the hope of creating the nucleus of a creditable Hanoverian episcopate. Now he asked for the cup to pass. He protested often enough, and sincerely, that he had had greatness thrust upon him. He was making a serious attempt, about which the Clerkship of the Closet was the chief step, to have the selection of the episcopate and other sought-after tasks transferred to Willis at Winchester. In these exceptional circumstances, with bishops dying like plague victims, he had given his best political, doctrinal and character judgements to see sound men into place, but he did not wish to become a career patronage secretary. As bishop at Lincoln and after translation to London, he had come down on the right side more by coincidental conviction than any sharp-eyed calculation. In consequence he had found Townshend and Walpole, both exasperated by Wake, suddenly turning to him and enforcing their embrace upon a man who stood on their side of the line.

Gibson made a strenuous attempt to get out. Either the powers should go to Salisbury as Clerk of the Closet and thus court confidant, or London should sit only in a three-man commission with Salisbury and Exeter. But Gibson's conscience fretted in vain. Having found a man they could work with, Townshend and Walpole took him enthusiastically on board. The message was Sam Weller's: '"He wants you werry particler and nobody else vill do", as the Devil's private secretary said to Dr Faustus.' And there was something very Faustian about it. Gibson was loyal to Church *and* state, but many servants of the state held the Church in contempt, so that the clergyman serving it became, against all his wishes, a lobbied and besought politician with the name of a Minister's creature. He was doomed to a life of combined solicitation and abuse as 'Walpole's Pope'.

A very odd situation had arisen. The Archbishop of Canterbury had been bypassed and ministers had decided not to trouble York, Sir William Dawes, who would shortly die, making way for Blackburne, the court favourite. Political sympathy had been the sole foundation for giving the leadership of the Church and custody of its fountain of honour and income to a junior bishop who had passed the loyalty test. So matters would remain until 1736. The relationship was like a marriage which gives something to one partner but much more to another. Walpole and Newcastle saw a reputable but safe upper clergy installed and the lower clergy denied the leadership with which to make them dangerous. Everything which had angered them in the days of Sacheverell and Atterbury had been routed.

But Gibson had a series of useful, unpolitical purposes for his quasi-papacy. He wanted better clerical education, indeed better education altogether. He recognised the gap in university education in respect of history and modern languages. The answer was to open new courses. He found a mild patron for the scheme, not in Walpole, but Townshend, and authorisation was obtained to establish an academic chair in each subject at both universities. At £400 a year, such a post compared well with the £300 pension which Samuel Johnson, forty years later, would think princely.

After Cambridge had made an enthusiastic reply to the proposal and Oxford a sullen acquiescence conveyed by its beadles,[18] occupants were sought, though with the usual concern for 'soundness'. With the chair were to go scholarships, twenty for each university. The early history of the chairs is one of perplexity, with the professors on the lookout for canonries, numbers of pupils dwindling and a general fizzling, if not out, then down, the sort of thing always liable to happen in the eighteenth-century public sector if it were not minutely supervised. But the Regius chairs existed and would have a splendid future, if not a very startling present, and Edmund Gibson is entitled to almost all the credit.

As far as the Church itself was concerned, his concern for making payment fairer to those drawing the short straw in preferment was quite alien to Walpole. Never a compassionate man, he applauded success and despised failure even in the form of a cure of souls sustained at £20 a year, a ghostly figure, often unattained. Being a poor clergyman was one of the forms which failure took. Walpole was a coarse man who did not believe in disinterested good intentions. 'He did not like him' says Plumb abruptly, of Gibson. A letter very early in the relationship, 6 September 1723, ends, 'He must be Pope, and would as willingly be our Pope as anybodies [sic].'[19] But he is sharply contradicted by someone placed to know. Francis Hare, Dean of St Paul's, later Bishop of Chichester, early critic, later friend, of Gibson, and, as Walpole's former tutor at Cambridge, close to the Prime Minister himself, was very clear in a letter to Gibson himself of August 1736 at the end of the affair. He thought that there had subsisted between the two 'an intimacy and a confidence such as no ecclesiastic had had with a Minister in his time, nor would any again, nor hardly any other person with him'.[20]

Nevertheless that comment 'He must be Pope' lies in the focus of Walpole's limited vision. He esteemed other men by his own standards. Most men in early Georgian England did indeed 'have their price'. It was therefore not possible for Gibson to be any different. Walpole would discover how untrue this was thirteen years later when, on good and bad grounds, his Church bullied, some of its presumptions more reasonably assailed, Gibson walked away from his papacy and concentrated upon his great diocese. Walpole's notion of erastianism was the Church underfoot or, at best, the Church valued only for its political use. The Whig command of the upper clergy quickly ceased to have any pretence of being a defence against Laudian or Jacobite threats, though in Cold War style, fears and threats would be invoked all the time.

The Church was a treasury of good things, deaneries were desirable residences, an archdeaconry a pleasant prospect, prebendal stalls in the richer cathedrals exquisite inducements to party loyalty. The rewards were wonderfully unequal, the bishoprics themselves a geology of ridge, plateau and declivity; the great See of Durham, with its £3500 a year, was some way above snug, a condition which starveling Bristol on £400 barely reached. There were deaneries which paid better than mediocre bishoprics, and much of the derided pluralism of that century was no more than the putting together of two modest incomes to make a decent one in a post heavy with overheads. The carrying over to a frugal promotion of an earlier, lesser, but paying post *in commendam*, as it was called, was crucial for the harder hit bishops.

It was not unknown for a needy diocesan to have a little lobby of his brethren do the asking. A very revealing undated message to Walpole from the Bishops of Chichester, Bangor and Gloucester on behalf of Smallbrooke, now translated to Lichfield, points out that his predecessor, Chandler, 'held the prebend in the Church [Cathedral] at Durham with this Bishoprick, and Bishop Chandler thought it a great hardship that he was not allowed hold the living of Wear with Lichfield after Lord Sunderland had encouraged him to hope for it'.[21] They therefore enquire for the current incumbent about the living of Withington 'which he did hold for two years, at the expiration of which, his Majesty was graciously pleased to give leave to apply for finalisation'. And the plaintive point follows 'that the two Bishopricks of Norwich and Lincoln which have about the same value with Lichfield, have commendams in perpetuity'.[22]

It reads demeaning even in a brazen age, but it was a peculiar advantage to a man like Walpole that bishops should demean themselves. The situation was one to diminish the Church and to emasculate men

who, having begged for its rewards, were badly placed to think of themselves as its princes. Demeaning was very useful. Gibson was conscious
of the hold which government patronage had, but he was stubborn and
always ready to dig in his heels. During all his exposure to ministerial
bullying, he remained preoccupied with retaining Church autonomy.
Some of his grounds for a quarrel sound narrow and doctrinaire, but
are better seen as a determination *not* to be demeaned.

Such tiresomeness was something which Lord Hervey found *ennuiant*.
As poor Archbishop Wake, his mind long erased, lay dying, Hervey
wrote seigneurially to Walpole, 'Sure, Sir . . . you have had enough of
great geniuses. Why can you not take some Greek or Hebrew blockhead that has learning enough to deserve the preferment, and not sense
enough to make you repent of it?'[23] The Church was one place where
Samuel Johnson's dictum 'Slow rises wealth by poverty oppressed',
though true, might still be accelerated through by talent – the talent of
Gibson himself who had entered Oxford as a servitor, the poor student's
half-menial scholarship, or that of Isaac Maddox, a former charity boy,
whom he raised to the Bench.*

Walpole, combining the automatic snobbery of the age with an understanding of its political application, complained that he gained too little
leverage from the bestowal of patronage upon plain men:

> It has not been customary for persons of birth or fortune to breed up their
> children to the Church by which means, when preferment in the Church is
> given by their Majesties, there is seldom anyone obliged but the very person
> to whom it is given, having no near relations either in the then House of
> Lords or Commons that are gratified or kept in dependence thereby. The
> only remedy to which is by giving extraordinary encouragements to persons
> of birth and interest whenever they seek preferment which will encourage
> others of the same quality to come into the Church and may thereby render
> ecclesiastical preferments of the same use to their Majesties with civil employ-
> ments.[24]

A more breathtaking candour about the entire Walpole system with
the Church as a nicely calibrated channel of money and moneysworths
does not exist. The poor or even middle-class cleric, given a job, had

---

* Slowly or not, Maddox rose a long way. His ultimate appointment was to Worcester, one
of the richest of all sees.

only his own gratitude for repayment, as with the Sternes busying them-selves at elections. The disposal of a rectory with £300 a year, or indeed a bishopric, to many such sterile persons was unavoidable, but was a poor investment. They stood outside the net of reciprocal obligation whose strings Walpole adjusted.

Persons of birth and interest would, however, be very fastidious about what place a younger son might take among the lower clergy. Despite many highly rewarded and gratifying exceptions, they were not called 'lower' for nothing. There were around 11,000 churches generating some sort of money. Just over a half, 5600, carried incomes of less than £50 a year.[25] The life of the unbeneficed was a scramble of small men after smaller curacies, perhaps a subsidy from Queen Anne's Bounty or a short-term locum post, with naval and prison chaplaincies at the melancholy base.

The power of Walpole and his allies was officially confined to a small fraction of the whole, but a fraction rejoicing in the very best. The Lord Chancellor, in obvious consultation with the head of govern-ment, held and distributed just over one thousand livings, the Church establishment had 36 per cent, while private men holding advowsons had 53.5 per cent.[26]

But this overstates the influence of the opposition and the room available for advancing independent, non-compliant men. With the crown and the Lord Chancellor commanding so much of everything worth having, all of it flatly denied to Tories or High Churchmen, such parsons depended on the Tory squires. But across the next two decades Tory squires would be led into temptation. In the early Whig days, they had defiantly accepted their own exclusion from good things by way of peerages, government service and, most painfully, the magistracy, a former place by right. But the want of political change, and consequent death of expectations, encouraged a new flexibility and accommoda-tion.

This in turn affected the colour of a clergy turning to whatever sun they could find. In Yorkshire, for which there are figures, and where Tory clergy and squires had predominated, the evidence is clear-cut. In 1742, the year of Walpole's fall, out of the 346 parsons voting in York in that year's county by-election, only a quarter gave their voice for the Tory.[27] Twenty years of Walpole had been brutally instructive in the charm of the winning side. Jacques Sterne had simply been ahead of the game.

It was a game played with some urgency. The correspondence crossing Sir Robert's desk, passed on by individuals who had, or thought they had, access through political loyalty, is eloquent. Most petitioners, or 'suppliants', are quick to the trigger, often beating Death to the draw: 'Stockingham Vicarage in the County of Devon and diocese of Exeter is a Crown living, the present incumbent being upwards of ninety, the next presentation is humbly requested by the Reverend Jas. Fox of Totnes in Devon whose brother is now mayor of the corporation.'[28]

Some drop dry little hints about the sender's influence: 'St Olave's, a Rectory in the gift of the Crown in the diocese of Winchester and Deanery of Southwark . . . computed to be worth about 300l per annum. The present incumbent, Mr Aiscough, aged 70, is very infirm and not likely to live out the winter. If given to Mr James Dunglas, it will very much oblige Mr Dunglas's friends and in particular, DUN: FORBES.'*[29]

From grand folk at Court the tone is, as here, imperious: 'Doctor Butts,† Chaplain in ordinary to his Majesty and Preacher of Bury, recommended by Lord Hervey, desires the first prebend that falls in the Church [i.e.Cathedral] of Worcester, Windsor or Canterbury which was expressly promised to him three years ago by Lord Townshend at the Solicitation of the Duke of Grafton.

Lord Hervey.'[31]

Ladies proved sometimes quite as peremptory as lords, even as they favoured the greengrocer's apostrophe: 'Lady Nicoll desires that Dr Philip Bunton, Canon of Christ's [sic] Church, who was Mr Charles Nicolls [sic] tutor at Oxford may be made one of the King's chaplains.'[32]

But they can, as in Henry Robinson's letter below, speak from the heart of need and ask for very little: 'All Saints within the Boro of Lynn. This application is made with the privity of Mr Pyle, the present incumbent, who though an ancient man, is very healthful at present. The value of it is under seventy pounds which is the most Mr Pyle has made of it for several years in the past.'[33]

---

* Duncan Forbes, who sat for Ayr Burghs, 1721–2 and Inverness Burghs, 1722–37, was sufficiently loyal, but a voice responsive to Scottish feeling, notably opposing a punitive bill against Edinburgh after the Porteous Riots of 1736. He left Parliament in 1737 to become President of the Court of Session. Having raised a regiment against the 'the Forty-five,' he offended the Duke of Cumberland as an advocate of clemency. Forbes, said His Grace, 'was no Jacobite, but was a Highlander and carried that to dangerous lengths'.[30]

† Robert Butts, a friend of Hervey, would later, in 1733, be advanced by him (and Queen Caroline), over Gibson's objections, to the See of Norwich at £1500 p.a.

And, speaking of himself in the third person, 'Littleton Bunton of Brackley in the County of Northumberland, Master of Arts and Rector of Credenhill in the County of Hereford, humbly begs to offer Your Majesty the Copy of a memorial in the same language and words as it was delivered to his late Majesty, King George . . .'

There follows a page of florid and grovelling French, before the claim that he 'had been offered the next vacant prebend in the Church either of Westminster or Windsor but that his Death . . .'. Then, recovering himself, 'Your suppliant humbly submits his cause to the great wisdom and Justice of your Sacred Majesty which so eminently appears in Every Act of your Majesty's Administration.'

He concludes by confiding 'that your suppliant is particularly known to the Lord Chancellor and Bishops of London and Salisbury who are Ready and willing to support his Character to your Majesty'.

For Gibson the price of exercising restraint on the Minister was to be caught up in the patronage game, besieged for his voice by the man seeking a living which, at £70, mocked the word, to bestow the income of a lush prebend upon a protégé of Pope's Sporus or satisfy the finger-clicking of a lady of birth and interest on behalf of her son's tutor. He was struggling never to become the fond lackey which a small litera-ture of abuse proclaimed him. Gibson was dogged, difficult, quietly proud and devoted, if in sometimes arcane ways, to the good gover-nance of the Church of England.

One way of demonstrating this was to pass up the good things dangled before him personally. He had needed commendams himself, but had confined them to short periods to cover the considerable costs of moving from his original post as Rector of Lambeth to Lincoln and again, in 1723, to London. In 1730 he was offered Durham, grander and better paid, and refused it. In 1734 the entice-ment was Winchester, a small heaven of emolument; again Gibson said 'no'. Both sees paid better than London, Winchester at £5000 splendidly so; either could be held jointly with the advisorship and its powers. Looking at the comments of Walpole and Hervey, one sees rationalisations of his conduct in terms of the only motives they recognised – low ones. But Gibson had recognised long before breaking with Walpole that they were working side by side for entirely different things.

However, through many difficulties they did work together. One problem they shared was Caroline von Ansbach. The Queen was a clever woman whose husband deferred to her, and she rather expected ministers and bishops to do the same. It was to Caroline that Walpole referred when he spoke of 'having got the right sow by the ear', opponents having spent, as we have seen, too many of the late years of George I cultivating Henrietta Howard, the rather improbably unpolitical mistress of the Prince.

As Lutherans the Hanoverians were always perplexed by the exalted rigidities of the Church of England. What shocked the English clergy often struck them as interesting and reasonable. But beyond this, Caroline followed Henry VIII and James I by indulging herself as a theologian. Naturally, she had a weakness, as a clergy fancier, for Latitudinarians, but she also liked the more presentable Tories, favouring Hoadly and Clarke in one category and the preeningly ambitious Thomas Sherlock in the other. Walpole's instinct was to give Caroline her way wherever it didn't matter. Left to himself, he would have thought that into this category the appointment of a bishop unsound on the Trinity fell comfortably.

Dr Samuel Clarke was a man of outstanding abilities and Queen Caroline was right to like him. Clever in the new scientific way, he had grasped Newton and rejected Descartes. The great book of his youth, *Discourses Concerning the Being and Attributes of God* (1704), was thought the most distinguished response to Hobbes and Spinoza. Clarke, the correspondent of Leibniz, was a great opponent of the deists, and a man of ardent, if good-humoured, morality. He did not precisely deny the Trinity, but in another work had entirely denied that the early Church had insisted upon such belief.

Gibson, given to excessive earnestness, was shocked. When Clarke's name came up in September 1727, with the Queen a keen supporter, for Bangor (from which Hoadley, surprisingly orthodox on the three-personed God, had long since moved up), Gibson told Walpole in his best works' convenor manner that the clergy wouldn't have it. They were outraged and felt that he was bound 'to declare his dislike of it in the plainest and most open manner and to show the sincerity of that conduct by his future conduct'.[34] Clarke, not anyway ardently ambitious for place, never did get the job, remaining in the pleasant precincts of St James, Piccadilly, before, two years later, dying too soon at fifty-four. In these conflicts, Gibson was engaged to get what, however narrowly, he thought right for the Church. Walpole wanted Hanoverian continuity and the consequent continuity of Robert Walpole.

When the two of them agreed about what mattered, Walpole, not a pious man, would indulge the Bishop in his area of expertise and prejudice. But when Gibson had protested that this appointment would embitter the clergy and stated his own readiness for industrial action, he was rocking the relationship. The Church/state entente stumbled at moments like that into large games of uncalled bluff. When, as here, Gibson won them, it was Walpole who had to attend court and explain, Walpole who had to displease the Queen. And keeping Caroline pleased, especially in the early, uncertain days of the reign, was a jewel of his system.

It would all be played out again in 1733/4, but with far more bitterness, over Dr Thomas Rundle. This clergyman lacked Clarke's intellectual pre-eminence, but his spiritual delinquencies were less central to Church doctrine. He had said, very sensibly, that Abraham's readiness to sacrifice his son was evidence of backward and ignorant desert ways, and that the patriarch was trying to gain cachet by pushing bloodthirsty piety to a new and ostentatious level.

The modern mind, including surely the best sort of Christian mind, would take this cool view of a mythical figure very calmly as psychological conjecture. But it discounted 'God's commandment to Abraham'. Gibson was dogged in his orthodoxy, and Rundle had anyway been a friend of Clarke, also of certain deists. When good court sources put it about that a more important friend, the Lord Chancellor, Talbot, intended advancing Rundle to succeed the dying Elias Sydal at Gloucester (his right in respect of this bishopric), Gibson was distressed and he poured out his heart to Walpole in a letter of 18 December 1733:

> I find myself in a very great difficulty in relation to the bishoprick of Gloucester which I suppose the Court designs for Dr Rundle. On the one hand, my own judgment and the regard I owe to my Character and the general sense of the Bishops and Clergy will not permit me to acquiesce in it; either of which in my present situation could be interpreted as sacrificing the cause of the Church to my own private Views, and this at a time when the Bishops have great reason to wish that no person may be brought among them whose affection to the congregation of the Church is not clear and unsuspected. On the other hand, I foresee that if I openly declare against it, as, for the reasons above mentioned, I must do, tho' with no probability of success; I shall greatly offend the Court

and draw upon me the displeasure of my Ld. Chancellor and all his friends.

Having set out his problem, Gibson moved into crisis mode:

In this perplexity, I see no refuge, but the withdrawing, beforehand from all concern in Church matters, except those of my own diocese. And if you think that this savours of Discontent, I beseech you to consider fairly and candidly what my condition is. I am of course on bad terms with the Tories for acting constantly against them; I have lost the goodwill of many of the Whigs by opposing their Designs against the Church and clergy; and the Dissenters are very angry with me for opposing the Test Bill. In these circumstances, my great comfort and refuge is the kind opinion of the Bishops and Clergy, and I cannot, either in judgment or prudence, do or submit to any thing which may endanger the loss of that.

The Bishops, on account of their dutiful behaviour to the Parlt. might hope for some regard to their inclination and good liking in the choice of every new member for the Bench; nor can they think it quite decent to have their successors fix'd and generally known while they are yet alive. [A certain Archbishop, if I am rightly informed, feels this in a sensible manner.] Why then may not this affair of Gloucester sleep and be understood to remain in suspense till the poor Bishop is dead? by which time I may either have nothing to do, or at least have nothing to expect?

I am Sir,

Your very faithful servt.
Edm. London.[35]

Whatever one thinks of the narrow theology which could not conscience Rundle, that is a rather splendid letter. It tells Walpole straightforwardly what the opposing pressures are. Without growing plaintive, it reminds him of the beleaguered position of the Minister's minister. And it says that, rather than stomach the appointment, he will walk away from his great unofficial office. It goes, in Beethoven's phrase, 'from the heart to the heart'.

Walpole was appalled by the crisis. This was 1734, and 1733 had been an *annus horribilis*, spent first in trying to pass an Excise Bill into law and failing, then in avoiding the political collapse which that calamitous defeat seemed to entail (see Chapter 14, *post passim*). In his fight for survival immediately after retreat, as Gibson hints in his letter, the bishops, broadminded at any rate about the Revenue, had, after a little wobble, rallied round. In modern trade-union parlance, they had delivered; he owed them. What after all were Whig bishops for if not to underpin a majority in the Upper House? He was vulnerable to their displeasure. For the unmentioned, indeed unmentionable, weapon behind Gibson's words was an adverse vote of the bishops on some crucial question after the recall of Parliament.

In the short term, Gibson would win at least a tolerable compromise, but at a hard price for the years ahead. He had drawn lines dividing Whig party from Whig churchmen. Walpole would have understood and, *strictly on political grounds*, done what he could to keep the Church happy. But brewing within Whig circles and at court was a vigorous and coarsely expressed anti-clericalism which wanted to make the Church as unhappy as possible. Gibson's threat over Rundle was precisely the sort of stiff-necked, doctrinal flapdoodle up with which such men of the world, and modern men at that, would not put.

To make life harder for Walpole, Talbot would not follow Caroline in her more or less graceful retreat over Clarke. Talbot was no lady. He was a big Whig politician whose constitutional right to nominate men to a bundle of higher clergy positions was, for reasons absurd to enlightened men, being resisted by a parson without birth or interest, the whole episode a deplorable demonstration of combined bigotry and counter-jumping. On top of all which, Caroline wanted Rundle appointed too. Gibson says that 'the court designs' Gloucester for Rundle. The prospect of an alienated Queen with influence over her husband, who hadn't liked Walpole much anyway, suddenly withdrawing her enormously important goodwill was horrid.

Between an episcopate, whose votes he needed, and a court, meddling as George I had never meddled, Walpole was trapped. And 1734 was election year, a bad time for doing anything decisive. His response was Fabian: he did nothing for a year, making no new decisions and no new enemies. But this, in French terms, had become *l'Affaire Rundle*. What followed was a public explosion, a whirlwind of pamphlets, some arguing a case, many drumming hard on the head of 'Dr Codex'. In the published flood were 'A letter to the Rev. Dr Codex on the subject of his modest instruction to the Crown'. This last, interestingly enough, was written by William Arnall, very much Walpole's in-house pamphleteer. Was he really operating simply on his own account? There were also 'Dr Codex no Christian' and, optimistically, 'The Case of Dr Rundle's promotion to the See of Gloucester impartially considered'.

Eventually, taking advantage of Rundle-fatigue, Walpole demonstrated his political class by blowing full-time on an inspired and glittering draw. Rundle would not go to Gloucester, given to a *different* friend of Talbot, the Archdeacon of Berkshire, Martin Benson. But he would become a bishop; a bishop, however, in Ireland which didn't count or, at any rate, was remote from the grieving English clergy. Gloucester, moreover, was a rotten see, worth only about £600.[36] Londonderry, to which the man of the moment would now be despatched, was, surprisingly, a financial catch, a very good thing. After all this tediousness and ill nature, Rundle would prove an excellent, devoted and decently paid bishop, winning the friendship of that great Tory and far higher Churchman than Gibson, Jonathan Swift, Dean of St Patrick's, Dublin.

Gibson had held his ground amid the Church's narrowest jealousies, the Court's active interest and the new secularism. Walpole's political fudge had been a piece of adult statesmanship. But if the Bishop of London had exasperated the Prime Minister, he had turned anti-clerical feeling at Westminster into a widespread anti-Gibson mood. The anger would find expression through two pieces of legislation, the Mortmain Bill of 1735 and the Quaker Tythe Bill of 1736.

Mortmain – literally dead-hand inheritance of money by institutions – was intensely disliked by those with an interest in great estates. The alienating of wealth outside the family line was, not surprisingly, unpopular among the heirs themselves, but the deeper sources of disapproval were historical, nationalistic, capitalistic and Protestant. Their roots lay in the days of the monasteries, enormous beneficiaries across the Middle Ages from speculative buyers of heavenly equity, making over good agricultural land to the praying brethren. The legislation cited by supporters of the bill had been written in the reign of Henry III when, in Catholic England, the struggle for wealth between sword and cloth had not been less bitter.

The argument was being revived now, though the trigger of legislation was the leaving by a Mr Mitchel of one very large landed estate to a university. Much of its effect fell, ironically, upon the Protestant Succession Church of England. Following that, in the dry words of Archdeacon Coxe, 'it was judged convenient for many reasons to put a stop to so growing an evil'. The essential purpose was that it should cease to be lawful to leave lands or money intended to buy land 'for charitable uses' if the conveyance were not executed twelve months before the testator's death.

One of the bill's advocates* stated:

> As the landed interest of this kingdom has always been our chief support against foreign enemies and the great bulwark for defending the liberties of the people against the attempts of ambitious encroaching power, therefore it has always been reckoned a most necessary and a fundamental maxim of our constitution not to allow any great share of our landed interest to be vested in societies or bodies politic, either sacred or profane.

If past legislation, the speaker continued, had only referred to religious houses, that was 'because alienation to them was at that time the only transgression of this maxim which had been felt or complained of'.[37] But hadn't a statute of Edward I expressly forbidden alienation of lands to any body politic whatsoever, and didn't another statute provide a writ against such delinquencies called 'Ad quod Damnum'? Lawyers would argue the statues of Henry II, indeed of Athelstan, down to the margins of the twentieth century. But the dispute here was close enough to the medieval norm for participants to quote medieval sources without anachronism.

The idea of lightly giving wealth without exceptional authority to Oxford, Cambridge or the Foundling Hospital or, if any such preposterous idea could have been suggested in the 1730s, a public art gallery, was offensive to received ideas and clenching fingers. But the bill grew very political and specific in so far as one of the 'bodies politic' standing protesting in the way of the accelerating legislation was Queen Anne's Bounty. This was the fund established in that Queen's reign to provide modest supplements to the stipends of clergymen, so many of whom lived nearer the ground than to God.

There was no way in which Gibson, always concerned for the poorer ministers, would not fight this, nor the Church with him. Like all the other threatened interests, they worked through petition. But, eloquently, whereas petitions from both universities, Eton, Winchester and Westminster schools, were accepted, the one on behalf of the Bounty

---

* No name is given in the record. This may be the address of counsel invited to speak in the House.

was debated, then, by 143 votes to 95, rejected. Also denied exception were the Charity for the Relief of Poor Widows and Children of Clergymen, the Greycoat School and the Trustees of the Charity Schools of London. It takes no very pronounced Marxist prejudice to see here class legislation of some ferocity. The poor clergy would be doubly victims, subject to the scorn reserved by the age for the poor and the contempt it felt for clergymen.

The debate was the occasion for reproach to them, reproach shading into abuse. Lord Hardwicke, Lord Chief Justice, remarked 'that the clergy already possessed a just proportion of the property of the nation which, although it was unequally distributed, nevertheless if pluralities were taken away and other regulations made which he hoped to see done, it would create preferments for those who were now the real objects of distress'.[38] Hervey spoke complacently of the bill giving 'the bishops and parsons very hard, as well as very popular, slaps',[39] and gloatingly observed that, in the Lords, 'the bishops had the mortification of having all the severe things said to their faces . . .'. Walpole made a show of disliking the hard words and cruel treatment, but the most accomplished political manipulator of the century did not stop or temper what he could have stopped or tempered. At best, he deferred to the mood of his party; he may well have shared it.

The second half of Parliament's two-part offering to the Church, the Quaker Tythe Bill, had justice and common decency on its side, perhaps reasons why it was ultimately defeated, despite Walpole's genuine goodwill. The Church of England was never more triumphalist and insufferable than in its claim to every farthing of the clerical tax of tithes from worshippers by other forms of faith or not at all. Old Dissent (Baptists, Independents and others), Catholics, Jews and unbelievers were all under legal obligation to pay up for the Church of England by law established, an inexplicable nonsense to our age, a shining commonplace in 1730.

The Quakers, whom the legislation was to have convenienced, did not even seek relief from payment. But they objected, where there was delay in payment – and not all Quakers were rich men – to being sued expensively even for small sums, in the Ecclesiastical Courts or in Westminster Hall under the rules of Equity. Current legislation, dating back to William III, allowed the option for sums under £10 (say £500 today) of going to the local magistrates. But the clergy, either to deter late payment or out of the particularist spite deforming Christianity

then and long after, were keen to punish the Quaker late in submission
with a stiff lawyer's bill.

A sense of this arrogance can be found in the speech of a layman,
Sir John St Aubyn, opposing the bill. There was no one more ready

> to give all reasonable indulgencies to the several unhappy sectaries among
> us; I think that in points of religious worship, compulsion should never be
> used, but truth is to have the fair opportunity of working by its own force
> upon the natural ingenuity of the mind, and the Supreme Lawgiver has the
> only right to interpose in such matters. But human authority has certainly
> a secondary power to restrain those wild excesses which under the false
> colour of religion would invade the order and discipline of civil society . . .
> What then is it that the Quakers want? Have not all their most intemperate
> desires been from time to time complied with? Are they not even exempted
> from applying to the great author of Truth in their legal testimony. [Quakers
> having a moral horror of an oath, had, after a great effort, been excused it.]
>
> But not contented with this, by a most strange abuse of the permissive
> liberty they enjoy, they send circular exhortation to their brethren to
> oppose the civil jurisdiction of our laws; and having thus cherished and
> strengthened an obstinacy, they approach the legislature itself with harsh
> revilings, unsupported by evidence, against the clergy of our established
> church.[40]

If this sounds like the Establishment with a vengeance, it wasn't. St
Aubyn, representing a county seat in Cornwall from 1722 until his
death in 1744, was a Tory Ultra and committed Jacobite in treasonable communication with the Pretender's court. He was someone of
whom Carte, a Jacobite agent, reported, 'Sir John has assured me he
does not doubt of putting himself at the head of 8 or 10,000 of these
[the tinners of Redruth and St Agnes] any day in the world, and they
are the best men we have in England'.[41] This then was an extreme Tory
speaking, but he was at no distance from majority opinion within the
Church. It was to the votes of such people that Gibson and his company
would appeal.

Together with Sherlock, Potter of Oxford and twelve other bishops,
Gibson opposed the bill, possibly with more vigour than they might
have, had this private proposal been official government business. But
vigorous they were, forming a sort of war cabinet and in St Aubyn's
words, 'sending circular exhortation to their brethren, firing up the

country clergy to represent their sense of it to their friends in Parliament and to petition to be heard by Counsel'.⁴²

They seemed to have succeeded when the bill was surprisingly defeated in the Lords by fifty-four votes to thirty-five after Lord Chancellor Talbot and Chief Justice Hardwicke had intervened with arguments about its practical application. It was, however, a Pyrrhic victory for the Bishop of London. Since, for reasons of sense and influence (the Quakers had weight in Norfolk), Walpole had quietly supported the bill, there had been a breach between Walpole's pope and that pope's political god. More important, since Walpole could readily make up such a difference, all the bitterness of the Rundle affair had come back. The court was furious, nobody more so than George II, who saw Gibson as the leader of a factional revolt. Hervey, who could be elegant as well as viperous, put it well: 'The King with his usual softness in speaking of any people he disliked, called the bishops, whenever he mentioned them in private on this occasion, a parcel of black, canting, hypocritical rascals.' Of Gibson he spoke 'in a style not to be mentioned'.⁴³

The operative word for Edmund Gibson facing the new political scene, was 'despair'. The only course tolerable to him was to leave. The warning in the December 1733 letter was invoked. In another, undated, letter, superscribed 'My last letter to Walpole', he said,

> I foresee that as long as this anti-church spirit prevails, vexations of the like kind are to be expected from session to session; the largest share of which has hitherto fallen upon me, as one who has been supposed to have the largest share in Church matters. I therefore choose to purchase my peace and quiet, or at least an abatement of trouble and vexation, by having it understood that I have no more share in the publick affairs of the Church than the rest of my brethren. They have had the happiness to go on undisturbed and at ease. While in the course of many years, I have been tossed about and insulted by people of almost all denominations, many of whom have been known to stand very well with the Court.⁴⁴

When, in January 1737, the body of William Wake followed his mind into oblivion, Gibson, presumed heir for a dozen years, declined the translation. He remained in post as an active, efficient and highly esteemed Bishop of London, working also at his schemes for education and a colonial ministry, until his death in 1748. So esteemed was he that, a year before his death at seventy-eight, Canterbury was offered again and civilly refused. Walpole would next have preferred Francis Hare, party man for sure, but of some substance. But the Queen, dabbling again, had her mistaken way. The See of St Augustine went to the smoothly minimal John Potter of Oxford. The judgement of the Reverend Henry Etough would have found few dissenters: 'A worse and more contemptible man could not have been selected from the Bench.'[45] Potter would describe himself, by way of pre-emptive cringe, as 'pusillanimous'.

Walpole had succeeded in his Church policy in the practical business of blocking off the overt enemies of Hanover seeking Church places from which to stone the government. He failed in the high aspiration, so far as Walpole ever aspired high, of achieving concord between exalted clerics and a sceptical political class which had lost its awe of men in black gowns. He had extended toleration in practical terms but not risked the comprehension of a very broad church or the open extension of Dissenting rights at the centre of Old Whig thinking.

Gibson had shown himself an outstanding man, abler than most occupants of the See of Canterbury, but not less rigid. He had been a politic idealist, understanding how politics worked while trying to sustain an elevated notion of the Church against the derisive grain of the age. The Anglican Ministry, overmanned and underpaid, its rewards dependent upon Walpole's understanding of obligation and the sporadic advancement of merit, remained a lottery tempered by social connection. Both men had done their imperfect best, but Gibson thought he had failed. The Walpole who could accept Potter had easier criteria.

EXCISE: SCANDAL AND REBUFF

At New Year 1733 Walpole might have been well contented. He had come through a perilous change of monarch six years earlier, yet, despite George II's early pungent dislike, the Prime Minister was now knit up with Queen Caroline and the King into something resembling a cosy triple alliance. In fact, that understanding stood on far stronger ground than any treaty Britain had signed in recent years. It rested upon shared sympathies and agreement. Abroad he was done with Townshend's fraught manoeuvrings promoting such treaties, done with the soldiers, costs and taxes they brought; and, blessedly, he was done with Townshend. The brother-in-law had sunk, departing for a breakthrough in progressive agriculture (cultivation of turnips for soil renewal and winter fodder).

The one reverse Walpole had suffered had been that Dunkirk affair of 1730 when French failure to destroy the harbour of Dunkirk under treaty terms had led to unpleasantness with France, and points scored by an alerted parliamentary opposition. Pulteney and Bolingbroke, with their sharp, derisive press, headed by *The Craftsman*, had become serious politics, playing up Dunkirk and everything else. But with the Treaty of Seville, pacific stability and the parliamentary majority of 1727 solid, there was no reason to think that new elections, due in 1734 under the leisurely requirements of the Septennial Act, would give trouble. With the owners of parliamentary seats, placed or pensioned, as voters to be paid on the nail, and the county seats and independent boroughs quiescent, Walpole did not contemplate a crisis.

But secure governments are rarely satisfied with security. They want to amaze posterity and get the leader's name on to the statute book.

The set phrase about Walpole 'letting sleeping dogs lie' is more accurate than most historical clichés, but in the matter of the Excise, a cosily set up Prime Minister would go around prodding them with a sharp stick.

The decision to introduce an Excise looked superficially like an uncontentious act of good administration. It flowed logically from what Walpole had been trying to do fiscally from the outset. In 1723, his year of vigorous innovation, taxes on coffee and tea had left him revenue to lighten the burden of the Land Tax. It had been brilliant Treasury practice and equally brilliant politics subject to a certain amount of later small print. Results for the first eight years showed £1 million more brought in compared with the previous eight. The shine of the idea had, however, been scuffed by a marked falling off over recent years, 1729–31.

An Excise was meant to benefit the country gentleman who paid the Land Tax at the expense of the merchant, the merchant who, moreover, had been avoiding duty due by way of illicit importation, smuggling (also illicit exportation, or owling, since we then had export taxes). Walpole, born the heir to a country gentleman, was familiar with the cheap cuts, turned jackets and other small economies to which his father, Colonel Robert, had been given. He also recalled from his early political days the grinding taxes raised for Marlborough's wars (which he had supported) and the success of Harley's Tories in promising to end war and cut taxes. Walpole was more Robert Harley's pupil than it would have been politic to admit.

Sweetening Sir John Brute with a diminishing Land Tax had been an obsession from the start. Voters who saw what had been a four shillings in the pound tax dwindle in this bold move from two shillings to one would be sweetly disposed to the getter-down. The urgency was, however, badly overstated. Seventy per cent of revenue at this time was raised from indirect taxes imposed on goods, and the taxes on essentials were higher in Britain than in France or Holland.[1]

But Land Tax reductions commanded a visceral conviction, rooted in the reclaimed soil of Norfolk. Walpole might spend money in a gaudy and arriviste fashion – Houghton, Orford House in Chelsea and a very flashy largesse in the way of entertainment given and figure cut – but at the bottom of the page he bought land. Houghton might be a showpiece, but the next five fields and the little farm across the way were sweet acquisition. Walpole embodied the English idea of the French peasant mentality. He hated the Land Tax because he paid it. It was the putting of shillings in the pound back on, to pay for the Hessian troops which the brother-in-law wanted to fight the Spanish or the Austrians, which had finished Townshend.

As for revenue lost on imported goods, smugglers brought in his wines. He had, as we have seen, used a government launch to carry uncustomed French luxuries to his property. But that was a venial sin from which the First Lord of the Treasury absolved Sir Robert Walpole. Smuggling done by other people in great volume was something else, a thoroughly bad thing, a question, perhaps, of moralities of scale. Smuggling deprived the revenue of its dues and put a further burden on the rural landowner. And heavily conducted it certainly was: lawbreaking on an industrial scale, the smugglers themselves 'arrived to such an intolerable Pitch of Insolence as to bid Defiance to the civil Magistrates'.[2] It was claimed in earnest that the illicit traffic through Falmouth alone would pay the Land Tax for two years together.

The Jamaica Inn sort of smuggling – goods run to obscure creeks and hidden in the eaves and cellarage of accommodating houses, all done under lamplight by characters to be played in the film by Robert Newton – was one thing and could only be fought by furious vigilance and laws ever more terminally retributive. But so much other smuggling was clerical and unromantic, a fraud on the bureaucracy, often with the remunerated connivance *of* the bureaucracy: false declarations, understated cargoes, the paying of duties on far smaller quantities of goods than were moving. Hitting that through an Excise was a good thing in its own right, independent of relieving the Land Tax. The Duke of Newcastle, with his brother, Henry Pelham, now rising in Walpole's command, certainly thought so. 'Excise will be the grand affair,' he wrote 'but as it is right in every respect, it gains every day and will certainly be carried by a great majority in both houses.'[3]

Such were the rewards expected from an Excise on key commodities that Walpole dreamed of reducing the Land Tax to zero, raising the necessary revenue by way of an inland operation, the requirement of all imported goods to be held in bonded warehouses and taxed at use. This would not end smuggling, but it would knock on the head the sham procedures by which imported goods, proclaimed for re-exportation, seeped into British consumption untaxed. It would, however, first have to clear Lords, Commons and that brute and unquantifiable thing, public opinion.

Walpole might have foreseen the dark wood into which he was jauntily travelling if in the previous years he had learned the right lesson about the Salt Tax. Duties on salt had been removed in 1730. At that time, having the means, he had wished to remove the tax on candles, an article purchased most heavily by the well-to-do. Reluctantly he had given way to strong feelings in Parliament. But regret lingered; the Salt Tax required 350 posts as Excise officers, favours in the crown's gift for friends, families and petitioners of peers and other borough owners, useful patronage. Unsurprisingly, finding himself short in 1732, he reimposed it.

Relating to the price of preserved meat, the Salt Tax fell hardest on the poor, for whom a higher proportion of income spent on necessities like food operated, then as now, as an economic original sin. By reimposting salt, a year before the Excise was put to Parliament, Walpole was stepping off the safe ground and making himself intensely unpopular with the general public while giving Pulteney, Sandys, Rushout and their Tory allies a populist drum upon which they would shortly beat his retreat.

Walpole was ardent to be cutting Land Tax (by half, to one shilling in the pound). And renewed salt duties gave him part of the financial leeway for such a reduction. The hammering of the general public with an indirect tax on a commodity in order to benefit a favoured minority was a triumph of prejudice over political judgement. Walpole, who could step into self-parody, proclaimed the salt duty as 'no burthen upon the people of England'.[4] The Land Tax was, by contrast, 'the most unequal, the most grievous and most oppressive tax' ever raised.[5] His speech of 9 February 1732 was full of his usual efficient detail, but also grandly complacent: 'Where every man contributes a small share, a great sum may be raised for the public services without any man being sensible of what he pays; whereas a small sum, raised upon a few, lies heavily upon each particular man, and is the more grievous in that it is unjust; for where the benefit is mutual the expense ought to be common.'[6] A remission of a shilling in the pound (5 per cent) was to be part paid for by an impost likely to run beyond 5 per cent on the poorer heads upon which it fell. It was 130 years before Gladstonian taxation, but there were plenty of people, especially Tories, in those days certainly warmer towards the poor than the Walpolians, to do the arithmetic and shout 'unfair'. But Walpole was majestic in his self-satisfaction: 'Of all the taxes I ever could think of, there is not one more general, nor one less felt than that of the duty upon salt.'[7]

The word 'general' was very unfortunate. The tax, itself a form of Excise, was resented over salt but why should it stop at salt? Why not a general Excise, punitive on all and most punitive on the poor? Walpole and the Salt Tax were confronted by Captain Edward Vernon, Member for Penryn, as something done 'only to ease the rich at the expense of the poor'. He added, 'This seems to be a step towards introducing a general Excise which is inconsistent with the liberties of a free people; and Sir, when life, liberty or property is concerned, it will be found that every man will fight; a country clown in hodden grey may perhaps shew as much courage and fight as well as a soldier in red.'[8] The key term was 'general Excise' and it would have enormous currency when the Excise Bill of 1733 was introduced. Eight years later, *Admiral* Vernon, otherwise 'Old Grogram' from his plain coat, would capture Portobello in the war with Spain and become a national hero, part of the naval pantheon. For the moment, *Captain* Vernon, warm-hearted and hot-tempered, was only speaking prophecy.

William Pulteney, effectively leader of the Commons opposition, carried on smooth where Vernon had started rough, recalling things said two years before when the Salt Tax had been remitted and when the King himself had 'expressed a compassionate concern for the hardships of the poor artificers and manufacturers; from which we must conclude that his Majesty's opinion then was that that sort of people laboured under the greatest hardships and were the first who ought to be relieved'.[9] Pulteney also pulled the stop marked 'general Excise' to perform with Handelian resonance. He took it that 'the meaning of a General Excise relates not to things on which it is raised, but to the persons from whom; and every excise is a general excise, if the whole body of the people, the poor, the needy, the most wretched are obliged to contribute thereto'.[10]

He also, amid the general elegance of a major speech, knew how to employ a homely touch. In the days before all-year foddering, never mind refrigeration, people lived if, they were lucky, on a winter and early spring diet of salt meat. Pulteney was understanding. 'I hope no farmer in England is as yet obliged to make his family dine upon bread and cheese or upon boiled cabbage without a bit of pickled pork, salt beef or bacon to give them a savour. I do not know what they may be brought to if we begin to multiply excises upon them.'[11] And from this homely, identifiable image, Pulteney went on to make calculations based on a farmer's extended family. This, including servants and board-found labourers, he reckoned at sixteen and estimated 'six pence a week for salt, according to the price at which it sold formerly when this duty was subsisting. At this rate there is scarcely a farmer in England but must pay above twenty shillings a year toward this tax.'[12]

With the general Excise went the extension of both political patronage and police interference in citizens' lives. Sir William Wyndham, arch-country gentleman that he was, preferred to keep up the Land Tax. 'One of the great evils of the Salt Tax, I may say the greatest because it strikes at our constitution, is the great number of officers which must be employed in collecting that branch of the revenue. These officers are named by the crown and being spread all over the country, must have a great influence in elections.'[13] And Wyndham declined to follow Walpole's flat-rate and regressive notions of tax. 'Liberty may be equally dear to every man, but surely he that has the largest property, ought to contribute most to the public expense.'[14]

Walpole was also exempting Scotland from the impost, and resenting 'Scotchmen' was an article high in the whole duty of English patriots. There was nothing, said Pulteney, in the Articles of Union which exempted the Scots from national taxes. Leaving them out made a nonsense of Walpole's view of a mild charge which people would never feel or notice. 'The only question is whether we ought, out of compassion, to indulge them with such an exemption, because the poor people of that country are not able to pay it; . . . I hope it will be allowed me, that we ought to have an equal compassion for the poor people of England: journeymen and day labourers who have no stock, no property, and are equally poor in all countries.'[15]

Walpole, in putting back an old and hated tax and drawing the threads of extra local patronage and obligation into hands already juggling so many, was awakening a feeling which the opposition, in the way of oppositions, would whip up into a vivid apprehension. It might be unfair, but Walpole was in politics and had never worried unduly about fairness when the boot was on his foot. And the tax was not even an effective one. For all the people it affronted, and all the people now playing on that affront, it brought in little enough revenue, one-third of a shilling's worth of Land Tax. It had been taken off, was now being put on again and did not meet the gap to be left by a projected concession to the landed gentleman. His own prejudice, his socially contemptuous view of an invisible poor, his identification with the rich or getting-rich, those owning land and buying more, for whom there should be 'compassion', lay behind a renewed Salt Tax. It was seen to do so and had started a debate in which Captain Vernon, getting in first, had shifted and heightened the issue by raising the question of a general Excise.

The phrase was on every tongue, professional politicians would play that theme long and large, angry feelings and fear of it would follow and transfer to any other Walpolian tax proposal, however rational. The poets were on to it already and were getting personal. Alexander Pope, friend of Bolingbroke, wrote in his *Epistle to Bathurst* (a Tory in the Lords):

> *Ask you why Phryne the whole Auction buys?*
> *Phryne foresees a general Excise.*[16]

Phryne was an Athenian courtesan who famously posed naked at the Eleusinian Games; she stood, and was known to stand, for Maria Skerrett, later Lady Walpole. It was getting rough and would get much rougher.

For Lord Hervey, the Prime Minister's recording partisan, 'Faction was never more busy on any occasion; terrors were never more industriously scattered, and clamour never more universally raised.'[17] He could only see the 'art, vigilance and industry of enemies' bringing on 'the epidemic madness of the nation'.[18] But Hervey, who gives only six lines to the Salt Tax, made no mention of the highly public failures in Walpole's judgement and sensibility which were doing his enemies' work for them.

For if the Salt Tax of 1732 gave Walpole an ill wind, the scandals of that year had turned it into a foul one. The Prime Minister was not implicated in the affairs of the Charitable Corporation, the York Buildings or the Derwentwater Trust. But they happened under his authority, they fitted comfortably with the reputation of the Minister who had screened the South Sea. And, where the conniver at fraud or theft was a useful ally, the Walpole machine had worked hard to mitigate consequences.

Back in 1730, Lord Perceval* wrote an invaluable diary, now identified as 'Egmont's Diary', Earl of Egmont being the (English) title to which

---

* John Perceval, Viscount Perceval, an Irish peer representing Harwich in the Commons, 1727–34.

he was elevated. A grumbling friend had already noted down a devastating general comment on Walpole's judgement of men. It was

> this meanness of his (the prostitution of the character of a first Minister in assisting and strenuously supporting the defence of dunghill worms, let their cause be ever so unjust, against men of honour, birth and fortune, and that in person too) that gains him so much ill-will; formerly when the first Minister appeared in any matter, he did so with gravity, and the honour and service of the Crown appeared to be concerned, but Sir Robert, like the altars of refuge in old times, is the asylum of little unworthy wretches who, submitting to dirty work, endear themselves to him, and get his protection first and then his favour . . .[19]

The case of the Derwentwater estates was dirty enough work. It concerned a dipping into supposedly secure funds held as trustees by commissioners. James Radcliffe, Earl of Derwentwater, had been one of the two Jacobite Lords beheaded out of the seven condemned, falling to Walpole's punitive resistance to the merciful instinct of George I which had retrieved four. A fifth, Lord Nithsdale, had saved himself by escaping from the Tower. Derwentwater's estates had been put into commission for his infant heir, John Radcliffe, as, similarly, were those of his brother Charles, also an attainted rebel, escaped to France.

The leading offender here was Denis Bond, Member for Poole, who with a single interval had sat in Parliament since 1709 and who had been made a commissioner of the estate. The commissioners were on a salary of £1000 p.a. tax free, in hope, forlorn here, of keeping them honest. Commissioners handling the estate had latitude to buy and sell to its intended advantage. On the strength of which, in 1723, Bond, together with the law-serjeant John Birch, MP for Weobley, concentrated on the parts of the estate, the remainder and the reversion, which had been confiscated and could be sold. They organised a one-bidder auction of the remainder, for a man of straw, a certain Smith, well known in the City as a rogue, for £1060. By further sleight of hand, they transferred the reversion to him as well, the whole deed made legal by the signatures of two other commissioners, which power, curiously among lifelong businessmen, had been casually given them, blank cheque-wise, in advance.

They next organised for themselves the annuity originally intended for the attainted Charles Radcliffe, worth £200 p.a. with the good prospect, via the reversion, given the infant heir's poor health, of the whole estate, worth £9000. All this came out when John Radcliffe died late in 1731, still a minor, with Smith holding the estates. This prompted an inquiry, after a private undertaking by the Irish peer and MP, Lord Gage, which discovered the essentials. Bond and Birch, beyond ministerial solicitude, were expelled the House.

But contingent fire was drawn upon another £1000 commissioner, Sir John Eyles, whose signature to unread documents had been freely available to Bond and Birch. Eyles was a paid-up Walpole man, entitled to the full Walpole cover. He had been trusted with running the residual South Sea Company after the crash and spoke for its interests in the Commons. A flavour of the Eyles outlook comes from his successful motion of 1725, reducing the franchise by raising the household rate requirement from twenty to thirty shillings.

Under attack in 1732 for, at very best, idly making a back for other men's fraud, Eyles appealed, not too humbly, to 'the great weight of business which the disordered affairs of the South Sea Company laid upon him' and assumed that, in its light, 'he can not but hope to find a generous apology from the breast of everyone before whom he is now in Judgement'. The syntax is sticky but he seems to be asking his critics to say 'sorry'. The admirable Captain Vernon declined the invitation and, according to a narrative in *The Gentleman's Magazine*, said plainly that 'directors of the Company had carried on a private trade contrary to their oaths and hurtful to the company . . . having his eye all the time upon Sir John Eyles'.[20]

This produced an eruption of the 'say that outside' kind from Eyles and the restraining intervention of the Speaker. Monumentally careless but far more likely involved to his discreet advantage, Eyles was declared 'to be guilty of an irregularity' and got away with a reprimand. Delivered at the same time as the Bond and Birch expulsions, by Mr Speaker Onslow, it told him, 'But happy for you, Sir, it appears to the House to have been a matter rather of evil example than of evil intention; for which reasons the Resolutions of the House on this occasion have a mixture of justice and mercy.' Few accessories to fraud have enjoyed so much tolerance.

The Charitable Corporation had been a wholesome good idea. Established in 1707 as a sort of poor man's bank to pre-empt loan sharks by offering small loans to small men at honest interest, it had operated since then on a modest scale. But in 1728, and again in 1730,

Sir Robert Sutton, a member of its managing committee, had succeeded in getting its capital-raising authorisation enlarged to, first, £300,000, then £600,000. About the chief villain of the Charitable Corporation, George Robinson, there were no difficulties. Originally a broker in Exchange Alley, and one with a bad reputation, as cashier of the Corporation he drew in three directors, desperate after market losses, contriving with even lower financial life, John Thompson, its warehouse keeper, to extract most of those reserves.

Fictitious schemes handled by Thompson served to take and drive away large quantities of money to 'stockjob and make fortunes by', and then 'return that money to the Company's account when their turns were served'.[21] Actually, Robinson bought heavily into the York Buildings Company and sold at a large profit, without telling his associates or returning the initial stake.

He had, in the usual manner, bought himself a seat, Great Marlow in Buckinghamshire, and a nearby estate; and, in the usual manner, never took it up, preferring an overseas destination never discovered, leaving to Parliament the superogatory duty of finding him 'guilty of being privy to and concerned in, many indirect and fraudulent practices in the management of the Charitable Corporation', formally expelling him on 3 April 1732. The money Robinson had invested in the estate at Marlow was recovered and doubtless there were overheads. Even so, owing the Corporation £46,000 as its agent, quite apart from what had been embezzled, he is likely to have lived on elsewhere pleasantly enough.

Robinson, his birth and death dates unknown, was one of those ghostly figures who sidle out of the shadows before disappearing in a flash of magnesium, furtive little sparrows in whose fall there is no great significance. Sir Robert Sutton was something else. Not particularly well connected by birth, but in deacon's orders, he had risen through the Church as an ambassador's chaplain, putting together a diplomatic and commercial career of some quality. British ambassador at Constantinople *and* agent of the Levant Company, before taking posts at Passarowitz for the treaty negotiations, then ambassador at Paris, he went pleasantly on to marry Sunderland's widow, and, in 1722, entered Parliament as county Member for his native Nottinghamshire.

Sutton had risen oddly perhaps and was *nouveau* certainly, but very big and very rich *nouveau*. And Sir Robert Walpole had no foolish

prejudices against such people. So few that Sutton was an early beneficiary of Walpole's personal ceremonial revival, becoming, in 1725, a
Knight of the Bath. He was also sub-governor of the Royal African
Company. Although by no means a total creature of the regime – he
opposed the government over Civil List arrears in 1729 and abstained
on the Pensions Bill defeated in February 1730 – he was customarily
a government supporter.

As spokesman for the Charitable Corporation in the Commons, he
had to defend it under fire. There was quite a lot to defend, Robinson's
crude theft having drawn uncalled-for attention, a committee of inquiry,
into the Corporation generally and wholly unrelated acts of dishonesty
committed by Sutton. He had not been part of the Robinson affair, but
one witness to the committee report, the Corporation's secretary, Higgs,
while clearing him of this, caught the wider mood of the directors, the
atmosphere in which that grand larceny had gone unnoticed. In 1725
and 1726 a number of meetings had been held 'to consult the opening
Houses to lend money upon pledges; That he [Higgs] sir Robert Sutton,
at the first, sir John Meres and Mr Gascoigne all along, were for lending
money in small sums to the poor, but the majority were for lending
money in the City for large sums; and Mr Bond who was in the majority,
said "Damn the poor, let us go into the City where we may get money"'.²²
That 'at the first' is eloquent of Sutton's and the whole Corporation's
frailty, if not so eloquent as 'Damn the poor'. Incidentally, the Mr Bond
who spoke then was the same Denis Bond MP met above.

Sutton's crimes were preliminary to the embezzlement. It emerged
that, in lobbying for an increase in permitted capital, he had given false
evidence about exhausted resources. Having given promises to cease
issuing notes, he had disregarded them. Much more seriously, Sutton
KB (when, in deacon's orders, described by Pope as 'Reverend Sutton')
had used his inside information about two new issues to buy early and
often. He 'kept secret for some months for the private advantage of
some of the committee and assistants and their agents, during which
time, great numbers of shares were bought by them'.²³ In an age when
petty theft could, and regularly did, lead to one of the thirteen hanging
sessions a year in which London rejoiced, Sir Robert Sutton's enrichment was resented.

The opposition smelled prey and fear. Samuel Sandys, Pulteney's
effective lieutenant, was on to him, first moving a succession of
resolutions condemning the acts which the House Committee had

disclosed, then directly accusing Sutton. The six-hour-long defence which Sutton had made did not impress Sandys or anyone else. As the indispensable Lord Egmont recorded, 'Mr Sandys, recapitulating the particulars to Sir Robert, showed the weakness of some and the falseness of others [and] made a motion . . . [that] Sir Robert Sutton had been guilty of promoting and abetting and carrying on the fraudulent practices of the Charitable Corporation.'[24] But Walpole, extraordinarily, set about organising Sutton's rescue.

On top of what he had done for sure – staging an issue on insider information, lying to Parliament over financial resources and breaking his promise on note issue – Sutton had been on the Board, as we would call it, throughout Robinson's raids, noticed nothing and done nothing. And such surprising incompetence was the foundation for the defence which Walpole mounted through his lieutenants, Henry Pelham and Sir Paul Methuen. He was actually a loser by those thefts, they said, and though fearfully negligent, he had a good character (something much disputed) and he had no part of the main fraud.

It was not good enough, certainly not for Sir John Barnard, the voice of small business in the City and a man much disliked by Walpole, who observed that Sutton

> was not only remiss and negligent, but the patron of the Corporation. That his application and credit alone obtained the two licenses for augmenting their capital . . . and his good character before is an objection to him in this case, since he made use of it to seduce numbers of people to trust him with their fortunes and then, not only betrayed them to others, but bought up their shares at low prices to sell them out dear, for which purposes he kept the licenses for augmentation of the capital secret for some months.

For Barnard 'the motion was rather too charitable than too severe'.

By any standards, including those of the flexible times, Sutton was a rogue, though, in the absence of anything worth calling company law, possibly not a punishable one. He deserved expulsion, and, on a motion that followed on 4 May, he and a co-conspirator, Sir Archibald Grant, were duly expelled. But the Walpole machine set about postponing the question of any other punishment. As the House was close to rising, nothing immediate was settled. Those involved were prohibited from leaving the country or moving their property into other hands. Otherwise, apart from a general declaration that the offenders 'should make just satisfaction', it was all left to be looked into in the next session.

But hopes of letting a scandal blow itself out simply prolonged it. Sandys had no intention of letting go. When the next session came, he was armed with a confession from Thompson, a leading conspirator. His new motion declared Sutton guilty of 'many notorious breaches of trust and many indirect and fraudulent practices'. As Egmont noted, 'Had this been carried, nothing had been bad enough for him and we should have moved for a bill of pains and penalties, to render him forever incapable of holding a place of profit or trust and to give his estate to the proprietors of the Corporation, sufferers by his breach of trust.'[25]

Such expropriation, which would have enabled the Corporation to resume in full its helpful dealings with small borrowers, engaged Walpole's compassion. Egmont again: 'Sir Robert Walpole, who thought this too severe, though he spoke not, yet influenced the court party to speak in Sir Robert Sutton's favour, who were likewise joined by some of the malcontents on account of relation or particular friendship . . . to him such as Sir Paul Methuen, Lord Morpeth etc.'[26]

It was enough to turn the axe. Sutton was simply declared, on a vote of 148 to 89, to have shown 'neglect of duty', and ordered to be reprimanded. At which understatement, and pulled punch, fifty MPs walked out. By ironical contrast, Sutton came back into the Commons in 1734 as Member for Great Grimsby, a seat notoriously owned by the defaulting Cashier of the South Sea Company, Robert Knight. Sutton had been expelled only in a Pickwickian (or Walpolian) sense. Birch, a hardy spirit, stood at the by-election caused by his expulsion, but was defeated, stood again in the general election of 1734 and was re-elected. Meanwhile, Denis Bond, having damned the poor, confined himself to upholding the law, as Recorder of Weymouth, Melcombe Regis, Poole and Wareham. And, from 1735, three years after expulsion from the Commons, he became Churchwarden of St George's, Hanover Square, a parish not too much troubled by them.

The timing of these episodes, bunched together with further irregularities at the South Sea and with the York Buildings affair, itself interlinked with the Charitable Corporation, fitted every hostile notion of Walpole's political circle. Pope's words, written in his third Moral Epistle (1732), spoke for a very broad public opinion indeed:

Perhaps, you think, the poor might have their part
Bond damns the poor and hates them from his heart
The grave Sir Gilbert holds it for a rule
That every man in want is knave or fool:
God cannot love (says Blunt with tearless eyes)
The wretch he starves – and piously denies.

Sir Gilbert Heathcote, Whig Member and former governor of the Bank (twice), was the pre-eminent City man. Blunt, of course, was the leading spirit of the South Sea, lucky not to be in jail. Pope made it clear that he was following the report and that '"Damn the poor", "God hates the poor", and "Every man in want is either knave or fool & c" were the genuine apothegms of some of the persons here mentioned.'

The idea of the Whig ascendancy as a near-conspiracy of rich, aggrandising men, turning the side of a shoe to the working citizen, and rotten corrupt with it, was general. The Salt Tax, reimposing upon poor, small and struggling men, a burden, at once irksomely new and unpleasantly familiar, completed the creation of the perfect wrong moment for establishing an Excise. Only someone too long in power, whose understanding of other men, however acute at Westminster and among the squires, extended no further, would have tried.

Whatever tribulations Walpole had laid up, he did not introduce the Excise fearing severe resistance. Like Margaret Thatcher after 1987, he had lost from government the contrary and restraining voices, in this case Townshend and Carteret, and was free to be truer to his own instincts than wisdom advised. There were less than two years of the septennial term to run, but Walpole was making schemes for expansion in the next parliament with unendearing assurance. The Excise would be hugely popular; Walpole men should go where they had not gone before. Back in Norfolk, Norwich, tenuously held, should have a Walpole triumph with brother Horatio replacing the current trusty, Robert Britiffe, leaving his own Yarmouth seat for Robert's unmeritable son, Edward. Meanwhile, one of the Whig-held county seats should enjoy apotheosis from the candidacy of the Prime Minister.

These plans and others for London, Gloucestershire and Hampshire, as Paul Langford points out in his superb study,* crept into newspaper

---

* *The Excise Crisis*, Oxford University Press, 1975.

stories and would be confirmed by the hurried slipping in of sacrificial substitutes, when the wind turned about. Triumphs are commonly planned ahead of victory; the Walpole who rose to outline the Excise Bill had anticipated nothing less.

He approached the task with less than his usual parliamentary craft. The Excise did not come as a furious surprise driven hard for quick accomplishment. The opposition had wind of it and the approach was sauntering. On 16 January 1733, the King's speech, short of details, made a pious injunction, echoed in the address of thanks (both presumably drafted by Walpole) that Members should 'avoid unreasonable heats and animosities and not suffer yourselves be diverted by any specious pretences from steadfastly pursuing the true interest of your country'.[27] Sir John Barnard, dogged but not factitious critic, rose to cast the first stone: 'I must say Sir, that the desiring such words to be put into address of thanks to His majesty, to me looks as if the gentleman was conscious that there is something to be brought before us in this session of parliament, which he foresees will be met with a warm opposition . . .' And 'if any thing should happen to be proposed in this House which evidently appears to be inconsistent with the liberties or the trade of the nation, I hope the indignation of every man that thinks so will rise against such a proposition . . .'. Barnard had looked 'without doors', and scented anxieties, or, in the language of the day, 'jealousies'. It seemed 'as if something were intended to be done in this session of parliament that may be destructive to our liberties and detrimental to our trade: from when this jealousy hath arisen, I do not know; but it is certain that there is such a jealousy among all sorts of people, and in all corners of the nation'.[28]

He was followed by Sandys, who found the official warning 'Derogatory to the honour of the House in general and that House in particular'[29]; and by Shippen, noting,

> at present a most remarkable and general spirit among the people for protecting and defending their liberties and their trade . . . from all quarters we hear of meetings and resolutions for that purpose; and the spirit is so general that it cannot be ascribed to any one set of men . . . the whole people of England seem to be united in this spirit of jealousy and opposition . . . such remonstrances are not to be contemned, a thorough contempt for them may produce the most terrible effects.[30]

There was, too, a rambling but enlightening speech from Sir Thomas Aston. Aston was the opposition Whig, whose election at Liverpool Walpole had attempted to kill by supporting the petition of his man, Brereton, provoking Egmont's comments about 'this meanness'. He spoke the new mood, lamenting the falling off of trade and damning the new finance embodied by Change Alley: 'And there Sir, there are such abominable frauds and such wicked impositions practised . . . Does not almost every session of parliament open us to some new scene of villainy and roguery?'[31] Walpole might not be getting the message; it was certainly being sent.

The Excise Bill not having been presented officially, opposition leaders obtained time to stage a debate 'in expectation of the Excise scheme being brought in'. Rushout, close to Pulteney, observed quizzically, 'For my part I know nothing about it, I cannot tell when we are to have the pleasure of seeing that famous project; but I wish that some gentleman who knows more of it than I do, would get up and fix a day when he thinks it will be brought in, and then move that the call of the House be put off till that day . . .'[32] It should have worried Walpole. The opposition were light on their feet and, in derisive good humour, they were teasing him.

The Prime Minister was relaxed in reply, but to the charge that the bill was being hurriedly changed he was blandly concessionary: 'As for the Scheme's having received alterations and amendments, I do not know but it may; I never thought myself so wise as to stand in no need of assistance.'[33] The debate provided new openings for talk of a general Excise and the charge of amendment. Barnard believed that 'this scheme in its first conception was for a general alteration of the method of collecting the revenue; it was for a general excise; but that, it seems, it was afterwards thought too much at once, and therefore we are now, I suppose, to single out only one or two of the branches, in order that they may be first hunted down.'[34]

Henry Pelham intervened to say that 'there never was any such thing intended as a general excise nor any design of making a general alteration in the method of collecting the public revenue'.[35] But, ominously, Pelham was followed by Micajah Perry. Walpole had talked of the frauds committed in the wine and tobacco trades. Perry is cryptically reported thus: 'Mr Perry, member for London, spoke in vindication of the merchants dealing in the wine and tobacco trade.' He was himself a leading tobacco merchant.[36] In the 1727 election the Whig monopoly of London had been mauled. A Tory won one seat and another had been taken for the Whigs – by Micajah Perry!

The getting in first of the opposition's case continued through other parliamentary business in March. The debate in early February on the army estimates had Shippen linking Walpole's unWhiggish standing army with political coercion. It might 'make wicked ministers more audacious than otherwise they would be in projecting and propagating schemes which may be inconsistent with the liberties, destructive to the trade and burdensome on the people of this nation'.[37]

The petition of the North American colony of Rhode Island against new sugar duties, one which the government refused to hear on the constitutional grounds that it was directed against a money bill, was latched on to by Barnard and Pulteney. Refusal, said Pulteney, relied on precedent which took no account of the vast expansion in recent years of taxes and tax legislation. It was 'monstrous, it is even frightful to look into the Indexes where for several columns together we see nothing but Taxes, Taxes, Taxes! . . . I cannot see why the receiving of this petition should be so much opposed, unless it be that the rejecting of this petition is to be made use of as a precedent for receiving no petitions against a certain scheme which we expect soon to be laid before us . . .' Aston intervened to say that, whatever the case about colonial sugar duties, 'there cannot surely be any objection against our receiving petitions that may be offered against a new and dangerous method of collecting duties already laid on'.[38]

They had every reason to make a to-do about petitions. Their friends were making ready to bombard Parliament with them. They would also be instructing their MPs. For the stir in the country, natural or lobby-stimulated, was already underway and not to be tempered. Walpole's loyal sheet, *The London Journal*, might soothingly assert, 'This *popular Fury* begins to abate; the Passions, at least of the better sort, begin to subside; and there seems a Disposition to hearken to the Voice of Reason and receive Advice.'[39]

Nothing could have been less true. *The Craftsman*, parodying such official self-assurance, wrote, 'Persons must have a very mean Opinion of the Understanding or Resolution of the Ministry to imagine they will be bullied out of their Reason or roared out of their Senses, or that they will be induced to depart from what is right or just through fear of a few Lob-headed politicians lifting up their voices and making a noise in the dark. No, if they are frightened, they are gone.'[40] It was an extraordinary putting of the writer's feet into ministerial shoes, bold assertion, underwritten by private acknowledgement, that the ice was very thin.

In London, the City, not then the citadel of the chalk-striped rich, but teeming with small and medium-sized merchant undertakings, meetings were called, City men invaded the parliamentary lobbies and had friends like Barnard and Perry giving the Excise relentlessly hostile attention in the Commons. As a Walpole ally, Colonel Howard, wrote in mid-March, 'The Court of Requests and the Lobby and the Stairs were filled with people from the City.'[41] So, soon, might the street be. The London mob in 1710 had been near-Jacobite, Church-in-danger, all for Dr Sacheverell, but at all times it was 'Agin the government'. Sophisticated political London, City and Westminster, was, in 1733, what might be called 'Old Whig', no friend of that standing army which Walpole called the Land Forces, fiercely and instinctively distrustful of central government, very much a repository of the parliamentary inheritance from Hampden and Pym. And public order, as ever more ferocious laws shrilly testified, was not a Georgian strong point.

When the debate opened, the mob was expected. In fact at first it was smaller and better behaved than expected but 'proper directions were given to justices of the peace, constables and civil magistrates to attend and keep the peace; and secret orders were likewise given both to the horse and foot Guards to be in readiness to march, in case of exigence and extremity, at a moment's warning'.[42] Walpole's introductory speech to the Commons on 12 March reflected the delays in bringing it in at all. Defensive and resentful in turn, it announced a scheme narrowed in focus. An Excise on wine had been much discussed and contemplated, but to the Commons Walpole said, 'My thoughts have been confined solely to the revenue arising from the duties on wine and tobacco.' It had been 'the frequent advices I had of the shameful frauds committed in these two branches and the complaints of the merchants themselves that induced me to turn my attentions to finding a remedy for this growing evil'.[43] However, he would confine himself 'entirely to the tobacco trade and the frauds practised in that branch of the revenue'.[44]

Tobacco was, of course, the thing for raising money. And speaking in moralistic terms to be adapted by generations of unconceived Chancellors, he apostrophised 'an article of luxury as depends for its use on custom or caprice, and is by no means essential to the support and real comfort of human life'.[45] The opposite had not troubled him in the case of salt meat. (Samuel Johnson, taxed about his regular sixpences to beggars, that 'they would only spend it on gin', would reply, 'And are they to be denied such sweeteners to their existence?')

The Craftsman, in high and sardonic fettle, recognised the space for a sword thrust. In particular, a bad-tempered remark of Walpole's about merchants as 'Sturdy Beggars' was taken hold of in No. 352 in the best dog-and-trouser style:

> We have lately been told that parliament does not sit to please the Merchants as they are really a band of STURDY BEGGARS who enrich themselves with the Plunder of the Nation, it must be acknowledged that they are so far from being gratified that the statutes against *Vagrancy* ought to be put in force against them; nay if all the foreign commodities which they import for the convenience of life in return for our surplus manufactures are to be ranked under the Denomination of Luxuries, as we are also told, I think that Trade itself ought to be suppress'd as well as the MERCHANTS.[46]

Even so Walpole had played to his technical and statistical strengths. And he had cases: Peele who on board the recently docked *James and Mary* of Maryland had bought 310 hogsheads of tobacco for ready money and the next month sold to a Mr Hyam 200 hogsheads for immediate re-export. By using debentures from a former cargo to certificate payments, Peele kept the official re-export volume below its true weight by 21,580 pounds.[47] Less sophisticated was 'socking', a cant term, said Walpole, for the theft 'chiefly carried on by watermen, lightermen, tide waiters and city porters, called gangs-men'.[48] Dumped in safe houses for later, uncustomed, import, it amounted to a useful piece of free trade. Fifty tons were reckoned to have been shifted during a year by the men subjected to one sustained investigation. The law being what it then was, he could record 150 dismissals and nine convictions, followed by six men being transported and three whipped, an interesting contrast to the fates of Bond, Birch and Eyles.

Less dangerous was cheating on the 'drawback'. This was the repayment of customs duty where goods appeared as intended for re-export. The cargo might be a dud, cases of tobacco stalks covered with a thin layer of leaves. Alternatively, the rogue trader collected the drawback on cargo, re-exported it only as far as a waiting ship in harbour at Ostend or Dunkirk, before relanding it in smaller parcels in England.

It was all reasonable and, as ever when Walpole spoke about finance, wholly lucid. Like Wood's halfpence, it was good sense incapable of being got across. Calmly enough, despite the syntax, the Prime Minister met the general Excise charge, one of 'the many slanders to which the report of this project has exposed me', head-on and in italics: '*I do most unequivocally assert that no such scheme ever entered my head, or for what I know, into* [sic] *the head of any man I am acquainted with*.'[49]

And he gave reasons why it should not have: 'In all plans for the benefit of government two essential points must be considered, justice and practicability; many things are just which are not practicable; but such a scheme would be neither one or the other.' And acknowledging the extent of feeling, he added, 'It would be a crime in me to propose, a crime in you to accept; and the only chance left to the House of retaining the favour of the people would be the unqualified rejection of the project.'[50]

Walpole's exasperation was very apparent:

> For myself, I shall only say I have so little partiality for this scheme, except what a real and constitutional love of the public inspires, that if I fail in this proposal, it will be the last attempt of the kind I shall ever make and, I believe a minister will not be found hardy enough to brave on behalf of the people, and without the slightest motive of interest, the worst effects of popular delusion and popular injustice.[51]

It was the antithesis of his fine exposition, petulant and sententious. Walpole had all sorts of 'motives of interest' – looking after that big battalion, the landed gentry, in which he served, achieving personal triumph at the next election, as private delusion had earlier told him the Excise and tax cuts would do.

But he was right about the advantages. He enumerated them: 'the great advantage to the public will be this, that no duty being paid on tobacco designed for exportation, an immediate stop will be put to the fraud on drawbacks, something sufficiently proved by the success and facility which attend the collection of the malt duty'.[52] And he argued impeccably that 'turning duties upon importation into duties on consumption is manifestly a great benefit to the merchant importer'. It removed a circuitous bureaucracy and the 'paying down of duties requires a treble stock to what would be requisite in trade'.[53] But what most benefited everyone was the fall in the duty.

Under the customs and drawbacks system, the merchant paid fivepence three farthings on 80 per cent of the tobacco and fourpence three farthings on the remaining 20 per cent. Walpole was proposing a single duty covering the whole import of fourpence three farthings. It was an admirable speech but one better made six months earlier or after an election. The lobby, the opposition politicians and everyone who distrusted Walpole had coalesced into a resistance which could not be passed.

Walpole was both losing support and gaining it. There were steady opposition men who saw the rationale of an Excise and voted for it. Sir William Lowther was one, Sir Joseph Jekyll another. Viscount Perceval, familiar here as Lord Egmont, indispensable diarist, also, after some hesitation, supported the bill. Perceval, though, counts as a friend of Walpole, periodically asserting himself, rather than opposition man coming over. Walpole had a majority in Parliament. The vote on 16 March on a consolidated group of resolutions was 249 in favour, 189 against. Not quite solidly comforting, but, in a full house with an opposition on full assault, by no means bad.

But Walpole had enjoyed the presumption of the all-powerful. *The Craftsman* derided such arrogance by way of what the law calls 'transferred malice', an assault on the pride and excesses of another famous man:

> The rise and progress of Mr Handel's powers and fortune are too well known to relate. No Music but his own was to be allowed, though every Body was weary of it and he had the insolence to assert that there was no composer in England but himself. No voices nor instruments were admitted but such as flatter'd his ears, and the best hands were kept out of the Orchestras in favour of the most wretched scrapers.[54]

It was a pretty trope. Handel, like Walpole, was going through a bad patch; *opera seria*, like indirect taxation, having become unfashionable, was being badly received.

But there were also, and very importantly, new opponents for Walpole at court, notably Lords Scarborough, Chesterfield and Stair, whose friends in the Commons now went with them. Stair, whom Hervey cattily described as 'the most thrifty Scotchman of them all', had turned bitterly against Walpole and tried unsuccessfully to convert the Queen. Three members of the Dalrymple family, showing more deference to

Stair than Walpole, left the column. Other Members suffered the penalties of sitting for open or semi-democratic constituencies, another clan trio, the Eyles brothers, splitting for this reason, two to one against the government.

Francis Eyles sat for Devizes, company property, and voted with ministers. Joseph and John represented Southwark and London respectively, both open and demonstratively independent boroughs. Notwithstanding the protection thrown over Sir John during the Derwentwater estates case, both deferred to 'popular delusion'. Broadly, men fearing the next election were up for defection, early movers being Hedworth in a Durham county seat and Milner at York. Others, like Sir Adolphus Oughton, warned off by trade interest at Coventry, and Sir Philip Parker in the port seat of Harwich, practised the inert shimmy of abstention, in Sir Philip's case with a sick note.

Another factor striking prudence into the hearts of marginal Walpolians was the by-election. In Kent, a Whig withdrew and a vacated county seat was taken uncontested by Sir Edward Dering, a sudden diehard opponent of Excise. At Chester, with any amount of contest, including picturesque corruption and violence, the government attacked a seat normally held by the Tory, if not yet ducal, Grosvenors. Chester was a freeman borough where the common trick was to swear in honorary freemen. Fifty years later, James Boswell would be made Recorder of Carlisle by Lord Lonsdale to approve three hundred of them.[55] At Chester, Malpas, Walpole's son-in-law, and Alderman Thomas Brereton backed their candidate, Richard Manley, arranging, ironically, for 'a swarm of excise, salt and customs house officers' to be sent in, along with 'common soldiers . . . detached from every quarter of the kingdom, to vote in favour of Mr Manley'.[56]

In the same spirit, the neighbouring Tory chieftain and Grosvenor ally, Sir Watkin Williams Wynn, despatched '8 or 9 hundred Welshmen . . . armed with clubs, staffs and other offensive weapons', bidden 'to beat the Whiggish rascals'. Allegedly, these activists 'knocked down every man that declared a Manley or for King George'.[57] The importation of unbonded excisemen as voters left Manley with 547 votes, precisely two more than the Whig total thirteen years before, while the new Tory candidate swept in with 811. Chester was a faraway city of which Westminster knew little, but the by-election was fought through and across the parliamentary Excise debate, and its result was declared on 21 March, five days after the Commons vote.

The mid-March voting would be the high point for the Excise Bill. The shift was sudden and drastic. Charles Delafaye, a close counsellor, wrote on 15 March, 'the House is now sitting upon the Report and fighting the Battle over again, but there is no manner of danger'.[58] Yet a few days later, Colonel Howard was writing to his father, 'It's inconceivable the clamour and spirit of opposition there is . . . It's thought we shall not have finisht the two Bills next month.'[59]

Whatever the effect of the by-elections, the hiatus of the Easter recess magnified all the manifestations of opposition. Public discontent, cheerfully worked on by the trade and the opposition, had made itself furiously felt before the House resumed. But public opinion was not the only influence. Walpole's status as the King's Minister cannot be overstated. He had invested his charm and intelligence in keeping George and Caroline onside, and, in fairness, they had been reliable good friends to him.

But the opponents at court – Scarborough, Stair, Chesterfield and Clinton – were not just voices at the ear of King and Queen contradicting Walpole and his man at St James, Hervey. They were a signal, a flag in a contrary wind. Then again, the Court opponents said such quotable things. Lord Scarborough told Walpole that soldiers expecting a rise in the price of tobacco were ready to mutiny, while he informed Queen Caroline, 'I will answer for my regiment against the Pretender, but not against the opposers of the Excise.'[60]

If these men, with votes and influence in the fluid Upper House, spoke out against the Excise, might they not have warrant for such outspokenness in royal backsliding? Back in February, the steady Perceval described a report that 'the Queen had told Sir Robert that though she thought his scheme the best in the world, yet seeing the people expressed such a dislike, she would not have them displeased . . .'. He added that he believed nothing of the story. But it made Hanoverian sense. Caroline was sensible that, for all the flummery of loyal addresses and clergymen cringing after benefices, she and the King were bloody foreigners in the most xenophobic country in Europe, tolerable only as lesser evils. 'She would not have the people displeased' rings true.

George II, who had the peppery flavour of any Lt. Colonel retd, sounded superficially more combative. According to Hervey, he called one defecting MP 'an Irish Blockhead' and another 'half mad' before later rhapsodising about Walpole: 'He is a brave fellow; he has more spirit than any man I ever knew.'[61] But the world went by gossip which tended to sensation and things getting worse. When a distressed Caroline called in Hervey for his best judgement, the thick-and-thin friend of Walpole advised her, 'the most zealous friends of the Excise began to be of opinion that considering what had happened at this end of the town, the clamour at the other grew too hot to be struggled with'. And George seems to be reaching similar conclusions. As Hervey recorded later, 'At every division showing a decrease in the majority, the King grew every division more and more uneasy.'[62]

And, of course, every division *did* show a general decrease in the majority. The actual government vote dropped, in that of 4 April, the first on Parliament's return, to fifty-six (232 to 176), with both sides thirty down. But while the opposition brought their numbers up later in the day for two further divisions, recording 199 and 200 in the lobbies, the government froze at 237 and 236 respectively. Majorities in the mid-thirties didn't happen in the parliament Walpole had bought. 'Ominous' was the only word. The impetus of defeat and the great wheel running downhill suggested themselves. On 5 April there was a string of low participation/low majority procedural measures, looking perhaps worse than they were. But Perceval, whose sympathies and vote were with the bill, noted, 'the minority gain ground so fast, that it is very doubtful whether this Bill will pass in any shape'.[63]

The opposition then, on 10 April, made an inevitable move. Recalling the arguments they had used quite recently over the Rhode Island petition, that it might be employed as a precedent against other pressingly relevant petitions, Pulteney and his allies called up the City artillery, a petition against the Excise proposal. As this was a money bill, which on strict form might not be petitioned against, the question was 'the strongest point for the government that had yet been debated in the whole of the Bill, as it was contrary to the rules and orders of the House'.[64] The petition was rejected, but, at 214–197, a dismaying majority. On the last properly attended vote, on 4 March, it had been thirty-six. Against a parliamentary precedent, reaffirmed less than a month before over the Rhode Island petition, the government had scrambled home sweating. The result, halving again a majority already halved, was generally seen as a coming defeat and the end of not just the Excise scheme, but the Walpole cosmos.

He was ready for the rebuff. He had seen King and Queen the night before, where, in principle, so Hervey tells us, 'the final resolution was then taken to drop the Bill'. That verb is cast in the passive voice.

Whether Walpole came to the Queen's drawing room with his mind made up for retreat or the decision was the result of discussion between sovereign, consort and first Minister remains conjectural. It was also decided then to wait 'till that petition was rejected, lest it should be thought to be done by the weight and power of the City'.[65] But the entire massive rebuke to Walpole *had* been done by the weight and power of the City – in conjunction with public manifestations on an unnerving scale, with the recognition of King and Queen and realistic politicians, that the Excise was a ship which was not going to sail. Walpole spoke calmly to his patrons. He and his friends were 'receding for prudential reasons from what they still think as right as ever'. But his quietus for the Excise was as final as eloquent: 'This dance, it will no farther go.'[66]

RESPITE AND AFTERMATH . . .

'Publick blessing naturally produces publick rejoicings' wrote *The Craftsman*, remarking crowds and fireworks on the streets, adding, 'I should think myself inexcusable if I neglected this opportunity of concurring with that general sense of festivity which hath manifested itself through all parts of the Kingdom on a late, ever memorable occurrence.'

Famously, William Whitelaw, catching the Labour Party embarrassed at something, reflected, 'It really won't do to gloat. Bad form gloating, simply mustn't do it. I'm gloating like Hell!' At the fall of the Excise Bill, Pulteney, Bolingbroke and Amherst felt much the same. Their leader page essayist of 21 April, having undertaken 'to leave the enemies of Trade and Liberty to humiliate themselves in sackcloth and ashes whilst we are wishing prosperity to both and drinking the health of THOSE HONEST GENTLEMEN who have preserved them to us', went on to gloat brilliantly:

It always goes against my Heart to insult the *unfortunate* and triumph over the *Vanquished*; though their Distress and Confusion have been entirely occasioned by themselves. I am rather inclined to compassionate the case of all those gentlemen (of whatever Rank or Station they may be) who have suffered themselves to be dragged through an horsepond and be mired to no purpose in pursuit of so Odious a cause. Even the Projector himself participates in my Pity.

The word 'Projector' was nicely chosen, a Change Alley word suggesting a South Sea man, not to mention Denis Bond or Sir Robert Sutton.

The giving of good advice was almost as enjoyable as gloating. 'As to the Projector Himself, I can only hope that this Rebuff will be at least Matter of Instruction to him to induce him to use a little more Caution for the Future how far he Provokes the Patience of the People. This will be the only way for him to sleep in quiet without being Hunted by continuous dreams of *Murder* and *Assassination*.'[1]

Celebration and better than celebration were reported by people better disposed to the Minister than *The Craftsman*. Oxford, according to a loyal don, writing to the adviser Charles Delafaye, on hearing of the Excise's fall, had reverted, town and gown, to recidivist type. 'The Spirit of Jacobitism that for some years has slept at Oxford', wrote Richard Meadowcourt of Merton,

> has been rowzed up again on the late foolish occasion. The night that the news came here that the Excise Bill was droppt, Bonfires were made, Moppetts*, with star and blue garter, were burnt and the University Bells, with the Bells of the Parish Churches, were rung all night.
>
> The next night the Mobb was entertained again with Bonfires and Moppetts; Great numbers of Gowns-men appeared openly in the streets, throwing money amongst the Rabble and reviving the old cry of 'Ormonde', 'Bolingbroke' 'King James for Ever' &c. On the third night, the same cries were repeated and the same Pranks began to be plaid till the vice-chancellor thought fit to send to the Mayor to keep his gowns-men in order, and the Proctors ventured abroad and dispersed the Academical Rabble.
>
> As I am sorry to see a Return of that foul, malignant Spirit that I once resisted almost unto Blood, so am I convinced from hence that some manner of treason is still permeating in this Learned Tump.[2]

Something distinctly less than riot would occur in the outer precincts of St Stephen's, Westminster, when Walpole's 'long and artful speech'[3] of 11 April announced the end of the Excise scheme. After Wyndham had engaged in a rather pointless and unsuccessful exercise, aimed at keeping back the discreet postponement so that the bill might be formally rejected, ministers left the chamber. They found the lobby and the adjoining Court of Requests full of enemies. Hervey and Colonel Charles Churchill had already walked through it, and, having collected

---

* Guys.

their own share of football abuse, alerted Walpole and advised another exit. No one ever accused Walpole of cowardice, and he declined, saying stoically, 'that there was no end of flying from such menaces and the meeting of such dangers was the only way to put an end to them'.[4]

The Prime Minister, according to Hervey, walked through a lane made for him through the crowd by 'forty or fifty constables'. Not for the first time the policing force seems to have got its retaliation in first: all the recorded injuries save three were taken by the crowd. The exceptions were Henry Cunningham, Walpole's son, Edward, and, not disagreeably, Hervey himself. Cunningham, 'a Scotchman' to his Lordship, had been in Parliament since 1708, representing Stirlingshire, and was reckoned the most honest commissioner for sequestered rebel estates. His valour that day would, three years later, be remembered with the Governorship of Jamaica.[5]

The so-called riot reads between the lines of Hervey's narration as a scuffle, crowd noise, some jostling and police brutality. But by the time henchmen had carried the tale to St James's, and the Commons, ready to cherish its affronts, had passed a series of shrill resolutions signalling general outrage, the propaganda victory was all Walpole's. Talk of attempted assassination flowed. Opposition Members were embarrassed and obliged to join in the indignation. An actual riot had taken place in the City on the previous night along Oxford lines: bonfires, illuminations and random disorder, with the addition of two figures* burned in effigy. This episode was conflated by government writers and spokesmen with the lobby affair and a general scare usefully worked up.

All governments in trouble are grateful for external threats, enemies within and general lowering menace. Hervey made a speech in his best supercilious manner, envisaging 'the Speaker at Charing Cross or the Stocks market, proposing laws to a tumultuous mob who, like the Roman plebeians, would enact, rescind, promulgate, and repeal, make and break laws, just as the caprice of their present temper and the insinuations of their present leaders should instigate and direct'.[6] It was high Castilian nonsense, but it caught the mood of the Commons (from which Hervey would shortly ascend) in an atmosphere of anxiety and, to a degree,

---

* One of these 'moppets' was, of course, Walpole; the other, a female form, was disputed as being either Queen Caroline or the recently executed murderess Sarah Malcom.

sympathy with the Minister whose schemes had just imploded. Lucky in his calamity, Walpole would now build on that luck.

His first move was to secure himself at court. The vote precipitating withdrawal had taken place on 10 April; Walpole struck on the 13th. George and Caroline had stayed true under fire from a dangerous alliance of courtier peers alienated for disparate reasons from the Minister. Insistence upon their dismissal was a natural reaction. 'The lenity, indolence, fear or policy that had prevailed so far as to make him acquiesce under such usage was now at an end,'[7] says Lord Hervey. Walpole didn't do lenity – or indolence; he was acting now because he was strong enough to act. Accordingly, the Duke of Grafton, low-calibre loyalist, was sent to demand Lord Chesterfield's staff as Steward and inform Lord Clinton of his dismissal as a Lord of the Bedchamber.

Agreeable as revenge, the sackings were more important as a vote of confidence by George in Walpole. In an age without fast public intelligence, the King's staunchness needed to be blazed forth. Hands were not letting go, the great wheel was not running downhill. Given that the King, vain and wayward as he was, had always to be watched and managed, seeking the dismissals was, very subtly, a vote of imperfect confidence in *him*. Even so, he had held up and the point has been made by Ian Gilmour[8] that, while George embraced the first Minister threatened by a modest scuffle and dismissed two opposition courtiers, Queen Anne's reaction to the much more serious Sacheverell riots had been to dispense with the ministers who had provoked them. It was the difference, perhaps, between a minor outburst which Hervey thought 'so well managed' and the real and furious thing. But Anne was a High Church Tory and George a frustrated beneficiary from the Excise.

Walpole was not, however, a man for token examples. A regular purge of court placeholders insufficiently loyal to the Prime Minister followed quickly, despatching the Dukes of Montrose and Bolton, together with Lords Stair, Marchmont and Cobham. Having made his point, Walpole was precipitated by events into rallying support in the Commons. The Opposition, directing their case more scientifically, were calling for a committee of inquiry into something running at a tangent from the Excise question, frauds thought to have been committed at the customs. Henry Pelham, loyal to Walpole and usually wary and efficient, agreed, unwarily and inefficiently, that this committee should be chosen by ballot.

This contradicted the very nature of the Walpole regime; Members owing obligation, hoping for advancement or fearing retribution, could be counted on under lights. Put the selection of inquisitors into the gratifying dark and they would surely decide wrong. At a meeting, or caucus, of the party, at the Cockpit, Walpole announced his list of trusties for the committee. To get his fluid assembly of many shades to vote the right slate, he played a whole hand, the patriotic card, the party one and the wild card of comforting fear.

Let Members examine the list in the last vote, he said:

> Let them see whether it is composed of discontented Whigs or equal parts of Tories and such as call themselves Whigs whilst they are doing the work of those who confess quite contrary principles. Let them reflect who, in the natural assemblage of this opposition has taken the lead in all debates and all measures – Whig or Tory? . . . consequently who would govern were they to become the majority? Let gentlemen, I say, reflect on these few self-evident truths, and then let them say whether the present contention for power is between Whigs and Whigs or between Whigs and Jacobites . . .

There were, of course, Tory names on the opposition list, and Walpole, treating all Tories as Jacobites, pushed second-generation guilt and guilt by association for all the ends of partisan rhetoric: '. . . if in this first step, I say, the Jacobites assumed authority and carried their point, can it be imagined but what they were able to do in a list for this committee, they would be able to do in an administration . . . What must become of this Government and this Family and the true Freedom, liberty, welfare and prosperity of this country?'

But they would have to face Robert Walpole first, and he would be properly indomitable, humble as well:

> . . . as for myself, I am but one, and what becomes of one man is of very little interest to the public or to any class of men; but as I have always fought on Whig principles, I will never desert them; as I have risen by Whigs, I will stand or fall with them; . . . it is in Whig principles I have lived, and in Whig principles I will die; it is by the assistance of Whigs, joined to a great deal of undeserved good fortune, that I am raised to height where I now stand; in gratitude I have always to the utmost of my power, obliged, maintained, and favoured the party to whom I could give nothing, because I owed everything . . .

He had, of course, no motives of personal interest:

> I am now therefore Gentlemen, not pleading my own cause, but the cause
> of the Whig party; I entreat you for your own sakes, for the sake of this
> Government and your own Family, for the sake and the cause of liberty,
> to exert yourselves with spirit and with unanimity on this occasion, that
> you may defeat and render abortive the scheme of those malevolent spirits
> which . . . have been long dormant and have now taken this favourable
> opportunity, as they think it to break forth; but with you it lies, and in
> your power it is, to disperse these hopes as fast as they gather and to
> render that assistance ineffectual with which the rage, malevolence, disap-
> pointment and revenge of some deserters from your cause have furnished
> these common enemies of the party, this country and this establishment.

Walpole confessed himself deserving reproach for one thing, the
restoration of Bolingbroke, 'who has made the lenity, indulgence and
mercy of this country the means of working its disquiet, if not its
destruction'. And he asked to be given leave 'to say so much in mitigation of this *much repented fault of mine* . . . I did not then believe it
was possible for any individual in human nature to be entirely devoid
of all shame, truth or gratitude . . .'[9]

Wyndham's Tory party was not Jacobite; Walpole had pursued a line
of independent personal power, with minimal regard for 'Whig principles'; Bolingbroke, granted no respite by Walpole, had purchased his
rights for cash from the Duchess of Kendal, Melusine herself. He was
engaged in the high crime of opposing a bill put before Parliament;
neither the Family (Hanover) nor the country was in danger, but at the
hands of a hostile committee, Sir Robert Walpole might very well be.
The speech was brilliantly judged, mingling patriotism, party feeling,
gratuitous smears and simple fear into an explosive whole. It deserves
the words of Enoch Powell about another speech, the one by which,
after the Suez fiasco which he had urged on, Harold Macmillan in 1957
won himself the premiership: 'one of the most horrible things I remember
in politics . . . The sheer devilry of it verged upon the disgusting.'[10]

Disgusting or not, it worked. The assembly of mixed Whigs who
heard it voted, in secret, for a committee wholly loyal to the government which returned correct conclusions. Pelham's blunder was
reclaimed and, in a corner excruciatingly tight, a demonstration given
of Walpole's courage, nerve and simple political effectiveness. He had

won in the Commons. But during the previous year or more the House of Lords had been making good-quality trouble. There had been acutely embarrassing debates about the election of representative Scottish peers, a simple coinage of legislative votes, which Lord Tweedale disloyally proposed subjecting to a ballot, another on the removal of officers in the armed forces, the political weapon Walpole was using against Cobham and Bolton, and now, late in March, one against stockjobbing.

One way of dealing with the House of Lords was to improve an institution too well balanced and short of ministerial talent. Hervey, sublimely contemptuous of colleagues, remarked that the Duke of Newcastle was 'simple enough not to be able to bear the receiving of assistance which the whole world knew he was simple enough to want'. Walpole struck against his enemies by getting from George some key elevations to improve his position in the Lords. Not only was Hervey, heir to a peerage, made a Baron by writ of acceleration, but, by pure luck for Walpole, his own loyal son-in-law, Malpas, had just succeeded his father as Earl of Cholmondeley.

At the same time, reliable party men came into the Judiciary and thus the Lords. The aggrandising Philip Yorke, now, on the death of the floor-crossing Robert Raymond, became Lord Chief Justice as Lord Hardwicke (the salary, at his insistence, increased). This was the Yorke who, joining Pelham and Speaker Onslow, had made a quartet of speakers with Walpole at the Cockpit meeting. Meanwhile, his friend Charles Talbot, who had resisted the City merchants' petition, became Lord Chancellor.

But any thought of actually routing Old Whigs and Tories was chimerical. The election of 1734 was to be one of the great distinguishable contests of the century. It came more than a year after the retreat over the Excise in June 1734, following the great event of 1733, which was a year spent in active and effective opposition. The opposition Lords, led by Scarborough, made a painful issue of the estates of the former directors of the South Sea Company. In the Commons there was a motion against the standing army, the not having of which was one of those Whig principles Walpole had amended. Walpole's parliamentary recovery was challenged on every issue. Division after division in the Commons was directed to discrediting the government in the public eye.

And the last months before the poll saw the assault sharpen.

Ominously, foreign policy was played as an issue with charges of weakness in government dealings with Spain. Spain and the quarrel to be picked in the southern hemisphere were good populist territory. All Walpole's best judgement would be directed to avoiding the futilities of war. But representing sense as cowardice is an easy tactic, most wars being popular before they happen. The method employed was a motion by Sir John Rushout, calling for papers relating to the Spanish treaties, Vienna and Seville. Using temperate language, it was directed at demonstrating, in Pulteney's words, 'that we are in a most calamitous situation . . . and that our present situation is owing to the mismanagement of those at home'.[11] It was bellicosity in the language of open government.

More creditably, the opposition, through a much-trumpeted petition to Parliament, presented by the indefatigable Sir John Barnard, went back to those Excises already in existence, notably Walpole's own prize achievement, the Excise on tea. It had been claimed, said Barnard, that the Excise had been proposed back in the early twenties on the grounds that 'the duty arising from Tea would be better secured to his Majesty and the interest of the fair trade be better supported, but we have fatally suffered the contrary effects; the clandestine importation of Tea being greatly increased to the damage of the of the public revenue and ruin of the fair trader . . .'. The effect of the Excise, he said, was to make tea relatively cheaper in other countries 'whereby the smugglers are enabled to purchase it abroad for less than half the duty paid here. One day this truth would take ministers to free trade. For the moment it was a useful way of identifying Walpole's entire policy as combining dearer goods and regularly denounced but flourishing illegal importation.

In the Commons on 13 February, Lord Morpeth* tabled that motion to prevent commissioned officers being removed except after a court martial or an address from either House of Parliament. Walpole had just used the royal route to dismiss two peers from regimental commands for voting the wrong way in Parliament. Walpole's defenders fell back upon the prerogative. For George, as a hot and angry supporter, had been a willing instrument of an exemplary (and vengeful) measure.

Morpeth quoted Holland and Sweden where such restraints on central

---

* Heir to the Earl of Carlisle and a commoner.

arbitrary powers existed. A Walpole spokesman, Clutterbuck*, a Lord of the Admiralty, struck a style of English sublimity about English perfection set to echo down the centuries: 'When we see other people more happy or more free than ourselves, it is then time for us to fly to other countries to seek example for our imitation.'[12] Clutterbuck thought that 'to invade the prerogative, or wantonly to rob the crown of any part of it, is certainly an invasion of our constitution . . . If once we begin, we may be carried to such lengths, as may intirely subvert that constitution which has rendered this nation so rich and so powerful and which makes us at present the happiest people upon earth.'[13]

In making temporary partisan points, the opposition sometimes stumbled into the considered liberalism of sixty years later. Samuel Sandys might be a factitious politician scoring a point, but he came very close here to anticipating Dunning's famous motion of 1780 that it 'had increased, was increasing and ought to be diminished'. Sandys's version went like this:

> It is certain that the prerogative of the crown has always been a very growing part of our constitution, and for this reason, our ancestors have been obliged to clip and pare it, otherwise all the liberties and privileges of the people would long ago have been swallowed up by the prerogative; and I believe it will be granted that the prerogative, even within these past 30 or 40 years, has grown pretty considerably. I believe every gentleman will admit the power of the Crown is now infinitely greater than it was for some years after the revolution; and I wish that those who now seem so tender of invading what they call the prerogative, would upon other occasions, appear as tender of invading the liberties of the people.[14]

Perhaps the speech, quite as much as it looked forward to Dunning, looked back to the ideas of Shaftesbury, father of the Whig principles with which Walpole had embellished his rhetoric in the Cockpit speech. Sandys was a player in current politics, but it is not necessary to follow Coxe and Sir John Plumb into dismissal of the Patriot case as mischievous factionalism obstructing Sir Robert's great work. Whatever the limitations of the men, the parliamentary debates preceding the 1734 general election, and notably this speech, make up a critique of what Walpole had created and remain important for any historical judgement upon him.

---

* Failing to get a post he coveted, Clutterbuck would desert in 1735.

In another motion two days later, on 15 February, critics aimed at the Walpolian system the long tail of job fillers whose employment guaranteed loyalty either as voter or Member. Sandys again, having deliberately framed a bill in sketch form, filled in its purposes. Self-sufficient country gentlemen were reckoned the best possible representatives.

> The people I believe, would always think themselves more secure in being represented by country gentlemen with whom they are well acquainted, and who can have no interest separate from them, than by clerks of offices, or such other persons . . . whom probably they may never see again until they return to ask the same favour; which every man here knows to be the case of many of the little boroughs in England.

But his chief concern was to make a mirror image of the bill against removing officers. Those officers had stepped out of their unacknowledged terms of employment. They had voted and argued against the crown. They were there to vote for it. Sandys thought that 'while men are men . . . there will always be a great number, by far I fear, the greatest number, who will rather vote according to the directions of the prime minister for the time being, than run the risk of being turned out of the lucrative post or office he holds at the pleasure of the crown'.

Edward Digby, a rather attractive and thoughtful Tory (Warwickshire), with a good record of independent conduct himself, added a compelling specific example. General George Wade had built roads and forts in Scotland and had exercised there the powers of a commander in chief. He had also sat in Parliament since 1715 and generally supported the government. But, said Digby, as Wade himself had recently told them, 'even he himself was threatened for daring to give his vote against one of the most destructive ministerial schemes that was ever brought into parliament'.[15]

The bill provoking General Wade's delinquency had been the one establishing the South Sea scheme. And, indeed, though he opposed the present motion on general grounds of discipline, his account of what had happened then was memorable:

> Though I have generally joined in opinion with . . . the Administration, yet I have on occasion differed from them . . . When the famous South

Sea scheme was in agitation in this House, though it was brought in
by a minister and strongly supported . . . yet I had the honour to be
one of the 55 who divided against it . . . I had upon that occasion
messages sent to me and was threatened to be stripped of my military
employments . . .'[16]

The opposition, busy running through the manual of Walpolian political mechanics, turned next to the parliamentary term and proposed
repeal of the Septennial Act. A creation of 1716, with George I just
settled into St James's Palace, this act had been justified on grounds of
reduced cost and increased stability. It had also given ministers five
years of voter-oblivious power instead of about eighteen months. The
distributor and withholder of place and favour relied on it. It was the
charter of centralised power, a reason why the opposition was making
such busy use of a year in which the charm of governmental authority
was briefly diminished.

The call for 'more frequent parliaments', made on 13 March by
William Bromley, son of the Secretary of State under Harley, exactly
anticipated a plea found a hundred years later in the central document
of the Chartists. And Bromley, in a slightly epigrammatic way, made
some hits: 'A farther mischief of long parliaments is that a Minister
has time and opportunity of getting acquaintance with members, of
practising his several arts to win them into his schemes.'[17] Also; 'Long
parliaments first introduced bribery because they were worth purchasing
at any rate.'[18] 'Despair naturally induces indolence, and that is the
proper disposition for slavery. Ministers of state understand this very
well and are therefore unwilling to awaken the nation out of its lethargy
by frequent elections.'[19]

He was met in Walpole's own 'enemies within' style by Conduitt of
Whitchurch who would, at another time, creditably move the abolition
of Jacobean legislation against witchcraft, but still believed in the Old
Pretender. One motive for bringing in the Septennial Act, he said, being

the great ferment the nation was then in . . . does not every gentleman know
what a spirit of discontent, nay I may say disaffection, was artfully raised
over the whole nation but last year? And can any gentleman say that spirit
has totally subsided? Or can any gentleman believe that there was not a
great deal of the spirit of Jacobitism at the bottom of these discontents . . .
I am persuaded that the ferment the nation is now in and the ferment it was

in when the Septennial Act was passed into law, proceed originally from the same cause . . .'[20]

Sir John Barnard feared that, as the Septennial Act settled down, 'by degree, the minds of the people will be debauched; they will be brought to think that selling their votes at election time is no crime, the representative who buy their seats must sell their votes . . .'. Then Pulteney joined in. First of all he acknowledged having voted for the original Septennial Bill arguing that, conceived a year after 'the Fifteen' and two years after George I's accession, it was emergency legislation:

> When a country, or the government of a country, is in any imminent danger, it often happens that people think regulations necessary, which when the danger is over, appear to be attended with as pernicious consequences as that very danger which they were made to prevent . . . Sir, I declare upon my honour, that of all the actions I ever did in my life, there is not one I more heartily and sincerely repent of than my voting for the passing of that law.[21]

Sir William Yonge, a ministerial henchman and Lord of the Treasury, put it cynically (and well) enough, remarking that it 'is now the last session of a Parliament, a new election must come soon on, and as this motion has an appearance of popularity among the meaner sort of electors, it may be of service to some gentlemen at the next elections'.[22] The opposition had hoped for a continuation of the Excise mood by way of a cry for shorter parliaments. But in an age of thin and random communication, the effect was marginal.

However, Walpole's own defence of the system was instructive. Pulteney had denounced seven-year parliaments as producing dishonest practice, parliments 'sunk to the lowest and vilest dregs of corruption'. In reply Walpole grew specious:

> To insinuate, Sir, that money may be issued from the public treasury for bribing elections is really something very extraordinary; especially in those gentlemen who know how many checks are upon every shilling that can be issued from thence and how regularly the money granted in one year for the public service of the nation must always be accounted for the next session in this House and likewise in the other, if they have a mind to call for any such account.[23]

This was nicely phrased. Bribery was done by his machine, not with funds direct from the Treasury, but secret service money. Proof of which sticky pudding would lie in subsequent scholarly discovery that the sums allocated from that source fell by half under Walpole's political heir, Henry Pelham, who bribed more moderately.

In this debate he offered a sophisticated version of the doctrine 'Every man has his price', treating the purchase of votes as a modest thing regulated by the character of the voter. And given that voter's high moral quality, such bribery was most unlikely to be accepted if it might occasion real harm.

> I will allow Sir, that with respect to Bribery, the price must be higher or lower, generally in proportion to the virtue of the man who is to be bribed; but . . . when no incroachments are made upon the rights of the people, when the people do not think themselves to be in any danger, there may be many of the electors who, by a bribe of ten guineas, might be induced to vote for one candidate rather than another.

It would be quite different of course, if the Court were doing anything wrong, if it were 'incroaching upon the rights of the people'. And of course, if it ever did, 'a proper spirit would, without doubt, arise in the nation, and in such a case, I am persuaded that none or very few, even of such electors could be induced to vote for a court-candidate, no not for ten times the sum'.[24] So if a Prime Minister ever offered bribes to destroy constitutional law, the voters would never accept them, evidence of the moderate and constitutional bribery of ministers. Not for nothing was 'Bob Brazen' one of the familiar names bestowed upon Sir Robert Walpole.

This was going to be an important election. The system, pocket boroughs, wide-scale bribery for which both sides had inclination but the government the larger means, combined with the ingrained practice of contesting so few seats, all meant that actual movement, seats lost and gained would always be small. But what the election would not provide was quiet evidence of the dumb content among the people, voters or not.

Perhaps the most inapt statement of the political mood had been made in the Commons back in January by Joseph Danvers: 'a rough rude beast but now and then mouths out some humour'.[25] He had 'never heard any man reproach the ministry; on the contrary they seemed all to think that the only dispute among us here was who should be minister; and as this is a dispute which the generality of the people of England are by no means concerned in, gentlemen are much mistaken if they imagine the people of England trouble their heads about it.'[26]

The election to celebrate the establishment of an Excise and slashing the Land Tax cut up far rougher than the Westminster brouhaha played up by the Whigs. The opposition carried on as in the Commons, as a combined opposition, doing everything to bury the old party lines. 'If anyone had told me in Queen *Anne's* reign that some time about the Year 1732 the invidious names of *Whig* and *Tory* of *High Church* and *Low Church* should be utterly abolish'd and forgot I should have consider'd him a false Prophet and/or a Dreamer of Dreams. And yet this thing has actually come to pass entirely owing to the excellent management of our Great Man.'[27] The passage comes from *Fog's Weekly Journal*, heir-at-law to *Mist's Weekly Journal*, after Nathaniel Mist, enterprising Tory journalist but fairly evident Jacobite, had fled abroad. *Mist/Fog* had had no trouble in the past distinguishing Whigs from Tories. But in January 1733, with the Excise still in hopes, the tightest coalescence of opposition parties yet could be cheerfully proclaimed.

In parallel with the parliamentary initiatives, a press and pamphlet war would be waged and country newspapers would abandon provincial quiescence to make war for party against party and each other.

For opposition papers one departure was the increasing importation of London-published material. Walpole had tried in the late twenties to confine them to submissive discretion using thoroughly despotic means. Edward Farley, John White and Samuel Farley, publishers of papers in Exeter, Newcastle and Bristol, were prosecuted for carrying material from *Mist's Weekly Journal* and *The Craftsman*. Edward Farley had been imprisoned for this offence in September 1728 and was reported 'loaded with irons'.[28] He petitioned Queen Caroline, complaining that his wife and children had been 'reduced to extreme poverty'.[29] Yorke (later Lord Hardwicke) as Attorney-General, recommended him to a pardon. In 1729 he died in prison.

Ministers also stood ready to prosecute provincial reports of proceedings in Parliament. Parliamentary secrecy, like the non-existence of an intelligence agency, lasted on paper and, *in terrorem*, long beyond its explosion. In practice, London editors like Edward Cave regularly printed reports. Cave's* *Gentleman's Magazine* became, from 1731, a hugely popular venture not least because of this feature. These 'Reports of the Proceedings in the Senate of Magna Lilliputia' used cod names for the participants, including a certain 'Waleop'. Cave and his reporters got away with it because the government knew a London prosecution would bring them into derision. The provinces were different. Robert Raikes had attempted in 1726 to reproduce another report in *The Gloucester Journal* and was taken into custody by the sergeant at arms for breach of parliamentary privilege.

Yet such repression soon lapsed in practice. By 1734 the government was not pushing its writ, so that, even in Norfolk, disrespectful things appeared in print. Henry Crossgrove of the Tory *Norwich Gazette* took on the Whig *Norwich Mercury* fiercely, with mere accuracy an early casualty.[30] But arguably the most useful thing provincial papers did was to print division lists of voters pro and con in the Commons, especially those voting for and against the Excise. This was centrally coordinated by *Fog's Weekly Journal* and *The Craftsman* from London. They did so in the conviction that the Excise was damned in the public mind and that a Member known to have voted for it and now seeking re-election in a seat not purchased outright, like the ghost boroughs of Cornwall, would have a harder time.

Some were feeling the heat anyway. John Scrope, the Secretary to the Treasury, heavily involved in bringing the Excise Bill to birth, was speaking to his furious Bristol constituents from his knees. He had taken, he insisted, 'all due care to observe the Dictates and Directions of his County; and if he had been short in any respect, he hoped they had Goodness enough in them to excuse him'. It was a Goodness they wholly lacked. Scrope, also Recorder of Bristol, was defeated and took refuge at Lyme Regis where the local magnate, Henry Holt Henley, at Walpole's urgent request, assembled enough honorary freemen to take what Bristol had declined. One of them in Lyme was Scrope's own coachman who 'came down from his box in his livery and voted for him'.[31]

Candidates, as *Fog's* had noted, now made far less of their status as Tory or Old Whig. In Kent they ran as 'zealous Opposers of the late Excise Scheme', in Leicestershire as 'Gentlemen of known Inclinations to oppose all excise and other Schemes which may tend to the destruction

---

* The most famous of Cave's parliamentary correspondents was the young Samuel Johnson who rewrote and improved material brought by the copy boy.

of the Liberty of the Subject'.[32] The absence of heavy party identification did not, however, stop violence with strong party colour. 'Riots in Shropshire' sounds like Lady Bracknell's 'grave disturbances in Grosvenor Square'. But in Bridgnorth, a Tory mob, encouraged by the candidate, besieged the town hall.

Thomas Whitmore, the Whig candidate, twenty-three, was due to inherit from his father, who had died nine years before, a seat kept warm for him in the interim. He and his family, who owned much of the town, enraged Tory feeling by putting in their own bailiffs, important men in an eighteenth-century election, something which provoked the riots, strongly encouraged by the rival, and Tory, family, the Actons.* Whitmore and his colleague wrote to Newcastle for troops, they came, and both Whigs were elected. ''Tis easy', wrote Walpole to Newcastle, 'to see what will be said, but the notoriety of the fact must and will justify the proceeding.'[33]

At the other, eastern, extremity of England, Great Yarmouth, the arrival of a son of Walpole as candidate ignited major disturbances, to which the Whig Mayor responded by flogging a rioter, for which he in turn was taken to court and fined. Rioters pursuing a ministerial candidate at Newcastle under Lyme promised to 'wash their hands in his blood'.[34] The conclusion was artlessly conceded by another Whig mayor of Yarmouth, looking back in 1747, that support for the Tories was 'the natural bent of the majority of the people, and has for many years been kept under by art, difficulty and expense'.[35]

Even where the candidate felt sure of being returned, as did Sir Henry Hoghton in Preston, messages warning of the difficulties were sent. 'I must not trouble you with a history of the violent proceedings here,' wrote Sir Henry to Walpole on 2 April: 'My enemies have offered their interest to several to oppose me, but I have the town in such spirit that nobody is yet named. Lord Derby, on account of the Excise and other unpopular votes this session which I now feel the weight of, is my declared Enemy and offers to be at the expense of Keeping me out if any one will undertake it . . .'[36] Hoghton was lucky. The local Tories never did agree on a candidate and he had a walkover, though one wonders about his keeping it 'in spirit'. Was this alcohol or cash?

At Harwich, Walpole resorted to the very device with which the

---

* One branch, being Catholic, did better for themselves in Naples, where Actons with names like Ferdinando would become Prime Minister.

opposition had taunted him during the Excise debates. Excise men, appointed by the crown and dependent upon it for continuance in employment, were called up for voter service. And much good it did him. Harwich was a model of baroque corruption, a borough of thirty-two voters, all serving the corporation. And as that corporation was augmented by customs officers and officers of the packet, or government mail boats, they could usually guarantee a ministerial majority.

The town had been represented by Perceval, alias Egmont, met as diarist, who made a great and irksome parade of his conscience and quasi-independence. In 1731, in the course of a Place Bill to exclude pensioners from Parliament, he had extolled his high motives to a government whip, 'telling him that my honour and conscience obliged me to be for it'. Against a similar bill, fired off by the opposition as pre-election artillery in 1734, he had recently been one of twenty 'friends of the court' who left the House rather than either oppose (or support) it.

The balance between conscience and Walpole's continuing goodwill was nicely managed, so nicely that the Prime Minister advanced this Irish peer to the sublimity of an English Lordship with a vote (for Walpole) in the Upper House. He was, of course, to be succeeded at Harwich by his son. The Perceval conscience had clear and happy limits and they descended to his heir. Young Perceval had published an anonymous pamphlet, attacking the Excise. But his note to the Prime Minister stated coolly 'that if he would be his friend, he would be his'.

Egmont, presenting his son's compliments to Walpole, did not mind doing the dirty work himself, begging 'that the servants of the government may be ordered to come to town and to that end that you will please only to write a line to Mr Carteret and also to Mr Hill for that purpose . . .'. A note spelled out the particulars. 'The servants under the Customs are Will. Philip, Sam Philips [*sic*], Under the packet, Capt. Fuller, Capt. Wimples. Capt. Dean. If you think it too much trouble to write . . . will you be pleased that I should tell them?'[37]

Walpole did not think it too much trouble, requesting 'That Mr Bell may order a proper person to go down tomorrow to acquaint the Officers of the Packet that Lord Perceval and Mr Leathes who are joined for the interest are the candidates for whom they must give their votes and no other . . .'.[38]

With so much stage villainy on furtive show, it seems sad that the Whigs should have lost. But even with government employees voting correctly, a private quarrel among Whig factions produced a certain

Charles Stanhope – the same Stanhope who had cut things so fine over the Bubble – who took nineteen votes to Perceval's thirteen and was elected with Leathes. And obedience to the all-powerful Minister does not seem to have done the local muster of staff any favours. Carteret and Leathes wrote at least two letters to Walpole, pointing out that the Samuel Phillips mentioned above and another customs man, Francis Coleman, had since been victimised. 'Mr Samuel Phillipps [sic] was appointed in April last by Warrant from the Treasury to the command of the Walpole sloop in the service of the Customs at Harwich without complaint or misdemeanour, and to his charge, an order was last week sent down from the Collector for him to deliver it up to another officer . . . whereby Mr Phillips is left destitute of bread.'

Leathes asked Walpole to do what he should 'to get the order reversed & Mr Phillips restored to his command'.[39] But in June he was still 'under the necessity of troubling you by letter to beg you would not forget your kind promise of restoring Mr William Phillips and Mr Francis Coleman to their places as tide surveyors of this port'. And while showing commendable concern for the two Phillipses and the other officer, he is speaking a language of networks which Walpole will have perfectly understood. 'My not having hitherto succeeded occasioned very cold greetings from my friends here, and of further apprehensions they are under of the Collector's success in another affair (Mr Anthony Dean)'. This must be the Captain Anthony Dean identified in the Walpole note as one of those to be told how to vote. The two Phillipses, Coleman and Dean, represented four votes in thirty-one, 12 per cent of the electorate, five thousand votes in a contemporary constituency. They deserved consideration.

In Walpole's own county disappointment deepened. When the Excise was still seen as a winner, he had, as noted, thought to fight the county seat rather than his customary King's Lynn (see *supra*, Chapter 14). He had retreated sharply from prospective humiliation. Norfolk had narrowly been a Tory seat. Sharp practice – in *this* county probably Walpole's sharp practice – had put it into Whig hands in 1715, when a petition by the narrowly defeated Tories Hare and Earle, that without the unqualified voters they had a majority, remained unheard.[40] Whigs had held the county unopposed ever since.

With Walpole himself shrewdly withdrawn, they still hoped to hang on. But the Tories, Bacon and Wodehouse, won a close contest over Walpole's men, Morden and Coke. With over six thousand votes cast, only six separated William Wodehouse in second place and elected from William Morden in third and not. The cost was so exhaustive that Whig and Tory parties fought shy of a contest for the next four elections, agreeing to the economical course of one member of each party walking over.[41]

Sussex was an important slice of Newcastle's territorial cake, and the Duke, anxious in easier circumstances, would take trouble and spend money there. The trouble involved personal fence-mending and goodwill-creating trips, much chivvying of his cousin, Henry Pelham, and his constituency colleague, James Butler, both on a county tour, and the opening of a coffee house for good party men in Lewes. With elegant irony, in an election preoccupied with the Excise, the Duke's seigneurial influence procured the release from prison of a smuggler, Thomas Newman, popular in that county of discreet shipments, as smugglers usually were.[42]

Newcastle was worried about Lewes. Even more than the rest of Sussex, it was the fief of his family, so much so that both Whig candidates for the town were called Thomas Pelham. They were distinguished as Thomas Pelham of Stanmer and Thomas Pelham of Lewes. Ill-disposed commentators remarked that Thomas of Lewes was idle and Thomas of Stanmer drunk. The Duke, Thomas Pelham-Holles, would stop at very little in assuring the return of the pair whom his biographer calls 'these two stooges'.[43] They were, after all, *his* stooges. The opposition saw their chance and put together a creditable slate, an eclectic alliance of Tories and Dissenters. Thomas Sergison, a landowner, and Nathaniel Garland, a 'rigid' Dissenter, put up together and came very close, in what had been thought of as bought-and-sold Pelham country.

The Lewes coffee house represented only a fraction of the money, spent like something better than water on entertaining and victualling the electorate. But local hostility to the Excise proved formidable. A Lewes merchant told the Duke's agent, William Hay, that he (Newcastle) had

> set out in the World with good Principles, and have acted upon them till the last affair; he says that he and all considerable Merchants have great Obligations to these Gentlemen that relived them against a Scheme which would have probed their Ruin; and they sought to express their Gratitude to them: that he would shew that he had some Interest in Lewes; and he thought Mr Garland a proper Person to represent it, because he understood Trade.[44]

That was serious opinion speaking; the two stooges were ultimately saved by the votes of the constables, returning officers appointed by other Dukes, Dorset and Norfolk, friendly to the patron.

However, in Nottinghamshire, another little kingdom, the Duke's influence had waned. The county seat had previously returned two Newcastle nominees. One of these, Howe, had taken a disqualifying office, the other was that same Sir Robert Sutton whom Walpole had protected from a bill of pains and penalties. Both had left in 1732 and been replaced by an acceptable, but non-dependent Whig, Thomas Bennett, and a Tory, William Levinz. In 1734, Newcastle, whose shares in East Retford, Nottingham and Newark, where he was lord of the manor, had held up, accepted the status quo.

Away from proprietorial boroughs, stipendiary voters and little fixes, it was possible for the opposition to make its point. Yorkshire, with 15,000 seats, was dangerously democratic and as potentially dear to fight. The Whigs had won one seat in a by-election in 1726 and, backed by the wealth of Sir Thomas Wentworth, had acquired the second in the general election of 1727. In 1734, although the Tories fielded only one candidate, Sir Myles Stapylton, against the two sitting Whigs, he topped the poll with 7896 votes. Meanwhile a splitting Whig, Edward Wortley Montagu, picked up nearly six thousand votes.

Middlesex, famously independent and, two decades later, enraging George III by returning 'that Devil, Wilkes', demonstrated public feelings in a way peculiarly painful to Walpole. As he had sat since 1700 for a family seat, so had Pulteney represented the 131 voters of Hedon, 'a venial borough'[45] in Yorkshire, at first by patronage, later in his own interest. Middlesex had three thousand accredited voters. Just as Walpole had planned to demonstrate, by leaving King's Lynn (three hundred voters) for Norfolk's six thousand voters, the popularity of the county's great man, so Pulteney abandoned Hedon for Middlesex. Carnarvon, heir to the Duke of Chandos, invited to stand against him, wrote back eloquently his view of a hopeless undertaking. The two county seats made up an eloquent episode, very much single-wicket cricket. Pulteney and the Tory, Sir Francis Child, were returned unopposed, Walpole hung on to nurse at King's Lynn and the Whig candidates, Morden and Coke, though lacking Walpole's personal opprobrium, lost Norfolk narrowly, at enormous expense all round.

It was not an election Walpole could actually lose. Too many seats were so secure in borough ownership as to be uncontestable, others were small enough to be corrupted in the through-produced factory-scale way of Newcastle or indeed for less. And freeman boroughs like Lyme Regis represented an alternative form of ownership. Honorary freemen were generally propertyless menials sworn in and written on to the roll by a pliant lawyer. The breakdown of the new house was 347 ministerialists against 232 opposition members, dividing into 145 Tories and 87 opposition Whigs. Newcastle was moderately pleased. 'Our Parliament,' he wrote to Horatio Walpole, 'is, I think, a good one; but by no means such a one as the queen and your brother imagine. It will require great care, attention and management to *sett out right*, and keep people in good humour.' He spoke with the quiet authority of a man who had chosen fifteen of them.

One aspect of the election proceedings in which Walpole could take pleasure concerned Scotland, not the Commons but the Lords. Here sixteen peers were nominated *au clair* by the rest under the guidance of Walpole's man in Scotland, Argyll. There had been a real risk that the foundations of loyalty, to wit bribes, pensions and inducements to the Scottish nobility, might not suffice. Chesterfield's defection had been followed by a determined attempt to divert Scottish Lords into revolt. If it had succeeded, then a hostile Upper House might have pursued a weakened Walpole, triggering the fatal departure of uncertain friends in the Commons.

But the government tie was tenuous. By the mid-thirties, with Walpole in diminished authority and the Excise again walking the streets, Argyll was strong enough to make Walpole oblige *him*. He had abstained over the Excise, and Walpole had been grateful for the abstention. But he had not succeeded, had not perhaps tried very hard, to keep all the Scots Lords in line. His brother, Islay, had given his support, but Lords Buchan, Haddington and Rothes had voted 'Not Content'. And the contentment of Scottish Lords was something Walpole cherished.

For the moment Scotland was safe, and its manager, though not precisely a friend, was onside. Like the Prime Minister's parliamentary majority, this was something to be enjoyed while it lasted.

'THESE SCRIBBLERS GROW SO BOLD OF LATE'

Walpole never did like writers. George II actively hated them. The King 'often used to brag of the contempt he had for books and letters, to say how much he hated all that stuff from his infancy; and that he remembered when he was a child he did not hate reading and learning merely as other children do, upon account of the confinement, but because he despised it and felt it was doing something mean and below him'.[1]

He did, however, enjoy music. We stand at the Hallelujah Chorus of *Messiah* because George, at the first London performance, also stood, thinking, like Handel himself, that at that moment he saw 'Heaven and Earth and the Great God himself'. Walpole employed agents, including his spy, Macky, to buy Flemish and Spanish masters to fill out his palace at Houghton. But he would confess in retirement that he 'could not bring himself to turn a page'. And a man who does not like books will not like authors.

Walpole had neither time nor patronage for Swift, Pope, Gay or Fielding.* As laureate he replaced the negligible Laurence Eusden with Colley Cibber. Cibber was a notable actor, the original Lord Foppington, and a capable playwright, as with *Love's Last Shift*. But no poet of any sort, he was hired as a wonderfully complaint, bad-verse, Hanoverian loyalist. Walpole's chief servant keeping newspapers puffing was a useful, unmemorable advocate, William Arnall. The only writer surviving in a modern anthology of the period to have been on tolerable terms

---

* Though, as we shall see, the case would be altered for Fielding.

with Downing Street was Edward Young, whose book-length epic, *Night Thoughts*, conveys ten thousand lines on death: 'Time flies, Death urges, knells call, heaven Invites, Hell threatens'.[2] We are also indebted to Young for 'Procrastination is the thief of time'.[3]

And if Walpole did not like 'the Wits' – playwrights, poets, essayists and novelists – they did not like him. Economics came into it, of course. The chances of making a living at writing anything worth writing, not good today, were worse then. The writers, like painters and composers, looked to patronage, royal, noble and political. Walpole and the Court disposed of pensions, sinecures, paid places, including, of course, that consolation of religion, the snug living. And they distributed such good things to people voting right in the Commons or who, while voting right in the Lords, induced family boroughs to vote right *for* the Commons.

If he had thought literature mattered, the Prime Minister could have shown writers disinterested favour, softening their dissent in a warm blanket of unspoken obligation and good manners. An Irish bishopric or an English deanery might have saved him the account of the rope-dancing Prime Minister, Flimnap, in *Gulliver's Travels*. For a decent court post, as gentleman-in-waiting rather than the preceptorship to a two-year-old infant Princess, offered as a studied insult, Bob Booty, the highway robber, would have been out of *The Beggar's Opera*. The £1000 a year as a commissioner of Forfeited Estates which kept Sir Thomas Hales of Canterbury loyal for twenty-six years would have left *Jonathan Wild* unwritten. Unlike Swift, Gay and Fielding, Alexander Pope, the only major writer actually to make large amounts of money by his genius, could not have been charmed with wealth and place. But the alienation from Court and first Minister of the greatest poet of the age is a case all to itself; and that assault, in the late epistles, was the most injurious of all.

The Wits, classicists to a man, looked back in the Age of George Augustus to a more interesting Augustus, the Roman Emperor proud to reward Horace, Virgil and Juvenal. They recalled his rich and open-handed minister, Gaius Maecenas, took notes and drew comparisons. A different comparison was made with the Ministry of Robert Harley. Harley had loved letters, read books as well as collecting so many valuable manuscripts and rare books that his Harleian Library became one of the foundations of the British Museum.

The Tory first Minister had made friendships outliving office, with

Defoe, Swift and Prior. Defoe, if anything a Whig and given to arguing back, had worked as his confidential political agent. Swift's pleadings on Ireland had at least been listened to. In opposition, he had been commissioned as the brilliant editor of *The Examiner*, railing against the Whigs, work for which he rebuffed payment. And though disappointed of Deaneries at Wells and Lichfield, against Queen Anne's censorious footdragging, that of St Patrick's, Dublin, was found for him. Swift's *The Conduct of the Allies* had been at the centre of the campaign leading to political victory and ending Marlborough's war. Meanwhile, negotiations for the peace had been put into the hands of the master of self-derisive verse miniatures, Matthew Prior, for whom, in the down days, Harley found a pleasant house in rural Essex.

As first Minister and Earl of Oxford, he became in January 1714 a member of the Scriblerus Club. This was a dining club devoted to mocking sham science, 'astrology, alchemy . . . millennialism, Cartesian vortices, medical quackeries and of course the abuses of language in bad writing'.[4] Its members, along with Dr Arbuthnot, the witty doctor to whom Pope addressed the great epistle thirty years later, and Thomas Parnell, a reputable Irish poet, were Swift, Gay and the twenty-five-year-old Alexander Pope. The nostalgia of the disaffected writers of Walpole's regime was for something better than emolument; it recalled friendship and good humour shared with the head of government. And though Oxford and Bolingbroke had been bitter and mutually destructive enemies, Bolingbroke too was a genuine lover of letters, an inhabitant of the world of imagination and ideas. And from the mid-1720s onward, he was back in circulation and active politics, offering at Dawley Farm, near Uxbridge, a running colloquium to the clever men out of political doors.

Close to Bolingbroke was Jonathan Swift, exiled, partly by his Irish deanery, partly by a complex commitment to Ireland, but also from a sense of having nothing to do or hope for in the London of the Whigs. An account has been given above of his assault on William Wood's copper coinage: a brilliant success and economic nonsense. It was Swift's achievement to have created a false market. A hundred iniquities were perpetrated against the Irish, but the sound small coin to help Ireland's poor little economy move goods around was not one of them.

Gulliver's Travels, a children's book but an adult classic from the day it left the presses of Benjamin Motte late in October 1725, is many things. In the Country of Houyhnhnms, land of equine virtue and human debasement, Gulliver, if not Swift, embraces misanthropy, a declaration of revulsion at the human race. But *Gulliver* is both discursive and complex, about politicians and about mankind. And in all four books, simply at the level of contemporary 1720s politics, there is quite enough to wound a contemporary 1720s Prime Minister – or King of England: 'The Emperor of Lilliput is taller by almost the breadth of my nail than any of his court, which is enough to strike an awe into the beholders'; while the King of Brobdingnag's inquiries of Gulliver about his native country, in Chapter five of Book Two, are straightforward attacks on the revenue, justice system and standing armies of Walpole's England.

As for Walpole himself, 'upon a slender white thread extended about two foot, and twelve inches from the ground', dance the Lilliputian candidates:

> for great office and high favour at court. They were trained in this art from their birth and were not always of noble birth or liberal education . . . Very often the chief ministers themselves are commanded to show their skill and convince the Emperor they have not lost their facility. Flimnap, the Treasurer, is allowed to cut a caper on the straight rope at least an inch higher than any other Lord in the Empire. I have seen him do the summerset several times together upon a trencher fixed on the rope which is thicker than a common pack thread in England.[5]

'Flimnap' was only one of the names given Walpole during his time in office, not as bitter as 'Bob Brazen' or 'Skreenmaster General' or, in one of Fielding's plays, 'Pillage'. But Flimnap, the supreme rope jumper, dishonest, scheming and ready to have Gulliver murdered, is all that the Opposition could have wished. Swift actually feared that Walpole's minions would kill him: 'I am advised by all my friends not to go to France (as I intended to for two months) for fear of their vengeance in a manner which they cannot execute here.'[6] As Swift's biographer, David Nokes, sensibly observes, 'The implication here is very sinister indeed. Yet though a ruthless opportunist, there is no evidence that Walpole went in for this kind of Jonathan Wild tactic.' Indeed not; there was no hint of it, while Bolingbroke is at least a suspect as chief mover behind the incendiary Sacheverell riots of 1710. This is Swift's paranoia talking.

Anything that Swift wrote generally in 1725 – about courts, monarchs, Lords, ministers and the apparatus, open and secret, of government –

was taken in his own lifetime as specific, concerning George I's court, Robert Walpole and the current filigree of rewards, spies, ciphers and surveillance. Which, of course, it was. A book may have the qualities of a classic such that, nearly three hundred years later, the sizzling-hot immediacies of here-and-now politics are left to painful spelling out in footnotes, read or, as the case may be, not read, by incurious posterity. Swift had, indeed, his own bleak and obsessive view of all mankind which generally affronted him, but for all that, he was out to get Walpole.

Book Three with its accounts of spying, looks universal and is specific:

> In the Kingdom of Tribnia, by the natives called Langdon, the bulk of the people consisted wholly of discoverers, witnesses, informers, accusers, prose-cutors, evidences, swearers, together with their several subservient and subaltern instruments, all under the colours and conduct of ministers of state and their deputies. The plots in that kingdom are usually the work-manship of those persons who desire to raise their own characters of profound politicians . . .

The last few words have perhaps a little contemporary resonance, but Swift was writing straightforwardly about Walpole, Walpole's spies and the triumph Walpole had brought off with the Atterbury Plot.

A few lines down, he lists the ciphers: 'For instance, they can discover a close-stool to signify a privy council; a flock of geese a senate; a lame dog an invader . . .' But, of course, a lame dog, poor Harlequin, had been sent to the Bishop of Rochester's wife as a friendly token by the agent of a French minister contemplating support for, precisely, an invasion. Writing three years after the event and without the long-subsequent evidence which proved Walpole's hunch and Atterbury's guilt, Swift is confident that the dog demonstrates Walpole's dishonest confections. This is pure contemporary politics, what a reader of the opposition press would cheer and a loyal backbencher resent.

Government publications paid Swift the compliment of affront and took it with a volley of abuse. The pamphlet, 'Remarks on the Response of the House of Commons to the King', attacking Pulteney, speaks of him as 'the Head of the Faction and assisted by some persons of wit; but they were chiefly Men of Desperate Fortunes or worse Characters'.[7] And, identifying Bolingbroke and Swift, it observed that 'the most noted of these were an attainted Lord who had before sacrificed his

Interests with all Parties, and an *Irish* Dean who, though one of a happy genius and some Learning, was such a debauched immoral Man that whatever was known to have come from him was of no Weight with the People'.[8] Another pamphlet, 'A letter from a Clergyman to his Friend', is slightly sinister, perhaps prompting Swift's fears. The author trying 'to create a Dislike in the People to those in the Administration' suggests that he was plotting dangerously with others and concludes 'there is no Honest man among us but would contribute the utmost in his Power to bring the Author *and those concerned with him* to exemplary punishment'.[9]

Oddly, the pro-government publications are keen to spell out allegory and unmask the aliases. Laboriously, they tell us that Flimnap is Walpole and his brother-in-law, Redresal, Walpole's brother-in-law, Townshend. The green, red and blue ribands distributed by the Emperor of Lilliput are spelled out to unheraldic folk as respectively Thistle, Bath and Garter. No contemporary reading *Gulliver's Travels*, remotely in touch with political debate, had any excuse for treating the book as either a fable or an assault upon generalised wrongdoing.

Swift had created a text for reference, a set of citable characters and a long-running opposition source text. The editorialist of *Fog's Weekly Journal*, probably Charles Molloy, wrote, tongue in cheek, eighteen months after publication, that 'if a Writer animadverts upon some fashionable Piece of Roguery, many a Man whom the Author never thought of, understands the whole Satyr to be levelled at him . . . It is for this Reason perhaps, that some People feel a Satyr in Captain *Gulliver's* Travels while the Rest of the World can read them over without finding the least Sting in any Part'.[10]

Walpole's men in the press, numerous, uninvestigated by postmasters and paid on the nail, were a ponderous lot, establishment artisans, everlastingly indignant, without style or light touch. If Molloy could dance round them, what could not Swift do? Their tone varies from abuse to menace, and is accompanied by a perpetual obbligato of fuming resentment. For a man dismissive of letters and literati, Walpole minded the flimsy art which showed him leaping upon a pack thread, no end. It had, after all, set the readers of successive editions laughing, and laughing at Robert Walpole.

Within Parliament, Commons and Lords, he knew what to do. To paraphrase a description by Simon Schama, in his 2002 television series *A History of Britain*, of the Premier's habit of dining every new MP:

'There you would sit, with a glass of claret in your fat little hand, while he sought your support and hinted at how very well you could do.' Although there were moments of contact with Swift and Pope, he was incapable of fashioning a subtler, suitable approach to the major writers, men not less susceptible by reason of their genius. Every man was supposed to have his price, but the price of the Wits was one he never knew, never tried seriously to find out, and one that cost him dearly for not knowing.

Of all the clever men Walpole neglected, the easiest, least fiercely political, was John Gay. A Whig rather than a Tory, he was friends with everyone except Colley Cibber. The actor, slow to realise he was being personally sent up, took the leading part in *Three Hours after Marriage*, written by Gay in 1717, together with his fellow Scriblerians, Pope and Arbuthnot, and marked the penny dropping by punching the author. Gay, a rackety, uncalculating man, had done quite well out of his writings. Another play, *What d'ye Call it?*, the light verse, *Trivia, or the Art of Walking the Streets of London*, and his *Fables*, characteristically invested the lot in South Sea stock nicely ahead of the crash. He, who eventually found patrons, guardians even, in the Duke and Duchess of Queensbury, would sooner please than wound. Indeed, the fables had been directed at the Court in hopes of a decent place whose remuneration would mend his rattled finances.

But Walpole had the instinct of so many politicians for dividing everybody else into those who were for him and those who, not being for, were necessarily against. He also had a bent for guilt by association. *The Craftsman* had been up and running hard at Walpole since the end of 1726. Gay was not a known contributor, but he was on amiable terms with *The Craftsman* circle, not least with Mrs Howard, patron of opposition. Swift and Pope were still civilly in touch, by correspondence or meeting, with the first Minister. But they had also been/ still were friends of another man of large culture, Francis Atterbury.

Neither was a Jacobite sympathiser, but both believed, strongly and mistakenly, in the Bishop's innocence. Consequently both had Walpole's ear and his mistrust. When they intervened to ask a court place for Gay, the response was that nicely calculated insult of a post in attendance on a toddler Princess. Swift wrote to Carteret, 'Your friend, Walpole', (he was no such thing) 'has lately done one of the cruellest actions I ever knew, even in a Minister of State, these thirty years past.'[11] Favour, put in Pope, was reserved for 'the mean, servile, flattering, and undeserving'.

There was no reason for Walpole to treat Gay well apart from rewarding talent and a prudential eye to that talent's capacity for trouble. The contempt shown was a serious mistake. The playwright was already at work on *The Beggar's Opera* when the slap in the face came. But plays are dishes easily savoured, and this text was heavily revised. The piece which John Rich produced in 1728 at Lincoln's Inn Fields Theatre notoriously made 'Gay rich and Rich gay'. It made Robert Walpole furious.

This was an excellent moment for a satire on Walpole. The first phase of his ministerial career was concluding. He had saved the nerve of the financial world and rescued its most hated and excoriated men from the revenge of an angry public and Parliament. Now, after ruling for six years almost unopposed and imposing his first Excises without trouble, he had easily won re-election in 1727. He seemed all-powerful and at the centre of a vast web of power. Two defining traits of Walpole's long Ministry – authoritative, calm political management and a defective sense of wrong – were already understood. The things for which he would be steadily satirised until 1742 and after were already in the cross hairs of satire.

Gay's plot does not follow a narrative drawn from Walpole's acts and policies. The assault, despite the insulting epithets, is generally derisive rather than narrowly political. But we have to distinguish intent from effect; and the effect was completely political. The idea Swift had tossed to him of 'a Newgate pastoral, among the whores and thieves there' touched Walpole in ways which every theatre-going citizen recognised.

The Beggar's Opera does not concentrate all its delectable invention upon a single Walpole character. Gay had ironies to spare. Peachum, the main Walpole figure, recurringly called 'The Great Man', is thief-taker, fence and impresario of larceny. He is disclosed early in the play reading through a personnel manager's check list of subcontracting robbers and thieves, concluding it on the climax of '*Robin of Bagshot* alias *Gorgon*, alias *Bluff Bob*, alias *Carbuncle*, alias *Bob Booty*'.[12] Robin of Bagshot is another allusion to the Chief Executive of the Robinocracy, but so, arguably, is Macheath. No one seems to have worried about duplication.

What people recognised was the concentration of power. Peachum is the head of a gang, his ally untrusted and untrusting. Visibly, they quarrel in the most satisfactory way:

PEACHUM: Lions, Wolves and Vultures don't live together in herds, droves or flocks – Of all the animals of prey, Man is the only sociable one. Every one of us preys on his neighbour yet we herd together. Peachum is my companion, my friend – according to custom he may quote thousands of Precedents for cheating me – And shall I not make use of the privilege of friendship to make him a return?[13]

This was 1728 when Townshend, having burdened Walpole with an expensive and baroque foreign policy, had lost his confidence and was being edged towards a new life of agrarian improvement.

But meanwhile the two rogues maintain discipline with rewards and punishments. The gang do the work but are pre-eminently dispensable creatures. But their names alone, especially after the South Sea with all its velvet-lined felony, could be distributed to taste among the Walpole gang:

> Crook-fingered Jack, Wat Dreary alias Brown Will; Harry Paddington, a poor petty-larceny rascal . . . will never come to the gallows with credit; Slippery Sam; Mat of the Mint . . . may raise good contributions from the publick if he does not cut himself short by murder, and Tom Tipple, a guzzling, soaking sot who is always too drunk to stand himself or make others stand. A cart is absolutely necessary for him.[14]

The Beggar's Opera attacked Walpole's world. 'Marriage', says Mrs Peachum, relaxed about her daughter confining herself to 'an intrigue', 'makes it a blemish.' And he replies, 'But money, wife, is the true Fuller's Earth for reputation, there is not a spot or stain but what it can take out. A rich rogue nowadays is company for any gentleman; and the world, my dear, hath not such a contempt for roguery as you imagine.'[15]

The idea of a Newgate pastoral marrying the world of our betters with that of the London rookeries took fire because, in the overcrowded, underfoot London of the 1720s, crime was a growth sector flourishing like financial speculation. And the captain of industry dominating this market was Jonathan Wild. Like so many Londoners, Wild was an incomer, a Wolverhampton buckle maker. With outstanding entrepreneurial flair, by impudence, nerve and a short way with anyone in his way, he had pulled lesser criminals together into a kind of delinquent cooperative. He organised or subcontracted burglaries, highway robberies and street thefts, paying low but assured fence money for goods submitted and either selling on or profitably returning them to their owners, a service which, with heroic nerve, he advertised in the newspapers.

At the same time, he proclaimed himself 'Thieftaker-general', at once keeping up discipline and assuaging the authorities by the periodic sacrifice of a thief. Wild was *Capo di tutti capi* of an English mafia, Al Capone up from the West Midlands. To give Walpole's enemies something else – hope perhaps? – Wild had finally come unstuck three years before the opera appeared, hanged in 1725. A government, long complacent about his useful activities, had turned against him. As a metaphor for what Walpole was and might be, the Wild story sat up and asked for satirical application.

Put together with a melange of traditional tunes, and some melodies of his own, by Johann Pepusch, an energetic, Berlin-born musician who felicitously added an overture based on the street ballad, 'Walpole, the Happy Clown',[16] *The Beggar's Opera* was wonderful entertainment, funny today, all short episodes and good-humoured disrespect. Full of good tunes, it turned another knife in the flesh of court and ministers by its anti-Handelianism when *opera seria* – *Otone, Giulio Cesare* and *Rodelinda* were flourishing at this time – was the high fashion. George and Caroline were devoted to it, and on-message politicians trailed dutifully along for four hours at a time.

And as English tunes, rollicking or sentimental, expressing satisfactorily low opinions, were belted out by sexually unamended English singers with little regard for tessitura, a long raspberry was blown at Handel's high-aspiring accounts of Paladins in Roman armour singing mezzo. The piece was a populist 'Damn you all' aimed at the foreign court and its hangers-on.*

The really subversive thing about *The Beggar's Opera* was its run. In the early eighteenth century, nine days was uncontested success, a hit. Peachum, Macheath, Polly and Bob Booty pulled people in for sixty-two nights, a political event! Certainly *The Beggar's Opera* was delightful, as certainly its sixty-seven songs were altogether charming. But seven times the gold standard requirement of a hit also intimated a public loathing for Walpole and the Walpole system. That was something which elections in seats controlled by the crown, the Duke of

---

* It hadn't stopped Gay back in 1718 from collaborating delightfully with Handel on *Acis and Galatea*, though this English-language piece was not performed until 1732.

Newcastle and assorted cash clients, would never show. The play was an opinion poll, the public voice. It was, whatever Gay's intentions, politics!

The opposition certainly thought so and, in newspaper essay and pamphlet, underlined the mood. *The Craftsman*, tongue clenched in cheek, deplored the disrespect shown to government. This was 'the most venomous *allegorical libel* against the G—t that hath appeared for many years past'.[17] And this essay appeared separately as a complete key to the characters, while a separate pamphlet, 'Memoirs Concerning the Life and Manners of Captain Macheath', undertook to explain the 'allegory'.

The opposition stressed allegory and political content. The government, not wanting to draw attention to either, was reduced to being shocked by the immorality. *The London Journal*, subsidised and loyal, found Gay 'debauching the nation's morals and encouraging the proliferation of robberies'.[18] A pamphlet, 'The Twickenham Hotch-Potch',* made a slashing attack on all the Scriblerians. Literature was clearly going to the dogs. Bacon, Milton, Spenser and Dryden had been superseded by 'an impertinent Scotch-Quack,† a Profligate *Irish* Dean, the Lacquey of a Superannuated Dutchess and a little virulent Papist'.[19] The fast-lane clergy joined in. Dr Thomas Herring preached at Lincoln's Inn against the indecent play performed nearby. Swift denounced Herring as 'a prostitute divine',[20] which preacher would in due course become Archbishop of first York, then Canterbury.

Walpole attended the first night, giving no display of anger for he was in no immediate position to suppress *The Beggar's Opera*. That would come later; meanwhile, he had to endure the vast popularity of a work everywhere perceived as the doing down and sending up of Robert Walpole. What he did do was to come brutally down against the sequel, *Polly*, concerned with the only creditable character in the *Opera*, and generally accounted milder and less brilliant. But though busy with *Polly* herself as Romantic Interest, a sequel in which both Macheath and Peachum are hanged hardly needed anything else. Grafton, the Lord Chamberlain, told Gay on 12 December 1728 that his play could not be performed. He had no legal authority but hardly needed any. Actors were held in contempt by the better sort and were

---

* An allusion to Pope's home and famous grotto in Twickenham, south-west of London.
† Dr John Arbuthnot.

vulnerable to every kind of pressure. Before the next decade was out they would be vagrants in form of law, if not protected by royal patent, liable to all the penalties, flogging among them, falling upon incorrigible vagabonds, a position in society giving the theatre much of its charm.

That charm clings to the life of Georgian theatre's bright, transient early star. Henry Fielding is known to most readers as a novelist, for *Joseph Andrews*, *Tom Jones*, *Amelia* and, something to grieve Walpole yet further, *Jonathan Wild*. But he was a man of the theatre before annoyance at Samuel Richardson drove him to narrative fiction.* He met *Pamela* (1740) with the novella *Shamela* (1741), the chaste servant girl become a manipulative minx with commercial flair. But he had made a complete reputation writing for the stage before changing direction for reasons soon apparent. Writing his first play at twenty-one, Fielding was effectively out of the theatre by thirty.

He always seems a young man. Born in 1707 when Walpole was an MP of six years' standing, and dying in Lisbon at forty-seven, he never had time to become old. Like Gay, profoundly unlike Swift and Pope, Fielding was light and easiness, by no means always wholly earnest. There was certainly a strong vein of moral sense and his personal attachments were deep. He turned his energies chiefly against the mean, the self-righteous and the unco' guid. Walpole, with his swaggering, ring-flashing political style, might have become attractive to Fielding, a wild young man in and out of scrapes. Indeed, there is an unconfirmed legend, based on a government source, that he was once helped out of such a scrape in the country, possibly in Norfolk, by Walpole himself.[21]

He went into the theatre, his plays performed variably at Lincoln's Inn, the Little Theatre in the Hay, Drury Lane and Goodman's Fields, for the money he always ran through and the fun he got out of most things. He began as he meant to go on, disrespectfully. *Tom Thumb* (1728) sends up heroic tragedy and was widened in an extensive revision as *The Tragedy of Tragedies*. Aimed at the great and grand, both works inevitably sent shell splinters toward the Prime Minister.

Sending up Walpole in *The Author's Farce* was a handy carrot in the stew; the matured inveteracy of Swift and the anger to which Pope came late were not there. And sending up is the furthest it gets in the early plays. There was once a notion of Fielding as highly politicised

---

* Richardson's *Pamela* was the first narrative to attract the firm title 'novel'.

and full-time scourge of Walpole. The American scholar Bertrand Goldgar, who seems to have read everything, and whose *Walpole and the Wits* is an essential source for Walpole and the hostile literary world, rightly scouts attempts to read serious political assault into such passages as this dialogue between a Scarecrow, a Grub Street hack and Bookweight, based upon the (successful) rogue publisher, Edmund Curll.

SCARECROW: Sir, I have brought you a libel against the ministry.
BOOKWEIGHT: Sir, I shall not bring anything against them [*aside*] for I have two in the press already.
SCARECROW: Then Sir, I have another in defence of them.
BOOKWEIGHT: Sir, I never take anything in defence of power.

Ironically, this exchange looks forward to the financially embarrassed Fielding of 1741 when he too would offer something in defence of power. Fielding's satirising of Walpole in the early plays is casual, part of the fashion and to do with making a little mischief. The inscription on Swift's tomb says that he now lies 'where savage indignation can no longer lacerate his heart'. Fielding didn't do savage indignation.

But one of his plays, *Rape Upon Rape*,* was triggered by something difficult to take lightly. Walpole had enjoyed the services as intermediary, informer and general dirty handsman, of a Colonel Francis Charteris, or Charters. In 1730, Charteris, a man of very villainous reputation but the best connections, had been convicted of raping his maid servant. Rape being a capital offence at that time, he was sentenced to death and confined to Newgate. But the sentence, regularly executed† upon small thieves, strikers of false coin and offenders against a capital code two hundred crimes strong, rape among them, was remitted after a cash payment. There is no hard evidence connecting Walpole to this burst of leniency, but the pardon flowed from the royal prerogative, upon which the first Minister had enormous influence, and Charteris was Walpole's crony. A furious public drew its own conclusions.

Fielding wrote, entwined with a muddling but entertaining farce, a morality play in which his central target is any man abusing power generally, and his villain a corrupt justice, Squeezum. Fielding would

---

* Produced with great success by Bernard Miles in a tidied-up version at the Mermaid Theatre in London in 1967 as *Lock Up Your Daughters*.
† However, the latest estimate is that only one in seven capital sentences was carried out.

later become an exemplary reform justice himself. His words, directed at Squeezum, 'your midnight intrigues, your protecting Ill-Houses, your bribing Juries, your snacking [sharing] fees, your whole train of rogueries', are targeted at legal chicanery generally rather than Walpole's role. But they seem to have penetrated. *Fog's Weekly Journal* speaks of 'many a Man whom the Author never thought of, understands the whole Satyr to be levelled at him . . .'; such comments were to be expected and potent for the future.

To keep up with Fielding's political excursions is like juggling quicksilver. He was capable of frantic opportunism, though Martin Battestin, author of the definitive life and probably better informed on Fielding than anyone, puts it best: 'he was unshakeable in his principles as a good Whig of the sound Lockean stamp. But he took a pragmatic view of his talents as a writer where politics was his subject.'[22] So pragmatic that the index to Professor Battestin's exhaustive biography has, under the heading 'favours Walpole' ten entries, and under 'favours Opposition' sixteen! The truth was that Henry Fielding did not take politicians seriously enough to afford them the consistency he applied to a general principle.

There were, though, principles which stuck. Fielding detested the Pretender and all his works. As editor of the thrice-weekly *The Champion* he would be a vigorous loyalist editor throughout 'the Forty-five'. In so far as Fielding did party attachments, he was an Old Whig, gravitating toward Pulteney and 'the Young Patriots', Lord Cobham's protégés, Lyttleton and Pitt. In 1735 he would contribute to *The Craftsman*. But two things influenced Fielding more: personality and money.

There was also what might be called enmity by association: Fielding hated Colley Cibber. As 'Conney Keyber', he is a character in *The Author's Farce* and present on the title page of *Shamela*. Any blows struck at the kingpin of Drury Lane also hit the on-draught loyalist. But *per contra*, since he was on good terms with his cousin, Lady Mary Wortley Montagu, whom Pope in the opposition camp would scarify in verse, Fielding, despite admiring the poet, felt obliged to hit back. But attacking the government and the Court was natural for a playwright when the short-lived stage piece functioned like a newspaper cartoon.

Witness *The Welsh Opera*, premiered on 22 April 1731, a quite funny and effective, if casual, afterpiece putting George II on stage as the Welsh squire, Sir Owen Apshinken, with a caricature of Queen Caroline as Lady Apshinken. We now know it, much amended and generally thought improved, under the title *The Grub Street Opera*. Members of the government make appearances as comic or dishonest servants: Thomas the Gardener for Newcastle (Thomas Pelham-Holles), Lord Hervey as John the Groom and, of course, Robin the Butler, locked into a running quarrel with William the Coachman. (Sending up Pulteney, too, was the sort of thing objected to as even-handedness.) The royal family are treated throughout with an amiable contempt, little political purpose, but no end of *lèse-majesté*. Sir Owen sets the tone:

> What a wretched life
> Leads a man with a tyrant wife
> While for each small fault he's corrected
> One bottle makes a sot
> One girl is ne'er forgot
> And duty is always neglected.[23]

It is met almost at once by a shrewish Lady Apshinken, remote from Queen Caroline's graceful cajolery: 'At your morning draft Sir Owen, I find, according to custom; but I shall not trouble myself with such a drone as you are.'[24] George, with all his faults of temper and intolerance, was neither sot nor idler. Caroline was a clever, managing woman but no harridan. The only canonical truth against the Hanovers was the Apshinkens' heartily shared low opinion of young Owen, their son, otherwise Frederick Lewis, Prince of Wales. But the Prince, though hardly celibate, could take legitimate offence in the compulsive, failed, adulterer pictured here.

The Welsh Opera/Grub Street Opera got the worst of all worlds; it makes very little political assault. But flicking all round, it gives general offence to people likely to take it. Robin's part of the plot, falling out with Sweetissa, his fiancée, because of a malicious letter sent by young Owen, is trifling and unconnected with anything on the political stage. But the dragging into the text of Moll Skerrett, instantly recognisable in Sweetissa, was gratuitous and a very good way of making an enemy – two enemies. Sweetissa being an almost ostentatious virgin and Robin a mere suitor would merely underline what London well knew, that Moll visited Walpole's Chelsea home most weekends as his acknowledged mistress. But Robin is allowed no false innocence. Thinking himself cheated, he proclaims in best low Restoration style, 'To lose a wife when you have had her is to get out of misfortune – to lose one before you get her is to escape it, especially if it be that somebody had had her before you. – He that marries pays the price of virtue. – Whores are to be had cheaper.'[25]

There is very little political satire in this text but what there is flies straight, especially if you produce a line like that of Parson Puzzletext (Bishop Gibson?): 'I think it is a difficult matter to determine which deserves to be hanged most; and if Robin the Butler hath cheated more than other people, I see no reason for it but because he hath had more opportunity to cheat.' Such moderation would not have been appreciated. And if Robin has this song:

> This world is crammed so brim-full of deceit,
> That if Robin be a name for a cheat
> Sing tantarara, Bobs all, Bobs all,
> Sing tantarara, Bobs all

which, set to 'The Madcaps of England', was just right for singing in the street, ministerial ill will should not have come as total surprise. Ministerial ill will took the form of a brusque suppression of the offending play's successor. But the heaviest action was almost certainly triggered by another man's work. *The Fall of Mortimer* by William Hatchett is 'a thinly disguised and abusive attack on Walpole',[26] and one with clear Jacobite overtones, a play, moreover, in which the Walpole figure is led away to execution.[27] To have put on across a period of three weeks (22 April–13 May) a lightweight political skit, short of real injurious commitment, but promiscuously offensive, and a piece of hard-core Jacobite propaganda, was not wisdom. To stage two attacks on monarch and first Minister looks like carelessness, and Fielding's problem was not political commitment, but precisely that – carelessness.

Consequences followed. The new draft, *The Grub Street Opera*, packed with further attractive melodies, several lifted from Handel, has been described as the best of the ballad operas written in the ten years after Gay's triumph, but, having been promised, it was not performed. A Grand Jury warrant over 'Mortimer', the Lord Chamberlain, the unsubtle Duke of Grafton – troubling the law no further – informed the management that the play would not take place. Rank and file actors involved in *The Welsh Opera* found themselves threatened with prosecution over *The Fall of Mortimer*, their Little Theatre in the Hay temporarily closed and the company effectively broken up. Fielding kept his head down, discouraging publication – though an unauthorised version did appear from the hedge printer, Rayner, and was generally pragmatic.

But while court and ministry could shut a theatre without clear legal authority, they could not avoid the judgement of the public, in claque-proof numbers, showing hostility to court and ministry. Foolishly they set up a riposte, *The Modish Couple*, a play not itself political but staged under glaring royal sponsorship, intended to afford a large and loyal turnout. Written ostensibly by a captain in the Coldstream Guards, Charles Bodens, also 'Gentleman Usher Quarter Waiter in Ordinary to His Majesty', the piece, according to rumour, had as its real authors Lord Hervey (imaginable) and Frederick, Prince of Wales (a likely story). Better opinion indicated the Reverend James Miller. The Court reserved a block of seats, Frederick was in attendance, Cibber in charge of the production, the Dukes of Richmond and Montague laid on pre-performance dinners for two hundred at two notable taverns, while Fielding, as an act of submission, wrote the Epilogue.

'Flop' hardly describes the theatrical production which, royal presence notwithstanding, with one half of the audience shouting down the other, makes it to a fourth night (and Miller's benefit) behind a dozen guardsmen with fixed bayonets. The theatre had the art to mock Court and government, incite heavy-handed retribution and trigger in the clumsy state an impulse to make a fool of itself. Parson Miller collected his benefit, Fielding cringed a little and picked himself up for further exertions.

He made his peace at Drury Lane with Colley Cibber who, acknowledging talent, wasted no time on resentment. The plays which Fielding wrote for the Lane are interesting, but, understandably, they gave the Duke of Grafton's master no excuses. *The Lottery* is a pleasant comedy plus love interest, soon after revised (for the better) and doing very well indeed for Fielding and Cibber – fourteen nights for the first version, fifteen for the revision,[28] serious commercial success in 1732. *The Modern Husband*, a serious play about libertinism, represented the other side of the playwright – Fielding, the passionately married and disconcertingly moral man. It ran for sixteen nights, winning four benefits and entailing no problems with the authorities. But then neither did *The Covent Garden Tragedy*, a comprehensive flop, possibly because it was set in a brothel. Fielding was always higher minded in substance than tone.

His career was next interrupted by extraneous events, ironically occasioned by the retirement of old Cibber from Drury Lane, a walkout by actors, in dispute with the new management of Charles Highmore. As the quarrel had been stirred up by young Cibber, Theophilus, whom Fielding (and everyone else) disliked more than his father, Fielding struggled along at the undermanned official Drury Lane, offering a revision of *The Author's Farce* which had, after all, been a satire upon Colley Cibber, then in 1735 *An Old Man Taught Wisdom*, otherwise 'the Virgin Unmasked', a short-term success of ten nights and holding the stage to the end of the century.

As a political satirist, Fielding came and went. But his bitterest critics at this time were writing for the near-Jacobite *Grub Street Journal*, which, in a controversy across the summer months of 1732, variously accused him of 'depravity', 'a scene of infamous lewdness', 'lewd dramatical entertainments' and characterised him as 'a venal and venereal poet'. Fielding was at once a sincere moralist and sexually frank, always likely to have as much trouble with decency crusaders as with St James's Palace or Walpole's circle. And the theatre was generally vulnerable to the resentments of puritans. In 1735 a volley was fired at the stage from a source remote from Robert Walpole.

Sir John Barnard is familiar here as an independent opposition man. Member for London from 1721 to 1761, wine merchant and marine insurer, Barnard was rich, turning down the Chancellorship as costing him, at £4000 p.a., too much loss of income, honest, pious and reactionary in a High Church way, strong against the Dissenters and Jewish naturalisation, and no fonder of the players. In March 1735, he presented a bill 'to restrain the Number and scandalous Abuses of the Play-Houses and particularly representing the mischief done . . . by the corrupting of youth, encouraging vice and debauchery, and greatly prejudicing industry and trade . . .'.[29] Interestingly, the bill was seconded by opposition figures like Pulteney and Sandys. It proposed allowing only royal patent holders to perform, restricted the number of playhouses, forbade anything 'profane, obscene or offensive to piety', stamped an unauthorised player as 'a rogue, vagabond and sturdy beggar' and froze all prices.[30]

The bill applied to Fielding since it was prompted by City of London resentment at the new Goodman's Fields Theatre there, whose manager,

Henry Giffard, would stage Fielding revivals. The playwright produced a sardonic essay in *The Craftsman*, clearly at odds with the piety affected by his usual friends in Parliament. But finally it failed, not least for infringing the royal prerogative, forbidding George to create new patents, but chiefly because Walpole added an amendment to confirm the powers of the Lord Chamberlain. Barnard's bill had specifically given powers to mayors and magistrates. The idea of the crown, meaning ministers, hugging to itself all power in the congenial business of suppressing disrespectfulness and stopping people enjoying themselves was unwelcome to an *independent* puritan.

Though the bill was dropped, the frightening thing for actors and playwrights lay in the entire absence of parliamentary or press opposition. English philistinism and sanctimony have deep roots, but the bill left the respectable theatres, Covent Garden, Drury Lane and the Opera House, secure. The message to Fielding and anyone like him offending Parliament was clear. There were no friends in high places, government or opposition. Stopping the mouth of the theatre would be easy. Perhaps Fielding, who in January 1736 had formed the ironically titled Great Mogul's Company at the Little Theatre, might have pre-empted censorship, writing plays clean beyond suspicion of political disrespect. But he always lived at the edge, hence his contempt for Colley Cibber declining the brilliance and risk of *The Beggar's Opera*. He also lived high, making large earnings across the decade and blowing most of them at the gaming table. Self-censorship, the best plays that could be written without dangerous opinions, was something to dry up the fountain of his creative, combative nature. Instead, he wrote his two best, least respectful plays and pulled down the pillars of the proscenium.

In *Pasquin* not only was he writing at the top of his form, once again he was annoying people in high places. It is, like *The Author's Farce*, a rehearsal play, part of a tradition, running from *The Rehearsal* through *Trelawney of the Wells* to *Noises Off*, of plays about players. It concerns the preparation for the stage of two pieces. One is a comic afterpiece, 'The Election', involving two country candidates, Squire Tankard and Sir Harry Fox-Chace, and two court men, Lord Place and Colonel Promise. 'I hate Bribery and Corruption', says Sir Harry; 'if this Corporation will not suffer itself to be bribed, there shall not be a poor Man in it.'

This is biting but general; Walpole used corruption, everyone in politics used corruption, such bantering, put in a worldly way, should not have given much offence. What followed the broadly aimed ironies of 'The Election' was the mock tragedy 'The Life and Death of Common Sense', which concerned the invasion of the land of Sense and murder of its Queen by her rival, Queen Ignorance. It was the morality tale, conflating with politics, invoked by Pope in *The Dunciad*. Indeed, Pope came, so did his opposition friends.

As with *The Beggar's Opera*, the run spoke the political content. Fielding had done well much more often than not in his apolitical plays, but sixty performances was sensational, almost level with the run of *The Beggar's Opera*. One report after the piece had hit its stride announced that it 'was acted the twentieth Time to a crowded Audience, amongst which were great Numbers of the Nobility, with Universal applause, and many thousands of People turn'd away for want of room'.[31] Dangerously, he was looking dangerous.

It is a fatal mistake to put Fielding in a box. But at the time of *Pasquin* he was as near to party commitment as this handful of artistic mercury ever would be. He did not spare the opposition and he would soon fall out with the Patriots, but he is making here a large statement indicting power and its holders. As a leading commentator puts it, 'The play quite clearly says that England is politically corrupt and culturally degenerate, but the message is conveyed in a roundabout way and softened by high jinks . . . Pasquin manages to be funny, boisterous, pointed, subtle and highly effective.'[32]

Pasquin did not need to be fatal. It concentrated no fire upon Walpole, triggered no immediate ministerial consequences. *The Historical Register for the Year 1736* was different. It has been characterised as a cabaret, a forerunner of the BBC television satire programmes of the 1970s and 1980s.[33] But where Walpole was concerned, sheer personal dislike, physical revulsion even, seem central. Its chief character is one Quidam who is shown bribing the Patriots onto his side and, doubling as fiddler, leading them in an out-of-tune dance and provoking the comment, 'Sir, every one of these Patriots have a Hole in their pockets as Mr Quidam the fiddler there knows, so that he intends to make them dance till all the Money is fall'n through, which he will pick up again, and so not lose one Half-penny by his Generosity; so far from it that he will get his wine for nothing, and the Poor people, alas! out of their own Pockets will pay the whole Reckoning.'

If that were not enough to set an affronted minister drafting administrative measures, the afterpiece, *Eurydice Hissed*, was even more scornfully imprudent. It links Fielding's own recent play, *Eurydice*, a rare but resounding flop, with Walpole's similar experience over an offering to the public, the Excise Bill of 1733. The Prime Minister will not have rejoiced that the Walpole character is called Pillage, and the intention of the whole thing is clear to the meanest intelligence. It was clear to the ponderous and godly Egmont, whose diary recognised 'an allegory on the loss of the Excise Bill. The whole was a satire on Sir Robert Walpole, and I observed that when any strong passages fell, the Prince, who was there, clapped, especially when in favour of liberty.'[34] Frederick was by this time (See *post*, Chapter 17) in open alliance with the Patriots. What will have pleased him were lines put into the mouths of the Patriots, vapid stuff all about preferring to starve

> Than vindicate Oppression for thy Bread
> Or write down Liberty, to gain thy own.

Unlike almost anything else Fielding wrote for the theatre, this double bill is at once anti-Walpole and pro-Patriot. It couldn't be tolerated and it wouldn't be. A piece appearing on 7 May in *The Daily Gazetteer*, a new amalgamation of three pro-Walpole papers, distinguishes between *Pasquin*, which, despite having 'laid the foundation for introducing POLITICKS on the Stage', could be lived with, since 'the Author was general in his Satyr', only mocking 'the practices of *Elections* without coming so near as to point *any person* out' and *The Register* whose object is 'to make a *Minister appear ridiculous to a People*'.[35] The people who wrote for Walpole knew his mind – they had been catering for it long enough – but one fears that here they may have parodied it. 'There are Things which from the good they dispense, ought to be *Sacred*; such are *Government* and *Religion*. No Society can exist without 'em: To turn either into Ridicule, is to unloose the fundamental Pillars of Society and shake it from its *Basis*.'[36] It also threatened the very fibre of all that we hold most dear.

Fielding, never prudent, had released all the furies of ministerial self-importance. Barnard's Licensing Bill had failed only through a demarcation dispute about who would do the gagging. The reckoning would follow, and the brave and stylish appeal to reason which he would place in the new opposition journal, Charles Molloy's *Common Sense* (financed, very quietly, by the Pretender), would spit elegantly into the wind. A new Licensing Bill was a certainty, but it is surprising that Walpole did not move on the strength of *Historical Register* and *Eurydice Hissed* alone. No doubt the obvious motive being Walpole's resentment at the ridiculing of Walpole, he might give a handle in Parliament to enemies who were Fielding's friends, if not the theatre's.

In Pulteney's stylish hands, the outrage of one of the chief 'fundamental pillars of society' could be shown as the private pique of Mr Pillage. Somebody other than Walpole must be mortally insulted, somebody altogether more sacred. But George II had been pretty much left out of Fielding's recent comedies. Indecency would help, given the impact Barnard achieved on that topic, but the double-hander was not notably rough-mouthed. A whiff of Jacobitism would be in order, but Fielding was a passionate opponent. What Walpole wanted was a pretext. How he came by one is a mystery but we have a notion of it.

The Golden Rump was news to Fielding. But this work, which does not survive, only ever existed as a manuscript sedulously waved around at Court and Westminster. His biographer thinks it might have been spun off from a rude allegory in *Common Sense*, of which an even ruder print exists showing the anal inspection of a figure of Pan conducted by George and Caroline. The piece was attributed[37] to Dr William King of Oxford, an extreme Jacobite. The official story is that the play text was brought to Walpole by a shocked Henry Giffard, manager at the Goodman's Fields Theatre, with which Fielding had connections.

Fielding was first into print, alleging in terms that Walpole had faked the whole case, commissioning an indecent piece, inexcusably abusive of the King, to give himself a pretext. Walpole rested everything, he claimed, upon an '*obscure piece* which was never exhibited upon the Stage, and pretended to be suppress'd; so that it may have been written on purpose, for aught we know with such a particular design'.[38] We don't know for sure but there are pointers. Giffard brought the text to Walpole. We know of no quarrel between him and Fielding, but all Giffard had needed to do was send the piece back with a shocked covering note. But Goodman's Fields had been in Barnard's sights. An obligation by the Prime Minister would see him all right or at any rate produce compensation. Was the piece actually recruited or was a screed of unsolicited rant from a blazing Oxford Jacobite simply an opportunist's opening, snapped up by Giffard in the knowledge that a greater opportunist would snap even harder?

Walpole's snapping was parliamentary, legislative and savagely swift, allowing no protest to get started. The bill declared anyone involved in performing plays for money without royal patent a rogue and vagabond liable to all the punishments, like whipping, reserved for rogues and vagabonds. It required 'a true copy' in the hands of the Lord Chamberlain two weeks before performance for his unreserved powers of refusal or cutting. Introduced by George Bubb Dodington, a boroughmonger commanding four seats who would later desert Walpole, and managed by the serene Henry Pelham, it passed the Commons in a little over a week and with Pulteney going through the motions, meeting no significant opposition, before reaching the Lords who, with only five peers not content, gave it a third reading on 6 June.

The only stand anywhere against executive censorship of the theatre and a monopoly for the patent theatres came from Chesterfield, elegant and supercilious perhaps, but a man with a strain of genuine liberality, standing aside from demands for 'strong measures', and a dedicated enemy of Walpole for many reasons, not all of them self-serving. Supporters had stressed a war against licentiousness. But, said Chesterfield, 'Licentiousness is the alloy of liberty; it is an ebullition, an excrescence; it is a speck upon the eye of the political body, which I can never touch but with a gentle and a trembling hand lest I destroy the body, lest I injure the eye . . .'

The bill was an arbitrary restraint on the liberty of the stage leading to an equally arbitrary restraint upon the press; it was indeed 'a long stride toward the destruction of liberty itself.'[39] The speech was long admired, Lord Hervey compared Chesterfield with Petronius, but as his biographer observes, 'The House listened to the Music provided for it with much pleasure and applauded loudly when the artist sat down; nevertheless it gave its vote to the rival artist, and the Bill became law.'[40] As for the manager's opportunism, if a tale told long after by the actor Tom Davies* is correct, it worked for Giffard:

Upon reflection, Mr Giffard thought it most honourable to make a merit of laying this farce before the minister. He waited upon Sir Robert Walpole: he acquainted him with his unhappy situation; He was reduced he said to the necessity of acting a dramatic piece, which would certainly fill his house

---

* Davies was the man at whose house James Boswell would first meet Samuel Johnson.

at a time when he was greatly distressed, but though he wished to mend his fortune . . . The Minister had no sooner perused this curious drama than he formed the plan of limiting the number of theatres and of suffering no plays, farces or any entertainment of the stage without the permission of a person appointed to license them . . . Sir Robert watched for the proper time, when he imagined the House of Commons would be in a humour to receive the impression which he intended to make. He informed the House that he had something to lay before them of great importance which he should submit entirely to their wisdom and determination.

He then desired that 'The Golden Rump' be read. The infamous scurrility contained in this piece alarmed every body . . . We are told that Sir Robert Walpole presented Mr Giffard with the sum of one thousand pounds. Thus, at a very cheap rate, the ministry gained the power of hindering the stage from speaking any language that was displeasing to them: and it has been said that the whole matter was the contrivance of Sir Robert Walpole.[41]

Opportunism would afford Walpole a final twist of the heel in the playwright's throat. Fielding would in law have been free to present an unlicensed play at the Little Theatre in the month before the Act became operative. He had been ready for a last fling with a version of Gay's forbidden *Polly* and a play by another hand, *The King and Titi*, about a king's highly topical ill use of his eldest son. But Potter, proprietor at the Little Theatre, came running for the same sort of reward as Giffard, telling Grafton by letter that 'In Order to prevent what was Intended to Be Represented' and hoping to 'find Incurragement to bear an honest mind', he would take steps. This involved taking the sets apart and turning the theatre into a store room for lumber. One wonders what form 'incurragement' took.

Walpole had put into the hands of a dullard with quarterings and an adviser, often a turncoat actor (like George Colman the Younger, fifty years on), the enforcement of political quietism and all the purity that a pious bureaucrat might demand. It was the dream of any politician. Chesterfield had invoked the dreaded Excise. He recognised wit as 'a sort of property'. So that 'by this Bill, wit is to be delivered out to the public by retail, it is to be excised my lords'.[42] It was, rather, an act in restraint of trade, and it took another politician, Sheridan (plus two other good writers, Goldsmith and Arthur Murphy), to write well for the stage in the 150 years of mediocrity enjoined by Walpole's revenge on his chief mocker.

The question has been asked why Fielding didn't make a fight of the issue; why didn't he write a brilliant pamphlet in defence of the stage? Another playwright, Henry Brooke, took on Walpole and made himself pleasing amounts of money by writing a defiantly anti-Walpole play *Gustavus Vasa*, seeing it banned and, amid the protest, publishing the text, something entirely legal, and selling a great many copies.

Henry Fielding, always chronically broke, was a deeply principled man in great things, a flippant cynic in lesser ones. He wrote modest protests in the standard places but made no great blaze. And by the turn of the decade, having fallen out with the Patriots, and short of money, he was actually writing dulcet words in a Walpolian publication. But then Fielding's swings of mood were likely to hit on the rebound anyone who came too near. In 1743 he would publish *The Life of Mr Jonathan Wild the Great*.

Alexander Pope was a different kind of enemy. Fielding was a wit, Pope wrote supremely witty things. But he wrote them while making deadly judgements; he was a serious man, whose attacks do not come as entertainment: they are brooded upon and uttered in deadly earnest. *The Dunciad*, walled in with explanatory footnotes as it is, represents, in both first draft and revision, Pope's response to accumulating affronts. Many of these are directed at the Walpolian propaganda machine and the machine minders, but it is not an assault on Walpole. The *Epistle to Dr Arbuthnot*, though concerned with other things, is rich in slaps at the same people – Colley Cibber, 'Orator' Henley and James Moore Smyth:

> And hath not Colley still his Lord and Whore
> His Butchers, Henley, his free masons Moore?

Pope was close to Swift, to Gay and, importantly, to Bolingbroke. But it is a mistake to think of him as a lifetime active enemy of ministry and Minister as it is to overstress his religion. His own account of just what his Catholicism was ought to have won him easy tolerance from a Whig government. In a letter to Swift in November 1717 he says, 'I am not a papist, for I renounce the temporal invasions of Papal power, and I detest their arrogated authority over Princes and States. I am a Catholick in the strictest sense of the word.'[43]

This, to all calm-judging men, was the test for Catholics in the Anglican state of the eighteenth century. Pope owed no foreign allegiance. And he underlined the fact in the same letter. 'In a word, the things I have always wanted to see are not a Roman Catholick or a French Catholick or a Spanish Catholick, but a true Catholick; and not a King of Whigs or a King of Tories, but a King of England. Which God grant of his mercy his present Majesty may be.'[44] It is statement of faith and outlook anticipating the Enlightenment and one which would have been heartily endorsed by George I, far less bigoted than the majority of his subjects. It would have been taken civilly but cynically by Robert Walpole, happily twitchy on the subject of an enemy within and appreciative of its political mileage.

Pope had enemies who were friends to, or creatures of, Walpole, and he could never have been a partisan of Walpolian finance-Whiggism, even less, after the state trial, degradation and exile of Francis Atterbury, whom he thought innocent, of its spying and punishing streak. It is probably best to see him as a Tory of the same humanitarian sort as Samuel Johnson, but no sort of political Catholic. He found Walpole and the Georges, especially the Second, altogether too much, but for a long time tried to rub along with the regime. In the first version of *The Dunciad*, published in 1728, this running assault on the world of hack letters and poetasting, many writers for the government press can be found. Bertrand Goldgar lists twenty, the busily pamphleteering Bishop Hoadley undeservedly among them.

But the political element is at one remove, not highlighted. Leonard Welsted, John Oldmixon, Theophilus Cibber, Matthew Concanen and the rest embody mediocrity, 'dullness', every kind of untalent and desperate hackery. However much the sullen foot soldiery winced, for some time to come Pope was not seen, at Court or Westminster, as an opponent. The idea of *not* making an enemy of him surely played its part. Unlike Fielding, Pope guarded his tongue, but, aroused by degree, he would use it as injuriously as Swift, without Swift's general and nagging misanthropy.

He had suffered since childhood from tuberculosis of the spine, he was spindly and undersized and endured serious ill health throughout 'this long disease, my life'.[45] He compensated by a life of pleasant withdrawal at Twickenham, building the famous grotto and happily entertaining a brilliant company. This was possible because Pope, unlike Fielding, was sensible about money. The idea, conceived in 1713, of a proper translation of Homer, *The Iliad* then *The Odyssey* – a volume a year over six years, sold by subscription at a guinea a year, with Pope essentially publishing it himself in partnership with Bernard Lintot – brought profits, from *The Iliad* alone, of above £4000, £200,000 of our money. The leading poet of the age was rich and a gentleman, however intelligent. (And he was not then an enemy of Sir Robert Walpole who on publication subscribed for ten sets of *The Odyssey* in 1724.)

With Pope so much was personal that his entry into political conflict, tangential in the early thirties, scaldingly direct towards the end of that decade, might seem rather surprising. His gift for feuding was balanced by another for tender and ardent friendship: Arbuthnot, Thomas Parnell, Congreve and Wycherley, John Gay, old Duchess Sarah, Samuel Garth, Bishop Warburton, David Mallet, and from his Catholic acquaintance, the Blount sisters and his neighbour, John Caryl, are names on a long list. These were intellectual or personal friendships. But lamentably, in the context of Walpole's judgement of who was 'one of us', there was also a group of friends, sharply political, and the wrong politics: Earls of Oxford, father and son, Swift, Atterbury, young George Lyttleton, and, with especial devotion, Viscount Bolingbroke. A discreet man, but given to identification with friends, could spend just so much time being discreet before the common views and ministerial provocations drew him into controversy. After which, epigrammatical mind and combative spirit would make him, in a string of epistles, follow the Swift of Gulliver as Walpole's bleakest enemy in print.

Alexander Pope had the rare gift of pronouncing without sounding inflated. His charge that Moll Skerrett (Phryne) was buying the whole auction because she foresaw a general Excise (see *supra*, Chapter 14) is deftly linked in the *Epistle to Bathurst* to his private quarrel with her friend, Lady Mary Wortley Montagu. Only a finger on Walpole's shoulder, it tells us in thirteen words that Moll is a whore (identification with an historical Greek courtesan), that Walpole and his lady live high, and that, up his sleeve, the Minister conceals heavier charges all round, *Dichtung* in action.

For the moment he generalised, attacked trends and derided attitudes. If this involved also spitting Court and government men like Denis Bond, Sir John Blunt and Sir Gilbert Heathcote, *they* were not Walpole. Blunt was at the heart of the South Sea and Bond was a generally execrated, fraudulent converter. But the brutal greed and minimalist ethics they exemplified were the Walpole world view. The *Epistle to Bathurst*, concluding with the devil's temptation of the rise and fall of a modern self-made, Walpolian man, Sir Balaam, is an attack on the times.

> Stocks and Subscriptions pour on every side
> Till all the Daemon makes his full descent
> In one abundant show'r of Cent per Cent,
> Sinks deep within him, and possesses whole
> Then dubs Director, and secures his soul . . .
> . . . His daughter flaunts a Viscount's tawdry wife
> She bears a coronet and pox for life.
> In Britain's Senate, he a seat obtains
> And one more Pensioner St Stephen gains.[46]

An attack on the times? Who had shaped those times, who more exultantly their trumpet and drum than Robert Walpole? Even so, this is the assault implicit, the sly injury best caught in a phrase deployed elsewhere by Pope himself: 'Just hint a fault and hesitate dislike.'[47]

Yet what more political in 1734 than to dedicate a poem to a former supporter of the government dismissed from his offices for opposing the Excise Bill? That was what the *Epistle to Viscount Cobham* did. The piece may mock modes and fashionable types, but this peer was emerging as patron of 'Cobham's Cubs', young and attractive opponents of the regime. Through accelerated anticipation in the last line, Cobham is offered, rather bathetically by Pope's cool standards, suitably heroic deathbed words: '"Oh Save my country, Heav'n!" Shall be your last.'

It is no accident that the Excise Bill moves Pope to identify, if still tangentially, with the opposition. The Excise, whatever its inherent merits, was at once the product of Walpole's overreaching and evidence that he could lose. He had roused the country against him and retreated before the uprising. Coupled with his recent second screening of the South Sea directors from investigation into subsequent frauds, this vivid affair put a spring into the step of the opposition and provoked Walpole to the parliamentary equivalent of shooting hostages, a string of dismissals readily parlayed into martyrdoms.

Pope was part of the reaction, but his great assault lay ahead. The poem was given a title to put off the classically challenged modern reader: *The First Epistle of the First Book of Horace Imitated*. But this was an age in which the educated classes were seriously schooled in at least the Roman classics, and the parallels were very rewarding: Augustus: George II; Maecenas, the generous patron: Walpole; Horace: Pope!

The First Epistle marks the point where open hostilities began. The Prime Minister would have been chiefly affronted by the dedication, 'To Lord Bolingbroke'. After years of controlled antipathy, he had declared a species of jihad upon Henry St John, effectively declaring him a public enemy. Having won the 1734 election, the Minister felt new strength and began a press campaign against his old enemy.

The Walpole press was not a thing of quality, but it understood hatred and it understood fear. The name of one pamphlet gets the sense: 'The Grand Accuser – The Greatest of All Criminals'. *The Daily Courant* had a series of pieces on 'The Reasonableness and Necessity of driving Bolingbroke out of the Kingdom'.[48] For financial reasons rather than flight from such fury, Bolingbroke would indeed eventually leave the country, settling in Amboise in Touraine. But first, while trying to sell Dawley Farm, for the best part of a year he stayed at Twickenham with Pope. And with his easy access to a press, Pope, in 1738, had had Bolingbroke's new book, *Letters on the Study of History*, printed and privately distributed.

And here he was, in April 1738, dedicating to Bolingbroke *The First Epistle*:

> Who counsels best? Who whispers, 'Be but Great,
> With Praise or Infamy, if possible with Grace,
> If not, by any means get Wealth and Place.
> For what? to have a Box where Eunuchs sing,
> And foremost in the circle, eye a King!'[49]

The box was at the Royal Italian Opera where Whigs and moneymen, following Walpole, following George II, went to be rapturous about castrati. That was the assault direct, but in contrasting the morality of Walpole's world with an older pattern, Pope directly acknowledged himself a signed-up Patriot. The young members of the opposition had assumed, anticipating Disraeli's Young England, a Gothic slant. They revered the days 'when chivalry lifted up its lance on high'. The choice of discourse, argued Pope, lay between

This new Court jargon or the good old song
The modern language of corrupted peers
Or what was spoke at CRESSY and POITIERS.[50]

The alternative to wealth and place, goggling at George II and listening
to *opera seria*, was an ancient (and imaginary) purity of purpose, from
which – thanks to we-know-who – political life had decayed. Splendid
satiric verse and bad history, it was what Pope had never done before,
straight party politics. It also characterises Bolingbroke, postal addressee
of this verse letter, in glittering terms:

That Man divine whom Wisdom calls her own;
Great without title, without Fortune bless'd . . .
In short that reas'ning high, immortal Thing,
Just less than Jove, and much above a King, . . .[51]

He was now in the open, and Walpole's men were authorised to hit
back. The first attack came in *The Daily Gazetteer* on 27 March 1738
and was followed by assaults on 6, 11 and 12 April.[52] But they concentrated less upon his picture of corrupt getters of wealth and place than
that effusive celebration of 'the Great Criminal'. Pope is patronised as
a literary and hence, *a fortiori*, irrelevant figure.

So may thy virtues tinkle in our ear
Thy *Honour spotless* and thy *soul sincere*
Safe from they Arts, so may thy harmless Praise
In harmless Song our *Doubt* and *Pleasure* raise.

And his judgement smiled at:

Our *Doubt, so true a Briton* e'er could be;
Our *Mirth* to find that B — ling — ke is He.[53]

It was pretty good by the standards of government propaganda, but
the suggestion to an artist that he doesn't count is something of an incentive. Pope came fighting back with *One Thousand Seven Hundred and
Thirty-Eight*, later published as Dialogue I in the *Epilogue to the Satires*.
     It contains, if only at the margin, a profound chance irony. A central
opposition cause, particularly for the Young Patriots, was a foolish

urgency for waging against Spain, over a trading dispute, the War of Jenkins's Ear (see *post*). The pickled ear of Captain Jenkins was already in circulation. Pope, so long discreet, endorsed this enthusiasm, mocking ministers' pacific imperturbability in the face of outrage:

And own the Spaniard did a *waggish thing*
Who cropt our Ears and sent them to the King.

(But very quietly, Bolingbroke agreed with Walpole.)

Pope is swivelling machine-gun fire around his targets, mingling a party puff for the Patriots with a kick at the Theatre Licensing Act:

A Patriot is a fool in every age,
Whom all Lord Chamberlains allow the stage
These nothing hurts; they keep their Fashion still,
And wear their strange old Virtue as they will.[54]

As for Walpole himself, the tone is more of sorrow than anger. The 'Friend' of the dialogue says: 'Go see Sir Robert', and receives Pope's melancholy reply:

See Sir Robert! – hum
And never laugh for all my life to come?
Seen him I have, but in his happier hour,
Of Social Pleasure, ill-exchanged for pow'r
Seen him uncumbered with the Venal tribe,
Smile without art, and win without a Bribe.
Would he oblige me? let me only find,
He does not think me what he thinks mankind.[55]

Disregard the misreading of foreign policy, the naïvety seeing only the good in Bolingbroke which, intellectually at least, was there. Consider only the tempered taking of Walpole's moral measure, and these are superlative lines, hitting exactly home and, in terms of historic reputation, doing mortal hurt.

From a letter of 31 July[56] we know that Pope had a meeting with Walpole, his biographer, Maynard Mack, thinks fairly soon after the publication of the first dialogue on 16 May. We do not know what was said, only that publication of the second followed on 18 July. And the central tone of these writings was struck finest of all in the second, dedicated to William Murray, later Lord Chancellor Mansfield. Despite the party politics and clear above the scarifying of courtiers, bawds and bubble-company directors, it is one of nobility. It concerns honesty when government is not honest. Pope had been deeply impressed with the reply of young Lord Cornbury, when offered a government pension by way of his brother-in-law: 'How could you tell, my Lord, that I was to be sold? Or at least, how could you know my price so exactly?'[57] He remembered that in the second dialogue in the laconic injunction:

> Would ye be blest? Despise low Joys, low Gains
> Disdain whatever Cornbury disdains.[58]

Pope is bright with animation. Asked by the 'Friend' why he goes to all this trouble:

> . . . Walpole guilty of some venial sin;
> What's that to you who ne'er was out nor in?'

he replies:

> Ask you what provocation I have had?
> The strong Antipathy of Good to Bad.[59]

He feels himself engaged in a good and truthful fight against an eighteen-year winning side:

> Yes I am proud; I must be proud to see
> Men not afraid of God afraid of me.[60]

Whatever Pope's mistakes, the pride is important. He is claiming not only the right of his side, a slight thing, but a continuing and imperative duty of honesty, which is not, and exalting the power of a despised art to champion it. The verse continues and, epitomising all the gilt-finished company of Walpole, rejoices at his art's power:

> Safe from the bar, the Pulpit and the Throne
> Yet touched and shamed by ridicule alone.[61]

Of course Pope was writing for the *Guardian* readership of his day, the highly educated, liberal-minded, politically preoccupied, but not politically powerful, elite of outside. The regime might flinch, but it did not, even in the very rough circumstances of 1737–8, fall. It sent its hacks out in numbers against Pope, but the real business lay in the clenched, excluding world of Lords and Commons where eventually, in February 1742, Robert Walpole would lose his authority. Pope had said what he had to say, he would take a cooler view of the opposition, even of the Patriots, though never a warmer one of Sir Robert. His function had been to write the man who could no longer turn a page into the canon of literature, not a mortal blow but a fearful epitaph.

The last assault on Walpole from the ranks of the Wits was made by the man he had silenced and who, in desperate financial straits, had paid him court despite the destruction of his first career. For Henry Fielding, it was only one career. Martin Battestin dates his first proper novel to late 1741/early 1742. It was published in a volume of miscellanies in 1743. This was *Jonathan Wild*, more precisely *The Life of Mr Jonathan Wild the Great*. 'Great' was a burr catching in Walpole's coat whenever the unhired writers brushed against him.

It is a brisk, vigorous read, darker than anything else by Fielding, having affinities with Swift. The idea is not new. The charm of identifying the King's first Minister with someone who had run a supermarket of stolen goods and kept his thieves in order by periodically betraying one of them had been evident when Swift had suggested that Newgate pastoral to Gay. In 1725 Wild had been hanged, in 1742 Walpole had been – next best thing – defeated in the Commons. In 1743 *The Life of Mr Jonathan Wild the Great* appeared. For the publishing press, despite serious fears after the theatre legislation, had not been subjected to a licensing act. This was literature's last, and by no means fond, farewell to Sir Robert Walpole.

SCOTLAND, RIOTS AND
READY MONEY

Sometimes you have a bad run. In 1736, abolition of the Witchcraft Act, a belated glint of enlightenment, was almost the only thing going right. Not that 'enlightenment' was a Walpole quality. Egmont has a startling cameo of the Prime Minister's view of justice. In January, the King and the relevant councillors hearing appeals 'of the Malefactors capitally condemned' dealt with a case of fraudulent conversion. It involved 'debate of three hours whether the King should pardon Wreathock, the attorney, or order his Execution'.

The conviction was very dubious, turning upon the evidence of Wreathock's business partner. For good legal reasons, the Lord Chief Justice, Hardwicke, and Mr Justice Reeves,

> were absolutely for pardon . . . Sir Robert Walpole argued with great earnest . . . saying among other things that the late King of France [Louis XIV] never pardon'd a criminal condemned by law, for he took it to be the duty of a king to see his laws punctually executed and not ennervate the force of them by suggesting to subjects that they, or the judges who pronounced justice, were too severe.

George was a peppery little soldier, but he had merciful instincts denied his Minister. At the end of a three-hour wrangle and in the teeth of Walpole's taste for shining and untempered authority, 'The King proposed transporting the criminal for life . . . to this the Council agreed.'[1]

Otherwise 1736 was the year when things began to go wrong in the most public fashion. Bitter wrangles over the Mortmain and Quaker Tithe Bills and the cool departure of Walpole's churchman, Gibson, have been related, as, with the last derisive plays of Henry Fielding, has the quarrel with the theatre. The period 1736–7 was almost unrelieved in conflicts.

But even political trouble has its sensational aspect. Gunpowder is more fun than normal politics and, in Westminster, with its memories of Captain Fawkes, has a dramatic ring, something widely appreciated when, in July, a small fire was started in Parliament. It was set in galleries built for the wedding of the Princess Royal to the dwarfish and deformed Prince of Orange. As Walpole wrote to his brother, Horatio, in Hanover with the King, 'the insolent affair at Westminster-hall' had involved 'a preparation which they call a *phosphorus* that takes fire from the air'. Being Walpole, he was quite sure who had done it, seeing 'no reason to doubt but the whole was projected by a sett of low Jacobites' who, he claimed, had talked of such a scheme. Walpole had an informer assuring him that it was so. He relied upon 'the same fellow that brought me these and many such sort of intelligencies. He has promised a more particular account, but declines giving evidence.'[2]

The arson turned out to be the act of a half-mad, non-juring parson called Nixon who, mercifully or otherwise, would be confined in an asylum. Walpole's same fellow does not seem to have brought him intelligencies of the riots against Irishmen also about to explode. It was a rough year for street trouble generally. If our contemporary response to immigration lacks sensibility, that of the mid-eighteenth century was on the rough side of virulent. Irishmen had been coming into the English countryside since the sixteenth century for limited seasonal work, mostly the harvests. By the 1730s they were coming to the cities, especially London – and staying. So were the Scots, but though the Scots were loathed, the feeling rested only upon resentment. For the poorer Irish, outworking and underliving so many natives, it stood upon a fearful contempt. The poor East End of London relied heavily upon weaving, the trade, originally, of immigrant Flemings and Huguenots. The new urban Irish took up weaving well below the (not very high) going rate. The provocation of their also being Catholics adding a final relish, it seemed reasonable to burn down the houses where they lived.

The riots broke out soon after the Westminster arson because, in Archdeacon Coxe's *douce* phrase, 'the weavers of Spittalfields took umbrage at an inferior rate of wages'.[3] Umbrage was also taken at

Shoreditch, Whitechapel, Southwark, Lambeth and Dartford and involved the burning or tearing down of Irish-occupied houses by crowds estimated at anywhere between two and four thousand people.[4] The riots raged around different parts of London for three nights together, countered by detachments of Grenadiers and a wholly ineffectual reading of the Riot Act. Walpole, set in his ways, blamed it all on the Jacobites.

But what happened next in Edinburgh, where the citizenry staged a riot so viciously dramatic that it has entered literature, was far more important and carried consequences, all to Walpole's political disadvantage. Eighty years later, Sir Walter Scott would recall the event in *The Heart of Midlothian*, describing a real night-time lynching, through his fictional character Reuben Butler, who 'at the opening into the low street called the Cowgate, cast back a terrified glance, and, by the red and dusky lights of the torches could discern a figure wavering and struggling as it hung suspended above the heads of the multitude, and could even observe men striking at it with Lochaber-axes and partisans'.[5] He was describing the climax of the Porteous Riots.

Andrew Wilson was a smuggler who had killed an exciseman. Smugglers were popular enough in England and even better regarded in Scotland, excisemen not. Wilson, said to have been ill treated in prison and admired for helping a comrade escape, was dangerously popular. The crowd assembled for his execution, came to mourn and stayed to riot. The officer commanding the guard, Captain Porteous, had a name for harshness. And his tight handcuffing of Wilson with the words, 'It signifies little, your pain will soon be at an end', met the eighteenth-century norm of military insensibility. After the hanging, the crowd threw stones, causing a number of injuries. Porteous, having been hit by one, took a musket, shot one man and told his troops to fire. A second volley fired during the return to the guardhouse, and without orders from Porteous, killed another three people, seven dying in all.

Scotland having a separate system of law and the public mood vividly apparent, the captain was prosecuted for murder – while a large crowd stood ominously outside the court. The charge of murder was bad law. He was acting at the least under gross provocation and, with men injured by stones thrown, could in a neutral court have probably successfully pleaded self-defence.* A charge of manslaughter was a reasonable

---

* Contrast Peterloo (1819), where eleven people were killed and scores badly injured by a sabre charge of mounted men for attending a meeting, with no provocation at all.

option, but a crowd nursing a wrong is not reasonable. The jury, fifteen men in Scotland, and semi-coerced, convicted him by a bare majority of eight to seven, and he was condemned.

Caroline, Regent in George's absence, scornful of indictment and verdict, quickly granted Porteous a respite of six weeks, to make time for further and successful legal appeals, with London's authority behind them. The response in Edinburgh was frightening. The mob, which came out on 7 September, set fire to the Tolbooth, dragged Porteous from his hiding place in a chimney, took him to the Grassmarket, the customary place of execution, and summarily part-hanged, part-hacked him to death. What was truly unnerving was that this crowd was stone-cold sober. As well it might have been. The Edinburgh mob had just done something which, over the long term, would help undermine the government of Sir Robert Walpole.

The Westminster and St James's reaction was also reconstructed by Scott: 'An express was despatched to London with the tidings where they excited great indignation and surprise in the council of regency, and particularly in the bosom of Queen Caroline ... Nothing was spoken of for some time save the measure of vengeance which should be taken.'[6] Porteous had been serving the legal authorities and dealing with a violent mob. His detention while the case was *sub judice* required the protection which had been fearfully abandoned. All mobs threatened all government, and the notion of a mob exacting the suspended capital sentence of a coerced court for a misjudgement doing loyal duty was not to be endured.

The political reaction was enormous. Caroline, Walpole and Lord Hardwicke had read an account, far more vivid than Scott's would be, in *The Gentleman's Magazine*, showing clearly the assurance and ceremony with which the law of Queen Regent and Lord Chancellor had been flouted:

Betwixt 9 and 10 at Night, a Body of Men entered the West Port of *Edinburgh*, seized the Drum, beat to Arms, and calling out *here! All those who dare avenge Innocent Blood*, were instantly attended by a numerous crowd. Then they seized and shut up the City Gates, and posted Guards at each to prevent Surprize by the King's forces while another Detachment disarmed the City Guards and advanced immediately to the Tolbooth or Prison ...

The piece went on to explain how, after Porteous was captured, the crowd

> drew him up, but having got his hands to the Rope, they let him down and
> tyed them and draw'd him up again, but observing what an indecent Sight
> he was without any Covering over his Face, they let him down and pull'd
> off one of the two shirts he had on and wrapped it about his Head, and
> hal'd him up a third Time with loud Huzza and a Ruff of the Drum. After
> he had hung till supposed to be dead, they nail'd the Rope to the Post, then
> formally saluting one another, grounded their Arms, and on t'other Ruff of
> the Drum, retired out of Town.[7]

What had increased royal and ministerial rage was the panoramic
ineptitude of those in immediate authority, legal, military and munici-
pal, an ineptitude which looked like connivance, if not conspiracy.
General Moyle, officer commanding in the city, had acted as Porteous
ought to have done, but as *he* should not. He refused to do anything
without written authority! The available MP, Lindsay, whom Moyle
thought drunk, refused to carry written instructions for fear the mob
found them on him. Another group of magistrates came to the scene,
took a look at the crowd, and went quickly and fearfully away. Lord
Islay, Argyll's brother, charging the magistrates with being 'wilfully
neglectful', described their behaviour as 'certainly worse than can be
imagined'.[8] The Reverend Henry Etough knew what he thought – about
the mob: 'The magistrates and principal inhabitants of Edinburgh, being
wellwishers, they acted with perfect security' – also about the Scots: 'It
was made a national point to palliate and defend all misdemeanours
and to excuse riotous and treasonable practices.'[9]

Walpole reckoned that he understood Scotland as far as it needed
or deserved to be understood. The foundation of his management of
all voters, Members and Lords, a cheerful and unplumbably low esteem
of humanity, extended to the Scottish nobility. In 1721, he had applied
it at annual but terminable rates: £3000 to the Earl of Hopetoun, £2000
to the Earl of Leven, as to the Earl of Orkney and the Honourable Mr
Ross; £1000 each to the Earls of Loudon and Marchmont, Robert
Sinclair, John Scot, John Hay and John Kerr and steady recurring sums
to sundry others, all drawn from the secret service fund.[10] Walpole
bribed retail, but he bribed widely. Noble loyalty had secured the interest
of Lords then, and in the difficult election of 1734 it would keep them

secured. If the price went up, it would be met. As Sherlock Holmes put it, 'You know my methods.'

Their loyalty, however, had never warranted complacency. The investment required a manager, in this case the Duke of Argyll and his family, the Campbells. They were Calvinists if not Puritans, wholly in favour of the Hanoverian succession, but not close to Walpole. Fortunately, in the mid-1720s, though disliking him and Townshend, they disliked Carteret more and Carteret's friend in Scotland, the Duke of Roxburghe, most of all. What existed between Westminster and Edinburgh was an alliance of dispassionate self-interest.

But the Argylls were managing Scotland on account of earlier riots (in Glasgow), riots which broke the power of Roxburghe and which turned, unsurprisingly, upon an Excise, in this case on malt. The riots had tempted Roxburghe to plot with the opposition at a time, 1725, when that opposition was miserably inadequate and Walpole at the full tide of power. Argyll had been Walpole's ally then and chief gainer afterwards. But that summer of 1736 his writ did not run in the streets of Edinburgh. What followed the riots would slacken the ties binding him to the Prime Minister, eventually contributing to his defeat.

Scottish populism would now be followed by English, with the opposition beating the drum. Edinburgh citizens had revolted atrociously; they should suffer humiliation. Lords and Members talked, with no government resistance, of Edinburgh being stripped of its charter and suffering formal degradation. The entire Porteous case involves a startling succession of wrong decisions. Prudence made it wrong in a febrile city to hang a popular citizen. The crowd was wrong to stone the soldiers, Porteous wrong to fire on them, the local court wrong to condemn him for murder, the civil authorities wrong not to transfer him to the security of the Castle, and the lynch mob wrong to murder him. Finally, confronted with all this, the opposition sought a humiliating and quite wrong revenge on the city which Robert Walpole, against all customary shrewdness, wrongly supported.

But given a train of error, the opposition could hardly be blamed for jumping on, and the case they made was not entirely factitious. Carteret, the old enemy, who was emerging with Chesterfield as the leader of opposition in the Lords, made judicious distinctions. Instead of blazing away at an outrage in the red-faced, Westminster way, he defined differing sets of circumstances. In the previous year in the west, notably Herefordshire, there had been riots against newly established turnpikes, riots against immediate charges for road improvements merely proposed. The Ministry had been promiscuously brutal in response, the military making themselves felt, one Herefordshire man sent to Tyburn through the Lord Chief Justice's twisting of the Black Act, a thing quite twisted enough anyway.[11]

Carteret deplored such executive bullying; indeed, he spoke almost tenderly of the turnpike rioters. The last thing he wanted was an extension of military control. There was already quite enough of that unEnglish sort of thing, notably 'the severe law which your lordships passed some time since against those who should be concerned in any such. To me it is amazing to see the civil power, armed with such a severe law, should not be able to prevent as well as to quell any such tumult without the assistance of the gentlemen of our army.'[12]

People had their legitimate wrongs and if they kicked up about something, they did not deserve repression. 'The people seldom or ever assembled in any riotous or tumultuous manner unless when they are oppressed or imagine they are oppressed.'[13] If they were mistaken, then the case should be put to them rationally by a magistrate. 'In common humanity he is obliged to take this method before he has recourse to such methods as may bring death and destruction upon any number of his fellow countrymen.' And as for circumstances where there *had* been oppression, 'you may hang them, you may shoot them, but till the oppression is removed or alleviated, they will never be quiet'.[14]

This opening was admirable and almost certainly Carteret's true conviction. But it was also an Olympic-standard springboard for assaulting that soberly murderous Edinburgh mob and urging exemplary measures. The Porteous Riots were smuggling riots and 'The Riots and Tumults which proceed from Smuggling, are, my Lords, of an old standing and of a very different nature; . . . I am afraid some extraordinary methods must be made use of for suppressing them.'[15] What had happened in Edinburgh, 'that wicked, that atrocious act, proceeded originally from smuggling . . . that tumult and the Murder they committed, was one of the most extraordinary that ever happened in any country, and it was, I think, one of the greatest indignities that ever was put upon a civil government'.

The lynching deserved especial concern 'because it was carried on with a sort of decency and order'.[16] Nothing was being done, yet it was impossible in that tight-packed town for the culprits not to be known. In which case, and Carteret quoted an earlier Edinburgh riot, the city magistrates had been warned in Queen Anne's time that 'if such tumult ever happened again, the courts of justice should all be removed from the city; from which I must conclude that the king has a power to remove them'.[17] And Carteret urged decisive action. The magistracy of Edinburgh had turned hedgehog. It knew one big thing – that if it moved against the ringleaders, the lives of magistrates would be threatened – so it made great play of knowing nothing at all. In which case, said Carteret, 'if they should protect or conceal the murderers, or if the magistrates of that city had, through fear or design, connived at the murder, they might be justly deemed to have forfeited their charter; and in such a case I do not know that it may be thought proper to divest them of some of their privileges by way of punishment, and as an example for other cities in time to come'.[18]

Nothing is more deadly to a minister in a fix than an opponent quietly urging him, at the very top of courtesy, to do something with the widest popular appeal, calculated to get him into a worse fix. But, anyway, even without Carteret, Walpole faced the horrified anger of Queen Caroline. Accordingly, he saw no alternative to the sort of bill which Carteret later moved, and gave it clear support. But if Walpole had problems, the Duke of Argyll and his brother, Lord Islay, had rather different ones.

It was one thing to manage the selection of Scottish representative peers and manage Scottish elections, transparently bogus even by Cornish standards, quite another to take on a killer mob shrewdly directed by cold-eyed Presbyterians with a continuing interest in cheating the revenue. Walpole thought he understood Scotland. Argyll and Islay understood it too well to risk provoking more and worse 'tumults'. Legislation to abolish the town guard, permanently bar from the magistracy the Lord Provost, Alexander Wilson, and pull down the city gates at the Nether Bow Port moved Argyll to 'an animated speech' against. He voiced a general Scottish protest, headed in the Commons by Duncan Forbes, the Lord Advocate!

Walpole found himself urged to pursue his hard course by the opposition and warned against it by customary and crucial supporters. Eventually, although the Porteous Bill, as it was generally called, passed the Lords fifty-four to twenty-two, on 11 May 1737, its thundering terms were eventually diluted to dismissal of Wilson and a £2000 levy on the city, to be paid to Porteous's widow. This, said Lord Hervey, gracefully, should make her 'with most unconjugal joy, bless the hour in which her husband had been hanged'.[19] The ministerial response had been an affair dragging and dwindling through almost a year before emerging as an anti-climactic legislative mouse.

Worse yet, although Argyll's opposition to collective and exemplary punishments had been right, his motives went beyond wise scruples. Eternally sullen, militarily underpromoted in his own eyes, the Duke saluted an excuse for what would slowly uncoil into a quarrel and withdrawal of support. But he played betrayal long. The Duchess of Marlborough, herself throbbing with malice towards the Minister, would observe two years on, in 1738, 'After all the great noise there was of the duke of Argyle being irreconcilably angry with Sir Robert; every thing passed in the house without his saying the least word to show it; *that* was no surprise to me.'[20]

Judging that the Walpole, who had proposed severe measures under Caroline's pressure and retreated from them under Scottish protest, was a falling stock, the Duke would sell Walpole futures steadily. His brother and eventual successor, Archibald, Lord Islay, a sounder man, did not follow him, and soldiered on beside Walpole, but the platoon of loyal Scottish nominees for each House was no longer assured. As for the English opposition, they would hold out garlands to Argyll. As Archdeacon Coxe deftly put it, 'He who was bitterly arraigned for political versatility, was now applauded for virtue and patriotism.'[21] But Edinburgh would not raise the only riot that year. The Gin Act,* put through Parliament in March/April, on the initiative of Sir Joseph Jekyll, came into operation in August. Though unanswerable in terms of facing up to a social catastrophe, it was, like American Prohibition, drafted in terms making it unenforceable, terms to bring out the London mob. During one eruption, Lord Egmont observed 'The Mob, disabled with putting down their beloved gin, exclaim publicly "No gin, no King"'.[22] And sentiments no kinder were expressed directly to the Prime Minister.

A letter in a decent hand of 24 September is superscribed 'Dreadful Year' and signed laconically 'Wellwisher'. It catches the mood:

> As the late pernicious and Enslaving Bill for the suppression of all distilled liquors affects trade in general and is the prelude to a general excise next session, several dealers agreed to buy large quantities of Gin and distribute

---

* Officially 'the Spirituous Liquor Act'.

[it] among the populace on Tuesday night, that being the eve of the day in which the said Act commences – This act of Public Spiritedness – Let town and country echo that night with Sir Robert and Sir Joseph, make bonfires and give loud huzzas in their honour.[23]

They were as good as their word. A letter to Walpole two days later announces:

I am just come from the view of one of the shops in Silver Street opposite the King Street by Golden Square. In the middle of the shop elevated a foot above the floor stands a large barrel covered with black cloths upon which is a coffin covered in the like manner; at the head of the Coffin lies a cushion with a little brass crest upon it. The Mimick Corps within (which they styled 'Mother Gin') is a barber's block dressed very whimsically; at the foot of the coffin, a large plume of feathers and on either side an undertaker's pole.

Nothing paid for what was drunk . . . they intended to bury her at 12 o'clock on Wednesday night at St George's burial ground & that she would be well attended to the grave.

They only copied one for a hundred and thirty in the town.[24]

The trade stood solidly behind the mob!

Walpole had never liked the legislation, though for reasons which parody one of the preoccupations running through his career. He remarked to the Commons that 'by an average of 9 years past, 6,775,000 gallons of spirits had been made in England from corn, 1,317,062 gallons from molasses. He therefore was not for totally destroying the distillers since the landed interest were so benefited from spirituous liquors made by them . . .'[25] Another problem might be the need to buy off George II. The King's income derived in part from the duties on gin. No bad thing for His Majesty for, according to Lord Egmont, when 'the monstrous encrease of drinking it was at its highest, this came to £70,000 per annum . . .'[26] If less of it were to be consumed, the King's glass would have to be topped up.

Not that George was creating a national mood happy about alternative revenues or making life easier for his Prime Minister. Unlike his father who, against English legend, seems to have managed in mature life to stick with one woman, Melusine, Graefin von der Schulenburg, George II had long visited Henrietta Howard on a basis regular enough to constitute clockwork adultery. But she was at any rate English. And the English public, nothing if not xenophobic, had a fresh occasion for taking umbrage when, on an interminable visit to Hanover, across most of 1736, George struck up with a German lady, the Graefin von Walmoden, and showed signs of being besotted.

Lord Egmont, not a ladies' man, remarked,

> Popular reports come to my ear occasioned by the King's absence in Hanover; as that the King kept Madame Walmoden's birthday with great magnificence, and I find the same spread maliciously in the Crafts man [sic] of this day. Again the people will have it that the King has writ for £200,000 from England to give her. Advertisements were given that the Elector of Hanover intended to visit his British dominion for two months and then return to his German estate . . . Others talk almost treason.[27]

But then the political sentiments picked up in time of riot did not encourage confidence. 'No gin, no King' just about said it.

George continued to give Walpole problems. Not content with getting Marianne von Walmoden pregnant, something nobody had told Lord Egmont, he marked his long-awaited return by putting his life at mortal risk. His escort at the Dutch port of Helvoetsluys was Admiral Sir Charles Wager, a fair judge of difficult seas. This one was quite difficult enough for Sir Charles who proposed keeping off it. The sea being as rough off the English coast as the Dutch, both court parties spent the interim thinking the unthinkable. In the case of Prince Frederick, it may also have been the delectable. He filled in the interim by accepting the freedom of the City of London at the Guildhall, something winced at by courtiers like Hervey as slumming. Caroline put it tersely. 'My God' says the Queen, 'popularity makes me sick; but Fritz's popularity makes me vomit.'[28]

Meanwhile, the King was trying hard to get himself killed. George II's single great talent was courage. He would show it in leading the charge at Dettingen six years later. In December 1736 it was singularly ill applied. The sea was too high, the danger too great for Wager who had spent his life being brave at sea, but George, who had never experienced a proper storm, imperiously wanted to. Letters from Horatio Walpole, present in fearful attendance, and Wager himself, made clear what happened, something soon after in wide circulation. If Wager wouldn't sail, he would 'go in a packet boat'. He had told Sir Charles *he would go*; that Sir Charles, in his laconic Spartan style, had told him that *he could not*; that the King had said 'let be what weather it will, *I am not afraid*'.

Wager's reply, 'If you are not, I am,'[29] should have been the end of it. Instead, George claimed the privilege of peremptory blockheadedness and endangered the lives of the sailors manning the royal yacht, *Charlotte*, and the four convoy ships. The yacht's captain, Charles Hardy, would save them, as well as George's own thick royal skin. In fact, it was necessary for Hardy to bring them back to Helvoetsluys with the King, as Wager put it, 'as tame as any about him'.[30] The King's unpopularity quickly achieved a new and yet lower mark.

When reports came of distress guns fired at sea off Harwich, Walpole's sixteen-year power structure trembled. The rift between Frederick and his parents had long been maturing into trench warfare. Caroline, watching what she saw as his casual assurance at this time, had felt something in her throat 'that swelled and half-choked me'.[31] It was going to get worse. When, as Hervey put it, 'the people of England were employed in nothing but looking at weathercocks'.[32] Walpole made no distinction from the Queen and served more as echo than counter influence. He spoke about Frederick in ways illuminating about Walpole.

He launched into a blast of adjectives aimed at the heir: 'A poor, weak, irresolute, false, lying, dishonest, contemptible wretch that nobody loves, that nobody will trust, and that will trust everybody by turns and that everybody by turns will impose upon, betray, mislead and plunder.'[33] When Hervey, after comparing the Prince to the Roman conspirator, Catiline, suggested that his mother would still have some influence for good, Walpole exploded. '"Zounds my Lord" interrupted Sir Robert "he would tear the flesh off her bones with hot irons."'[34]

But Walpole was hardly disinterested. He had reached the sulphurated George through the influence of Caroline. And, as neither mother nor sister now had any influence upon Frederick, the Prince was now playing (rather seriously) the role of patron to the opposition Whigs. If George had died, Walpole would have died too, stripped of all office which, in his obsessive case, was much the same thing.

Lady Anne Irwin, lady-in-waiting to the Princess of Wales, together with a bleak picture of royal rejection, lays serious blame upon Walpole. Writing to her brother, Lord Carlisle, on 15 March 1737, she reports, 'The Prince goes to the King's Levy, the Queen's Drawing Room and Church, but, I believe, has never been spoken to by the King or Queen since the Affair happened. The Ministry, I am afraid, is not desirous to reconcile the unhappy difference . . . 'tis generally thought the King is more moderate in the affair than either the Queen or Minister.'[35]

However that might be, George's absence had made the Street's heart anything but fonder. Hervey tells of a man pledging soldiers in an alehouse, 'Here is damnation to your master', adding things about the King 'hating the English nation' and 'going to Hanover only to spend English money there and bring back a Hanover mistress here'. When the platoon's politic sergeant took this tale to Walpole, he was paid, as informers reliably were, and told to make out an affidavit, but to 'leave out the account of the English money and the Hanover mistress'.[36]

No such discretion guided the people who refused to take their hats off to the King's returning coach, and Caroline's hatred of popularity was gratified by being hissed as she left the opera. Meanwhile, Fritz's popularity was running wild. While his father was making a fool of himself, the Prince managed on a small scale to emulate Charles II. That master of public management had made friends all round by his courageous presence and direction of action in the Great Fire of 1666. On 4 January 1737, in response to a raging fire in the Temple, Frederick came out at nine at night to pass buckets with all and sundry, staying till it was out at five next morning.

Whatever his faults, the Prince had a flair for doing, and being seen to do, creditable and popular things beyond the instincts and competence of the lecherous, long-vacationing, life-endangering little colonel, his father. For Walpole, the two episodes, coming so close, constituted wormwood with a side order of gall. His patron was now held in a degree of public contempt never felt for his father. George I was a damned foreigner and not easily approached, but he had dignity and the cool art of keeping it. Meanwhile the thirty-year-old upstart, on whom Sir Robert had wasted seven spitting adjectives, was a general hero. And when the Prince's role as volunteer fireman was celebrated in a painting by Richard Wilson,[37] the capacity of friendly and grateful artists to promote the political prince was underlined.

Incidentally, the historical image of Frederick embodied in the malice of Hervey, the prejudices of the Reverened Etough and the *parti pris* opinions of Walpole reflected by his son, Horace, are almost certainly off target. There is enough evidence of Frederick's real interest in painting, theatre and literature, his fluency in Italian and ability to play the cello, to suggest his grandfather's grandson than a true child of his culture-averse parent. Again, the man investing time in a visit to the greatest poet of the age at least knows what he ought to be doing. If the five-hour afternoon call on Alexander Pope was only politics, it was in vivid contrast to the back-turning and kicking of other people's shins familiar in the discourse of George II.

Frederick put up £500 towards the release from prison of a number of debtors. Calculated it might be, but it was a calculation which neither George nor Walpole could manage. The nickname with which history has saddled him, 'Poor Fred', is terse rhetoric at its most deadly, but on the strength of recent inquiry, grotesquely unfair.[38] The hatred felt by his mother and father might be judged in the light of their pride in his brother, William Augustus, whose open-handed slaughter of prisoners after Culloden earned the equally terse epithet 'Butcher'!

Quite simply, Frederick had the wit and inclination to advance himself by behaving well to people, a further instance of trying to be as unlike his father as possible. Frederick Lewis, Prince of Wales, had been left in Hanover aged seven in 1714, for an education by Hanoverian preceptors, and kept four hundred miles away from the country to whose crown he was second heir. Coming late to England and shown very little sympathy at home, he had tried harder than any member of the family before to adjust sympathetically to all things English, finding his own friends and educating himself among them.

If Opposition figures didn't need to be asked and had neon-lit motives of their own, Carteret, Chesterfield, Cobham and the younger men, Lyttleton, Pitt and Cornbury, were at least excellent company. Excitingly detested by his father, they were better read and more interesting than almost any of Walpole's ring of butter and oil, Henry Pelham, Sir William Yonge, Newcastle, Grafton and Horatio Walpole. Their attentions flattered him, his sympathy as a mainline Prince of Hanover made nonsense of Walpole's tired mantras about covert Jacobitism. With the expected Frederick I backing the opposition, talk about the shadow of James III looked as silly as it was.

Among the new friends, 'the Universal Criminal', Bolingbroke, was prominent, and his ideas of a patriot King influential on the young man. Bolingbroke's thinking did contain, beside protogothic historical projections, at least the *idea* of a prince governing in the wider interests of the nation. And for all his opportunism, he was arguing for an idea, less selfish and *evidently* less selfish than the static, remote and huddled status quo of King, Queen and Sir Robert.

Frederick's connection with Pope explains a good deal. We have seen the poet blazing at the commercial arrogance and social contempt of Denis Bond and 'grave Sir Gilbert', and speaking of clean government, honour and the decent provision for the poor which Samuel Johnson, drawing at the same well, would proclaim. Where earnest conviction left off and nice calculation began in, respectively, Bolingbroke, the Young Patriots and Frederick, is a large question and not for present discussion. But at the lowest level of image and good feeling, the Prince and his friends were running rings round Court and Prime Minister.

Not the least of his achievements, despite the Hanoverian upbringing and lateness to the language, was Frederick's grasp of the importance of Englishness. It was, as *Pravda* would have said, no accident that Fritz took up and enthusiastically played cricket.* Some part of the febrile loathing of King, Queen and younger sister surely derived from professional jealousy. They might speak of the 'wretch' being 'caressed by the multitude', but to any public person the public is a potential lover and 'Fritz's popularity' showed who was walking her out. In consequence, 'neither of them made much ceremony of wishing a hundred times a day that the prince might drop down dead of an apoplexy – the Queen cursing the hour of his birth and the Princess Caroline declaring she grudged him every hour he continued to breathe'.[39] 'Dysfunctional' is hardly the word.

Frederick and the Patriots would inflict the greatest injury upon Walpole through a request for money, the doubling of the Prince's allowance, an ironical and inadvertent turning upon Sir Robert of his own maxim. 'Every man has his price,' the Minister had famously and complacently said. Frederick's was £100,000 a year, and Walpole was not placed to meet it.† The Prince's money would help make 1737 as unhelpful to Walpole as 1736. It caught him between three lines of fire, the opposition (now augmented by the Prince's Duchy of Cornwall MPs), public opinion – and the King.

George's detestation of Frederick was not the sole cause. The King was by every instinct stingy. The young man had some claim on good treatment. He had not contradicted or opposed his father when, in 1736, he had become engaged with some enthusiasm to Augusta of Saxe-Coburg-Gotha. It was a perfectly reasonable and indeed conventional

---

* By a sad irony it would be the death of him, from an abscess some days after being hit by a cricket ball. No detail survives but one imagines him fumbling an off drive in the covers.
† In fact as Lady Irwin told her brother less would be done: '£80,000 would be gratefully accepted, but he won't bait one farthing of the Princess's joynture.'[40]

choice from the German small courts, but Frederick had been treated, in the best royal way, without consideration. Protracted plans for a match with the Princess Royal of Prussia had been terminated over his head for reasons of foreign policy. But after understandable unhappiness and resentment, he managed to fall young-mannishly in love with the official replacement. For which George, full of Pooh-Bah-ish references to 'the respect due to me', showed neither grace nor appreciation.

The opposition noticed the coolness of the King. And in the debate on the Congratulatory Address of 29 April, a promising young politician made a speech mock-heroically praising George's open-hearted pleasure at his son's choice and exalting Frederick for statuesque virtues, 'a generous love of liberty' and 'a just reverence for the British constitution', which might be true, and 'filial duty to his parents', which wasn't. The oration was compared with Demosthenes, Cicero and other orating ancients, but reads cold like simple grandiloquence. But Cornet William Pitt MP lost his military sinecure for cheek, not verbosity. It was a stupid, spiteful act, confirming a critic in his hostility, getting the speech reprinted, transmitted more widely and giving Pitt the priceless gift of victimhood.

Professor Paul Langford believes the squabbles over marriage may have been the turning point which took the Prince out of trying to please into skulking antipathy and ties with the Bolingbroke circle. But it took money to go political, and *party* political at that. Heirs receive an independent financial settlement on marriage, means for the separate establishment and cutting of a figure expected. Money there would have to be, and, thinking himself handsome, George proposed turning his discretionary £50,000 a year into an autonomous £50,000, everywhere recognised at once as an insult and too little.

There had been notice of the coming problem. In February, Hare, Bishop of Chichester, told Walpole from the episcopal grapevine that Frederick was looking for private finance, finance involving the disgraced Chancellor of South Sea days. 'I hear that the Prince is falling into Mr Aislabie's hands and that he is to be his Peter Walters.'[41] Walters was the ubiquitous moneylender, regularly flicked at by Pope, thought to have stripped out a number of noble clients.

Everything was being done as badly as ever could be, with Walpole, faced with the self-destructive instincts of George, proving surprisingly anaemic. On 19 February 1737, he announced the £50,000 to a ministerial group of Newcastle, Grafton, Devonshire, Scarborough, Horace

Walpole, Islay, Sir Charles Wager and the brand-new Chancellor, Hardwicke,* saying that 'he had, though not without the greatest difficulty, prevailed upon the King to render the prince's allowance independent and to settle the princess's joynture'.[42]

What happened next shows Walpole doing business under pressure. Hardwicke, the most sensible man present, warned that doing this without telling Frederick before it was announced in the Commons was asking for further and better trouble. Walpole said simply that it was hopeless to ask the King to show such tact when Frederick had put him into a rage. Hardwicke stuck to his guns and Walpole went to the King and came back with a paternal message full of affronted self-importance about 'the undutiful measures which his majesty is informed your royal highness intends to pursue'.

If ever a man needed a good lawyer, George did. Hardwicke suggested deleting 'undutiful' as calculated to make Frederick spit. But with Walpole shuttling between him and the Cabinet, the King insisted upon it, though the Chancellor did manage to replace 'intends' with 'hath been advised to pursue'. Nobody, especially a Lord Chancellor on his first day in the job, wanted to deliver this mildly amended poison to the Prince. All helpfulness, George told Walpole to take the whole Cabinet. Having escaped the Presence, the Prime Minister passed on the message, adding that it was frightfully late, and that he and Admiral Wager really were needed in the Commons. Islay, taking Sir Robert as model, slunk discreetly away. The Cabinet went nervously to tell Frederick about his undutifulness and new, confined income. The Prince behaved far better than his father, speaking with grave irony of 'his majesty's goodness' and 'gracious intention', but he remained quietly implacable. Hardwicke and the rest were told politely that the fight was on. 'Indeed my lords, it is in other hands, I am sorry for it.'[43]

Frederick's resentment came gift-wrapped to the Opposition. Consultations made it clear that, as he would privately explain, 'the measure was fixed'. Talking with a new friend, George Bubb Dodington, a Walpole man so far and four-seat boroughmonger, now ominously uncoupling, Frederick discussed allies. 'That he was resolved and wanted no advice, but he would not send to him [Argyll] nor Lord Scarborough, but to the duke of Dorset and lord Wilmington, he would send, being

---

* Talbot had died.

resolved that it should come into the House of Lords the same day, or soon after, let the fate be what it would in the House of Commons.'[44]

When Dodington warned him that there was little chance of carrying the vote, Frederick said there was 'none at all', but that there were precedents, and

> that all the opposition and all the Tories were engaged in it; that as it was his own determination, and he had been advised by nobody, when he had resolved it in his own mind, he thought it necessary to speak to people himself; he had done so, to Mr Pulteney, lord Carteret, lord Chesterfield, master of the Rolls [Jekyll] and sir William Wyndham, that they were all hearty in it; that Mr Pulteney at the first notice so expressed himself so handsomely that he should never forget it: but said he could answer for himself, not expecting the proposition, but begged leave to consult with some of his friends . . . and he had, since, assured him they were unanimous.[45]

Frederick went on to assure Dodington that one emissary, Lord Winchelsea, had gone to Petworth to round up the Duke of Somerset, that Samuel Sandys and other prominent Whigs were on board and that it was possible that Sir John Barnard would move the motion. (He would second it.) Frederick had involved himself against his father with the parties opposing Walpole's government. The Ministry was known as 'the Court', but Frederick was turning the opposition Whigs into an Anti-Court. They, now and delightedly, had a royal patron, with seats to dispose, peers to summon and perhaps his own Chief Whip. The strategy was to make a motion for a supplement to be paid, separate from the Civil List, leaving Walpole to defend George's tightfistedness, alienate the heir further and generally make himself more unpopular.

On 22 February, in a full house, Pulteney led ('very sparkling, strong and learnedly' according to Egmont).[46] He began formally, alluding respectfully to 'his present Majesty's happy accession to the throne', before getting down to the disrespectful arithmetic. They had found then

> that a civil list revenue even of £700,000 a year as it had been managed, had not been sufficient to support the honour and dignity of the crown and to pay £100,000 to the then Prince of Wales; for which reason, several additional sums had been granted in that reign to the civil list, amounting in

the whole to £1,300,000, which made the civil list during that reign amount at an average to £803,000 a year.[47]

The implication was clear and injurious. The going rate had been established for Prince George, extra money found by Parliament to cover him. Frederick, on his father's decision, would be confined to half. The King was able to pay and was not paying. Walpole, game but horribly embarrassed, could only say that the younger George already had a family and Frederick did not. Egmont could foresee only 'dismal consequences'.[48]

Everybody knew and nobody said that rational comparisons didn't come into it. *Seriatim*, George was three things: mean about money, permanently enraged at his son and incapable of graceful flexibility. The less now offered was tendered with all the offensiveness of which the King was a steady practitioner. Pulteney could, with an innocent manner, advance his proposals for Parliament making up the difference. He was doing what good parliamentarians had done since Magna Carta – seeking powers they hadn't had before. He was also blowing cayenne up the King's nostrils.

The opposition came out in force. Frederick's own Treasurer, John Hedges, pointed out that the estimated minimum costs of his establishment were £73,000. His Duchy of Cornwall revenues were supposed to have increased his income to £59,000. But after paying the Land Tax, even with them, he would have only £52,000. It would all involve 'a vile pecuniary dependence upon his father's ministers and servants'. Hedges had privately, at Walpole's request, warned Frederick against raising the question, 'by telling him that it was impossible he could ever get the money'.[49] But debate continued past midnight and when, at 1 a.m., it came to a vote, although the First Court party had a majority, at 234 to 204 it was a thoroughly depressing one. 'Never was more solicitation or more anxiety about any vote in Parliament, and highly disagreeable', wrote one habitual ministerial supporter.[50] In the Lords the motion failed by 103 to 40.

In the Commons it was nearly much worse. Sir William Wyndham had originally been strongly onside. He 'had long desired an opportunity of showing his regard and attachment to his Royal Highness by their zealous and hearty appearance in support of his interest how far they were from being Jacobites . . .'.[51] But Wyndham left at the vote, taking forty-five supporters. The Tories, for all the Jacobite smears, had shown the ruling house a picturesque constitutional rectitude. Specialists in not so much missing open goals as regarding them as ungentlemanly, they could not bring themselves to win.

As parliamentarians, they treated a thoroughly sordid royal dispute about butter and jam with their own ancestral non-resistance. Wyndham had felt that he must abstain with his friends. Tory piety was enough to save Walpole from a terminal crisis. Had Tory Members been less high minded, another phosphorus, of a political sort, would have taken hotter fire than the Reverend Nixon's.

But Frederick's friends were confident that society, high and/or political, approved his claim. Lady Anne wrote to her brother at Castle Howard, 'Everybody agrees, even those who voted against the prince, in wishing him £100,000 p.a. and make no scruple of saying it, therefore 'tis plain the only reason that kept them from voting it was their dependency.'[52]

But Walpole had on his hands, almost at once, a more intrinsically important if less glittering question. Different trouble began in March, peaceably enough (in the sense that a splitting headache is still peaceful), with a financial scheme from the eternal Barnard. Rich, clever, if narrow-minded, influential in the City, indifferent to office and less impressed by Walpole than most, Sir John knew at least as much about finance as the Prime Minister. If he said that the interest on the National Debt could be reduced by a quarter – from 4 to 3 per cent – there should be something in it.

Barnard was a fully paid-up moneyed man, someone able to lend the government money. If *he* proposed a reduced reward for doing so it carried conviction. And the proposal gained wide support – in the Commons and among members of the government like Pelham. But it lacked charm in St James's Palace. Also receiving state paper were the King and Queen. They stood to lose if the state borrowed for less and lacked Sir John's larger vision. They were against it.

That vision was an early draft of the nineteenth-century Liberal mantra of 'Peace, Retrenchment and Reform'. Money was very necessary to the corruption by place and inducement through which Walpole worked. He operated a species of private interest/public expenditure mini-welfare state for anyone able to elect a Member or persuade one to vote right. Reduce the cash and politics might grow honest by illiquidity. But Barnard's plan involved telling investors that the state would pay them less. This created a lobby of interested parties crying national ruin.

Walpole had obvious motives for resisting, not least of reputation. These savings outreached in imagination those expected from the Excise scheme in which Walpole had sailed and foundered; and who had spoken more incisively against the Excise than Sir John Barnard? His scheme was the sort of large thinking to excite the young, quick-minded Walpole. It was almost a career reproach, and it came from the man who had recently turned down the Exchequer, disdaining the top of Walpole's line in emolument.

Speaking for his motion, Barnard argued that his sinking fund would, given current demand for 3 per cent stock at a premium, raise an estimated £1,600,000, ending the need to tax necessities, one of the fixed iniquities of eighteenth-century finance. Untaxed coal, leather, candles and soap represented a large benefit to poorer people, a slashing of their cost of living. Walpole, of course, had demonstrated his view of the poor when seeking to excise salt.

Barnard became the object of rumour, smear and panic-inducement. His insurance business would be ruined 'by a combination of the merchants, for they have agreed not to insure their ships with him, and his whole fortune lost, they say, but £6,000, having had great losses of late, besides an extravagant son'.[53] It was said that the City men would keep him from the Lord Mayoralty. His business carried on as usual, he became Lord Mayor and was given at the end of his terms an unprecedented testimonial.

Walpole claimed that the bill could not be countenanced because it offended the money men. If it pleased MPs, Sir Robert would stop it by putting up Thomas Winnington, a laughing man of some arts, bought out of his family Toryism long before, of whom young Horace Walpole wrote, 'It was impossible to hate or to trust him.'[54] He urged that proposals, limited in Barnard's motion to National Debt borrowing, should apply to all redeemable debts. Barnard knew that this was impracticable and he quoted the proverb 'Grasp at all and lose all'.

Unwisely, he tried to make the best of it and adduced arguments about the effect of indirect taxes on the poor to which the eighteenth-century House of Commons was not responsive. But he ended by saying of Walpole's easy arguments against the new expanded version, that

> every gentleman that hears me knows it is very different from what I offered; and every one likewise knows that the new model which is the model we have before us, if it was not offered by the honourable gentleman himself,

it was at least offered by some of his friends; . . . and it is very remarkable that all objections made to the bill, are only to those articles and clauses of it which relate to the improvements and additions made to my scheme by the honourable gentleman's friends.[55]

Rejection by 249 votes to 134 followed inevitably.

That Walpolian victory after Barnard had handsomely won earlier votes on his basic principle was typical. Through Winnington he swamped an idea near to carrying the Commons with a frightening scheme to embrace and smother the original. It was the assembling of a straw man and setting fire to it, good politics but only good politics. Henry Pelham, eventually Walpole's successor, admired what Barnard was trying to do. As Prime Minister, Pelham in 1747, replaced the backstage fixes by which government debt was sold with an open auction. And, in 1750, Pelham set up an eight-year process of reducing the effective National Debt rate *from 4 per cent to 3 per cent*. He would carry it and be advised and supported in the undertaking by Sir John Barnard. Routing the 1737 proposal must be seen as petty guile employed in fearful retreat before the rich interests. It is also a measure of the sterile sameness of the later Walpole's thinking.

There would be only a few months' respite from royal unpleasantness. The fallout from the Allowance debate proved bad enough. The King severed relations with his son, before turning upon his friends. The second crisis followed the birth labour of the Princess. Frederick wanted his first child born at St James's; his father ordered the couple to Hampton Court, in itself a sensible, healthier choice, but another instance of George giving unnecessary commands. Showing less sense than at any time so far, Frederick gave counter-orders and on 31 July, running serious risks to wife and child, he dragged Augusta into a coach and across north Surrey, a bridge and central London, to St James's.

In the wrong and told so by his new friends, Frederick tried to apologise. George, though invoking Augusta and her new daughter's safety, was chiefly concerned with George. The unannounced flight, said Lord Essex, was 'looked upon by the king as such a deliberate indignity, offered to himself and to the queen, that he has commanded me to acquaint your royal highness that he resents it in the highest degree'.[56] Attempts by Frederick to elaborate the apology and seek a meeting with his mother were met with all the pettiness in which royalty delights. Silence on the first point, refusal on the second were followed by George and Caroline boycotting the christening. A Saxe-Coburg grandmother and the unlucky Hardwicke were told to stand proxy as godparents for grandmother and grandfather, affronted Queen and King. George followed this up with the nearest a Protestant layman could get to excommunication. He made, says Archdeacon Coxe, 'the violent resolution of making a total separation between his family and that of the Prince, by dismissing him from his residence in the palace of St James'.

Walpole's Latin phrase *Quieta non movere* is commonly translated 'Let sleeping dogs lie'. Having on his hands a dog barking furiously, the Minister's reaction was to descant a growl himself. Hardwicke ran through with him all the longer-term injuries which a running fight would engender: the future of the Prince's children if the King insisted on control, experience of the last royal breach plaguing Sunderland's Ministry, deepening divisions among the Whigs and the handle given to enemies if this dispute intensified. Perhaps, he thought, Walpole should try to activate womanly sense in the Queen, if she shelved her own affront and played peacemaker in a quarrel between men.

But for the moment Hardwicke was the only grown-up on the scene. Walpole commented later that the Lord Chancellor had 'talked like an angel', and ignored him completely. Walpole would be a statesman on occasion, but his natural, comfortable position was as partisan politician. Calm the storm be damned! If the opposition were playing politics against the King, he would stand beside George. Even Coxe, a friendly biographer, is dismayed. Frederick had been in the wrong, 'yet it must at the same time be lamented that the Minister involved in the interests of party, the feuds of the royal family'.[57] Unrestrained by his Minister, George's 'violent resolution' was put into effect. Frederick, ordered henceforth from the Palace, set up new HQ at Norfolk House which, unsurprisingly, became a sort of superior coffee house for the Old Whig leaders and anyone else against George and Walpole.

The response dug the hole deeper. An edict of September barred anyone attending Norfolk House from admission to every royal palace. It was a miserable episode and, however provoked, very much the King's fault. Those who were not against his son could not be for *him*. It was a high, formal message exactly expressing George's favourite gesture towards anyone out of favour, of turning his back. Frederick had apologised, sought a meeting, apologised again, and explained his predicament to Hardwicke who was sympathetic. But George who, by long absence and its busy sexual employment, had lately shown country and wife no respect and behaved without discernible dignity, demanded the one and stood upon the other.

The futility of it all would soon be demonstrated. For two years, Caroline, afflicted with recurrent pain, had concealed its immediate cause, a ruptured abdomen. By autumn 1737, no concealment was possible and she almost certainly endured a carcinoma. On 9 November she was in the library recently built for her in St James's Park and, never a complainer, began to complain – of unbearable pains. Attended by Tesier, her German physician, she took medicines and soon after threw them up. Characteristically, she refused George's suggestion of cancelling her 'Drawing Room' or reception, spoke lightly of 'this nasty cholic that I had at Hampton Court come again',[58] then soldiered on until she could bear the pain no longer. Plied with snakeroot, Sir Walter Raleigh's cordial, Daffy's Elixire and, more sensibly, whisky, she was violently sick.

At which, the surgeon, Ranby, who had dismissed the medicines as quackery, was ordered by the doctors to take twelve ounces of blood from her. The King, wiser in his distress, told his daughter that the doctors were irrelevant. Caroline was going to die. Hervey, reaching similar conclusions, wrote to Walpole, away in Norfolk, telling him to come at once, since his absence would be played up by the opposition. Walpole, not receiving the message until the evening of the 12th, set out next day. The medical futilities continued, the Prince tried to call on his mother, occasioning a volley of fatherly abuse about 'his whining, cringing tricks' and giving instructions that 'the puppy' should 'get out of my house'.[59]

The depth of hatred stands tragically in the Queen's words concerning any visit from the Prince. She told the King:

> sooner or later I am sure one shall be plagued with some message of that sort, because he will think that it will have a good air in the world to see me; and perhaps hopes I shall be fool enough to let him come, and give him the pleasure of seeing my last breath go out of my body, by which means he would have the joy of knowing I was dead five minutes sooner than he could know it in Pall Mall.

If she grew worse, added Caroline, 'and should be weak enough to talk of seeing him, I beg you sir, to conclude I doat or rave.'

Ranby who, like Hardwicke in a different context, sounds like the only sensible person present, insisted on a full examination, reached the vagina and, on finding something, spoke quietly to the King. Caroline 'started up and, sitting in her bed, said to Ranby with great eagerness, "I am sure now, you blockhead, you are telling the King I have a rupture." "I am so" said Ranby "and there is no time to be lost: your majesty has concealed it too long already; and I beg another surgeon may be called in immediately."'[60]

After argument with two elder surgeons, an operation took place on Saturday the 12th. The wound, which, following the overwhelming pattern of surgery before chlorate of lime and sterile instruments, was found gangrenous on Sunday the 13th. There was then some respite in symptoms and pain, encouraging Walpole to talk vapidly about recovery. But on the Thursday vomiting came back and 'the running at the wound was immense'.[61]

Walpole needed optimism. Caroline had been his voice at the heart of the Court and, as she died slowly of a mortified wound, he contemplated politics without her. 'Oh my Lord,' said Sir Robert, 'if this woman should die, what a scene of confusion there will be! Who can tell into what hands the king will fall? Or who will have the management of him?'[62] He was assured by Hervey that he would actually be stronger since the King would never be influenced by any other woman as he had been by Caroline.

Walpole, who knew more about this strange ménage than anyone outside it, explained that the role of the Queen had been to persuade the King to listen to his first Minister when, as so often, he would not see him. Caroline, who never contradicted any opinion of George, would, he said, talk him round to attention or, better, sometimes into thinking Walpole's view his own. The wracked and suppurating life dragged on another week while squabbles about prayers and the sacraments and who should inherit Richmond Park – fears that it might go to Frederick were assuaged: it reverted to the King – were finally brought to an end when on the night of Sunday the 20th, an attendant, Mrs Purcell, heard a rattle in the Queen's throat. Caroline asked for a window to be opened, said the word 'Pray', and died.

Sir Robert had lost his ally. He had also lost someone he genuinely cared for. But according to Hervey, who never speaks well if it can be avoided, he was heard calculating the next move like a stage heavy.

Under the page caption 'Walpole's Coarseness',* he has him saying, 'I'll bring Madame Walmoden over, and I'll have nothing to do with your girls: I was for the wife against the mistress, but I will be for the mistress against the daughters.' He is also quoted as calling, *on health grounds*, for an interim mistress, Lady Deloraine, to be brought in since 'people must wear old gloves till they could get new ones'. The remark was said to have alienated the princesses, Emily and Caroline, for ever. But Walpole had no practical use for them anyway. As for Frederick, having never been admitted to his mother's death room, to George and by extension, Walpole, he remained the enemy.

1737, like 1736, had been a miserable year for all the skill Walpole had used to stay afloat. And it was not going to get any better.

---

* Probably added by the editor of the 1848 edition of Hervey's *Memoirs of the Reign of George II*, John Wilson Croker.

THE LONG DESCENT

'All hands leave go when the great wheel runs down hill.' It says so in *King Lear*. Walpole was no Lear though he would soon drink enough personal sorrow. But the last years of the decade would replace the intermittent tribulations of Excise, riot and opposition manoeuvre with a running crisis. And as he twisted and turned in adversity, hands would reliably leave go. Walpole was about to be dragged against all the staples of his good judgement into war; and war, as he had probably suspected, was one thing he wasn't very good at.

But the first sorrows of the season were private. Walpole and Molly Skerrett had been together on a weekend-visiting basis since 1724. Ill-natured people might call her 'Walpole's whore', but she had outlived the malice of Hervey who in his endlessly spiteful way had hinted at a cash relationship. In reality, she, the daughter of a substantial merchant, is reported as bringing Walpole money. Horatio spoke of her as 'a very sensible, well-behaved, modest woman', and thought his brother's 'happiness . . . very deservedly wrapt up in her'. Sir Thomas Robinson reckoned that 'Everybody gives her a good character both as to her understanding and good nature.'[1] Walpole's first marriage had long been exhausted. Only the impossibility of divorce had prevented the pious regularities. Catherine's death at fifty-five in August 1737 ended that.

The marriage ceremony was performed in February 1738 by Henry Etough, whose manuscript yearbook of historical events is a handy minor source. There was already a daughter born out of wedlock, but another child was due. On 4 June, with everything set for happiness, the new Lady Walpole, thirty-six years old, miscarried and died – 'of a fever', presumably puerperal fever, midwife's dirty-hands disease. It was the savage termination of a marriage far longer than its legal three months. Walpole had called himself a widower when the estranged Catherine died. He was now a true widower, bereaved and alone in the part of life outside politics.

And politics was turning sour. 'Spanish depredations' was the catch phrase, the happy opposition response to arrested ships, rough-handled sailors in the West Indies and South Americas. Under the *Asiento* there was a right to bring an annual ship of 5000 tons with cargo to Spanish overseas territory; and the trade in slaves was admitted by the Spaniards because it was convenient for them.

Spain alleged that the annual ship was craftily quantified by *unauthorised* ships moored nearby, from which, like the bottomless cup of coffee, the cargo was indefinitely refreshed. But when diplomatic communication proceeded *andante maestoso*, precise responsibility was impossible to place. Undoubtedly there were high-handed, perhaps brutal acts by the *Guardas Costas*; and assuredly, merchant ships of the nation which invented the privateer got in all the illicit trading they could. Beyond that, Elizabeth Farnese, still Queen (and usually King) of Spain, was as keen on a fight as ever, while behind her stood Cardinal Fleury, ancient, twinkling, benign and mindful of opportunities.

As to legal rights, some antedated the *Asiento*, a general treaty from 1667, and another three years later, much vaguer, specific to English trade with New Spain. But that was before Philip of Bourbon had gained his crown. As France's enemy, England had done well with Spain, her treaty rights read very broadly. But with the world differently configured, 'The letter of the American treaty was now followed and the spirit by which it was dictated, abandoned.'[2] As Archdeacon Coxe succinctly put it, 'Spain was governed by a sovereign connected to France by blood and policy'.[3]

Embarrassment had been regular. Sir Benjamin Keene, Minister in Madrid, had to make cases on behalf of complaining merchants but had his own view of the merits:

> Then my God what proofs! At most they can be regarded as foundations for complaints but not for demands for restitution . . . Are the oaths of fellows that foreswear themselves at every custom-house in every port they come to, to be taken without any further enquiry or examination, what should we say to a bawling Spaniard who had made a derelict of his ship

at Jamaica & afterwards swore blood and murder against the English before the Mayor of Bilbao?[4]

In 1738 discontent came to a head at a time when relations between the governments were no better than they should have been. The Farnese had made a bid for British help in 1735 during the War of the Polish Succession. She was outraged that Tuscany, and Parma with it, looked to be going to the Austrians. If British naval power were exerted, would she give up claims on Minorca and Gibraltar and take a more open trading position? It would have been a return to 1670, military gestures and presences rewarded by trade accommodation. With the active, meddling foreign policy favoured by Townshend and Carteret, a valuable deal might have been made. We had alienated the Emperor anyway. Walpole, wedded to virtuous inactivity, declined the pass made at him.

But beyond that, the government's legal position over Spanish trade had been confounded by a serious mistake. In November 1737 Newcastle had despatched a haughty statement of our rights, based on the 1667 treaty. He took great trouble, he always did; Walpole saw the paper, the Cabinet discussed it. The paper was wrong. We had, it claimed, citing the 1667 document, 'an indisputable right' to sail in American seas, one making the searches and arrests illegal. We didn't. The proper source was the much less conclusive 1670 treaty. Words in the 1667 document had been drawn to Newcastle's attention by the West India lobby, delighted that it forbade searches beyond a ship's papers. But its commercial clauses had nothing to do with the Americas.[5]

Spain knew her rights. Keene reported to Newcastle on 13 December 1737 that local Spanish officials 'presume that they have a right of seizing, not only the ships that are continually trading in their ports, but likewise of examining and visiting them on the high seas in order to search for proof of fraud which they may have committed'.[6] The government, obliged, said Horatio Walpole, 'to scramble out of it as best we can',[7] shifted its case to the vaguer agreement of 1670 and nebulous talk of 'the law of Nations'.

British obtuseness in pursuit of self-interest was matched by Spanish delusion. Keene, fair-minded towards Spain as he was, described Spanish ministers as 'three or four mean, stubborn people of little minds and limited understandings'. They were readers of 'speculative authors who have treated the immense grandeur of the Spanish monarchy, people who have vanity enough to think themselves reserved by providence to rectify and reform the abuses of past Ministers and ages'.[8] The searches went on and incidents multiplied.

Meanwhile, the provocations of the *Guardas Costas* were matched by the lobby of the 'West Indians', as they were called then, the investors behind the trading ships, commonly traders in slaves outraged at being treated like servants. The government, caught between fires, made warlike gestures, shifting ships to Minorca whose great harbour was a pivot of threatening British strength in Spain's home waters.

Contradictions rattled around, Walpole telling Keene to soften the discourse with the Spanish Foreign Minister, La Quadra, and Newcastle accepting in April a right of search within specific distances of the islands. Yet letters of reprisal were promised on request to British merchants seeking them. The conduct of the business was the overture to an unrehearsed tragicomedy.

On 3 March, the West Indians brought in a petition. A motion was entered for their counsel to be heard. Alderman Robert Willimot, moving it, was a City member of the most mean-spirited kind.* His ranting invocation of 'free-born Englishmen' was the model for the vast yardage from opposition mouths in the months ahead. He had a sheet of paper to wave at the House: 'This letter gives an account of that seventy of our sailors are now in chains in Spain. Our countrymen in chains! And slaves to Spaniards! Is that not enough to fire the coldest? Is it not enough to rouse all the vengeance of national resentment?' As Samuel Johnson remarked of American patriots thirty-five years later, 'The greatest yelpers after liberty are the drivers of negroes.' But the yelping worked; the merchants were heard in the Commons in person and by counsel.

Robert Walpole is nowhere more attractive than when resisting the snarling clamour of the war crisis. He had a contempt for war, less humanitarian than rational. War was a stupid surrender to primitive emotions, the indignation was humbug, and the thing itself never examined for its immeasurable consequences. War and patriotism suited opposition politicians who never had to think beyond rhetoric. To the following debate on Barnard's motion demanding release of all correspondence with Spain, he replied in his soothing way that,

It is, without doubt, a very popular way of arguing to talk highly of the

---

* He was outraged at Irish wool being unofficially exported to Lisbon, opposed a bill to check insurance fraud and, in the interests of the City, voted against building Westminster Bridge.[9]

honour, the courage and power of the action, as any man can or ought to have; but other nations must be supposed to have honour as well as we, and all nations have a great opinion of their own courage and power. If we come to an open rupture with Spain, we might in all probability have the advantage; but victory and success do not always attend upon that side which seems the most powerful. Therefore an open rupture or declared war between two potent nations, must always be an affair of the utmost importance to both; and as this must be the consequence of our present deliberations, we ought to proceed with great coolness, and with the utmost caution.'[10]

He rehearsed the technicalities, delays and misunderstandings attending foreign policy. Madrid to the West Indies was a long way, the insolence of local governors something independent of the Spanish court; there had been cases enough where ships had actually been released. As to documents, he was all compliance, though not releasing everything at once. The last reply from Madrid had indeed not been helpful, but there were new proposals sent from London which might lighten matters. Let ministers proceed along those lines, then, if Madrid was no less difficult; the release of all papers would follow and he, Walpole, would move it.

Walpole seems almost never to have blustered. Reasoned speech, softly expressed, was his natural style, and at the end of a long debate he won a signal victory, one which, at 164 to 99, kept the war party under a hundred. Unfortunately the petitions, like Claudius's sorrows, came not as single spies, but in battalions. The decision to authorise reprisals simply put down a powder trail from the fires lit by the West Indians.

The story of Robert Jenkins, captain of the *Rebecca*, dated from 1731. Allegedly during an arrest, a Spanish officer, one Fandino, had seized Jenkins's 'left Ear and with his Cutlass slit it down; and then another of the Spaniards took hold of it and tore it off, but gave him the Piece of his ear again, bidding him carry it to his Majesty, King George'.[11] Walpole thought he had put this story to bed. He had summoned Jenkins to Chelsea, talked to him, sent him on to Newcastle and forwarded his deposition to Keene to raise with the Spanish court. After which, Jenkins himself had been placed in a merchant command sailing to the Spanish-free East Indies.

But it was a good story to recycle. The City, not content with serial petitioning, hired the best counsel available; Murray, a future Lord Chancellor, would become the most distinguished of lawyers. But here and now he evidently played Serjeant Buzfuz. Although the erratic parliamentary record of the time gives no detail beyond Jenkins being summoned on 16 and 17 March to give evidence, give it he clearly did, producing a piece of human tissue wrapped in cotton wool, and declaring it to be the famous ear, depredation as morbid anatomy. The atrocity went gaily round, and to the war party was added that familiar, toxic thing, a war press.

The Craftsman of 18 March invoked Our Boys, more precisely 'our Seamen', stating that 'the Depredations of the Spaniards and their Barbarity to our Seamen required only a full and clear Representation to raise the Antient British Spirit, and fill every Breast with the highest Indignation and Resentment against all our adversaries, their Aiders and Abettors'. Rolling the drums, they described men 'loaded with Irons and fed with Provisions neither sufficient nor wholesome being nothing more than salt Fish and dry'd Beans full of Worms'.[12] *Common Sense* announced that 'the Nation calls loud for War'.[13]

But the government's incoherence for which Walpole, despite his sane views, takes final responsibility, was partly culpable along with the fire raisers. The law of unintended consequences obtained. The Ministry had ordered its ships to Minorca, hoping to intimidate the Spaniards. Newcastle's biographer, Reed Browning, believes that Spain was uneasy about pushing the quarrel. Relations with France had been queasy and a one-to-one war with Britain had limited appeal. But in May the appearance in the Mediterannean of Admiral Nicholas Haddock was followed by reports of a British regiment despatched to Georgia in the American territories to pre-empt any possible Spanish assault from Florida. Spanish ministers, assuming a high manner with Keene, sent another wrong message, that they wanted a fight.

The corresponding British overreaction advised British merchants to leave and ships to avoid Spanish ports. Neither Walpole nor the Spanish Ministry wanted a war, both were scared of it, but there was every risk of ignorant armies eventually clashing by night.

Briefly, good sense and mutual terror got both sides out of trouble. In May also, Walpole made an impressive speech to Parliament, pointing out the disadvantages, in low, political terms, of war:

I could never see any cause, either from reason or from my own experience, to imagine that a minister is not as safe in time of war as in time of
peace. Nay if we are to judge by reason alone, it is the interest of a minister,
conscious of any mismanagement, that there should be a war; because by
a war the eyes of the public are diverted from examining into his conduct;
nor is he accountable for the bad success of a war as he is for that of an
administration.[14]

That is a cynic's insider view of cynicism and a running historic
truth. Walpole had also valiantly tied himself to the bowsprit of his
own pacific policy: 'It is but a mean excuse for a minister, when a
wrong step is made in government, to urge that he is not accountable
for the events of measures that were never advised by him and in which
he was overruled by his superiors.'[15] He said this to acknowledge the
war option, counter the charges of fear and send a message to Madrid,
itself notably jittery. Between speeches serious talking went on. The
Spanish envoy, the expatriate Irish gentleman Thomas Fitzgerald, otherwise Geraldino, stopped making trouble with the opposition, moving
officially – he had been in touch anyway – into Walpole's world of
negotiation. There were charges and countercharges, Spanish and British
depredations, wrongful arrests and confiscations against actual smuggling. The grown-ups were bent on getting a credible number written
down and signed so that nothing worse happened. Keene and the
President of the (Spanish) Council of the Indies, Montijo, worked at
this.

But the psychology had to be right. None of the ranters should be
allowed to cry outrage. £200,000 as net Spanish obligation had been
mooted by Britain back in choleric March. It was modified in calmed-
down July to £140,000 but Madrid still cavilled. Keene came down to
£95,000 on his own authority. Newcastle saw this as a mistake. But it
was July and Molly had died on 4 June. Walpole, said his brother, was
in a 'deplorable and comfortless condition'. Horatio hoped to 'divert
his melancholy by business'. Keene had taken a brave decision which
won him the nickname 'Don Benjamin' because, knowing his subject,
he was certain that Britain would not get authorisation for the next
two annual ships unless the issue was settled.[16] And Walpole agreed
with him. 'Business' meant putting Keene's conclusions to the Privy
Council and having them endorsed.

Unhappily, Spain now turned to offsetting claims, a fearful pushing of luck. The monies now demanded were against the South Sea, alleged to have outstanding obligations over uncustomed trade worth £68,000. And tidying up the books nicely but giving maximum offence, Spain proposed that if the Company lent King Philip another £27,000 to pay off the residue of the agreed £95,000, all parties should stand quits. It was better than it looked. Spain actually had a case for £60,000 over the ships taken near Sicily by Byng in 1718, one recognised in the Madrid treaty, confirmed at Seville, but never actually paid. And Spain was conceding that there had been wrongdoing against British traders. With the air cleared and ancient grievances met, the going should have got easier.

But nobody pushed luck harder than the South Sea. In August 1738, while talks were going on, they went back into their books to losses during Spanish conflicts in, respectively, 1727 and 1718–19, and demanded £484,000. It couldn't be proved and Spain wouldn't have paid even if it could. Walpole was having no more of the long wrangling. Taking foreign policy into his own hands, he decided to harden the agreement by further serious talks, establishing an agreement, the Convention of the Pardo, named for Philip III's seventeenth-century palace, ten miles north-west of Madrid. This undertaking, reached in January 1739, dismissed the South Sea claim and left Keene's settlement intact.

It also made arrangements for a side issue, the borders of Georgia, as the business of commissioners. The possibilities of an agreement on the territory upset Mr Perceval, member of the Georgia Committee, who observed 'it being suspected that Georgia is to be given up to the Spaniards, Sir Robert has refused to give the House satisfaction on this point'.[17]

The trouble with the Pardo was the opportunities which both long negotiations and conclusions gave for raising the temperature. Press and opposition wanted insults so that young Mr Pitt could make another patriotic speech. As the ministerial *Daily Gazetteer* put it, 'the good old Cause of Minister-Hunting' required 'a War, a bloody War!' and they would have one 'right or wrong'.[18] And indulging a burst of *hidalgo* affront, Philip V had been no help at all. This monarch, intermittently out of his mind, said after formal Pardo business, that if the Company didn't pay him, he reserved the right to suspend the *Asiento*, 4,800 slaves a year.

It was said too late for Keene to refuse his signature, as Newcastle

wished. For an outburst, it was nicely timed. But pacific British judgement, Walpole's and Keene's, was that the King and Company were
both blustering and were best ignored. In May 1738, Walpole had
spoken his deepest convictions: 'I remember when I was a young man,
nothing gave me greater pleasure than voting for a war with France; I
thought that it sounded well, that it was heroic and for the glory of
my country. But sir, how fatal in some respects have the consequences
of that war, just and necessary though it was, been for Britain.'[19] He
now had to sell the Pardo to Parliament. The speech from the throne
said that the King of Spain

> upon consideration had of the demands of both sides . . . has obliged himself
> to make reparation to my subjects for their losses, by a certain stipulated
> payment; and plenipotentiaries are therein named and appointed for regu-
> lating within a limited time, all the grievances and abuses which have hith-
> erto interrupted our commerce and navigation in the American seas; and
> for settling all matters and disputes in such a manner as may for the future,
> prevent and remove all new causes and pretences of complaint by a strict
> observance of our mutual treaties and a just regard to the rights and priv-
> ileges belonging to each other.'[20]

The principle was perfect wisdom, the interpretation a hopeful gloss,
but not a misrepresentation, and the essence of Walpole's purpose in
the whole convention undertaking. It was Walpole's speech from the
throne. His own speech combined closely argued detail and unreserved
praise for the convention. It also contained an emotional appeal, taking
Members back to the previous May and his personal responsibility.
Carrying the address was the easy part – it went through 234 to 141.
But the convention itself would become a sort of St Sebastian, shot at
from all directions, not least the offices of City petitioners.

Horatio Walpole's painstaking and detailed justification the next day,
8 March, could not deflect the dominant mood – of men who, feeling
themselves horribly wronged, wanted action. It was a time for patriotic blowhards, of whom Pitt was a superior version. 'The address was
proposed for no other end than to extort an approbation for the convention.' It took sanctuary in the royal name instead of meeting Parliament's
judgement. 'Is this,' Pitt thundered (and he liked to thunder), 'any longer
a nation? Or where is an English parliament, if with more ships in our
harbours than in all the navies in Europe, with more than two millions

of people in the American colonies, we will bear to hear of the expediency of receiving from Spain an insecure, dishonourable convention which carries downright subjection in every line.'[21]

The slogan gracing opposition press and backbenches was 'No Searches'. Lyttleton had just said that 'The Grievances of England admit but of one remedy, a very short and simple one; that our ships shall not be searched on any pretence',[22] an argument dear at all times to the felonious element. British ships did trade unlawfully, did carry goods beyond *Asiento* terms. Until we had free trade, that would be an offence against the treaty agreement and only enforcable by searches. Pitt despised such pettyfogs when the case was so simple. We saw 'on the part of Spain an usurpation, an inhuman claim exercised over the American Seas'. *We were British* and simply had a right. It was 'an undoubted right by treaties and from God and nature, declared and asserted in the resolution of parliament . . .'. This undoubted right was now to be discussed and regulated, '. . . by the express words of the convention, to be given up and sacrificed; for it must cease to be anything from the moment it is submitted to limits'.[23]

This was frightening stuff, very contemporary American, national particularism, contemptuous of duty between nations or law among them. And Pitt did his best to start a war by declaring 'from my soul' that the convention was 'nothing but a stipulation for national ignominy, an illusory expedient to baffle the resentment of the nation; . . . the complaints of your despairing merchants, the voice of England has condemned it; be the guilt of it upon the head of the adviser; God forbid that this committee* should share the guilt by approving it'.[24]

To return to Walpole in the same debate is to step down from the balcony into the assembly chamber, from flushed exaltation to sense. The Prime Minister would be honoured and proud 'to be mentioned as the minister who had endeavoured by this convention to prevent the necessity of making war upon a nation with whom it was our greatest interest to be at peace'. He answered Pitt's manic exclusivity by pointing out that we were signatories to treaties, which, by way of the *Asiento*, gave a measure of trading to us. Should we 'have no regard to common justice, to those treaties, the observance of which has been so justly contended for? These treaties prohibit all trade with the Spanish West Indies, excepting that carried on by the annual *Asiento* ship. In contra-

---

*The House stood resolved into committee.

diction then to these express stipulations, are our ships never to be searched?'[25]

In the middle of military swagger, Walpole asked if it were quite so certain that we would actually win. There were other countries in the world; might we not find ourselves drawn into a war with one or more of them? The idea of free trade did not exist in 1739. The criers after 'No Searches' and a persistence with illicit trading were, like Willimot, the barrers of Ireland from exporting its own wool. Any Spanish attempt to do surreptitious business in a British area of trading privilege would have been met with rage . . . and British searches. Walpole wanted everything settled by law and consensus, law here being that of treaty. It actually protected us. 'We are therefore in danger of suffering from the Convention, because it is admitted that all we ought, in reason to claim, is the observance of those treaties.'[26] Walpole got his majority, but it was disturbingly small: twenty-eight (260 to 232).

At this, the Tory party, not quite for the last time, wandered up to the nearest cliff edge and jumped off. No reference to Sir William Wyndham, their long-term leader, is complete without words like 'honourable', 'upright', 'decent' and 'respected'. All of which were true, but he was also a complete tactical and strategic dunce and unlucky with it.* He had previously trailed behind his followers in a withdrawal denying the opposition a divisional victory. He now led a walkout in person.

It was a walkout after a division. Wyndham got up and solemnly announced, 'I have seen with the utmost concern, this shameful, this fatal measure, approved by a majority of but 28, and I now rise to pay my last duty to my country as a member of this house.' Government MPs had let the side down by not doing what Sir William wanted. He had hoped that 'the many unanswerable arguments urged in this debate against the convention might have prevailed upon gentlemen . . . for once to have distinguished themselves from being a faction against the liberties and properties of their fellow subjects'.[27]

The rumour attributing the move to Bolingbroke's advice maligned him. He thought it an abandonment of the field, but argued that, having done the wrong thing, Wyndham should busy himself getting constituencies to send in remonstrances applauding it.[28] The departure had embarrassed

---

* The measure of Wyndham's gift for misfortune was established when the newly formed, and specifically Tory, White's club managed that year to blackball the party leader.

the opposition Whigs into similar departure rather than vote in risible numbers. This played deeper into Walpole's hands. Pulteney and Wyndham were barely speaking and certainly not cooperating. Walpole responded to the actual walkout by pulling back Pelham, uncharacteristically angry enough about the 'faction against the liberties' remark, to intend charges against Wyndham.

Instead, the Prime Minister did his tired but safe speech accusing everyone opposite of being a Jacobite at heart. It was nonsense, but such counter-patriotism got the House away from 'No Searches' and an overdose of heroics. And having no one to argue with in the next few weeks, he got down to sensible domestic legislation: on the wool trade, stone instead of wooden construction for Westminster Bridge and, topically enough, carriage of West Indian sugar in British ships free of London duties. He also won easy approval for subsidising that jobbing military handmaiden, Denmark, something embarrassingly confusable with George II's private interests in that country.[29]

But if the Tories had provided a useful breathing space, the South Sea Company now spoiled everything. It was understood that what was agreed between Britain, Spain and the Company would be duly performed. The South Sea, however, now chose to take Philip V's words about cancelling the *Asiento* at face value. Due to pay Spain £68,000, it sulkily refused. Philip, treating a tantrum as high policy, responded with one of his own. Spain would not now make *its* first payment on the stipulated date. He followed this up by suspending the *Asiento*, breaking the terms of the Treaty of Utrecht and giving the war party, however meretriciously, a legal handle for war.

All Keene's efforts and all Walpole's understanding of the folly impending were confounded. The British Cabinet, meeting in June, did not actually declare war, but it took those 'strong measures' the commercial interest and war fanciers sought. The long drift into war had begun. On Newcastle's proposal, poor Haddock, eternally sent to and recalled from Minorca, was shuttled out again, to Cadiz actually, and told cryptically to 'commit all kinds of hostilities at sea'.[30]

Mutual incomprehension ruled. Even Newcastle, the keenest ministerial supporter of war, tried jointly with Walpole to have the Spanish ambassador understand the orders to Haddock as home market rhetoric, not an intimation of war. However, such was the state of 'order, counter-order, disorder', that Geraldino couldn't believe them. Hardly surprising since Newcastle was also asking Spain to abandon the right to search, an echo of the rant in the opposition press. The slide went on; in July, Edward Vernon who, for his attacks on Walpole as an MP, had earlier been stood down from his vice-admiralship, sought a command providing he was reinstated. Both requests were met.

Walpole was not a free agent. With Caroline gone there was no one to hose down a King red hot for war. It was his *métier*, and he would soon have a delightful chance at Dettingen to jump on a horse and charge the enemy. Handel would compose a Te Deum to celebrate the fact. George, in his maddening but rather endearing way, first urged Walpole, against all his judgement, into war, then, when he tried to resign, burst into tears and asked if he were now to be deserted.

Newcastle was also a factor. The Secretary of State favoured military action. He has been accused of conspiring against Walpole, but such a charge misses the nuances and misunderstands the man. Thomas Pelham-Holles had neither the shabbiness nor the nerve to stab anyone in the back. He *disagreed* with Walpole and had conversations with the like-minded Carteret. But Newcastle was both an honest, if dithering, member of the war party and a consistent friend to Austria. With better reason, he had favoured helpful intervention in the Polish conflict. Spain was France's client; what was good for Spain was good for France and bad for Austria. So obscurely, and in the longer term, it would be bad for Britain. A further concern was that France and Spain had made another marriage pact, the Spanish King's younger son marrying the eldest daughter of Louis XV. This persuaded some ministers, in the jittery way of such things, that a deal with Spain would strengthen France, actually far more cautious than anyone suspected.

Again, Newcastle was temperamentally ill-equipped to resist clamour. Even Walpole had partly won the debate with emphatic words about no yielding over Georgia. If the rabblement could shake Walpole, it could command Newcastle. His dispirited comment was 'We must yield to the times'.[31] In such a mood of despair and exaltation at dice being cast, the British now committed themselves to seizure of Spanish bullion, larceny as high policy and military expansion by eight Irish regiments. Things said and meant as bluff were turning into cannon and dead men. Delay over a formal declaration owed more to making ready than any belief that Keene and his Spanish counterparts could find a way out.

It followed on 19 October 1739, proclaimed at the Royal Exchange. Naturally 'huzzas and acclamations resounded on all sides'.[32] The heralds signalling it were followed by a mob, the funds rose, the Prince of Wales, still working on his public relations, drank triumph to it in the doorway of the Rose Tavern, Temple Bar. And, of course, the bells were rung. Whether Walpole actually said 'They are ringing their bells, soon they will be ringing their hands' is not certain, but they were his sentiments. And if he had heard Sellar and Yeatman's twist on the phrase, 'Now they are ringing their bells, soon I shall be ringing their necks', he would have laughed out loud. But Walpole had lost. It was not his war; he would wish his colleagues 'joy of it'. And now, only tenuously, was it his government.

Why did the Prime Minister not now resign? He was right and knew it. He would make little effort to run the campaign. From Houghton he would have been free, over the marmalade, to read of naval reversals and the raising of fresh supply while drinking deep of *Schadenfreude*. But in pursuit of an undertaking he despised, conscious that he no longer controlled the government in the coolly certain way of eighteen years, he trudged on, a ploughman behind the wrong horse. The answer is simple. Walpole was into politics as some men are into business, women or drink. Politics entirely occupied and vitalised him. Politics defined him. There were twenty-eight scrambling months to go.

The war got off to a brilliant and misleading start. It had been Newcastle's dubious judgement to fight in American waters where we had fought them last time in 1726, and Admiral Hosier had won a famous victory. Hosier had done well but had not taken the coastal town of Portobello; indeed, he had died there, with most of his men, trying. Vernon, who had served under him, was convinced in his hearty way that he could capture it. And the wise instinct of Newcastle and Hardwicke was to let the commanders make tactical decisions without political second-guessing.

Vernon was as good as his word: the vice-admiral sailed, Portobello fell, more bells were rung. He was promoted full admiral and, out of Parliament since the 1734 election, found constituencies queuing up for his candidacy in 1741 (Ipswich won). If things had gone on like that, the war would have been velvet and primroses. They didn't. Dr Tobias Smollett, ship's surgeon on the *Chichester*, wrote a direct report of the conflict, *An Account of the Expedition against Cartagena*, and incorporated its events into his vivid classic, *Roderick Random*.

The *Chichester* joined the flotilla under command of Rear-Admiral

Sir Chaloner Ogle, which meant that for a long time the large, thirty-six-year-old third-rate went nowhere. As Newcastle dryly put it, 'If you ask me, "Why does not Sir Chaloner Ogle sail?" I cannot answer, because he is not ready. If you ask another question – "Why is he not ready?" – to that I cannot answer.'[33] Ogle, intended to reinforce Vernon in the West Indies, spent a year until October 1740 off the Isle of Wight, supposedly repairing and victualling his twenty-five ships, before sailing clean into a ferocious Channel storm.

The objective was the capture of Cartagena on the modern Colombian coast. It remained the objective. The military commander, Lord Cathcart, died the day the fleet reached Dominica. His successor, Wentworth, and Vernon were soon quarrelling and holding separate councils of war. The admiral, for Pulteney 'the most popular and best loved man in *England*,' shrivelled in the astringent eye of the Scottish surgeon. A 'man of weak understanding, strong prejudices, boundless arrogance and over-boiling passions' was Smollett's view. He was little kinder to Wentworth: 'wholly defective in point of experience, confidence and resolution'.[34] As for his soldiers, they were 'taken from the plough's tail a few months before'.[35]

Smollett was almost professionally uncharitable, but events do not contradict him. Taking the Spanish flagship *Galicia* did not diminish the complex and heavy fortification of the town under a capable commander, Don Blas de Leso. An attempt made to use the Spanish ship and its sixteen guns as a floating battery to assault the citadel of Cartagena, San Lazaro, was no substitute for taking the fleet's warships into the harbour. The land assault, made in the hot, rainy season with ladders too short for the walls, failed miserably. But health in the tropics was the chief anxiety.

The *Chichester*, typically, had lost 110 men sick, a sixth of the crew, on the journey. Hosier's siege of Portobello had ended in the death of five-sixths of the men and Hosier himself. Fear that Cartagena would produce a similar contagion hung over the expedition. The fighting was expensive enough with the San Lazaro assault costing two hundred dead and four hundred wounded. Continuous rain was accompanied by such non-stop lightning that 'one might have read a small print all night by the illumination'.[36] Men went in fear of the local killing disorder, the African slave's revenge, having come originally on the slave ships.* Yellow fever was named for the sudden change to complexion

---

* Wager, knowing this, wanted the Spanish ships to arrive first and be hit by the fever.

and eye colouring, reddening of parts of the skin, vomit mixed with blood and haemorrhages from every orifice.[37] Flesh and blood suffered horribly on this campaign, and, fearing Hosier's experience, flesh and blood turned away.

Vernon had enjoyed other victories beside Portobello (which the Spaniards would later take back). He had destroyed Spanish ships and taken the forts of St Louis and St Philip which Smollett in the reinforcement fleet had missed. 'Old Grogram', who had invented 'grog' by watering rum to stop his men killing themselves, deserves better of posterity than the crabby genius of Smollett would give anyone. But whether by quarrels, disease or weather, combined with terrible provisions (another Smollett charge), the siege failed. Haddock and Norris could not prevent Spanish and French fleets breaking through to relieve the Americas. The news midway through 1740 was of frustrated withdrawal in a war not to be won or readily ended, which went expensively on.

Now, for extraneous reasons, Austria was about to come into the picture in ways to add a rationalising layer to the conflict. The imperial anxiety for the last decade had been the succession. Would Charles VI's daughter, Maria Theresia, acknowledged Queen of Hungary, also become Empress? The Pragmatic Sanction was pragmatic because its signatories agreed to break the Empire's Salic law against female heirs in the interests of peace and continuity, pragmatism enough. Charles died in October 1740, all deals done.

Certainly they were done straightforwardly with Kurfurst Georg August of Hannover, done also with the abominable, old flogging corporal, the King of Prussia, Frederick William. No trouble was expected from his dilettante, flautist son, now Frederick II, whom the old monster had wanted to behead for running away. Promptly, lightweight, no-account Frederick took his father's collection of soldiers, too precious for use, and invaded Austrian Silesia with them. Progress toward the title of 'the Great' had begun. And however bruised the British links with the Empire, Britain was inevitably involved.

But nobody was involved the way George II was. Anyone thinking the homosexual flautist unsuited to war was stopped short by brilliant victory early next year at Mollwitz. New men in France saw their chance, overruled Fleury and proclaimed their own imperial client the Elector of Bavaria. George might strike chivalric poses towards Maria Theresia, might feel loyal sentiments to the Habsburgs. But if Frederick brought cold-eyed opportunism into repute by winning, it would be essential to avoid a peace conference where bits of Hannover were annexed.

Klein-Schnellendorf does not resonate in English history, nor is it an honourable name in the record of the Guelph-Windsors. There it was that George declared his and the Electorate's neutrality against Prussian aggression and joined France in endorsing the Bavarian. But Maria Theresia was popular in England for sentimental but not discreditable reasons. Firm commitments had been made. Doing anything was expensive and tended towards a wider war. Doing nothing was impossible.

George feared being dragged as Elector into the consequence of policies which the King accepted. The signatory of Klein-Schnellendorf could be heard in Westminster on 8 April informing Parliament that the support requested by Maria Theresia would be forthcoming. She had asked for 'twelve thousand men, expressly stipulated by treaty; I have therefore demanded of the king of Denmark and the king of Sweden as Landgrave of Hesse Cassel, their respective bodies of troops, consisting of six thousand men each, to be in readiness to march forthwith to the assistance of her Hungarian majesty'.[38] The Patriot opposition at least was delighted, with Pulteney and the young Henry Fox making budget-free speeches about standing by our allies.

Pulteney expanded on long-term projections (which would come true) about forming 'a confederacy' and seeking 'to unite the powers of Europe against the house of Bourbon, that ambitious and restless family by which the rest of the world is almost daily interrupted . . .'.[39] We were back in the classic Whig territory of the wars against Louis XIV. This was a doctrine which Walpole had once proclaimed then steadily tried to bury. But if only as paymaster and troop hirer, he was now into his second war and trapped. On 13 April, Parliament voted £300,000 to Maria Theresia.

Patriotism of this sort was not something the Tories did. William Shippen, now seventy, was growing dangerously fond of Walpole, sensing the affinities between two anti-war men. Sardonically, he condemned the immediate undertakings as 'inconsistent in my opinion with that important and inviolable law, the Act of Settlement!'. He pointed out, 'It was expressly determined that this nation should never be involved in a war for the defence of the dominions on the continent . . .'[40] Shippen might be making mischief, but Walpole's assumptions were not very different. The keen supporters of a war policy in the government were

Newcastle and his inseparable friend, Hardwicke. Walpole, listening behind the Speaker's chair to a war speech by Hardwicke murmured audibly 'Bravo! Colonel Yorke'.

Opposition and government were both split. Walpole and his circle of supporters were opposed to the policy he was carrying out and which Newcastle's thought essential. Pulteney and his Old Whigs were for war, the Patriots, and their friends in the Lords like Carteret and Chesterfield, if possible even more so. The Tories were cool at best. This would show a little later when the chance arose to bring down Walpole by the vote of a united opposition. Militarily speaking, Britain was caught up in the War of the Austrian Succession, Part 1, what Carlyle called 'a huge and unintelligible English and foreign delirium'. What matters here is its effect as the war went ever less well and the bills came in, upon the internal politics of Walpole's government.

The opposition had demonstrated their power in 1740 with a Place Bill. Place Bills, opportunities to detail the Walpole system of using office as valuable exchange, were the commonplaces of the Outs. Nothing came of them. The Patriot/Tory governments of the 1760s hung comfortably on to practices which Patriots, Tories and Pulteney's men now excoriated. Assault came only in the early – mid-1830s, immediately after the Reform Act. But a Place Bill was a good speculative flag to run up the Westminster pole. When a government was struggling, as now, MPs often saluted it.

In February 1740, the bill registered a startling vote of 222 to 206. Walpole was mindful of great wheels and the contagious effect of a government thought to be losing control. He was now reaping the consequences of alienating Argyll and the Prince. Both had MPs, in Scotland and Cornwall respectively. Argyll could not be relied upon; Frederick, all too emphatically, could. The base was slipping. Walpole now suffered a melancholy stroke of luck. Wyndham died on 17 June 1740. Chancellor of the Exchequer at twenty-five (the doing of his patron, Bolingbroke), he had been sent to the Tower at twenty-seven. Even now he was only fifty-two, though everything about his grave and dignified irresolution suggested a man twenty years older.

What mattered about Wyndham was that he had stayed Bolingbroke's man, a protégé guarding a flame across a quarter of a century's opposition. And Bolingbroke had been giving the Tories responsible advice. They should stay in Parliament, forget Jacobite dreams, work with Pulteney or any other calculating politician willing to work with them.

Wyndham tried with imperfect success to follow. With Wyndham gone, the Tories were always liable to give way to what Aneurin Bevan called 'an emotional spasm'. They didn't trust Pulteney; he was out for himself. So he was, but he could do them mighty favours in the process. But they didn't want favours from a fellow like that. Up against Sir John Brute, Walpole watched adverse majorities go sullenly astray.

Tory resentment would undermine the Whig opposition's boldest move yet, motions in February 1741 to both houses of Parliament recommending to the King Walpole's dismissal from office *sine die*. The motion was put by Carteret in the Lords and Samuel Sandys in the Commons. Sandys's speech, as we have it from Henry Fox's notes, quoted by Coxe, was largely factual, sticking to everything which had gone wrong in foreign policy, especially Walpole's closeness to the French and how little Britain had gained by it. It was a broad indictment going back to at least 1731.

The Prime Minister had misread the balance of power to vindicate his France-friendly Hanover treaty:

> We then guaranty'd the Pragmatic Sanction and engaged to support the emperor in all his dominions, but saw him lose Sicily and Naples, saw France get Lorrain, and the power of Austria, which had been ridiculously magnified . . . pulled down and brought into its present low and miserable situation. That great man, Admiral Vernon, saw all this and advised against France in this house, for which reason it was contrived that he should not be in the next parliament.

Apart from overselling Vernon, that was a fair enough case, remote from Pitt's floridities. Walpole's overall foreign policy *had* sold the Emperor short and traded heavily on Fleury's compliance. It could fairly be called miscalculated. With some domestic points and the marking up of immediate failures as in not supplying Vernon with decent provisions (confirmed by Smollett) and bomb vessels, it was, however extravagant the penalty sought, a decently made case.

It was, of course, politically motivated in all four suites. But the case was strengthened by Sir John Barnard. He argued that though things going wrong and mistakes being made were commonplaces in any government, the trouble came from Walpole being a sole Minister. Having concentrated power, he stood all the more vulnerable to receiving all blame. If a Minister had the King's support and had corrupted

Parliament, 'I should be glad to know what controul [*sic*] he is under, or by what legal means our constitution could be restored. This unlucky situation we may fall into by having the same minister too long continued in power.'[41]

The drama of thirty years was marked by the intervention of Edward Harley, later Third Earl of Oxford from 1741. Nephew to Oxford, no fool and universally respected, he was now a force in opposition politics. Harley's objection to the Sandys bill was that it struck at Walpole by way of a quasi-impeachment without reference to law and the courts. Harley's family and friends had been sent to the Tower by Walpole in the same bad, extra-legal way. Magnificently, he disdained it:

> A noble lord to whom I had the honour to be related, has often been mentioned in this debate. He was impeached and imprisoned; by that imprisonment, his years were shortened; and the persecution was carried on by the honourable person who is now the subject of your question, though he knew at that very time that there was no evidence to support it. I am now, Sir, glad of this opportunity to return good for evil, and to do the hon. gentleman and his family that justice which he denied to mine.[42]

It was mortal chivalry, a killing grace.

Walpole's own defence was, as ever, highly competent. These criminal good relations with France which he had developed had done British merchants no injury. But it is the style – light, good-humoured, assured and assuring – which shows Walpole's command of the Commons, bribed or not. He had a light-hearted dig at 'Patriotism' in its new form. 'A Patriot Sir! Why patriots spring up like mushrooms! I could raise fifty of them within the four and twenty hours. I have raised many of them in one night. It is but refusing to gratify an unreasonable or insolent demand, and up starts a patriot.' And there was a bitter thrust at his Old Whig enemies, addressed directly to the Tories, about whose uneasiness Walpole was fully informed. 'There is not a man amongst them whose particular aim I am not able to ascertain, and from what motive they have entered into the lists of Opposition.'[43]

That is a very large statement and spoke Walpole's vast professionalism. He was saying to the Tories, 'These are very clever fellows. But we know, don't we, you and I, that for all the gestures they strike and all the patriotic stuff, they want jobs, and in particular my job. And whatever you think of me, is there really any point in making the change?' Indeed, his actual words were an overture. The opposition to him, he said, 'may be divided into three classes, the Boys, the riper Patriots and the Tories. The Tories I can easily forgive, they have unwillingly come into the measure and they do me honour in thinking it necessary to remove me as their only obstacle.'[44] But what of Pulteney and the ambitious, younger men 'in long cravats' (Shippen's phrase)? They had denounced his 'long continuance in office. This is the heinous offence which exceeds all others: I keep from them the possession of that power, those honours and emoluments to which they so ardently and pertinaciously aspire.'[45]

Coming from Walpole, a charge of wanting office was chutzpah of a high order. As to events, the war had indeed, in Carteret's elegant term, 'been conducted in a languid manner' . . . warranting his injunction, 'if one physician cannot cure a fever, take another'.[46] But the Tories heard Walpole, and in large numbers they agreed. It had been a bitter and drawn-out affair, begun at eleven a.m. and not extinguishing the candles until four in the morning. Direct as ever, Shippen encapsulated the Tory position. He 'would not pull Robin down for republican principles'.[47] And as *The London Magazine* reported it, 'Mr Shippen withdrew and was followed by 34 of his friends.' That understated it; all in all, fifty-five Tories and friends abstained while twenty-eight such folk actually voted for Walpole (or against Pulteney).

The motion should have done well enough, not to drive Walpole out but to burn him badly. It failed by 290 to 106, a grotesque majority by the House arithmetic. It was a demoralising defeat for the Opposition and a staggering recovery for a Minister fighting an unsuccessful war against his own judgement, after making a thorough mess of foreign policy. The Tories had missed the point. They disliked Walpole, but then he was on the other side. Pulteney was an ally and they *loathed* him. Sir John Brute detested calculating professional politicians, so he kept Robert Walpole in office.

It was the resurrection but hardly the life. Not only did the war go on, and badly, but 1741 was election year and Walpole was not defending a majority of 150. He was defending his credibility in the swivelling eyes of boroughmongers like Bubb Dodington. If the wheel rolled downhill, hands *would* leave go. In the mixed constitution of 1741, with some seats contested by an independent electorate, others tucked away by assorted grandees, yet others up for trade, along with their owners, voting shifts mattered chiefly as triggers. The question, when the House returned, concerned how many names among Walpole's paper majority would move, or be moved by patrons, following electoral setbacks. 'Four columns will march on Madrid,' said General Franco, 'the fifth is already there.'

The Prince and his Cornish seats were already gone; so was Argyll's Scottish interest, losses of ten and twelve respectively. But Newcastle, for all his differences, remained actively loyal. His political equity in Sussex, Nottinghamshire and Yorkshire was kept in line. In what we might anachronistically call the democratic parts of the country, Walpole had lost a little, but in normal circumstances could have been sanguine. Only in Kent, Berkshire and Dorset, where the Court had lost three seats apiece, Hampshire where they picked up six, and Wiltshire, where they took four, did mobility go beyond one or two seats. Indeed, the Ministry had gained ten seats outside Cornwall and Scotland. Walpole finished overall with a majority of eighteen, down from the previous forty-two.[48]

The opposition was, as we have seen, badly split. But the government was hardly united. Hervey lived in reciprocal hatred with Newcastle, and Walpole had recently promoted Hervey to Lord Privy Seal with embittering ministerial precedence over the duke. In any test of Parliament the majority was there, but crumbling almost from the start. When it met on 1 December, a new chronicler appeared. Young Horace Walpole had been returned for the family borough of Callington (acquired through marriage); and now, to friends like Horace Mann, he wrote amusingly of events from Downing Street. The gossip, dismissively passed on, includes one report that Admiral Haddock had shot himself and two that Sir Robert had had an apoplectic seizure. More certainly, 'The Parliament met the day before yesterday and there were four hundred and eighty-seven members present. They did no business, only proceeded to elect a Speaker which was unanimously Mr Onslow . . .'[49]

The issue might now be decided on the address. Pulteney, remembering the Removal debate, deftly talked the Tories out of forcing a division. When Shippen said that he loved them, Pulteney gaily returned that 'dividing is not the way to multiply'.[50] The debate itself, on 9 December, got good notices. 'A warm battle between Sir R. and Mr Pulteney', Horace called it. Dispassionately, he admired Pulteney's effort: 'a fine speech, very personal, on the state of affairs'.[51] Joseph Danvers was cooler all round. As he gracefully put it, the encounter resembled 'two old bawds debauching young members'.[52]

But, clearly, 'Sir R.' had been in best genial/sardonic mode. 'He had been taxed with all our misfortunes; but did he raise the war in Germany? Or advise the war with Spain? Did he kill the late Emperor or King of Prussia? Or was he first minister to the King of Poland?'[53] And when Walpole flung out an invitation to a debate on 'the state of the nation', an odd phrase which American presidents have institutionalised, Pulteney accepted. But Pulteney the next day, Wednesday, brought in a huge parchment of signatures, the election petition from democratic Westminster.

The very first petition was heard the same day. A ministerial claim for less democratic Bossiney, in corrupt Cornwall (twenty to twenty-five voters) seated their defeated candidates, John Sabine and Christopher Tower, in place of the opposition men, Richard Liddell and Thomas Foster, but not by anything like enough. The vote was 222 to 215. The opposition was delighted and Horace knew why: 'one or two such victories, as Pyrrhus, the Member for Macedon, said, will be the ruin of us'.[54] The size of the early votes in the new Commons was everything.

Whips knew well enough in close terms their paper support. The question was who would rat and how many. It was terribly important from the start to look like the winning side. Successive small majorities for the Ministry were a fearful incentive to the rats. And to activate them, Pulteney chose his ground very shrewdly. Bossiney, handled before the appointment of a committee chairman, went to the government. Another ministerial petition over Denbighshire succeeded despite the sheriff's spectacular misconduct.* Perhaps the procedures themselves might be probed.

'They [the opposition] intend to oppose Mr Earle's being Chairman of the Committee, and to set up a Dr Lee . . .'[55] 'The Committee' examined the petitions alleging irregularities brought by defeated candidates against successful ones, an important aspect of eighteenth-century electoral politics and something conducted in a thoroughly partisan fashion. Gyles Earle, Member for, and controller of, Malmesbury, had been Chairman of the Elections Committee since 1727, and, where ministerial candidates were petitioned against, would be entirely helpful. He was a Walpole man, not a creature, but 'with an odd, violent way of speaking', more of a heavy, a ruffian on the stair. Hervey hated him,

---

* After Walpole's departure, this was reversed and the sheriff sent to Newgate.

always a recommendation. But a man of some wit, 'which he has dealt out largely against the Scotch and the Patriots',[56] Earle had made enemies. As opposition candidate, Pulteney's clever choice, Dr Lee, a Church lawyer, was genial and uncontroversial where Earle was biting and rough.

No vote could be more important. Horace watched the machines working the pay roll:

> In short, the determined sick were dragged from their beds: zeal came in a great-coat. There were two vast dinners at two taverns, for either party; at six we met in the House. Sir William Yonge, seconded by my uncle Horace, moved for Mr Earle: Sir Paul Methuen and Sir Watkyn Williams Wynne proposed Dr Lee – and carried him, by a majority of four: 242 against 238, the greatest number, I believe, that ever *lost* a question.'[57]

Lee's geniality was of no account now; the matter of disputed elections was in the hands of the enemy. Horace and his father did not despair: 'Sir R. is in great spirits, and still sanguine. I have so little experience that I shall not be amazed at whatever scenes follow.'[58]

But in the fluid, adaptive world of the mid-eighteenth century, all crowd psychology was against Walpole. Mr Pickwick's advice about the right response when there were *two* mobs – 'Shout with the largest' – applied to politicians. There were some absentees from the vote of 16 December and eight outright desertions.[59] One of these, James Oswald, embodies shameless, almost heroic opportunism, the sort of man whom, in an earlier year, Walpole would have weighed and bought. He had come forward for Dysert Burghs and its eighty-eight voters as a ministerialist. On the vote of 21 January, Oswald deserted. 'Sir R. sent a friend to reproach him; the moment the gentleman who had engaged for him came into the room, Oswald said, "You had like to have led me into a fine error! Did you not tell me that Sir R. would have the majority?"'[60] Where Oswald led, others, less brazen, would furtively follow.

Walpole might keep up the front of sanguine good spirits. The measure of his actual desperation showed in the overture he now made to the Prince of Wales. When Frederick had raised the question of getting his father's £100,000 a year as Prince, Walpole had deferred to current authority, George II. £50,000 was all there could be. Now, with eight clear deserters and a run of dangerous petitions coming up, Frederick's

Cornish seats might charm the likes of Mr Oswald and transform the landscape.

The messenger, sent by Walpole's son-in-law, Cholmondeley, on the order of the King, was no less a lackey than the Bishop of Oxford and future Primate, Dr Secker. Not only would the missing £50,000 be paid if the Prince came up with the votes, said His Grace, but there would be a full rebate of £200,000 for the four underpaid years. It was good cash politics, but Fritz, cherishing his popularity, intimated that so long as Sir Robert remained Minister, he would decline the *Kreutzer* and withhold the *Schweitzer*. The dimension of the crisis lay in George's engagement. Walpole was the King's Minister, and his fall would register the limitations to kingly authority, an excellent constitutional talking point and a mighty humiliation.

On 18 January, the Berwick petition went against the Ministry and in favour of the son of Lord Marchmont, noted opposition figure. Walpole was done for. Surely he was? But this Minister died hard and died brilliantly. On 21 January, Pulteney proposed the reference to a twenty-one-man select committee, of all the papers on the war which the House had seen. Bluntly called a 'Committee of Accusation', this was prospectively the kill. By all accounts, the debate as debate was outstanding, Pulteney and Walpole both speaking to the height of their abilities. 'There were several glorious speeches from both sides', wrote the fair-minded Horace, 'Mr Pulteney's two, W. Pitt's and Grenville's, Sir Robert's, Sir W. Yonge's, Harry Fox's, Mr Chute's and the Attorney General's.'[61]

Pulteney's wit delighted the connoisseur in Horace:

> I have heard this committee represented as a most dreadful spectre; it has been likened to all terrible things; it has been likened to the King; to the Inquisition; it will be a committee of safety; it is a committee of danger; I don't know what it is to be! One gentleman I think called it a cloud . . . I remember, Hamlet takes Lord Polonius by the hand and shows him *a cloud* and then asks him if he does not think it is like a whale.[62]

The picture we get from him shows good humour and mutual respect between professionals, rather as footballers shake hands after ninety minutes of kicking each other about. 'Mr Pulteney owned that he had never heard so fine a debate on our side and said to Sir Robert "Well nobody can do what you can." "Yes," replied Sir R. "Yonge did better."

Mr Pulteney answered "It was fine, but not of that weight with what you said."' Yet the young man was also reporting gossip that Robert and his brother Horatio 'were to be sent to the Tower, and people hired windows in the City to see them pass by . . .'.[63]

The debate had been in earnest enough. Men had come in on crutches. Sir William Gordon, a dying man who would hang on only until June, came 'with a blister on his head and flannel hanging out from under his wig', and looking, said Horace, 'like Lazarus at his resuscitation'. Gordon's son had just been given a ship. But it was a measure of expectations that bought men should stay bought that this dying man came to vote against the government.[64]

Defeat would have started a formal investigation and with it, Walpole's ministerial demise. As it was, at eleven at night, thanks to the exertion of Lord Hartington bringing two Tories from the Lowther clan into the government lobby, he survived (253 to 250). But the petitions were taking their toll. Dodington boasted that he had brought seven men across. This professional renegade was also writing in glutinous terms to Lord Wilmington, the Spencer Compton who had fluffed the succession in 1727, to prepare for heading an administration.

Reluctant rats consulted on the details and timing of betrayal and stayed away. As Hartington put it, 'we have a parcel of shabby fellows who will not attend . . .'. That was out of a majority of fourteen on his reckoning, 'and the others make a great point of it, they will, I really think, get the better of us by determining all the elections in their own favour'.[65] A technical point over the Chippenham petition had already involved a single-vote defeat for the government on 28 January. It had convinced more than Hartington. Walpole drew his brother, son and close friends around him to discuss the dismal future. And on the 31st it was resolved to end resistance.

But nothing was said, and on 2 February the Chippenham vote proper came on. The constituency with its 130 burgage holders had declared for two opposition men, Edward Bayntun Rolt and Sir Edmund Thomas, but only, it seems, after they had visited upon the town 'a considerable number of armed men . . . to terrify and intimidate the voters' as well as trumping up charges against the Whig sheriff, demanding £10,000 bail and holding him in Devizes 'until the morning after the poll'.[66] The Whig candidates, John Frederick and Alexander Hume, had an excellent case which, in the febrile circumstances of a deserting majority on 2 February, was neither here nor there. The vote went against them by the startling margin of sixteen. Walpole invited Bayntun Rolt to come and sit beside him, said something about people whom he had done favours who were now voting against him, then 'declared he should never again sit in that house'.[67]

He went to the King who wept, sincerely; George was an honest man. But he was obliged on 3 February to adjourn the House for two weeks while the detail of a new government was arranged. On the 9th, Walpole was offered, and accepted, an earldom, reviving the East Anglian title which had died with his mentor, Edward Russell. He was Earl of Orford, and, when he formally resigned on 11 February, Britain's first and longest Prime Ministership had ended.

CONCLUDING AND CONCLUSIONS

The coalition which had defeated Sir Robert and become a new Ministry was broad but uneasy. It was not the government of an incoming opposition, but a coalition formed to fight the war to which sentiment and necessity had committed the country. Its justification was its majority in Parliament, as good as that and no better.

Walpole's grouping had stood at a maximum of 286. Of these, 124 members were in crown places, 28 were unrewarded adherents, while a further 134 are categorised as independents.[1] Under the very serious pressure operating from 1739 onwards, this ostensibly safe majority in a House, theoretically 558-strong, would flake. Great patrons like Argyll defected, the flexible arbitrageurs of politics like Dodington knew where their duty lay. Among rankers, James Oswald was the poster-paint model of unabashable self-interest, though Oswald's came in more delicate shades. All this would be true in reverse; any new Ministry went in fear of the mobility creating it.

The former Opposition, now in government, involved 130 Whigs, eighty of them country Members more or less reliably in that column, and a further fifty endorsing Walpole's judgement of every man having his price. The new disposition of leadership was complex. Carteret, soon, by inheritance, to become Granville, was associated with Pulteney. Argyll was associated with someone who could *not* come into government, the Prince of Wales. As the King remarked, 'I saw that I had two shops to deal with.'[2] The Pelhams, Newcastle and his cousin, Henry Pelham, were the historic Walpole faction, the 'Old Corps', coalescing with Sir Robert's opponents and enemies. Still outside government, apart from two brief minor appointments, were the Tories, crypto-Jacobites or sullen ruralists, whom Walpole had turned into untouchables.

Pulteney had put himself out of the running for the Lord Treasurership. Accused so often, even beyond his deserts, of careerism, he had felt the need over the previous months to disavow the highest office. It went consensually to Spencer Compton, who had refused the fence in 1727. Now Earl of Wilmington, two years older than Walpole and with sixteen months to live, he stood as low as common denominators get, a Pope to delight an ambitious conclave. Samuel Sandys, 'the motion maker' and Pulteney's man, went to the Exchequer Walpole had clutched close, supported there by the other Pulteney lieutenants, Rushout and Gybbon. Harrington, Walpolian regular, made way as Secretary of State for Carteret. Pulteney sat in the Cabinet, but without formal office. The Pelhams kept a large equity in the government, Newcastle retaining the other Secretaryship, while Henry Pelham, cooler toward the opposition Whigs than his cousin, retained the Paymastership which he still declined to plunder.

This was not a drastic change of government. The men establishing it showed little of the grasping ruthlessness marking Walpole in his opening years. Pulteney talked world-weariness and, in a fatal impulse, practised it. He might have created a Ministry dominated by supporters and allies, with the Pelhams sitting at the back. He settled for five friends in the Cabinet against thirteen of Walpole's. Worse, in July 1742 he accepted the earldom of Bath. A brilliant Commons debater, taking on, often matching, Walpole across a dozen years and observing his methods, he did not grasp the need for personal control of the Commons. By no means indolent, he seems, despite so much effort in opposition, to have lacked Walpole's demon to command power with colleagues subordinate or obliged. Arguably, his approach may be a measure of Walpole's political excess, something abnormal even among politicians.

Walpole himself, before moving to Arlington Street, lingered for a few months in 10 Downing Street, the house bestowed upon him as Prime Minister, which he chose not to retain. But by the mid-year he would be preoccupied, facing the same prosecution he had inflicted upon Harley. Except that, for all young Horace's fantasising about the Tower, he would not spend years of deteriorating health there contemplating the axe edge. The new men were vindictive but not as vindictive as Robert Walpole.

The charge was not treason but essentially larceny. Money or moneysworth had been the blood of his regime. A great many men did indeed have a price and from the secret service fund Walpole had paid it, his delightful grip on power mightily subsidised by state revenue. The question for Parliament was whether he had enriched himself. He was very rich, probably more in assets than cash. But Houghton, its rooms handsomely furnished with an international collection of Old Masters, was quite an asset. He lived very high, and, since his earliest days as a young MP, had been lavish and reckless with the stuff, getting, spending and getting more, notably in two terms as Paymaster. And he had, of course, in Tory times, been sent to the Tower after the Commons convicted him of selling that contract.

Pursuing him by way of investigation was not fundamentally unfair, but it was a mistake. David Hume's observation put things best: 'I would give my Vote for removing him from St James, but should be glad to see him return to Houghton Hall to pass the Remainder of his Days in Ease and Pleasure.'[3] Pulteney was accused of lacking zeal. His daughter having just died, he probably did. But on 15 March he came to the Commons seeking a Secret Committee. Horace made his maiden opposing it, with much credit. Following a further motion by the Irish peer, Lord Limerick, on the 29th, the Commons, by an ominously modest margin, 252 to 245, commanded the committee.

Some people were better at this sort of thing than others, notably William Pitt. This strange young man had said during the 2 February debate that Walpole deserved to be 'deprived not only of his honours but his life'.[4] One of Pitt's biographers, Sherrard, observes that 'it is sad to read his speeches at this time', and thinks his contributions to the inquiry 'smell of resentment and revenge'. Like the Walpole of 1717, Pitt seriously wanted his quarry sent 'to a lodging at the other end of the town [the Tower] where he cannot do so much harm to his country'.[5]

Probably the most useful fact turned up was proof of Walpole having subsidised the pro-Ministry press (a more virile approach than today's habit of briefing it). As proof in action, *The Daily Gazetteer*, gatherum of three ministerial sheets, now unsubsidised, subsided, collapsing into neutral reports.[6] But the heavy claims of the million and more, said to have moved lightly about by way of persuasion, would run into the political equivalent of solicitors advising clients not to reply. Richard Edgecumbe, the quintessence of crony, was to have helped the committee with its inquiries. Long on £3000 a year as vice-treasurer of Ireland, intermediary with Sunderland and George Augustus in 1720 and

Walpole's hardly empty-handed 'Grand Tourist of Cornwall' (his own phrase) for the 1727 elections – 'success in every place where I have been'[7] – he was a prime money-handling source for everything that concerned the committee, a bagman. Suddenly, on 20 April, by royal fiat, he became Baron Edgecumbe, immune from questioning, and, insultingly to ministers, Lord-Lieutenant of Cornwall.

Nicholas Paxton, Treasury solicitor, was asked unpleasant questions about the conduct of an election in Wendover. Rather than answer he went to jail, and, in the absence of *peine forte et dure*, weights on the chest facilitating interrogation in Tudor times, there was nothing the committee could do about it. Old John Scrope, 'a most testy little old gentleman' according to Horace, who, as Secretary to the Treasury since 1724, knew more about secret service money than anyone except Walpole himself, had no intention of talking about it. 'Pulteney himself has tried to work on him; but the old gentleman is inflexible and answered "that he was fourscore years old and did not care if he spent the few months he has to live in the Tower or not; that the last thing he would do should be to betray the King and next to him the Earl of Orford."'[8] He had ten years to live and told nobody anything!

The committee was anyway badly constituted for single-minded pursuit of Walpole's wrongdoing. It split four ways: six opposition Whigs, five New Whigs, five Tories and five Old Whigs, with many keen enemies excluded. Having lost ground over its composition, the new Ministry lurched into a toughness which backfired. The bill giving immunities to whichever tainted birds would sing passed the Commons and failed the Lords. By this time, the will to push the Lords again had worn thin and the slender majority registered the resilient strength of loyalists, its effective veto on proceeding further against wrongdoings, by which, after all, so many Members had profited.* Sir John Hynde Cotton for the Tories spoke for most in concluding that the inquiry was going no further.

Ministerial change of policy was concentrated in foreign affairs and the war. Accordingly, the new government was dominated by Carteret who, better than Pulteney, knew what he wanted. Carteret was a King's man, but also a foreign affairs man. And where, over Hanover interests, Walpole practised cautious accommodation, with the adjective dominating the noun, Carteret was in candid agreement with George.

---

* Of that profit, Newcastle drily observed that 'there were too many beasts and not enough pasture'.

What happened in Europe next was vital and there were no reservations about looking after Hanover. Speaking German has always been thought a semi-treasonable eccentricity in British politicians, witness the First War experience of Haldane who read Hegel and saved the British army. Frederick of Prussia might be happiest in French, but conversational German gave Carteret better access and deepened empathy with George.

He was not pandering to the King so much as understanding larger European complexities. And for some time he succeeded, brilliantly knitting an international alliance together which, given good soldiering, might achieve victory and settlement. But the war was filthy dear, annual military costs rising from between £1.5 and 3 million from 1714 to 1739 to £5.5 million in 1742, reaching £8 million in that exceptional year, 1745.[9]

Meanwhile, George's generalship did not help his ministers. The battle of Dettingen, won in June 1743, did his courage and field skills great credit. But his failure to exploit what Newcastle called 'the providential advantages we got at Dettingen' probably stopped Carteret getting from France those good peace terms for which critics and taxpayers yearned. It might be right – it *was* right – to stop either Frederick and/or the French, together or separately, from reshaping the Continental map to their own ends at Britain's longer-term peril. But the taxes were here and rising, the war there and interminable. In particular, the subsidies, to Hanover and Austria, were British money into foreign hands.

Everything that Harley and the Tories had said in 1709/10 could be said now. And the barely latent xenophobia of the English was up and running, with Carteret stigmatised in a little scream of Pitt as the 'Hanoverian troop minister'. Hanover and Hanover's interests and their costs were the foundation of debilitating resentment and parliamentary desertion. It was a bad basis for a majority. Carteret was a high and sophisticated intelligence but a terrible politician. Wilmington, in a flash of perception, said, 'Had he studied parliament more and Demosthenes less, he would have been a more successful minister.'[10]

The Commons was where he had to be for control, but Carteret had been a peer at five. With far more social compassion than Walpole, he had none toward politicians, no arts to soothe them. It would have been wisdom to cultivate and confide in Cabinet colleagues. Carteret bought no drinks, helped nobody on with his coat, failing comprehensively in what the century called 'caressing' those colleagues. He spoke of Pelham as 'Walpole's clerk' and expected Bob Cratchit-like compliance. Newcastle spoke of his 'insufferable silences'. Again, the war and the King's active part in it kept him abroad longer than was good for a main Minister.

Cerebral, preoccupied, impatient, Carteret was also grieving at the sudden death of his wife, news brought to him in Germany on the day after the false dawn of Dettingen. Ultimately, as the war ground on, as plans for a grand alliance with Austrians, Dutch, Hanover and Savoy sucked in subsidies without finding a Marlborough to win the battles, Carteret lost his colleagues. When Wilmington died on 2 July 1743, he did his loyal best to have Bath (Pulteney) take his place, but he (and Bath) lacked the goodwill of colleagues.

His troubles brought forward Robert Walpole, increasingly ill with the stone, to play a last and gratifying political hand. Walpole was a good hater and he hated Carteret with an intensity probably heightened against someone he had injured. When Newcastle, seconded by Hardwicke, urged George to give Henry Pelham the post, the King, who liked him and disliked Bath, agreed. Walpole is not known to have directly influenced the King, but there was no need. George's prejudices already tended that way. What he did do was counsel and stiffen up Pelham himself.

As successor to Wilmington, *pro forma* head of government, he might easily be no more than Bob Cratchit in office. Walpole wrote, setting out the state of play and indicating what was to be done. He must not underestimate the strength he now had: 'the defeat of Lord Bath upon an avowed and declared attack is more decisive against him than a battle of Dettingen'. George must be kept sweet but not overinformed. So he should 'write to the king, full of duty and acknowledgement; without reserve, approve what he has done for the present, because he has done it; assure him you will endeavour to carry on his business in the way he judges proper . . .'. Carteret, 'the great man abroad', must be oiled over too. Though half a sentence in, Walpole breaks into italics, better characterised as ironics:

> You will treat the great man abroad too in his own way; give him as good as he brings; and desire him as an earnest of that *cordial affection which he bears to you and your brother*, and as a proof *he will endeavour to support you as much as he can*, to prevent any changes or engagements to be made in the province where you now preside, detrimental or disagreeable to you and your interest.

Bath might well come over for a meeting 'to protect his creatures in their present possessions and encourage them, upon that presumption, to hold together. If they purchase their peace of you, it will be false and deceitful.' He must instead advance his own creatures and split the other side:

> Your strength must be formed of your own friends, the old corps and recruits from the Cobham squadron [the Young Patriots] who should be persuaded, now Bath is beaten, it makes room for them if they will not crowd the door when the house is on fire, that nobody can go in or out . . . [But] if they still meditate the fall of the great man, the attempt, instantly, will be in vain, which time, management and opportunity may bring about . . .
>
> Dear Harry, I am very personal and very free, and put myself in your power.[11]

Essentially that was how it would be. There would be humps and declivities, but Henry Pelham would progress from Wilmington's formal place in 1744 to Prime Minister in substance by 1746, and stay there until he died in 1754. Walpole could take satisfaction in the defeat of enemies and creation of what might be called the continuation of Walpole by other means. Gentler and less suspicious, cutting the bribery bill, but shrewd enough, Pelham inherited and ran the Walpole system, a console of obligations and adherences which successor Ministers with varying degrees of success would imitate.

As for Lord Orford, that had been a good, characteristically vengeful, note upon which to fall silent. He was sixty-seven years old. His retirement to Houghton had to be made the best of. But Walpole had no hinterland, no capacity, as he acknowledged, for reading books. His chief activity lay in planting. A letter to Charles Churchill at the time of Dettingen indulges a little Horatian rhapsody at retreat: 'My flatterers here are all mutes. The oaks, the beeches, the chestnuts, seem to contend which best shall please the Lord of the Manor. They cannot deceive, they will not lie . . . With these I am satisfied as they gratify me with all I wish, and all I want, and expect nothing in return.'[12]

William Coxe was right to say that talk of loyal beech trees does not deceive. It rings not so much false as self-deluding. Retreat was for intervals between politics and politics; as a fixed condition it was intolerable. Walpole *died* of going back to London. George, concerned at a crisis involving Carteret and the Pelhams, sent a message through

Walpole's son-in-law, Cholmondeley, asking him to come up ten days before Parliament opened in November 1744. Gratifyingly, Carteret lost the contest, resigning his seals on 16 November. But Walpole did not have long to enjoy vicarious victory. The journey proved excruciating.

Travelling over four days from King's Lynn to London in a horse-drawn coach over an unmade road while suffering acutely from gall-stones is a horrid business. In agony over the twenty miles of the last lap, Walpole was dosed by a temporary medical adviser, Jurin, with what Coxe calls 'a powerful solvent'.[13] This produced laceration of the bladder itself and intensification of pain, even though the stones were diminished. The only sensible thing to do was to take opium and take it heavily, escaping for six weeks into 'a constant state of stupefaction'.[14] He hung on long enough to give the young royal Duke, so soon to become 'Butcher' Cumberland, good advice about marriage.

George wanted to marry his younger son to a deformed Danish Princess. Walpole advised submission providing the money was right, advising a very high financial settlement, adding, 'Believe me when I say the match will no longer be pressed.' Walpole knew his stingy George. It wasn't. Humorously shrewd and, by his doctor's account, full of the fortitude the century prized, Robert Walpole, 1st Earl of Orford, died, aged sixty-eight, on 18 March 1745, and was buried at Houghton. He had got out, as one would have expected, ahead of the game.

At the end of his life narrative, what are we to make of Walpole? Certain things should be said at once. The words of his letter to Henry Pelham are those of a supremely lucid and practical politician. And Robert Walpole *was* a practical politician, a man of the highest intelligence, endowed with relentless application. He had an excellent grasp of practical finance. As a parliamentary speaker when Parliament valued debate, he was clear, plain, effective and is still a pleasure to read. By means, creditable and otherwise, he dominated his times. But beyond gifts and winning, is he to be admired?

Sir John Plumb, his biographer, was a partisan, rightly admiring the managerial skills and unpompous lucidity. He was correspondingly (and excessively) brusque with opposition. He winces occasionally, as over the brutal abandonment of the no-longer useful Sir John Fryer. But he is ardent to see sensibility in the private life and supremely concerned, something expanded in a famous essay, to claim that Walpole had underpinned the state and given the country stability. I do not know why Sir John, after producing the second volume in 1960, and with decades to live, never undertook an account of events after 1734. It could hardly have been squeamishness at the hero's fall. Walpole, the enemy of facile patriotism and uncovenantable wars, emerges from that defeat as well as or better than from his triumphs. Walpole, the knower of risks and limitations, Walpole, whose every instinct was to keep troops in barracks, money unspent, war rhetoric unuttered, is the best of him, a triumph of things not done.

But at the end of Plumb's text there is a hint of what may be troubling him: 'By 1734, his life, his attitudes, his methods had been clamped into an iron mould; the years had hardened and coarsened the fibres of his personality; and as his vision narrowed into a desire to retain power for its own sake, as intolerance of criticism grew, as the fluid, sensitive feeling of the realities of men and politics were smeared by success and calloused by power, so too did Nemesis creep upon him.'[15]

That is a fine judgement, beautifully expressed. It may imply a growing distaste which he did not want to pursue. But over all, Sir John was kind to Walpole. The coarseness had always been there, likewise the ruthlessness. The searching of Atterbury's coffin, the collective fine upon Catholics for being Catholics, the drafting of the Black Act, the long, spiteful pettifog through Horatio in France, by which Carteret was undermined, are events of the 1720s. An act of 1736, the attempt across a three-hour Privy Council to hang a man against the legal understanding of Hardwicke and the moderation of George II, belongs to the 'coarsened fibre' period, but how is it any different? My impression is of a lifelong urge to peremptory command and brutal overreaction, underlined again.

And it is this authoritarianism, otherwise the concentrating of every line of power into his hands, which makes one cavil at following Plumb too far on stability. The idea is of England saved from the squabbling and backbiting of a lot of other politicians by Sir Robert's sticky-fingered but decisive conduct. There was, though, a lot of stability in Stanhope's time and what were Walpole and Townshend, as they encouraged George Augustus's quarrel with his father and promiscuously attacked ministerial legislation, but squabbling and backbiting politicians?

We should look sharply at what distinguishes stability from power-hoarding. Pope's phrase about one who could 'bear, like the Turk, no brother near the throne' is simple truth. Walpole could not, with the single exception of Hardwicke, endure first-rate men about him. (Hardwicke, anyway, came late and was fenced by his legal offices.) Newcastle, Harrington, Horatio, even Henry Pelham, were modest men, no threat to the Turk and safe from the bowstring. Carteret, the early Pulteney and Chesterfield were large talents to be intrigued against, demoted, got rid of. By stability of power, Walpole meant not the crown but Walpole. And it is doubtful that a period of solitary power, of 'a sole minister', *does* create stability. Walpole wanted everything. Other men wanted their piece of everything. The virulence and extravagance of late opposition, as seen particularly in *Common Sense* and the shrilling speeches of Pitt, was rage at a monolith.

How unstable was Britain anyway without Walpole? The Hanoverians were there. They might be satirised and sung against. Even today one can read John Buchan's *Midwinter* and buy Jacobite wine glasses. But James Edward, in Avignon, Rome or Urbino, was never going to be King. The rising of the 'Fifteen' was openly supported by a single, inconsequential English political figure, Thomas Forster of Newcastle. Atterbury, playing with fire and consumed, was going against his own rule, accepted by every thinking Jacobite, that restoration could only come from a serious foreign military commitment. The 'Forty-five', supposed to validate Walpole's preoccupation, was a French confection whipped up in a war with France. English support was trivial. Probably Walpole's fear of the Jacobites, as of the Church Militant, was real. He was the child of his younger days, of Sacheverell and the latent hysteria of 1712–14. But zealous belief commingled with relentless, cool-eyed exploitation of fear and defined him.

The idea of a Walpole who saved dynasty and order as bastions against the Pretender is historical back-formation, a taking of credit for something happening anyway. The screening of the South Sea men has been quoted in its cause. But that screening, the tempering of the wind to the shorn wolf, sparked at least as much hatred for the new regime as the ruin the South Sea wrought. As for its effect on Walpole, the screening was invoked in Walpole's bitterest nickname, 'Bob Brazen'. Again, as Plumb brilliantly demonstrated, Walpole categorically did not resolve the financial crisis of the Bank. Like so many crises, it slowly sorted itself out, getting better through a sort of financial homeopathy. A scrupulous, non-lynching investigation would have made fewer enemies and denied propaganda weapons to Jacobites and the mob.

But then Walpole did protect King and politicians from a truth harder to be sanguine about. He also put himself to mighty advantage.

Admirers must face the fact that Walpole was about power – acquisition of power, keeping of power and getting rich by power. The fibre was always coarse, the vision low. Walpole did not invent English political corruption, but he turned it into a public company. The politics of Queen Anne's time, passionate and dangerous, rested emerging parties upon the disputing opinions of crown, local nobles and gentlemen able to create Members, and, in the open seats, upon whoever could vote. There were bribes, of course, but nothing to touch the systematic rottenness, talley lists of hard cash, military and civil places, the benediction of snug livings to younger sons, the outright purchase of power in a myriad of little deals which was Robert Walpole.

Another leader, Stanhope, say, would have required a measure of such business done. But it was in Walpole's nature to do dirty work *à l'outrance*. He was, beyond the norm of rough politics, amoral. And, importantly, he did it beyond necessity. Henry Pelham ran the same system but cost the secret service half the money drawn by minions like Nicholas Paxton for Walpole. Politics was not going to be shining bright in anyone's hands, but we must not so fear false projection and anachronism as to think bribery, suborning and enrichment natural eighteenth-century things taken in everybody's stride. The milking of the Paymastership had been frowned upon, had indeed begun to be abandoned before Walpole took his full pailful. Again significantly, Henry Pelham in the same post took nothing.

If all this seems harsh, it is meant to offset a too great tolerance. For Walpole created the politics of the next hundred years. The rotten boroughs, the bought and sold MPs sustaining government under the Younger Pitt and pathetically defended on the eve of Reform by Sidmouth and Eldon as the most perfect constitution in the world, were Walpole's system. And blindness to the power, hoarded and cherished by a long-lived oligarchy, is not something to celebrate.

Against this, there is one mighty virtue, more evident to our age than his – Walpole's contempt for the game of war. 'Fifty thousand men dead in Europe last year and not one Englishman' – the attributed statement suggests a humanity to which a sheaf of new capital offences makes sufficient rebuff. But Walpole was free of the figure-cutting vainglory of too many politicians. He had no wish to be an equestrian statue in his own lifetime. The stupidity and expense of invading a territory for the glory of this monarch or that nation, the sheer teenage bombast of it, left Walpole in creditable disbelief. 'Now God be thanked who has matched us with this hour' was folly quite beyond him. He was a commercial civilian who understood profit and loss and derided trumpet and drum. If corrupt, he was at least a corrupt adult.

It took a formidable man to make what Walpole made and passed down. One wouldn't deny, even momentarily, the will, personality and intelligence which made him formidable. Admiring the man requires discrimination and distinction-making, liking him is too difficult. Enough to say that Robert Walpole was a great man in all the senses, affirmatory and satirical, by which contemporaries understood the term.

NOTES

Chapter 1: The State of Play (pp. 5–23)

1 David Ogg, *England in the Reigns of James II and William III* (Oxford University Press, 1969), p. 145.
2 J. D. Kelly, ed., *The Oxford Dictionary of Popes* (Oxford University Press, 1986), p. 288.
3 Gilbert Burnet, *History of His Own Times*, pp. 492–3. Quoted in J. P. Kenyon's editorial introduction to *Halifax: Complete Works* (Pelican, 1969), p. 35.
4 Ogg, *op. cit.*, p. 173.
5 Geoffrey Holmes, *The Making of a Great Power*, p. 176 *et seq.*
6 Lord Halifax, 'Letter to a Dissenter (1687)', published in Kenyon, *op. cit.*, p. 106.
7 Quoted in Pierre Goubert, *The Course of French History* (Routledge, 1988), p. 128.
8 Sermon at St Ethelburga's, 30 January 1708, quoted in J. P. Kenyon, *Revolution Principles*, pp. 76–7.
9 Introduction to *Patriarcha* (Oxford University Press, 1949). Quoted *ibid.*, p. 63.
10 Holmes, *op. cit.*, p. 341.
11 Quoted in Geoffrey Holmes, *The Trial of Dr Sacheverell*, p. 52.

Chapter 2: 'I was in hopes you would have . . . payed' (pp. 24–38)

1 J. H. Plumb, *Sir Robert Walpole*, vol. I, p. 82.
2 *Ibid.*, p. 81.
3 *Ibid.*, p. 86.
4 *Ibid.*, pp. 57–8.

5 Prideaux Letters 195, quoted in James M. Rosenheim, *The Townshends of Raynham*, p. 194.

6 Quoted *ibid.*, p. 194.

7 C(H) 307.

8 C(H) 275.

9 C(H) 271.

10 C(H), 277.

11 Plumb, *op. cit.*, note, p. 106.

12 *Ibid.*, p. 109.

13 C(H), 319.

14 C(H), 279.

15 C(H), 307.

16 C(H), 300.

17 C(H), 305.

18 *Ibid.*

19 Julian Hoppit, *A Land of Liberty?*, p. 433.

20 Plumb, *op. cit.*, p. 110.

21 C(H), 268.

22 C(H), 305.

23 C(H), 661.

24 Quoted in Rosenheim, *op. cit.*, p. 196.

25 Blenheim MSS E.26, quoted in Geoffrey Holmes, *British Politics in the Age of Anne*, p. 234.

26 Plumb, *op. cit.*, p. 118.

27 *Ibid.*, p. 126.

28 *Ibid.*, p. 120.

29 HMC Portland MSS, quoted in Holmes, *op. cit.*, p. 234.

Chapter 3: The Consequences of Dr Sacheverell (pp. 39–52)

1 Alexander Cunningham, quoted in Geoffrey Holmes, *The Trial of Dr Sacheverell*, p. 150.

2 Thomas Hearne, quoted *ibid.*, p. 50.

3 Oxford Assize Sermon, quoted *ibid.*, p. 54.

4 Leicester Assize Sermon, quoted *ibid.*, p. 54.

5 'The Character of a Low-Church-Man', 1702, quoted *ibid.*, p. 55.

6 *Ibid.*, p. 54.

7 All at, or quoted in, Holmes, *ibid.*, p. 54.

8 'A Review of the State of the British Nation', Defoe, December 1709, quoted *ibid.*, p. 76.

9 Holmes, *op. cit.*, the indispensable modern source *passim*.

10 Bishop Atterbury correspondence, quoted *ibid.*, pp. 31–2.

11 'A True answer to Dr Sacheverell's sermon before the Lord Mayor', quoted *ibid.*, p. 77.

12 Plumb, *op.cit.*, vol. I, p. 148.

13 *The Tryal of Dr Henry Sacheverell before the House of Peers for High Crimes and Misdemeanors et.*, published by order of the House of Peers. Printed for Jacob Tonson, 1710, pp. 90–1.

14 *Ibid.*, pp. 91–2.

15 *Ibid.*

16 *Ibid.*, p. 93.

17 *Ibid.*, p. 92.

18 *Ibid.*, p. 93.

19 *Ibid.*

20 *Ibid.*, p. 94.

21 *Ibid.*

22 State Trials XV, 126–34. Quoted in Basil Williams, *Stanhope*, p. 124.

23 *Tryal of Dr Henry Sacheverell*, p. 105.

24 C(H), MSS 6, quoted in Plumb, *op. cit.*, p. 150.

25 Burnet, *op.cit.* p. 11.

26 *Ibid.*, p. 11.

27 Lord Dartmouth, quoted in Burnet, *ibid.*, p. 9.

28 *Ibid.*, p. 10.

29 *Ibid.*

30 Walpole MSS A.1 quoted in Plumb, *op. cit.*, p. 160.

31 Williams, *op. cit.* p. 126.

32 Quoted in Rosenheim, *op. cit.*, p. 218.

33 Dyer correspondence 14 October 1710, quoted in Holmes, *op. cit.*, p. 252.

Chapter 4: Go to Jail (pp. 53–65)

1 The Review VIII 491, 3 January 1712, quoted in J. P. Kenyon, *Revolution Principles*, p. 179.

2 'Four Last Years', Swift, quoted in William Cobbett, ed., *Parliamentary History of England from the Norman Conquest in 1066 to the Year 1803* (hereafter *Parl. Hist.*), vol. VI, col. 1074.

3 C(H), quoted in J. H. Plumb, *Robert Walpole*, vol. I, p. 176.

4 BM Loan 19/127/7, quoted in Geoffrey Holmes, *British Politics in the Age of Anne*, p. 267.

5 All Parliamentary Record, quoted in Cobbett, *Parl. Hist.*, vol. VI, cols 1067–8.

6 Willard Connely, *Sir Richard Steele*, pp. 154–5.

7 Chandler, quoted in Cobbett, *Parl. Hist.*, vol. VI, col. 1236.

Chapter 5: 'The Old Order Changeth' (pp. 66–96)

1 Harold Williams, ed., *Correspondence of Jonathan Swift*, vol. II, p. 101.
2 Quoted in Julian Hoppit, *A Land of Liberty?*, p. 389.
3 State Papers, Kemble, p. 451, quoted in Ragnhild Hatton, *George I, Elector and King*, p. 116.
4 *Ibid.*, p. 131.
5 Quoted in Hoppit, *op. cit.*, p. 388.
6 Plumb, *op.cit.*, vol. I, p. 208.
7 *Ibid.*, p. 212.
8 Elizabeth Hamilton, *'The Backstairs Dragon': A Life of Robert Harley, Earl of Oxford*, p. 269.
9 Quoted in *ibid.*, p. 274.
10 *Ibid.*, p. 274.
11 *Ibid.*
12 Plumb, *op. cit.*, p. 217.
13 *Ibid.*, p. 214.
14 Hatton, *op. cit.*, p. 122.
15 *Ibid.*, pp. 179–80.
16 Paul Fritz, *The English Ministers and Jacobitism*.
17 Quoted in Hatton, *op. cit.*, p. 179.
18 *Ibid.*, p. 178.
19 Quoted in Fritz, *op. cit.*, pp. 6–7.
20 Quoted in B. W. Hill, *The Growth of Parliamentary Parties*, p. 159.
21 B. W. Hill, *Sir Robert Walpole*, p. 83.
22 Quoted in Hatton, *op. cit.*, p. 190.
23 *Ibid.*, p. 196.
24 *Ibid.*, p. 199.
25 Hill, *op.cit.*, p. 162.
26 *Ibid.*, p. 201.
27 *Ibid.*, p. 162.
28 Cobbett, *Parl. Hist.*, vol. VII, col. 505.
29 Quoted in Williams, *op.cit.*, p. xxx.
30 Cobbett, *op. cit.*, vol. VII, col. 507.
31 *Ibid.*, col. 522.
32 *Ibid.*, cols 522–3.
33 *Ibid.*, col. 523.
34 *Ibid.*, col. 544.
35 *Ibid.*, cols 597–8.
36 Quoted in Basil Williams, *op. cit.*, p. 391.
37 *Ibid.*, p. 391.
38 Quoted in Hill, *op.cit.*, p. 174.

39 Basil Williams, *op. cit.*, p. 393.

40 *Ibid.*, pp. 393–4.

41 *Ibid.*, p. 398.

42 'Thoughts of a Member of the Lower House', quoted *ibid.*, p. 407.

43 *The Plebian*, No. 1, quoted in Willard Connely, *Sir Richard Steele*, pp. 347–8.

44 Quoted *ibid.*, p. 412.

45 William Coxe, *Memoirs of the Life and Administration of Sir Robert Walpole, Earl of Orford* (hereafter *Life*), vol. I, p. 608.

46 *Ibid.*, p. 608.

47 Speaker Onslow's account, quoted in Connely, *op. cit.*, p. 415.

48 Coxe, *op. cit.*, p. 608.

49 Quoted in Cobbett, *op. cit.*, cols 618–19.

50 *Ibid.*, col. 623.

51 *Ibid.*

52 *Ibid.*

53 *Ibid.*, col. 619.

54 *Ibid.*, col. 621.

55 *Ibid.*, col. 622.

56 *Ibid.*, col. 621.

57 Quoted in Hill, *op. cit.*, pp. 177–8.

58 Portland MSS, quoted in Basil Williams, *op. cit.*, p. 422.

Chapter 6: 'I was offer'd a present by the South Sea Company' (pp. 97–123)

1 Geoffrey Holmes, *The Making of a Great Power*, pp. 266 *post*.

2 *Ibid.*, p. 268.

3 Quoted *ibid.*, p. 269.

4 Julian Hoppit, *A Land of Liberty?*, pp. 266–7.

5 John Carswell, *The South Sea Bubble*, p. 29.

6 *Ibid.*, p. 44.

7 *Ibid.*, p. 46.

8 *Ibid.*, p. 65.

9 *Ibid.*, p. 71.

10 Letter (no. 412), to Charles Montague, Earl of Halifax, 30 November 1714, in Walter Graham, ed., *The Letters of John Addison*, p. 306.

11 *Ibid.*, letter (no. 412).

12 *Anatomy of Exchange Alley*, p. 39, quoted in Carswell, *op. cit.*, p. 75 (no author given).

13 *Ibid.*, p. 87.

14 *A Nation a Family*, 26 February 1720, quoted in Connely, *op.cit.*, p. 368.

15 Quoted *ibid.*, p. 92.
16 William Coxe, *op.cit.*, vol. II, pp., 182–3, quoted in J. H. Plumb, *op.cit.*, vol. I, pp. 302–3.
17 *Ibid.*, pp., 182–3, quoted in Plumb, *op. cit.*, p. 303.
18 Quoted in Romney Sedgwick, *The House of Commons 1715–1754*, vol. II, pp. 202–4.
19 Brodrick quoted in Plumb, *op. cit.*, p. 303.
20 *The Family Memoirs of the Reverend William Stukeley*, quoted in Hoppit, *op. cit.*, p. 335.
21 Harold Williams, *The Correspondence of Jonathan Swift*, vol. II (Letter 14 April 1720), pp. 341–2 and note, p. 342.
22 Plumb, *op. cit.*, p. 309.
23 Harold Williams, *op. cit.*, p. 422.
24 *Ibid.*, p. 422.
25 *Ibid.*
26 For the complex detail of this, see Appendix B of Carswell, *op. cit.*
27 Carswell, *op. cit.*, p. 130.
28 *Ibid.*, p. 113.
29 Cobbett, *Parl. Hist.*, vol. VII, cols 657–9.
30 Carswell, *op. cit.*, p. 131.
31 *Ibid.*
32 Ragnhild Hatton, *George I, Elector and King*, p. 253.
33 *Ibid.*, pp. 252–3.
34 Carswell, *op. cit.*, p. 149.
35 *Ibid.*, p. 150.
36 Plumb, *op. cit.*
37 C. B. Realey, *The Early Opposition to Sir Robert Walpole*, p. 10.
38 *Ibid.*, p. 10.
39 Carswell, *op. cit.*, p. 162.
40 *Ibid.*, p. 164.
41 Plumb, *op. cit.*, p. 332.
42 Carswell, *op. cit.*, p. 166.
43 *Ibid.*, p. 170.
44 *Ibid.*

Chapter 7: 'Odious inquiries' (pp. 124–148)

1 Carswell, *op.cit.*, p. 159.
2 Cobbett, *Parl. Hist.*, vol. VII, cols 660–1.
3 Sedgwick, *op.cit.*, vol. II, p. 262.
4 Cobbett, *op. cit.*, vol. VII, col. 683.
5 *Ibid.*, col. 766.

6 *Ibid.*, col. 769.

7 *Ibid.*, col. 768.

8 Richard Ollard, *Pepys: A Biography* (Oxford Paperbacks, 1984), pp. 196–204.

9 Cobbett, *op. cit.*, vol. VII, col. 683.

10 C(H), MSS 88, 26/1, quoted in J. H. Plumb, *Sir Robert Walpole*, vol. I, p. 330.

11 Quoted *ibid.*, p. 329.

12 Carswell, *op. cit.*, p. 180.

13 *Ibid.*, p. 185.

14 All at Realey, *op.cit.*, p. 22.

15 Carswell, *op. cit.*, p. 184.

16 *Ibid.*

17 Sedgwick, *op. cit.*, pp. 392–3.

18 Quoted in Carswell, *op. cit.*, p. 190.

19 Quoted in Sedgwick, *op. cit.*, p. 436.

20 Quoted in Williams, *Stanhope*, *op.cit.*, p. 441.

21 *Ibid.*, p. 434.

22 *Ibid.*

23 Sedgwick, *op. cit.*, p. 425.

24 *The Journals of the House of Commons*, XIX, quoted *ibid.*, p. 462.

25 Realey, *op. cit.*, p. 25.

26 Carswell, *op. cit.*, Preface, pp. xii–xiii.

27 Quoted in Carswell, *op. cit.*, p. 199.

28 Carlisle MSS, quoted in Plumb, *op. cit.*, p. 343.

29 Quoted in Sedgwick, *op. cit.*, p. 534.

30 HMC 14th Report, quoted in Sedgwick, *op. cit.*, p. 592.

31 *Ibid.*, p. 592.

32 Cobbett, *op. cit.*, vol. VII, col. 755.

33 Brodrick, letter to Lord Middleton, quoted in Cobbett, *op. cit.*, vol. VII, col. 756.

34 *Ibid.*, col. 756.

35 *Ibid.*

36 Carswell, *op. cit.* p. 210.

37 Quoted *ibid.*, p. 211.

38 *Ibid.*, p. 211.

39 *Ibid.*, p. 215.

40 Quoted *ibid.*, p. 217.

41 Sedgwick, *op. cit.*, p. 192.

42 Plumb, *op. cit.*, p. 363.

43 Carswell, *op. cit.*, pp. 230–1.

44 Cobbett, *op. cit.*, vol. VII, cols 903–4.

45 *Ibid.*, cols 904–7.
46 *Ibid.*, col. 909.

Chapter 8: 'Treason doth never prosper' (pp. 149–176)

1   Linda Colley, *In Defiance of Oligarchy*, p. 34.
2   Geoffrey Holmes, *British Politics in the Age of Anne*, p. 279.
3   *Ibid.*, p. 279, citing Macpherson, original papers, 1775.
4   PRO SP35/8, quoted in Paul Fritz, *The English Ministers and Jacobitism*, p. 23.
5   Cobbett, *Parl. Hist.*, vol. VII, 21 February 1717, col. 423.
6   Quoted in Fritz, *op. cit.*, p. 32.
7   *Ibid.*, p. 33.
8   J. D. Kelly, *The Oxford Dictionary of Popes* (Oxford University Press, 1986), entry on Clement XI, p. 292.
9   Stuart MS V11644, quoted in Fritz, *op. cit.*, p. 49.
10 Fritz, *ibid.*, pp. 49–50.
11 *Ibid.*, p. 56.
12 *Ibid.*, p. 57.
13 John Dryden, *Absalom and Achitophel*, 1: 150–1.
14 Romney Sedgwick, *op. cit.*, vol. II, p. 422.
15 *Ibid.*, p. 423.
16 Quoted in Fritz, *op. cit.*, p. 45.
17 G. V. Bennett, *The Tory Crisis in Church and State*, p. 224.
18 Quoted *ibid.*, p. 224.
19 Fritz, *op. cit.*, p. 70.
20 Royal Archive, Stuart 65/10, quoted *ibid.*, p. 71. (Full complement of names in Appendix 2.)
21 HMC Portland v552, quoted in Sedgwick, p. 494.
22 Bennett, *op. cit.*, p. 230.
23 *Ibid.*
24 *Ibid.*, p. 240.
25 Royal Archive, Stuart *op.cit.*, 58/140, 6 April, NS 1722, quoted *Ibid.*
26 William Coxe, *Life*, vol. II, pp. 22–4, quoted *Ibid.*, p. 250.
27 Fritz, *op. cit.*, p. 88.
28 Bennett, *op. cit.*, p. 254.
29 Cobbett, *op. cit.*, vol. VIII, col. 272.
30 All *ibid.*, cols 272–4.
31 Morrice to Atterbury, 28 September, quoted in Colley, *op. cit.*, p. 33.
32 Colley, *op. cit.*, p. 34.
33 C(H), 1053.
34 C(H), 1067.

35 C(H), 1082.

36 C(H), 1087.

37 C(H), 1091.

38 Edward Thompson, *Whigs and Hunters*, p. 305.

39 Quoted *ibid.*, Appendix 1.

40 Leon Radzinowicz, *A History of English Criminal Law and its Administration from 1750*, p. 77, quoted *ibid.*, p. 22.

41 *Ibid.*, p. 23.

42 Quoted *ibid.*, p. 48.

Chapter 9: Plotting in France, Stumbling in Ireland (pp. 177–197)

1 Quoted in Reed Browning, *The Duke of Newcastle*, p. 28.

2 C(H), 1465.

3 Basil Williams, *Carteret and Newcastle*, p. 12.

4 *Ibid.*, p. 11.

5 David Nokes, *Jonathan Swift: A Hypocrite Reversed*, p. 283.

6 Cobbett, *Parl. Hist.*, vol. X, col. 1047, quoted in Williams, *op. cit.*, p. 45.

7 *Ibid.*, p. 46.

8 Romney Sedgwick, *op. cit.*, vol. II, pp. 456–8.

9 C(H), 1035, letter to Townshend.

10 J. H. Plumb, his own words, not Horatio Walpole's, in *Sir Robert Walpole*, vol. II, p. 64.

11 Williams, *op. cit.*, p. 45.

12 Plumb, *op. cit.*, p. 56.

13 Ragnhild Hatton, *op. cit.*, p. 135.

14 C(H), 1034.

15 *Ibid.*

16 *Ibid.*

17 *Ibid.*

18 C(H), 1035, letter to Townshend, 1 December 1723.

19 Coxe, *Life*, vol. I, p. 184.

20 C(H), 1035.

21 C(H), 1037.

22 C(H), 1084.

23 C(H), 1057, 26 December 1723.

24 *Ibid.*

25 All *ibid.*

26 C(H), 1084.

27 C(H), 1091.

28 C(H), 1101.

29 C(H), 1103.

30 *Ibid.*

31 *Ibid.*

32 *Ibid.*

33 Williams, *op. cit.*, p. 53.

34 Quoted *ibid.*, p. 54.

35 Quoted in Herbert Davis's introduction to Swift, *The Drapier's Letters*.

36 Nokes, *op. cit.*, p. 280.

37 Quoted in Williams, *op. cit.*, p. 70.

38 C(H), 1048.

39 *Ibid.*

40 C(H), 1055.

41 C(H), 1048.

42 *Ibid.*

43 *Ibid.*

44 Entry in S. J. Connolly, ed., *The Oxford Companion to Irish History* (Oxford University Press, 2003), p. 53.

45 Swift, *op. cit.*, p. 11.

46 *Ibid.*, pp. 23–4.

47 *Ibid.*, p. 9.

48 *Ibid.*, pp. 19–20.

49 Quoted in R. F. Foster, *Modern Ireland 1600–1972* (Allen Lane/Penguin Press, 1988), p. 173.

50 *Ibid.*, p. 173.

51 Coxe, *Life, op. cit.*, vol. I, p. 216.

52 C(H), 1084.

53 *Ibid.*

54 Nokes, *op. cit.*, p. 291.

55 *Ibid.*

Chapter 10: 'Sir Blue-String' (pp. 198–217)

1 Quoted in Charles Realey, *The Early Opposition to Sir Robert Walpole*, p. 179.

2 *Ibid.*, pp. 194–5.

3 Quoted in J. H. Plumb, *Sir Robert Walpole*, vol. II, p. 99.

4 Both quoted *ibid.*, pp. 193–4.

5 Sedgwick, *op. cit.*, vol. II, p. 375.

6 *Ibid.*, p. 375.

7 Cobbett, *Parl. Hist.*, vol. VIII, col. 414.

8 All at *ibid.*, col. 414.

9 *Ibid.*, col. 416.

10 HMC, Various VIII, 15 March 1724/5, quoted in Ragnhild Hatton, *George I, Elector and King*, p. 369, note 24.
11 Cobbett, *op. cit.*, vol. VIII, cols 417–8.
12 Sedgwick, *op. cit.*, p. 406.
13 Cobbett, *op. cit.*, col. 453.
14 *Ibid.*, col. 454.
15 *Ibid.*
16 *Ibid.*
17 *Ibid.*, cols 454–5.
18 John, Lord Hervey, *Memoirs of the Reign of George II*, vol. I, p. 21.
19 Quoted in H. T. Dickinson, *Bolingbroke*, p. 147.
20 *Ibid.*, p. 151.
21 Quoted *ibid.*, p. 178.
22 Harcourt papers II, 109–10, 22 March 1726, quoted *ibid.*, p. 181.
23 *Fog's Weekly Journal*, 3 January 1729.
24 Realey, *op. cit.*, p. 201.
25 *The Daily Courant*, 30 January 1733.
26 Portland MSS VII, 464, quoted in Realey, *op. cit.*
27 Linda Colley, *In Defiance of Oligarchy*, pp. 211–2.
28 Quoted in Dickinson, *op. cit.*, p. 217.
29 Gerrard, *The Patriot Opposition to Walpole*, p. 164.
30 *Ibid.*, p. 117.

Chapter 11: Oh, Death, Where is thy Sting? (pp. 218–229)

1 John, Lord Hervey, *Memoirs of the Reign of George II*, vol. I, p. 31.
2 Sedgwick, *op. cit.*, vol. I, p. 568.
3 Hervey, *op. cit.*, pp. 32–3.
4 HMC Onslow, quoted in J. H. Plumb, *Sir Robert Walpole*, vol. II, p. 166.
5 C(H), 1448.
6 *Ibid.*
7 C(H), 1450.
8 C(H), 1453.
9 Add. MSS 32688, f.15, quoted in Sedgwick, *op. cit.*, p. 25.
10 C(H), 1458.
11 Sedgwick, *op. cit.*, p. 381.
12 See Sedgwick, *op. cit.*, vol. II, p. 65.
13 *Ibid.*, p. 65.
14 C(H), 1472.
15 C(H) 1468.
16 Quoted in Sedgwick, *op. cit.*, vol. I, p. 273.
17 C(H), p. 1476.

Chapter 12: Wars and Rumours of Wars (pp. 230–256)

1 Plumb, *op. cit.*, vol. II, p. 117.

2 *Ibid.*, p. 120.

3 David Bayne Horn, *Great Britain and Europe in the Eighteenth Century*, p. 117.

4 *Ibid.*, pp. 285–8.

5 Townshend to Newcastle 12/24 August 1725, quoted in G. C. Gibbs, 'Britain and the Alliance of Hanover, April 1725–February 1726', *English Historical Journal*, vol. 87, January 1961, p. 271.

6 *The Craftsman*, 16 January 1727 [OS], quoted in Gibbs, *ibid.*

7 All at Cobbett, *Parl. Hist.*, vol. VIII, col. 500.

8 *Ibid.*, col. 494.

9 *Ibid.*, cols 504–5

10 *Ibid.*, col. 501.

11 *Ibid.*, col. 502.

12 *Ibid.*

13 Horn, *op. cit.*, pp. 121–2.

14 All at Cobbett, *op. cit.*, vol. VIII, col. 531.

15 Plumb, *op. cit.*, vol. II, p. 185.

16 Horn, *op. cit.*, p. 290.

17 *Ibid.*, p. 290.

18 *The Craftsman*, 16 September 1727.

19 *Ibid.*

20 *Ibid.*, 21 October 1727.

21 *Ibid.*

22 *Ibid.*, 28 October 1727.

23 *Ibid.*, 23 December 1727.

24 *Ibid.*, 10 July 1728.

25 H. T. Dickinson, *Bolingbroke*, pp. 231–2.

26 Newcastle to Armstrong, C(H), *op. cit.*, April 1728.

27 Armstrong to Horatio Walpole, C(H), *ibid.*, 9 September 1728.

28 Armstrong to Newcastle, C(H), *ibid.*, 5 September 1728.

29 *Ibid.*, 25 April 1730.

30 *Ibid.*, 27 April 1730.

31 Quoted in Basil Williams, *Carteret and Newcastle*, p. 67.

32 Reed Browning, *The Duke of Newcastle*, p. 53.

33 Coxe, *Life*, *op. cit.*, vol. II, p. 623, quoted *ibid.*, p. 53.

34 Dickinson, *op. cit.*, p. 231.

35 Williams, *op. cit.*, p. 68.

36 *Ibid.*, p. 94.

37 *Ibid.*, pp. 98–9.

38 Add. MSS 32776, f.441, quoted *ibid.*, p. 95.

39 *Ibid.*, p. 96.

Chapter 13: To Heel but Snapping: Walpole and the Church (pp. 257–284)

1 Ian Campbell Ross, *Laurence Sterne: A Life*, pp. 46, 66, 133–5.

2 Sedgwick, *op. cit.*, vol. II, p. 487.

3 Quoted Ross, *op. cit.*, p. 69.

4 All at *ibid.*, pp. 72 *passim*.

5 *Ibid.*, p. 90.

6 Geoffrey Holmes and Daniel Szechi, *The Age of Oligarchy*, p. 104.

7 Quoted *ibid.*, p. 63.

8 Quoted in Norman Sykes, *Edmund Gibson*.

9 Diary of Nicholson, Bishop of Carlisle, quoted in Sykes, *op. cit.*, p. 72.

10 *Ibid.*, p. 6.

11 *Ibid.*, p. 74.

12 *Ibid.*, p. 75.

13 *Ibid.*, p. 73.

14 Ballard MSS, quoted *ibid.*, pp. 73–4.

15 Quoted *ibid.*, p. 77.

16 Add. MSS 32686, f.316, quoted in Reed Browning, *The Duke of Newcastle*, p. 26.

17 Holmes and Szechi, *op. cit.*, p. 107.

18 Quoted in Sykes, *op. cit.*, p. 97.

19 Add. MSS, quoted in J. H. Plumb, *Sir Robert Walpole*, vol. II, p. 96.

20 Sykes, *op. cit.*, p. 144.

21 C(H) Miscellaneous Ecclesiastical Matters 48 (Cholmondeley/Houghton 78 Papers, hereafter MEM)

22 *Ibid.*

23 John, Lord Hervey, *Memoirs of the Reign of George II*, vol. II ed. Sedgwick, p. 546.

24 Letter from Walpole to Ms Clayton, quoted in Plumb, *op. cit.*, vol. II, p. 97.

25 Holmes and Szechi, *op. cit.*, p. 110.

26 *Ibid.*, p. 104.

27 *Ibid.*, pp. 104–5.

28 MEM 39, 16 October 1733.

29 MEM 4, 1733.

30 Sedgwick *op. cit.*, pp. 43–4.

31 MEM 4.

32 MEM 15.

33 MEM 18.

34 Sykes, *op. cit.*

35 C(H), 106.

36 Holmes and Szechi, *op. cit.*, p. 395.

37 All at Cobbett, *Parl. Hist.*, vol. IX, col. 1121.

38 Sykes, *op. cit.*, paraphrase and quotation of Carlisle MSS.

39 Hervey, *op. cit.*, vol. II, p. 94.

40 Cobbett, *op. cit.*, vol. IX, cols 1161–2.

41 Sedgwick, *op. cit.*, p. 401.

42 Quoted in Sykes, *op. cit.*, p. 169.

43 Hervey, *op. cit.*, p. 93.

44 Quoted as Appendix D in Sykes, *op. cit.*, p. 413.

45 Add. MSS 9200, Yearbook of Reverend Henry Etough.

Chapter 14: Excise: Scandal and Rebuff (pp. 285–309)

1 Ian Gilmour, *Riot, Rising and Revolution* (Hutchinson, 1992), p. 85.

2 *The London Magazine*, 1732, p. 37, quoted in Paul Langford, *The Excise Crisis*, p. 27.

3 Add. MSS, ff. 95, 125–6, quoted in Reed Browning, *The Duke of Newcastle*, p. 65.

4 Cobbett, *Parl. Hist.*, vol. VIII, col. 968.

5 *Ibid.*, col. 968.

6 *Ibid.*, col. 944.

7 *Ibid.*

8 *Ibid.*, col. 949.

9 *Ibid.*, col. 971.

10 *Ibid.*, col. 972.

11 *Ibid.*, col. 983.

12 *Ibid.*

13 *Ibid.*, col. 953.

14 *Ibid.*

15 *Ibid.*, col. 976.

16 Quoted in Gilmour, *op. cit.*, p. 86.

17 Hervey, *op. cit.*, p. 159.

18 *Ibid.*, p. 161.

19 HMC Egmont Diary I, pp. 85–6, quoted in Langford, *op. cit.*, p. 21.

20 *The Gentleman's Magazine*, 1733, p. 44, quoted in Romney Sedgwick, *The House of Commons*, vol. II, p. 21.

21 HMC Egmont Diary, quoted in Sedgwick, *op. cit.*, p. 386.

22 Cobbett, *op. cit.*, vol. VIII, col. 1120.

23 Quoted in Sedgwick, *op. cit.*, p. 457.

24 Quoted *ibid.*, p. 457.

25 *Ibid.*, p. 458.

26 *Ibid.*

27 Cobbett, *op. cit.*, vol. VIII, cols 1168–9.

28 *Ibid.*, cols 1170–71.

29 *Ibid.*, col. 1172.

30 *Ibid.*

31 *Ibid.*, cols 1175–6.

32 *Ibid.*, col. 1224.

33 *Ibid.*, col. 1232.

34 *Ibid.*, col. 1234.

35 *Ibid.*

36 *Ibid.*, cols 1234–5.

37 *Ibid.*, col. 1186.

38 All at *ibid.*, cols 1264–5.

39 HMC Egmont Diary, 17 February 1733, quoted in Langford, *op. cit.*

40 *The Craftsman*, No. 353, 7 April 1733.

41 HMC Carlisle, p. 104, 15 March 1733, quoted in Langford, *op. cit.*, p. 65.

42 Hervey, *op. cit.*, p. 179.

43 Cobbett, *op. cit.*. vol. VIII, col. 1270.

44 *Ibid.*, col. 1270.

45 *Ibid.*

46 *The Craftsman*, No. 352, 31 March 1733.

47 Cobbett, *op. cit.*, vol. VIII, col. 1273.

48 *Ibid.*, col. 1274.

49 *Ibid.*, col. 1270.

50 All at *ibid.*, col 1270.

51 *Ibid.*, col 1270.

52 *Ibid.*, col. 1277.

53 *Ibid.*

54 *The Craftsman*, No. 353, 7 April 1733.

55 Adam Sisman, *Boswell's Presumptuous Task: The Making of the Life of Dr Johnson* (Penguin, 2002), pp. 190–5.

56 Quoted in Sedgwick, *op. cit.*, vol. I, p. 203.

57 All at 'A Letter from a Freeman', *The Gentleman's Magazine*, 1733, p. 87, quoted in Sedgwick, *op. cit.*, p. 203.

58 Add. MSS 23787, f.303, quoted in E. R. Turner, 'The Excise Scheme of 1733', *English Historical Review*, XLII, January 1927, p. 31.

59 Carlisle MSS, quoted *ibid.*, p. 31.

60 'Life of Chesterfield', Maty, quoted in Turner, *op. cit.*, p. 31.

61 All at Hervey, quoted in Langford, *op. cit.*, p. 80.

62 All *ibid.*, quoted in Langford, *op. cit.*, pp. 84–5.

63 Egmont Diary I, p. 354, quoted in Langford, *ibid.*, p. 79.

64 Hervey (Croker edition, 1848), *op. cit.*, p. 195.

65 All at Hervey, *ibid.*, p. 188.

66 *Ibid.*, p. 198.

Chapter 15: Respite and Aftermath . . . (pp. 310–330)

1 *The Craftsman*, No. 355, 21 April 1733.

2 Letter of Richard Meadowcourt of Merton College to Charles Delafaye C(H), 21 April 1733.

3 Hervey, *op. cit.*, p. 198.

4 *Ibid.*, p. 200.

5 Romney Sedgwick, *The House of Commons*, vol. I, p. 597.

6 Hervey, *op. cit.*, p. 204.

7 *Ibid.*, p. 207.

8 Ian Gilmour, *Riot, Rising and Revolution* (Hutchinson, 1992), p. 90.

9 All quoted in Hervey, present at the meeting, *op. cit.*, pp. 215–21.

10 Quoted in Edward Pearce, *The Lost Leaders* (Little, Brown, 1998), p. 100.

11 Cobbett, *Parl. Hist.*, vol. IX, col. 211.

12 *Ibid.*, col. 289.

13 *Ibid.*, cols 288–9.

14 *Ibid.*, col. 291.

15 *Ibid.*, col. 377.

16 Quoted in Sedgwick, *op. cit.*, vol. II, p. 502.

17 Cobbett, *op. cit.*, vol. IX, col. 404.

18 *Ibid.*

19 *Ibid.*

20 *Ibid.*, col. 408.

21 *Ibid.*, cols 467, 470.

22 *Ibid.*, col. 452, quoted in Langford, *The Excise Crisis*, pp. 103–4.

23 *Ibid.*, col. 476.

24 All *ibid.*, at col. 475.

25 Horace Walpole, quoted in Sedgwick, *op. cit.*, vol. II, p. 604.

26 Cobbett, *op. cit.*, vol. IX, col. 213.

27 *Fog's Weekly Journal*, 13 January 1733, quoted in Langford, *op. cit.*, p. 107.

28 Quoted in Jeremy Black, *The English Press in the Eighteenth Century*, p. 137.

29 *Ibid.*

30 Langford, *op. cit.*, p. 111.

31 Diary of Lady Sarah Cowper, 5 May 1734, quoted in Sedgwick, *op. cit.*, vol. II, p. 413.

32 Quoted from the *St James's Post* and the *Northampton Mercury*, in Langford, *op. cit.*, p. 110.

33 Quoted in Sedgwick, *op. cit.*, vol. I, p. 310.

34 Quoted in Gilmour, *op. cit.*, p. 91.

35 Sedgwick, *op. cit.*, vol. I, p. 290.

36 C(H), 2146.

37 C(H), 2160.

38 C(H), 2161.

39 C(H), 3182.

40 Sedgwick, *op. cit.*, vol. I, p. 289.

41 *Ibid.*

42 Browning, *op. cit.*, p. 70.

43 *Ibid.*, p. 70.

44 Hay to Newcastle, Add. MSS 32688, f.379, quoted in Langford, *op. cit.*, p. 114.

45 Sedgwick, *op. cit.*, vol. I, p. 359.

Chapter 16: 'These Scribblers grow so bold of late' (pp. 331–363)

1 Hervey, quoted in Maynard Mack, *Alexander Pope: A Life*, p. 574.

2 Edward Young, *Night Thoughts*, 2, 292.

3 *Ibid.*, 3, 393.

4 Mack, *op. cit.*, p. 237.

5 Jonathan Swift, *Gulliver's Travels*, Book One.

6 Williams, *Correspondence of Jonathan Swift*, vol. III, p. 207, quoted in David Nokes, *Jonathan Swift: A Hypocrite Reversed*, p. 312.

7 Quoted in Bertrand Goldgar, *Walpole and the Wits*, p. 56.

8 *Ibid.*, p. 56.

9 *Ibid.*, p. 53.

10 *Fog's Weekly Journal*, 25 July 1730, quoted *ibid.*, p. 61.

11 *Ibid.*, p. 66.

12 John Gay, *The Beggar's Opera*, Act 1, Scene 3.

13 *Ibid.*, Act 2, Scene 2.

14 *Ibid.*, Act 1, Scene 3.

15 *Ibid.*, Act 1, Scene 9.

16 D. M. Greene, *Biographical Encyclopaedia of Composers* (Collins, 1985), p. 611.

17 *The Craftsman*, 17 February 1728, quoted in Goldgar, *op. cit.*, p. 69.

18 Quoted *ibid.*, p. 72.

19 *Ibid.*

20 *Ibid.*, p. 71.

21 See Martin Battestin, *Henry Fielding: A Life*, pp. 68–9.

22 *Ibid.*, p. 115.

23 *The Grub Street Opera,* edition of Strahan, Rivington *et al.*, Act 1, Scene 1.

24 *Ibid.*, Act 1, Scene II.

25 *Ibid.*, Act 1, Scene XI.

26 Battestin, *op. cit.*, p. 114.

27 *Ibid.*, p. 114.

28 *Ibid.*, p. 120.

29 Cobbett, *Parl. Hist.*, vol. IX, col. 945.

30 *Ibid.*, passim.

31 Quoted in Battestin, *op. cit.*, p. 193.

32 Robert D. Hume, *Henry Fielding and the London Theatre 1729–1735*, p. 213.

33 *Ibid.*, p. 234.

34 Egmont, vol. II, 390, quoted in Battestin, *op. cit.*, p. 221.

35 *The Daily Gazetteer*, 7 May 1733, quoted *ibid.*, p. 223.

36 Quoted *ibid.*, p. 223.

37 *Ibid.*, p. 225.

38 *The Craftsman*, 28 May, quoted *ibid.*, p. 229.

39 W. H. Craig, *Life of Lord Chesterfield* (John Lane, 1907), pp. 159–60.

40 *Ibid.*, pp. 160–1.

41 Thomas Davies, *Memoirs of the Life of David Garrick*, vol. II (1780), pp. 214–7, quoted in Battestin, *op. cit.*, p. 227.

42 *Ibid.*, pp. 228–9.

43 Quoted in Mack, *op. cit.*, p. 339.

44 *Ibid.*, p. 339.

45 Alexander Pope, *Epistle to Dr Arbuthnot*.

46 Pope, *Epistle to Bathurst*.

47 Pope, *Epistle to Dr Arbuthnot*.

48 Both quoted in H. T. Dickinson, *Bolingbroke*, p. 245.

49 Pope, *The First Epistle of the First Book of Horace Imitated*.

50 *Ibid.*

51 *Ibid.*

52 Goldgar, *op. cit.*, p. 167.

53 Quoted *ibid.*, p. 167.

54 Dialogue I, in Pope, *Epilogue to the Satires*.

55 *Ibid.*

56 Mack, *op. cit.*, p. 715

57 *Ibid.*, p. 688.

58 Dialogue II, quoted in Pope, *op. cit.*, p. 688.

59 Dialogue II, quoted in Goldgar, *op. cit.*, p. 171.
60 *Ibid.*
61 *Ibid.*

Chapter 17: Scotland, Riots and Ready Money (pp. 364–389)

 1 Add. MSS 47065.
 2 All at Sir Robert Walpole to Horace Walpole, letter, London 29 July–29 August 1736, quoted in Coxe, *Life*, vol. III, Appendix, p. 413.
 3 Coxe, *ibid.*, vol. III, p. 272.
 4 Quoted in Ian Gilmour, *Riot, Rising and Revolution* (Hutchinson, 1992), p. 94.
 5 Walter Scott, *The Heart of Midlothian*, chapter 7, pp. 72–4.
 6 *Ibid.*, p. 74.
 7 *The Gentleman's Magazine*, September 1736, p. 8.
 8 Quoted in Gilmour, *op. cit.*, p. 96.
 9 Add. MSS 9200, Etough, *op. cit.*
10 Blenheim MSS D113, quoted in J. H. Plumb, *Robert Walpole*, vol. II, p. 105.
11 Gilmour, *op. cit.*, p. 93.
12 Cobbett, *Parl. Hist.*, vol. IX, col. 1288.
13 *Ibid.*, col. 1289.
14 *Ibid.*
15 *Ibid.*, col. 1290.
16 All at *ibid.*, col. 1291.
17 *Ibid.*, col. 1292.
18 *Ibid.*
19 Gilmour, *op. cit.*, p. 96.
20 Quoted in Coxe, *op. cit.*, vol. III, p. 105.
21 *Ibid.*, pp. 104–5.
22 Add. MSS 4706, Egmont Diary, 28 September 1736.
23 C(H), 2630.
24 Letter from H. Hitch, 26 September 1736, C(H), 2631.
25 Add. MSS 47068, *op. cit.*, 7 April.
26 *Ibid.*, 7 April.
27 Add. MSS 4706, *op. cit.*, 13 November.
28 Hervey, *op. cit.*, vol. III, p. 7.
29 All at *ibid.*, p. 21.
30 *Ibid.*
31 *Ibid.*, p. 8.
32 *Ibid.*, p. 3.
33 *Ibid.*, p. 6.

34 *Ibid.*

35 HMC Report XV, Carlisle, MS 941, p. 180.

36 All in Hervey, *op. cit.*, vol III, pp. 21–2.

37 HMC Report XV, *op. cit.*, p. 196.

38 See Gerrard, *op. cit*, pp. 56–7, for a full account of Frederick and the arts.

39 Hervey, *op. cit.*, vol. III, p. 53.

40 HMC Carlisle, letter of Lady Anne Irwin, 15 March 1737, *op. cit.*

41 C(H), 2667.

42 Coxe, *Life, op. cit.*, vol. III, p. 336.

43 *Ibid.*, p. 342.

44 Appendix to fourth edition of Dodington's diary, quote in Cobbett, *op. cit.*, vol. IX, cols 1364–5.

45 *Ibid.*, col. 1366.

46 Add. MSS Egmont, 22 February 1737, *op. cit.*

47 Cobbett, *op. cit.*, vol. IX, col. 1391.

48 *Ibid.*

49 Hervey memoranda quoted in Sedgwick, *op. cit.*, vol. II, p. 125.

50 HMC Carlisle, *op. cit.*, Colonel Charles Howard to Lord Carlisle, 24 February 1737.

51 Dodington, *op. cit.*, quote in Cobbett, *op. cit.*, vol. IX, col. 1365.

52 HMC Carlisle, Lady Anne Irwin to Lord Carlisle, 6 April 1737, *op. cit.*

53 Egmont (11), p. 366, and Hervey memoranda, pp. 726–8, quoted in Sedgwick, *op. cit.*, vol. I, p. 436.

54 H. Walpole to H. Mann, 25 April 1746, quoted in Sedgwick, op. cit., vol. II, p. 550.

55 Coxe, *op. cit.*, vol. III, p. 305.

56 *Ibid.*, p. 353.

57 *Ibid.*, p. 360–1.

58 Quoted in Hervey, *op. cit.*, vol. III, p. 295.

59 *Ibid.*, p. 303.

60 All *ibid.*, p. 309.

61 *Ibid.*, p. 331.

62 *Ibid.*, p. 139.

Chapter 18: The Long Descent (pp. 390–416)

1 All quoted in W. T. Laprade, *Public Opinion and Politics in Eighteenth-Century England*, pp. 392–3.

2 Coxe, *Life*, vol. IV, pp. 6–7.

3 *Ibid.*, p. 7.

4 Waldegrave MSS, Keene to Waldegrave, 13 December 1737, quoted in Richard Pares, *War and Trade in the West Indies*, p. 25.

5 Browning, *op. cit.*, p. 90.

6 *Ibid.*, p. 90.

7 *Ibid.*

8 State Papers 94/128, Keene to Newcastle, 13 December 1737, quoted *ibid.*, p. 33.

9 Romney Sedgwick, *The House of Commons*, vol. II, p. 546.

10 Chandler's parliamentary record, quoted in Coxe, *op. cit.*, pp. 36–7.

11 *The Daily Advertiser*, 1737, quoted in Laprade, *op. cit.*, p. 332.

12 *The Craftsman*, 18 March 1738, quoted *ibid.*, p. 394.

13 *Ibid.*

14 Tindal's Reports, quoted in Coxe, *op. cit.*, vol. IV, p. 55.

15 *Ibid.*, p. 54.

16 Pares, *op. cit.*, p. 55.

17 Add. MSS 47069, Egmont Diary, 7 February 1739.

18 Quoted in Laprade, *op. cit.*, p. 399.

19 Quoted *ibid.*, p. 393.

20 Commons report, quoted in Coxe, *op. cit.*, vol. IV, pp. 64–5.

21 Chandler's report, quoted *ibid.*, pp. 82–3.

22 *Ibid.*, pp. 83–4.

23 *Ibid.*, p. 82.

24 *Ibid.*, p. 83.

25 All at *ibid.*, p. 86.

26 *Ibid.*, pp. 86–7.

27 *Ibid.*, pp. 88–9.

28 H. T. Dickinson, *Bolingbroke*, pp. 266–7.

29 Coxe, *op. cit.*, vol. IV, pp. 93–6.

30 Quoted in Browning, *op. cit.*, p. 95.

31 Add. MSS 35406, f.111, quoted in Browning, *ibid.*, pp. 94–5.

32 Coxe, *op. cit.*, vol. IV, p. 112.

33 Quoted in Jeremy Lewis, *Tobias Smollett*, p. 42.

34 Quoted *ibid.*, p. 45.

35 *Ibid.*

36 *Ibid.*, p. 47.

37 *Ibid.*

38 Chandler's report, quoted in Coxe, *op. cit.*, vol. IV, p. 218.

39 *Ibid.*, pp. 221–2.

40 *Ibid.*, pp. 226–7.

41 Cobbett, *Parl. Hist.*, vol. XI, col. 1268.

42 Coxe, correcting Tindal's misattribution, quoted Cobbett, *op. cit.*, vol. XI, col. 1269.

43 Walpole's own speech notes, quoted in Coxe, *op. cit.*, p. 1296.

44 Cobbett, *op. cit.*, vol. XI, col. 1284.

45 *Ibid.*
46 Secker MS, cited in Coxe, *op. cit.*, vol. IV, quoted in Cobbett, *op. cit.*, vol. XI, col. 1050.
47 Quoted in Sedgwick, *op. cit.*, vol. II, p. 432.
48 John B. Owen, *The Rise of the Pelhams*, p. 7 and note.
49 Paget Toynbee, ed., *The Letters of Horace Walpole*, 16 vols (Oxford University Press, 1903–5), vol. I, no. 53.
50 Owen, *op. cit.*, p. 19 note.
51 Toynbee, *op. cit.*, vol. I, no. 55.
52 Owen, *op. cit.*, p. 19.
53 Toynbee, *op. cit.*, vol. I, no. 55.
54 *Ibid.*, no. 55.
55 *Ibid.*, no. 54.
56 *Ibid.*, no. 56.
57 *Ibid.*
58 *Ibid.*
59 Owen, *op. cit.*, p. 23.
60 Toynbee, *op. cit.*, vol. I, no. 61.
61 *Ibid.*
62 *Ibid.*
63 *Ibid.*
64 *Ibid.*
65 Devonshire MSS, Hartington to Devonshire, 30 January 1742, quoted in Owen, *op. cit.*, p. 33.
66 Quoted Sedgwick, *op. cit.*, vol. I, p. 344.
67 Coxe, *op. cit.*, vol. IV, p. 354.

Chapter 19: Concluding and Conclusions (pp. 417–428)

1   W. A. Speck, *Stability and Strife*, p. 239.
2   Quoted *ibid.*, p. 240.
3   Quoted in W. T. Laprade, *Public Opinion and Politics in Eighteenth-Century England*, p. 433.
4   Quoted in O. A. Sherrard, *Lord Chatham*, vol. I, p. 84.
5   *Ibid.*, pp. 84–5.
6   Laprade, *op. cit.*, p. 435.
7   Sedgwick, *op. cit.*, vol. II, p. 3.
8   Paget Toynbee, ed., *The Letters of Horace Walpole*, vol. I, p. 240.
9   *Ibid.*, p. 241.
10 Quoted in Speck, *op. cit.*, p. 241.
11 Letter, Orford to Pelham, 13 July 1743, originally quoted in Coxe, *Life*, pp. 182–4. Quoted here in Owen, *op. cit.*, pp. 171–2.

12 Quoted in Coxe, *Life*, vol. IV, p. 377.
13 *Ibid.*, p. 242.
14 *Ibid.*
15 Plumb, *op. cit.*, vol. II, pp. 332–3.

BIBLIOGRAPHY

Printed and Published Books

Battestin, Martin with Ruth Battestin, *Henry Fielding: A Life* (Routledge, 1989)

Bennett, G. V., *The Tory Crisis in Church and State: The Career of Francis Atterbury, Bishop of Rochester* (Clarendon Press, 1975)

Black, Jeremy, *Natural and Necessary Enemies: Anglo-French Relations in the Eighteenth Century* (Duckworth, 1986)

—*The English Press in the Eighteenth Century* (Croom Helm, 1987)

—*Robert Walpole and the Nature of Politics in Early Eighteenth-Century England* (Macmillan, 1990)

Browning, Reed, *The Duke of Newcastle* (Yale University Press, 1975)

Burnet, Gilbert, *History of His Own Times* (Oxford University Press, 1833)

Butterfield, Herbert, *The Whig Interpretation of History* (George Bell, 1968)

Campbell Ross, Ian, *Laurence Sterne: A Life* (Oxford University Press, 2001)

Cannon, John, ed., *'The Whig Ascendancy': Colloquies on Hanoverian England* (Edward Arnold, 1981)

Carswell, John, *The South Sea Bubble* (Alan Sutton, 1993)

Colley, Linda, *In Defiance of Oligarchy: The Tory Party 1714–60* (Cambridge University Press, 1982)

—*Britons: Forging the Nation 1707–1837* (Pimlico, 2003)

Colman, George, *Dramatick Works*, vol. II (T. Becket, 1777)

Connely, Willard, *Sir Richard Steele* (Jonathan Cape, 1934)

Connolly, S.J. ed., *The Oxford Companion to Irish History* (Oxford University Press, 2003)

Coxe, William, *Memoirs of the Life and Administration of Sir Robert Walpole, Earl of Orford*, vols I and II (Cadell and Davies, 1798); vols III and IV (separate ordering) (Longman Hurst et al., 1816)

Dabydeen, David, *Hogarth, Walpole and Commercial Britain* (Hansib, 1987)

Dickinson, H. T., *Bolingbroke* (Constable, 1970)

—*Walpole and the Whig Supremacy* (Hodder & Stoughton, 1973)

—*The Politics of the People in Eighteenth-Century Britain* (St Martin's Press, 1995)

Fielding, Henry, *The History of the Life of Mr Jonathan Wild the Great* (Everyman, 1932)

Foord, Archibald S., *His Majesty's Opposition 1714–1830* (Oxford University Press, 1964)

Freeman, William, *The Incredible De Foe* (Herbert Jenkins, 1950)

Fritz, Paul S., *The English Ministers and Jacobitism Between the Rebellions of 1715 and 1745* (University of Toronto Press, 1975)

Gerrard, Christine, *The Patriot Opposition to Walpole* (Clarendon Press, 1994)

Goldgar, Bertrand A., *Walpole and the Wits* (University of Nebraska Press, 1976)

Goubert, Pierre, *The Course of French History* (Routledge, 1988)

Graham, Walter, ed., *The Letters of Joseph Addison* (Clarendon Press, 1941)

Hamilton, Elizabeth, '*The Backstairs Dragon*': *A Life of Robert Harley, Earl of Oxford* (Hamish Hamilton, 1969)

Harris, Michael, *London Newspapers in the Age of Walpole: A Study of the Origins of the Modern English Press* (Fairleigh Dickinson, 1987)

Hatton, Ragnhild, *George I Elector and King* (Thames & Hudson, 1978)

Hervey, John, Lord, *Memoirs of the Reign of George II*, vol. I (John Murray, 1848); vol. II, separate edition (Bickers, 1884)

Hill, B. W., *The Growth of Parliamentary Parties 1689–1742* (George Allen & Unwin, 1976)

—*Sir Robert Walpole* (Hamish Hamilton, 1989)

Holmes, Geoffrey, *British Politics in the Age of Anne* (Macmillan, 1967)

—*The Trial of Doctor Sacheverell* (Eyre Methuen, 1973)

—*The Making of a Great Power: Late Stuart and Early Georgian Britain 1660–1722* (Longman, 1993)

—and Speck, W. A. *The Divided Society* (Edward Arnold, 1967)

—and Szechi, Daniel, *The Age of Oligarchy 1722–83* (Longman, 1993)

Hoppit, Julian, *A Land of Liberty?: England 1689–1727* (Oxford University Press, 2000)

Horn, David Bayne, *Great Britain and Europe in the Eighteenth Century* (Clarendon Press, 1967)

Hume, Robert D., *Henry Fielding and the London Theatre 1728–1738* (Clarendon Press, 1988)

Hutton, Ronald, *Charles II* (Clarendon Press, 1989)

Kemp, Betty, *Sir Robert Walpole* (Weidenfeld & Nicolson, 1976)

Kenyon, J. P., *Revolution Principles: The Politics of Party 1689–1720* (Cambridge University Press, 1977)

Kramnick, Isaac, *Bolingbroke and His Circle* (Harvard University Press, 1968)

Langford, Paul, *The Excise Crisis: Society and Politics in the Age of Walpole* (Oxford University Press, 1975)

—*A Polite and Commercial People: England 1727–1783* (Guild Publishing/Oxford University Press, 1998)

Laprade, W. T., *Public Opinion and Politics in Eighteenth-Century England* (Macmillan, 1936)

Lewis, Jeremy, *Tobias Smollett* (Jonathan Cape, 2003)

Macaulay, Lord, *The History of England* (Penguin, 1980)

Mack, Maynard, *Alexander Pope: A Life* (Yale University Press/Norton, 1985)

McLynn, Frank, *Crime and Punishment in Eighteenth-Century England* (Oxford University Press, 1991)

Mitchison, Rosalind, *Essays in Eighteenth-Century History: from the English History Review* (Longman, 1966)

Nokes, David, *Jonathan Swift: A Hypocrite Reversed* (Oxford University Press, 1985)

O'Gorman, Frank, *Voters, Patrons and Partners* (Clarendon Press, 1989)

—*The Long Eighteenth Century* (Edward Arnold, 1997)

Olland, Richard, *Pepys: A Biography* (Oxford, 1974)

Owen, John B., *The Rise of the Pelhams* (Methuen, 1957)

Pares, Richard, *War and Trade in the West Indies 1739–1763* (Oxford University Press, 1936)

Plumb, J. H., *The Growth of Political Stability in England* (Macmillan, 1957)

—*Sir Robert Walpole: The Making of a Statesman*, vol. I (Cresset, 1956); vol. II (Cresset, 1960)

Pope, Alexander, *Poetical Works*, ed. Herbert Davies (Oxford University Press, 1966, 1978)

Porrit, Edward and Annie, *The Unreformed House of Commons*, vol. I (Cambridge University Press, 1903)

Realey, Charles, *The Early Opposition to Sir Robert Walpole, 1720–27* (University of Kansas Press, 1931)

Rogers, Nicholas, *Crowds, Culture and Politics in Georgian Britain* (Clarendon Press, 1998)

Rosenheim, James M., *The Townshends of Raynham* (Wesleyan University Press, 1980)

Scott, Walter, *The Heart of Midlothian* (1818) (Penguin, 1994)

Sedgwick, Romney, *The House of Commons, 1715–1754*, 2 vols (HMSO, 1970)

Sherrard, O. A., *Lord Chatham*, vol. I (Bodley Head, 1952)

Speck, W. A., *Stability and Strife* (Edward Arnold, 1977)

Swift, Jonathan, *The Drapier's Letters to the People of Ireland* (Clarendon Press, 1985)

—*Gulliver's Travels* (1725) (Penguin, 1994)

Sykes, Norman, *Edmund Gibson, Bishop of London 1669–1784* (Oxford University Press, 1926)

—*From Sheldon to Secker: Aspects of English Church History 1660–1768* (Cambridge University Press, 1959)

Thompson, E. P., *Whigs and Hunters: The Origin of the Black Act* (Allen Lane, 1975)

Williams, Basil, *Stanhope: A Study in Eighteenth-Century War and Diplomacy* (Oxford University Press, 1932)

—*Carteret and Newcastle* (Frank Cass, 1966)

Williams, Harold, ed., *The Correspondence of Jonathan Swift*, 5 vols (Oxford University Press, 1963–5)

Primary Sources and Printed Primary Sources

The Cholmondeley (Houghton) Manuscripts C(H)

Additional Manuscripts (Add. MSS) at the British Library and

Historic Manuscripts (HMC)

Carlisle

Egmont

Etough

Hastings

Portland

Waldegrave

The Burney Collection at the British Library

The Craftsman

The London Journal

The Corn Cutter's Journal

The Champion

The Daily Gazetteer

Common Sense

All Printed Primary Primary Sources

The Tryal of Dr Henry Sacheverell before the House of Peers (Jacob Tonson, 1710)

William Cobbett, ed., *Parliamentary History of England from the Norman Conquest in 1066 to the Year 1803* (Longman, 1810), vols VI, VII, VIII, IX, X, XI

John, Lord Hervey, *Memoirs of the Reign of George II*, vol. I, ed. J. W. Croker (1848); vol. II, Bickers edn (1884); ed. and revised in 3 vols by R. Sedgwick (1931)

Mrs Anthony Thompson, ed., *Memoirs of Viscountess Sundon, Mistress of the Robes to Queen Caroline*, 2 vols (Henry Colburn, 1847)

Henry Fielding, *The Grub Street Opera* in *Works*, vol. II (Strahan, Rivington et al., 1784)

Mrs Paget Toynbee (ed.), *The Letters of Horace Walpole*, vol. I 1732–1742

INDEX